WILLIAM F. BUCKLEY, JR.

Patron Saint of the Conservatives

John B. Judis

A TOUCHSTONE BOOK
Published by Simon & Schuster Inc.
New York · London · Toronto · Sydney · Tokyo

Touchstone
Simon & Schuster Building
Rockefeller Center
1230 Avenue of the Americas
New York, New York 10020

First Touchstone Edition, 1990

TOUCHSTONE and colophon are registered trademarks
of Simon & Schuster Inc.

Designed by Anne Scatto/Levavi and Levavi
Manufactured in the United States of America

10 9 8 7 6 5 4 3 2 1

10 9 8 7 6 5 4 3 2 1 Pbk.

Library of Congress Cataloging in Publication Data
Judis, John B.
   William F. Buckley, Jr., patron saint of the conservatives / by
John B. Judis.

      p.   cm.
Includes index.
1. Buckley, William F. (William Frank), 1925–   . 2. Journalists—United
States—Biography.   3. Conservativism—United States—History—20th
century.   I. Title.
PN4874.B796J83   1988
070'.92'4—dc19
[B]
                                                                    87-28797

ISBN 0-671-45494-3
ISBN 0-671-69593-2 Pbk.

For Susan

Contents

CONTENTS

Prologue

Every year the retiring editors of the *Yale Daily News* held a banquet. Usually the banquets were modest affairs at which an alumni speaker was highlighted, but in February 1950, the retiring chairman, William F. Buckley, Jr., proclaimed that the banquet would be held to honor retiring Yale President Charles Seymour and he invited the presidents of the major East Coast universities to attend. By allowing each of the presidents to assume that the others had already accepted, Buckley secured the attendance of Dwight Eisenhower of Columbia and Harold Stassen of the University of Pennsylvania, both potential presidential contenders, James B. Conant of Harvard, the most respected educator of his day, Harold Dodds of Princeton, and James R. Killian, Jr., of the Massachusetts Institute of Technology.

The banquet was held at the Law School Auditorium. The editors, clad in black tie and tails, were seated at the head table with the guests. Buckley was between Conant and Seymour; and Thomas Guinzburg, the managing editor, between Eisenhower and Stassen. Buckley's younger brother, Reid, who chatted with Eisenhower at the reception, said later of the general, "For about four heady hours I was in the palm of his hand." Guinzburg kept thinking that the rest of his life would be an "anticlimax." But Buckley was not awed.

Slightly over six feet tall, with light-brown hair, sardonic blue eyes, and a small round mouth from which slightly Anglicized inflections sallied forth, Bill Buckley had little respect for established authority. And as chairman of the *Yale Daily News,* he had developed a reputation around the Ivy League as a right-wing firebrand. When Harvard's Conant got up to speak that evening, he remarked, "In all my years in education, I had come to the conclusion that most bright young men were liberals at twenty or twenty-five and conservatives at thirty-five or forty, but I wonder what will happen to William F. Buckley, who is more conservative at twenty or twenty-five than most Harvard graduates I have known at thirty-five or forty."

After Conant and the other guests had given short speeches in praise of Seymour, Buckley was supposed to give a short speech and then to introduce the guest of honor. His guests and the audience expected him to eulogize Seymour, but when he rose to speak, he astounded them by giving a substantial address on the state of university education in which he criticized the way the presidents, including Seymour, had run their schools.

Buckley lectured the retiring president and his colleagues on the dangers of allowing communism and atheism a free rein in their classrooms. He urged the presidents to defend free enterprise against its detractors on the faculty and to foster "active Christianity" among the students. If their faculties refused to heed them, the presidents should lay aside their qualms about academic freedom, Buckley said, adding: "Since it is [the college presidents] who establish policy, their associates will cooperate with their program if they conscientiously do so; and if they cannot, Godspeed on their way to an institution that is more liberal." [1]

Afterwards, there was polite applause, but according to a reporter from the *Daily Princetonian,* "the guests were shaken." [2]

Buckley's speech displayed a defiance of authority that would be common on college campuses in the late 1960s but that was unheard of in 1950, especially from someone on the political Right rather than the Left. It was the opening salvo in a career that would soon make him the "enfant terrible" of the eastern intelligentsia and that would bring to American conservatism a philosophy of radical dissent rather than accommodation with the status quo.

Thirty-five years later, more than seven hundred American conservatives gathered at New York's posh Plaza Hotel to pay homage to him and to *National Review,* the magazine that he had founded in 1955. Buckley, his sister Priscilla, the managing editor of *National Review,* and his brother Jim, the former senator from New York and the president of Radio Free Europe, stood to receive the guests as they arrived. Buckley's hair had turned gray, but it still fell boyishly over his brow. His face was lined, the flesh on his long neck sagged; the features that had seemed perfectly regular at age twenty-four had assumed a life of their own; his chin jutted; his eyes tended to bulge as he raised his eyebrows to emphasize a point or signal disbelief; his tongue darted out of a small pursed mouth; his left eye twinkled, while his right gauged reactions and plotted future sentences. But then, a child's grin would spread across his face and his discordant features would collect themselves into a buoyant chorus. Buckley had always smiled, but in 1950, his public smile had been tinged with sarcasm; it was a defense against the scorn of his elders. Now he was himself an elder, and those who had once ridiculed him now paid tribute. The establishment that Buckley had once attacked had become his own.

Among the guests at the banquet were corporate heads like Roger Milliken, who had been an important financial backer of *National Review* and of Barry Goldwater; repentant liberal intellectuals like Irving Kristol; and numerous administration officials, including the CIA director, the White House director of communications, and the President's chief speech writer, who had first learned their conservatism from *National Review;* and of course President Ronald Reagan, who for more than twenty years had been Buckley's friend and close political associate.

When the President spoke that evening, he recalled how, as a Democrat, he "picked up my first issue of *National Review* in a plain brown wrapper." Then he said of *National Review*'s founder:

> I think eventually the pundits and analysts are going to catch on to the enormous force and deep roots of the conservative movement. . . . And when that happens, they are going to realize something not only about this journal, but about its founder and editor; that Bill Buckley is perhaps the most influential journalist and intellectual in our era—that he changed our country, indeed our century.[3]

Afterwards, Buckley got up to speak. When he had first spoken in public as a college student, he used to stand on his tiptoes, stretched taut by the sublimated fury of his delivery. But now he dallied at the podium and joked with his audience. He had become convivial. If Buckley betrayed a darker side, it was not that of the malcontent, but rather of the celebrity's uncertainty about his public status.

The heart of Buckley's speech was an assessment of the President's contribution to the conservative cause. The man who had once excoriated Eisenhower from the Right now defended Reagan against his right-wing critics. He brushed aside conservative complaints of the President not doing enough. The President, Buckley said, "is not powerful enough to do everything that needs to be done." But "the conclusive factor in the matter of American security against ultimate Soviet aggression, is the character of the occupant of the White House, the character of Ronald Reagan."[4] Buckley's role had been transformed from establishment critic to its defender.

During the fifties and sixties, Bill Buckley *was* American conservatism. In his writings, in *National Review,* and in his television and campus appearances, he created the style and the politics that have come to be identified as conservatism. "He, more than any single figure, has made conservatism a respectable force in American life," wrote journalist John Chamberlain,[5] who moved from Left to Right in the late thirties, and himself was one of the founders of the modern conservative movement.

For conservatives who came of age during the late fifties and the sixties, Buckley provided the model. "Buckley was the spiritual father of the movement," columnist and White House Communications Director Pat Buchanan said. "To the conservatives of the silent generation, Buckley was a real beacon. He was as responsible as anyone for my being part of the conservative movement. I read *National Review,* and that's the first magazine I took a real interest in. It expressed, with a sense of humor and intelligence and wit, exactly the things I felt I believed."

All the major political figures of conservatism, including Barry Goldwater and Ronald Reagan, owed much of their politics to Buckley and *National Review.* After Reagan's landslide victory in November 1980, columnist George Will summed up Buckley's contribution:

> . . . all great Biblical stories begin with Genesis. And before there was Ronald Reagan, there was Barry Goldwater, and before there was Barry Goldwater there was *National Review,* and before there was *National Review* there was Bill Buckley with a spark in his mind, and the spark in 1980 has become a conflagration.[6]

It is impossible to understand American politics today without understanding the rise of American conservatism. And it is impossible to understand American conservatism without understanding Bill Buckley's extraordinary life.

PART ONE

The Enfant Terrible

He has the outward and visible signs of the campus radical, and the inward and spiritual qualities of the radical's wealthy grandfather.

—Dwight Macdonald,
"God and Buckley at Yale"

CHAPTER 1

The Counterrevolutionary

In 1925, the year Bill Buckley was born, Calvin Coolidge, the dour New Englander known for his eighteenth-century apothegms, was just beginning his second term in office. Coming from the ranks of the Republican Right, Coolidge epitomized the conservative of his day. He believed unquestioningly in the power of the free market to achieve prosperity. During his time in office, he reduced taxes for business and the wealthy; he vetoed two bills to provide relief to farmers; he sent the Marines to Nicaragua to protect American interests. But when the European countries sought to renegotiate their crippling war debt, like the isolationist that he was, Coolidge quipped, "They hired the money, didn't they?"

Coolidge had won a landslide victory in November 1924, and his former Secretary of Commerce, Herbert Hoover, scored an even greater landslide in 1928. But the Great Depression, which began in 1929, discredited the Republican Party and the policies on which it had been based. During Bill's boyhood, a new political era began, in which the Democrats, led first by Franklin Roosevelt, dominated the nation's politics for almost four decades, and in which a new politics of welfare capitalism and internationalism, called "liberalism," provided the framework for policy making and political debate.

Bill Buckley grew up in this period of liberal ascendancy when even the children of the wealthy were expected to flirt with left-wing radicalism. But from the moment he began to have political opinions, they were right-wing rather than left-wing. For the most part, they were the conventional opinions of the Republican Right of the twenties and thirties. At age seven, while a day student at a London Catholic school, he wrote a letter to King George demanding that Britain pay its war debts. At age thirteen, he was an outspoken foe of the New Deal and an isolationist. When he got his first sailboat, he named it *Sweet Isolation.* After the war, as the chairman of the *Yale Daily News,* he conducted a personal crusade against "collectivism" and atheism among the faculty.

But while many of young Bill Buckley's opinions were the same as those of Ohio Republican Senator Robert Taft or of former President Coolidge, the framework of his opinions was different. Buckley didn't see himself defending the verities of small-town America, but rather arresting the global assault of Soviet Communism. And he didn't see himself as a defender of the status quo (a stance that defined a conservative in an earlier day), but as a rebel against it.

The key to Bill's incongruous political views and temperament was the influence of his father, William (Will) F. Buckley, Sr. Born in Texas of immigrant Irish Catholic parents, Will Buckley was a man for, but not of, the Right. His convictions did not date from the battle over the League of Nations and against the New Deal, but from his experiences as a Catholic boy in Protestant Texas and as an oilman during the Mexican Revolution. He held his views in defiance of his immediate environment: whether in revolutionary Mexico or in moderate Republican, internationalist, Yankee Connecticut. And he saw himself as a counterrevolutionary rather than a conservative.

He transmitted these views to Bill and his other children through dinner-table conversation and lengthy memoranda that he sent them from abroad. He created a world unto itself for them, centered at the family estate, Great Elm, in Sharon, Connecticut, and staffed by an army of tutors and governesses. But most important was his own example. He was a man continually at odds with prevailing opinion and custom; and his children, identifying with him, grew up with a sense of themselves as embattled warriors, sallying forth on behalf of unpopular but righteous causes. They didn't think of rebelling against him, because they saw him as a rebel. Bill Buckley said later, "Perhaps the reason we did not rebel was that Father was a dissenter all his life. Had he been an establishmentarian, there might have been a greater impulse to rebel."[1]

I

Will Buckley was born in Washington, Texas, in 1881 and was raised in San Diego, a small, hot Texas town just a hundred miles north of the Mexican border. His father, John, had emigrated to Texas from Canada, to which John's father, a native of County Cork, Ireland, had come in the 1840s. The parents of Will's mother, Mary Anne, had emigrated from County Limerick to the U.S. at about the same time.

Will later told his children a story of how the first of these Buckleys had come to the New World. According to Will, his grandfather had been an Irish Protestant in County Cork, on the southwestern coast of Ireland, who had married a Catholic in the 1840s. The annual Orangemen's Day Parade, organized by Irish Protestants in the early 1800s to mark their ascendancy over Irish Catholics, had always cut across the Buckley farm, but after he was married, Will's grandfather, out of deference to his wife, asked the parade leaders to bypass his farm. When they refused, he bashed in the head of the first man who set foot on his land. He was released from jail when the man recovered, but the Buckleys had become sufficiently unpopular with their neighbors that they decided to emigrate. According to Will, they sailed to Canada, where they raised their children.*

This story is highly implausible.† But even if Will's story of his grandfather were entirely false, it indicates the kind of life and identity that he and his father, from whom he presumably got the story, valued. The first of these Buckleys to emigrate from Ireland was a Prot-

---

* See F. Reid Buckley, "Retold Tale," in *WFB: An Appreciation,* eds. Priscilla Buckley and William F. Buckley, Jr. Reid Buckley is the unofficial family historian, having once even begun a family chronicle. When I relayed to him the doubts that historians had raised about his father's tale, he insisted that the tale was "in the main accurate."

† On Will's story of his grandfather, I consulted Anne Culinaine, a specialist in Irish history, at the University of Maryland, and at Culinaine's urging, Mary Daly, professor of modern Irish history, University College, Dublin, and the leading authority on nineteenth-century Ireland. Both historians thought that Will's story was implausible. By the 1840s, the Orangemen's Society was in disarray, and it is very unlikely that an Orangemen's Day Parade could have taken place in County Cork at that time. Two different things might have impelled the Buckleys to emigrate. They might have joined the million other Irish who fled the famine of the 1840s, many of whom came from County Cork. Or they might have run afoul of sectarian tensions, either because John's father converted to Protestantism, or because he, a Protestant, married a Catholic. In this case, some less dramatic version of the events told by John Buckley to his son might have impelled his father to sail across the Atlantic.

estant rather than a Catholic—a contention important not for its religious but its social meaning. He was a dissenter and a rebel who fought for his individual beliefs against prevailing custom and opinion and who was moved to emigrate not by material factors but by principle and conviction. According to Will's story, his grandfather was not a poor Catholic who fled the famine, but a Protestant pilgrim— much like those who sailed on the *Mayflower*—fleeing religious bigotry. But where Pilgrims and the average Irish Catholic immigrant sought religious community in the New World, the first Buckley sought individuality.

Will's parents, John and Mary Anne Buckley, had moved to San Diego to help relieve John's asthma. Most of San Diego's two thousand inhabitants were Mexicans, but the two hundred Americans were an unusually cosmopolitan collection of asthma victims, who in between cattle roundups played string quartets in each other's houses. According to Will, his father was a sheep rancher who became county sheriff, and who did not make enough money to pay his sons' way through college. But Will's own registration documents at the University of Texas, which he entered in 1899, reveal that John also sold insurance and that he was financing Will's education.

Will's early education was closely supervised by his mother—a devout Catholic—and by the Basque-born parish priest, who schooled Will in Latin, history, and Catholic doctrine. From Padre John Peter Bard, Will learned a continental Catholicism that was far more private and aristocratic than the democratic and highly public Catholicism that most Irish émigrés practiced in the New World. Will also learned to speak fluent Spanish, which he put to use teaching for a year at the local high school before enrolling at the University of Texas. He graduated with a Bachelor of Science in 1904—the year his father died—and with a law degree the following year.[2] In 1908, after working for two years in Austin, he left for Mexico City to practice his profession and, in the process, to make his fortune.

In the early 1900s, Mexico was enjoying the beginning of its oil boom, and American oil speculators, encouraged by dictator Porfirio Díaz and his advisers, the *científicos*, were eagerly signing long-term leases. Fortunes were being made and lost overnight in both oil and real estate. Business regulation was practically nonexistent; and one of the principal functions of lawyers was to cajole and, if necessary, bribe corrupt judges and other officials. In a letter to a friend, Will

Buckley later described the Mexican oil business as a "jungle [where the] only law was devour or be devoured."[3]

It was also a time of increasing political discontent with the Díaz dictatorship. Mexico's emerging middle class resented Díaz and the wealthy landholders' monopoly of political power and their concessions to American and British investors. (By 1910, two Americans and an Englishman owned 98 percent of Mexico's oil output.) And the impoverished peasants yearned for land of their own. In 1911, with Díaz's overthrow by Francisco Madero, the scion of a wealthy manufacturing family, the Mexican Revolution commenced. For almost a decade, revolutionary and counterrevolutionary armies roamed over the countryside, alternatively claiming control of the nation.

For the first five years that he was in Mexico, Will stayed out of politics. During that time, he and his brothers set up a law firm in Tampico, which was about to become the center of the Mexican oil business. Will's firm won the accounts of the major oil companies there, and while his brothers handled the legal business, Will, aided by his gambler's instincts, knowledge of Spanish, and his Catholicism (which endeared him to the Mexicans in Tampico), branched off into real estate and oil, undisturbed by the political unrest. By 1914, Will's property, which included his own island, was worth at least $100,000; and he had become one of the most prominent Americans in Mexico, looked to for advice both by the Mexican government and Wilson's Secretary of State, William Jennings Bryan.

Although Will admired the Díaz regime because of its encouragement of American investment and because of its close ties to the Catholic hierarchy in Mexico, he was not very concerned when Madero ousted Díaz and the pro-Díaz general Victoriano Huerta overthrew Madero, seeing these first stages of the revolution as adjustments within Mexico's ruling class. It was only in 1914 when the revolutionary forces of Generals Venustiano Carranza and Álvaro Obregón and peasant revolutionaries Pancho Villa and Emiliano Zapata began defeating Huerta's forces that Will became alarmed. The rebel armies demanded tolls from the oil companies to feed their men. Zapata called for the outright confiscation of foreign lands. And Obregón, resentful of the Church's support of Díaz and now Huerta, described the Catholic Church in Mexico as a "cancerous tumor" and threatened retribution against pro-Díaz priests.[4] With other American oilmen, Will began working with the Huerta government to try to ensure its survival.

Will's support for Huerta threw him, however, into conflict with his own government. American President Woodrow Wilson was no revolutionary, but he believed that Mexico would remain at war until some measure of land reform and democracy was achieved.[5] In 1914, the U.S. Navy landed at Veracruz, south of Tampico, to head off a German arms shipment for Huerta. The American admiral asked Will to become one of the four civil governors during the American occupation, but he refused. When talks were held that summer at Niagara Falls to try to end the crisis, Will attended as a legal adviser to the Huerta regime, and lobbied the Wilson administration on its behalf.

After Huerta was overthrown, Will became an active counterrevolutionary. He joined an underground that hid priests whose lives were in danger and that concealed Church artifacts to prevent their being looted by revolutionary armies. In 1919 he helped Tampico General Manuel Pelaez organize an abortive coup against the bourgeois nationalist Carranza, whom he accused of being a Bolshevik when testifying before the Senate Foreign Relations Committee. In 1921, he walked out of the major oil companies' increasingly conciliatory National Association for the Protection of American Rights, and founded his own lobby, the American Association for the Protection of American Rights, to oppose recognition of the new Mexican government. That fall, he organized a counterrevoltionary coup against Obregón, who had been elected to office the prior year. The coup attempt collapsed when the man in charge of bringing the weapons across the border got lost and ended up getting arrested for smuggling while trying to cross back from Mexico to the U.S. By this time, Obregón had had enough of Will Buckley. In November 1921, he expelled him from Mexico and, over the next year, confiscated his properties.[6]

Will came back to the United States without most of the fortune he had made, but with an insider's knowledge of the oil business, and a seething hatred of revolution. Equating Carranza with Lenin, he believed that he had seen in Mexico the first stage of a worldwide Communist revolution against capitalism and Christianity. In New York, Will met with exiles from the Díaz and Huerta governments and lectured on Mexican politics.[7] But he drew away from what he realized was increasingly futile counterrevolutionary activity. He devoted the bulk of his energy to making back his fortune and to raising a family. He didn't lose his desire to affect history; he projected it onto his children. They would be raised to undo the evils of revolution.

II

In 1917 Will had married Aloise Steiner, a tiny, vivacious woman who would be the mother of his ten children. Marjorie Otis Gifford, who taught the Buckley children piano and became a friend to Aloise and her children, described her as a "capricious, delightfully spirited, enchanting, willful, endearing Southern belle," adding, "Young and beautiful she was at 39, profound and thoughtful she was not."[8]

Aloise was in many ways Will's opposite. While he was an extremely judgmental person—Will could be witheringly sarcastic in describing political adversaries or business rivals—Aloise was always kindhearted in her opinions. "She never said a bad word about anybody," her daughter Jane Buckley Smith recalled. While Will could be cold and distant at times—even to his closest associates he remained "Mr. Buckley"—she was warm and effusive. She was the one who always put her children's friends at ease when they came to Great Elm. Bill's friend Alistair Horne described her as "one of the sweetest, warmest and gentlest women whom I ever met."

Their children describe Will as an introvert and Aloise as an extrovert. "My father played it two ways—either I am going to be alone tonight with my wife and nobody is gong to disturb me, including you children—or he would have a dinner party for forty-eight people," John Buckley said. "My mother just liked people. She enjoyed being around them."

The difference between Will and Aloise was evident in the way they practiced their religion. Although both were devout Catholics, Will's faith was as private as it was militant. He prayed on his knees every morning by himself and attended Mass every week. But he never spoke publicly of his belief in or commitment to God. "My father would fight if anybody said anything about the Catholic Church," Patricia Buckley Bozell said. "But his religion was where his introvertedness came in. He didn't blare about it. Mother did. It was so much a part of her it wasn't a private thing.

Aloise's religion was more emotional. "She prayed for everything," Priscilla Buckley recalled. "Good weather, bad weather. She had a very personal relationship with God. She said nothing was too unimportant for God." Will's Catholicism was Old Testament, his God stern and unforgiving. Aloise's was the merciful God of the New Testament. Describing the sense of Christ that he had gotten from his mother, Bill once wrote that he found Jesus Christ "endearing" and the God of the Old Testament "a horrible, horrible person, capricious and arbitrary."[9]

Aloise Steiner was born in new Orleans in 1895, the daughter of a successful banker. The Steiners had come to New Orleans from Switzerland before the Civil War, and Aloise prided herself on being a "Daughter of the Confederacy." As a child, she displayed some literary talent. She was the editor of her high-school newspaper and the only Steiner daughter to attend college. She wrote both short stories and poems, some of which may have been published in newspapers and magazines.* Later she would exercise her talent at storytelling for her children, who regularly trooped up to her room before bedtime to listen intently to stories of Revolutionary America that Aloise would improvise on the spot.

At Christmastime 1916, Will met Vivian, one of Aloise's sisters, in Mexico City when she was visiting her uncle, a banker with whom Will was friendly. Several months later, on a business trip to New Orleans, Will called on her, only to discover that she had become engaged. He did meet, however, her older sister Aloise, to whom he proposed after several days. They were married that Christmas and went to live in Mexico.

They had, by all descriptions, a happy and fruitful marriage. It would survive more than forty years, the first half of which Will scrambled, often with little success, to recoup the fortune that he had lost in Mexico City, leaving Aloise alone—sometimes without money to pay the bills—to manage the affairs of their growing and demanding family. In 1918, they had their first child, Aloise, then six others in quick succession—John in 1920, Priscilla in 1921, James in 1923, Jane in 1924, Bill in 1925, and Patricia in 1927. Reid would come in 1930 and Maureen in 1933, when the Buckleys were living abroad, and Carol in 1938.

As the children began to learn what was expected of them in the world, the examples most often came directly from their mother. "It was Mother who was with us day in and out." Jim Buckley recalled. "Hers was the dominant influence when it came to such essentials as faith, love of country, and consideration for others." [10]

But it was invariably Will Buckley's word that Aloise was conveying. "Father was the unchallenged source of authority," according to

---

* In *Reminiscences of Aloise Steiner Buckley,* edited by Aloise Harding Buckley, Jimmie Steiner, Aloise's younger brother, claims that she had stories published in *Collier's,* including one called "Burl's Spring Time," but I could not find any story by Aloise Steiner or of that title in *Collier's.* According to her daughter Priscilla, Aloise Steiner also had poems published in the *New Orleans Times-Picayune.*

Bill.[11] Aloise's role was not to counter his authority but to mute its potentially harsh impact. "If Father was in an authoritarian mood, Mother would try to soften it," Patricia recalled. There were never any important differences of opinion between them. Aloise clearly saw her role as ally and supporter of her husband in his business, his political causes, and what would become his greatest cause of all: the education of his children.

III

Will Buckley was forty-four by the time Bill was born—an age more characteristic then of a grandfather than a father. He was a commanding presence. He had a broad forehead and piercing cobalt eyes that looked out from behind pince-nez that rested on a long, pointed nose. His graying hair was parted back in the middle. He was elegantly tailored and formally attired in starched white shirts even when he was relaxing at home.* "He was like a gentleman of the World War I period," Sheridan Lord, one of Bill's college friends, remarked.

Of only medium height, Will so impressed people who met him that they exaggerated his stature. Stewart Hoskins, the former editor of the *Lakeville [Conn.] Journal* and an old foe of the Buckleys, recalled Will Buckley as having been "very tall." He could at times strike terror into the minds of his children and of innocent visitors to the Buckley home at Great Elm. The Buckley children, Jim Buckley said, were "in awe of him." [12]

Will was capable of both kindness and generosity, but in a manner dictated by an extreme shyness and formality. When he died, in 1958, his children discovered a network of indigent widows of former employees that he had secretly supported over the years. When he disciplined his children, he would invariably feel remorse—but he would express it by sending them a present through the mail the next week. And while he felt great affection for his children, he communicated with them primarily through letters rather than in person. These letters displayed a certain distance and stuffiness, but also a dry, teasing wit, as when he wrote his children complaining of their overuse of the family cars.

---

* There is a striking resemblance in manner and style between Will Buckley and Edward Doheny, the leading American oilman in Mexico when Will was there. Invariably formally attired in pince-nez and English suits, Doheny was an Irish Catholic who affected the style and manners of the English upper class.

Memorandum to the Buckley Children:

I have been much concerned of late with the apparent inability of any of you at any time to go anywhere on foot, although I am sure your Mother would have informed me if any of you had been born without the walking capacity of a normal human being.

A few of the older children, notably Priscilla, occasionally walk a few hundred yards behind a golf ball, but all the others "exercise" exclusively by sitting on a horse or a sailboat.

Concurrently, I have noticed that the roads around Sharon are crowded with Buckley cars at all hours of the day and night. . . . All the cars are left out every night in all kinds of weather, undoubtedly because of the dangerous fatigue involved in walking from the garage to the house.

I think each of you should consider a course of therapy designed to prevent atrophy of the leg muscles if only for aesthetic reasons, or you might even go to the extreme of attempting to regain the art of walking, by easy stages of course. The cars might then be reserved for errands covering distances of over 50 yards or so.[13]

Will valued the well-delivered wisecrack and smart remark, and he loved to laugh. He savored the Marx Brothers' and Ritz Brothers' movies. He enjoyed teasing his wife and children. And he was not above staging practical jokes. Once, in South Carolina, Will stole the cherished vase from the garden of a priest whom he knew and then sold it back to him at lunch, claiming that it was the twin of the original that the priest had often bragged about.

His children would inherit, in varying degrees, both sides of Will's personality. They would be capable of kindness and generosity, but also of withering hauteur and iron defiance. They would value wit and cherish a good laugh, but they would also remain unwavering in their political and religious convictions.

Will's politics were those of the conservative southern Democrats among whom he had grown up and the conservative Republicans who dominated national politics in the 1920s. Will was a proponent of laissez-faire capitalism, believing that anyone with sufficient ambition could work his way to the top of the American system. His faith in unfettered free enterprise, his son John recalled, was "an emotional feeling verging on the quasi-religious." Like many Republicans and southern Democrats, he was an isolationist who had opposed Woodrow Wilson's attempt to "make the world safe for democracy" and would later oppose American intervention in the European war of 1939–41.

Will also reflected the social attitudes of his class and region. He regarded blacks and Indians as inferior beings unworthy of the same rights and privileges as whites, and would frequently rail against the Jews as interlopers within a Christian nation. "He thought of the American Jews of the twentieth century as culturally unintegrated," Bill said.*

But at the heart of Will's political convictions lay his Catholicism and his opposition to communism and revolution. Will's religious faith was itself a politics. As a result of growing up among Protestants and then seeing the Church threatened by Mexican revolutionaries, Will's Catholicism came to have the fervor of the English Jacobites—English Catholics G. K. Chesterton and Hilaire Belloc were among his favorite authors—and of the early American Congregationalists.

His Catholicism informed his deeply felt opposition to communism. Communism was not merely a foreign ideology—like socialism or fascism—but a Satanic faith that threatened the soul of Western civilization. According to John Buckley, his father regarded communism as the "anti-Christ." It could invade the spirit of peoples unexpectedly and in disguise, as it had in Mexico. Will's isolationism was based ultimately on his anticommunism rather than upon his principled opposition to intervention. He opposed Wilson in 1914 because he thought Wilson was aiding the Mexican Revolution. And he opposed American intervention in the European war of 1939–41 because he wanted to see Nazi Germany defeat the Soviet Union. To the Buckley family, "Bolshevik Russia was an infinitely greater threat than Nazi Germany," Bill's childhood friend Alistair Horne later recalled.[14]

Will's Catholicism and his anticommunism conditioned his view of democracy. He believed that few countries were capable of sustaining it (Mexico was "incapable . . . of a democratic form of government," he had told a congressional committee investigating the revolution).[15] He saw the demand for political democracy in countries like Mexico, Venezuela, and Spain as a cover for communism and anticlericalism. In the thirties, he backed Catholic counterrevolutionary Francisco Franco's attempt to overthrow the Spanish Republic. "Father didn't think that democracy was the right political system for Spain," his daughter Patricia Buckley Bozell recalled. "He understood Spanish politics, and he knew the Republic meant, if not out-and-out communism, then one of these accommodations which would become communism."

---

* Describing his father's prejudice, Buckley recalled a well-known figure who had "once told me that he would leave the room if ever someone in it said something about the Jews which he had heard routinely at his own dinner table. That exactly expresses the situation in my home."

Even his view of American democracy was somewhat jaundiced. He rarely voted. He liked to describe politicians as "mountebanks." He ceased to identify himself as a Democrat after Roosevelt's New Deal, but he never became a Republican, and his favorite politicians remained southern Democrats like Mississippi Senator John Sharp Williams.

Will's overall views fit none of the existing political categories. His economics were thoroughly Protestant American, but his view of communism and democracy was much closer to that of a European Catholic. Through the years of the Great Depression and New Deal, when unemployment exceeded 25 percent, he doggedly maintained his belief in the wisdom and justice of the free market. And in the same years, he maintained that the greatest threat to peace and liberty was not Nazi Germany but Communist Russia. These seemingly incongruous convictions became the lens through which Will's children viewed the world.

Will also conveyed a distinctive set of personal and moral values to his children. In the 1920s, a conservative was the narrow-minded provincial described by Sinclair Lewis in *Babbitt* and *Main Street* and parodied by H. L. Mencken as a member of the "booboisie." The conservative was dull and unlearned, obsessed with money and status, and fearful of appearing different from his fellows. Will could not have diverged more sharply from this stereotype. He was an avid reader, with a wide knowledge of Mexican and world history. He was constantly recommending books to his children, from Van Wyck Brooks's studies of American culture to Albert Jay Nock's writings on education and the state. He was fascinated by architecture and helped to design his family homes in Connecticut and South Carolina.

Will loved the adventure of business, but he despised men for whom commercial profit and economic status became ends in themselves. His letters to his children were filled with warnings against what he called "materialism." In one memorandum from abroad, he wrote:

I have just read *Prairie Avenue* by Arthur Meeker, an impressive novel about wealthy families in Chicago during the Golden period of 1885 to 1918. These people were pure materialists, without morals and religion, although uniformly contributing members of churches. Notwithstanding their conviction that they were establishing families that would last forever, these had disintegrated entirely by 1918.[16]

Will scorned many of the conventional tokens of success. He once paid a public-relations man to keep his name out of *Who's Who*, and he had no interest in presenting his children to high society. (None of the Buckley daughters "came out.") He sent them to elite colleges, but only out of a conviction that they could get the best education there.

Will's aspiration for his children was that they excel intellectually and morally. Except for his oldest son, he had no interest in forcing his children to follow his own path. Instead, he saw the wealth that he had acquired as freeing them to follow higher pursuits. He stressed that they should use their education for broader moral and political ends.

Will's training showed. Of his ten children, only his son John, who secretly yearned to be an archeologist, followed him directly into business. Jim also worked at the family oil business, but fled it for public service at the first opportunity. And the rest of the children became, to one degree or another, writers and editors committed to spreading the gospel that they had first heard from their father. Like him, they came to see themselves as members of what Will's friend the Tory anarchist Albert Jay Nock called "the Remnant," a small select group of individuals who are carrying aloft the flame of civilization in the face of an encroaching Dark Age.

IV

After leaving Mexico, Will moved his family to New York, where he was raising funds to launch a new oil venture in Venezuela. But he didn't think children should be brought up in the city, and within a year he had bought a forty-seven-acre estate in Sharon, a rustic town of two thousand in the northwestern corner of Connecticut. Sharon and neighboring Lakeville were both Revolutionary-era towns, many of whose inhabitants could trace their families back to before the Revolution. The New England colonial house he bought, called Great Elm because the state's largest elm tree stood in its front yard, had been built in 1763 and had briefly housed the governor of Connecticut.

Will's decision to raise his family in such a place expressed distaste for the Irish Catholic subculture in America. Like other upper-class Irish, Will insisted that he was an American rather than an Irish-American, and he defined himself against the stereotype of the immigrant Irish Catholic. "An Irishman should not drink," he would tell his children. Probably his distaste for electoral politics stemmed in part from its identification with immigrant Irish.

In situating his family in Sharon, Will was also re-creating for his children—perhaps unconsciously—the cultural and social alienation in which he himself had been raised and in which he imagined his Irish grandfather had grown up. He would raise his children to be highly cultured and individualistic Catholic reactionaries in Yankee Protestant Connecticut.

Will and his family were bound to stand out and to arouse a certain amount of resentment in Sharon. The modest farmers and shopkeepers who lived there resented the wealthy commuters who built houses along Sharon's main road; fourth- and fifth-generation Yankee Protestants, they also looked askance at a large half-Irish Catholic family from the South.* But instead of trying to assimilate, Will carved out a distinct world for his children. According to Peter Coley, one of their neighbors, "The Buckleys were elite and self-isolating."

Will trampled Great Elm's storied past. He enlarged and redesigned it, blending its colonial lines with his own Catholic and Mexican background. Each room became a shrine, containing a religious painting and a portrait of his family. American colonial and Mexican artifacts coexisted. In the late thirties, when he had finally struck oil in Venezuela, he built an extension, almost as large as the original house, which contained a three-story glassed-in Mexican patio, inlaid with tiles that he had sequestered after fleeing in 1921. Entering what Will called "El Patio" was like leaving Concord for Cuernavaca.

Rather than educating his children in local schools, he designed an elaborate program for them that set them off from other children. It provided them not only with the rudiments of a liberal education but also with athletic and social skills. Believing that younger children were best equipped to exercise their mnemonic capabilities, he hired Mexican *nanas* to teach the youngest children Spanish, and French governesses to teach French to the children over five. As a result, all the Buckley children were fluent in French, Spanish, and English by the time they reached thirteen. (Bill and Reid both spoke fluent French and Spanish before English.)

He wanted his children not only to learn what he had learned, but

---

* There is some question about how much hostility the Buckleys incurred simply because they were Catholic. Peter and William Coley, the Buckley's neighbors, insist that it was not Catholicism but their "elite and self-satisfied" attitude that made local people distrust and dislike them. But in interviews with Sharon and Lakeville residents who had lived there when the Buckleys had, one finds recurring echoes of anti-Catholicism. For instance, one longtime Lakeville resident drew a distinction between the "very so-called orthodox" priests who had formerly been active in the area and the "very good Catholic priests around recently," the implication being that priests who were serious about Catholic doctrine were not "very good."

to excel at acitivities he never mastered. He hired music teachers to instruct each child in an instrument and in musical appreciation. And he hired rhetoricians to teach his children to speak in public.

His oldest daughter, Aloise Buckley Heath, later described her father's penchant for education.

> There was nothing complicated about Father's theory of child-rearing: he brought up his sons and daughters to be absolutely perfect. To this end his children were, at one time or another, given professional instructions in: apologetics, art, ballroom dancing, banjo, bird-watching, building boats in bottles, calligraphy, canoeing, carpentry, cooking, driving trotting horses, French, folk-dancing, golf, guitar (Hawaiian and Spanish), harmony, herb-gardening, horsemanship, history of architecture, ice-skating, mandolin, marimba, music appreciation, organ, painting, piano, playing popular music, rumba, sailing, skiing, singing, Spanish, speech, stenography, swimming, tap-dancing, tennis, typing, and woodcarving.[17]

Until his children reached age thirteen, Will often hired private tutors for them rather than send them to local schools. From 1929 until 1933, when, seeking to raise money in France to finance his oil holdings, Will moved his family to Paris, he set up a school in the Buckleys' four-story house there. He installed a French tutor on the fourth floor, a Latin teacher on the third, an English teacher on the second, and a music teacher on the first, and the children would troop up and down the stairs of the house on the hour. When the family returned to America, Will organized his own school at Great Elm, with two full-time teachers, tests, grades, class hours, and requirements for graduation. Besides the Buckley children, several neighborhood children also attended the school.

What education did not take place in the classroom took place at the dining table, which Will presided over when he came home from New York City on the weekends. He used the dinner hour not only to quiz his children about their work at school, but to acquaint them with his political views on the European payment of war debts or the Spanish Civil War. William Coley, who, as a friend of Jim Buckley, sometimes came to dinner at Great Elm, recalled the scene:

> At table, their father made them defend their intellectual and political positions. He would catechize them, so to speak, on the various things they had learned. The dinner table was his place for checking them out, a place where he could keep in touch with them and where, if someone had something bright to say, it could be offered

up for the family—and perhaps the guests—to pick apart. You had
to be on your mettle.

Will's dinner-table examinations encouraged a certain kind of performing intelligence among his children. They succeeded or failed not
simply by saying the right thing, but by saying it well—with wit and
with style. "Exhibitionism rather than intimacy was the way you
came to the attention of the father," Coley commented.

Within this setting, Will's children grew up with a strong sense of
being different from and resented by other people. In Sharon, they
saw themselves slighted for being Irish, Catholic, and southern. In
France, and in England, where Will took them to live briefly, they
were looked down upon as Americans. Even when Will bought a
winter house in Camden, South Carolina, in 1939, his children were
still not spared. "In the North, we were the southern Catholics and
the New Rich," Reid Buckley explained. "In the South, we were
Yankees. Our experience was always that we had to hold together
ourselves."

The Buckley children developed a defensive clannishness. "I remember they had a very strong family feeling," Adelaide Emory, a
friend of Jane Buckley Smith, said. "There would be squabbles
among themselves, but if an outsider entered in, then everything
turned against the outsider." Reid's friend Peter Coley recalled their
boosterism. "They were self-promotional. They were always speaking in extravagant terms of the feats of each other."

They often expressed their identification with their father and their
dissatisfaction with the world around them through pranks. One
neighbor, Robert Lewis Taylor, remembered them as "outright hel-
lions." [18] Some of their pranks were Halloween tricks, but others had
a thinly veiled social content. For instance, one Thanksgiving evening
the children sneaked into the Sharon Public Library and turned all the
titles upside down. They would also jumble the letters on the sign
outside Sharon's Congregational church announcing that week's
sermon.

Other pranks reflected their father's religious intolerance. When Bill
was nine, his older brothers and sisters burned a cross on the lawn of
a Jewish resort near Salisbury. "I unquestioningly would have gone
along if I had been permitted," Bill acknowledged. His brothers and
sisters also sent the town's Protestant ministers to the top of a nearby
mountain to visit what they thought was a dying man—only to discover that the man was in perfect health.

The most notorious Buckley prank took place on a weekend in May 1944, when Jane and Priscilla Buckley came down from Smith College with two friends who wanted to be a part of one of the "mad escapades" for which the Buckley children were famous. On Saturday night, the four of them and Patricia Buckley sneaked into the Reverend Mr. Cotter's Episcopal church. (Cotter had led the opposition to isolationism in Sharon.) They smeared honey onto his chair and inserted risqué cartoons into his Bible. When Cotter discovered the prank the next day, he called in the state troopers, who were led by rumor to Great Elm. The Buckley girls pleaded guilty in court and were each fined $100. "The incident," as the family came to refer to it, caused Will to send his daughters to secretarial school that summer as a punishment.

As they became older, the children became politically combative, invariably on behalf of their father's convictions. They saw a responsibility to spread light among the benighted, even if it meant an unpleasant battle in which they found themselves isolated from the rest of Sharon and Lakeville. "Each one of us seemed to get involved, maybe because Father was always involved," Patricia Buckley Bozell recalled. "We couldn't keep out of [political] fights. There was a right and a wrong."

In the summer of 1940, they became embroiled in the debate over whether the U.S. should aid Britain against Nazi Germany. Most of the Sharon-Lakeville area, with its ties to England, was strongly in favor of aid. In September 1940, a local branch of the Committee to Defend America by Aiding the Allies organized a town-hall meeting in Sharon to support Roosevelt's decision to lease destroyers to Britain. The prior summer, the Buckley children had begun their own local newspaper, *The Spectator,* to spread their father's opposition to intervention in the European war. *The Spectator* became the local voice of America First, the organization led by Charles Lindbergh and the *Chicago Tribune*'s Robert McCormick that opposed American intervention in the European war. On the eve of the meeting, *The Spectator* came out with an unsigned "open letter," written by Will, accusing the meeting's organizers of trying to "high pressure this country into war."

Afterwards, the *Lakeville Journal* printed the open letter under Will's signature along with responses from the townspeople. Some of these responses contained barely veiled references to Will's Irish Catholicism. "Those of us who claim Anglo-Saxon lineage, and who inherit the English tongue, find it very hard to close our eyes and ears to England," Theodore Sedgewick wrote. John Buckley replied on behalf of his father. "My father, with a few others, is an exception to the average person in that, although he despises Hitler, the prevalent fear of him has not affected him to the extent that he can no longer think straight." [19]

The children themselves carried their father's battle into the Lakeville Country Club. At the weekly dances, the Buckley children would defend their father's isolationism against all comers. "Instead of everyone dancing to Frank Sinatra records," Patricia Buckley Bozell remembered, "you'd find us in every corner surrounded by controversy because we were the only conservatives and America Firsters."

All the Buckley children became eloquent defenders of their father's unpopular views, but none was so outspoken as Bill. Bill became his father's foremost disciple and the most militantly political of the Buckley children. He was quick to challenge the opinions of other children, often with unpleasant consequences. "Bill paid the least attention to being liked, and the most to being the ideologue of the group," Peter Coley said.

And, while all the Buckley children dutifully followed the course of study their father set out for them, Bill alone succeeded at mastering each part of the curriculum. He became a proficient pianist. He learned to speak in public. And he quickly became the most outspoken proponent of his father's conservative views. "He was always molding us," Jane Buckley Smith, one of Bill's older sisters, said, "but with Bill it took. Of all the children, he was the one who took most advantage of the opportunities [father] gave us."

CHAPTER 2

The Young Mahster

For five years, Will Buckley had resisted Aloise's entreaties to name a son after himself. He was worried that by doing so he would be favoring one of his children over the others; and he also feared the precedent of his own older brother John, who had been named after his father and who was killed in a Texas saloon. But when the sixth child was a boy, Will gave in. Born November 24, 1925, he was christened William Francis Buckley, Jr. According to his sister Priscilla, he was named Francis, not Frank like his father, because there was no saint named Frank.

Bill—or Billy, as his parents called him—spent much of his first years on ocean liners to and from Venezuela, where the Buckleys lived in 1926, and to and from Europe, where they lived from 1929 through 1933. Bill's home was Sharon, but until he was eight, he hardly lived there. His world was not defined geographically, but by the self-enclosed realm of his family.

In these first years, Bill's most immediate contacts were with his mother, his younger sister Patricia, and his Mexican *nana*, whom he called Pupita. They lent a feminine cast to his life. In the early portraits that his parents commissioned, Bill could be mistaken for a

35

pretty little girl. In one portrait, painted when he was three, he is
dressed in a pale-blue-and-white open-necked blouse; and his brown
hair, parted in the middle, frames his forehead and blue eyes in wavy
bangs. In another portrait, done when he was five, he is unmistakably
a little boy, but he stands in a field holding a flower rather than a
baseball bat.

He loved music and books, and he liked to ride horses and to sail,
but he had no interest whatsoever in team sports like baseball and
football or in his brother John's passions, fishing and hunting. When
he came back to Sharon in 1933, the children in the town regarded
him as a "mama's boy." "A lot of us thought he was a little bit
effeminate," William Coley said. "He went around mainly with his
sisters, and the others didn't. He wasn't very active in sports. He
didn't do anything physical that we could see."

From these early years, he acquired his mother's religious faith. He
was more demonstrative about his Catholicism than his older brothers
and sisters. Like his mother, he came to have a very personal relationship with God, to whom he communicated in prayer and to whom he
credited his personal successes. When the Buckleys toured Europe,
little Bill would sometimes go off by himself to pray in a cathedral.
Later, when he went away to school, he would ask his mother to pray
to God that he succeed in his exams. When he was sixteen, he wrote
her, "Probably the greatest contribution you have given me is your
faith. I can now rely on God in almost any matter."[1]

He displayed a warmth and protectiveness toward the women in his
life, defending them against their natural adversaries—Patricia against
her older brothers when they tried to push her into the swimming pool
at Great Elm and his Pupita against the other Mexican nurse, with
whom she was constantly quarreling. Patricia recalled how Bill fretted
over his *nana:*

> We shared our Mexican *nana* and as little children I took her for
> granted. She was very shy, almost illiterate, and she must have been
> desperately lonely. Bill would do everything in the world for her.
> He would make sure that things were right. When she went on her
> few vacations, he would always make sure that everything was
> right. He would go into New York with her on the train, take her to
> the ship.

I

But as Bill reached school age, his life became centered on winning
the approval of his father. One act perfectly symbolized the change.

When Bill was five, he announced to his family that he would henceforth be called William Frank rather than William Francis Buckley,
Jr. He told them that he thought Francis was a "sissy" name; and he
wanted to have exactly the same name as his father. He began to
mimic his father's gestures and attitudes. Even though he was just "a
little thing with a high falsetto voice," Patricia recalled, he "pontifi-
cated" just like his father, and spoke with the same "edge of sarcasm" toward opinions that did not conform to his own. Like his
father, "he would brook no opinion that was not his own."

Toward his older brothers and sisters and toward other children,
Bill became ferociously competitive and often arrogant—as if they
were all rivals for his father's favor. His older brothers and sisters
found him somewhat obnoxious. "He was cocky, brash, bright, and
witty. These were not endearing qualities if you felt you were not as
bright as he," his older sister Jane recalled.

His attempt to win his father's favor took this form partly because
he was the sixth child and third boy. "Bill was number six in a large
family of very bright and very active kids, and if anyone was going to
pay attention to number six, he had to be obstructive," Priscilla Buckley said. "It was part of being a younger sibling that he spent a great
deal of time scrambling for the attention of his parents."

Within the Buckley family, even the competition among the brothers and sisters was institutionalized. When Bill was growing up, the
children were divided into two groups, with Aloise, John, Priscilla,
and Jim in the first, Jane, Bill, Patricia, and Reid in the second. The
groups were initially segregated during meals—the children in the top
group ate with their governesses and parents at the main table while
the younger children ate with their *nanas* and spoke Spanish at a
separate table. The top group tended to exclude the lower group from
its activities, and when forced to mingle with their other brothers and
sisters, demanded proper deference from them. The younger siblings
were constantly in rebellion. "The upper four, we thought, considered
themselves the *crème de la crème,* and they considered us the up-
starts," Reid recalled. "So we had to fight to be heard. We were all
brought up intellectually battling each other. We would get into fero-
cious arguments."

Bill was most resentful of this arrangement, and spent much of his
youth defying his older brothers and sisters, particularly his brother
John. "He thought he was quite as good as they were," Patricia
recalled. "Whenever John tried to act big brother, Bill would not
stand for it." John confirmed this description. He recalled Bill as
having been "totally and absolutely stubborn. He had simply no re-

spect for me as an older brother." Aloise, mocking her younger brother's imperiousness, dubbed him "the young mahster." [2]

Bill could turn the most minor incident into a test of superiority. A typical battle took place, John recalled, one Sunday night in Sharon when John was thirteen and Bill eight. On Sundays, the cooks and maids would take the day off; Will Buckley would cook Mexican food for his family; and the children would take turns cleaning up. That night John and Bill were assigned to do the dishes, and there was an uneven number of dishes, so John told Bill that since he was the youngest, he would have to wash the odd dish. Bill refused, and the brothers argued heatedly for half an hour, until John picked up the dish in disgust and started washing it.

Other disputes were of more consequence. In the summer of 1939, when the older children started *The Spectator,* they excluded Bill and Patricia, who demanded to be put on the staff. When Aloise and John, the editors, told them they could make coffee, they stomped out. Will Buckley finally had to make peace by proposing that if Bill and Patricia learned how to touch-type, they should be allowed to work on the paper. When they mastered the typewriter in two weeks, Aloise and John were forced to let them take part. Bill did proofreading, but when he took the paper to the post office, he announced to the postmaster that he was the managing editor.

Patricia saw how much even a stray criticism from his older brothers and sisters or parents could wound him. During these years, she saw Bill creating a "wall" that hid his deepest feelings from the outside world—even from his other brothers and sisters. "I think he had to build up a wall to protect himself," Patricia said. "Bill was always so sensitive as a child to criticism. He would never show it on the outside and he would come out fighting, but he would be raw, and at night he'd say something. He'd show you that he'd been cut to the quick."

Toward other children, whom Bill thought of not merely as rivals but as contemptible aliens, he displayed even greater arrogance and competitiveness. Jim's friend William Coley described Bill as being obsessed with besting others. "I found him very easy to dislike," Coley said. "He was extremely competitive. He seemed to most of us to have to win everything. And most of what he said to people was designed to put the people down and to insure his own sense of self-importance."

Stories of Bill putting down other children were legion. Once his sister Jane, who was a year and a half older than he, had invited a guest to dinner. Bill, who was not yet a teen-ager, arrived late for dinner and after briefly listening to the guest's opinions on world affairs, proclaimed, "Look here, you are entirely too young to have such positive convictions, and besides I am going to tell you something that will surprise you—you are mistaken in every statement that you have made."[3]

Other children both feared and disliked him. According to William and Peter Coley, Bill as a youth did not have any close friends in Sharon outside his family. Even his brother Jim's sponsorship failed to win him a place in the Black Widow Spider Club, the local boys' club.

"Bill was seen as a Little Lord Fauntleroy type. He wasn't one of the fellows," Peter Coley recalled. But unlike the typical boy whom others think is a "sissy," he was feared and disliked rather than pitied. One of the boys from Sharon recalled, "Somehow he didn't belong with us kids in the hayloft of the neighborhood barn where our club met. But he wasn't the kind of little spoiled brat with a nanny that you wanted to beat up. He had a tongue and a wit that could cut, even then, and we just wanted to walk away from it."[4]

But while Bill failed to make friends as a boy, he succeeded in winning his father's favor above his brothers and sisters. Will was amused by little Billy's displays of hauteur, but what he valued above all were his son's intellectual abilities.

Will's testing ground was the dinner table, and even when his older brothers and sisters were present, Bill was often the clear winner among the children: the first to get the right answer, the first to fire back a witty riposte. By the time he was a teen-ager, Bill was dominating the dinner-table discussion, displaying the kind of performing intellect that his father loved. "At dinner, their father would feed the issues," William Coley recalled. "A lot of the feeding went to Bill."

Empowered by an inexhaustible energy and driven by an insatiable curiosity, Bill succeeded at everything he tried. Of all the children, he and his younger brother, Reid, became the most accomplished linguists. Bill was constantly introducing new words into his vocabulary, sometimes with results that amused his older brothers and sisters. Even as a child he was capable of a "bon mot" that his father could later quote to his friends. Bill and Patricia were the only children to excel musically. When he was thirteen, Bill even thought of becoming a concert pianist and conductor. And while Bill was by no means an athlete, he won prizes at horse shows for his riding and became an accomplished sailor.

Bill followed his father's education injunctions to the letter, even to the point of a certain absurdity. In 1938, when Will Buckley sent his younger children to private Catholic schools in England during Aloise's last pregnancy, he told them that he was sending them abroad to cure them of mumbling. Bill took his praise of English speech patterns so seriously that when he returned to Sharon, he had what seemed like a pronounced English accent. "Everyone was flabbergasted when he came home with an accent," Adelaide Emory said.*

"Bill became the apple of his father's eye," Jane Buckley Smith remarked. Reid Buckley concurred:

> Father had a very special love of Bill. He had a tremendous respect for Bill's innate mental faculties and Bill's moral control over himself. Bill disciplined himself from the earliest age. He disciplined himself to learn the piano. He disciplined himself to do his schoolwork. Father loved us all, he respected us for our various talents, but Bill combined the intellectual brilliance with the moral control.

Bill's success at winning his father's favor was undoubtedly the basis for the self-confidence that he would display for the remainder of his life. It gave him an ability to endure harsh and even reckless criticism without accepting the terms and a willingness to take political, intellectual, and financial risks. But his success would also reinforce a sense of superiority over his brothers and sisters and over other boys his age that would make it hard for him to make friends in his early school years.

II

The Buckley children were raised to be their own best friends and enemies. They were also raised to think of themselves as different from and superior to other children. They accepted no standard of judgment other than that of their father. One could say that they had no respect for authority outside of God and their father. When they ventured out into the world—at age thirteen or fourteen—they were like acolytes from a monastery going out amidst the infidels.

Reid Buckley described the spirit in which his father sent his children to boarding schools and colleges. "He felt he could throw us to

---

* Bill himself attributed his accent to his learning English at an English school in 1933, when his parents lived in London for a year, while Garry Wills attributes Bill's accent to the influence of one of his teachers at Yale, Willmoore Kendall, but Emory's memory of the change is confirmed by Jane Buckley Smith.

the wolves and our faith would not be shattered in any dimension, religious or political. He felt it was good for us. We had an obligation to bring America back to herself."

The first time Bill went away to school was when his father packed him, Jane, Reid, and Patricia on a boat to England in 1938, when Aloise was pregnant with Carol. He was enrolled at an exclusive private school, St. John's Beaumont, which was the upper-class Catholic version of the English "public" school.

Bill entered St. John's on the same day that British Prime Minister Neville Chamberlain met with Hitler in Munich. As fear of war swept Britain, Bill carried on his father's isolationist crusade. He draped an American flag across his bed and once, while the rest of the boys were at afternoon athletics, lowered the British flag that flew over the school and replaced it by a small American flag. He also made a point of never saying "sir" more than once in a conversation with one of the masters.[5]

The most important impact of St. John's was on his already strongly held Catholic belief. Bill was aware that his mother's life was threatened by her pregnancy and prayed fervently during his time in England. Patricia, who saw her brother sometimes on weekends, said, "Bill would kneel during Mass every day. It was a very difficult thing to do because Masses were long, and the benches in those days didn't have those nice soft rubber things. It was just one of the things as a Catholic that you did if you really wanted something."

The fear of his mother's death as well as his own intellectual awakening probably made him more receptive to his Jesuit instructors. For the first time, he thought about theology, and the impression was lasting. "When you're thirteen, certain things begin to become curious," Bill said later. "One begins to sense that there are depths in a position that one tended to accept rather two dimensionally. That happened to me at St. John's."

III

Will pulled his children out of English schools in the spring of 1939 to tour Italy, then under Fascist rule. Bill and his family returned to Sharon that summer, and he spent the next year being tutored at Great Elm. In September 1940, he followed his brothers John and Jim to Millbrook, a small Protestant preparatory school fifteen miles across the New York state line from Sharon. Will chose the little-known Millbrook over the more socially prestigious Hotchkiss, located in neighboring Lakeville, primarily because Millbrook's headmaster,

Edward Pulling, allowed Will's sons to come home on weekends.
There is no indication that Will even considered sending his children
to Canterbury, the exclusive Catholic boarding school in nearby New
Milford.

Pulling, who had been born in England but educated at Princeton,
had taught at Groton and Avon Old Farms before founding Millbrook
in 1931. In Millbrook, he combined the educational experimentalism
of Avon, a school influenced by John Dewey's view that education
and practical experience should go hand in hand, with the austerity
and moral rectitude of Groton. Students at Millbrook not only conju-
gated Latin verbs but studied biology in the school's small zoo. They
were also expected to do "community service," which ranged from
waiting on tables to picking apples.

When the Buckleys began coming to Millbrook, there were only a
few scattered buildings set on rolling hills. Chapel services were held
in Pulling's home, and the students themselves slept in partitioned
cubicles. Most of the sixty students were drawn from Pulling's and
his wife's personal contacts. They were a mixed lot, some bright and
ambitious, but others were reclamation projects that would not have
been accepted at Hotchkiss or Groton. The Buckleys—and Bill in
particular—stood out in such a setting.[6]

Bill excelled academically at Millbrook. He was so far ahead of his
classmates in English, languages, and music that Pulling allowed him
to skip a year. He was the first student to whom Pulling awarded an
"A" in English; and he founded the school yearbook and shone in
debate. But while Pulling and the music teacher, Nathaniel Abbott,
were fond of Bill, other teachers and students found him arrogant and
difficult.

He displayed little deference toward teachers whose opinions he
disagreed with. He defiantly championed America First even though
Pulling, a British World War I veteran, and the other teachers and
students strongly favored intervention.* And at a Protestant school,
he noisily proclaimed his Catholicism. Bill recalled later, "I don't
deny that I have a tendency to be attracted to combatant positions, so
that to the extent other people were Protestant, I became sort of
obnoxiously Catholic."

His classmates remember him as having been "haughty" and

---

* Buckley claimed that one other student, Philip Jessup, advocated America First. Jessup
denied this in an interview, but the fact that Jessup's father was a prominent America
First supporter suggests that Buckley's memory may have been more accurate. Buckley
and Jessup remained on friendly terms after Millbrook until Buckley attacked Jessup's
father in *McCarthy and His Enemies*.

"aloof." Classmate Philip Jessup remembers him as having been a "loner" who "wasn't anybody's close buddy." His brother Reid, who followed Bill to Millbrook, recalls his having been unhappy there. "He formed some close friendships, but was not generally popular, mostly because of politics," Reid said. "He was very outspoken about it, and to his masters he was very obnoxious. Nobody likes to be talked politics to by a fifteen-year-old." Nathaniel Abbott thinks that at one point Bill contemplated leaving Millbrook.

Even his father seems to have worried about Bill's attitude toward other students and teachers. When Bill was a sophomore, his father wrote him several letters expressing concern about his "attitude." While the context of Will Buckley's remarks has been lost, their thrust is clear from this letter.

My dear Billy,
    In thinking over my letter to you it may have appeared very critical and I hope you did not take it that way. Your mother and I like very much your attitude of having strong convictions and of not being too bashful to express them. What I meant was that you would have to learn to be more moderate in the expression of your views and try to express them in a way that would give as little offense as possible to your friends.[7]

Bill did make one important friend at Millbrook. Alistair Horne, a tall, thin, brown-haired boy whose father had sent him to Millbrook as the war began in England. With a dry wit and interest in history, Horne was one of Bill's few peers at Millbrook. They shared a distaste for organized athletics and an unwillingness, in Horne's words, "to suffer fools gladly." But Horne was strongly in favor of America joining the war on the side of Britain, and during his first year at Millbrook, he was frequently at odds with Bill. According to Horne, they were "outrightly hostile to each other."

After the Japanese attack against Pearl Harbor and the American declaration of war against the Axis powers, Will and his children tacitly accepted the necessity of war, although they continued to reject the claim that America was fighting for democracy in Europe. While Bill still quarreled with Horne about the Soviet Union and the Spanish Civil War, the main point of contention between them was somewhat removed, so they could begin to see what they had in common. Horne became Bill's first close friend outside his family. And with Horne, Bill showed a side of himself that only his sister Patricia and brother Reid had known. Horne later said about their friendship, "I don't think I had one single friendship that I could count an affectionate relationship until I met Bill. The outstanding thing about Bill, as I remember him at age sixteen or seventeen, was an unashamed ability to show affection and to *care* about his friends."

IV

At Millbrook, Bill became a more skillful pianist and debater and probably improved his writing skills, but none of the teachers appear to have had an impact on how he thought about the world. He did, however, discover a writer who became one of the most important influences on his thinking.

In his last year at Millbrook, he began to read, at his father's urging, the writings of Albert Jay Nock. Nock's *Memoirs of a Superfluous Man,* which came out in Bill's senior year, became his favorite book, and one from which he drew quotations for the rest of his life.

Nock, born in 1870, was a man of Will Buckley's generation, and, like him, had had two distinct lives. After nearly twenty years as an Episcopalian minister, Nock left the clergy and his family to become a professional writer and editor. In the 1910s and early 1920s, as a contributor to *The Nation* and as the editor of his own short-lived magazine, *The Freeman,* Nock was a left-wing anarchist and bohemian: a champion of free love, an opponent of American entry into World War I, a defender of the Russian Revolution, a critic of commercialism and materialism, but above all, an enemy of authority, whatever form it took. Nock remained an enemy of authority, but during the twenties, he became disillusioned with the ordinary American. Where he had previously believed that the state held in thrall "that possible Socrates in each man's breast," he came to believe that the masses were "structurally immature."[8] Influenced by Spanish philosopher Ortega y Gasset's *The Revolt of the Masses,* Nock now argued that the mass-man held the state in thrall and that only by abolishing state power would the civilized, enlightened few be able to exert their influence over the many.

Borrowing from the Book of Isaiah and from Matthew Arnold, Nock described the enlightened few as part of a "Remnant." In a 1933 essay in *The Atlantic,* Nock distinguished between the "mass-man . . . who has neither the force of intellect to apprehend the principles issuing in what we know as the humane life, nor the force of character to adhere to those principles steadily and strictly as laws of conduct" and "the Remnant . . . who by force of intellect are able to apprehend these principles, and by force of character are able, at least measurably, to cleave to them."[9]

In the last years of his life, having become virulently anti-Semitic—a position that undoubtedly informed his opposition to American participation in World War II—and unable to write for *The Atlantic* and other respectable publications, Nock turned toward Merwin K. Hart's National Economic Council for support. But in his mock autobiography, *Memoirs of a Superfluous Man,* published only two years before his death in 1945, Nock, like Henry Adams, was able to gather together his literary and political ingenuity for a brilliant summation.

Nock's *Memoirs* contained little of Nock's life and much of what it did contain was false. Rather, it was a rambling, spirited Rabelaisian polemic against everything Nock despised about the modern world: democracy ("an ochlocracy of mass-men led by a sagacious knave"); politics ("something remote, disreputable, and infamous, like slave trading or brothel-keeping"); the modern states ("Communism, the New Deal, Fascism, Naziism, are merely so many trade-names for collectivist Statism, like the trade-names for toothpaste which are exactly the same except for the flavoring"); marriage ("a quasi-industrial partnership, a business-enterprise"); organized Christianity ("a pattern set not by Jesus, but by Gresham's Law"); and the relentless pursuit of material success, which Nock called "economism." Economism, Nock wrote,

> interpreted the whole of human life in terms of the production, acquisition and distribution of wealth. . . . [It] can field a society which is rich, prosperous, powerful, even one which has a reasonably wide diffusion of material well-being. It cannot build one which is lovely, one which has savor and depth, and one which wields the irresistible power of attraction that loveliness wields.

Nock's ability to charm and influence Will Buckley—Will befriended Nock and periodically invited him to lunch at Great Elm—is interesting in itself. Nock was a libertine and an agnostic who had little patience with organized religion. But both Will and Bill overlooked Nock's views of the Catholic Church and marriage for the rebellious anti-authoritarianism and anti-egalitarianism that were at the core of Nock's teachings. It was here that Nock and the Buckleys found common ground.

Nock also provided Will and his son with an understanding of how they fit into the modern world. Eccentric, individualistic, even superfluous, they were part of Nock's "Remnant," and while they might not be able to sway the mass of men in their generation, they had important work to do for future generations. It was this conviction that Bill and the other Buckley children took with them when they left Great Elm to go to school and college.*

Nock's view of society and the state and of democracy and politics would run through Bill's politics over the next four decades. He would gain other influences and adopt contrary and competing views, but he would never entirely abandon Nock's jaundiced view of democratic America.

V

Bill graduated from Millbrook in June 1943. His brother John had joined the Army and his brother Jim the Navy after they had graduated from Yale. Bill, who was seventeen, was not subject to the draft until he was eighteen. That summer, Will moved his family to Mexico City so that Bill could take Spanish lessons at the University of Mexico. Bill thought that courses at the university might help him qualify for the Army's or the Navy's advanced language training programs. In November, he was drafted, but he was not inducted until July 1944 because of a sinus condition.

Bill asked to be placed in the infantry rather than the Navy because, as he told his father, "there will be more chance for me to land a desk job of some sort." [10] He was sent to basic training at Camp Wheeler, just outside Macon, Georgia. At the same time, he applied to both the Army and Navy language schools and to Officer Candidate School.

Bill had a difficult time at Camp Wheeler. Only eighteen, he was tall but not muscular. He was unprepared not only for the discipline and physical regimen of basic training but for the rough egalitarianism of barrack life. He wrote his mother, "My chief complaint is that intelligence is neither recognized nor appreciated." He felt "a natural tendency toward recalcitrance," he wrote, "when I am bossed around by a person of no education." He also found it difficult to share his quarters with men of inferior manners and intelligence, but he was

---

* Nock and his *Memoirs of a Superfluous Man* also had an enormous impact on two other men who would become important conservatives in the 1950s. Russell Kirk, the author later of *The Conservative Mind,* read Nock's *Memoirs* while stationed during World War II at the Great Salt Lake Desert and began a correspondence with him. Sociologist Robert Nisbet "practically memorized" Nock's *Memoirs* while he was in the South Pacific in World War II. See George H. Nash, *The Conservative Intellectual Movement in America,* 15.

learning how to maintain a veneer of friendship. In the letter, he cited lessons from Camden's priest, Father Burke:

> By far my greatest achievement . . . has been my success in social relations. I follow every day a formula outlined to me by Father Burke. Be quiet, kindhearted, generous, interested in other people's problems, helpful and *inconspicuous*. It works like a charm. There are sixty men in the two floors of my barracks and with a solitary exception, I am friendly with all of them and could make my relations with them as warm as I should wish.

But Bill explained to his mother that he was spared the need to do so. "I have not had to associate with any one of them in my free time because I am the close friend of two other intelligent boys from another platoon." [11]

After several weeks at Wheeler, Bill was summoned to camp headquarters because he had omitted his mother's maiden name from his OCS application. When the company clerk handed him the application to complete, he failed to remove the recommendation sheet that had been filled out by the company commander. Bill saw that while his captain recommended Bill for OCS, he had given him a "very good" rather than an "excellent" in both efficiency and character. Bill wrote his father: "I don't mind his not giving me the top rating for efficiency as an infantry soldier because I am not excellent as an infantry soldier. . . . But I was and am furious about the fact that he did not rate me as excellent in character." [12]

The next week, Bill had his interview for OCS, and, as he told his father, he fully redeemed himself before a colonel who, he discovered, shared his own values and perceptions. When the colonel asked him what he thought of his noncommissioned officers, Bill replied:

> Well sir, I think some of them are fine men, and I think others are crude, coarse, vulgar and highly objectionable in some respects. However, providing they teach me what I need to know to make a good soldier, I can tolerate them, because I realize that the Army is not a sociable organization, and that personal likes and dislikes don't come into the picture. [13]

In January 1945, he joined two hundred other officer candidates for the eighteen-week officer training course at Fort Benning in Georgia. He was extremely nervous about OCS. On the eve of going to Fort Benning, he had had a terrible attack of pimples that almost led to his being disqualified in the first medical examination. And as a boy of southern parents who had spent part of each winter in the South, he had trouble adjusting to the fact that blacks and whites ate in the same mess hall and sometimes slept in the same rooms.

Bill was part of a platoon of fifty, only half of whom were expected to graduate. As at Wheeler, Bill found the physical regimen demanding. "This is one of the most grueling courses man's sadistic ingenuity has ever constructed," he wrote his mother. But as at Wheeler, what Bill found more difficult was not the physical but the social aspect of camp life. Although he did make two friends, Bill was not generally popular among the men in his platoon, many of whom were older than he. One of his friends, Charles Ault, thought the word that best described him was "effete."

Where he encountered most difficulty, however, was with his commanding officers, because he was unwilling to act suitably deferential.* According to Ault, the officers came to see Bill as a "smart-ass." He was also typically outspoken in his political opinions. "He was very vocal about his feelings about the Democrats in general and Roosevelt in particular," Ault recalled. "He would express those feelings very vociferously." These political views were also "not well received by the commanding authorities."

Bill's commanding officers didn't think that he took his training as seriously as the other men, some of whom had already served in combat. Once, when leading a group of men in a training exercise, Bill stopped in order to pick a flower, suspending maneuvers for ten seconds and costing his group a victory in the competition.

But Bill was brought up short in the fourth week of OCS. Presiding as duty officer one night, he looked in the drawer of a desk for a pencil. Inside were the lieutenant's weekly ratings of the platoon, on the basis of which, officer candidates were passed on or failed out of Officer Candidate School. To Bill's dismay, he was fiftieth out of fifty. "I was absolutely heart-struck. I couldn't stand the thought of failing, and so I developed a very inquisitive concern for what it was that the guy who made these ratings had against me," he said later.

Lieutenant John Lawrence told Bill that his "definite air of superiority which alienated a tremendous number of people might easily be a barrier between [himself] and success as a commissioned officer." [14] Bill could not easily dismiss the opinion of Lawrence, who had gone

---

* In his *Memoirs,* Nock wrote that when he saw a file of soldiers, he wondered "why the sound of a drum does not incite them to shoot their officers, throw away their rifles, go home, and go to work."

to Yale and was engaged to a woman who had gone to Smith with Bill's sisters Priscilla and Jane. Bill seriously began to question the way that he appeared to other people. In a letter to Patricia, he confided his doubts. She recalled the letter: "Bill sensed that his attitude of superiority was not what these people were used to. And he asked me what he should do to right this in himself. I wrote back that before you ever say anything put in I think or I believe or In my opinion. So he went at that." Patricia believed that the Fort Benning experience left its mark on Bill. "I think the army experience did something to Bill," she said. "He got to understand people more."

But Bill's lieutenant continued to doubt whether he was officer material. The problem, Lawrence explained later, was that Bill "didn't exhibit much in the way of field presence. He was sort of a boarding-school type, and that really didn't work too well when you are in control of troops." Lawrence also felt that Bill didn't take his responsibilities seriously enough.

I don't think he ever came to grips with what was going on. Perhaps because of his age it didn't have much meaning, but it did to us, because during the period when we were graduating officers from Fort Benning, they were getting two weeks' leave, and then in another week or so we would hear that they had been killed in action.

At the end of the eighteen weeks, Bill was brought up before a special hearing to determine whether he should be made an officer. He spent "hours and hours" rehearsing his answers to anticipated questions. The hearing itself was an ordeal, and afterwards, according to Lawrence, Bill's commanding officers had a protracted and painful debate before deciding to pass him. "I think that riled a lot of people," Lawrence said of the decision.

Bill's remaining time in the Army was largely uneventful. For the next five months, he served as an infantry training officer at Fort Gordon in Georgia. Then, because of his knowledge of Spanish, he was sent to Fort Sam Houston in San Antonio to engage in counterintelligence acitivities. He arrived in San Antonio, however, on the day the Japanese surrendered. In the resulting confusion, he was initially assigned to teach sex hygiene to Mexican recruits.*

---

* At Fort Benning, when his platoon leader suggested that the men take condoms with them on their leaves, he had responded indignantly that *he* didn't need them.

Toward his superiors, he displayed the same lack of deference that he had at Fort Benning. Soon after his arrival, he wrote the commanding officer a letter suggesting ways in which the War Department should handle men whose discharges were being delayed.

But at Fort Sam Houston, he showed himself better able to get along with the men around him. He made a close friend of his immediate commanding officer. And he had his first serious romance—with a local San Antonio college girl, Gloria Huddelston. (The relationship dissipated after Bill went to college the next year, and Huddelston eventually married a Texan.)

When Bill entered the Army, he was an obnoxious brat incapable of forming friendships except with a select few whose background, beliefs, and intelligence he approved of. When he left the Army two years later, he had learned a certain humility and had become capable of appreciating people who didn't share his background and beliefs. He explained what he had learned in the Army in a long letter to his father.

I don't know whether you were aware of this while I was in Millbrook, but I was not very popular with boys. After a good deal of self-analysis, I determined that the principal reason for this revolved around my extreme dogmatism—particularly in matters concerning politics and the Catholic Church. I could not understand another point of view; it seemed to me that anyone who was not an isolationist or a Catholic was simply stupid. Instead of keeping these sentiments to myself, I blurted them out and supported them upon the slightest provocation. I was intolerant about all kinds of things. I would not sit in on sex conversations or trivial gossip because I considered them wrong. Because I was intellectually able to support most of my arguments, my opponents would normally lose out in any discussion. The result of this was that my company was very little sought for except by a few close friends.

When I went to the Army, I learned the importance of tolerance, and the importance of a sense of proportion about all matters—even in regard to religion, morality etc. Some friends I made whom I really prized were atheistic, and even immoral. But I learned, nevertheless, that regardless of the individual's dogmas, the most important thing as far as I was concerned was the personality: would his friendship broaden your horizon or provide you with intellectual entertainment? I found that there were actually very few prerequisites to the good friend: he had to have a good sense of humor, a pleasant personality and a certain number of common interests.[15]

Bill had not abandoned his political or religious convictions, nor the sense that he had a mission to defend these beliefs in a world that was hostile to them. But in the Army, he had learned to distinguish the rules of personal friendship from those of political combat.

CHAPTER 3

A Pleasing Vanity

When Bill Buckley entered Yale in September 1946, after having been discharged from the Army, he was no longer a gangly teen-ager afflicted by pimples. At twenty, he had filled out and had regained the jaunty good looks that he had had when he was a child. His freshman class, swelled to fifteen hundred by returning veterans, was the largest in Yale's history. Bill, three other students, and Bill's piano were assigned to a suite meant for only two. But after the Army, Yale's wood-paneled rooms, with daily maid service, had to appear a luxury.

Bill's decision to attend Yale had been made for him a decade earlier by his father. Will Buckley had chosen Yale for his sons because of its educational reputation and proximity to Sharon. But Will had imparted to his sons a strongly ambivalent attitude toward Yale, which he saw as part of the liberal establishment that was corrupting America. Thus, Bill was determined to succeed at Yale at the same time as he challenged Yale.

With its imitation Gothic and Georgian ivy-covered buildings set in the midst of an old New England manufacturing town, Yale had served as a transmission belt to Wall Street and corporate boardrooms for upper-class graduates of eastern prep schools. It was more socially homogeneous than Harvard or Columbia—a Catholic chapel for students was not constructed until 1938 and there were no Jews on its faculty until 1946.

Yale was also considerably more conservative politically than other Ivy League schools. In 1948, the *Yale Daily News* found that 88 percent of the students supported Republican Thomas Dewey for President, 4 percent Democrat Harry Truman, and 4 percent Progressive Henry Wallace. The same year, the *Yale Banner,* the class yearbook, showed 50 percent of the students considered themselves Republicans, 30 percent Independents, 17 percent Democrats, and 3 percent Socialists.

But Bill and his brothers espoused a different kind of conservatism. Bill's militant Catholicism distinguished him from the average student, who tended to be Protestant and nominally Christian. He was a reactionary among mainstream Republicans whose conservatism consisted of upholding the status quo that he wanted to subvert. Like his father, Bill saw himself as a counterrevolutionary in the midst of a complacent America threatened by socialism from within and a virulent communism from without.

Bill's political differences were most pronounced with those students and professors who shared his intense preoccupation with broader political issues. The students who worked on the *Yale Daily News* and the politically active professors at the Law School tended to be the most liberal people on campus. Thus, even at Yale, Buckley and his brothers could imagine themselves to be politically isolated. "It took us just about five minutes at the Yale campus," Reid Buckley, who entered Yale in 1948, said, "to realize that what the establishment there stood for was radically opposed to what we had been brought up to think was correct."

But although Bill realized from the beginning that he was on enemy ground, he had learned in the Army not to let religion and politics dictate the scope of his friendships and associations. He was a more open and friendly person than he had been at Millbrook. Classmate Frank Harman, who met Bill their second day at Yale, as they sat together in a class in classical civilization, was impressed. "He had very strong views, but he was charming and gregarious," Harman said.

I

From the moment he arrived at Yale, Bill's one overriding ambition was to be the chairman of the *Yale Daily News*. He wrote his father, "I have never run across anything I wanted so much in all my life as the chairmanship of the *News*."[1] His ambition was fueled in part by the success of his popular brother Jim, who had been vice-chairman of the *Yale Daily News* and a member of Skull and Bones, the most prestigious of the secret senior honor societies. But it also reflected his view of what he could accomplish at Yale. Being chairman was not only the surest token of success at Yale—in the absence of a student government, the *Yale Daily News* chairman was the *de facto* class leader—it also would provide him with a platform from which to make his views known.

Students had to try out for the *Yale Daily News* in the fall of their freshman year. There was an eight-week "heeling period" that William Ottley, another freshman, compared to "being in a Russian prison camp." Freshmen had to write stories, sell ads, fetch drinks, and sweep the floor for the senior editors. They were given points for how many stories they wrote (with extra credit for stories they originated) and for how many ads they sold. At the end of eight weeks, about ten of the freshmen were chosen from more than sixty who initially tried out.

Buckley quickly established himself as the best of the freshmen. Aided by his experience on the *Millbrook Silo* and *The Spectator,* and by his ability to touch-type and take shorthand (a skill he had acquired from tagging along when his father sentenced the Buckley girls to summer secretarial school for defacing the Reverend Mr. Cotter's church), he easily produced more stories than the other freshmen. William Carlin, another one of the heelers, found Buckley's performance "unnerving."

Buckley's only competition was Thomas Guinzburg, the tall, handsome son of the publisher of the Viking Press. Guinzburg, a Jew, had gone to Hotchkiss and then into the Marines. When the heeling period was nearly over, he and Buckley went out for a drink together. Buckley asked him what he wanted to do on the *News*. Guinzburg replied that he wanted to be the managing editor rather than the chairman because he was more interested in getting out the news than in writing editorials. "That's good," Buckley replied, "because I want to be chairman, and we'll make a terrific team."

At the end of eight weeks, Buckley finished well ahead in points, making him the odds-on choice to be chosen chairman when his classmates on the paper voted the next year. But Buckley, seeing himself surrounded by liberals, couldn't accept the fact that his selection was assured. "He was afraid he wasn't going to be elected because of the prejudice against him," his sister Patricia, then at Vassar, recalled. He was also afraid that his sense of personal superiority was alienating his classmates on the newspaper.

I will definitely stand out, by virtue of ability, industry, experience, conscientiousness, and self-confidence as the next logical chairman [he wrote his father]. But I am so terribly afraid that because of the remnants of the difficulties I have in arousing spontaneously friendly relations, I will not be elected. Were it an appointive position, I would most certainly get the office. However, as you probably well know, there is a tendency in human beings to resent obviously superior ability, a tendency, translated into terms applicable to my situation, to resent my having won the competition so overwhelmingly, to resent my being looked upon by the older members of the board as the obvious choice for chairman, a tendency to be reluctant to vote for the man who so obviously should have the job.[2]

II

Buckley tried out for the freshman debating team. He had been drawn to debating by the public contest of ideas. Debating permitted questions to be resolved, political enemies to be defeated, and audiences to be won over within the space of an afternoon or evening.

Buckley was selected along with two other freshmen, Arthur Hadley, a flamboyant former tank commander, and Brent Bozell, a tall, red-haired boy from Omaha with roughhewn Lincolnesque features who had been in the Merchant Marine during the war. Bozell and Buckley made a particularly devastating combination. Bozell was a brilliant orator, who would beat out Buckley for the Ten Eyck Award for public speaking their last two years at Yale. "He had great skill in the selection of just the right word and just the right phrase," Rollin Osterweis, the debate team coach, recalled.

Buckley's platform presence was far less satisfactory. "I remember him as a freshman as a charming, amusing sort of boy who could never stand still on the platform and who was forever raising himself up on his toes when he spoke in what I called in those days the Buckley bounce," Osterweis said. But Buckley was a "terrific infighter" who knew how to go for his opponent's jugular. Osterweis usually assigned Bozell to give the opening address and Buckley "to handle the heavy oar as far as the rebuttal was concerned." Buckley also acquired what Osterweis called a "flair for the dramatic." He could disarm an opponent during the opponent's rebuttal by pretending he was playing the violin while his opponent was speaking or by removing his handkerchief in a disdainful manner.

Buckley and Bozell's style of debate was English rather than American. While American debaters invariably relied on the rapid-fire marshaling of facts, English debaters relied far more on "sarcasm and biting humor." At some debate tournaments, judges declared their displeasure with Buckley and Bozell's style (one judge wrote on his ballot, "You'll never persuade me by your sarcasm and your denigrating references to your opponent"), but in most settings, Buckley and Bozell were highly effective.

Buckley's debating style was probably influenced by his brief experience at St. John's in England. But it also stemmed from his peculiar understanding of his situation. Seeing himself politically isolated from his audience as well as his opponents, he directed a special scorn at both. It was, by his own admission, a form of "protective covering." [3]

> My point of view was so generally disdained that it probably acquired, for that reason, a kind of stylistic pretension [Buckley later explained]. It was very important for me in those days publicly to disdain the judgment of the audience. That is, I knew they would find me wrong, but that made little difference to me given the fact that I knew I was correct. I have a feeling that affected my style on into the future.

Buckley saw debating as a means of defending his own views, and when he had to defend the liberal side of an argument, he "wasn't particularly effective," Osterweis recalled. But when Buckley and Bozell were defending a position they espoused, they were unbeatable, the best that he would see in two decades of coaching debate at Yale.

Buckley and Bozell were as different as people as they were as debaters. Buckley was far more gregarious than Bozell, who preferred discussions with one or two friends to parties. Buckley also tended to acquire his own ideas through talk and argument, while Bozell was much more prone to reading and reflection. Bozell was also more liberal politically than Buckley. His parents had been Democrats, and he was far more sympathetic to the welfare state and civil rights than Buckley was. When Buckley met him, he was president of the campus branch of the World Federalists, a left-of-center organization championing the United Nations and world government. But Bozell was one of the few students Buckley met at Yale who was both as intense and intelligent as he was. The two young men shared a hatred of communism and a passionate interest in political, moral, and religious questions.

After their freshman year, Buckley and Bozell became inseparable. Every evening, they would meet for tea at the Elizabethan Club, or for drinks at George and Harry's or the Fence Club, and on weekends Buckley took Bozell to Great Elm or to visit his sister Patricia at Vassar. When he realized Patricia was interested in Bozell, he avidly encouraged the match, even informing Bozell to Patricia's consternation that she was "deeply in love with him." The two friends spent summers together, including one summer working in Canada for one of Will Buckley's oil companies.

From their first year, they became known as a formidable political team, both in debating and in the Political Union, the campus organization in which members were grouped according to parties and debated the merits of candidates and issues. Alan Finberg, who was president of the Political Union during Buckley and Bozell's senior year, said of them, "They were extremely effective and dedicated, and [it] struck some of us as rather unusual that people of their relatively young years could be so fiercely ideological. Many of us wished that we could be as certain about anything as they were about everything."

Bozell initially appeared even more talented than Buckley. He was not only a better speaker, he was also a better student. Paul Weiss, who had both of them in class, thought that Bozell "was more intelligent, better focused and clearer." But Buckley quickly established himself as the dominant person in the relationship. Even though Bozell continued to differ politically on some points from Buckley, he abandoned his allegiance to the World Federalists and became closely indentified with Buckley's politics. Bozell, a Protestant by birth, also converted to Catholicism.* And in 1949, he married Patricia Buckley.

By the spring of his freshman year, Buckley had already established himself as a "big man on campus." And he had drawn around himself a wide circle of friends that included Guinzburg, Bozell, and Harman.

---

* Bozell later claimed that he had decided to convert to Catholicism in 1946, before he had met Buckley, but had postponed the decision because of his father's death and fear of upsetting his mother.

In contrast to his experience in Sharon, at Millbrook, and in the Army, he made friends easily at Yale; his room, in which he had a piano, became a kind of salon that his friends would visit to party and sing; and acquaintances eagerly sought weekend invitations to visit Great Elm.

At Yale, Buckley succeeded in drawing a distinction between his public, political style, which remained deeply influenced by his father's attitudes, and his personal and private manner of being. His political style was highly abrasive. He would give no quarter in debate. Law professor Thomas Emerson, who frequently debated Buckley on the *Connecticut Forum of the Air,* a radio show, said, "He was really vicious. I was no match for him at all." But Buckley had learned to temper his public arrogance with a willingness to laugh at himself. Off stage, even his political opponents found him an attractive person. William Sloane Coffin, who was in the class ahead, was invariably at odds with Buckley, but he still liked him. "He was a very arrogant guy, but there was a kind of pleasing vanity," Coffin said. "He was a *prima donna,* and he knew it, but he could be kidded about it. He wasn't a 'WASPy,' smug, arrogant type. He was just cocky arrogant, which was a lot more becoming."

Buckley's close friends at Yale recall him in terms that formerly only his sister Patricia might have used. "He was warm and generous without guile," classmate Evan Galbraith recalled. Frank Harman even came to believe that there was a trade-off between the public and the private Buckley. "He was unmellow in his debating, in his public arguing," Harman recalled. "It was as though he got rid of all his aggressions that way and what was left over, among friends, was very mellow."

Like his father, Buckley also began to help friends—or even bare acquaintances—in financial need. When a friend's mother had a nervous breakdown and could not afford the cost of hospitalization, Buckley arranged through his own father, and without his friend's knowledge, to have the bills paid. Hired along with another classmate, Theodore Pichel, to teach beginning Spanish, Buckley later insisted to Department Chairman Thomas Bergin, when it looked as if one of them would be laid off, that it should be he and not Pichel, because Pichel "needed the money and spoke better Spanish."

In private, he was tolerant of others' opinions and religious beliefs, and was free of his father's virulent anti-Semitism. Buckley not only became close friends with Tom Guinzburg, but when the Fence Club, Yale's most exclusive fraternity, rejected Guinzburg because he was Jewish, Buckley threatened not to become a member himself. Guinzburg, who was then admitted, recalled that "Bill's role was pretty forceful."

Buckley later brushed aside any explanation of why he had not followed his father's example in this regard. "In my own experience, anti-Semitism is not a communicable disease," he quipped. But he was clearly affected both by his experience in the Army and by the revelations about Nazi death camps. These revelations changed anti-Semitism from a quasi-acceptable and very typical social attitude among Gentile businessmen to a genocidal political doctrine.

Buckley's ability to reject his father's anti-Semitism while retaining the core of Will's counterrevolutionary convictions was the first clear indication that he would be able to transcend the disabilities of the Old Right.

III

Buckley might have excelled as a student at Yale, but he was not interested in scholarship or even in the play of ideas. He liked debating with his professors in class, where the response was immediate, but even during his first two and a half years at Yale, before he was consumed by the *Yale Daily News,* he never read beyond what was assigned in class. He regarded his education as an instrument—as a means of buttressing his existing convictions and strengthening his hand in public debate. When his freshman composition teacher, Richard Sewall, suggested that he take a challenging metaphysics course, Buckley replied, "I have God and my father. That's all I need."

But during his sophomore year, Buckley discovered a professor whom he could learn from. In September 1947, Buckley enrolled in a demanding political science seminar taught by Willmoore Kendall, who had come that fall to Yale from the Central Intelligence Agency. Kendall was a tall, blue-eyed Oklahoman who parted his hair down the middle like the actor James Cagney and spoke alternatively with a prairie drawl and an Oxford inflection. He was one of the most brilliant political scientists of his day and a deeply committed teacher who conducted his small seminars according to the Socratic method. In his class, Kendall encouraged the kind of spirited argument with which Buckley was familiar from his childhood. "It was no holds barred. Everybody insulted everybody. But you didn't take your arguments out of the classroom," recalled Edward "Ned" Chilton, who took Kendall's seminar with Buckley.

In his relationships with his colleagues and in political debate on campus, Kendall displayed both an arrogance and a rebelliousness that was familiar to Buckley. Writer Dwight Macdonald once described Kendall as a "wild Yale don of extreme, eccentric and very abstract views who can get a discussion into the shouting stage faster than anybody I have ever known."[4]

Buckley became a political disciple and a close friend of Kendall, learning from him to read political theory with rigor and with the same single-minded attention to the text that the literary New Critics like Yale's Cleanth Brooks championed. And Buckley also became influenced by Kendall's peculiar political views, which ran decidedly counter to those of the other Yale political scientists.

Like other men who would later influence Buckley, Kendall was a refugee from the far Left. The son of a blind itinerant preacher from rural Oklahoma, Kendall had been a child prodigy who graduated from college at eighteen. In 1932, he had gone to Oxford as a Rhodes Scholar, where he studied with political philosopher R. G. Collingwood and became a follower of Leon Trotsky, the Soviet Socialist exile who had broken with Soviet Premier Joseph Stalin. Kendall became a bitter foe of Soviet Communism when he went to Spain in 1935 to cover the Spanish Republic for United Press and saw the Communists attempting to destroy other left-wing parties.[5]

When Kendall returned to the U.S. to finish his Ph.D. at the University of Illinois, he developed a political theory called absolute majoritarianism. In his doctoral dissertation on Locke and in a series of articles for scholarly journals, Kendall argued that the rule of majority should take precedence over individual rights, including those spelled out by the American Bill of Rights. He didn't believe that the majority was always "right," but that the survival of societies depended upon the existence of a "public orthodoxy" to which the members adhered and to which the majority would brook no exceptions.

In economics and politics, Kendall was an opponent of laissez-faire philosophies. A follower of John Maynard Keynes, he didn't believe that firms, if left to compete freely, would automatically create prosperity. Nor did he believe that if ideas were simply left to compete with one another, the truth would win out. He thought societies had to protect themselves against the ideological movements like Naziism and communism, against which, history had shown, truth did not necessarily prevail.*

---

* John Stuart Mill was a repeated target of his barbs. "Start out with Mill's principles," Kendall wrote in 1946, "and you end, as Mill himself did, with the anarchistic view that there are no limits whatever upon the degree of diversity a society can stomach and still survive (wherefore we must today tolerate, for instance, anti-Semitic utterance by our neighbors, because prohibiting would infringe upon their 'rights' to freedom of speech)."

In the late thirties, Kendall's absolute majoritarianism led him to back Roosevelt in his battle with the Supreme Court. In the late forties, it inclined him to support legislation for outlawing the Communist Party, whose principles, Kendall believed, violated the public orthodoxy necessary to the country's survival.

When Buckley first met him, Kendall still described himself as "an old-fashioned majority-rule Democrat." In November 1948, he would vote for Harry Truman rather than Dewey. But Kendall shared Buckley's political intensity, and he was equally fervent in his hatred of communism. Kendall even advocated a preventive nuclear war against the Soviet Union. And like Buckley, he considered himself at the core to be a counterrevolutionary rather than a conservative.*

Buckley wrote later of Kendall, "He was a conservative all right, but invariably he gave the impression that he was being a conservative because he was surrounded by liberals; that he'd have been a revolutionist if that had been required in order to be socially disruptive." †

Kendall became a notorious character on campus, outspokenly opposed to most of his colleagues' beliefs; a heavy drinker and philanderer, from whose advances few faculty wives were safe; and an eccentric genius who attracted a devoted corps of students. Kendall also became a looming presence in his students' lives. Charles Lichenstein, who became Kendall's graduate student when Buckley was at Yale, and who later was an ambassador to the U.N. for the Reagan administration, said of him, "Willmoore had an incredibly dominating personality. He always wanted to be in command and in general he was. It was largely force of intellect."

In his classes, he encouraged his students to read political texts extremely carefully. He counseled them to allow the conclusions "to leap out of the page" at them. Buckley, who had read primarily for entertainment, learned from Kendall how to follow a written argument closely. He learned how to focus his mind on perplexing intellectual questions. "Bill learned an enormous amount from Willmoore," recalled Lichenstein. "Bill always had so much intellectual energy that he threatened to run off in too many directions simultaneously. Will-

---

* Gerhart Niemeyer recalled a conversation with Kendall that he had in the early fifties. "In Washington I was having a long discussion with Willmoore, and he said, 'Now we're coming to a revolution.' That upset me. I had looked upon him as a conservative."
† Reid Buckley made the same point about the Buckley children: "Had we not been inclined to conservative politics for reasons *qua* politics, we would have been inclined temperamentally to espouse the cause that least obtained."

moore helped him enormously to focus that energy, target that energy, to encourage a higher degree of discipline."

Kendall encouraged his best students to become his friends, and insisted that they call him Ken. Lichenstein recalled:

> With Willmoore, it was almost impossible to have one kind of a relationship. He almost always tried to draw you into his personal and private life. You became a personal friend as well as a student, and you became a disciple. He just started making incredible inroads on you. And that was one of the problems, because he kind of wanted to consume you.

Like Lichenstein and Chilton, Buckley became a disciple of Kendall. He took him to Great Elm to meet Will Buckley, who enjoyed talking with Kendall in Spanish about the Communist threat in Latin America. He deferred to Kendall in public, according to Charles Lindblom, a colleague of Kendall. "When I'd see him in Kendall's suite, he would say practically nothing. He would act very self-effacing." In class, Kendall used to needle Buckley about his views on economics. "He would kid Bill unmercifully," Ned Chilton recalled. "Bill would get this sheepish grin on his face, and Kendall would say, 'You don't know a damn thing about economics.'"

But Kendall's relationship with Buckley was more complex than Kendall's relationship with his other students. While Buckley looked up to Kendall for his theoretical brilliance, Kendall was equally drawn to Buckley. He saw in Buckley's large family and Great Elm both the family that he had lacked as a child and the communal ideal that he sought in his works. "Willmoore had a yearning for something that had not been his," Lichenstein said. "The fabulous family context, the Buckley family, all of these kids, and this wonderful, powerful man, the warm woman, the servants, the hangers-on, it was a whole community, a whole universe."

Kendall also saw Buckley as his "ticket" into class and power. "Bill was going to offer him an entrée that he had never had. Prominence, and the ability to bring power effectively to bear," Lichenstein recalled, noting that as Buckley advanced on the Yale campus, "Willmoore took inordinate satisfaction from it being recognized that he was Bill's very special mentor."

IV

From his first year at Yale, Buckley sought to make his political views known, even if doing so meant incurring the wrath of students and faculty. "Bill looked upon himself and Brent Bozell and a few conservatives as the Dutch boy with his finger in the dike. After us, the deluge," Richard Sewall recalled.

Indeed, Buckley liked being the center of controversies. Evan Galbraith said, "I think it was part of his makeup. He got wounded when people went after him, so it was not without pain, but I think he had a certain compulsion to be an outspoken public advocate for his point of view." It was as if he were reaffirming at the same time as he was challenging the basis of his father's and then his family's political alienation. "There was a certain allure to being provocative," Buckley later acknowledged.

During the first semester of Buckley's freshman year, he and Frank Harman led a fight against the establishment of a student council at Yale, which they believed would become a liberal redoubt. Then in the second semester, Buckley defiantly attacked the annual Yale Budget Drive for charity, because it allocated its surplus funds to a scholarship fund for blacks. Buckley insisted that before giving the money the Budget Drive Committee should have to win the unanimous consent of the students.

In his sophomore year, Buckley got embroiled in a broader political issue—Henry Wallace's campaign for the presidency in 1948. Wallace had been Truman's Secretary of Commerce, but Truman fired him in 1946 because Wallace publicly opposed the administration's attempt to unite America's Western allies against the Soviet Union. Wallace wanted to draw the Soviet Union into the Western capitalist orbit (and, he hoped, temper its aggression) through conciliatory economic policies. Wallace was by no means a Communist, but he became the leader of the left-wing opposition to Truman, which included the American Communist Party and its front organizations. In 1947, he formed the Progressive Citizens of America (PCA), and by that fall, he was already planning to oppose Truman for the presidency. As the campaign neared, Truman successfully drew away most of Wallace's liberal supporters, leaving him increasingly dependent upon the Communists.

The fact that Buckley became intent on discrediting Wallace reflected his own political priorities. To many Republicans, Wallace had no chance of winning in the fall, but promised to take votes from Truman. He was, in short, a godsend. It was liberal anti-Communist Democrats like Arthur Schlesinger, Jr., and Dwight Macdonald who saw Wallace as a threat. Buckley was not concerned, however, about the final vote tally, but about Wallace's connection to the Communist Party; to Buckley, that made his candidacy a paramount threat.

In October of 1947, Buckley and Frank Harman put together a special protest for Wallace's appearance in the New Haven Arena. Along with Buckley's sisters Patricia and Jane, they dressed up in leftist garb—the girls wore dark suits and no makeup and the boys dark suits, loud ties, and greased hair—and they carried signs declaring, "Let's Prove We Want Peace—Give Russia the Atom Bomb." They also planned to release a dove of peace in the arena, but were foiled when the light system went off, bathing the seating area in darkness.

That fall Buckley and Bozell toured neighboring campuses debating Wallace supporters. Then at a January 1948 forum on the Wallace campaign, Bozell charged that the PCA's actions were "much like the group I think they support, that is, the Communists." When Yale's PCA chairman, Pasquale Vecchione, charged Bozell with "smearing" his organization, Buckley got the *Yale Daily News* to sponsor a debate between the two.[6] He and Bozell spent the next month drawing together an indictment of the PCA's Communist connections, which they published under Bozell's name in the *News*.

In April 1948, Buckley and Kendall appeared on the *Connecticut Forum of the Air* to debate two Wallace supporters from Yale, whom Kendall accused of having "in fact transferred their loyalty to the Soviet Union."[7] When one of them, law professor Nathaniel Colley, threatened to sue, Kendall wrote a retraction in the *Yale Daily News*, but Buckley took relish in appending a statement of his own challenging Colley to sue him instead of the improvident Kendall. "The undeniable facts are: Nathaniel S. Colley, through his support of Henry Wallace, is—be it unwittingly—furthering the ends of the Soviet Union." Colley did not rise to the bait.

Through their sophomore year, Bozell was far more widely known as a right-wing political activist than was Buckley, who was still devoting much of his time to the *Yale Daily News* in preparation for the election of chairman that would take place in the spring of that year. Buckley worried that his politics and personality would damage any chance that he had of winning the election. Before the vote was to take place, he asked his brother Jim whether, given the prospect of a close vote, it would be proper that he vote for himself. Jim assured him that it was.

Buckley's fears reflected the view of his life he had drawn from his childhood rather than the reality of his situation at Yale. Far from being resented, he was widely admired by the other students on the *Yale Daily News*. Garrison Ellis, who would succeed him as chairman, was in awe of him. "He was an overpowering personality," Ellis said. And Ottley saw him as a kind of "cosmic-charismatic superintelligent personality."

The vote was taken by secret ballot in the *News* boardroom. Afterwards, the outgoing chairman, Samuel Sloan Walker, Jr., returned to announce the results. The new chairman chosen was, Walker said, "William Buckley . . . unanimously."

CHAPTER 4

Into the Limelight

Buckley began his one-year term as chairman of the newspaper on February 1, 1949. Guinzburg was elected managing editor, in charge of the news pages of the paper; Bill Carlin, the vice-chairman, to help the chairman with the editorial page.

They inherited what was a typical college newspaper. Like other college newspapers, the *Yale Daily News* had largely confined itself to reporting fraternity elections, college sports, and administration business. Editorials plugged the college charity drive and cheered on the football and basketball teams. The newspaper was cursorily read by students and faculty and little discussed. But Buckley and Guinzburg widened the scope and increased the seriousness of the *Yale Daily News*. They sent reporters to New York and Washington to cover national stories. And Buckley editorialized not only on the effectiveness of Yale's educational program, but also on the relevance of Christianity, the evils of communism, and the follies of Truman. "There was never a time during the years I was at Yale when the paper was read so eagerly," Paul Weiss recalled.

I

During Buckley's first months, he wrote editorials on the importance of religions banding together "in their struggle against the godless materialism whose headway in the last 30 years threatens
civilization," and on the desirability of convictions in the Smith Act
trials of eleven Communist leaders. He attacked the hypocrisy of
liberals who protested the appearance in the U.S. of musicians who
had performed in Nazi Germany, but not the appearance of Soviet
composer Dmitri Shostakovich. But the editorials that caused the
greatest furor were not on the Communist threat, but on the teaching
techniques and beliefs of a popular Yale anthropologist, Raymond
"Jungle Jim" Kennedy.

Kennedy, a colorful teacher, taught a heavily attended class that
Buckley had begun auditing that semester. What offended Buckley
was Kennedy's view that religion was a "matter of ghosts, spirits, and
emotions." In a March editorial, "For a Fair Approach," Buckley
attacked Kennedy's views:

Professor Kennedy, who year after year addresses several hundred
freshmen and sophomores in Sociology 10, has made a cult of anti-
religion. It is a waste of breath to assert the obvious truth that he is
entitled to his own belief in regard to the Existence of God; it is
similarly obvious that in undermining religion through bawdy and
slap-stick humor, through circumspect allusions and emotive in-
nuendoes, he is guilty of an injustice to and imposition upon his
students and the University.[1]

The editorial created an extraordinary uproar. What made it so
provocative was not merely Buckley's view of Kennedy, which was
shared by some students, but the lack of deference with which he
expressed his view. In those days, students were not supposed to
criticize their professors publicly. "An undergraduate newspaper attacking a respected professor was itself highly provocative," Bill Carlin recalled.

Over the next week, advertisements had to be pulled to make room
for the letters to the editor, protesting Buckley's editorial. They included an angry letter from the chairman of the Sociology Department
and from Kennedy himself. Kennedy warned Buckley that his views
would eventually get him into trouble: "I hate to criticize a young
man . . . but the Chairman is growing up now, and he should learn
that in the world of adult men attacks upon the integrity and honesty

of another man will not be excused on the ground of youthful brash-ness.''[2]

The protest was not limited, however, to the readers of the *Yale Daily News*. Vice-Chairman Carlin wrote a letter to the editor com-plaining that "at this time where there is a tendency to be intolerant of opinions with which we don't happen to agree, it is vital we take pains to safeguard the free exchange of ideas.''[3] And among the other editors, a revolt began to stir. Features editor Arthur Milam described the scene:

> The Kennedy editorials seemed to some at the time to be the last straw. Tom [Guinzburg] sat at his desk and looked twenty degrees blacker than usual. [Business manager] John [Macomber] started plotting the slump in advertising returns that he was certain would follow in its wake. Hazy liberals . . . walked around shaking their heads and saying, "Aww, ah disagree.''[4]

One of the "hazy liberals," sports editor Fred Stannard, called a meeting of the editors to discuss whether the chairman should have to submit his editorials for approval.

Undaunted by the uproar from readers, Buckley was upset by the reaction within the newspaper. The evening before the meeting he told his brother Jim, who had joined a New Haven law firm, that he was even considering resigning. Jim, horrified that Bill was about to give up a Yale undergraduate's highest achievement, persuaded him that it was much too early in his term to do so.

When the meeting began the next day in the newspaper's board-room, Stannard tried to press the question of whether the chairman alone or the whole board was responsible for the editorials. But Buck-ley immediately called for a vote of confidence. "He just changed very cleverly the whole issue," Stannard recalled. Stannard countered by asking him whether he would resign if denied a vote of confidence, and when Buckley said he would not, Stannard rejected taking a vote. Buckley finally agreed that he would announce in the newspaper that the editorials represented his views alone and that he would post for comment any future editorials that he thought might be controversial. He had won, but his victory did not quiet the grum-bling over his editorials.

II

Buckley and Brent Bozell spent the summer between their junior and senior years working for one of the new oil companies that Will

Buckley had started in Saskatchewan and Alberta, Canada. Over the July fourth weekend, Buckley arranged to meet his sister Patricia in Vancouver at the home of Pat Taylor, a friend she had met at Vassar and whom he had dated several times.

During her sophomore year at Vassar, Patricia Buckley had lived across the hall from Taylor. Almost six feet tall, with dark-brown hair framing classical features, Taylor was strikingly beautiful. She was also like the Buckley women: extremely witty and very imperious. By her own description, she and her family were several degrees to the right of the Buckleys politically. She came from one of the wealthiest families in Canada—her father, Austin Taylor, had major holdings in gold, oil, and timber—and had quickly dismissed her surroundings at Vassar as a "slum." While the other Vassar girls wore the usual uniform of a dirty raincoat, Pat preferred her mink coat and complained bitterly that her closet wouldn't hold her collection of hats.

Patricia Buckley had become convinced that Taylor was the girl for her brother. "Pat looks like a queen, she acts like a queen, and is just the match for Billy," she had reported to her family.[5] Patricia had set up one date between Bill and Pat that year, and they had hit it off well enough to write a few letters back and forth, but over spring break that year, Pat injured her back in a horseback-riding accident and never returned to Vassar.

Patricia Buckley had been invited to visit Pat in Vancouver the summer of 1949 when Bill and Brent were nearby, and she had convinced Bill to meet her at the Taylor home, which took up a square block of downtown Vancouver, for July 4. The visit was an extraordinary one. Buckley arrived on Sunday and by Thursday evening—having postponed his return to Regina by a day—had decided that he wanted to marry Pat, but he was worried that Pat, who had turned down numerous suitors before, would reject him. He asked Pat's sister to fetch her from a canasta game. Pat's sister told her that Bill, acting strangely, wanted to talk to her. Pat put down her cards and joined Buckley in the library. He was pacing up and down the floor, smoking. "Bill, what do you want?" she asked. And he said, "Patricia, would you consider marriage with me?" She said, "Bill, I've been asked this question many times. To the others I've said no. To you I say yes. Now may I please get back and finish my hand?"

Buckley wrote his mother that night that he had become engaged to Pat. "She is without a doubt the most charming, lovely, sensitive girl that I have ever met," Bill wrote. "As you know I am not susceptible to heart flurries except of the deepest nature—the type that I experience for Tish and for you. I am in love with Pat, and I am going to marry her within a year."[6]

Pat Taylor did, however, swear Bill to secrecy until she got up her nerve to tell her mother, a High Church Anglican of Northern Irish descent who did not care for Irish Catholics. When she did tell her four days later, Mrs. Taylor, Pat recalled, went into "total shock" at the thought that her daughter wanted to "marry an unknown Catholic from the farthest reaches of Connecticut."

Bill's family was also surprised to hear that he was engaged. "Here was a handsome guy who had no time for women at all; nobody could have been more surprised than his own family when he announced his engagement to Pat Taylor," Reid Buckley recalled. But Will Buckley —taken aback by Pat's mother's reaction to *his* religion—voiced no objection to his son's marrying an Anglican. After six months of negotiations, the two families worked out a way of accommodating both religions at the wedding.

When Buckley returned to Yale that September, his classmates were astounded to hear that he had become engaged. They were even more surprised when they met Pat, who visited Buckley in new Haven that fall. "We were all over there to meet the bride-to-be," Francis Donahue, the faculty adviser to the *Yale Daily News,* recalled. "She came into Buckley's room with a mink coat on, and she just let it fall off her shoulders onto the floor. All the students were in love with her." Bill Ottley had a similar memory. "Pat Taylor walked in and she absolutely mesmerized everyone."

III

Buckley's fall semester as chairman of the *Yale Daily News* was marred by a personal rift between himself and Guinzburg. Guinzburg and Buckley's sister Jane had met the year before and fallen in love, and they had announced to Buckley's parents that they wanted to marry. Will Buckley had peremptorily refused to allow one of his daughters to marry a Jew. He insisted that Jane break off the engagement and, according to Guinzburg, "tried to put barriers in front of our seeing each other."

But Guinzburg and Jane continued their relationship in spite of Will's edict. "Like many youthful romances, if left to our own devices, we'd probably have separated a lot sooner," Guinzburg said. "But it was only because people made it so difficult for us to get together that we became more intent on maintaining our intimacy."

Buckley took his father's side in the controversy. "It was my feeling that the marriage would not have worked for religious reasons primarily," he recalled. As a result, Guinzburg ended his friendship with Buckley, and their working relationship deteriorated. "It affected the atmosphere of the newspaper," Guinzburg recalled. "It tended to isolate the city room from the editorial department."

In effect, the rift with Guinzburg made political conciliation with the other editors impossible. "It seemed to be the mood of the other editors whatever Buckley said to go against it," Francis Donahue recalled. For his part, Buckley simply ignored them. If he needed to talk about his editorials with anyone, he consulted Bozell and Kendall.

That fall, Buckley editorialized frequently on the subject of the Soviet threat. The Soviet Union had few defenders at Yale; there was no campus Communist Party; and the John Reed Club, the Communist-organized student group, had at most five members, none of whom were open party members. On the *Yale Daily News* itself, the other editors were liberal anti-Communists. Where Buckley differed from the other editors and from most Yale students was in the vehemence of his hatred and the extent of his fear of communism. He believed that the U.S. was not only on the verge of attack, but of defeat. He wrote in one editorial following the announcement in September of the Soviet explosion of an atom bomb:

> Today (for a while at least) two thoughts will occupy the average undergraduate mind: the game against Connecticut and the Russian acquisition of the atomic bomb. . . . Will Russia have too long to wait before she spurns her nose at conference and diplomacy and invades Finland and Yugoslavia and maybe even Western Germany and France? . . . At worst, we might consider if this time next year Yale will be a garrison for soldiers and sailors, preparing for the next far-reaching struggle in history.[7]

Buckley became embroiled in a debate with law professor Tom Emerson on the Smith Act convictions that October of eleven Communists. Emerson wrote in the *News:* "I wonder if any thoughtful person seriously believes that the convictions of the Communist leaders will protect us, in any degree, from the dangers of Communism."[8] Invoking Kendall, Buckley responded:

> To begin with, we probably differ with Mr. Emerson on the "dangers of Communism." He could probably count the dangers of

Communism on the joints of his big toe. For us they are legion. . . .
All in all, the best comment was Professor Kendall's. After reading
the statements of the trial, he sighed, "Yes, things have come to a
hell of a pass when you can't conspire against your country and get
away with it." [9]

Buckley was willing to abandon the canons of objective journalism
when communism was the issue. In June 1949, the *Harvard Crimson*
had published a series of articles charging that the FBI, hunting for
Communist sympathizers, had "moved in on Yale University." [10] The
Crimson reported that Yale physics professor Henry Margenau had
been chastised by an FBI agent for speaking at a pro-Communist
forum in New Haven and that a philosophy professor, Robert Cohen,
had initially had his appointment blocked by Provost Edgar Furniss
because an informant, who was probably sent by the FBI, had linked
him with the Communist Party.

Margenau and Furniss had repudiated the *Crimson*'s assertions, but
not in an entirely convincing manner. Margenau, under pressure from
the FBI, had offered contradictory versions of what had happened,
and his subsequent conduct appeared to bear out the *Crimson*'s contention that he had been intimidated; Dean Furniss had acknowledged
that an informant did try to prevent Cohen's being hired, although he
refused to identify the person.

In September, the *Yale Daily News* assigned a reporter to look into
the story, but when Special Agent John J. Gleason of the FBI's New
Haven office heard about it, he enlisted the FBI's "liaison officer" at
Yale, H. B. Fisher, to get the story killed. According to Robert
Cohen, Buckley spent a few hours at Cohen's house discussing the
charges. Cohen says that he was able to convince Buckley that the
Crimson story was accurate and that it had been an FBI man who had
fingered him.

According to Cohen, Buckley told him later that he had decided not
to run an article on the *Crimson*'s charges because "it's not news to
repeat what has already been put in the newspaper." But Buckley
told the Yale administration and the FBI that he had killed the article
because he believed that the *Crimson*'s charges were false. Subsequently, Buckley made an appointment to see Gleason.* He told Glea-

---

* Buckley doesn't remember visiting Cohen or killing the story. It is clear from the FBI files
on the affair that Buckley was aware at least that the story had been killed. In a letter to
FBI Assistant Director L. B. Nichols, Gleason writes that Buckley assured him that the
story "was killed prior to any contact" Gleason had had with him. It is also likely that

son that he believed that the *Crimson* reports were "vicious and insidious in addition to being journalistically poor" and he offered to be of assistance to the FBI by arranging a forum, sponsored by the *Yale Daily News,* at which the bureau could rebut the *Crimson*'s charges.[11]

In October the forum was held before a packed Law School Auditorium, with Buckley as moderator and Gleason and Assistant Director L. B. Nichols responding to questions from a panel of students and professors. As he boasted to Nichols afterwards, Buckley stationed *Yale Daily News* reporters around the room to jostle the writing arm of the *Crimson* reporter who had come to New Haven to cover the event.[12] Afterwards, he wrote glowingly of Nichols and Gleason's performance. They had demonstrated, Buckley wrote, that the *Crimson*'s charges "have not the remotest resemblance to the truth." Of Nichols, he wrote, "We are not in the least bit hesitant to take our hats off to an officer of the Federal Bureau of Investigation who . . . demonstrated his devotion to duty, his enlightened sensitivity to criticism, and his anxiety to reveal and to unfold every detail in the functioning of an organization with which he is justly proud to be associated."[13]

Buckley printed a letter of protest to his editorial from Cohen, but refused to print a letter from *Harvard Crimson* chairman John Simon and even forwarded copies of Simon's correspondence with him to the FBI. Simon telegrammed and then called Buckley, urging him to print his letter, but Buckley refused. "John, there is no chance we will run that," Buckley told Simon over the phone. "We here at the *Yale News* know the truth about the *Crimson*."

Gleason and Nichols were highly appreciative of Buckley's conduct. Nichols wrote afterwards to Clyde Tolson, FBI Director J. Edgar Hoover's assistant: "I was very much impressed with William Buckley, editor of the *Yale Daily News*. I have a very definite feeling that we will hear from this young man in years to come. I would say very definitely that he is pro-FBI."[14]

With the struggle against communism at stake, Buckley showed a lack of objectivity and a kind of personal ruthlessness that he didn't show in his personal relationships. If Cohen's account is correct, Buckley acted deceitfully. At best, Buckley, who recalls being sur-

---

Buckley talked to Cohen about the story. Paul Weiss, a friend of Buckley and a colleague of Cohen in the Philosophy Department, vouches for Cohen's trustworthiness on this matter.

prised to learn that the FBI had a "liaison man" at Yale, was simply unwilling to voice publicly any doubt and suspicion where the FBI was concerned.

IV

Buckley continued to participate in debates even after he became chairman of the *Yale Daily News*. That fall, Oxford University had sent a team on tour of the Ivy League colleges, with Yale as the last stop. The Oxford team of Robin Day and Anthony Wedgwood-Benn had defeated all its opponents easily, and it was widely expected that they would dispatch the Yale team in the same manner. On the Yale campus, the debate attracted the same attention as a football game. At Strathcombe Hall, where it took place, "a throng . . . filled all available seats downstairs and in the balcony, sat in the aisles, and stood in rows three or four deep in the outside hall." [15] Included in the audience were Bill's father and his sister Patricia.

The Oxford team provided their challengers with a list of seven topics on which they were willing to take either the affirmative or negative position. Buckley and Bozell chose the negative on "Resolved: the Americans should nationalize all their non-agricultural industries." "This was a subject made to order for Buckley and Bozell if there ever was one," Rollin Osterweis said. "If there was anything they despised, it was the idea of the U.S. socializing its basic industries."

The two teams were different not only in their views but in their appearance. "The Oxford team was too cocky, too neat, all the best tailoring you can think of, beautiful haircuts, and Bill and Brent looked like they always did, hair pulled back, clothes falling apart, buttons missing," Partricia Buckley Bozell recalled.

Osterweis designated that Bozell speak first in order to "win audience rapport and the judges' favor with his charm and pleasantness and felicity of language," and he designated Buckley to "handle the heavy oar as far as the rebuttal and the infighting were concerned." Bozell warned that "Britain was in danger of being enslaved" and Buckley argued that socialism was obsolete in America.[16] But Buckley and Bozell's main strength was not their arguments.

> I think the thing that set the British aback the most was that they were up against a team that was doing their style of debating [Osterweis said]. The British were past masters of wit and humor and a deliberate manner of speaking and the arousing of a lot of audience

rapport. And these were the areas where Buckley and Bozell were the most effective.

According to *Yale Daily News* adviser Francis Donahue, the debate turned on a single theatrical gesture. As the first British debater was reaching the climax of his argument, Buckley flamboyantly extracted his handkerchief from his pocket and waved it to the audience—a gesture that Yale students made before singing their school song. Buckley's ploy amused the audience and upset the British team. By the end, the debate was a rout. To the cheers of their fellow students, Buckley and Bozell were declared the winners by three to zero.

The debate made Buckley and Bozell campus heroes. Buckley was exhilarated. Evan Galbraith, who saw him afterwards, remarked on how he had appeared to thrive under the pressure of an audience's attention. "It was a lot of limelight. He took to it and liked it," Galbraith said.

As the end of his term as chairman of the *Yale Daily News* drew near, Buckley wrote a series of four editorials attacking the effect of "publish or perish" on faculty teaching of undergraduates and calling for "student opinion of teachers" to be "solicited more regularly." [17] Then in a closing series of editorials—"What to Do?"—he called for Yale and other universities to defend free enterprise against the challenge of socialism. Like the editorials on Kennedy, these contained a veiled attack on the doctrine of academic freedom.

The battle to retain free enterprise as the fundamental economic philosophy for America is being lost, and there are those of us who mind [Buckley wrote]. The battle is even being lost at Yale. . . . We are losing the battle for a variety of reasons. Perhaps the most influential is the spirit of restlessness, of iconoclasm, of pragmatism that is intellectually *au courant* and that is warmly embraced by so many evangelistic young intellectuals who find . . . their most enthusiastic disciples in the cloistered halls of a university, where everything goes in the name of the search for truth and freedom of inquiry. [18]

Buckley argued that "the collectivist movement in America is largely dependent on its umbilical cord to the universities," but instead of advocating that it be cut, he called for Yale and other colleges to set up "Adam Smith chairs of Political and Economic Philosophy" in which the proponents of free enterprise could hold forth. [19]

In the last issue, Buckley's fellow editors made their own feelings about his editorials known. Guinzburg authored a poem on their behalf that summarized the year and then addressed the chairman:

> And then to the chairman, William Frank Jr.
> We render with love one aged petunia—
> On the subject of edits, we're 100 percent,
> Stopped reading them last year, at the beginning of Lent—
> Not once have we agreed, not one single time,
> And a statement like that doesn't need any rhyme.[20]

The Yale administration was more supportive of Buckley than his fellow editors were. While the administrators did not share Buckley's editorial views, they thought that he had been a valuable chairman.* Yale President Charles Seymour had requested that the newspaper collect Buckley's columns so he could send them to alumni who protested that Yale had become too "liberal." Dean William DeVane had written him that he had never seen a "more successful" college newspaper than the *Yale Daily News* under Buckley's tenure. And the college secretary, Carl Lohmann, had asked him if he would be the student speaker at Yale's Alumni Day celebration, February 22, an honor that had gone to William Sloane Coffin the year before.

V

By the beginning of his last semester at Yale, Buckley had achieved exactly what he had set out to do four years before: he had succeeded on Yale's terms, winning the administration's and his classmates' acclaim, while carrying on a crusade against communism and atheism. He had been the first choice of Skull and Bones, the secret senior honor society, many of whose members went on to high government positions while maintaining their ties with fellow "Bonesmen." His own success had convinced him of Yale's tolerance: he could do anything, he believed, and if he did it well, regardless of his slant, he would be rewarded.

In composing his Alumni Day speech, Buckley flouted convention.

---

* Yale Dean William DeVane and President Charles Seymour, who had met with Buckley weekly during his tenure, regarded him as an oddball, but as a talented one. When writer John Chamberlain visited Yale in the spring of 1949 to research a story for *Life* on Yale's coming 250th anniversary, DeVane boasted to him, "There is a remarkable thing here. We have a conservative heading the *Yale Daily News*, the son of an oilman." "DeVane's attitude," Chamberlain later recalled, "was that it was very strange and incomprehensible that this should happen."

The purpose of Alumni Day was to inspire the alumni to give money to Yale; and the highlight of that year's event was to be the commemoration of a plaque to Yale's war dead. The student speech was a formality designed to give the alumni some taste of the current generation. But Buckley wrote a speech that condemned Yale for failing in its responsibility as an "educational leader" and for leading her students "only to confusion."[21] And he called upon the Yale administration to restore a sense of purpose by requiring its faculty to foster active Christianity and free enterprise, even if this meant disciplining professors like Kennedy.

Drawing on Kendall's attack against the laissez-faire view of politics, Buckley placed the blame for Yale's failure on what he called the "laissez-faire theory of education." According to laissez-faire theory of education, the university presents every side of a question "with equal vigor" on the assumption that in the "arena of public and conflicting opinion . . . the best thought [will] win." This meant, Buckley pointed out, that socialists and atheists were on an equal footing with capitalists and Christians, regardless of the Yale administration's or corporation's opinions on these questions. "Although the members of the Corporation of Yale believe that modified free enterprise is the best course for Americans," Buckley wrote, "their opinion is of no more value than that of Professor Jones, who urges modified socialism upon his students."

Advocating that both the laissez-faire theory of education and the doctrine of academic freedom that sustained it be abandoned, Buckley called upon the university to declare "active Christianity the first basis of enlightened thought and action" and "Communism, socialism, collectivism, government paternalism inimical to the dignity of the individual." The university, Buckley suggested, should demand of its faculty, like Kennedy and political scientist Charles Lindblom, a Keynesian Buckley considered a socialist, that they adhere to these principles and "not *sustain*" those who refuse.

A week before he was to appear, he got a call from Yale Secretary Carl Lohmann asking him whether he would be willing to rehearse his speech in private before he gave it to the alumni. Suspecting that Lohmann might try to tone down the speech, he refused. Instead, two days before the event, he defiantly deposited a copy of the speech at the Yale News Bureau, which handled press releases for Yale events. When Buckley handed it in, the head of the News Bureau, Richard Lee, who later became the mayor of New Haven, quipped, "What are you saying in it—nothing I hope." But when Lee read it, he took it

immediately to Alumni Director Carlos Stoddard, who after reading it
passed it on to Lohmann and Seymour. They were appalled. Seymour
later described his reaction to the speech in a letter to his successor,
Whitney Griswold: "Mr. Buckley's manuscript was conceived in a
vein that amounted to an attack upon the Yale faculty. It was strongly
controversial as well as inaccurate. In my opinion there could not
have been a less appropriate introduction to a commemorative service." [22]

Stoddard tracked down Buckley on the campus and conveyed to
him the president's "deep disappointment" in his speech and Lohmann's conviction that it was an "indictment of the administration." [23]
He asked Buckley to revise the speech to make it more acceptable to
Seymour. That evening, Buckley consulted his brother Jim. When he
told Jim that he was only willing to make cosmetic changes in the
speech, Jim advised him to offer to withdraw it entirely if the revisions
were not acceptable. "My theory was that it was their party," Jim
Buckley recalled. But both Bill and Jim assumed that because the
speech was to be delivered in a day, the administration would accept
it rather than try to recruit a new speaker at the last moment.

The next day he gave a new version of the speech to Stoddard in
which he removed specific references to errant Yale faculty members.
Stoddard insisted that Buckley was "absolutely free to make the
speech," but promised to forward his offer to withdraw to Seymour. [24]
To Buckley's surprise, Seymour immediately accepted his offer.

Buckley was chagrined by Seymour's rejection. He wrote Stoddard
a curt note: "I believe the President's decision to accept my offer
bespeaks a curious fundamental attitude toward the alumni." [25] Bozell
and Kendall shared Buckley's feelings.

> They were indignant, as were a lot of people [Buckley recalled]. It
> was an immature act, an act of a university not entirely confident of
> itself. They never would have dared do it had the criticism been
> from the Left. That's in part because alumni are more accustomed
> to that criticism, and they tend to discount it more. But a Right
> criticism they might be more harmed by.

The administration's rebuff shattered Buckley's belief in the university's tolerance. What he had taken for tolerance he now saw as
hypocrisy. The experience strengthened his conviction that he was
part of a political "Remnant" whose purpose was to keep the torch of
truth lit during the encroaching Dark Ages. More than any single
experience he had at Yale, it shaped his future course of action.

VI

During his senior year, Buckley had to decide what he would do after leaving Yale. His friend Professor Tom Bergin recalled, "He was very ambitious. He had enormous drive. But I don't think he was ambitious for a particular spot like President of the United States. I think he wanted to have an impact. It was a curious kind of ambition. It was not particularly egocentric, but he wanted people to listen to him."

Galbraith, who became close friends with Buckley in Skull and Bones, sized up Buckley's ambition in very similar terms. "He wanted to influence public opinion at a very young age," Galbraith said. "He wanted to continue on in some way to be a spokesman for the conservative movement."

Buckley's father encouraged him to continue at Yale as a graduate student in political science under Willmoore Kendall. And Buckley did apply to and was accepted by both the Yale Graduate School and the Law School. But his heart was not in being a scholar. He had learned to enjoy the public light of controversy. And he retained the view that knowledge was purely instrumental.

On one weekend, Buckley's classmate William MacLeish took him and Galbraith to visit his father, the poet Archibald MacLeish, and as Galbraith recalled:

> Bill asked Archibald if he thought it was a good idea if he, Bill, went to graduate school to study political science. And MacLeish said, "That would be very good, it would be very helpful in causing you to know what you think." But Bill said, "No, I know what I think. The question is whether this will be helpful to me as a salesman. Will this credential help in getting heard?"

In May, Buckley, still bristling from his rejection by the Yale administration, resolved that he would write a book laying out his case against Yale education and the doctrines upon which it was based. He decided that after getting married that summer, he and Pat would return to New Haven, where he would spend several months writing the book.

But his plans were complicated by the threat of a new war. Buckley dreaded having to go back into the infantry. In January, he had written to resign from the Reserves, but he had not heard back from his Unit Headquarters in Hartford. As the Korean War broke out in June, Willmoore Kendall suggested that Buckley join the CIA as an alternative. He offered to introduce Buckley to James Burnham, who was then a consultant to the Office of Policy Coordination, the CIA's covert action wing.

The CIA was a popular haven for Yale and other Ivy League graduates. William Sloane Coffin had joined, and of Buckley's classmates and close friends, Frank Harman, Dino Pionzio, and Evan Galbraith would all eventually join the CIA. Its attraction to both liberals and conservatives was a combination of intellectual challenge, high adventure, and moral crusade.

In June, Buckley went to Washington, where he met Burnham, a quiet, urbane man whose professorial demeanor concealed a political and intellectual intensity that had carried him from the leadership of the Trotskyist movement in the thirties to becoming after World War II one of the chief architects of America's Cold War policy. Kendall idolized Burnham. (When he talked about Burnham in class, Buckley recalled, it was as if he were "describing Wotan.")

At Burnham's apartment, Buckley met Howard Hunt, a Brown University graduate who had already had a storied career as an OSS member, a best-selling novelist and journalist, and was now about to join the CIA's covert action wing. Hunt had the jutting jaw and square physique of an amateur boxer, but the sad, contemplative eyes of a romantic who had decided to devote his life to slaying the Communist dragon. Hunt was slated to take over the CIA's operations in Mexico City, and Burnham had already mentioned to him that the young Yale graduate spoke fluent Spanish and had lived in Mexico City. Buckley, Burnham had told Hunt, was "a committed and articulate anti-Communist looking for the optimum way of working against the Stalinists."[26]

Hunt recalled their conversation:

> We were talking about student matters and he described some of the problems at Yale that had incited him into writing a book, and I found that interesting. I knew the student situation in Mexico City was crying out for some corrective attention, and I thought here was a young man just out of college. I was going to be in the embassy myself, and I needed somebody on the outside who could make contacts and deal with the younger people.

At Buckley's graduation, his classmates chose him to deliver the Class Day Oration. It was his last chance as a Yale undergraduate to score points off his political enemies and he didn't balk. Standing before his classmates and their parents, he began, referring to the right-wing publisher of the *Chicago Tribune,* "Greetings from Colonel McCormick and from the archangel." And then he launched into an assault against the position, popular among liberal Yale faculty and students, that the best way to defeat communism was by improving American democracy.

That month, after writing a complaint to his congressman, Buckley finally heard from Reserve Headquarters that his resignation had been accepted, but he remained interested in joining the CIA if it would have him. First, however, he wanted to write a book about Yale.

CHAPTER 5

A Fiery Cross on a Hillside

With Pat having agreed to raise their children as Catholics, Bill and Pat were married in Vancouver in July in a church ceremony presided over by the archbishop of Vancouver. Afterwards, at a reception for more than a thousand guests on the Taylor family lawn, they were blessed by Vancouver's Anglican bishop. Bill's brother John, who attended the wedding, was impressed by the Taylor family's wealth, which easily exceeded that of his own family. When John arrived at the airport, he had been met by Pat's brother Austin. Driving back to the Taylors' home, he had asked Austin where he could buy some English shoes that he had seen advertised at the airport. "You wouldn't want them. They're mass-produced," Austin replied.

After the wedding, Bill and Pat honeymooned in Hawaii, where Bill read James Burnham's *The Coming Defeat of Communism*, while Pat basked in the sun. After a detour in Vancouver, they set off for New Haven. They rented a house in Hamden, a suburb of New Haven, and Buckley took a $120-a-month job teaching Spanish at Yale. Brent Bozell, who was attending Yale Law School, and his wife, Patricia Buckley Bozell, rented a house nearby. Buckley spent the morning teaching, and the rest of the day writing. He wrote quickly. By the spring of 1951, he had finished the book.

When he began, Buckley had briefly considered writing a general book about American college education, but he didn't want to do the research that such a book might require. Always the debater, he was more comfortable casting his ideas in the polemical framework of a critique of Yale education. He called the book *God and Man at Yale* ("For God, for country, and for Yale . . . in that order," the dedication read); and in it, he charged that Yale had abandoned both the religion of God—Christianity—and the economics of man—free enterprise, or individualism.

I

In *God and Man at Yale,* Buckley took the argument that he had made in his Alumni Day speech several steps further. He charged faculty members like Raymond Kennedy, Paul Weiss, and Keynesian Charles Lindblom by name with fostering atheism and socialism. And he called outright for firing such teachers. "Let us survey the situation of Mr. John Smith, a socialist professor of economics at Yale," Buckley wrote. "Let us bar him from teaching because he is inculcating values that the governing board at Yale considers to be against the public welfare." [1]

He urged that Yale fire not only Marxists, but followers of John Maynard Keynes and the Truman administration's tepid Fair Deal. He grouped the ideas of Thomas Huxley's Darwinism, Harold Laski and Sidney and Beatrice Webb's Fabian Socialism, and John Dewey's Pragmatism with those of Marx and Hitler. "While reading and studying Marx or Hitler, Laski or the Webbs, Huxley or Dewey, I should expect the teacher . . . to deflate the arguments advanced," Buckley wrote.[2] The only thinkers he commended were John Locke, Thomas Jefferson, Adam Smith, David Ricardo, Jesus, and St. Paul.

The argument of *God and Man at Yale* was, however, more sophisticated than that of his earlier editorials and speeches. In the book, he took aim explicitly at the connections between the laissez-faire theory of education and the doctrine of academic freedom. In doing so, he rejected the underlying philosophy not only of Yale but of the modern university.

The modern American university had taken shape in the late nineteenth century, when the industrial revolution and modern science had swept aside the church-based college. The industrial revolution broadened the scope and purpose of university education—it was no longer solely to acquaint would-be ministers with a received body of knowledge—and the development of modern science had challenged the preeminence of religious knowledge and the theory of truth upon which it was based. By the mid-nineteenth century, educators like Harvard's Charles W. Eliot were putting forth a conception of knowledge and education drawn from the scientific method and modeled on the economic marketplace. According to this view, knowledge was best acquired through the widest and freest competition of ideas; and education consisted of exposing a student to this marketplace, or arena, of ideas. The goal of education was no longer to acquaint students with certain received truths, but rather to train their minds to discover truths for themselves.

This view was most clearly stated by Cornell professor Edward Kirkland in a passage that Buckley cited in *God and Man at Yale:*

> An academic institution is an arena. Into it ride different contestants. They may uphold different causes, some perhaps wholly or partially wrong. They may be differently armed. But all must meet the test of conflict, of argument, and of performance. We believe that in this free and open contest truth will be victorious and error defeated over the long time.[3]

The doctrine of academic freedom was a corollary of the laissez-faire theory of education. Developed in the early twentieth century partly in response to dismissals of scholars who advocated Darwin's theory of evolution or unorthodox economic theories, the doctrine of academic freedom upheld the scholar's right to be judged by his competence rather than his beliefs. By the 1940s, it was accepted by all Ivy League administrators and faculty. Even disputes over whether universities should hire Communists were argued within the assumed context of academic freedom: the question was whether Communists, by their commitment to place party above truth, had forfeited the protections of academic freedom.

In *God and Man at Yale,* Buckley rejected both the doctrine of academic freedom and the laissez-faire theory of education. Buckley charged that the doctrine of academic freedom was a "hoax" to which administrators gave lip service, but which they periodically ignored. He noted that Yale had dismissed a theologian in 1937 for his opposition to capitalism and that Seymour had declared he would not knowingly hire Communists. "I should be interested," he wrote, "how long a person who revealed himself as a racist, who lectured about the

anthropological superiority of the Aryan, would last at Yale. My prediction is that the next full moon would see him looking elsewhere for
a job."[4]

Buckley contended that Yale "*does subscribe to an orthodoxy:*
there are limits within which faculty members must keep their opinions if they wish to be tolerated." He insisted that he was not arguing
that "limits should be imposed, but that existing limits should be
narrowed."[5]

Buckley rejected the conception of the university as an educational
marketplace; he believed that the purpose of education was not to
acquaint students with the means of discovering the truth, but with
received truths and the means of defending them. Commenting on
Kirkland's image of education as an arena, he wrote:

> More properly, the teaching part of a college is the practice field on
> which the gladiators of the future are taught to use their weapons,
> are briefed in the wiles and strategems of the enemy, and are in-
> spired with the virtue of their cause in anticipation of the day when
> they will step forward and join the struggle against error. This is
> important since the most casual student of history knows that, as a
> matter of fact, truth does *not* necessarily vanquish.[6]

Buckley's view of education was similar to that of the eighteenth-
century clerics who had founded Yale, as well as to that of many
Catholic educators.* While he did not believe that students should
spend most of their time studying Latin and reading the Bible, he did
believe that the goal of education was to familiarize students with an
already-existing body of truth, of which Christianity and free enterprise, or individualism, were the foundations. "Christianity may not
be truth," he said, "but . . . in the eyes of Christians it is at least the
nearest thing to unrevealed and perhaps inapprehensible ultimate
truth . . . Individualism is, if not truth, the nearest thing we have to
truth, no closer thing to truth in the field of social relations having
appeared on the horizon."[7]

Buckley's view left two major questions unanswered, neither of
which he had faced in his senior-year editorials or his Alumni Day

---

* Contrary to many of his later critics, Buckley's view of education was not similar to that
of Cardinal Newman, whose views were actually more liberal than Buckley's. Buckley
read Cardinal Newman's *The Idea of a University Defined* when he was writing *God and
Man at Yale* but had realized that Newman's conception of knowledge for its own sake
was entirely foreign to his own. "I recognized about three-quarters of the way through
that it would be of no particular use to me," Buckley said of Newman's book.

speech. First, if the function of the university was to indoctrinate students in received wisdom, how could it also perform its modern function of advancing knowledge? Second, who in the university would decide what constituted the received wisdom and what constituted falsehood and heresy?

Buckley acknowledged that his view of education might impede the advance of social and natural science where new truths tend regularly to replace old, but he proposed a novel situation—separating research from teaching so that researchers whose ideas differ from the prevailing orthodoxy would seek funding separately from the teaching faculty. Buckley's answer to the question of who will decide what is truth was equally novel. In his Alumni Day speech, he had implied that the administration should, but in *God and Man at Yale,* he turned to the alumni—whom he assumed to be a conservative body—as the final arbiter of educational orthodoxy. Buckley contended that the alumni, who elected the Yale Corporation that, in turn, appointed the president, were in charge by right; as the consumer-purchasers of Yale's product, who supported Yale through their contributions, they should enjoy the same sovereignty as the consumer supposedly enjoyed in the marketplace. "Every free citizen in a free economy . . . must defer to the sovereignty of the consumer," Buckley wrote.[8]

God and Man at Yale could not be fit into any of the existing political categories. Buckley's proposals for separating teachers from researchers and putting the alumni in charge distinguished *God and Man at Yale* from the theories of conservative critics of education such as Nock and Irving Babbitt, who wanted, if anything, to protect teachers from the dictates of the public. Buckley's proposals were not so much reactionary as radical. By subjecting teaching and research to the dictates of the alumni and the market, Buckley plunged the university into an unknown future, dominated by the political marketplace in one case and the economic in the other.

Applying Kendall's populist majoritarianism to Yale, Buckley believed that the alumni were both the rightful majority and the repository of conservative wisdom. *God and Man at Yale* assumed a liberal "establishment" of administration and faculty ruling without clear mandate over a conservative majority. It sounded the clarion of revolution, calling upon the conservative majority to rise up and overthrow the liberal elite.

When Buckley showed the manuscript of *God and Man at Yale* to his friends and teachers at Yale, he got a mixed response. Kendall went over the entire manuscript carefully, honing the style and even adding some sentences of his own. One statement that Kendall added, explaining the importance of educational theory "in the context of a world-situation that seems to render totally irrelevant any fight except the power struggle against Communism," became a target of reviewers, but it expressed perfectly Buckley's as well as Kendall's underlying views: "I myself believe that the duel between Christianity and atheism is the most important in the world. I further believe that the struggle between individualism and collectivism is the same struggle reproduced on another level."[9]

According to Charles Lichenstein, Kendall admired *God and Man at Yale,* but he had some reservations about it.

He said that the book had great brilliance, great flash [Lichenstein recalled]. He had very great admiration for this kid's talent for which he took some credit and rightly so. But at the same time, he had the scholar's reservation: [Bill's] not really ready for that, he can't quite come to grips with what he's got in the palm of his hand. The book is a shooting star, but it is not a fixed planet.

What Kendall—and Bozell, who also went over the first draft carefully—objected to most was the section on alumni control. Bozell thought that the alumni were simply not qualified to judge what was true. According to Buckley, Kendall didn't object to the proposal itself, but to its inclusion in a book that was otherwise a report on Yale education. He thought the chapter on alumni control violated the "poetry" of the book. But Lichenstein believes that Kendall—in spite of his communitarian views—was "a true believer in the old original honorable academic freedom."

Buckley also showed the entire manuscript to Rollin Osterweis, his former debate coach and friend. Osterweis advised him to put the book aside for ten years and to see then if he still wanted to publish it. Buckley replied, "You know as well as I do that if I wait ten years I won't publish it. If I wait ten years, I'll lose the specifics, the indignation, all the things I care about now. I rather think you're trying to persuade me not to publish it at all." "You might be right," Osterweis replied.

In spite of these criticisms and warnings, Buckley decided to publish *God and Man at Yale* in exactly the form he had written it. But now he had to find a publisher.

Buckley never even considered getting one of the large New York publishers to put out *God and Man at Yale.* "It didn't occur to me that any of them would publish it," he said later. "It was very hard for a conservative, meaning someone of my stripe, to be published." But there were only three right-wing publishing houses at the time, Caxton Printers of Idaho, Devin-Adair in New York, and Henry Regnery Company in Chicago. Caxton and Devin-Adair emphasized defenses of laissez-faire capitalism, while Regnery had concentrated on isolationist, pro-German, and anti-Communist authors.

In April 1951, Buckley's father took him to lunch with Devin Garrity of Devin-Adair, but Garrity did not show much interest. Buckley then sent the manuscript to Henry Regnery.

Henry Regnery was a slight, shy, blond-haired Midwesterner of German-Catholic extraction, the son of a wealthy textile manufacturer, who displayed at an early age far more interest in ideas than in making money. After receiving an engineering degree from MIT, he studied philosophy at the University of Bonn and economics at Harvard. Initially a liberal and a supporter of Roosevelt's New Deal, Regnery went to work for the Resettlement Administration and then the American Friends Service Committee. But his isolationism and pro-German sentiment made him oppose American entry into the European war; and his opposition to Roosevelt's foreign policy gradually led him to question the Democratic domestic policy as well.

In 1945, Regnery met Frank Hanighen, an Omaha businessman, who with two other isolationists, Felix Morley and William Henry Chamberlin, had started a weekly broadsheet in Washington, *Human Events*. Regnery became a co-owner and the treasurer of the paper, but he was unwilling to leave the Midwest. In 1947, with his father's help, he founded Henry Regnery Company. The first two books he published were anti-Nazi but pro-German attacks on the Nuremberg Trials. Neither of these nor the subsequent books Regnery had published made money, and by the time Buckley sent *God and Man at Yale* to Regnery in April 1951 the firm was barely solvent.

Regnery had already heard of Buckley from Frank Chodorov, Nock's disciple who was a friend of Bill and his father, and from Frank Hanighen (Buckley had published an article in *Human Events* that spring, "Harvard Hogs the Headlines"). When *God and Man at Yale* arrived, he gave it to his editorial assistant, Kevin Corrigan, to read. Corrigan was wildly enthusiastic about the manuscript, comparing it to Cardinal Newman's *Tracts*. And Regnery, after reading only several chapters, wrote Buckley accepting it for publication. But there was a hitch.

Buckley and his father wanted *God and Man at Yale* to come out by the end of October—probably so that its publication would coincide with Yale's celebration of its 250th anniversary—but Regnery insisted that he could not afford to bring the book out that quickly. To persuade Regnery to go ahead, Buckley had to advance him a $3,000 loan. To gain publicity, Will Buckley's consulting firm, Catawba Corporation, bought the rights to *God and Man at Yale* from Bill for $16,000. Bill then gave $10,000 to Regnery to publicize the book and kept $6,000 to fund his own publicity tour. Regnery would have published the book anyway, but without the financial help from the Buckleys, it might have been less timely and have received little notice.

After Regnery agreed to publish *God and Man at Yale*, Buckley asked John Chamberlain to do the introduction. Chamberlain, a highly esteemed journalist, had graduated from Yale in 1925. Originally a socialist, he had achieved renown for his 1932 study of the progressive movement, *Farewell to Reform*, but after joining Henry Luce's *Fortune*, Chamberlain moved steadily to the Right. In 1950, he left Luce's Time Inc. to help found *The Freeman*, a revival of Nock's old magazine. He had first heard of Buckley when he visited Yale in 1949, and he had heard about him again from *The Freeman*'s managing editor, Suzanne La Follette, who was encouraging Buckley to write for the new publication. "He was about the only bright young college graduate that we had come across," Chamberlain recalled.

Chamberlain readily agreed to do the introduction to Buckley's book. He was not sympathetic to Buckley's critique of Yale's religious education—as a student there, he had campaigned against compulsory chapel—but he concurred wholeheartedly with Buckley's critique of Yale's Economics Department, and he wanted to encourage the young author.

II

In April, just as he was finishing *God and Man at Yale*, Buckley heard that he had been accepted for the CIA and that after three months' training in Washington, he would be assigned to Mexico City. Bill and Pat left New Haven in May. After living as postgraduates in New Haven, they looked forward to the romance of a secret agent's life. "I thought it would be fascinating," Patricia Buckley recalled.

The Buckleys got an apartment in Northwest Washington over a grocery store. While Buckley was learning from other agents about safe houses and how to enlist foreigners in a CIA operation—a process he described in his first spy novel, *Saving the Queen*—he covered himself by claiming to be doing research on academic freedom for a sequel to *God and Man at Yale*. Buckley had told Pat and his father what he was going to be doing, but no one else. When he saw his classmate Frank Harman in Washington that summer, Harman confessed to him that he had joined the CIA, but Buckley merely repeated his own cover story.

While he was in Washington, Buckley also worked on *Human Events*. In one issue, he wrote that the CIA

> appears to be heavily staffed by young Ivy Leaguers, who seek to serve their country outside the armed forces; a welter of young Ph.D.s . . . and a liberal sprinkling of middle-aged business executives. . . . All those men and women . . . are earnest about their work. . . . Unfortunately, an appraisal of their efficacy is on the face of it impossible.[10]

During his CIA training, Buckley had to fend off an attempt by Yale's new president, Whitney Griswold, to get him to withdraw *God and Man at Yale* from publication. Buckley had called Griswold that summer to inform him that the book would be published, and Griswold had thanked him, promising that he respected his rights to make his views known, but a week later Buckley received a phone call from William Rogers Coe, a wealthy alumnus who had funded Yale's American Studies Department. Coe told Buckley that Griswold had assured him that he would "clean up" Yale by getting rid of Thomas Emerson and "shutting up" left-wing law professor Eugene Rostow. (Rostow, who would later join the Republican Reagan administration, was then a New Deal Democrat.) Coe insisted that there was no longer any reason for Buckley to publish his book. "I gasped at the blend of naïveté and effrontery," Buckley wrote later.[11]

Refusing to withdraw his book, Buckley wrote Coe: "By telling me that they will clean up at Yale, you are implying that they will betray their principles as they have publicly upheld them." Buckley insisted that he was a "loyal Yale alumnus," but added, "I consider myself to be loyal to the Yale tradition to an extent very few people at Yale are."[12]

The Buckleys arrived in Mexico City in early September. They stayed in the beginning at a sprawling house owned by friends of Buckley's father, and Buckley proceeded, on the instructions of Howard Hunt, who was already installed in the embassy, to begin setting up an import-export business. That was a cover for his CIA work, which involved, among other things, learning about the Mexican student movement.

Hunt was the first covert agent in the Western Hemisphere. His brief in Mexico was to encourage anti-Communists to challenge Communists for leadership in the trade unions, professional and artistic organizations, and student organizations. Hunt accorded special importance to Mexican student organizations. "The students in Mexico had a great deal of power," Hunt explained. "In Mexico, there were parliamentary seats reserved for students. One of the things we did was to help support non-Communist students toward gaining parliamentary seats in the legislature, hoping that would be a springboard for them to some kind of political influence in the country."

Buckley reported to Hunt three or four times a week, often over lunch at a French restaurant they both enjoyed. Hunt put very little pressure on Buckley for results. "My policy as chief of station was always to get the right man, tell him what to do and what was expected of him, and wait for him to report," Hunt said. "I was never a close supervisor."

Hunt also assigned Buckley to work with Eudocio Ravines, a former Chilean Communist who had helped organize Chile's Popular Front government in the 1930s, but who, disillusioned by the Nazi-Soviet Pact of 1939, had broken with the Communists. Ravines had written an anti-Communist book entitled *The Yenan Way*. Buckley's job was to help edit *The Yenan Way* so that it could be circulated in Latin America.

According to Hunt, Buckley "was very comfortable in Mexico." He introduced Hunt to Will Buckley's old friends, and he quickly made inroads in the Mexican student movement. He also got Ravines's book edited in several months. Hunt was very impressed. "He was good," Hunt said.

Hunt was also greatly impressed by Buckley's mind. "I hadn't realized in my first dealings with him how well read and politically educated he was," Hunt said. "His reading, his political tutelage, were vastly greater than mine." Within several months, their relationship, which began as one between senior and junior intelligence officers, had become one of "operational equals."

Bill and Pat also became close friends with Hunt and his wife, Dorothy. When the Hunts drew up a will that fall, they asked the Buckleys to become the legal guardians of their children in case they both died. The Buckleys agreed—a decision that would become important two decades hence.

But while Buckley enjoyed his friendship with Hunt, he was quickly becoming disillusioned with the life of an agent. His work involved making hundreds of phone calls and contacts, of which only one or

two would bear fruit. Buckley was learning that "the romantic inter-
ludes in the life of an agent were very infrequent." Hunt began to
notice his restlessness. "When we went for an operational luncheon,
or went off in a corner in a social event to talk, he would talk about
other things that were of more interest to him. The proportion between business and general talk just shifted positions completely."

Buckley's restlessness with the life of a CIA agent was exacerbated
by the publication of *God and Man at Yale*, which plunged him into a
raging controversy.

III

God and Man at Yale appeared in late October 1951. Regnery had
ordered a first printing of five thousand, most of which he hoped to
sell. But the day the book came out, Regnery received a frenzied call
for help from the manager of the Yale Co-op Bookstore. According to
the manager, a line of students had formed outside the bookstore that
morning waiting to buy copies, and there were far more students than
there were copies. The interest in *God and Man at Yale* wasn't just
confined to Yale. In November alone, Regnery sold twelve thousand
copies and the book made number sixteen on *The New York Times*
best-seller list. In December, the *Buffalo Courier-Express* listed it as
one of the five best-selling nonfiction books in the Buffalo area. By
the spring, it had sold thirty-five thousand copies. And no one was
more astonished at the book's reception than its author.

The sales of *God and Man at Yale* were aided in part by Chamberlain's introduction and by a few favorable reviews in popular publications. Former leftist Max Eastman, writing in *The American Mercury,*
dismissed Buckley's chapters on religion ("To me it is ridiculous to
see little, two-legged fanatics running around the earth fighting and
arguing on behalf of a deity they profess to be omnipotent"), but he
called Buckley's critique of the Yale Economics Department "devastating" and praised Buckley for his "arrant intellectual courage." [13]
Buckley drew expected raves from the *Chicago Tribune* and *The
Freeman,* and he got an unexpected boost from critic Selden Rodman
writing in the prestigious *Saturday Review*. While dissenting from
Buckley's conclusions, Rodman hailed Buckley's challenge to "that
brand of liberal 'materialism' which, by making all values 'relative,'
honors none." [14]

But what made *God and Man at Yale* an instant success was the
seething controversy that it provoked. Buckley was, of course, not
the only American to look askance at Ivy League schools. As numer-

ous favorable reviews from papers in the South and the Midwest showed, there was considerable distrust of "eastern establishment" education. But Buckley's criticisms were different because they came from the inside rather than the outside: from an outstanding graduate of the Yale Class of 1950, a member of Skull and Bones, and the chairman of the *Yale Daily News*. Both Yale and the eastern press could not discount Buckley as a "yokel" or a "hick."

The source of most of this controversy was, directly or indirectly, the Yale administration and loyal Yale alumni. The Yale administration, having failed to get Buckley to withdraw *God and Man at Yale*, tried to ward off the blow. Reuben Holden, Griswold's assistant, wrote Irving Olds, the chairman of the board of U.S. Steel and a Yale trustee, "We intend to take the offensive in this matter and not sit by waiting for complaints to roll in when the book is published in November." [15]

To inquiries about the forthcoming book from alumni who heard rumors of its publication from Yale faculty and administrators, Griswold and other administration officials responded that the book was an expression of Buckley's "militant Catholicism." In a June letter to a prominent alumnus, Griswold described the book as "attacking academic freedom and advocating from the standpoint of a militant Catholic, religious controls that we got rid of a couple of hundred years ago." In answer to another inquiry, Holden wrote that Buckley's proposals "would make this institution [into] a small town parochial academy." [16]

Griswold and Holden worked closely with McGeorge Bundy, a Yale graduate and a Harvard professor, who had been commissioned by *Atlantic Monthly* editor Edward Weeks to review *God and Man at Yale*.* At the end of September, Bundy spent a day at Yale with Griswold going over the points of the review. Afterwards, he wrote Griswold that he had taken a "kind of savage pleasure in the composition" and hoped that Griswold would "find it of some help to Yale and her officers." [17]

Bundy's review, which Weeks ran as a major article in the November *Atlantic* (and of which the Yale administration ordered two thousand reprints), was laced with bitter invective. Bundy described Buckley as a "twisted and ignorant young man" and *God and Man at Yale* as "dishonest in its use of facts, false in its theory." But Bundy

---

* From Bundy's correspondence it appears that Griswold might have even inspired the review and the choice of reviewer. Bundy wrote Holden, "Ted Weeks is, of course, delighted to have a chance to strike a blow for his favorite Yale professor." (Griswold Papers.)

also made some telling points. He noted the "distinctly capitalist" bent of the Democratic and moderate Republican views that Buckley had labeled "collectivist" and had lumped indiscriminately with Naziism and Stalinism; he pointed out that in construing Seymour's promise not to hire Communists as being inconsistent with academic freedom, Buckley had failed to "understand the vital difference between standards for hiring a professor and standards for firing him."

Bundy followed Griswold in insinuating that Buckley's real motive in writing *God and Man at Yale* was to impose his Catholicism on Yale.

> Most remarkable of all, Mr. Buckley, who urges a return to what he considers to be Yale's true religious tradition, at no point says one word of the fact that he himself is an ardent Roman Catholic. In view of the pronounced and well-recognized difference between Protestant and Catholic views of education in America, and in view of Yale's Protestant history, it seems strange for any Roman Catholic to undertake to define Yale's religious tradition.[18]

In effect, Griswold and Bundy were trying to establish that Buckley was not an "insider" after all, but the representative of an alien faith.*

Other prominent "Old Blues" took the field against Buckley's book. In an editorial accompanying *Life*'s story on Yale's 250th anniversary celebration, Henry Luce described *God and Man at Yale* as a "brilliant but not quite honest polemic," and Buckley as "the brat who comes to the party and tells the guests that their birthday boy is secretly a dope addict."[19] Yale trustee Frank Ashburn, the headmaster of the Brooks School, raised the specter of the totalitarian Right in a *Saturday Review* article paired with Rodman's positive review.

> *God and Man at Yale* stands as one of the most forthright, implacable, typical and unscrupulously sincere examples of a return to authoritarianism that has appeared. . . . The book is one which has the glow and appeal of a fiery cross on a hillside at night. There will undoubtedly be robed figures who gather to it, but the hoods will not be academic.[20]

---

* When Dwight Macdonald interviewed Griswold for an article that he was writing on the controversy, Griswold told him that Bill's mother had a private chapel on her estate, which she did not. Macdonald later took Griswold's word for the story about Aloise Buckley's private chapel and included it in his story in *The Reporter*, May 27, 1952. (Dwight Macdonald Papers.)

Reviewers in other major publications echoed the charge that *God and Man at Yale* was an expression of militant Catholicism and neo-fascism. *The New Republic*'s Robert Hatch wrote: "It is astounding, on the assumption that Buckley is well-meaning, that he has not realized that the methods he proposes for his alma mater are precisely those employed in Italy, Germany, and Russia."[21]

Buckley himself had expected a certain amount of hostility from the Yale administration and alumni, but nothing approaching Bundy's or Ashburn's reviews. It was only six years since the United States had been totally mobilized against fascism; and to accuse someone of being a Fascist was a very serious charge. It was also unusual for a writer to be subjected to *ad hominem* attacks because of his religion. Buckley was very taken aback. "He took it all pretty seriously," Regnery recalled.

Buckley's reaction was to fight back in print and on the lecture platform. Responding to Bundy in the December *Atlantic Monthly,* he matched him insult for insult. He denounced Bundy's "appalling insincerity" and "arrogance." The word " 'Fascist,' " he wrote, "has been used carefully to describe persons and points of view. But it fits with unusual precision Mr. Bundy's advocacy of irresponsible, irreproachable education by an academic elite."[22]

He later described his method of responding to criticism: "When I set about to comment on statements from the Opposition, I look at their latest as I would a sort of wriggling eel. I then search out the tenderest spot and do my best to impale it with a bright and lethal pin."[23]

With some reviewers, Buckley even threatened libel suits. When Dartmouth's *Vox Populi* charged that Buckley was "selling Christianity and capitalism down the river," Buckley enlisted his father's attorney to write the editors a threatening letter accusing them of making an "irresponsible and unsupporting [*sic*] statement."[24]

All in all, the success of *God and Man at Yale* combined with its bitter reception hardened him for the battles to come. It showed him what he would have to endure if he sought, on his terms, "to bring America back to herself." As a result of the experience with the book, Reid Buckley said, "Bill became a tough polemicist, like the young Cassius Clay."

The wildly hostile and adulatory reviews of *God and Man at Yale* revealed more about the reviewers' political and educational views than the author's. It was only those reviewers who refused to join one side or another of the barricades who were able to grasp what was unusual about the book. They understood that *God and Man at Yale* bore distinct traces of Catholic educational doctrine, but was also a strange hybrid of religious traditionalism and libertarian and individualistic economics.

Most Catholic journals, while commending Buckley's support of Christian education, rejected his defense of laissez-faire capitalism and his opposition to the welfare state as contrary to the Church's teachings on the state's responsibilities for the poor. These Catholic journals could cite with good authority encyclicals by Popes Leo XIII and Pius XI affirming the state's role and condemning unregulated capitalism.

"The trouble with Mr. Buckley," the Jesuit magazine *America* editorialized, "is that he does not judge [Yale economics] in the light of Catholic social doctrine. . . . His unawareness of the moral authority of the state to regulate economic society seems fairly complete."[25] Writing in *Catholic World*, Christopher E. Fullman remarked, "Now it is surely quite obvious that Christ and Adam Smith have very little in common."[26]

Buckley's response to the Catholic attacks was far less strident and more cautious than his response to Bundy and other critics. Having read relatively little Catholic theology or doctrine, he knew that he was not on firm ground. In responding to Fullman, he accused him of arguing that "God is on the side of the New Deal." But he admitted that he was "confused by some of the statements that appear to be social encyclicals."[27]

Buckley's book was also criticized by a group of intellectuals who called themselves the "new conservatives." They included Bundy, poet Peter Viereck and *New York Herald Tribune* editorialist August Heckscher. Claiming to be influenced by the European conservatives Edmund Burke, Benjamin Disraeli, and Klemens von Metternich, they saw conservatism as a politics of gradual rather than abrupt change, and defended the welfare state as a means of stabilizing capitalism. They were most clearly identified with the moderate Republicanism of the Northeast.

In *The New York Times Book Review,* Viereck praised Buckley for his insistence that "man has a moral nature," but criticized him for identifying morality with the anti-welfare-state economics of the National Association of Manufacturers (NAM) and "Old Guard Republicanism." Viereck asked, "Is there no selfish materialism at all in the NAM?"[28]

In an exchange of letters, Buckley treated Viereck's criticisms respectfully, but he rejected not only the new conservative's argument, but his political approach. If conservatism meant defending what existed, then Buckley was not a conservative.

Buckley understood that his ideas did not fit any existing political tendency, including that of conservatism. In *God and Man at Yale*, he referred to the "so-called conservative" who is "uncomfortably disdainful of controversy." [29] In describing his economics, he preferred the Nockian term "individualist" to "conservative."

In an article he had written in June 1951 for the Buckley family newspaper, *Grelmschatka*, Buckley had also expressed his dissatisfaction with being called a "conservative." Taking issue with a conservative critic who had called his proposals "impractically reactionary," Buckley wrote, "Since no one doubts that in the past 18 years radical changes have taken place, then one cannot despair of more radical changes. It cannot be said of anything that it is 'impractically reactionary.' " "Radical" and "reactionary," Buckley argued, are not antonyms by synonyms. "Too many conservatives are holding back because they regard as futile the espousal of any radical measure." [30]

One critic who understood the author of *God and Man at Yale* was maverick journalist Dwight Macdonald, a Yale graduate and a rebel of the Left, who had been a Trotskyist and then an independent Socialist. In an article describing the controversy over the book for *The Reporter,* Macdonald portrayed Buckley as being both a radical and a reactionary. "He has the outward and visible signs of the campus radical, and the inward and spiritual qualities of the radical's wealthy grandfather," Macdonald wrote. *God and Man at Yale* exemplified this paradox.

> It was an earnest, extreme, and irreverent book, a book that, in its mockery of authority, its relentless logic, followed the old familiar script: CAMPUS REBEL FLAYS FACULTY. But the script was all balled up, for the author was more reactionary than any of the dignitaries in their black robes, and his book damned Yale as a hotbed of atheism and collectivism.

Macdonald denied that Buckley's Catholicism was important to his critique of Yale. "Buckley is indeed a Catholic, and an ardent one," Macdonald wrote. "But oddly enough this fact is irrelevant, since his book defines Christianity in Protestant terms, and his economics are

Calvinist rather than Catholic." And while Macdonald held little brief for Buckley's religious or economic views, he believed that "Buckley's medieval lance struck Yale officialdom in the most vulnerable joint in its armor: the gap between ideology and practice." Yale had reacted to *God and Man at Yale,* Macdonald wrote, "with all the grace and agility of an elephant cornered by a mouse."[31]

IV

As *God and Man at Yale* climbed onto the best-seller lists, invitations to speak poured in. And both *The American Mercury* and *The Freeman,* the two most important right-wing publications of the day, asked Buckley to become an editor. Bored with the CIA, he wanted to take one of the two offers.

Pat Buckley also wanted to leave Mexico. She had suffered an ectopic pregnancy in 1951, and was pregnant again. She didn't want to have a child in Mexico City, where Dorothy Hunt had nearly died in childbirth.

In February, during a luncheon at their favorite French restaurant in Mexico City, Buckley told Hunt that he was going to resign from the CIA. Hunt was not surprised. "I felt Bill had a great deal of drive to excel, to become a figure with a capital *F,* and a spokesman, a man who wanted to present his ideas and his philosophy in very broad and significant forums," he recalled. "Obviously, this wasn't possible given the limitations of the CIA."

That spring, after only nine months with the CIA, Bill and Pat left Mexico City for New York, where Buckley planned to continue his crusade to "bring America back to herself."

PART TWO

The Editor in Chief

What matters, verily, is personality substance. And the good Lord, it seems, has made them in two versions—"ins" and "outs." Now the "ins" are people who'd rather die than be out of step; . . . What makes them, at the core, is their "optimism"—their do-gooding, go getting stick-to-iting optimism which hates nothing more than the "apocalyptic hunch." The "ins" are, in other words, born for the exercise of power. . . . The "outs" . . . not only despise but dread power; are actually incapable of exercising it. . . . The outs have indeed the "apocalyptic hunch," a respectful notion that there is an end as surely as there is a beginning, an organic reverence for the grown rather than the manufactured, the private rather than the public, the small rather than the big, the old rather than the new, the beautiful rather than the strong. The "outs" can never get in, and it's a good thing, too. In their hands power would crumble. . . . Needing both types, the world is in good shape so long as the "outs" can project their mood into society. Our world is about to burst because the "outs" have been virtually suffocated. . . . There are, I suspect, more "outs" in this country than we know; but they get nowhere near the "in" market. How do you reach them? . . . By publishing a magazine. This, my friend, is the ceterum censeo *of our day: . . .* [1]

—Willi Schlamm, letter to
Henry Regnery, 1953

CHAPTER 6

McCarthy and His Friends

In the spring of 1952, when Bill and Pat Buckley returned to New York from Mexico City, Ohio Republican Senator Robert Taft was engaged in a last-ditch struggle with General Dwight Eisenhower for the Republican presidential nomination. His defeat in Chicago that summer would spell doom for the wing of the Republican Party that he had represented for two decades: isolationist, anti-New Deal, white Protestant, small-town Midwestern. Taft himself would die the following year. But Taft's defeat would not leave the Republican Right without a national leader.

For two years, the junior Republican senator from Wisconsin, Joseph McCarthy, had been leading a crusade against Communists in government. Although many of the Taft Republicans supported him, McCarthy was not a Taft Republican. He was a transitional figure between an old and a new Right. A supporter of both the United Nations and NATO, McCarthy was obsessed with fighting communism rather than with preventing foreign entanglements.

McCarthy's anti-Communist crusade also had consistent echoes of anti-establishment populism that were foreign to the Taft Republicans. McCarthy never hesitated to contrast his own background—he was an Irish Catholic from a modest farm family and had graduated from Marquette—with that of the lawyers and investment bankers who staffed the higher reaches of government.

A burly unkempt man, who had been a boxer in college, McCarthy had a trial lawyer's flair for the dramatic and a small-town overachiever's hunger for publicity. After three undistinguished years in the Senate, McCarthy won national attention in February 1950 when, speaking in Wheeling, West Virginia, he claimed to know the names of 205 "men at the State Department who have been named as members of the Communist party and members of a spy ring."[2] Challenged by Senate Democrats to back up his charges, McCarthy had upped the ante with more fabulous charges—for instance, calling State Department consultant and China scholar Owen Lattimore "the top Russian agent" in government and charging former Secretary of State General George Marshall with treason. With the Republicans about to win control of the Senate and the country in the midst of a second great "Red Scare," McCarthy was on the verge of becoming the most powerful politician in America.

Among conservative intellectuals, McCarthy provoked a crisis of conscience. Many of them agreed with their liberal counterparts that McCarthy was a boor and an opportunist more interested in gaining publicity than in combating communism, but they believed that because of the importance of McCarthy's ostensible objective—combating the Communist threat—he had to be defended. Former Socialist Max Eastman confessed privately that "McCarthy is a misbehaving and sloppy-minded person functioning in a place where the prime demand was for a well-behaved and extremely accurate and exact mind." But Eastman insisted that McCarthy was "doing badly a job that has to be done."[3]

Buckley shared the conservative intellectuals' doubts about some of McCarthy's wilder charges, but he believed that they were the result of overzealousness. He also couldn't help but identify with McCarthy. He saw McCarthy as a Catholic who had the same burning hatred of communism that he had. And he saw that McCarthy had earned the undying wrath of the same eastern liberal elite that had tried to pillory him. Buckley's first nationally published article—appearing in *The Freeman*, May 1951—was a defense of McCarthy.[4] And his next book after *God and Man at Yale* would be an extended defense of the controversial senator.

I

Buckley returned to New York in March 1952 a minor celebrity, a status he clearly enjoyed. His father, who could hardly contain his joy over the success of *God and Man at Yale* ("Our bloodlines clicked," Will told Aloise), and Henry Regnery both wanted him to spend a year or two studying politics and economics.[5] Regnery suggested studying under economist Friedrich von Hayek, who was then at the University of Chicago, and Will Buckley recommended that his son attend Oxford or Cambridge. "What this country needs is a politician who has an education and I don't know of *one,*" he wrote Bill. "If you are going into politics, or if without going into politics, you want to continue to discuss public questions, you should spend a couple of years in study."[6] But Buckley, having had his first taste of national controversy, was anxious to plunge back into the fray. He decided to join one of the magazines that had approached him with job offers.

Buckley chose *The American Mercury* over *The Freeman* because the *Mercury's* latest editor, William Bradford Huie, was steering the magazine to the Right and he promised Buckley considerable autonomy as associate editor. In addition, *The American Mercury,* which had had its heyday in the 1920s under H. L. Mencken, still enjoyed a readership of 90,000, while *The Freeman's* circulation was only around 20,000.

The Buckleys, who were expecting a child, settled outside of Stamford, Connecticut, where after a month's search they found a three-story, fifteen-room house on exclusive Wallacks Point, overlooking Long Island Sound. To buy it, Will Buckley authorized Bill to liquidate $65,000 from the capital that he had already begun to bestow upon his children. The house had terraced gardens going down to the seashore, and the location fit Buckley's specifications: it was within commuting distance of New York and on Long Island Sound, where he sailed. The Buckleys also kept a small apartment in New York City. That fall, on September 28, Christopher was born.

When Buckley went to work on *The American Mercury* in May, he discovered that the job was not quite what Huie had described. The magazine was in a financial crisis, and Huie had to spend most of his time on the road raising money. When Huie was gone, the other associate editor, Martin Greenberg, "maneuvered himself, in a few short weeks, into the position of exercising (through Huie) virtual control of the magazine," according to Buckley.[7] Buckley and Greenberg quarreled repeatedly, and when Greenberg refused to print his article on the hegemony of liberalism—ironically titled "The Plight of the Liberals"—Buckley quit.

Buckley's reason for leaving was his unhappiness with Greenberg, but he would probably not have lasted long at anyone else's magazine. "He couldn't work for someone else," *National Review* senior editor Joe Sobran said later. "He is a man who wants to control the situation, who wants to do things on his own terms."

When Buckley quit *The American Mercury,* John Chamberlain, Suzanne La Follette, and the other editors at *The Freeman* repeated their offer, but Buckley declined. At that point, *The Freeman*'s editors and board members were hopelessly divided. Editor in chief Forrest Davis had numerous enemies on the board and among the editors. And the editors could agree neither on their presidential choice—they were split between Taft and Eisenhower—nor on whether the magazine should support McCarthy.[8]

Working out of the garage that he converted to a study, Buckley began to look around for another book to do. Henry Regnery had written him suggesting a book on the educational ideas of Robert Hutchins, and Buckley had countered with a proposal for a book that would "examine the claims of Peter Viereck, August Heckscher *inter alia* to representing the 'legitimate conservatism.' "[9] But Buckley was drawn to the controversy swirling around McCarthy. He and Bozell were already organizing an independent campaign in Connecticut to defeat Senator William Benton, a foe of McCarthy, who was running for re-election that November against Prescott Bush. They ran anti-Benton newspaper advertisements that were financed by Connecticut millionaire and future *American Mercury* owner Russell Maguire. Benton later blamed his defeat partly on Buckley's ads, which he described as "scurrilous." He wrote former Maryland senator Millard Tydings, "Buckley is a smart, able, aggressive young man. Yes, he is a potentially dangerous young man."[10]

Buckley and Bozell, who was still in law school, also began drafting a long article on McCarthy for *The Freeman.* When Regnery suggested that they turn it into a "short book," they readily concurred.[11] McCarthy himself, with whom Buckley had become friendly, agreed to cooperate by making his staff and materials available to the authors.* That fall, before Bozell returned to school, the coauthors di-

---

* According to Buckley, McCarthy was visiting his house in Stamford in October 1952 when Senator Henry Cabot Lodge's campaign manager called to ask McCarthy to come to Massachusetts to back Lodge against Democrat John F. Kennedy. As McCarthy told Buckley, he decided not to intervene out of loyalty to John Kennedy's father, who had been a staunch supporter of his own career. (*National Review,* October 9, 1962.)

vided the chapters of the book between them and began writing. But the book, which they called *McCarthy and His Enemies*, kept growing as they tried to defend a man many of whose actions were indefensible.

Buckley and Bozell wanted to write a credible book that took account of what they thought was legitimate in liberal objections to McCarthy, but at the same time warded off the brunt of those charges and reaffirmed McCarthy's crusade against Communists in government. They also wanted to write a book that reflected their own loyalty to McCarthy.

They tried to salvage McCarthy's crusade by distinguishing between McCarthy and McCarthyism. They admitted that McCarthy had "committed an egregious blunder" in his Wheeling speech and had been "guilty of exaggeration" in defending himself against his Senate detractors. They rejected the *ex post facto* reasoning that had led McCarthy to accuse Marshall of treason. "In assessing a man's primary loyalties, we cannot thus base our deductions on the *effects* of that man's behavior," they wrote.[12] In all, one critic counted sixty-three critical references to McCarthy in the text.[13]

But while they criticized McCarthy, they unequivocally supported what they described as "McCarthyism." "McCarthyism," Buckley and Bozell wrote, "is primarily the maintenance of a steady flow of criticism . . . calculated to pressure the President, Cabinet members, high officials, and above all the political party in power, to get on with the elimination of security risks in government."[14] In the present historical juncture, they argued, such a program is necessary. "We cannot avoid the fact that the United States is at war against international Communism and that McCarthyism is a program of action against those in our land who help the enemy." They added, "An Alger Hiss, critically situated, can conceivably determine the destiny of the West."[15]

They dramatically summed up their case for McCarthyism:

> To the extent that McCarthyism, out of ignorance or impetuosity or malice, urges the imposition of sanctions upon persons who are *not* pro-Communist or security risks, we should certainly oppose it. . . . But as long as McCarthyism fixes its goals with its present precision, it is a movement around which men of good will and stern morality can close ranks.[16]

Buckley and Bozell vindicated McCarthy's reckless crusade by justifying McCarthyism. In the process, they took McCarthyism politically far beyond McCarthy's own stated intentions. McCarthy had framed his charges within the prevailing legal definition of disloyalty —persons who belonged to the Communist Party or who actively and knowingly participated in Communist-organized front groups. But Buckley and Bozell argued that the threat posed by Communist subversion justified removing from government not merely Communist conspirators, but also policy makers who advocated measures that, in Buckley and Bozell's opinion, benefited the Communist cause. "When we look closely at the matter," Buckley and Bozell wrote, "we find that we are interested in talking, not about 'who is loyal?' but about *who favors those policies that are not in the national interest as we see it.*' "[17] According to Buckley and Bozell, officials or consultants like Lattimore and John Stewart Service, who recommended that the U.S. come to terms with the Communist Chinese, should have been discharged regardless of whether they were Communists.

> When we speak of personnel who frustrate the advancement of American interests, we speak of a group that includes some men who are *not* traitors, men whose only fault may be that they are incompetent political analysts, men of bad judgment. And if the ultimate objective of the security program is to remove from government service all who frustrate the advancement of American interests, the merely incompetent men must go out along with the traitors.[18]

Willmoore Kendall, who went carefully over every chapter with the authors, and Bozell wanted to take McCarthyism even further. According to Buckley, they wanted to make McCarthyism into a new "public orthodoxy" through legislation outlawing Communist ideas as well as Communists. Buckley thought that the Communist Party should be outlawed, but he wanted to eliminate Communist ideas through social pressure rather than legislation. After several heated arguments at Great Elm and at Austin Taylor's New York apartment, where they had holed up to finish the book, Buckley and Bozell finally agreed to fudge their differences. They described their proposal as a "balanced libertarianism" in which social sanctions would be given precedence over legal sanctions unless society were faced with a "clear and present danger" from a body of ideas.[19] "McCarthyism," they wrote, "involves an orthodoxy still-in-the-making; and therefore, as with all imperfect conformities, some coercive sanctions are being exercised in its behalf."[20]

Buckley and Bozell's "balanced libertarianism" bore little resemblance, however, to the libertarianism of Frank Chodorov or Albert Jay Nock. Beginning with the assumption that the United States was locked in a life-and-death struggle with communism, Buckley and Bozell opted for what amounted to a balanced authoritarianism. Their proposals for government loyalty tests would have entailed the abandonment of the civil service and its replacement by a docile bureaucracy hired and retained on ideological and partisan grounds, while their suggestions that "coercive sanctions" should be used to enforce a public orthodoxy would have meant the abandonment of First Amendment guarantees. Like *God and Man at Yale, McCarthy and His Enemies* was a radical rather than a conventionally conservative book, designed not to preserve the existing order, but to uproot it. It was bound to create a great deal of controversy and to gain its authors no small measure of public attention.

II

Buckley had hoped and expected to have a large family as his father had. In May 1953, while Buckley was writing *McCarthy and His Enemies,* Pat had her second ectopic pregnancy. When she had had her first, Pat had had one of her Fallopian tubes removed, and now she had to have the second removed, making it impossible for her to have more children. "Pat was broken up," Patricia Bozell recalled.

Bill stayed by Pat's bedside, and then close to her during her recuperation. It took several weeks before the full import of what had happened hit him. "It was a terrible blow," he said later.

Not being able to have a large family had few immediate but many long-term repercussions. While having only one child made it easier for the Buckleys to shuttle between homes in New York, Wallacks Point, and Gstaad, Switzerland, and to undertake a wide range of activities, many of them requiring travel, not having a large family deprived them of a certain stability and sense of self-worth. It threw them upon the world, making them more dependent for emotional sustenance upon a far-flung network of friends and associates and more dependent for self-satisfaction upon public acclaim.

III

Buckley and Bozell finished *McCarthy and His Enemies* in the fall of 1953, but the manuscript they sent Henry Regnery was 250,000 words, about three times the length of a "short book, " and Regnery insisted that they cut 75,000 words from it. To do the cutting and to write an introduction to the book, they hired Willi Schlamm, an Austrian émigré who had been Henry Luce's foreign-policy adviser at Time Inc., and whom Buckley had met at *The Freeman,* where Schlamm had been writing a column, "Arts and Manners."

In December 1953, Buckley and Bozell sent *McCarthy and His Enemies* to McCarthy for his approval. They wanted McCarthy's endorsement not only to help promote the book once it was published, but to help them raise money to defray its publishing costs. Regnery was planning to sell *McCarthy and His Enemies* for $6.50, a prohibitively high price in those days, and he had agreed that if the authors could arrange the sale of six thousand copies in advance, he would lower the price to $5.00. Buckley and Bozell believed that if they could get McCarthy's advance endorsement, they could obtain the advance sales from several of the senator's fervent supporters in Texas and the Midwest.

McCarthy was already operating in an alcoholic daze and couldn't get through *McCarthy and His Enemies.* He told Patricia Bozell, "I don't understand the book. It is too intellectual for me." But when his wife, Jean, read the galleys of *McCarthy and His Enemies,* she became furious at the criticisms of her husband and advised him not to endorse the book. Buckley later wrote of Jean McCarthy, "She stood resolutely in the way of any author, film-maker, or television writer who undertook to grapple with Joe McCarthy and failed at the outset to declare him indistinguishable from St. Francis of Assisi."[21]

To mollify Jean McCarthy, Buckley and Bozell spent two evenings in Washington going over the galleys with her husband. Buckley later described the meetings: "Joe had really lost his capacity for sustained concentration at that point, and although we sat next to each other at a table looking over the galleys, you could see his mind was wandering. He never really gave us any constructive criticism." Buckley and Bozell finally agreed to rewrite several passages that the senator thought were "too stridently anti-McCarthy."

McCarthy was satisfied with the changes, but his wife was not. On Jean's advice, he still refused to help Buckley and Bozell raise money, but he did agree to attend the party that was to be held March 30 at New York's Waldorf Astoria to celebrate the book's publication.* At

---

* Will Buckley threw the book party for his son, but, being an unqualified admirer of the senator, he had expressed some reservations about the criticisms of McCarthy in Buckley and Bozell's book. Trying to mollify him, Henry Regnery wrote him, "I understand how you feel about Bill's new book, but if you consider the circumstances under which it is appearing and the audience for which it is intended, I think you will agree that it is a first-

the lavish party, attended by a host of right-wing and anti-Communist luminaries, reporters asked McCarthy what he thought of *McCarthy and His Enemies*. Seated between the two authors, he remarked cagily, "It is the only book ever written about me not written by an enemy or by McCarthy."

With *God and Man at Yale,* Buckley had created a raging controversy. With *McCarthy and His Enemies,* he joined one. The publication of *McCarthy and His Enemies* in March 1954 occurred one month before the nationally televised Army-McCarthy hearings. These hearings marked the height of McCarthy's notoriety, but also the beginning of his precipitous decline. As a result of the publicity McCarthy generated, Buckley and Bozell were besieged with invitations to speak and debate and to talk on the radio.

Buckley, who had been treated as a black sheep by his alma mater since the publication of *God and Man at Yale,* was invited back with Bozell to debate two Law School professors, Vern Countryman and Fowler Harper. Buckley's return was a triumph. Speaking to several thousand students crammed into Woolsey Hall, Buckley and Bozell routed the law professors. The *Yale Daily News* reported the next day:

> [Buckley] faced a hostile audience which had been left, by Harper, eager for the kill. He was greeted with a smattering applause and spoke quietly, with an impassive expression. Slowly building on the background of his McCarthy facts, he made a logical case for his side. He drew with him an audience that was first relaxed, then attentive, then mellow, and finally enthusiastic. When he sat down, he was greeted with a long and loud burst of applause.[22]

In April Buckley had been invited to address the Women's National Republican Club in New York, but its Board of Governors, alerted to the administration's growing opposition to McCarthy, rescinded the club's invitation. Mrs. Preston Davie, chairman of the Women's Auxiliary of the County Republican Committee, arranged, however, for him to speak at the National Republican Club under its auspices. Ten chartered buses brought interested listeners. More than a thousand people jammed the club's auditorium, while a thousand gathered outside to hear Buckley's speech on loudspeakers that had been mounted

---

rate job and just the sort of book that is needed. I don't think it has been Bill's intention to write only for those who agree with and admire McCarthy. . . ." (Buckley Papers.)

on sound trucks. In his speech, Buckley roasted the Republicans who
were turning their backs on McCarthy.

> Far from suffering from a reign of terror, it is my contention that we
> are living in an age when particularly the cowards speak up. Men
> who have never had the spirit to face up to their mothers-in-law are
> suddenly aware that they can now earn a badge of courage by de-
> nouncing Senator McCarthy, and what is more their heroism is sure
> to be immortalized by the *New York Times*.[23]

In defending McCarthy, Buckley also came in contact with a large
audience of conservative Catholics. At the Catholic seminaries, conservative clerics looked to Buckley as a Catholic who understood
McCarthy. "We used to listen to Joe McCarthy on television, and we
used to read the *Times* the next day, and say to ourselves, 'That
couldn't have been what we heard,' " Msgr. Eugene V. Clark, later
Cardinal Spellman's secretary, remembered. Middle-class Catholic
Action groups organized in Queens, New York, and in the suburbs of
other eastern cities called upon Bill to speak. "He was taking invitations constantly," recalled Kieran O'Doherty, who met Buckley at
one of these meetings in Forest Hills. These meetings represented a
new audience for the American Right.

McCarthy and His Enemies did not get quite as widely reviewed as
God and Man at Yale had been. Both *Time* and *Newsweek* ignored it.
This may have been partly because of its style. Where *God and Man
at Yale* had the tactlessness and breathless enthusiasm of a young
man's polemic against his elders, *McCarthy and His Enemies* read
like a courtroom document. Dwight Macdonald described it as "a
laborious piece of special pleading which gives the effect of a brief by
Cadwalader, Wickersham & Taft on behalf of a pickpocket caught in
the men's room of the subway."[24]

Primarily, though, *McCarthy and His Enemies* was ignored because
of the bitterness of the controversy that it joined. The nation was
sharply polarized over McCarthy, and the editors of the eastern establishment magazines and newspapers were so violently against him that
they simply didn't want to give any publicity to a book that tried to
defend him. The only major review was in *The New York Times*. One
of its own political journalists, William S. White, described *McCarthy
and His Enemies* as "the most extraordinary book [about McCarthy]
yet to come. . . . Here, at any rate is proof that it is the young who
are infinitely more deadly—in purpose at least—of the species."[25]

If *God and Man at Yale* had given Buckley the reputation of an enfant terrible among the eastern intelligentsia, *McCarthy and His Enemies* made him a pariah. When Sol Stein, the executive secretary of the American Committee for Cultural Freedom, agreed to serve on an anti-Communist committee that Buckley was helping to organize, Daniel Bell, a member of the ACCF's board, warned Stein that "officers of the ACCF should not collaborate with an apologist for Senator McCarthy." [26]

IV

McCarthy himself quickly disintegrated that spring under the glare of the Army-McCarthy hearings. He was destroyed by his own alcoholic ineptitude and by the calm that President Eisenhower had brought to the country. By July his approval rating in opinion polls had plummeted.

Both Buckley and Bozell were aware of McCarthy's decline. Buckley remembered McCarthy as "drugged by the velocity of events." In December, when Buckley and Bozell were negotiating the final approval of *McCarthy and His Enemies* with McCarthy, McCarthy had told Buckley that of the fourteen hundred "security risks" who had been fired during 1953, only a "tiny faction" were "security risks in the political sense." But then he claimed at a press conference that "the overwhelming majority of the 1400 were loyalty risks." [27] Buckley concluded that McCarthy was no longer committed to fighting communism. "I never questioned McCarthy's integrity," he said later, "but I came to question his seriousness, using that word in the French or Spanish sense. It gradually became clear to me that he was not any longer concerned about the leverage of disloyal persons in the administration."

In a manner reminiscent of his behavior at Yale during the looming FBI scandal, Buckley did not let what he knew of McCarthy color his public portrayal of or his political loyalty to the man. Far from dissociating himself from McCarthy, Buckley—and also Bozell—remained fiercely loyal to the senator. Buckley wrote a speech for McCarthy in July 1954 on "Investigating Committee Methods." [28] And Bozell, after a fling at private practice in San Francisco, went to Washington to work for lawyer Edward Bennett Williams on McCarthy's censure defense. Then he became McCarthy's chief speech writer, contributing the infamous speech that insured McCarthy's Senate censure the next December. (In the speech, McCarthy accused a Senate committee of being the "unwitting handmaiden" of the Communist Party.)

The Buckleys and Bozells and McCarthys remained personally friendly. McCarthy was particularly fond of Pat Buckley, whom he called to give stock tips.

Buckley's behavior and attitude were influenced by a kind of familial loyalty to McCarthy, but he was also moved, as before, by the overarching importance he attached to the struggle against communism. Whatever damage McCarthy had done—from ruined reputations and lost livelihoods to suicides—paled in comparison to what communism had already done and might still do.

McCarthy's censure left the Republican Right without any heroes. Its remaining champions were lackluster men of the past like California Senator William Knowland and Indiana Senator William Jenner. There was a political vacuum on the Republican Right.

There was also a certain kind of intellectual vacuum. Both *The Freeman* and *The American Mercury* had ceased to be vital political publications. In January 1953, the battle among *The Freeman*'s editors and board had climaxed with the resignations of Chamberlain, La Follette, Davis, and the treasurer and major contributor Alex Hillman. The next year, *The Freeman* was bought by Leonard Read's Foundation for Economic Education and was converted into a monthly under Frank Chodorov's editorship. Many of the same writers continued to write for it, but without a sense that they were making an impact on the national political debate. The magazine, in Buckley's words, became "staid and academic."

The American Mercury suffered an even worse fate. In December 1952, the editor, Huie, fell out with his principal supporter and acquired a new backer, Connecticut millionaire Russell Maguire. Maguire was a notorious anti-Semite, who had previously funded Merwin K. Hart and Allen Zoll's anti-Semitic American Patriots Inc. Except for Huie, the magazine's top editors resigned immediately in protest, and Huie himself resigned six months later when Maguire took editorial control of the magazine and began publishing anti-Semitic articles.

With these magazines courting oblivion, there was no major national right-wing publication, a fact that Buckley was well aware of.

CHAPTER 7

The Ins and the Outs

At no time did the fortunes of the American Right appear as dim as they did in 1954. Taft was dead; McCarthy had been discredited; the Democrats had recaptured Congress; Eisenhower, by his hostility to McCarthy and acceptance of the New Deal, had repudiated the Republican Right. The principal right-wing organizations were anti-Semitic and neo-isolationist throwbacks to the thirties and forties like Gerald L. K. Smith's Nationalist Christian Crusade and the Congress of Freedom.

To claim to be a right-wing intellectual was to court ridicule. In 1953, when Michigan State College instructor Russell Kirk submitted his pathbreaking history of Anglo-American conservatism to Henry Regnery, he provisionally titled it *The Conservative Rout*. Only at Regnery's insistence did he change the title to the less pessimistic *The Conservative Mind*.

But during what appeared to be the collapse of the American Right, Buckley set out on the boldest political and intellectual venture of his life.

I

In the spring of 1954, after *McCarthy and His Enemies* had come out, Buckley joined the family business at his father's suggestion, going to work at the Catawba Corporation office on 37th Street in New York City. Will Buckley had formed Catawba in 1948 as a combination holding company–consulting business that both managed and partly owned the companies that he set up. It was a complex arrangement designed to shield Will and Catawba from angry stockholders. Buckley worked at Catawba for about four months. His brother Jim, who had joined the firm in 1953, said of Bill's tenure, "I do recall he had some positive, good ideas, but also some ideas that were not practical, a reflection that he hadn't learned yet what you can and can't do."

But Buckley was increasingly distracted by the prospect of starting his own magazine—an idea that he had toyed with for at least two years. When he left the CIA in the spring of 1952, he had told Howard Hunt that he wanted to buy a magazine. When he went to work on *The American Mercury,* Evan Galbraith recalled, "even at that time he was thinking of his own magazine." The split in *The Freeman* and the degeneration of *The American Mercury* opened a space on the Right that Buckley believed he could fill.

Buckley first tried to buy *Human Events* in order to expand the weekly broadsheet into a magazine. But while editor Frank Hanighen was amenable to a deal, the other owners balked at turning the newsweekly over to him.* Buckley also corresponded with Regnery and his assistant, Kevin Corrigan, about starting a magazine. In September 1953, Regnery had written Buckley suggesting that he edit a new "monthly magazine" with the assistance of Russell Kirk. But Regnery's conception was more scholarly than Buckley's, and he also insisted that the magazine "be edited and published outside New York."[1]

In the summer of 1954, Buckley found someone who was as eager to start a new right-wing magazine as he was: Willi Schlamm, who had helped him and Bozell with *McCarthy and His Enemies.* While Buckley would eventually have embarked on a magazine without Schlamm's prodding, it was largely because of Schlamm that Buckley threw himself into the project.

---

* In 1955, Buckley tried to buy *The Freeman* in order to take over its mailing list and turn it back into a weekly, but *The Freeman's* directors balked at Buckley's proposal.

Schlamm, then fifty, was a small, dark man, who wore his black hair slicked straight back. One newspaper account described him as "the incarnation of the Viennese coffeehouse literati."[2] He was a brilliant conversationalist who could hold forth on any subject, a passionate polemicist, and an inveterate factionalist. "Life with Willi was a nonstop conversation," Buckley recalled. The son of a Jewish merchant in Galicia, Schlamm had joined the Austrian Communist Party and visited Moscow as a sixteen-year-old, where he suffered his first disillusionment with communism when a Moscow party member offered to procure a prostitute for him. While only in his twenties, he became the editor of a Communist newspaper, but he quit the Communist Party in 1930, as Stalin veered in a sharply sectarian direction both at home and abroad. (During the "Third Period," Communist parties attacked Social Democrats with the same fervor that they attacked Fascists—a particularly disastrous policy in Germany.) Schlamm then became an editor of *Die Weltbuhne,* a left-wing avant-garde magazine opposed to both Stalinism and Naziism.[3] When Hilter took power, Schlamm and *Die Weltbuhne* moved to Prague, and then in 1938, when Hitler seized Czechoslovakia, Schlamm fled to the United States. After writing for *The New Leader,* he was hired, on John Chamberlain's recommendation, as an editorial assistant to Henry Luce.

At Time Inc. Schlamm rose quickly to become Luce's chief adviser on foreign policy. With Chamberlain, Whittaker Chambers, and John Davenport, he became part of an anti-Communist faction at Time Inc. Like Chambers and other ex-Communists, Schlamm turned toward the Right because he had become disillusioned with Stalin's Soviet Union. He had little interest in right-wing economic doctrine, and he had nothing but contempt for the right-wing isolationists and libertarians who had opposed fighting Hilter and now opposed the Cold War. He even attributed the Right's McCarthyism to nativism and anti-Semitism. Remarking on the support for McCarthy's investigation of Irving Peress, a Jewish dentist from the Bronx, Schlamm wrote Chambers, "In their deepest emotional commitments, Americans even (and particularly!) on the Right prefer to fight a Bronx dentist to fighting [Soviet Premier Georgi] Malenkov."[4]

Even when he was one of the most important people at Time Inc., Schlamm dreamed of running his own magazine. Chambers once described him as having "the worst case of magazinitis" that he'd ever seen. In 1949 he left Time Inc. on Luce's promise to fund a new intellectual journal called *Measure* that Schlamm would edit. Schlamm had already assembled more than forty articles for the first few issues when a recession dampened Luce's enthusiasm for the project and left Schlamm stranded. He and his wife moved to Vermont where they planned to run an inn and where he wrote the "Arts and Manners" column for *The Freeman.*

But Schlamm hadn't given up on *Measure.* Luce had sold the name to the University of Chicago, which sold it to Regnery. In spring 1953, Schlamm wrote Regnery a long letter explaining that a new magazine was necessary to give the congenital "outs," whom Schlamm identified with conservatives, a way of pressuring the "ins," the people "born for the exercise of power." Schlamm's "outs," his "dispersed," were precisely the Remnant that Albert Jay Nock had described and that Buckley had been raised to think himself a part of.

But Regnery never seemed to trust Schlamm—he balked at financing a book by Schlamm, let alone a magazine—and he was interested in a more scholarly, less *au courant,* journal. By the beginning of 1954, Schlamm had given up any hope of interesting Regnery in the project and had turned to Buckley for help. As John Chamberlain put it, "He saw Buckley had money and ambition, so he went to work on him."

It would be hard to imagine two more different people than Buckley and Schlamm, but in 1954 the two men's personal differences paled before their common conception of what needed to be done. Both men thrived on the adversity of the times. Both men had arrived at similar conceptions of the Remnant to which they belonged and to which they wanted to speak. Both men believed that the threat of communism was the paramount threat facing America and the West. Buckley's conception of the threat was more religious and Schlamm's more philosophical, but both men deeply feared that the West was on the verge of being swallowed by the Communist behemoth and both had been outspoken defenders of McCarthy.

Both men were philosophical idealists. Buckley believed that intellectuals determined what people thought, and that the ideas of intellectuals shaped events rather than vice versa. "It is the *dominant* intellectual group which calls the tune to which society dances," he had written in 1953.[5] Both men believed that the way to change politics in the country was to challenge the reigning intellectuals. Both men had come to the conclusion that a magazine was the key to doing so.

Buckley and Schlamm approached beginning a new magazine not as though they were creating something entertaining or even illuminating, but as though they were about to change the country itself through the power of their argument. "Schlamm viewed the projected magazine as a magnetic field with which professional affiliation could no more be denied by the few to whom the call was tendered, than a call to serve as one of the twelve apostles," Buckley recalled.[6]

Buckley's willingness to work with Schlamm was significant. By joining forces with Schlamm, a cosmopolitan Jew who had more in common with Dwight Macdonald or Daniel Bell than with Robert McCormick, Buckley was turning his back on much of the isolationist and anti-Semitic Old Right that had applauded his earlier books and that his father had been politically close to.

In the early summer of 1954, Bill and Pat visited the Schlamms' house in Vermont. During that visit, Schlamm proposed to Buckley a weekly magazine that, like *The Freeman* of the early fifties, would cover politics and the arts and be pitched at "opinion makers" rather than the general public. Its purpose would be to exert pressure from the Right on the liberal establishment.

Schlamm insisted, however, on two conditions. First, he wanted Buckley to be the undisputed editor in chief.

> I remember Willi announced it to me as definite that I was going to start it [Buckley recalled]. Willi was capable of flattery, but the point was not flattery. It was much easier for a 29-year-old to be editor in chief of a magazine with these giants than for a 39-year-old or a 49-year-old, because people are willing to do favors and be condescending toward someone who was 25 years younger than they. They would not consent to be in a situation that was organically competitive.

Schlamm's second condition was that Buckley own the voting stock so that factional disputes would not be able to destroy the new magazine as easily as they had destroyed *The Freeman*. "*The Freeman* had splintered as a result of too many people owning stock. There are any number of difficulties that you don't have if you own all the stock," Buckley said.

By elevating Buckley to be editor and sole owner of the magazine, Schlamm didn't believe that he was reducing his own role in the project. According to John Chamberlain, Schlamm believed that he could dominate the magazine from behind the scenes as a kind of "éminence grise." "He was confident, of course, that he could maintain his influence over a young man who was all of twenty-nine years old and was just feeling his way amid the complexities of a Stalin-dominated world."

Schlamm foresaw little supervision from the editor in chief. The senior editors, Schlamm explained in a letter to Whittaker Chambers, would "establish satrapies in the magazine, domains in which each of us editors is acknowledged as the supreme authority (though all of us, in technical ultimate decision, will listen to the editor-publisher who hires and fires us)."[7]

Schlamm's proposals for making Buckley the formal and legal head of the new magazine enabled the magazine to survive periodic internal disputes. But the worst of those disputes was precipitated by Schlamm's not taking his own proposals seriously.

Buckley got his father's enthusiastic backing, including a pledge to contribute $100,000. That summer he and Schlamm worked out the initial details. They chose the name *National Weekly,* which they had to change to *National Review* a year later when they found that the *National Liquor Weekly* copyrighted the name "National Weekly." Buckley had William Casey, a Wall Street lawyer whom he had met through Regnery and who would later achieve renown as head of the Securities and Exchange Commission and the CIA, draw up the papers for *National Review,* and he and Schlamm wrote a prospectus to attract both financial contributors and writers.

The prospectus exhibited what Buckley later called Schlamm's capacity for "hype," but it also reflected their mutual view of the magazine's role. Echoing their idealism, the prospectus declared that the "political climate of an era" was fashioned by the serious opinion journals. "The New Deal revolution, for instance, could hardly have happened save for the cumulative impact of *The Nation* and *The New Republic,* and a few other publications, on several American college generations during the twenties and thirties," Schlamm and Buckley wrote.

The opportunity now existed, the prospectus declared, for a rightwing journal to make its mark by uniting opponents of the regnant liberalism. "New Deal journalism has degenerated into a jaded defense of the status quo," the prospectus stated. "If we competently and resourcefully attack it at this time with the vigor of true conviction, we can rout it intellectually."[8]

Buckley and Schlamm described their own "convictions" in terms of a synthesis of the "libertarian," "conservative," and "implacably anti-Communist" right wing. Their synthesis was based in part on a genuine ecumenical strategy and in part on opportunism. They believed that the different strands of conservatism—represented by the libertarian Chodorov, the conservative Kirk, and the anti-Communist

Burnham—had to be unified. But they were also carful not to offend either the isolationists or the pro-Eisenhower conservatives among their propective wealthy donors.

While they did not attack NATO, nor "interventionism" and "internationalism," they made the obligatory swipes at the United Nations. And while they charged that "clever intriguers [were] reshaping both parties in the image of Babbitt, gone Social-Democrat," they made no reference whatsoever to the Eisenhower administration. Writing to former leftist Max Eastman, Buckley explained that in order "to attract the investor," he had made "no mention of the fact that I intend, in an early issue, to read Dwight Eisenhower out of the conservative movement."[9]

Buckley and Schlamm also made no mention of the anti-Semitic Right in their prospectus, but they saw the politics of their magazine as an alternative to the Congress of Freedom and *Facts Forum*. Lunching with Yale professor Thomas Bergin in New York, Buckley tried to explain the purpose of the new magazine. "I can give the Right the kind of decent image it needs instead of the image that some people are giving it now," Buckley told Bergin.

II

To get *National Review* off the ground, Buckley and Schlamm had to raise money and recruit a staff. Neither proved to be easy.

Buckley estimated they would need $450,000 beyond the $100,000 that he had gotten from his father to meet the deficits of the first two years before *National Review* began to break even or make a profit.

Buckley dreaded fund raising. In September 1954, he wrote his father's business associate Dean Reasoner:

> I think I also told you that I am a rotten salesman, and that I have always conceived of Hell as the place where people of my temperament are required to spend eternity going from person to person selling something. But there is no apparent way of circumventing this gethsemane, so I shall have to spend the next months in importuning people and making a terrible nuisance of myself.[10]

Buckley's initial experiences largely confirmed his fears. The two groups that had funded right-wing activities and publications in the past were the old isolationists, typified by the *Chicago Tribune's* Colonel McCormick, and extreme right-wing Texans like H. L. Hunt. Buckley had little success with either group. Some of the old isolationists distrusted the politics of a magazine that promised to feature interventionists like Schlamm and Burnham. But most of them had simply lost hope after Taft's defeat and death. DuPont Vice-President Lammot duPont Copeland was typical of those who turned Buckley down.

> Probably I am wrong and I hope so [Copeland wrote Buckley], but I have very grave doubts as to whether a new weekly can have any influence upon the country's thought leaders at least for many years after its organization, and in the interim, it will probably be so labeled as being of the right that it will have little effectiveness with those who do not wish to see the truth.[11]

Buckley was too Catholic, too eastern, and too moderate for most of the Texas Right, which had funded McCarthy and would later back the John Birch Society. Buckley tried repeatedly to work out an arrangement with oilman Hunt, either to have Hunt contribute directly to *National Review* or pay for articles to be excerpted in his *Facts Forum,* which was being edited by former FBI agent Dan Smoot. Hunt would not budge, however, even after Buckley had agreed to write for *Facts Forum* and to appear on Hunt's radio show. Hunt's son Bunker Hunt promised $10,000 to the new magazine through a mutual associate of his and Buckley's, but then ignored Buckley's requests to make good on his promise. Buckley said later about his failure in Texas, "I had the feeling subsequently on the basis of a highly informed source that anti-Catholicism was part of the problem in Texas."

Karl Hess, a former *Newsweek* reporter whom Buckley hired to help him with fund raising, saw the problem in political terms. "I talked to Hunt about *National Review,* and he just wouldn't do anything," Hess said. "Dan Smoot was Hunt's ideologue. People like Smoot didn't really want to change anything. They wanted to lay a curse upon the benighted. Buckley really wanted to change things."

Buckley did have some success among two groups that had not contributed greatly to the Right before. In Southern California, he met a group of wealthy businessmen and Hollywood actors and writers through humorist Morrie Ryskind, a sharp-tongued, balding man who had written many of the Marx Brothers' movies. A former leftist, Ryskind had moved to the Right in the late 1940s during the battles over communism in the Hollywood unions. Ryskind bore the same relationship to the liberal Hollywood intelligentsia that Burnham or Eastman did to the New York literary intelligentsia.

Buckley met Ryskind in the fall of 1954 when he and Brent Bozell had gone to Los Angeles to speak about *McCarthy and His Enemies*. Ryskind, who shared the dais with Buckley and Bozell, took an immediate liking to Buckley, whom he assumed to be an improvident young writer trying to make good. "I knew nothing about his money. All I knew was he needed a haircut," Ryskind said. Ryskind invited Buckley and Bozell to stay at his house, and offered to hold a reception for Buckley to help him raise money for *National Review*. As a result, Buckley met sympathetic individuals who contributed at least $50,000 to the magazine's founding and continued to contribute over the next decades. They included men like Henry Salvatori and Frank Seaver, who were among those who would later fund Ronald Reagan's political career.

Buckley also discovered a group of wealthy Yale alumni who had been impressed with *God and Man at Yale*. They included Lloyd Smith, a Houston oilman who had been an editor of the *Yale Daily News*, South Carolina textile magnates Roger and Gerrish Milliken, and New York financier Jeremiah Milbank. The Millikens had been related to a Sharon family, the Hatches, and Milbank had been a classmate of John Buckley and a friend of both John and Jim. But both the Millikens and Milbank were moved by politics rather than friendship to fund the new enterprise, and they became, over the years, not only its steadiest backers, but also important contributors to the conservative wing of the Republican Party. The Millikens were largely responsible for elevating Barry Goldwater to national prominence in 1960, and Milbank served several terms as the GOP's national finance director.

By September 1955, with the help of these people, and some friends and associates of his father, Buckley had still raised only $290,000. And he had found recruiting editors as difficult as raising money.

III

Buckley and Schlamm hoped to recruit James Burnham, Whittaker Chambers, and Russell Kirk as senior editors and either David Lawrence of *U.S. News & World Report* or Ralph de Toledano of *Newsweek* as the managing editor. Russell Kirk demurred primarily because of geography. After the success of *The Conservative Mind*, Kirk had resigned from Michigan State College and moved to the small snowbound town in north-central Michigan where he had grown up. There, he wrote books and articles and received occasional visitors. Kirk refused to leave Mecosta, and he didn't want to take editorial responsibility from afar. He also had some political qualms about *National Review* but Kirk did agree to write a fortnightly educational column. Chamberlain (who had joined *Barron's* as an editor after *The Freeman* split), Lawrence, and de Toledano did not want to leave secure and remunerative positions for a magazine that appeared to them very chancy. Chamberlain agreed, however, to write a fortnightly book review and contribute editorials.

Buckley and Schlamm had better luck with James Burnham, whose situation was almost the opposite of Chamberlain's. While Chamberlain had been welcomed back into the mainstream media after his fling on *The Freeman* with literary bohemianism, Burnham had recently been ostracized from the higher circles of the eastern intellectual establishment for his views on McCarthy. He needed *National Review* as much as it needed him.

When Buckley had last seen Burnham in 1951, the noted author of *The Managerial Revolution* was still part of the liberal—and anti-Communist—intelligentsia, although at its right-wing extreme. Burnham's views on "rolling back" rather than "containing communism," his support for outlawing the American Communist Party, and his estimation of imminent danger from internal Communist subversion were seen as extreme, but arguable. He was a consultant for the CIA, at that time a bastion of liberal anti-Communism. He was on the editorial advisory board of *Partisan Review,* the principal liberal journal of its day, and he was a founder of the International Congress for Cultural Freedom and its American affiliate. The Congress was a liberal anti-Communist organization in which, according to Buckley, Burnham probably served at the behest of the CIA. While he was fully appreciative of Buckley's anti-Communist credentials, Burnham probably would not have imagined being on the same magazine with him.

But Joe McCarthy's anti-Communist crusade split the anti-Communist camp into what became liberal and conservative wings. While Schlesinger, Macdonald, Richard Rovere, and Daniel Bell condemned McCarthy unequivocally, Burnham, Eastman, and Chamberlain either equivocated or refused to make any public statement against a man whose cause they believed to be just, even if they disapproved of his methods. Burnham did not defend McCarthy himself, but he attacked his critics and he defended the congressional investigations into internal subversion. That was enough to put him squarely at odds with liberals like Schlesinger and Rovere.

In 1953, Burnham became embroiled in a dispute with members of the American Committee for Cultural Freedom over an introduction he had written to a McCarthy-style book accusing American scientists of relaying secrets to the Soviet Union. Scientists in the ACCF demanded Burnham's expulsion. In July 1954, Burnham resigned, declaring that while he was not a McCarthyite, he was an "anti-anti-McCarthyite." Burnham wrote to the ACCF's director:

> In my opinion those anti-Communists who consider themselves to be anti-McCarthyites have fallen into a trap. They have failed so far to realize that they are, in political reality, in a united front with the Communists, in the broadest, most imposing united front that has ever been constructed in this country.[12]

That same year, the editors of *Partisan Review* asked Burnham to resign from its editorial advisory board because of his "neutralism" toward McCarthy.[13]

Burnham's neutrality on McCarthy may have led to his being discharged by the CIA, which was itself under attack from McCarthy. Howard Hunt, who had worked with Burnham in the CIA, said, "I received a notice from [CIA official] Frank Wisner tht henceforth there was to be no contact with James Burnham, and the implication was that violations of this order would be severely dealt with." *

Burnham retired to the pre–Revolutionary War house that he had bought in Kent, Connecticut, about twelve miles from Sharon, where he wrote a book for the *Reader's Digest* defending the congressional investigation of internal subversion. He had some inherited income to live on—which had been augmented by a canny decision to invest heavily in an airplane manufacturer at the end of World War II—and his wife supplemented that by working as a real-estate broker, but by the time Buckley visited him in Kent in late 1954, Burnham had been cut off from the intellectual world in which he had thrived for more than two decades and he was anxious to find a new place for himself.

Coincidentally, Burnham had also been thinking about a new magazine along lines very similar to those of Buckley and Schlamm. In 1953, Regnery's assistant Kevin Corrigan had visited Burnham in Washington. Corrigan later described the conversation in a letter to Buckley:

---

* Buckley believed that Burnham's neutrality on McCarthy in the Cultural Freedom committees precipitated his firing. McCarthy was then attacking the CIA. Burnham, Buckley recalled, "was a principal organizer of the Congress for Cultural Freedom and disagreed with the governors on what the official position should be on McCarthy, he talking a hard line [against denouncing McCarthy]."

When I asked [Burnham] what he thought was the most urgent of all anti-Communist tasks, he replied without hesitation, "A magazine." "What is needed," he said, "is a weekly, something that, like *The Nation* and the *New Republic* of the '30s, would be on the desks of professors, bureaucrats, editorial writers, legislators, in short, of opinion-makers all over the country every week." [14]

Burnham received Buckley enthusiastically and accepted his offer to work as a senior editor on the magazine. The only condition that he laid down was that he not be involved in the administrative or financial aspects of the magazine. He was Buckley's first and would become his most important recruit.

Buckley was even more anxious to recruit Whittaker Chambers. In 1952, he had been enthralled by *Witness,* Chambers's autobiographical account of his time as a Communist spy and of his successful courtroom duel with former State Department official Alger Hiss, whom Chambers had accused of being a Communist agent. What struck Buckley about *Witness* was its fusion of the spiritual and the political, the struggle for God and against communism. The struggle between communism and capitalism was a "great war of faith," Chambers wrote, in which communism was the anti-Christ and the Cold War Armageddon.[15] "I was shaken by that book," Buckley later recalled. "I saw there a conjunction of style, analysis, romance, and historicity. I wasn't shaken into a position I hadn't already occupied, but if possible I felt more passionate about the responsibilities of people who dissented against a particular trend in Western history."

Buckley had also become a close friend of the older man. They had met when Henry Regnery had sent Chambers the galleys of *McCarthy and His Enemies.* Chambers had been enthusiastic about the book, but not about its subject, whom he described to Regnery as a "heavy-handed slugger who telegraphs his fouls in advance." [16] When Buckley asked him to write a blurb that could be used for promoting the book, he had refused. He wrote Buckley that the one way he could "most easily help Communism is to associate myself publicly with Senator McCarthy; to give the enemy even a minor pretext for confusing the Hiss Case with his activities, and rolling it all into a snarl with which to baffle, bedevil and divide opinion." [17]

Undaunted by Chambers's rejection, Buckley had asked if he could visit Chambers. In April 1954, accompanied by Willmoore Kendall, he paid his first visit to Chambers, who was living on a farm in Westminister, Maryland. Chambers surprised people who knew him only from his brooding meditations on the decline of the West. A large, heavyset man who always looked as if he had slept in his clothes, Chambers loved to put his hands on his large belly and laugh uproariously. He was as jolly in private as he was glum in public.

Chambers responded warmly to Buckley's proffered friendship. He wrote him after his visit:

> In general, I make friends with grudging slowness, and my true intimates are few. But perhaps four times in my life I have had this experience: I sat down with a stranger, and, with the first words, had the sense, not of beginning, but of resuming a conversation that had been going on for years, and might well go on without effort for the rest of our lives.[18]

In August 1954, while Buckley was in Europe, Schlamm, who had known Chambers from Time Inc, went down to Chambers's Maryland farm to talk him into joining *National Review*. During the last decade, Chambers had had two heart attacks, and had not appeared eager to rejoin the political fray, but to Schlamm and Buckley's surprise, he was willing to discuss becoming an editor of *National Review,* although he postponed his decision until he had talked to Buckley.

Chambers had political and tactical reservations. While he shared an apocalyptical, quasi-religious view of the Cold War with Buckley and Schlamm, Chambers did not view politics in the same manner. As a Communist, Chambers had lived through both the futility of the "Third Period," in which the Communists tried to organize workers directly for a Soviet America, and the successes of the Popular Front, in which the party backed the labor movement and the New Deal. He realized that a political organization had to weigh long-term goals against short-term realities. Just as the revolutionary often had to settle for mere reforms, the conservative, whose goals were equally, if not more, remote, had to settle for minimal gains.

During Schlamm's first visit, Chambers expressed concern that Schlamm and Buckley were too enamored of McCarthy and too negative toward Eisenhower and his Vice-President, Richard Nixon. Writing after his visit, Schlamm tried to reassure Chambers, saying that the editors would have to decide "how to handle Ike—and how to handle Joe—week by week."[19] But Schlamm's attempt to brush aside Chambers's doubts led Chambers to open up the larger issue.

Writing after Labor Day to Buckley and Schlamm, Chambers intimated that a "much more serious" difference might underlie their disagreement about Eisenhower and McCarthy. In his letter he contrasted his own "conservative" view with their more reactionary and radical position. Chambers evoked his revolutionary past and the examples of both Lenin and Disraeli (Lord Beaconsfield). "I remain a dialectician," Chambers wrote, "and history tells me that the rock-core of the Conservative Position . . . can be held realistically only if conservatism will accommodate itself to the needs and hopes of the masses—needs and hopes, which, like the masses themselves, are the products of machines. . . . This is, of course, the Beaconsfield position." *

By saying he was a "dialectician," Chambers meant that he still believed that social and political change was determined by events outside the control of any individual—by the inevitable advance of technology under capitalism and by the evolving needs and sentiments of the majority of people, that is, the "masses." The role of conservatives, Chambers argued, was not to try to block change—a politics that would foredoom conservatives "to futility and petulance"—but to "maneuver" within its compass, as Disraeli had been able to do.[20]

In a memorable passage, Chambers summed up for Buckley and Schlamm the difference between the conservative and the merely reactionary positions.

> Escapism is laudable, perhaps the only truly honorable course for humane men—but only for them. Those who remain in the world, if they will not surrender on its terms, must maneuver within its terms. That is what conservatives must decide: how much to give in order to survive at all; how much to give in order not to give up the basic principles. And, of course, that results in a dance along a precipice. Many will drop over, and, always, the cliff dancers will hear the screaming curses of those who fall, or be numbed by the sullen silence of those, nobler souls perhaps, who will not join the dance.[21]

In reply, Schlamm balked at Chambers's contention that conservatives must accommodate themselves to the "essentially socialist needs and hopes of the masses." "Being of free will, the writer realizes that he, too, holds a franchise to cast a vote in this continuous ballot," Schlamm wrote. "He does *not accept at the start* what, most likely, is going to be the upshot of all that painfully universal suffrage."[22]

---

* Disraeli, the founder of modern British conservatism, changed the Conservative Party from a party of the past, defending landed interests against worker and businessman alike, to a party of gradual change, championing political and economic reform in the interests of long-term stability. (*Odyssey*, 79.)

Buckley was much closer to Schlamm's position, but being in awe of Chambers, he tried to be conciliatory. He even suggested that if his own participation were any obstacle to Chambers joining *National Review,* he would remove himself as an editor—a suggestion that he never would have made for anyone else. During one drive that Chambers and Buckley and his wife took to the country, Buckley tried to quiet Chambers's doubts. Chambers kept asking Buckley to define "what it is *National Review* desires to cause to survive." An exasperated Buckley finally asked Chambers, "What is it that you want to hear from me, because I doubt very much if it is at war with anything I actually want to say."

IV

In April 1955, the month Buckley and Schlamm had originally designated for *National Review*'s first issue, Will Buckley underwent surgery in a Charlotte, North Carolina, hospital for a malignant tumor. While he was in surgery, he suffered a massive stroke that left him in a coma. Aloise summoned the family to Charlotte for Will's last rites. Bill and his brothers and sisters chartered a plane from New York.

But Will lingered in his coma. The children moved into a nearby hotel, where, Patricia recalled, everyone but Bill congregated on the porch and talked. Bill "kept to himself," concealing his own grief. Patricia was reminded of when they were children and Bill never showed his grief or anger in public. "He felt more deeply than any of us," Patricia said.

On the fourth day, Will showed his first signs of consciousness. Aloise, sitting at his bedside, was reading to him the Book of Psalms, from the Old Testament, and Will opened his eyes and exclaimed, "Boy, could those Jews write!"[23] He lapsed again into a coma, but soon afterwards he came out of it.

Will never fully recovered from the stroke. His left side remained paralyzed, and he lost some of his mental faculties. Aloise, concerned about his morale, never told him that he had cancer. His children, assured that he would survive, returned home. Buckley was shaken by his father's illness, but he resumed fund raising and recruiting a staff for *National Review*. He and Schlamm decided, however, to postpone *National Review*'s publication date until November.

V

In September 1955, an event occurred that caused Chambers to make a final decision about *National Review:* President Eisenhower suffered a heart attack that at the time appeared to rule out his running for re-election the next year. The debate among the prospective editors over who should succeed Eisenhower brought the differences between them and Chambers to a head.

Chambers had already watched with considerable skepticism as Buckley, Schlamm, and Burnham courted California Senator William Knowland, the former majority leader and a man known primarily for his vociferous defense of the Taiwanese. In February 1955, the three editors had gone to Washington to have lunch with Knowland in the Senate Dining Room. With Eisenhower apparently out of the 1956 race, they urged Knowland's candidacy, and had already lined up an article by Knowland for their first issue.

Chambers's objection to Knowland's candidacy was based both on his low opinion of the senator and his high opinion of Vice-President Richard Nixon, who would have been expected to run if Eisenhower withdrew. Nixon had championed Chambers before the House Un-American Activities Committee and had stood by him through the two years of his ordeal, and Chambers retained both an appreciation of his loyalty and a respect for his anti-Communism. The editors' preference for Knowland bore out, in Chambers's mind, their failure to understand the "Beaconsfield position."

In mid-September, Buckley and Schlamm drove down to Chambers's farm to try to obtain a final commitment from him. Schlamm, who was certain that he could convince anyone of anything, was crippled by laryngitis. Buckley later described the scene:

> It was an awesome moment. A climaxing disappointment. It was rendered tolerable by one of those masterstrokes of irony over which Chambers and I were to laugh convulsively later. My companion Willi Schlamm is a Viennese, volatile, amusing, the soul of obduracy, and a conversational stem-winder. He had been in on the negotiations with Chambers from the very first, and was modestly certain he could bring his old pal Whit along by the terrible cogency of his arguments. But as we drove down to Maryland from New York, Schlamm got progressively hoarser. Two minutes after we arrived, laryngitis completely closed in. Whittaker was wonderfully attentive—aspirin, tea, lemon, whiskey, bicarbonate, all that sort of thing. But at one point he turned to me, when Willi was out of sight, and gave me a huge conspiratorial wink.[24]

After that visit, Chambers wrote Buckley declining the invitation to become a senior editor. Chambers assured him that their "area of agreement seems to me to be organic, beyond reason or dogma, in the sense that both of us hold that socialism is death to what we feel makes life worth living" and that "the differences lie wholly within the area of operations, what one makes of a real situation and what to do about it." But these differences were sufficient to prevent him from joining the magazine. "I am passing no moral judgement on your project," Chambers wrote, "I am appraising certain tactical, or, if you prefer, practical considerations that divorce me from it." [25]

Buckley didn't understand the depth of those "practical considerations." Indeed, Chambers himself had made it almost impossible to understand them by counseling gradualism, on the one hand, and proclaiming that "socialism is death," on the other. Buckley attributed Chambers's withdrawal entirely to the editors' doubts about Nixon. Buckley wrote, "His true reason was his fear of association with a journal whose editors entertained doubts about Richard Nixon's fitness to succeed Eisenhower." [26] It would take another decade, if not longer, before Buckley understood Chambers's critique of reactionary "escapism" and his insistence that conservatives understand the "Beaconsfield position."

Chambers's letter came just six weeks before *National Review* was targeted to appear. Along with Buckley's failure to raise the entire $450,000, Chambers's defection seemed to suggest that the enterprise might be premature. Buckley, Schlamm, and Burnham met in New York to decide whether to postpone publication of *National Review*. Buckley and Burnham were inclined toward another postponement, even if that meant losing some of the staff they had recruited, but Schlamm was adamant that the magazine go forward. Schlamm argued that if the magazine succeeded politically and intellectually in attracting a readership, then it would not fail. "Willi's point was that if you get twenty-five thousand readers, your subscribers won't let you die, and that proved almost exactly accurate," Buckley recalled.

Schlamm won the day. Buckley decided to go ahead in November.

VI

That fall, Buckley and Schlamm hired Suzanne La Follette to be the managing editor. La Follette, a flamboyant feminist with a raspy voice and an imperious manner, had been a young assistant to Albert Jay Nock on the original *Freeman*. They also recruited Willmoore Kendall to be a senior editor in charge of the book section and to write a fortnightly column. They got Brent Bozell, who was still working for McCarthy, and publicist Sam Jones to write Washington columns. And they recruited a prominent group of writers whom they planned to list as "Associates and Contributors."

With Schlamm, La Follette, and Chamberlain, there was continuity between *National Review*'s staff and that of *The Freeman* of the early 1950s. But *National Review*'s masthead was heavily weighted with former leftists preoccupied with fighting communism. Besides Burnham, Kendall, and Schlamm, the contributors included Max Eastman, Morrie Ryskind, Ralph de Toledano and former Communists Frank Meyer, Freda Utley, and Eugene Lyons. Meyer himself would become a senior editor in 1957. Except for Chodorov, who was a Buckley family friend, none of the right-wing isolationists were included on *National Review*'s masthead. While this point of view had been welcome in *The Freeman*, it would not be welcome, even as a dissenting view, in *National Review*.* *The Freeman*'s editors had been divided on whether to back McCarthy, but on *National Review*, support for McCarthyism, if not McCarthy himself, bound together the senior editors and shaped the list of contributors.

In its choices of editors and contributors, *National Review*, like *The Freeman*, represented a cosmopolitan conservatism at considerable distance from the anti-Semitic and paranoid Right. None of the editors had belonged to the far-right organizations or written for Merwin K. Hart's National Economic Council. Schlamm, Meyer, Lyons, Ryskind, Chodorov, and Toledano were Jewish—a fact that would later prompt attack from Gerald L. K. Smith and the Liberty Lobby.

In addition, Buckley and Schlamm went out of their way to recruit a group not represented on *The Freeman* and sometimes attacked in its pages—traditionalists and southern agrarians. Richard Weaver, the author of *Ideas Have Consequences*, readily agreed to be listed and to contribute regularly to the magazine. Erik von Kuehnelt-Leddihn, a monarchist, became *National Review*'s correspondent in Vienna. Having earlier rejected becoming a senior editor, Russell Kirk balked at being listed even as a contributor, because he didn't want to appear on the same masthead with Meyer, who had savaged his book in *The Freeman*, but he agreed to write a regular column.

In September, Buckley rented and furnished a floor in an office building on East 37th Street in Manhattan, a block away from the

---

* When Buckley was negotiating to buy *The Freeman* in 1955 and convert it into *National Review*, he offered to assume responsibility for Frank Chodorov's livelihood—the aging Chodorov was then an editor of *The Freeman*. The deal fell through, but Buckley still supported Chodorov financially for the rest of his life, and the two remained close.

headquarters of the Catawba Corporation. William Rusher, who became publisher in 1957, called the first *National Review* office a "rabbit hutch." Associate Publisher Jim McFadden, who came to *National Review* in 1956, described it as "dingy quarters." There was, McFadden later wrote, "a medium sized room, called the 'bullpen,' surrounded by cubicles indescribably tiny. Only three had windows and they looked out on a dirty courtyard."[27] Buckley took the largest of the three windowed cubicles for himself, Schlamm the next, and then La Follette. The editors and business staff shared the others. It was set up so that everyone was aware of anything happening in the office, from a quarrel to a love affair.

The editors immediately began planning the first issue. Burnham suggested that *National Review* might kick off by backing Knowland. "Ought *National Review*, in its very first issue announce its support of Knowland for president?" Burnham wrote Buckley. "Assuming ultimate support of Knowland, the most dramatic way, and journalistically the most sensational, would be to state it at the start. Also, it might give *National Review* a place in the national scene, a *root*."[28]

But Buckley and Schlamm wisely demurred. Assuring Burnham that they agreed that *National Review* should eventually throw its support to Knowland, they disagreed that they should do so in the first issue. "Buckley and I agree that it would be dangerous to announce our candidate in the first issue of *National Review*," Schlamm wrote Burnham. "If we did, we would be suspected, not only by our enemies, to be simply a journalistic tool of one among several factions in the Republican party."[29] But Schlamm and Buckley did think that *National Review* should feature an article by Knowland in its first issue.

In the second week of November, the editors sent the first issue to the printer.

CHAPTER 8

Standing Athwart History

Liberal social scientists dubbed the fifties the Age of Apathy and Conformity. Sociologist C. Wright Mills, bemoaning the absence of protest politics, described the decade as "The Great American Celebration," while USIA Director Arthur Larson, the Eisenhower administration's chief ideologue, wrote: "[Americans] have greater agreement than ever before. . . . on fundamental issues. . . . We have an administration whose philosophy and actions reflect, more accurately than before, this general agreement."[1]

However, there were undercurrents threatening to disrupt the consensus that the administration sought to maintain. In the South, the Supreme Court's 1954 decision outlawing racial segregation in public schools had inspired both a civil rights movement and white racist backlash. Public disquiet about the threat of Soviet Communism lessened after McCarthy's censure, but was periodically rekindled by insurgencies abroad and Soviet advances in space and military technology.

Buckley and *National Review* challenged the Eisenhower administration's claim of consensus. In their prospectus, Buckley and Schlamm had written:

Middle-of-the-Road, *qua* Middle of the Road, is politically, intellectually, and morally repugnant. The most alarming single danger to the American political system lies in the fact that an identifiable team of Fabian operators is bent on controlling both our major parties—under the sanction of such fatuous and unreasoned slogans as "national unity," "middle-of-the-road," "progressivism," and "bipartisanship."[2]

Buckley and the other editors condemned the administration's concessions to communism and the welfare state, and they defended the South's resistance to racial integration. By the end of its first year, the magazine would stake out new ground on the American Right while thoroughly enraging its liberal opponents.

I

In the first issue's statement of the "Magazine's Credenda," the editors claimed to represent the libertarian, traditional, and anti-Communist tendencies of the Right. They promised to oppose the "growth of government," defend the "organic moral order," and fight "the century's most blatant force of satanic utopianism."[3] The choice of articles in that issue reflected, however, how their priorities were ranked. The first issue featured an attack by Knowland on the Eisenhower administration for negotiating with the Soviet Union and columns by Burnham, Kendall, and Bozell on the Soviet threat. There was nothing on economic policy.

National Review's format was exactly like that of *The Freeman,* but its tone was very different. Like other opinion journals of the time, *The Freeman* was serious verging on dull. But Buckley, drawn by the example of Mencken's *American Mercury* and of the British weeklies, insisted that *National Review* be biting and witty as well as serious. When Max Eastman had urged him to use discretion in what he published, he had replied, "All I can say to satisfy you is that I want discretion in the sense that I want intelligence, and no crackpottery. But I want some positively unsettling vigor, a sense of abandon, and joy, and cocksureness that may, indeed, be interpreted by some as indiscretion."[4]

The first issue featured humorous pieces by Aloise Buckley Heath and Morrie Ryskind. Heath's article, "How to Raise Money in the Ivy League," deftly poked fun at the result of her own efforts to expose Communists on the Smith faculty. "The day the gods smiled on Smith was the day a number of her graduates received a letter from me," Heath wrote. Editorials were laced with sarcasm. In the second issue, the editors remarked upon the administration's willingness to travel to Geneva to negotiate with the Soviet Union, "One wink from a Soviet diplomat and they are ready to rush halfway across the world to get kicked in the teeth."[5]

Some of the humor was madcap. In each issue, there was a contest. One announced that the first person who sent in $7 would get a subscription to National Review donated in his name to U.N. Secretary-General Dag Hammarskjöld, a particular target of the magazine's scorn. The second person would get a subscription donated to Eleanor Roosevelt. Other times the humor was adolescent and had no particular bearing on the politics of the magazine. In the January 7, 1956, issue, the editors offered a free copy of Mahler's First Symphony to the first person who solved the following:

There must have been a dearth of eligible young ladies in Newport, for each of five men there has married the widowed mother of one of the others. Johnson's stepson, Jackson, is the stepfather of Harrison. Johnson's mother is a friend of Mrs. Richardson, whose husband's mother is a cousin of Mrs. Harrison. What is the name of the stepson of Olson?

National Review's tone offended some conservatives like Russell Kirk who saw it as "sophomoric." But its humor—and its collegiate snideness and silliness, recalling the Buckley children's infamous pranks—made it a far more interesting and lively journal than its predecessors or other right-wing publications. Its humor situated National Review in the cosmopolitan world of wit and punditry rather than in the grim crypt occupied by Facts Forum or the latter-day American Mercury. Its humor leavened the political statement and made it harder to characterize National Review as fanatic and its editors simply as zealots.

II

Most political commentators of the time regarded the fifties as a conservative decade and Eisenhower's as a conservative administration. In reviewing Kirk's The Conservative Mind in 1953, Time described the United States as "the citadel of conservatism in a tumult of innovation."[6]

But Buckley and National Review's editors disagreed. While Time and the "new conservatives" saw America as "conservative" in comparison to Europe's experiments in state capitalism and social democracy, Buckley and the *National Review* editors identified the acceptance of the New Deal and the willingness to seek accord with the Soviet Union with liberalism. They therefore saw the leading opinion journals as liberal; and they saw the Eisenhower administration, which was maintaining the welfare state intact and which had already negotiated with the Soviet Union at Geneva, as acting in a liberal rather than conservative manner. Whether Eisenhower was himself a liberal was irrelevant.

Writing in 1962, journalist Richard Rovere credited Buckley and *National Review* with introducing the concept of the liberal establishment into American journalism.[7] Like many of Buckley's and *National Review*'s inventions, it was the result of Burnham—and in this case, Kendall as well—adapting the Marxism of their youth to the needs of a new conservatism. The establishment was Marx's ruling class whose rule extended to the realm of ideas as well as things. But in a departure from Marx, Buckley, Burnham, and Kendall accorded the producers of ideas—the professors, journalists, and editors—preeminence over the class for whom their ideas were produced. In a note appended to Kendall's first column, which was to be a dissection of the liberal media, the editors declared "that there *is* a liberal point of view on national and world affairs . . . that the nation's leading opinion-makers for the most part share the liberal point of view—that we may properly speak of them as a huge *propaganda machine*."[8]

Buckley saw conservatism as a radical and dissenting philosphy. He made the point in a "Publisher's Statement" that he wrote for the first issue:

> Let's face it: Unlike Vienna, it seems altogether possible that did *National Review* not exist, no one would have invented it. The launching of a conservative weekly in a country widely assumed to be a bastion of conservatism at first glance looks like a work of supererogation, rather like publishing a royalist weeky within the walls of Buckingham Palace. It is not that, of course: if *National Review* is superfluous, it is so for very different reasons: It stands athwart history, yelling Stop, at a time when no one is inclined to do so, or to have much patience with those who do.

Borrowing from left-wing critics like Dwight Macdonald who decried the period's bland conformity, Buckley placed *National Review* on the bohemian fringes of intellectual society. "Conservatives in this country," Buckley wrote, "are non-licensed non-conformists; and this is dangerous business in a Liberal world, as every editor of this magazine can readily show by pointing to his scars.''

Buckley's declaration echoed Nock's concept of the Remnant, and it also recalled his father's defiant individualism. Buckley's conservatives rejected the status quo. They were rebels who defied authority and were willing to risk isolation and ridicule for the sake of the truth. They were "radical conservatives."[9]

The editors were utterly contemptuous of Eisenhower and his policies. In the second issue of *National Review,* they mocked the suggestion by *U.S. News & World Report* editor David Lawrence that both parties nominate Eisenhower in 1956. They lamented "the spirit of blind submission whose political expression is the attempt to Caesarize Dwight Eisenhower, with or without his cooperation." Eisenhower, they wrote, "is a man more distinguished for his affability and skills in reconciling antagonisms than for a profound knowledge of his country's political institutions."[10]

In March, Eisenhower announced that he would run for re-election; in an editorial about the decision, Buckley described Eisenhower's program as "undaunted by principle, unchained to any coherent ideas as to the nature of man and society, uncommitted to any estimate of the nature or potential of the enemy."[11]

When Buckley's friend, British historian Alistair Horne, visited a *National Review* editorial board meeting that spring, he was amazed to hear from both Buckley and the other *National Review* editors "an unremitting flow of criticism about President Eisenhower." Buckley himself told Horne, "Above all, Eisenhower is a man unguided and hence unhampered by principle. Eisenhower undermines the Western resolution to stand up and defend what is ours."[12]

During *National Review*'s first month, Buckley solicited a review of Arthur Larson's *A Republican Looks at His Party* from the isolationist John T. Flynn. But when Flynn's review came back criticizing Eisenhower for prolonging the Cold War, Buckley turned it down, ending his relationship with Flynn and severing his last tie with his father's isolationist past. Kendall, who did not object to Eisenhower's economics, but only his foreign policy, reviewed the book for *National Review*. His review, unlike Flynn's, got at the heart of what bothered Buckley and the *National Review* editors about Eisenhower's policies.

I think the administration has played a positive role in inducing a material prosperity without precedent in history. . . . In fact, I am prepared to believe, having read this book, that when the Communist glacier finally overtakes us, it will find the best-fed, best-clothed, best-housed, best-traveled population in the whole history of mankind.[13]

III

In his "Publisher's Statement," Buckley attempted subtly to distance *National Review* from the existing right wing. *National Review*'s intention, he wrote, was to present a "responsible dissent from Liberal orthodoxy," and he assured his readers that *National Review*'s editors had "a considerable stock of experience with the irresponsible Right." In his correspondence, Buckley protested the influence of anti-Semitism within organizations like the Congress of Freedom. But in its first years, *National Review* did not explicitly criticize any right-wing organizations and it praised some anti-Communist and segregationist groups that to many Americans certainly appeared to be irresponsible.

Buckley's initial reluctance to criticize right-wing anti-Semitism stemmed, it appears, from an unwillingness to cast *National Review*'s political project in a sectarian light. But his unwillingness to criticize other organizations resulted from the fact that *National Review* continued to occupy the same political orbit as they did.

National Review gave its support to the most hysterical anticommunism of the fifties. The magazine praised Dr. Fred Schwarz's Christian Anti-Communist Crusade—Schwarz warned that Communists had a blueprint for world domination by 1973—and printed political reports by Revilo Oliver, a future John Birch Society member. In an account of a National States' Rights Conference, Oliver concluded:

> Most conservatives profess to make no predictions concerning the future, but some, both in the North and South, admit that they foresee no future but a few years of accelerated socialism and corruption, of constant decay in the international position and security of the country. Then the inevitable war against terrible odds and conscription of the whole nation. And finally, whoever is victor, naked dictatorship, the rule of uniformed thugs, and the concentration camp for all who obstinately believe in human freedom. Fantastic? I *hope* so.[14]

National Review also lost few chances in its first years to come to McCarthy's defense. In 1956, its main investigative piece was on Paul Hughes, who had been hired by Americans for Democratic Action attorney Joseph L. Rauh and other liberals to spy on and discredit McCarthy.

In 1957, when McCarthy died, the magazine devoted two issues of tributes to him. In his editorial, Buckley described the charges that McCarthy was an enemy of freedom of thought as "superstitions . . . brewed by liberal intellectuals." Bozell's tribute, entitled "This Was a Man," attributed to McCarthy "a vivid moral sense" and "an iron will" and claimed, against Bozell's private testimony, that even in his last years McCarthy was "still able to concentrate, ruthlessly, on the central problem of our time." [15] Even Burnham praised McCarthy. "McCarthy was the symbol through which the basic strata of citizens expressed their conviction—felt more than reasoned—that Communism and Communists cannot be part of our national community, that they are beyond the boundaries," Burnham wrote in his column. [16]

The editors tried to make their case against school integration and black voting rights on the quasi-constitutional grounds of states' rights employed by Georgia Senator Richard Russell and the other Bourbon Democrats, and to avoid the racist populism of the White Citizens Councils, Willis Carto, and Gerald L. K. Smith. But Buckley, who had been raised to think that blacks were inferior to whites, injected a racist note into National Review's appraisals.

National Review's first editorial on the issue clearly distinguished constitutional from racial objections to integration. In opposing school integration, the editors insisted that their "support for the Southern position rests not at all on the question whether negro and white children should, in fact, study geography side by side, but on whether a central or local authority should make that decision." [17]

But an editorial written by Buckley in August 1957 crossed the line between constitutionalism and racism. In this case, the issue was not school segregation, but voting rights, which, in violation of the Fifteenth Amendment, were being systematically denied southern blacks. In an editorial entitled "Why the South Must Prevail," Buckley posed the question directly:

> The central question that emerges . . . is whether the white community in the South is entitled to take such measures as are necessary to prevail, politically and culturally, in areas in which it does not predominate numerically. The sobering answer is *Yes*—the white community is so entitled because, for the time being, it is the advanced race. . . . The question, as far as the white community is

concerned, is whether the claims of civilization supersede those of universal suffrage. . . . *National Review* believes that the South's premises are correct.[18]

In his defense, Buckley would claim that he was asserting the *de facto* rather than genetic inferiority of blacks. But the inescapable point was that he was willing to cite an individual's membership in a "race"—regardless of that person's educational background or intelligence—to disqualify him from voting. It was a racist and unconstitutional position. Buckley also identified "the South" with the white South, as if blacks were newcomers.

Brent Bozell, who was more favorably disposed to the civil rights movement than the other editors, dissented from the editorial in the next issue, because it condoned the South's violation of the Fifteenth Amendment. In an "Editorial Clarification," Buckley conceded Bozell's point and suggested that instead of disenfranchising blacks, the South should deny the vote to the uneducated, blacks and whites alike: "The South should, if it determines to disenfranchise the marginal Negro, do so by enacting laws that apply equally to blacks and whites, thus living up to the spirit of the Constitution, and the letter of the Fifteenth Amemdment."[19]

Buckley had retreated to Nock's elitism. The clarification distanced Buckley and *National Review* from Carto and the White Citizens Councils. But like Buckley's proposal for alumni control of Yale education, his proposal for disenfranchising whites as well as blacks satisfied his requirements of logic, but was irrelevant politically. In the political divisions of the fifties, the magazine lined up squarely with the southern segregationists.

IV

On the Right, *National Review* was greeted positively. The second issue was filled with congratulations from prominent right-wing businessmen and columnists including former Roosevelt brain truster Raymond Moley and former New Jersey governor Charles Edison. More important, it provided a voice to a younger generation of conservatives who had grown up idolizing McCarthy and General Douglas MacArthur, but had lacked a political context for their views.

Like Buckley, many of them were Irish Catholics, although from considerably more modest backgrounds. At St. Bonaventure, Kieran O'Doherty, who, with his brother-in-law Daniel Mahoney, would later found the New York Conservative Party, "devoured each issue of *National Review* within twenty-four hours of its receipt." At Georgetown, Patrick Buchanan, later a columnist and an aide to both Presidents Nixon and Reagan, discovered in *National Review* "the first magazine [that] expressed, with a sense of humor and intelligence and wit, exactly the things I felt I believed."

McCarthy was a key figure not only in uniting *National Review*'s editors, but in uniting its early readers. When *National Review,* which in 1957 had a circulation hovering around 18,000, did a subscription mailing based on condolences sent to Jean McCarthy, it got the greatest return of any mailing in its history. By 1958, circulation had climbed to 25,000.

There was, however, considerable grumbling on the right wing about the magazine's elevated tone and language. Financier E. F. Hutton, who had given money to the magazine, complained in a column, "There is a magazine put out by a young Yale man and his friends. But they don't speak the homely language of Americans who work and sweat on the farms and factories. It is too highbrow to be effective." [20] In a letter to columnist Ruth Alexander, who had complained that the magazine was pitched too high for the ordinary American, Buckley explained his editorial strategy.

We aim to revitalize the conservative position. . . . We believe that the only way to do this is to abjure the popular and cliché ridden appeal to the "grassroots." . . . We are very consciously aiming at thoughtful people, at opinion makers . . . we feel that before it is possible to bring the entire nation around politically, we have got to engage the attention of people who for a long time have felt that the conservative position is moribund. Once we prove that we can take any comer, once we have engaged in hand-to-hand combat with the best the Liberals can furnish, and bested them, then we can proceed to present a realistic political alternative around which we hope the American right, at present so terribly disintegrated, can close ranks. [21]

V

Buckley defined *National Review* in opposition to the ideas of the liberal intelligentsia, but from the beginning he sought to create ties with leading liberal intellectuals. As he had done in Yale, he refused to make political agreement a condition of friendship. Liberals like Murray Kempton, whom he debated, discovered a sharp contrast between the private and the public Buckley. Kempton, a *New York Daily News* columnist, first debated Buckley in 1953, and afterwards they became friends, largely at Buckley's initiative. "There was always a contrast between the way he operated in debate and the way he acted before or after a debate," Kempton recalled.

Buckley also tried to find areas of agreement with Kempton and other liberals. He invited them to the weekly lunches that the editors had at the Catawba headquarters, before their Wednesday afternoon editorial meeting, and he solicited from them articles on subjects where he believed there was room for conservative debate. When he met Ernest van den Haag in 1956, he suggested to the lawyer-economist-psychoanalyst that he write for *National Review*. When van den Haag submitted an article defending the ideas of Keynes, he printed it without any alterations.

In the spring of 1956, after *National Review* had been published for only six months, *Commentary* (then a liberal publication), *Harper's,* and *The Progressive* each featured reviews of the magazine. Not surprisingly, the liberals responded in kind to *National Review*'s attempt to depose them. The strategy of these reviews was at once to dismiss the magazine as dull and to pigeonhole it with the more fanatic right wing.

Both Murray Kempton in *The Progressive* and Dwight Macdonald in *Commentary* bemoaned how boring *National Review* was. Kempton in his review called it a "national bore" and complained of *National Review*'s "grey patches."[22] "Journalistically," Macdonald wrote, "the *National Review* actually manages to be duller than the liberal weeklies."[23]

Macdonald and *Harper's* editor John Fischer accused Buckley and *National Review* of being radical rather than conservative. Citing *National Review*'s "conspiracy theory of liberal control" and "its grave doubts about freedom," Fischer wrote that it was not "an organ of conservatism, but of radicalism."[24] Macdonald wrote, "The McCarthy nationalists—they call themselves conservatives, but that is surely a misnomer—have never made so heroic an effort to be articulate. Here are the ideas, here is the style of the *lumpen*-bourgeoisie, the half-educated, half-successful provincials . . . who responded to Huey Long, Father Coughlin, and Senator McCarthy."[25]

Kempton was the most generous to Buckley himself. "In the grey patches of *National Review,* there are occasional pebbles with a certain shine, and most of them are left by Buckley himself in those moments when his sense of irony breaks its conscious check."[26] Macdonald's review, on the other hand, was in places vitriolic. Compared to his wry assessment of *God and Man at Yale,* this review displayed the bitterness created during the McCarthy era between liberals and the senator's defenders on the Right. Macdonald lumped even the erudite Burnham, who had been his idol fifteen years before, with the "half-educated."[27]

Buckley was disconcerted by Macdonald's attack. "I confess to being a little out of sorts," he wrote Russell Kirk. "I have just seen Dwight Macdonald's review of the magazine in *Commentary.* That, sir, is an attack—mean, and more clearly concerned to discredit certain people (particularly myself) than a position."[28] In *National Review*'s "Report from the Publisher," he struck back, trading Macdonald *ad hominem* for *ad hominem.* Referring to a frequently married playboy, Buckley described Macdonald as "the Tommy Manville of American politics; he has been married to just about every political faith."[29]

He even took a few swipes at Kempton, wondering aloud how Kempton could "associate himself with a newspaper [*New York Daily News*] that feeds on butchery and prurience."[30] He rejected Fischer's claim of a conspiracy theory. "*National Review*'s position," Buckley wrote, "is that our society behaves the way it does because the majority of its opinion makers, for various reasons, respond to social stimuli in a particular way—spontaneously, not in compliance with a continuously imposed discipline."[31]

The three reviews showed that *National Review* was being taken seriously by the very opinion makers at whom it had been aimed, and that rather than boring them, it exerted a certain fascination. But in ridiculing the marginality of some of *National Review*'s articles and ideas and in describing the magazine's politics as radical rather than conservative, the three reviewers were not entirely off the mark.

CHAPTER 9

The Eisenhower Axioms

During the first year of *National Review*, Buckley devoted almost all his time to the magazine. He wrote more than half of the editorials and a monthly column on education, "From the Ivory Tower." He hired and very occasionally fired staff. He supervised the magazine's finances and did his best to defray its substantial deficit, not only by fund raising but by donating the fees from numerous speaking engagements. He put aside a plan to write a new book attacking the presumptions of liberalism. And he spent little time at home, leaving the raising of his son to his wife and to a French governess. "My dad is said to have visited me once in the Nursery while I was eating and was so revolted by the sight that he did not repeat the experience," Christopher Buckley later joked.

Buckley devoted himself to *National Review* partly because he was excited by the novelty of putting out his own magazine and by the controversy that *National Review* provoked. He was also forced to resolve financial crises and political and personal disputes that threatened its very existence. The most serious of the political disputes occurred right after the magazine began publication.

I

In February 1956, Soviet First Secretary Nikita Khrushchev gave a speech to the Twentieth Congress of the Soviet Communist Party condemning Stalin's terror and his "cult of personality" and initiating a process of "destalinization," which included significant relaxation of internal repression.

The editors believed that Stalin's terror had not been an aberrant departure from communism—or in Trotsky's words, a "betrayal" of communism—but its essence. Burnham, who along with Chambers was singularly responsible for the way the Right viewed Soviet Communism, had made this point in a series of books and articles during the late 1940s. In *Partisan Review,* Burnham, the former Trotskyist, had argued that "under Stalin, the communist revolution has been, not betrayed, but fulfilled."[1] In *The Struggle for the World,* published in 1947, Burnham had argued that the terror is "integral to Communism."[2]

But Burnham had always been willing to adjust his ideas in the face of contradictory experience. Writing in his *National Review* column, "The Third World War," he greeted Khrushchev's speech with skepticism. Treating the speech as part of a further factional fight within the Soviet leadership, Burnham wrote in April, "Before this new fight is over, there may be many who will sigh for the good old days of Josef Vissarionovitch."[3] Buckley echoed this opinion in a *National Review* editorial. "Surely the soundest measure would be to change Khrushchev's name to Stalin, in which case the map of the Communist world would remain unchanged," he wrote.[4] But in August, Burnham changed his mind. " 'The thaw' is modest in degree," he wrote. "Nevertheless it is real."[5]

The other editors sharply disagreed with Burnham. In a symposium, which appeared in October, Frank Meyer and Schlamm insisted that destalinization was an elaborate ruse. For Meyer, the Twentieth Congress demonstrated "the firm continuity of Communist aims and essential policies." And Schlamm declared, "Now at last the Communist Party consists of Stalinists only. The incorrigibly naïve West does not understand that Stalinization was the *prerequisite* for any 'denial of Stalin.' "[6]

The editors clashed again over whether to back Eisenhower in the 1956 election. All the editors had been critical of Eisenhower's administration, but when Burnham was in San Francisco attending the Republican Convention, he wrote Buckley a long letter explaining why

he thought the magazine should endorse Eisenhower. Burnham enclosed with his letter a copy of a publication called "Convention
News" that declared, "Ike Renominated in Spite of His Red Record"
and that accused Eisenhower of being "a tool in the hands of certain
unnamed subversive forces." The choice, Burnham wrote Buckley,
was between making "National Review a serious (whether or not
minor) force in American life" or a "fancier form of 'Convention
News.' "[7]

But Buckley was not ready to endorse Eisenhower. In April, he had
backed a far-Right third-party challenge and had signed a night letter
from a right-wing organization, For America (which was chaired by
Sears, Roebuck chairman General Robert E. Wood and H. L. Hunt
protégé Dan Smoot), "launching [an] intensive campaign to place independent Presidential electors on November ballot." The telegram
declared that "this is [the] sole Constitutional method whereby [a]
conservative All American could be elected President and thereby
defeat international Socialism which has captured both political parties." *

As he had done with Khrushchev's speech, Buckley decided that
the magazine run a symposium, "Should Conservatives Vote for
Eisenhower-Nixon?," with Burnham pitted against Schlamm. In this
debate, Schlamm called on conservatives to abstain from voting in
order to "break [Eisenhower's] firm control of the Republican Party."
Burnham reminded National Review's readers that American political
parties were not "ideological or class organizations," but "coalitions
[formed] before general elections" whose choice of President "must
be a 'compromise.' "[8]

Buckley himself had stayed out of the Khrushchev debate, but he
could not avoid taking a position on the November election. His statement, "Reflections on Election Eve," showed that Burnham had
moved him some distance from his radical stance that spring. While
denouncing the Eisenhower administration for its "easy and wholehearted acceptance of all that came before, of the great statist legacy
of the New Deal," Buckley admitted that compared to Stevenson's
program, "the program of the Republicans, which is essentially one
of measured socialism, looks wonderfully appealing to the conservative." But he went on:

---

* For America was largely a throwback to the isolationist (Wood had been a prominent
America Firster) and nativist past of the American Right. Although the term "All American" can be understood ideologically to contrast with "international Socialism," it also
echoes the plaint of the Midwestern WASPs faced with invasions of Eastern European
immigrants. (A copy of the night letter is in Buckley Papers.)

My reasoning becomes inadequate, and perilously so, only when, in my zeal to stress the relative merit of the less exacting master, I find myself speaking approvingly, enthusiastically about him. . . . The danger posed by the Republican Party today lies bare-breasted in its universal emblem, I like Ike. It should read, I prefer Ike.[9]

Burnham's argument had influenced Buckley, but his heart was still not where his mind was. On election day, he followed Schlamm's and not Burnham's advice and abstained.*

II

After the first six months of publication, it was obvious to Buckley that while some editors had been brilliant choices, others had not been. Buckley found Jonathan Mitchell's writing uninspiring. "He had lost that little secret of how to engage people's attention," Buckley said. By the spring, Buckley had resolved to fire him—the first and one of the few staff members that Buckley would discharge. "I went through the most awful agonies of my entire life when I had to fire him," Buckley said. "I don't like firing people, especially such nice people."

Buckley and the other editors also found Willmoore Kendall's choice of book reviews too academic for National Review. In the summer of 1956, Buckley proposed to Kendall that he yield the book section to Frank Meyer, while continuing to write his column and editorials. Kendall agreed amicably at the time, although later his resentment would surface.

The addition of Meyer was important to the staff's makeup and to the magazine's political perspective. Meyer was a small, pale, gaunt man, with high cheekbones, a long, thin nose, and protruding lips, who rarely left his book-lined house in Woodstock, New York. Meyer did all his business on the phone, and liked to stay up all night and sleep during the day.

Meyer had entered Princeton at the same time as Burnham, but had left after two years to study at Oxford. While a graduate student at the London School of Economics in 1932, he had joined the Communist Party. When he returned to the U.S., he became the educational director of the Communist Party in the Illinois-Indiana region, but he

---

* Buckley didn't recall what he did in 1956, but the next year, asked by Alfred Kohlberg to join a group of other Eisenhower voters in urging the President to break relations with the Soviet Union, Buckley replied, "I could not have signed your letter to the President in any case, given the fact that I did not support, nor vote for, Eisenhower in 1956."

drifted away from communism in the mid-forties and by the early fifties was debating the nature of conservatism with Russell Kirk.

In summer 1956, he took over editing the book section and also began to write a column, "Principles and Heresies." As a book editor, he was surprisingly flexible in what he covered and whom he asked to cover subjects. Literary critic Hugh Kenner's first article for *National Review* was a review of a book on the Marx Brothers assigned him by Meyer. Kenner said later of Meyer as a book-review editor: "Frank was a dyed-in-the-wool ideologue. At the same time, Frank had a sense of intellectual variousness that no ideologue is entitled to have. And that is the way he orchestrated the back of the book." *

Meyer was trying to provide the new conservatism with the philosophical grounding that it lacked; in a series of columns and essays, he had developed a theory of freedom and virtue that eventually became *National Review*'s and Buckley's *de facto* philosophy. This theory, which Brent Bozell, one of its critics, labeled "fusionism," sought to combine the libertarian defense of economic and political freedom with the traditional and Christian emphasis on virtue as the end of society. In a debate over the merits of classical liberalism with Russell Kirk, Meyer summed up his position: "Although the classical liberals forgot that in the *moral* realm, freedom is only a means whereby men can pursue their proper end which is virtue, they did understand that in the *political* realm freedom is the primary end." [10]

For Buckley, this provided a way to reconcile his two doctrinal legacies from his father: Catholicism and laissez-faire capitalism. And for the magazine, this provided a way to unite its diverse and fractious readership.

From the beginning, Buckley sought to involve his brothers and sisters in *National Review*. Aloise, the most talented writer besides Bill, began doing several pieces a year for *National Review* while raising a family of ten in Connecticut. Reid, who had joined *The Freeman*'s staff after graduating from Yale, also began to contribute occasional pieces; and both Priscilla and Maureen Buckley joined the regular staff.

Priscilla Buckley, who was four years older than Bill, had gone to

---

* As a columnist, Meyer could be predictably blind and dogmatic. He could read his own fantasies into reality, as when he would insist well into the fall of 1964 that Barry Goldwater was going to win the presidency. And he could be an unabashed Philistine in his assessment of contemporary culture. Reviewing Norman Mailer's essay "The White Negro," Meyer was so offended by the article's theme that he failed to mention the article's title or its central argument.

work for United Press after graduating from Smith in 1943. She had quit UPI in 1951 to take a job with the CIA in Washington, but returned two years later when offered the chance to be a general assignment reporter in Paris. Right after the magazine's first issue, Buckley asked Priscilla to come work on the *National Review*. He told her that he wanted someone with real newspaper experience. "He told me that he had lots of professors and no journalists," Priscilla Buckley said.

Priscilla was a lot like her father: quiet, somewhat shy, with a dry wit that made her adept at writing headlines and catchy news items. She was also extremely efficient and well organized, and as the chaos mounted in the *National Review* office, she began to assume more editorial responsibilities.

Maureen, eight years younger than Bill, joined *National Review* several months after Priscilla did. Initially, Maureen, who had graduated Phi Beta Kappa from Smith in 1954, did office work and answered crank mail, but after a year on the job she became one of the magazine's regular staff writers. Maureen was gay and effervescent and mischievous. One of her stunts was decorating Willi Schlamm's office with pictures of Eisenhower. She was also imperturbable. "Her sense of the ludicrous was almost perfect, and what would make anybody else mad only seemed to charge the cells of her funnybone," said Jim McFadden, who came to work at *National Review* in the fall of 1956.[11]

Bill was reassured by having Priscilla at *National Review*. She was enormously competent and he trusted her absolutely. But Maureen was almost as important. Though Buckley had barely known her as a child, he became extremely fond of her. She carried within her the lighter side of Great Elm. "He enjoyed Maureen so much. She perked him up, she pleased him, she enlivened him," Patricia Bozell said.

Among the senior editors, Buckley had initially relied most on Schlamm. During the summer of 1956, when he and Pat went on a brief vacation, he left Schlamm in charge of the magazine. But his relationship with Schlamm had begun to deteriorate from the first issue. He turned down several of Schlamm's editorials because of their melodramatic formulations and florid style, and Schlamm grew increasingly resentful. "Willi wasn't disposed to accept Bill's decisions when they went against his decisions," Chamberlain said.[12] After six months, Schlamm stopped doing any editorials.

Buckley began increasingly to seek out Burnham's advice and assistance. Burnham was quiet and authoritative. When his advice ran counter to Buckley's inclinations, he never pressed his points or subtly threatened to resign if Buckley did not accept them. "Jim was never obtrusive," John Chamberlain recalled. "He was there willing to work for Bill. He didn't want to run the magazine by himself. Bill came to appreciate that."

Burnham also wrote quickly and clearly and had an encyclopedic knowledge of world events. Buckley noted the difference between Schlamm's and Burnham's writing: "Burnham was more professional than Willi. His columns and editorials were brilliant and usable." Buckley began to ask him to write the editorials that he couldn't do himself.

Burnham had differed with Schlamm not only over political questions but over what kind of stories the magazine should run. "Willi wanted to make it a more crusading magazine than Jim Burnham did," Chamberlain recalled. Initially, these differences had not threatened their working relationship, but as Schlamm became estranged from Buckley, he began to take out his resentment toward Buckley on Burnham. Schlamm exaggerated their political differences and tried to impugn Burnham's character. At the beginning of November, Schlamm brought his dispute with Burnham to a head. The issue was how the magazine should respond to the Soviet invasion of Hungary.

III

Inspired by Khrushchev's destalinization campaign, the Hungarians had ousted their pro-Stalin regime and installed a new government, which had announced its withdrawal from the Warsaw Pact. In response, in the last week of October, Soviet tanks, already stationed in Hungary, went into action, and the Soviet Union set up a government of its own. *National Review* immediately called for breaking relations with the Soviet Union and with any country that condoned the Soviet repression, but the editors stopped short of recommending that American troops drive the Russians out of Hungary.

Like Khrushchev's speech, the Hungarian uprising and the Soviet reaction posed questions that threatened the basis of the editors' world outlook. Burnham, in particular, had been responsible for developing what was called the "liberation" or "rollback" doctrine. According to this view, the purpose of American foreign policy should not be to contain Soviet Communism, but to roll it back by attacking it at its weakest link, Eastern Europe. In *Containment or Liberation?*

Burnham had contemplated the prospect of an uprising in Eastern Europe and drawn the obvious theoretical conclusion: the U.S. would have to go to war. Burnham wrote:

> What if in a captive nation a broad mass uprising against the regime began? Or what if one of the communist governments, supported by the majority of the people, decided against Moscow? And, in either case, what if help were then asked from the free world? . . . Would not passivity under such circumstances be a final proof of the irreversibility of communist world victory? [13]

But faced with the grim reality of revolt in a landlocked country bordered by the Soviet Union and Soviet allies and by the Soviet development of a nuclear deterrent, Burnham reconsidered his own strategy.

In the first week of November, Burnham submitted a column in which he argued that the Hungarian uprising was the "initial phase" in "the breakup of 'the Yalta pattern' according to which Eastern Europe has been organized as a satellite area of the Moscow-dictated Soviet empire." But rather than calling for the U.S. to accelerate the breakup by actively defending the embattled Hungarians, Burnham called for the United States and West Germany to negotiate a solution modeled upon the Soviet-American agreement to neutralize Austria. Noting that Eastern Europe was kept within the Soviet camp not only by force of arms, but by fear of a rearmed, reunified Germany, Burnham called on the U.S. and West German chancellor Konrad Adenauer to negotiate the reunification of Germany along with the neutralization of Central and Eastern Europe. Burnham insisted that by forcing the withdrawal of Soviet troops and allaying Eastern European fears of a rearmed Germany, the new proposal could accelerate the breakup of the Soviet empire. It could achieve the independent "Eastern European federation" that Burnham called for in *Containment or Liberation?* without resort to American arms and the risk of a nuclear war. [14]

Burnham's proposal was rejected by the other editors, including Buckley, as tantamount to abandoning his own liberation doctrine. But Schlamm, with the support of La Follette, went further. In a heated meeting with Buckley, he charged that Burnham's column violated *National Review*'s most basic principles and threatened to resign if Buckley printed it.

Buckley rejected Schlamm's claim that Burnham's column was a major break with the magazine's premises. He even more firmly rejected what he took to be Schlamm's attempt to bully him and to force Burnham to resign. That afternoon, Buckley wrote Schlamm and La Follette an angry memorandum.

> James Burnham was asked to write a weekly column presenting his analysis, not yours or mine, of the developments in the strategic situation within which the third world war is being fought. He was asked to do so because his essential premises are the same as my own. He is free, in his column, to think out loud, free from censorship and, I should hope, free also from sniping. As of the moment that, in my judgment, he accepts premises which I find intolerable, I shall cancel his column. . . . It is not my opinon that Burnham has rejected those premises that I deem essential, but evidently it is your own, in which case I think we should reconsider the masthead, possibly abandoning the category of Editors and listing all of you as contributors. . . . It is my present mood, after months of deliberation, and a reservoir of patience all but exhausted, to reconsider very seriously the viability of *National Review* in the light of the present tensions. Perhaps we should devote some attention to exploring a rearrangement within which such episodes as that of this morning will not recur.[15]

Burnham offered to calm the tensions with Schlamm by not participating in editorial work, but Buckley rejected such a proposal out of hand. Buckley was concerned, however, about losing Schlamm, who remained one of *National Review*'s most popular columnists. The next day he wrote a memorandum to Schlamm in which he assured him that his angry memo had not signified "reduced esteem."[16] When Schlamm went away on vacation that December, Buckley wrote him a letter encouraging him to reply to Burnham, but imploring him to "keep out of the exchange not only what is obviously undesirable, i.e. personalized references, but any rhetoric whatever. I think we have serious tactical questions to discuss between people who agree on the relevant fundamentals, and I think it would be a mistake to use rhetoric as one of the weapons in our arsenal."[17]

IV

As the conflict between Schlamm and Burnham was growing more heated, *National Review* was running out of money. Expenses had run higher than Buckley had expected, and subscriptions were suddenly dropping—from 18,000 to 14,000. The editors believed that it was because anti-Semitic readers were protesting the magazine's support for the Israeli attempt, backed by Britain and France, to seize the Suez Canal. But Jim McFadden, who had been shifted from the editorial to the business department to help resolve the crisis, discovered that no renewal notices had been sent to the original subscribers. "There was a kind of general expectation that once you subscribed to *NR* you were one of the upward plus numbers, and very little attention had been paid to renewing these people," McFadden said.

The immediate cash-flow crisis was eased by a fund-raising letter to *National Review*'s subscribers—Schlamm's prediction that its subscribers would not let it die proved correct. The magazine's prospects were also improved by a decision to change from a weekly to a biweekly schedule. But Buckley knew that the magazine still faced large annual deficits; and he decided that the magazine needed another business that could provide a regular source of funds. He discovered an Omaha radio station that was for sale and proposed to William Casey, who was acting as the magazine's lawyer, and the *National Review* board of directors that the magazine borrow the money to purchase it. In a letter to the board of directors, he wrote, "I really think we have got hold of something which will take care of *National Review* in the foreseeable future."[18] But others, including Casey, were dead set against the venture. "I told him that Todd Storz, the owner of the radio station, made a lot of money because he was a genius at running radio stations and devoted all his time to it," Casey recalled. "I told Bill, you'll have to decide whether to run a magazine or a radio station. You can't count on the revenue."

Buckley was intrigued by the idea of starting a business, and he went ahead and bought the radio station anyway, with $150,000 from his family and $500,000 from a bank. The disagreement over the purchase led to Casey's withdrawal as the magazine's lawyer. "I stopped being his lawyer because I gave him advice he didn't like," said Casey.

V

As the debate between Burnham and his critics commenced in January, Buckley was in a difficult position. While he admired and respected Burnham more than he did Schlamm or Meyer, his view of communism and politics was much closer to theirs.

In January, Buckley wrote a short editorial introducing the debate over Burnham's proposal. Its purpose was both to insulate Burnham from the most violent attacks and to indicate to *National Review*'s anxious readers that the magazine's official position was different.

Does *National Review* buy [Burnham's] proposal?'' [Buckley wrote]. Certainly not on the strength of what we have heard to date. But we shall not close our minds on the subject. We shall encourage serious discussion of the proposal in future issues. . . . Such a discussion will surely be fruitful, for it will be a discussion of means between men who share the relevant fundamental assumptions: that coexistence is immoral, undesirable, and, in the long run, impossible. . . .[19]

In two columns, Burnham tried to clarify his position. Burnham defended the Eisenhower administration's unwillingness to intervene militarily. He explained that in refusing to risk war through an ''ultimatum or any comparable move with military implications,'' Eisenhower was following ''liberal humanitarian'' axioms that ''are a part of the reality of our time.''

Burnham protested that he was not repudiating his own liberation doctrine. If the Soviet Union agreed to neutralize Central and Eastern Europe, Burnham wrote, ''world communism would have suffered a defeat that might remain for a while hidden—even from Moscow— but would, as Austria proves, soon become known and marked.''[20]

Schlamm led off the offensive against Burnham; in subsequent issues, he was joined by Meyer and by Bozell. Schlamm argued that the effect of Burnham's proposal would be to abandon Europe to the Soviet Union by disarming Germany. Schlamm rejected what he called Burnham's ''Titoist'' assumption that the Eastern European Communist countries, if left to themselves, would drift out of the ''Soviet-Communist orbit'' and weaken world communism. Schlamm rested his refutation—ironically—on China and Czechoslovakia.[21]

As had happened in the controversy over Eisenhower's re-election, Buckley was finally forced to take a position on behalf of the magazine. In a carefully worded essay, he sifted through the arguments of Burnham and his critics. He concluded that short of American willingness to use force to back up an ''Austrian solution,'' ''the Burnham plan should be rejected on tactical grounds,'' but he granted important parts of Burnham's argument. Noting that ''we must resist the temptation to order our thinking on fixed conclusions of the kind that time and tide are capable of undermining,'' he rejected Schlamm's view that ''Titoism . . . is the more pernicious form of the worldwide Communist assualt on the West'' and endorsed the possibility of Communist internal opposition, described by Burnham:

Though the Communist deviationist is to be reckoned more importantly Communist than deviationist, we should not as a matter of dogma exclude the possibility that events might bring him to be, in strategic terms, rather a net loss than a net gain to the International Communist movement.[22]

Buckley also rejected the way in which Schlamm, Meyer, and Bozell had dismissed the "Eisenhower axioms." He accused them of misconstruing Eisenhower's position as one of sheer unwillingness to go to war, when the position was one of unwillingness to go to war to liberate Eastern Europe. Eisenhower and his advisers, Buckley wrote, "would not willingly exchange freedom-and-war for subjugation-and-peace. . . . [Eisenhower] would go to war tomorrow to resist the occupation of Long Island by a foreign power." The problem was that Eisenhower and Americans in general did not see the occupation of Eastern Europe as a threat to their freedom. And the challenge was to persuade the Free World "to extend Eastward the line that marks the effective boundary this side of which the West is prepared to act upon its preference for freedom over slavery."[23]

Buckley had rejected Burnham's plan, but he had accepted the analytical method that had led Burnham to propose it. He had accepted that even the most hallowed assumptions of the Right—the inevitability of war between the West and the East, the monolithic character of the Communist world, and the identification of Stalin's terror with communism—could be subjected to empirical examination. And even more important, he had accepted that policy alternatives had to be weighed against prevailing popular needs and assumptions.

But he had stopped well short of revising his overall view of Soviet Communism or American foreign policy. While in the specific case he was learning to weigh options and to assess alternatives, he still adhered to the quasi-religious view of the Cold War that he had inherited from his father and that had been reinforced by Chambers's *Witness*. What he had acknowledged was that, short of convincing a majority of this view, conservatives could not insist that American foreign policy follow their own dictates.

VI

Buckley tried to maintain a spirit of camaraderie among the editors. The weekly meetings at *National Review* were usually preceded by lunches, held at the Catawba headquarters down the street, to which the editors would invite honored guests, ranging from Murray

Kempton to Otto von Hapsburg. The editors also had quarterly meetings, some of which were held at Buckley's home in Stamford. In the
week before Christmas, Buckley invited the entire staff to Stamford
to listen to *The Messiah,* a tradition dating back to his college days.
Pat was a brilliant hostess, overseeing each detail of the elaborate six-
course meals that were served to the guests.

There was nothing, however, that Buckley could do to alleviate the
growing tension on the staff. The Wednesday editorial meetings, held
in his small office, became painful ordeals. Outside the meetings,
Schlamm began to complain about Buckley and Burnham both to
other staff members and to several people on *National Review*'s board
of directors. He claimed that Buckley had become hostile to him
because Pat Buckley didn't like him. When he tried to enlist one of
National Review's board members, Mrs. Cynthia Castroviejo, in an
open revolt against Buckley's leadership, Buckley decided to put his
foot down.

At the end of April 1957, Buckley informed Schlamm in a tersely
worded memorandum that he wanted him to work at home in Vermont
rather than in the New York office, limiting his contribution to
National Review to his "Arts and Manners" and "Foreign Trends"
columns.

> The disagreements that have moved you to your position of despair
> are procedural and tactical [Buckley wrote]. You have insisted that
> they are substantial and organic, and call into question the maga-
> zine's purpose. . . . I continue to believe that that which separates
> the individual editors of *National Review* is, by contrast with the
> faith that binds us together, in the class of a dispute among monks.[24]

Schlamm wrote Buckley that he didn't want to limit his participation on the magazine, and he demanded a meeting of the editors to
discuss Buckley's order. "*National Review* is as much my creation
and my life's central concern as it is yours," Schlamm wrote.[25] Buckley agreed to the meeting—to be held not in his office but at the
Commodore Hotel.

Buckley described it as a "long, agonizing, horrible, tumultuous
meeting" during which he repeated his demand that Schlamm limit
his participation in the magazine. Schlamm, recounting his own contribution to the birth of *National Review,* exclaimed, "You can't fire
me." As Schlamm drove himself farther into a corner, John Chamberlain, Schlamm's oldest friend among the editors, and a man not given

to emotional displays, began to get tears in his eyes. The meeting broke up inconclusively, with Schlamm refusing to indicate what he would do.

Afterwards, Buckley went to dinner with Burnham, who had barely been affected by the meeting's Wagnerian pathos. As Buckley recalled, he was in a sort of "philosophical whimsical mood." He told Buckley, "I've seen a lot in my life that is crazy, but I've never seen anybody say you can't fire me, when you are the undisputed boss of the enterprise." As he had done eight months before, Burnham volunteered to remove himself if Buckley thought that doing so would improve the atmosphere on *National Review*. But Buckley had already decided that Burnham was indispensable.

The next day, in a letter to Schlamm, Buckley laid down the conditions under which he would agree to his remaining on *National Review*. If he wanted to remain, Schlamm could not discuss *National Review*'s affairs outside of the office, could not threaten to resign in editorial debates, would have to understand that his authority did not exceed that of the other senior editors, would have to acknowledge Buckley's authority as editor in chief, and could not try to enlist others to resign on his behalf if Buckley were to modify his role in the future. Schlamm agreed. He began coming into the office for several hours once or twice a week, writing his columns, and then leaving without speaking to anyone.

VII

That summer, Buckley took a more important step to resolve the magazine's financial crisis: he hired a publisher who would have full-time responsibility for the magazine's business affairs. The new publisher, Bill Rusher, a lawyer who had been serving as associate counsel to Senator Pat McCarran's Internal Security Subcommittee, had originally asked Buckley to lunch to see whether he could work for the Buckley family oil business. But, to Rusher's surprise, after a few minutes' conversation, Buckley asked him to join *National Review*. As he would often do, Buckley made personnel decisions on the basis of immediate intuition rather than résumés and recommendations. And more often than not, his decisions were brilliant.

Rusher, a bachelor who loved fine wine and eighteenth-century English literature, was the kind of eccentric to whom Buckley was drawn. But Rusher also had the makings of a publisher. A square-jawed, gray-eyed Princeton and Harvard Law School graduate, Rusher had a cold efficiency, an inbred caution and fear of disorder, and an unerring eye for detail that stood him well in managing *National Review*'s finances. Over the next decades, he would consistently oppose Buckley's impulsive spending sprees, including the expansion of the magazine's radio holdings.

Rusher also contributed his own political outlook to *National Review*. Unlike the other editors, he was fascinated by and had considerable experience in Republican politics, and he became the magazine's link to the conservative upsurge then taking place in young Republican ranks. Republican political consultant Clifton White said later, "Buckley was a conservative philosopher, writer, and pamphleteer when he started, and I think one of the things that Rusher did for him was to introduce him to the world of organized politics, and in a manner that Buckley found acceptable."

Rusher's arrival in July precipitated Schlamm's departure. Buckley decided to give Rusher the office that Schlamm was using only one or two days a week and to move Schlamm into an office with one of the other senior editors. When Schlamm came in and learned that he had been moved out of his office, he gathered together his things and walked out. He wrote Buckley a note declaring that "we need a long and, while it lasts, total separation." And that summer, he left for Europe on leave, never to return to *National Review*'s offices again.*

Buckley made one other impulsive and brilliant hiring decision that summer. In June, he got in the mail a parody of *Time* magazine, "Timestyle," from Garry Wills, who was a graduate student at Xavier University in Ohio, and who had never published anything before. Both Buckley and Burnham were enthusiastic about the article. "He writes in places as only a true writer can," Burnham informed Buckley in a memo.[26] Buckley called up Wills in Ohio to accept his piece for publication and to invite him to New York at the magazine's expense.

When Wills entered his office, Buckley was "astonished," he told Burnham, to discover that the rosy-cheeked, rawboned Wills was only twenty-three.[27] After a brief conversation, in which he found out that Wills was a practicing Catholic, admired Chambers's *Witness*,

---

* Schlamm began writing from Europe for *American Opinion*, the magazine of the John Birch Society. He eventually proposed a reconciliation with *National Review*, which Buckley accepted, and in 1965, he began writing from Europe for *National Review*. In 1969, commenting on one of Whittaker Chambers's posthumous letters that Buckley had sent him, Schlamm wrote to Buckley, "You and I were so insane as to let the 'essence' of our 'affinity' . . . go to the dogs—literally to the dogs. I could not read Whittaker's letters without thinking of you and him and me; and of the mess we all keep doing of friendship and essence and affinity." (Buckley Papers.)

and did not know whether he was a conservative (he called himself a "distributionist"), Buckley asked him if he would stay in New York and review plays for *National Review*. "We have just lost our drama critic," Buckley, referring to Willi Schlamm, told Wills.[28] Wills excitedly agreed, and over that summer became a close friend of Buckley and a regular contributor to *National Review*.

CHAPTER 10

The Two Lighthouses

In August 1957, after Schlamm had resigned, Chambers wrote Buckley that he wanted to join *National Review*. Although Chambers never said so, his timing was probably dictated by Schlamm's departure: Schlamm was the ardent opponent of the kind of realistic conservatism that Chambers advocated, and with Schlamm out of the way, Chambers believed that he could have considerable influence over the magazine.

Fearful that any delay would cause a change of heart, Buckley rented an airplane and flew down to Westminster to make the final arrangements. According to the plan they worked out, Chambers would write reviews and articles and attend meetings at his own pace. And he would be paid $125 a week. In the August 31, 1957, issue, the editors announced that "Mr. Whittaker Chambers will resume his career as a journalist to join the staff of *National Review*."

Some of the younger staff members expected that Chambers would impart a note of brooding solemnity to the offices, and that Chambers and Burnham would soon be at each other's throats. But as they soon learned, Chambers was a jolly and very friendly man. "I was astonished to discover that he was this great corpulent ho-ho sort of guy,"

Bill Rusher confessed. And Chambers and Burnham, who had never met, discovered that they were not only admirers of each other's work, but also shared an interest in the work of beat-generation novelist Jack Kerouac. "It took them about two or three minutes to become fast buddies," Jim McFadden recalled.

Chambers had not agreed with Burnham's proposals for a neutralized Central Europe, but he shared Burnham's approach to concrete political questions and he had enthusiastically endorsed Burnham's re-evaluation of Soviet-American reality. In July he had written Buckley:

> The plain fact is that history's latest turn has forced Burnham, exactly as it has forced me, to re-examine reality, and therewith our own position with respect to it. What are we to do—act as if nothing has happened? Abdicate intelligence on what grounds? What do the Burnham critics say: that what is happening in Communist lands is just more of the same, that Khrushchev is a new edition of Stalin? Perhaps he would like to be. Unhappily, for him and for those who will not probe reality coldly, circumstances will not let Khrush be another Stalin.[1]

Chambers wrote irregularly for *National Review,* starting but not finishing many articles. His columns on foreign policy were mediocre. He was not so much interested in reiterating the threat of communism as in examining what he believed to be the spiritual crisis of the West. His most impressive articles were a critique of Ayn Rand's didactic novel *Atlas Shrugged* and a defense of Alger Hiss's right to travel. In both cases, he was trying to challenge the assumptions of his readers and fellow editors about the nature of conservatism.

Rand, a Russian émigré, had used her novels to proselytize for a philosophy of economic individualism that she called "objectivism," and she had assembled a devoted intellectual following. On purely economic issues, she differed little from *National Review,* but unlike *National Review*'s editors, who tried to balance their economic individualism with a traditional conservatism, she made her economic views the basis of a psychology and politics that extolled selfishness and damned religion. Her movement's emblem was a gold brooch with a dollar sign, rather than a cross, dangling from it. (The first time she had met Buckley, she had not endeared herself to him by remarking, "You are too intelligent to believe in God!"[2])

Chambers, like the other *National Review* editors, had come to the

Right as a counterrevolutionary idealist. Like Schlamm and Burnham he had no particular fondness for the rich. He saw economic freedom and capitalist individualism not as a path to wealth, but as the antithesis of Communist totalitarianism. Individualism was not good in itself, but only as a means to civic and religious virtue. Chambers condemned objectivism as a cousin of Marxism. "Randian man, like Marxian man, is made the center of a Godless world," Chambers wrote.[3]

Rand and her followers were stung by Chambers's attack. Rand's young disciple, economist Alan Greenspan, who later became President Gerald Ford's chief economist, wrote Buckley, "This man is beneath contempt and I would not honor his 'review' of Ayn Rand's magnificent masterpiece by even commenting on it."[4] Rand herself complained aloud, "What would you expect from an ex-Communist writing in Buckley's Catholic magazine?"[5] She never talked to Buckley again and refused to enter any room in which he was present.

But Buckley was not moved by their protests. For Buckley, Chambers's essay revealed a way to reconcile conservatism with the Catholic critique of laissez-faire capitalism. Chambers had not demonstrated that individualism was wrong, but only that it was wrong if taken as an end in itself. He applauded Chambers's attempt to "read Miss Rand right out of the conservative movement." "Her exclusion from the conservative movement," he wrote later, "was, I am sure, in part the result of her desiccated philosophy's conclusive incompatibility with the conservative's emphasis on transcendence, intellectual and moral."[6]

Chambers's Rand essay, written soon after his becoming an editor, was precisely what Buckley had hoped for when Chambers joined *National Review*. It merged organically the libertarian and traditional tendencies in *National Review*'s politics that had previously merely been juxtaposed.

I

Buckley continued to spend a lot of his time giving speeches and appearing on radio and television. He did so partly to defray the magazine's deficit, but also because he loved public combat and controversy and enjoyed performing, and he was much in demand by both conservative and liberal audiences. While conservatives saw him as a champion of their cause, liberals saw him as an entertaining and formidable adversary. Buckley responded to the latter's interest by stressing what was most extreme and provocative in his own views. In December 1957, appearing on Mike Wallace's television interview show in New York, Buckley described himself as a revolutionary.

> WALLACE: Are you for majority rule in the U.S.A.?
> BUCKLEY: Yes, unless the majority decides we should go Communist. I would try to subvert any Communist society.
> WALLACE: You mean you would turn revolutionary?
> BUCKLEY: Yes. I am already a revolutionary against the present liberal order. An intellectual revolutionary.
> WALLACE: What would you like to overthrow?
> BUCKLEY: Well, a revolution in the U.S.—or a counterrevolution —would aim at overturning the revised view of society pretty well brought in by FDR.[7]

Buckley's speaking style had continued to improve. One of his most brilliant performances came that same December at Hunter College, on the East Side of Manhattan, where *National Review* regularly staged debates. In this instance, Buckley took the affirmative against Tex McCrary, a pro-Eisenhower television and radio newsman who had staged a massive rally for Eisenhower at Madison Square Garden. Buckley debated McCrary on the provocative question, "Should the Republican Party Repudiate Eisenhower?"

The debate attracted almost two thousand persons to the Hunter College Auditorium. Most of them were fervent *National Review* supporters who came to see the opponents of conservatism impaled by their champion. One Hunter College student remembered the well-to-do East Side audience as "very vociferous and very nasty." They cheered the conservative and booed and hissed at the liberal. Buckley opened the debate by sketching an imaginary scene on Eisenhower's airplane while the President-elect is returning home from his December 1952 visit to the Korean front.

> The scene is the main cabin of the great plane. It is midmorning. The engines are purring. At the back, the President-Elect sprawls relaxed, reading a Mickey Spillane. [Adviser] Mr. C. D. Jackson and [future Secretary of State] Mr. John Foster Dulles are seated opposite each other. Mr. Jackson is lost in his thoughts. But something gradually intrudes into his consciousness. He becomes uneasily aware that somebody is staring at his feet. It is Mr. Dulles. "Where," he asks at last, "do you have your shoes made, C.D.?"

"Church's—Madison and 48th Street," says Mr. Jackson. "Oh," Dulles answers. Silence closes in again.

That silence, five years later, is unbroken.[8]

To the delight of the conservatives in the audience, Buckley contrasted Eisenhower's blandness and complacency with the evil that was Soviet Communism.

The sin of Eisenhower is the sin against reality [Buckley declared]. His sin against reality is due to deficient understanding; and his occupancy of high office is the result of raging national ignorance. . . . I sometimes feel that it takes a tainted mind to understand—to really understand—the threat of communism. To *really* understand communism is to have touched pitch: one's view of man is forever defiled.

Buckley concluded with a peroration that brought the audience to its feet.

Let us, as far as Mr. Eisenhower is concerned, take the pledge. I hereby serve notice on Mr. McCrary that next time he stages one of those high masses in Madison Square Garden urging Mr. Eisenhower to run for a seventeenth term, I shall be lurking in the shadows, and anyone who reads my lips will know that I am muttering a subversive prayer to our Lord to grant Washington another leader, and Gettysburg another squire.

II

Since his stroke in 1955, Buckley's father had largely retired from business, leaving day-to-day affairs to his sons John and Jim and to his daughter Aloise's husband, Benjamin Heath. Paralyzed on one side, he was confined to a wheelchair. While he still retained his wit and intelligence, his ability to concentrate was impaired. He lived largely for his children, and particularly for Bill. Although he despised publicity, he insisted upon keeping a scrapbook of Bill's clippings, and he regaled his associates with stories of Bill's accomplishments. "At business meetings we'd have," Ben Heath recalled, "Mr. B. would come and start talking, and he would say, 'By the way, did I tell you what Bill did?' We'd never get around to the rest of the business discussion. His eyes would light up, and he would say, 'Isn't that wonderful.' "

Will Buckley loved to attend Bill's speeches, and when he did, he forced himself to walk to his seat supported by the chauffeur and Aloise rather than be wheeled in. When Jim McFadden once asked why Will Buckley had endured the pain of walking, Aloise Buckley told him, "He just wanted to do it for Billy."

Bill visited his father at Great Elm, and they had long talks, mostly about what Bill was doing. Earlier, Bill had gone to his father for advice, but now he went to show his devotion. "Bill absolutely adored his father," his wife, Pat, recalled.

At the end of September 1958, on an ocean liner returning from Europe to America, Will Buckley suffered a massive stroke and went into a coma. Aloise cabled New York, and Bill arranged to take a Coast Guard cutter out to meet the boat. Will was rushed to Lenox Hill Hospital, where he died five days later, without ever regaining consciousness.

Even though Buckley had believed after his father's first stroke that his death was imminent, he was stricken. "He was deeply, tragically affected. It was a major loss of his life up until that time," Pat Buckley said. Usually unwilling to display his grief or anger, he wept in front of Pat and his brothers and sisters.

Will Buckley's body was sent to a midtown funeral parlor to be prepared to be sent to Camden for burial. At the funeral parlor, Bill, cognizant of his father's wishes, said to the directors, "Show me your plainest coffin." When they resisted, arguing for a more luxurious and ostentatious coffin, Bill repeated sharply, "Show me your plainest coffin." For the burial in Camden, the mayor, who six months earlier had presented Will Buckley with a silver bowl in recognition of his generosity toward the town, postponed a city parade so that the funeral procession could wind through downtown.

In an obituary, *The New York Times* reported that Will Buckley was worth $110 million at his death, but this figure appears to have been based on the total value of all the oil and mining firms in which Catawba held a controlling but not necessarily majority interest. Will was probably worth somewhere between $15 and $25 million by the mid-1950s, and in the years prior to his death he had disbursed most of that among his family, with each child receiving $1 million. It was a fortune, but not enough to justify the family's inclusion in Ferdinand Lundberg's book *The Rich and the Super-Rich*.

Buckley wrote an obituary in *National Review*—one that portrayed his father as a man of learning and morals.

He worshipped three earthly things: learning, beauty and his family.
. . . Here in America was the beauty, the abundance, that he re-
vered; here in the political order was the fruit of centuries of learning; here his wife, and his ten children, and his 31 grandchildren,
would live, as long as he lived and years after. So he encouraged us
to stand by our country and our principles.[9]

Buckley's obituary omitted, however, the remarkable man of business
whose gambler's instinct and ability to reassure wary investors had
permitted him to make, lose, and then remake a fortune. It was as if
he thought that by acknowledging that part of his father, he would
degrade the rest.

After his father's death, Buckley paid special attention to his
mother, who was plunged into depression. "His immediate reaction
was to take care of Mother," Patricia Bozell recalled. "Mother began
to visit Father's graveside two or three times a day. Bill took her aside
and told her that Father would have wanted her to go on living her
life."

Buckley's grief did not immobilize him, but the feeling of loss
stayed with him. "Not a day goes by when Bill does not mourn his
father," Pat Buckley said almost three decades later.

III

One month after Will Buckley died, Whittaker Chambers was felled
by a heart attack. From his bed, Chambers began to retrace the line
that separated him from other conservatives, including Buckley. He
was moved to do so in part by gloom, but in part by a continuing
difference between his perception of events and that of some of the
other editors at *National Review*.

In the November 1958 elections, the Republicans had suffered their
worst defeat in the House and Senate races since the Great Depression. *National Review*'s editors had been divided in interpreting the
election. Burnham saw the defeat of "Old Guard" Republicans (William Knowland in California and Senator John Bricker in Ohio) and
the defeat of right-to-work referenda in four states as a repudiation of
conservatism, while Buckley and Bozell, focusing on the gross nu-
merical results—roughly a two-to-one Democratic majority in both
Houses—insisted that the election was a repudiation of Eisenhower
and Larson's "modern Republicanism."[10]

In his letters to Buckley, Chambers emphatically took Burnham's side in the debate. "It was the Old Guard the voters wiped out in the last election," Chambers wrote Buckley. "If the Republican Party cannot get some grip of the actual world we live in and from it generalize and actively promote a program that means something to masses of people—why, somebody else will. . . . The voters will simply vote Republicans into singularity." [11]

Then, as Christmas neared, Chambers began to dwell on the particular differences between himself and Buckley, including those that separated the Quaker Chambers from the Catholic Buckley.

> First, you stand within a religious orthodoxy. I stand within no religious orthodoxy. . . . You also stand within, or, at any rate, are elaborating, a political orthodoxy. I stand within no political orthodoxy. You mean to be a conservative, and I know no one who seems to me to have a better right to the term. I am not a conservative. . . . I say: I am a man of the Right because I mean to uphold capitalism in its American version. But I claim that capitalism is not, and by its essential nature cannot conceivably be, conservative. This is peculiarly true of capitalism in the United States, which knew no Middle Age; which was born, insofar as it was ideological, of the Enlightenment. [12]

Four years before, Chambers had distinguished between a reactionary and a conservative politics that he called the "Beaconsfield position." Now making the same point but changing the names, Chambers distinguished between a conservative (i.e., reactionary) politics and a right-wing politics. The conservative was unable to understand American capitalism. "Capitalism, whenever it seeks to become conservative in any quarter, at once settles into mere reaction—that is, a mere brake upon the wheel, a brake that does not hold because the logic of the wheel is to turn," Chambers wrote Buckley. The man of the Right cannot seek to "brake" the ever-changing reality of capitalism, but only to "retard [it] for an instant." [13]

Buckley could understand Chambers when he cast the world in a religious or moral light, but he could not understand Chambers when the former Communist tried to make political distinctions. Chambers's distinction between the conservative and the man of the Right eluded Buckley just as his distinction between the reactionary and conservative had eluded him four years before. Buckley asked himself how Chambers could draw a distinction between his and *National Review*'s politics when he had never written a piece "that was out of harmony with the thrust of *National Review*'s position." [14]

After Chambers recovered, in the spring of 1959, he returned to work on the magazine, but his differences with the editors, including Buckley, grew more pronounced. It was only a matter of time until an issue crystallized those differences and made them unresolvable.

IV

Ever since he had worked for *The American Mercury* in 1952, Buckley had been trying to develop a set of ideas about liberal hegemony. In the summer of 1952, he had proposed a book on the subject to Regnery, and he made it the subject of a set speech on "The Default of the Intellectuals" that he gave to intellectual audiences like the Catholic John Carroll Society in Washington. Inspired by his correspondence with Chambers and perhaps also by the importance his father attached to writing books, he decided to put these ideas into a small volume.

In the winter of 1959, the Buckleys went to Switzerland, which Buckley described as the "way station to paradise."[15] With Alistair Horne and his family, they rented a two-story chalet in Saanenmöser, near where Will Buckley had taken Bill and his brothers and sisters in the early 1930s. The main activities in the nearby Gstaad area were skiing and having dinner parties, but while Buckley skied every afternoon and accompanied Pat in the evening to dinner invitations, he used his vacation for writing. He assembled past editorials, articles, and speeches into a book, which he called *Up from Liberalism* (after Booker T. Washington's autobiography, *Up from Slavery*). When Regnery, judging it too slight, refused to publish it, Buckley gave it to another conservative publisher, McDowell, Obolensky of New York.

Up from Liberalism, while serious in intent, was the book of a man unwilling to devote more than several months to its composition. It was organized as a running argument with successive liberals and liberal positions, and the style was rent by bursts of youthful pomposity and quasi-academic convolution that a careful rewrite might have eliminated. (An example: "I shall not, here, be contending what Miss Sayers, whose dismay is shared by many observers of American education, contends, namely that the faculty for logical thought is a skill of which the entire contemporary generation has been bereft; I note, but do not press the point.") But for all its flaws, *Up from Liberalism* was the fullest statement of Buckley's political philosophy that he would ever make, and its argument marked a milestone not only in his own political development but in that of the conservative Right. It bore out his attempt to come to terms with Chambers's criticisms.

Buckley's principal targets in *Up from Liberalism* were liberals and the Eisenhower administration. Buckley identified the "Liberals" with intellectuals like Arthur Schlesinger, Jr., and television newsman Edward R. Murrow, publications like *The Nation* and *The New Republic*, and institutions like the Americans for Democratic Action. Buckley conceded that most Americans were neither consistently liberal nor consistently conservative, but he contended that liberalism was the "predominate" political philosophy of the intellectual elite and therefore the "dominant voice in determining the destiny" of America.[16]

Some liberal critics found Buckley's insistence that liberalism was the dominant philosophy in America ludicrous, especially in view of Eisenhower's landslide victory in two elections over the liberals' favorite, Adlai Stevenson, but Buckley argued that despite the Eisenhower administration's attempts to differentiate itself from Roosevelt and Truman's New Deal liberalism, "modern Republicanism," through its dogged commitment to the "middle of the road" and "blandness," had allowed liberalism a free ride.

In *God and Man at Yale*, Buckley had shown how the liberal focus on the method of inquiry—epitomized in the laissez-faire theory of education and the doctrine of academic freedom—had provided a convenient cover for Socialists and atheists. In *Up from Liberalism*, Buckley argued that the liberal preoccupation with the method of politics—democracy—was justifying the enlargement of government power at the expense of individual freedoms and states' rights. Liberals, he charged, had mistaken a mere means to a just, virtuous, and harmonious society for an end in itself. Echoing Frank Meyer, Buckley wrote:

> The democracy of universal suffrage is not a bad form of government; it is simply not necessarily nor inevitably a good form of government. Democracy must be justified by its works, not by doctrinaire affirmations of an intrinsic goodness that no mere method can legitimately lay claim to.[17]

Buckley gave two examples of how this obsession with democracy warped the liberals' judgment. In the white South, he contended, liberals who pursued the "absolute right of universal suffrage" for the Negro were endangering existing standards of civilization, which were maintained by the superior "cultural advancement" of the white community.[18] And in Africa, by acceding to black demands for independence and one man, one vote, whites were inviting a return to barbarism.

We see in the revolt of the masses in Africa the mischief of the white man's abstractions: for the West has, by its doctrinaire approval of democracy, deprived itself of the moral base from which to talk back to the apologists of rampant nationalism. The obvious answer to a Tom Mboya [the Kenyan nationalist] is: Your people, sir, are not ready to rule themselves.[19]

By appealing to democracy and academic freedom, Buckley argued, the liberals got what they wanted, a Socialist economy and a secular society, and by attacking ideology per se—one of the period's most influential books was Daniel Bell's *The End of Ideology*—they discredited their opposition on both the Left and the Right. But they paid a price, Buckley charged, for their approach to politics. By making method supreme, liberals deprived Americans of a political goal and a vision worth fighting for at a time when they needed it most. "Liberalism cannot sustain our civilization on the little it has to offer," Buckley wrote. And he noted: "It is not lost on the undergraduate or on the adult public that there is no Liberal vision. And so long as there is not, there is no call for the kind of passionate commitment that stirs the political blood."[20]

Buckley attributed the apathy prevailing on the campuses of the fifties to the predominance of liberalism. Student apathy was

a reciprocal infidelity that Liberalism itself invites. Liberalism cannot care deeply, and so cannot be cared about deeply. . . . There is nothing there of ultimate meaning to care for, though there is much there to despise. The large majority of students, angled as they are toward Liberalism, are silent, reflecting the great emptiness of their faith.[21]

In the next decade, students on both the Left and the Right would echo Buckley's analysis of liberalism's shortcomings and of the Eisenhower decade. One critic, Irving Kristol, perceived the affinity between Buckley and the emerging corps of New Left intellectuals. In a review of *Up from Liberalism,* Kristol wrote: "Far from being recognizably conservative, Mr. Buckley is a gay dissenter, having more in common with [New Left sociologist] C. Wright Mills than any other contemporary writer one can think of."[22]

Chambers's influence on Buckley was most evident in Buckley's analysis of contemporary conservatism. Buckley blamed conservatives themselves for the failure to win popular support for a challenge to liberalism. His case in point was the "Old Guard" conservative opposition to the social security system.

Buckley contended that conservatives had undermined their credibility by insisting the social security laws

> toll the knell of our departed freedoms, or that national bankruptcy will take place the month after next. Conservatives have not "proved" to the satisfaction either of the public or of the academy that the moderate welfare state has paralyzing economic or political consequences for the affluent society. Our insistence that the economic comeuppance is just around the corner (not *this* corner, *that* one. No, not *that* one, *that* one over *there* . . .) has lost to conservatism public confidence in its economic expertise. And on the matter of liberty, conservatives have not been persuasive . . . in their contention that the freedoms they have been forced by the welfare state to do without add up to humiliation, let alone privation.[23]

Buckley acknowledged that the value of social security had been "politically secured."[24] He acknowledged that social security had contributed real security to Americans and that "political opposition to deeply imbedded welfarist carbuncles is futile."[25]

These were important admissions, equivalent to Burnham's admission that trying to free Eastern Europe by war was politically futile. But in *Up from Liberalism* Buckley stopped short of Viereck's or Bundy's "new conservative" position that social security was part of the status quo that must be defended. Instead, he held out for conservatives being able to persuade Americans over the long run that by its compulsory character social security limited economic freedom and that "economic freedom is the most precious temporal freedom."[26]

He described the modern conservative by using a sailing metaphor:

> A navigator for which two lighthouses can mark extreme points of danger relative to his present position, knows that by going back and making a wholly different approach, the two lighthouses will fuse together to form a single object to the vision, confirming the safety of his position. They are then said to be "in range." There is a point from which opposition to the social security laws and a devout belief in social stability are in range: as also a determined resistance to the spread of World Communism—and belief in political non-interventionism . . . a respect for the omnicompetence of the free market place—and the knowledge of the necessity for occasional interposition.[27]

While admitting for the first time the short-term political futility of railing against social security or calling for world war, Buckley still sought a means of reconciling these long-term goals with a politics of the present.

In *Up from Liberalism,* Buckley acknowledged Chambers's influence. In the concluding chapter, he quoted at length from the letter on the "Beaconsfield position" that Chambers had written him and Schlamm in 1954. But his explanation of Chambers's position showed that he had still not understood the heart of Chamber's argument.

Buckley quoted with approval Chambers's statement that "the Conservative Position . . . can be held realistically only if conservatism will accommodate itself to the needs and hopes of the masses— needs and hopes, which, like the masses themselves, are the products of machines." But he contended that while the elimination of social security and of "socialized agriculture" might appear "antiquarian and callous" in a "modulated age," the "machine" had not by any means permanently invalidated these planks in the conservative platform. If properly anchored—by a persuasive argument about the primacy of economic liberty—they could one day become the basis of a realistic politics.

This was a misunderstanding of what Chambers meant by the machine. Chambers, a former Marxist, was using "machine" to mean "capitalism," and when he spoke of the machine's effects on the masses, he meant the inexorable effects of capitalist development on the needs of human beings. Thus, one could not go back to the economic policy of the 1920s any more than one could go back to the economy of the 1920s. But Buckley mistook Chambers's deeper point for a simpleminded technological determinism.

In May, Buckley sent Chambers the galleys of *Up from Liberalism.* Realizing that Buckley hadn't understood him, Chambers wrote him a letter tactfully expressing his disagreement with the book's final conclusion. Chambers began:

> I have finished your book, and suppose (with a good chance of being mistaken, of course) that I understand some of your problems in winding it up. It seems to me that they must swarm a little around the chapter which (in my copy) excerpts a letter of mine and indicates only that commentary cometh. . . . But I think you know what lies on the other side of that excerpt, whose meaning remains constant, in the sense that I hold the machine to the enemy of Conservatism. As I have said ad nauseam, I hold capitalism to be profoundly anticonservative. . . . The result is the oddest contradiction in terms.[28]

Buckley had still not abandoned the radicalism of his youth: it was present in the fixture of the fused lighthouses that betokened the end of both social security and the cataclysmic destruction of world communism. He had still not arrived at what Chambers had called the "Beaconsfield position," in which objectives were weighed against historical possibility. But he had moved significantly away from the purely radical position that he had brought to *National Review*. Like the navigator in his own metaphor of the two lighthouses, he was now poised between radicalism and reform, a reactionary and a genuinely conservative politics.

V

Immediately before he had left for Switzerland that year, Buckley had hired a Harvard dropout, John Leonard, as an editorial assistant. Buckley hired Leonard, as he had hired Wills, on the basis of his writing style—he had seen an article of his in a college literary magazine—rather than on the basis of his politics. Leonard was a liberal, but Buckley thought that he could be brought along. As he was leaving for Switzerland, he advised Burnham that Leonard's first assignments "should stay away as much as feasible from those for which we require either ideological sophistication or ideological steam."[29]

Leonard's hiring proved to be the last straw for Suzanne La Follette, whose relationship with Buckley had been strained ever since she and Schlamm threatened to resign over Burnham's column. La Follette had wanted to hire Morrie Ryskind's son Allan, who had just graduated from the University of Southern California, and she took Buckley's decision to hire Leonard as another slap against her own authority as managing editor. In a terse letter to Buckley, she resigned. When Buckley asked her to reconsider, she replied, "While I do not think *National Review* can or should be an egalitarian enterprise, it seems to me to leave something to be desired as a dictatorship."[30]

Buckley replaced La Follette with his sister Priscilla. In the new quarters at 35th Street to which *National Review* had moved the year before, she took the office beneath his, and they sent articles to each other by a connecting dumbwaiter. Priscilla's promotion gave the magazine a cohesive and effective leadership. Priscilla Buckley and Burnham not only got along well, but agreed on the kind of magazine *National Review* should be—witty, erudite, but also detached from the political passions of the moment. Together, they were to run *Na-*

tional Review's day-to-day affairs for the next twenty years, permitting Buckley to devote more time to other kinds of activities.*

That spring, as Buckley returned from Switzerland, he faced another entirely different challenge. In the "Publisher's Statement" in the first issue of *National Review,* Buckley had warned against the "irresponsible right," and in the Introduction to *Up from Liberalism,* he had reiterated that "conservatism must be wiped clean of the parasitic cant that defaces it."[31] In the first three years of *National Review,* however, Buckley and the editors had expressed their antipathy to the "irresponsible right" by ignoring rather than criticizing it. But that spring, he was forced to go further.

The issue was *The American Mercury,* which, ever since Russell Maguire bought it, had been embroiled in controversy over its owner's anti-Semitism. After Huie resigned in protest in 1953, Maguire brought in John Clements, and stayed clear of trying to influence the magazine himself, but in 1955, he reasserted his control over the editorial process and again began publishing anti-Semitic diatribes. Clements and the other top editors resigned. After that, the magazine became increasingly bilious, and in January 1959, Maguire published an editorial endorsing the theory of a Jewish conspiracy to take over the world promulgated by the fraudulent *Protocols of Zion.*

Morrie Ryskind and Alfred Kohlberg, the founder of the Taiwan lobby and a financial supporter of *National Review,* both pressed Buckley to dissociate *National Review* from the magazine. When Buckley discussed *National Review*'s position in a board of directors' meeting, however, both Rusher and Mrs. A. E. Bonbrake, a Forest Hills housewife whom Buckley had promoted to the board as a representative grass-roots activist, argued against *National Review* taking a public stand against the *Mercury.* Bonbrake and Rusher both warned that *National Review* would lose hundreds, or even thousands, of subscribers if it did so. "Since when is it the job of *National Review* to attack supposedly anti-Semitic publications?" Bonbrake wrote Buckley.[32]

But Buckley felt hypocritical at remaining silent. He wrote Bonbrake, "I do not feel comfortable criticizing Liberals as I do repeatedly in my new book for not disavowing objectionable Liberals, when I do not myself [disavow objectionable conservatives]."[33] In April,

---

* In an August 1971 letter to *New York Times* editor A. M. Rosenthal, Buckley described *National Review* as "me, my sister, and James Burnham." (Buckley Papers.)

Buckley took a compromise stand. He circulated a private memo to the magazine's writers informing them that "*National Review* will not carry on its masthead the name of any person whose name also appears on the masthead of the *American Mercury*. The editors of *National Review* have individually resolved not to write for *The Mercury* until management changes hands."[34]

The memo was shown to Maguire—probably by former MacArthur aide General Charles Willoughby, who was on both mastheads and who protested bitterly Buckley's decision—and in July, Maguire accused *National Review* of sectarianism on the Right. *National Review* also received some subscription cancellations, although fewer than Rusher and Bonbrake had feared. But Buckley's stand prompted other prominent conservatives and Republicans, including New Hampshire Senator Styles Bridges and radio commentator Fulton Lewis, Jr., to dissociate themselves from *The American Mercury*. Instead of seriously damaging *National Review,* Buckley's memo destroyed whatever remaining claim to respectability Maguire's magazine had.

Both Burnham and Chambers strongly supported Buckley's stand. Chambers called the memo a "liberation." "How good, and how strong, it is to take a principled position," Chambers wrote Buckley. "It defines, and defining, frees. Now what is good and strong outside us can draw to us, about whom there is, in this connection, no longer question, equivocation. The dregs will be drawn to the dregs, and sink where they belong."[35]

VI

On *National Review,* the debate over the Cold War that had split the editors in 1956 and 1957 had never been resolved. Since Chambers had joined the board, he, Burnham, and Buckley had repeatedly quarreled with Bozell and Meyer over how aggressive the U.S. should be in pressing liberation and in denouncing any accommodation with the Soviet Union. Buckley had refused to print an article from Meyer and Bozell calling for a preemptive nuclear strike against the Soviet Union.* And, in June 1959, he had insisted that a column by Meyer ruling out any negotiations with the Soviet Union over Berlin be

---

* According to John Leonard, Buckley, Burnham, and Chambers were the only editors on *National Review* who did not believe that the reported launch of a Soviet satellite, Sputnik, into outer space, was an elaborate ruse.

printed in the special section devoted to replies to editorials rather than as a column.*

But there were important underlying differences over the Cold War that separated Buckley from Chambers. Buckley saw a nuclear first strike and a refusal ever to negotiate as impolitic rather than unprincipled. But Chambers viewed the use and threat of force as at best irrelevant to the Cold War. Chambers saw the struggle between East and West as fundamentally spiritual, and he believed that what the West needed was not a greater nuclear arsenal but what, in a letter to Buckley, he had called "justifying energies."

Chambers never shared the illusion—so common among conservatives and liberals of the fifties—that the Soviet Union was militarily superior to the U.S. If he exaggerated the Soviet Union's strength, it was the spiritual and ideological strength of communism that he exaggerated. And he thought that waging the Cold War on any other terrain was destructive to the fundamental cause of spiritual renewal. He wrote Buckley in August 1958, "The West keeps piling up weapons systems, which lead, of course to two bad alternatives: (1) to retreat whenever there is any danger of using the weapons; (2) the temptation to use them, which is catastrophic." [36]

This difference over the nature of the Cold War rose to the surface in August 1959, when Eisenhower announced that he was inviting Khrushchev to the United States, and the Soviet leader responded that he would visit for ten days in September. Eisenhower's invitation to Khrushchev stirred Buckley's most visceral feelings about Soviet Communism. Buckley convinced Rusher and publicist Marvin Liebman to pull together a Committee Against Summit Entanglements (CASE) and to begin organizing an anti-Khrushchev rally for New York's Carnegie Hall on September 17. In the press conference announcing the rally, Buckley threatened to dye the Hudson River red so that when Khrushchev entered New York it would be on a "river of blood." [37] *National Review* editorialized, "The President will meet with Khrushchev as Chamberlain and Daladier met with Hitler at Munich, as Roosevelt and Churchill met with Stalin at Yalta." [38]

Even on brief notice—the $1 tickets had been put on sale the same morning—twenty-five hundred protestors filled Carnegie Hall, just

---

* This elicited a harsh memo from Bozell to which Buckley, in a private response, revealed the problem he faced keeping peace among the warring factions: "It makes sense, I feel, not to be sarcastic in a serious communication for consideration by a board of high strung editors (serving for the most part in a harmonious relationship) each one of which is himself a virtuoso in the arts of elenchus and rhetoric." (Buckley Papers.)

two hundred short of capacity. They wore black armbands and waved black flags—to symbolize their grief for the victims of communism. Rusher opened the meeting by calling for the audience to rise and sing "that outmoded classic, 'The Star-Spangled Banner.' "[39] This was followed by an organist playing a Bach fugue—a special touch that Buckley had contributed. The speakers included Buckley, Brent Bozell, columnist Eugene Lyons, and Mrs. Joseph McCarthy, but the highlight of the evening was Buckley himself.

In his speech, Buckley bemoaned the widespread public support for Eisenhower's invitation to Khrushchev. "If indeed the nation is united behind Mr. Eisenhower in this invitation, then the nation is united behind an act of diplomatic sentimentality which can only confirm Khrushchev in the contempt he feels for the dissipated morale of a nation far gone, as the theorists of Marxism have all along contended, in decrepitude."

Buckley brought the crowd spontaneously to its feet when he noted that "the social history of the White House" would record that Eisenhower had invited Khrushchev to the White House but had snubbed the late Senator Joseph McCarthy. He provoked laughter and applause when he remarked upon the irony of New York Mayor Robert Wagner's willingness to receive Khrushchev but not Saudi Arabian King Saud, whom he snubbed because of his discrimination against Jews.

> Nikita Khrushchev not only discriminates against Jews, he kills them [Buckley noted]. On the other hand, he does much the same thing to Catholics and Protestants. Could this be why Mr. Wagner consented to honor Khrushchev? Khrushchev murders people without regard to race, color, or creed, that is on straight FEPC [Fair Employment Practices Committee] lines; and therefore, whatever he is guilty of, he is not guilty of discrimination.[40]

In an editorial on the proposals for trade and disarmament that Khrushchev presented in his United Nations speech, the *National Review* editors accused Khrushchev of asking for American help "in accomplishing our downfall." In his column, Bozell blamed Americans' willingness to receive the Soviet leader on an inordinate fear of war and he blamed America's defeats in the Cold War on an unwillingness to use or threaten to use force. "Let the rhetoric be that of *battle* and *victory*—and the West may yet live," Bozell wrote. "A new leadership . . . would have the power and will to drop the Bomb, but, by the same token, it would have the power and will to wage an extended war of attrition against Communism."[41]

Chambers wrote Buckley that in its handling of Khrushchev's visit, "*National Review,* faced with a great test, did not serve its readers very well." Chambers was most upset by *National Review*'s dismissal of Khrushchev's speech and its insistence that he was simply a reincarnation of Stalin. Khrushchev "is no monster," Chambers wrote Buckley, "in the sense that Stalin *was* a monster; and it does much disservice to say he is. It blurs where we need clear windowpanes. His speech to UN was also a de-Stalinization speech." [42]

Chambers objected even more strenuously to Bozell's and the other editors' call for a strategy of victory against the Soviet Union:

> The danger that *NR*'s handling of recent events incurred is not being taken seriously. Its enemies could not ask for more. The logic of *NR*'s policy, as no doubt I have said to you before, is: War. If gentlemen hold that war is what is necessary, I, for one, wish they would say so simply, clearly, courageously, stating their reasons for believing so. It is not an easy position; it would take courage to set it forth at all. But it would be an intelligible position, and popular, I am told, with SAC [Strategic Air Command], though I doubt that it would be so with wider circles. But short of this forthrightness, shouts of "Russia go home!" and the like lack coherence, meaning, gravity. [43]

At the end of September Chambers resigned from *National Review.* Chambers said he needed to devote more time to study—he had enrolled in classes in Greek and natural science at Western Maryland College—but he did not hide that political differences with the magazine were the real reason. "I think my separation from *NR* is in order," Chambers wrote Buckley. "I dare say it will be an occasion for relief, if not rejoicing, with all but you and Jim." [44]

Refusing to understand that Chambers's view of the Cold War was profoundly different from his own, Buckley wrote Burnham that he would not accept Chambers's resignation "unless he forces me to. I regret very much to say that I think his defense of the visit, greatly impelled by his thralldom to Nixon, has rendered him virtually incoherent on the subject." [45] But Chambers persisted and in November wrote an official letter of resignation, asking that his "name simply be dropped from the masthead without any comment whatever." [46]

Buckley was deeply troubled by Chambers's resignation. He wrote about it four years later.

In the five-year history of the journal, Chambers was the only man to resign from its senior board of editors explicity because he felt he could no longer move within its ideological compass; and yet he never wrote a piece for us (or in the last dozen years of his life, that I know of, for anyone else) that was out of harmony with the thrust of *National Review*'s position.[47]

VII

The political stasis in which Buckley found himself at the end of the fifties was borne out by his response to the 1960 election. In marked contrast to 1956, Buckley did not endorse a far-Right third-party effort. Like other conservatives, he was encouraged by the emergence of Goldwater at the Republican Convention as the right-wing Republican alternative to Nixon. But he found himself paralyzed by the subsequent choice between Nixon and Democrat John F. Kennedy.

From Buckley's standpoint, the choice was even more difficult than that between Eisenhower and Stevenson. During the election year, Nixon had steadily moved to the center—a stategy that climaxed with his agreement at a preconvention meeting to support Nelson Rocke-feller's platform planks on civil rights and welfare. And Kennedy had run on a Cold War platform accusing the Eisenhower administration of allowing the Soviet Union to create a "missile gap" and promising retaliation against Castro's Cuba.

On the magazine, Rusher, Meyer, and Bozell urged abstention. Goldwater, Meyer wrote in a memo before an editorial meeting, was "the only candidate conservatives can support."[48] In another memo, Rusher wrote Buckley that he planned to abstain. "When the candidates are as similar as Nixon and Kennedy, how can it possibly be contended that a serious conservative is effectively registering his opinion."[49] Privately, they also talked of forming a third party that would challenge both the Democrats and the Republicans.

Burnham urged support for Nixon, and wrote to Buckley in October, stating his views.

> The public, objective, conservative position in this election is and must be, Vote Nixon. The Rusher withdrawal stance is an example not of conservatism, but of what . . . Marxists would call "subjectivism" or "sectarianism." . . . The matter of individual characteristics of the candidates is a very minor concern. . . . But in support of Kennedy are virtually all the forces, groups, tendencies and individuals that *National Review* is not merely against, but recognizes as its primary targets.[50]

However, Buckley reasoned that "the gravity of the historical situation demands that someone—something—concern itself with maintaining the paradigm. . . . We actually increase our leverage by refusing to join the parade."[51] In the editorial he wrote that month, he announced that *National Review* would neither endorse a candidate in the election nor counsel abstention. Instead, he gave the arguments of both sides, and concluded, "*National Review* was not founded to make practical politics. Our job is to think and write."[52]

Having refused to back Nixon, Buckley still took Kennedy's victory as a defeat for conservatives, and at *National Review*'s fifth anniversary celebration in December, he invoked the magazine's continuing responsibilities to the Remnant. Significantly, the dinner's sponsors were Herbert Hoover, Douglas MacArthur, and Lewis L. Strauss, three men whom history had passed by. Hoover had presided over the Depression wreck of the Republican Party; MacArthur had been fired by Truman; and Strauss had been denied confirmation as Commerce Secretary. "The sponsors of this dinner," Buckley told the black-tie audience that had gathered at New York's Plaza Hotel, "know that we are probably destined to live out our lives in something less than a totally harmonious relationship with our times."

Echoing his founding statement in *National Review,* Buckley concluded:

> We are all of us in one sense out of spirit with history, and we are not due to feel those topical gratifications which persons less securely moored will feel as they are carried, exhilarated, in and out with the ebb and flow of events. But ours is the ultimate gratification. I believe Mr. Hoover and General MacArthur and Admiral Strauss are happier men than they would be had they taken a different course when the tidal wave roared up before them. And I expect they and all of you . . . must be happy, as I am, to know that for so long as it is mechanically possible, you have a journal, a continuing witness to those truths which animated the birth of our country, and continue to animate our lives.[53]

Buckley's view of himself was ironically echoed by the mainstream media. In January 1961, *Esquire* ran a profile of Buckley entitled "W.F.B. Jr., Portrait of a Complainer." The article itself, published by a popular men's magazine, testified to Buckley's growing celebrity, which he had achieved both through *National Review* and his books and through his frequent appearances on the college and radio-TV debate circuit. He had become the acknowledged spokesman of the "hard Right." But the author, Dan Wakefield, contended that, except on the Right itself, his politics were not taken seriously. He was an oddity—a conservative with wit and intelligence—and appreciated for that very fact rather than for what he espoused.

He is becoming "incorporated" into the public rituals of the society he attacks. In a sense, the process Buckley has undergone is similar to the experience of Jack Kerouac—first attacked by the majority voices of the society he is criticizing; then, after more books offering the same violent criticisms come forth, the rebel is treated with increasing "tolerance," detachment, even wry amusement and patronizing camaraderie; and increasingly the rebel becomes a favorite performer before audiences who wholly disagree with what he says, but would defend to the death his right to entertain them by saying it—and the louder he says it, the louder they applaud.

PART THREE

The Public Man

For some people, politics is the ultimate concern. Of them, it can be said that they are serious about politics, in the sense in which Mr. John Lindsay is serious about politics. He is as serious about politics as, for instance, a flagpole-sitter is serious about flag-poles. Politics sustains Mr. Lindsay, even as the flagpole sustains the flagpole-sitter. Others care less for politics than for the end of politics. We climb flagpoles, but only in order to look at the horizon.[1]

—William F. Buckley, Jr., 1965

CHAPTER 11

Mater Sí, Magistra No

In the early sixties the liberal and left-wing movements in the country, which had dozed through the Eisenhower years, revived. New leaders like Martin Luther King and Malcolm X surfaced; new organizations like Students for a Democratic Society were formed; and older magazines, like *The New Republic,* which had lost readers during the fifties, experienced a revival. The liberal awakening was reinforced by developments abroad. Of no small interest to Buckley and *National Review* was the election of Pope John XXIII, who put the weight of the Church behind a Soviet-American accord and the struggles against poverty and colonialism in underdeveloped nations.

To the immense surprise of Buckley and the other *National Review* editors, the American Right also emerged from the cocoon in which it had slumbered since the early fifties. If Kennedy's and King's idealism inspired a new liberal movement, and if Malcolm X stimulated a radical Left, these developments also provided Buckley and the Right with the visible enemies and burning issues that they had lacked in the bland Eisenhower years.

In 1961, Goldwater protégé John Tower was elected to the Senate from Texas. Goldwater, who had been little known outside conservative circles before the Republican Convention, was touted by *Time* as "the hottest politician this side of John Kennedy."[2] A new organization, Young Americans for Freedom, founded with Buckley's and *National Review*'s assistance, gained several thousand members in its first year. *National Review*'s circulation shot up from 34,000 in 1960 to 54,000 in 1961.

But not all of the growth on the Right reflected *National Review*'s influence and accorded with its wishes. In the South, the segregationist movement swerved sharply in a populist and openly racist direction. And a retired candy manufacturer from Boston set up a fanatic anti-Communist organization, the John Birch Society, that by 1962 claimed as many as 100,000 members. If Kennedy in Washington threatened to solidify the liberal hold over the government, the new southern segregationists and the John Birch Society threatened to make a responsible opposition impossible.

I

Buckley, along with Burnham, initially took a wary but hopeful view of Kennedy's presidency. While he preferred Eisenhower's economics to Kennedy's, he preferred Kennedy's emphasis on military spending and military counterinsurgency. He also couldn't help feeling a sympathy for America's first Catholic President. But in the spring of 1961, Buckley broke sharply and permanently with Kennedy over his approach to the Third World.

In Asia, Africa, and Latin America, movements and parties had sprung up committed either to ending colonial rule, as in Portuguese Africa, or to ridding their country of corrupt, pro-Western oligarchs, as in Cuba. In 1954, the Vietnamese Communists defeated the French at Dienbienphu; in 1959, a Cuban nationalist, Fidel Castro, who was not yet a Communist, toppled the Batista regime. In Portuguese Africa, liberation movements, aided by the Soviet Union, fought to end colonial rule. In South Africa, the African National Congress was revived to press for political power for blacks. These struggles became the new terrain on which the Cold War conflict between the U.S. and the Soviet Union was being fought.

Kennedy, influenced by liberal social science, believed that the U.S. had to identify with and support the anticolonial and antifeudal revolution taking place in the Third World. From his first day in office, he sought to encourage democratic "third forces" in countries torn between right-wing dictatorship and Communist-led insurgency in order to keep these countries within the American orbit. Through the

Alliance for Progress, Kennedy backed Christian Democrats in Venezuela and Chile. In the Congo, abruptly granted independence by Belgium, Kennedy supported the U.N.-sponsored regime rather than Moise Tshombe's pro-European separatist movement; and in one of his first acts at the U.N. he joined a Third World call for an investigation of Portuguese colonialism in Africa.

Buckley and *National Review* fought Kennedy's policies in the Third World. Burnham bemoaned "the flight of the West" from Africa and described colonialism as "that brilliantly conceived structure."[3] The editors condemned Kennedy for opposing Portuguese colonialism and scorned the administration's support for the U.N. in the Congo. "What the evidence of the Congo has provided," Buckley editorialized in March 1961, "is that 1) black Africans, with some but insufficient exceptions, cannot handle their own political and economic affairs; 2) they tend to revert to savagery."[4] In his interview in *Esquire* with Dan Wakefield, Buckley had quipped that Africans would be ready for self-government "when they stop eating each other."[5]

Buckley, like his father, appeared to identify the world's darker races with both revolution and backwardness.* When Buckley described the Congolese as "semi-savages" in a speech for YAF at the 1961 National Student Association meeting in Madison, Wisconsin, the NSA's Congress voted officially to censure him for racism. But Buckley was amused rather than troubled by the fury his opinions evoked. Noting the resolution, he somewhat disingenuously remarked in *National Review,* "I think people can be savages irrespective of race, color, or creed."[6]

Buckley did not greet with similar equanimity the response to his criticisms of Pope John.

II

Buckley had always been a serious Catholic. He attended Mass every Sunday in Stamford at St. Mary's Church and felt inferior to his mother and sister Patricia who went to church every day. His Catholicism was the one aspect of his life that he would not joke about.

---

* Will Buckley saw Third World revolution as a threat to religion and capitalist property. He also believed that revolution represented a form of racial rebellion by the mixed and black peoples against the white. In a memorandum he wrote on Venezuela in 1947, he characterized both the Mexican Revolution and the Venezuelan reform movement in racial terms. "In Mexico, it was a revolt of the Indian against the white, whereas in Venezuela it is a revolt of the Negro against the white." (Lucille Cardin Crain Papers.)

When Bill Ottley, his classmate at Yale, visited him at Wallacks Point once, Ottley tried to argue with him about whether the Virgin Mary had really been a virgin. "Bill suddenly got quite stony-faced," Ottley recalled.

Buckley's religious belief informed and underlay his opposition to communism and to unbridled individualism and materialism. Russell Kirk said of Buckley, "The economic question is incidental to his conservatism. He is not an economist. His conservatism is a product of his religion rather than of his economic views." But Buckley's Catholicism was rooted in his conception of God's rather than Rome's authority, and when the political—or even moral—priorities of Rome differed from his own, Buckley expressed his disagreement, sometimes harshly. This was particularly the case when he didn't think Catholic officialdom adequately appreciated the threat of communism.

Buckley's books and articles had given him a significant following among Catholic priests, but for his stands on general political rather than doctrinal issues. "We didn't think of him as a champion against the Catholic Left," Msgr. Eugene V. Clark said. "We thought of him as someone articulating the profound problems of liberalism." Likewise, *National Review*'s substantial Catholic readership did not stem from the magazine's infrequent comment on specifically Catholic issues, but from its advocacy of causes important to the growing number of right-wing Catholics. However, with the publication of Pope John's *Mater et Magistra,* Buckley was drawn into a heated controversy with Catholic liberals.

Pope John's *Mater et Magistra,* issued in July 1961, reiterated the Church's commitment to the world's poor and oppressed. But unlike past Church documents, this one devoted much attention to the problems of the developing countries, and it contained a call to end colonialism. In a July editorial, *National Review* commented that "the large sprawling document" released by the Vatican "must strike many as a venture in triviality coming at this particular time in history. The most obtrusive social phenomena of the moment are surely the continuing and demonic successes of the Communists, of which there is scant mention." [7]

In the next issue, the magazine noted in its opening column, "For the Record": "Going the rounds in Catholic conservative circles: '*Mater sí, Magistra no.*' "

This remark—a play on the Cuban "*Cuba sí, Yanqui no,*" which Buckley had gotten from Garry Wills—mobilized Catholic liberals against Buckley and the magazine. Leading the charge was the magazine *America*.

Since *National Review*'s founding it had had a running feud with *America*, the liberal Jesuit weekly that prided itself in representing educated Catholic opinion in the U.S. In 1955, after *National Review* had listed *America*'s former editor along with Eleanor Roosevelt, Dag Hammarskjöld, and other liberals to whom *National Review* readers could donate a free subscription, *America* returned articles by Russell Kirk and Erik von Kuehnelt-Leddihn that it had accepted for publication on the grounds that it would not publish anyone listed on *National Review*'s masthead.

America denounced *National Review*'s crack about *Mater et Magistra* as "slanderous." It went on to accuse *National Review* of disloyalty to the Church. "So-called Catholic conservatives, like the rest of us, may be honestly mistaken in their judgment of modern trends . . . but they are not disloyal. . . . The *National Review* owes its Catholic readers and journalistic allies an apology."[8] *America's* editor, Rev. Thurston N. Davis, S.J., commented: "Mr. Buckley is no ordinary person. It takes an appalling amount of self-assurance for a Catholic writer to brush off an encyclical of John XXIII as though it has been written by [columnist and former *Commonweal* editor] John Cogley."[9]

America's denunciation was echoed by other Catholic commentators. The Reverend William J. Smith described Buckley as a "hypercritical pygmy." Donald McDonald wrote that "true conservatives must stand aghast at this latest display of anti-intellectual temper tantrums by the men at *National Review*."[10]

America's response raised questions not only about Buckley's political and religious views, but about the propriety of *National Review* publishing a critique of a papal encyclical, even though encyclicals were not covered by the mantle of papal infallibility. Buckley sought to reply in *America*, but Davis informed him that *America* would not run his reply and would accept no further advertising from *National Review*. Buckley printed his reply in *National Review*. He prefaced his letter by explaining that *National Review* was not itself a Catholic magazine.

I gently remind the editors of *America* that *National Review* is no more a Catholic magazine because its editor is a Catholic than the present administration is a Catholic administration because its head is a Catholic. The editorial in question represented the position of

the editorial board of *National Review,* on which the three major
religious faiths are represented, Catholic, Protestant, and Jew.[11]

Buckley distinguished flippancy from infidelity. "Proceed, if you
like, publicly to despair over our insouciance or frivolity—but to edge
us over into infidelity is more than uncharitable; it is irrational, and,
in the true sense, scandalous." [12]

Buckley urged *America* to reconsider its hostility to *National Review.*

I hope you will, from time to time, review the grounds of your new
anathema. When we stand together, as well we may, in that final
foxhole, you will discover, as we pass each other the ammunition,
that all along we had the same enemy; and that if we had acted in
concert, we might have spared ourselves that final encounter, under
such desperate circumstances.[13]

Buckley believed that what really bound Catholics together was
opposition to communism. In the Catholic journal *Ave Maria* he drew
an analogy between Lincoln's subordination of all issues to that of
preserving the Union and the need for Catholics to subordinate all
issues to the defeat of communism. But Buckley's anti-Communist
platform, meant to unite Catholic liberals and conservatives, tran-
scended rather than drew together the immediate concerns of liberal
and conservative Catholics. And it bore out the extent to which Buckley himself was not really part of the debate in which *America* had
tried to engage him, but rather a Catholic with a platform around
which political conservatives, regardless of religious belief, could
unite.

III

In the early sixties, Buckley and *National Review* took on a new
role, not merely as opponents of the liberal establishment, but as
tribunes of an emerging movement. Some of the magazine's editors
like Rusher and Meyer became organizers and day-to-day leaders of
the movement. But Buckley, who disliked meetings and faction fighting, preferred to play an inspirational rather than an organizational
role.

Buckley's role in founding the Young Americans for Freedom—an
organization with which he is often identified—typified his relationship to the new movement. The three people most responsible for

YAF's creation were two college students, David Francke and Doug Caddy, and public-relations expert Marvin Liebman. Liebman, a former Communist who had moved to the Right during the Cold War, had advised Buckley about fund raising for *National Review* and had organized the Carnegie Hall rally. The two had become fast friends. Liebman later credited Buckley with completing his conversion to conservatism. "He opened my eyes," Liebman said.

Buckley and Liebman had gone to the 1960 Republican Convention together. While Buckley was planning to write about it, Liebman was organizing on behalf of Walter Judd for Vice-President. Judd for Vice-President's headquarters at the Pick Congress Hotel were next to those of the Youth for Goldwater organization, which had been set up by Caddy and other conservative student leaders from the East and the Midwest.

Liebman and Buckley were impressed by the students and decided to take the two leaders, Francke and Caddy, under their wing, with Francke going to *National Review* as an intern and Caddy to Liebman's PR firm. At a luncheon the day after the convention, Liebman suggested to Caddy and the other students that they set up a new student organization. They responded enthusiastically, and one of Caddy's first assignments was to organize the meeting—to be held with Buckley's encouragement in September at Great Elm.

On the weekend of September 9, about 80 conservatives from the East and the Midwest arrived in Sharon. For most of them, Buckley was a model. "He was a hero to all the young conservatives," Scott Stanley, who later became the editor of the John Birch Society's *American Opinion,* recalled. "His presence, having it at his family home, lent a flavor of glamor to the event," young conservative and journalist Lee Edwards said. "I was particularly under his spell," Edwards recalled, "because I wanted to be like this brilliant young writer, editor, speaker, orator, debater, thinker."

Buckley let Stanton Evans and the younger conservatives make the decisions at Sharon. His and *National Review*'s influence were exercised through them. Evans wrote a declaration of principles that Buckley looked over and made minor changes in. Later called the Sharon Statement, it expressed *National Review*'s and Frank Meyer's attempt to fuse traditionalism, libertarianism, and anticommunism.

Buckley was enthusiastic about the event. He recognized that the young conservatives represented a new generation that might be capable not merely of enunciating *National Review*'s ideas but of putting them into the political mainstream. Buckley wrote about the Sharon meeting in *National Review:* "What is so striking in the students who met at Sharon is their appetite for power. Ten years ago, the struggle seemed so long, so endless, even, that we did not dream of victory. . . . It is quixotic to say that they or their elders have seized the reins of history. But the difference in psychological attitude is tremendous.'' [14]

Liebman set up Caddy, who was elected national director, in his offices on Madison Avenue. While YAF's growing membership provided the energy and zeal, Liebman brought to bear on YAF the talents he had first developed in the Communist Party. In January 1961, YAF members staged a counterpicket in Washington against demonstrators protesting the House Un-American Activities Committee. In March, they packed Manhattan Center for a rally at which Goldwater spoke. Both *The New York Times* and *Time* magazine covered the rally. Liebman and Caddy told *Time* that YAF already had twenty-one thousand members at 115 campuses, but even Stan Evans's considerably more modest estimate of several thousand members was very impressive for an organization only several months old. [15]

Buckley did not take an active role in YAF, but he was kept constantly abreast of what was happening in the organization by Liebman and Rusher and made speeches for YAF when called upon. According to Lee Edwards, who was the editor of YAF's magazine, *New Guard,* during its first year, Buckley "looked to Marvin for guidance. He sort of expected Marvin to say, 'We need you at this particular point to do this,' and he'd go ahead and do it." If he couldn't, he sent Rusher, whom YAF member and future congressman Robert Bauman described as being "the proconsul for the Emperor."

Buckley played a similar catalytic but not organizational role in the founding of the New York Conservative Party. In January 1957, Buckley had met with a Brooklyn conservative, Eli Zrake, and Michael Mooney, the son of a former General Motors president, to see whether a conservative party could be founded in New York that would play the same role in moving Republican politics to the Right that the Liberal Party had played in moving the Democrats leftward. Buckley wrote a memorandum to Bill Casey, former New Dealer Rayond Moley, Gerrish Milliken, the brother of Roger, and Jeremiah Milbank, trying to stir up interest in Zrake and Mooney's project. When Rusher became publisher, he took over the negotiations for the new party, but plans were cut short the next year by Zrake's death.

In July 1961, two Irish Catholic conservatives, Kieran O'Doherty and J. Daniel Mahoney, sent out a prospectus for a Conservative

Party. Mahoney and O'Doherty were lawyers and brothers-in-law. Both had been inspired by Buckley's example. As an undergraduate at Columbia in 1955, Mahoney had gotten Buckley to come speak on the campus and had maintained an acquaintance with him ever since. O'Doherty had met Buckley the previous year when he drove him to speak at a Catholic Action meeting in Queens.

Their plan, like Zrake's, was not really for a conventional "third party." Since New York allowed candidates for office to appear as the candidates of more than one party, a Conservative Party, like New York's Liberal Party, could use its endorsement power to influence rather than destroy the Republican Party. The party's goal, O'Doherty and Mahoney wrote, was not to supplant the Republican Party but to "bring down the liberal Republican *apparat* in New York State." [16]

Before sending out the prospectus, O'Doherty and Mahoney met with Buckley, Liebman, and Frank Meyer. Meyer agreed to write a "declaration of principles" for the organization and Liebman to provide fund-raising assistance. Buckley agreed to send out the prospectus with a covering letter to prominent conservatives. In August, after getting negative or no replies from Rayond Moley, General Electric vice-president Lemuel Boulware, and financier Frederic Coudert, Buckley wrote Mahoney, "My only position is to go ahead anyway. The older generation hardly qualifies, on the basis of their performance, as preceptors." [17]

IV

In the early sixties, Buckley played an equally important role in trying to discourage certain kinds of movements and organizations on the Right. Even if he did not succeed in stemming the growth of these movements, he did succeed in defining them out of the conservative coalition that *National Review,* YAF, and Goldwater were constructing. This would prove decisive to conservatism's political success in the decades to come.

Buckley's disenchantment with southern segregationism was partly the result of a change in his own attitude toward blacks. Under prodding from Bozell, Buckley had moved away from the racist position he had espoused in his 1957 editorial on black voting rights to a more elitist stance against uneducated voters. But under the influence of conservative proponents of civil rights like Wills and the heated debate about civil rights taking place in the country, Buckley began to distinguish *National Review*'s and the conservative position from that of southern racists, whose politics rested on the assumption of blacks' genetic inferiority to whites.

Buckley's position was that genetic inferiority was both unproven and irrelevant. In 1960, a Georgia lawyer wrote him to complain of a sentence in *Up from Liberalism* where Buckley denied that blacks were congenitally inferior to whites. Buckley replied:

> I have no objections whatever to continuing research on the question of the relative congenital superiority or inferiority among the races. But what conclusions of a political kind I should be prepared to draw from the fruits of such research, I am not prepared to say. My own notion, for instance, is that the Jewish race can probably be demonstrated to be more intelligent than the Gentile, on the average; as Gentiles might be shown to be superior to Negroes in intelligence. I guess another way of saying the same thing is that I believe a) there are as yet no conclusive grounds for such generalizations . . . and b) the whole situation is not, frankly, one of my principal concerns.[18]

Buckley's disenchantment with segregationists was also the result of a shift in the southern movement. In the early sixties, the leadership shifted from Bourbon politicians like Georgia's Richard Russell, who cloaked their segregationism in constitutional arguments, to the openly racist White Citizens Councils and to a new generation of populist and racist southern Democrats typified by Mississippi Governor Ross Barnett and Alabama Governor George Wallace.

In his articles, Buckley made clear that he rejected the politics of the southern racists. "No one who has contemplated a man brandishing a fiery cross and preaching hatred needs help from social science to know that the race problem has debasing effects on black and white alike," Buckley wrote in a 1961 article in *Saturday Review*. But insisting that the federal imposition of integration was a greater evil than the temporary continuation of segregation, he held out for voluntary, gradual change. "If it is true that the separation of the races on account of color is nonrational, then circumstance will in due course break down segregation."[19]

In 1962, when Ross Barnett refused to allow black student James Meredith to enroll at the University of Mississippi, Buckley attacked Barnett's motives. Recalling that Barnett had been thrown out of a Hartford restaurant a dozen years before for protesting the presence of a black diner, he denounced the Mississippi governor as a hypocrite who was more interested in excluding "the Negro" than in "states' rights." [20] But he still defended Mississippi's right to decide on the basis of race who would enroll at its university.

Buckley's attitude toward the right-wing anti-Communist movement had not shifted significantly from the first days of *National Review,* but the movement itself had become even more hysterical. Buckley had always exaggerated the Soviet military and diplomatic threat to the United States, but he had never shared the view of McCarthy's most rabid followers that American Communists posed a serious threat to the nation's survival. Buckley and the other *National Review* editors believed that, besides the Soviet Union, the main danger came from American liberals, who, although sincerely anti-Communist, underestimated the Soviet threat.

Buckley and *National Review* had tolerated and even praised organizations like Fred Schwarz's Christian Anti-Communist Crusade, which wildly magnified the Soviet threat. But they drew the line when the John Birch Society and its founder, Robert Welch, began to maintain that the American government was itself being run by Communists rather than liberals. Such a position not only ran directly counter to that of *National Review;* it also threatened to cast the Right into what Burnham called "crackpot alley."

Welch founded the John Birch Society in 1958. By 1961, the Society had recruited at least twenty-five thousand members, including numerous city officials and two California congressmen, into a secret, monolithic organization. Welch believed not only that Communists were at the root of whatever ailed America, but that America's leaders were actually Communists. In his book *The Politician,* which he handed out to Society members, he accused Dwight Eisenhower and his brother Milton of being Communists. Welch wrote:

> While I think that Milton Eisenhower is a Communist and has been for over 30 years, this opinion is based on general circumstances of his conduct. But my firm belief that Dwight Eisenhower is a dedicated, conscious agent of the Communist conspiracy is based on an accumulation of detailed evidence so extensive and so palpable that it seems to put this conviction beyond any reasonable doubt. [21]

Buckley had known Welch since 1954, when Henry Regnery, who published two of Welch's books, introduced them. They had complimented each other on their work. In 1955, Welch pledged $1,000 to *National Review* and in 1957 gave another $1,000, but he chided Buckley for not understanding that Eisenhower was "on the other side."

It was Buckley's first inkling that Welch's anticommunism had gotten out of hand.

The next fall, Welch sent Buckley a typewritten copy of *The Politician,* enclosed in a loose-leaf binder numbered 58. Buckley gave it to Jim McFadden to read. McFadden sent a memo to Buckley. "My conclusion was that this guy was a nut," Mc Fadden recalled. After he read the book, Buckley wrote Welch that he did not find his "hypotheses" plausible.

> I find them—curiously—almost pathetically optimistic. If Eisenhower were what you think he is, then the elimination of Eisenhower would be a critical step in setting things aright. In my view things will get not better but very possibly worse when Eisenhower leaves the White House. And the reason for this is that virtually the entire nation is diseased as a result of the collapse of our faith.[22]

In replying to Buckley's letter, Welch assured him that of all the people who had read *The Politician* he was the only one who "completely disagreed" with his hypotheses. In January, he wrote Buckley again—this time to inform him "off the record" that he had had a founding meeting of the John Birch Society in Indianapolis.[23] Buckley became alarmed when he learned that the Society's National Council included Spruille Braden, Adolphe Menjou, Clarence Manion, and Revilo P. Oliver, all of whom had been close to *National Review.* Both Willi Schlamm and *National Review* writer Medford Evans, the father of Stan Evans, were on the editorial board of *American Opinion,* the Birch Society journal. And one of the Society's members was textile magnate Roger Milliken, *National Review*'s chief financial supporter.

Buckley decided that he and *National Review* should criticize the Birch Society's views. His initial inpetus was more intellectual than political—he was offended by the conceptual lunacy of Welch's charge that Eisenhower was a Communist and that the course of American government was set by Communists. That spring he decided to print an attack on Welch and his magazine—by former Communist Eugene Lyons.

Welch and *American Opinion* had charged that Moscow had merely made a pretense of censoring Pasternak's novel *Doctor Zhivago* in order to fool the West into accepting an anticapitalist work. In his essay, Lyons lumped together *American Opinion*'s view of *Doctor Zhivago* with its refusal to accept the Tito-Stalin split or the authenticity of Yugoslav dissenter Milovan Djilas's critique of Communist society, *The New Class.*

Certainly there are elements of deception . . . in all manifestations
of Communist internal troubles. But to write them all off as propaganda devices . . . is to concede to the Communist world a monolithic perfection, a superhuman cleverness, which does not and
could not exist outside a fiction *1984*. Those who see Communism
in such Sophoclean terms might as well give up the fight, since the
odds against mere mortals would be too steep to overcome.[24]

Buckley wrote Welch in March informing him that he was printing
Lyons's essay and that he agreed with it. "Probably a little friendly
controversy among ourselves every now and then is not too bad an
idea," he wrote. Welch replied, "I shall not mind in the least your
publishing Gene Lyons' criticism."[25]

But after Lyons's essay appeared in April, angry letters poured in
from Birch Society members. Medford Evans wrote Buckley, "My
view on the subject is that *National Review* should refrain from making any criticism of other conservative periodicals except in the one
case when we earnestly feel that a spokesman for conservatism has
made a grievous error."[26] And Welch admitted several months later
that he had found "one or two aspects of that [article] annoying."
The article, Welch wrote, "consisted of holding up to complete and
sarcastic ridicule a theme to which we had given careful and considered argument, in which we still believe future history will prove
us to have been entirely correct."[27]

Buckley replied to Welch: "I do not encourage in *National Review*
editorial sniping at other conservatives. I ok'd Gene Lyons's project
because I believed that its central purpose was the rectification of a
grievous conservative mistake."[28]

By 1961, Buckley was beginning to worry that with the John Birch
Society growing so rapidly, the right-wing upsurge in the country
would take an ugly, even Fascist turn rather than leading toward the
kind of conservatism *National Review* had promoted.

His fears were crystallized by an analysis of the John Birch Society
by Alan Westin. Westin predicted that if Rockefeller defeated Goldwater for the nomination in 1964, Goldwater would turn to the "fundamentalist right." * Even Rusher began to fear the results of the
right-wing upsurge. In a private memorandum to Buckley, Rusher
wrote, "My own hunch is that we are in the early stages of a conser-

---

* In the margin of Westin's article, Buckley wrote: "(1) On mechanics, Goldwater loses.
(2) Result: An American Raskol'niki. (3) How does *National Review* avoid being trade
journal of Raskol'niki?" (Buckley Papers.)

vative trend which is going to grow and harden and quite possibly get
out of hand as the scope and pace of the free world's collapse becomes
apparent to the American people and desire for a scapegoat takes
hold."[29]

Buckley thought that this time *National Review* would have to attack Welch and the Birch Society more directly. But at the magazine's
quarterly editorial meeting in March 1961, Buckley encountered stiff
resistance from Rusher and Meyer. Neither of them had any respect
for Welch's conspiracy theories, but Rusher wanted *National Review*
to focus on developing an organized alternative to the John Birch
Society rather than on criticizing it. Rusher expressed his doubts
about criticizing the John Birch Society in a memorandum to Buckley.

> It seems to me that you are trying very hard indeed to persuade
> yourself and others of the validity of some such syllogism as the
> following: Robert Welch is incurable; Welch has absolute control of
> the John Birch Society; therefore the John Birch Society is also
> incurable. . . . I rather suspect that your insistence upon your syl-
> logism is based rather more upon your impatience with an organi-
> zation of conservatives that is not obediently following *our* lead,
> rather than upon a conviction that all of these people are somehow
> irretrievably tainted.[30]

Frank Meyer thought that the magazine had to "dissociate itself
from" the John Birch Society, but he wanted it done without alienating its members. "Some of the solidest conservatives in the country,"
Meyer wrote Buckley, "are members of the John Birch Society, and
we should act in such a way as to alienate them no more than is strictly
necessary from a moral, political, or tactical point of view."[31]

Buckley finally decided to write an article in question-and-answer
form rather than an editorial about the Society, and to aim the brunt
of his criticism at Welch's philosophy rather than the Birch Society
itself. In it, he tempered his criticism of Welch ("I have always admired his personal courage and devotion to the cause") but noted that
"every issue of *National Review* stresses a different analysis of the
cause of our difficulty" than that put forward by Welch in *The Politician*. Buckley suggested that Birch Society members also didn't share
their founder's view that Communists were in "effective control" of
the U.S. government.

> I myself have never met a single member who declared himself in
> agreement with certain of Mr. Welch's conclusions. If our govern-

ment is in the effective control of Communists, then the entire educational effort conducted by conservatives in this country . . . is a
sheer waste of time. . . . The point has come, if Mr. Welch is right,
to leave the typewriter, the lectern, and the radio microphone, and
look instead to one's rifles.[32]

Buckley's temperate attack won praise from supporters as well as
opponents of the John Birch Society. Birch Society Executive Council member T. Coleman Andrews wrote Buckley, "I appreciate the
very objective manner in which you handled the editorial on the John
Birch Society." When Frank Meyer spoke in New Orleans, Phoenix,
and Dallas to groups "where three-fourths of the best people I met
were John Birch members," he found "no dissatisfaction with the
editorial." Even Welch sent Buckley a friendly letter. "Despite the
differences of opinion between us, which remain and are stressed, I
think the article is both objectively fair and subjectively honorable,"
Welch wrote.[33]

V

In the last half of 1961, one event after another occurred that con-
vinced Buckley that he would have to mount a stronger attack on the
John Birch Society. By that fall both Liebman and Rusher were at
their wits' ends over the factional warfare in YAF, which they be-
lieved was being subverted from two directions: first, by its director,
Caddy, who was drawing YAF close to the Rockefeller forces in New
York, and second, by board of directors member Scott Stanley, who,
Rusher and Liebman had learned, was a member of the John Birch
Society. Every question was becoming a factional test, with the
Caddy and Stanley forces united against what they regarded as the
"*National Review* faction."

Lee Edwards shared Leibman and Rusher's suspicion of Stanley.
"I think there is no question that in the early years Scott Stanley was
trying to take over Young Americans for Freedom," Edwards recalled later. Edwards thought that *National Review*'s criticisms of
Welch as well as Liebman and Rusher's discomfort with Stanley were
perfectly justified. "We were beginning to get into the real world of
national politics, dealing with people like John Tower and Barry Goldwater and others. It was just obvious that we couldn't carry around
baggage from the John Birch Society."

The New York Conservative Party was also being threatened by
the specter of the John Birch Society, as New York Republicans tried

to discredit the new party by linking it to the Society. In November, barely three months after the prospectus was circulated, *The New York Times* had reported that "certain of the reputed sponsors of the new conservative group are said to have Birch Society association."[34]

The factional battles in YAF and the embarrassment that the Birch Society created for the New York Conservatives convinced Buckley that he and *National Review* would have to "dig in on the subject." In January 1962, he and other prominent conservatives met with Goldwater at the Breakers Hotel in Palm Beach. At the meeting, Buckley attached special importance to converting Goldwater, whom he considered to be the magazine's "most prominent constituent," to his view of the John Birch Society.

General Motors executive Jay Morton Hall had arranged for Buckley, Russell Kirk, and William Baroody, who was the director of the American Enterprise Institute, to spend two days talking with Barry Goldwater. Hall had judged Buckley's participation sufficiently important to schedule the meeting during the one gap in Buckley's crowded speaking schedule.

The five of them met during the afternoon and then had dinner together. Goldwater refused to commit himself to running in 1964, but it became apparent to Buckley that "while he would not admit that he was, it was by no means ruled out, and that the meeting itself was the beginning of an experiment with a kitchen Cabinet." Buckley steered the discussion toward Goldwater's stand on the John Birch Society. Arguing that it was a "menace" to the conservative movement, Buckley wanted Goldwater to join *National Review* in publicly dissociating himself from it. Kirk heartily agreed ("Eisenhower isn't a Communist. He is a golfer," Kirk had quipped), but Baroody didn't think that Goldwater should force a confrontation with Welch and the Society.

Goldwater admitted that he was sometimes embarrassed by the Birch Society's statements and actions, but he thought that there were both "nice guys" and "kooks" in the Society and that it would be unwise to denounce them publicly.[35] As Rusher later summarized Goldwater's reaction, he insisted that "the society supported him, not he the society."[36] But Goldwater promised that he would consider the issue, and he wrote Buckley that he would like to see Welch resign or the Society disband.

Buckley decided to follow up the meeting with an editorial on the John Birch Society. Rusher, Bozell, Meyer, and new senior editor William Rickenbacker opposed the decision on the grounds that *Na-*

tional Review should direct its fire at Communists and liberals rather than fellow conservatives, even if their political beliefs were deeply mistaken, but with Burnham's and his sister Priscilla's support, Buckley went ahead anyway. (In a letter to Buckley, Rickenbacker complained that Burnham "fiercely desired to annihilate Welch."[37])

Like the first statement, this one was directed at Welch rather than the John Birch Society, but unlike the first, it was run as an editorial and was far sharper in its criticism of Welch. Titled "The Question of Robert Welch," the editorial charged that Welch was "damaging the cause of anti-Communism. . . . Why?" the editorial asked. "Because he persists in distorting reality and in refusing to make the crucial moral and political distinction . . . between 1) an *active pro-Communist,* and 2) an *ineffectually anti-Communist liberal."* The editorial warned, "There are bounds to the dictum, Anyone on the right is my ally."[38]

In reponse to the editorial, Buckley solicited favorable comment from both Goldwater and Tower. Tower described the editorial as "a courageous and responsible analysis."[39] *Time* magazine and the *Washington Post* also praised *National Review'*s attack on Welch.

According to Scott Stanley, Welch felt "personally hurt and personally betrayed" by Buckley's attacks on him, but he dealt with *National Review'*s editorial obliquely by affirming his own belief in *"pas d'ennemis à droit* [no enemies on the right]." Welch wrote in *American Opinion:* "Let us repeat: we care about fighting the Communists—and nobody else! To avoid adding fuel to all of the friction among the anti-Communist forces, we shall even refrain from defending ourselves against the slings and arrows from the Right."[40]

However, many John Birch Society members and supporters among *National Review'*s readers did not turn the other cheek. One major contributor, James Lewis Kirby, declined to stand for re-election to *National Review'*s board of directors and made no further financial contributions to the magazine. Buckley had a "wrenching telephone conversation" with Birch Society member Roger Milliken, who did not, however, terminate or even lessen his financial support for *National Review.*

In response to a letter from one Birch Society supporter in Pasadena accusing him of weakening the Right through his criticisms, Buckley gave his most eloquent defense of the anti-Birch editorial:

> It was precisely my desire to *strengthen* the ranks of conservatism that led me to publish the editorial. Our movement has got to govern. It has got to expand by bringing into our ranks those people

who are, at the moment, on our immediate left—the moderate, wishy-washy conservatives: the Nixonites . . . I am talking . . . about 20 to 30 million people . . . .If they are being asked to join a movement whose leadership believes the drivel of Robert Welch, they will pass by crackpot alley, and will not pause until they feel the warm embrace of those way over on the other side, the Liberals.[41]

The immediate effect of Buckley's attacks against the John Birch Society was a loss in subscriptions and financial support for the magazine. In a letter to Buckley in Switzerland, Rusher reported that in all *National Review* had received 350 letters, almost all of them critical, including about seventy cancellations and twenty disavowals of support from $100-plus donors. For several years afterwards, both Buckley and Burnham wondered whether they had been effective at all.

But Buckley's attack on the John Birch Society was an important step forward for Buckley, *National Review,* and the conservatives who looked to them for leadership. By dissociating conservatism from the John Birch Society, Buckley showed that he, *National Review,* and the Goldwater conservatives accepted the legitimacy of their political opponents, even if they differed from them on every major question. The attack established them as the "responsible Right" and moved them out of the crackpot far Right and toward the great center of American politics, even though Buckley's and the magazine's own positions on the major issues—from the threat of communism abroad to the danger of welfare socialism at home—had changed very little over the first six years of the magazine.

Buckley's attack on the John Birch Society also transformed him as a public figure. He was no longer the pariah of the McCarthy days. He was a public representative of the new conservatism that television producers and college deans could invite to appear without provoking an outcry. Whether intentionally or not, Buckley's attack on the John Birch Society prepared the way for his own celebrity.

CHAPTER 12

The Big Book

When Buckley and Schlamm decided to start *National Review,* Buckley pledged that he would devote himself single-mindedly to it for at least ten years, but by the early sixties, he was beginning to wonder how long he wanted to spend working primarily on the magazine.

The problem was not the strain of conflict nor the threat of failure, but that *National Review* had become a success, and it no longer needed his constant attention to survive. Its subscriptions were higher than even Buckley had hoped. Rusher and McFadden had the business side under control. And Burnham and Buckley's sister Priscilla were capable of running the magazine day to day without his supervision.

Like his father, Buckley thrived on the anxiety of risk and creation, but became quickly bored after he had accomplished what he set out to do. Just as Will Buckley began thinking about exploring for oil in Florida's coastal waters soon after he had struck oil in Venezuela, Buckley began looking at new intellectual ventures once *National Review* had overcome its early obstacles.

Buckley thought about taking a leave from *National Review* to write a major theoretical work like Kirk's *The Conservative Mind*. He had always believed that an intellectual's highest calling was to write a book that would challenge an era's most basic assumptions. His father, his brother Reid, Henry Regnery, and Burnham and his other associates on *National Review* had long urged him to undertake what they called a "big book." And Buckley agreed. At dinner, Rusher had asked him what his ambition was. "He said that the thing he would most like to do in life was make an original contribution to political science," Rusher recalled. "I think he mentioned [political philosopher] Leo Strauss."

In a long evening conversation with Burnham in early 1960, Buckley pondered abandoning *National Review* for an academic career. While Buckley, on Burnham's advice, dropped the idea of leaving *National Review,* he committed himself to writing a scholarly treatise. In 1961, he signed a contract with Putnam's for "an untitled book on conservatism."[1]

But even though he wanted to think of himself as a theoretician and philosopher of the Right, Buckley was inexorably drawn toward a career as a popular journalist and political personality. Already, he had begun to write for popular magazines like *Coronet* and *Esquire*. In 1960, after *Up from Liberalism* was published, he signed his first contract with a large commercial publishing house, Putnam's, to do an anthology on the House Un-American Activities Committee, *The Committee and Its Critics*. And the renewed interest in American politics and the revival of a right wing were opening up for him opportunities in public life that Buckley could not resist.

I

Buckley had planned to spend his 1962 winter in Switzerland working on his "big book," but before he left, he was distracted by public controversy and the promise of popular journalism. In December 1961, the North American Newspaper Alliance had asked Buckley to write an article on the American Right, which it syndicated along with an opposing view from Gore Vidal. The week after Buckley's article appeared, a representative from NANA called him offering to syndicate a weekly column. Buckley was intrigued. He liked the idea of doing a column, and he also welcomed the extra money it would bring. During the late fifties, he had lost some of his inheritance on *National Review* and bad investments and, even with Pat's substantial trust, he was feeling unusually hard pressed to maintain the luxurious style of life—a staff of servants, a house in Stamford and an apartment in

Manhattan, as well as a rented chalet in Switzerland—to which he and Pat were accustomed.

But his colleagues on *National Review,* fearing that a column would detract from his time on the magazine, urged him not to take it on. He heeded their pleas, in effect, by demanding a guarantee of $200 a week, far more than a beginning columnist could normally expect. NANA turned him down, and he gave the matter no more thought.

Then a week before he was scheduled to leave for Switzerland, Harry Elmlark, the head of the George Matthew Adams Syndicate in Washington, called him. When Buckley's secretary, Gertrude Vogt, suggested to Elmlark that he talk to Buckley after he returned from Switzerland that spring, Elmlark, a voluble man who prided himself on his salesmanship, refused to get off the phone. Vogt, Buckley recalled, "who seldom spoke sternly to me during the fifteen years she was my secretary, told me that if I did not take this call from a man, Elmlark, of the George Matthew Adams Syndicate, she had to assume, from his persistence, that he would be waiting to meet me at the Geneva airport." [2]

Elmlark, a liberal, thought of Buckley as a "nut" and a "crackpot," but when, at the urging of a young assistant, he had sent out queries on a Buckley column to several newspaper editors, he had received enthusiastic responses and had resolved to sign up Buckley that month. Buckley found Elmlark's aggressive cajoling oddly charming and agreed to do the column on a guarantee of $125 a week and of $200 a week if the column grossed that much.*

The same week, Buckley received a hurried invitation to appear on *The Jack Paar Show.* Paar had succeeded Steve Allen as the leading attraction of late-night television, and an invitation to his talk-and-music show was highly coveted by politicians and writers as well as by entertainers. Former Vice-President Nixon had appeared on Paar's show, and President Kennedy watched Paar regularly.

Paar was known for his whimsy and his dry, understated humor. He did some stand-up routines, but primarily sat behind a small desk and engaged in light banter with his guests, most of whom were show-business people. Liberal authors Gore Vidal and Norman Mailer had already become regulars on Paar's show, and Buckley's invitation was owing indirectly to Vidal, who, as a guest that month, had told

---

* There are conflicting versions of how much Elmlark offered Buckley. According to Buckley, Elmlark met his $200-a-week demand at the outset. But according to Elmlark, he agreed to $200 a week only *if* the column grossed that much—still an extremely generous offer. Given the economics of publishing, Elmlark's account is slightly more plausible.

Paar that Buckley had "attacked" the pope as being "too left wing."
The spectacle of a Catholic writer attacking the pope had piqued
Paar's interest.

Buckley himself was extremely uneasy about appearing on Paar's
show. "I didn't know whether I could survive a half-comic talk
show," Buckley recalled. But before the show began, Paar did everything he could to remove any fears Buckley might have of an ambush.
He told Buckley in the dressing room:

> I want you to leave this show feeling good—that's what I want. You
> know one of the reasons why people think we give more breaks to
> Liberals and left-wingers is because we have more of them on the
> show. But that's only because there are more of them around, more
> of them who are interesting people, as people. On the other side,
> there's just Goldwater and you.[3]

During the half hour he was on the show Buckley discussed, among
other things, *National Review*'s editorial on *Mater et Magistra*, the
John Birch Society, and McCarthy. His eloquence on the air unruffled
Paar, who could hardly find an opening for repartee. Buckley left the
studio feeling that his appearance had been a "stunning success." But
as soon as Buckley had left, Paar began to attack him. He mimicked
his expressions and speech and then joined his next two guests in
deriding Buckley and his politics.

The next morning, one of Paar's assistants called Buckley to ask
him how he liked the show. He replied, "I thought it was fair enough
while I was on, but it's a pity Mr. Paar turned it into a Hate Buckley
session for the rest of the evening after I had gone."[4] That evening,
Paar made a pretense at apologizing to Buckley, only to continue to
attack him. He also invited Vidal back that evening to flay Buckley's
opinions of the pope. Vidal, who had taken a strong dislike to Buckley, criticized not only Buckley's political opinions—suggesting no
difference between his political views and those of the John Birch
Society—but he also made several personal cracks about Buckley and
his family, and implied that Buckley "had never worked for a
living."[5]

Buckley was incensed by Paar's and Vidal's attack, the more so
because it was before a national television audience to which he could
not reply. That night he couldn't fall asleep and called Jim Burnham
in the middle of the night to ask if he should cancel his trip to Switzerland so that he could demand to refute Paar and Vidal on the air. On
Burnham's advice, he decided to leave for Switzerland, as planned,
but he left a telegram at the office to be mailed to Paar.

Please inform Gore Vidal that neither I nor my family is disposed to receive lessons in morality from a pink queer. If he wishes to challenge that designation, inform him that I shall fight by the laws of the Marquis of Queensberry [a reference to the case of Oscar Wilde]. He will know what I mean. William F. Buckley, Jr.[6]

By the time he arrived in Switzerland, he had thought better of sending the telegram. Instead, he wrote a long article recounting his experience on the show, and he instructed his lawyer, C. Dickerman Williams, to explore whether he could sue Vidal for libel. (Williams and Rusher later convinced him that there were insufficient grounds for a suit.)

In his article, published later that year in *National Review,* he detailed Paar and Vidal's treachery and also tried to justify his decision to go on the show. Citing the record number of letters Paar had gotten from his appearance—more than seventeen thousand, the most ever —Buckley insisted that he had succeeded in getting his message across to Paar's audience even if he had failed to convince Paar.

I distinguish between Paar's audience and himself. It is probably true that one cannot succeed with Paar without that unctuous self-ingratiation which is the trademark of so many of his most successful guests; but the audience doesn't seem to mind a few minutes' serious talk, cast at an adult level. . . . [7]

Buckley's controversy with Paar, far from discouraging him from further appearances on television, only whetted his appetite to vindicate himself before a national television audience.

II

That winter in Switzerland, Buckley began writing his newspaper column. Entitled intitially "A Conservative Voice," it was supposed to represent not merely Buckley's opinion but that of an emerging political movement, of which he and Goldwater were the main voices. He wrote very quickly—a thousand words rarely took him more than a half hour to write. Elmlark read everything that Buckley wrote, and frequently demanded that he clarify a statement, but he refused to print only two columns—one an attack on Winston Churchill on the occasion of his death and the other an attack on the *New York Post,* which had just begun running Buckley's column.

Buckley's column gave him a readership and influence well beyond that of *National Review,* and he used it to fly in the face of prevailing opinion. After Kennedy in October 1962 humiliated Khrushchev by forcing him in a nuclear showdown to remove his missiles from Cuba in exchange for an American promise not to invade the island, Buckley alone among commentators condemned the deal. Kennedy, Buckley wrote, "has formally given our bitterest enemy a pledge that we will enforce the non-enforcement of the Monroe Doctrine!"[8]

He denounced the popular Kennedy as a creation of Madison Avenue advertisers. "It happens that the President of the United States is primarily a political technician. Nobody has the slightest idea of what the President really believes."[9] Or even more sharply: "Our President emerges as the ultimate man in the gray flannel suit: the great accommodator, the weather vane on the perfect ball bearings—soul-free, immune from any frictions of reality."[10]

But Buckley also kept his audience off balance by distinguishing his own voice from that of paranoid anti-Communists and southern racists. He criticized General Edwin Walker, who, fired from the Army for his Birch-like views, had become a hero of the far Right. Walker's "views," Buckley wrote, "were poorly thought out, grossly stated, and preposterous on their face."[11] He wrote that George Wallace's views "weave together a kind of philosophical and opportunistic ambiguity from which statesmanship is seldom cut."[12]

His best columns displayed his personal generosity as well as his defiance of public opinion. In a special column the day that Kennedy was assassinated, when rumors were rife of Kennedy assassin Lee Harvey Oswald's ties to Cuba and the Soviet Union, Buckley insisted that the assassination should not be blamed on either the Right or the Left. And he wrote of Kennedy, "Even his most adamant political opponents acknowledged the personal courage Mr. Kennedy showed during his young and dazzling lifetime."[13]

Two weeks after Kennedy was assassinated, Buckley called for a period of "dignified mourning for a graceful human being who passed through our midst with style and energy" but also insisted that the issues that had divided the country during Kennedy's tenure continue to be debated. "John F. Kennedy lived a life of tough controversy, and while it is correct that an individual's weaknesses should be buried with him, it is not ever possible to bury the public issues on which a public figure committed himself."[14]

Some of Buckley's weakest columns were those in which he attempted to run interference for conservative politicians and right-wing governments. During 1963, he used his column to promote Goldwater's presidential candidacy. In April, he wrote, "I am for him, and I do believe that if, in due course, he would declare himself, and go to the people, and tell them why he was running, if not for his own good for theirs, in no time at all he'd knock those crazy figures of Mr. Gallup into shape, and dispose them to say, 'Yes, Mr. President.' "[15]

Buckley's newfound influence as a columnist attracted the attention of right-wing regimes that were under attack from the Kennedy administration and were desperately looking for favorable publicity in the United States. Buckley was actively courted by Chiang Kai-shek's Taiwan, Franco's Spain, South Africa, Rhodesia, and Portugal's African colonies, and went on expenses-paid trips to some of these countries.

When he returned from Mozambique in 1962, Buckley wrote a column describing the backwardness of the African population over which Portugal ruled: "The more serene element in Africa tends to believe that rampant African nationalism is self-discrediting, and that therefore the time is bound to come when America, and the West . . . will depart from our dogmatic anti-Colonialism and realize what is the nature of the beast."[16]

In the fall of 1962, during a visit to South Africa, arranged by the Information Ministry, Buckley wrote that South African apartheid "has evolved into a serious program designed to cope with a melodramatic dilemma on whose solution hangs, quite literally, the question of life or death for the white man in South Africa."[17] When he returned from South Africa, he wrote of his trip in a manner calculated to win over liberals. In describing his visit to a Bantustan, he dwelt upon the weaknesses of apartheid before justifying its necessity. When the South African Minister of Information complained of the article's "peppery parts," Buckley assured him that he was merely trying to win over potentially hostile audiences. Buckley told him that he had "a knowledge of how to reach Americans." *

Buckley did not seem concerned that he might be violating his readers' trust in the way that he wrote about these regimes. As he had done before, he placed politics above the imperatives of journalistic objectivity.

---

* Buckley would use the same technique later in writing about such diverse subjects as California's newly elected governor Ronald Reagan and Chile's Pinochet regime. Writing to Nancy Reagan in 1967 about his portrayal of her husband, he explained, "It is cagily executed and purposely critical here and there in order to increase its effect." (Buckley Papers.)

III

Buckley was one of a small group of extremely articulate intellectuals that the new interest in politics elevated to celebrity status.
Buckley, Mailer, Baldwin, and Vidal became better known than sen-
ators or congressmen. Magazines eagerly sought interviews with them
—in the early sixties, *Mademoiselle,* a mass-circulation young wom-
en's magazine, ran a series of interviews, entitled "Disturbers of the
Peace," with Buckley, Vidal, Mailer, Ayn Rand, and others. Television talk shows clamored for their appearances and their debates became major public spectacles.

In 1962, when Buckley debated novelist and essayist Norman
Mailer at the Medinah Temple in Chicago, the crowd filled the hall to
capacity. Thirty-six hundred people paid $2.50—the price of an ex-
pensive movie—to see the two debate, and afterwards *Playboy* magazine, with a circulation of more than a million, published the debate
in a two-part series that it featured on its January and February 1963
covers. When Buckley debated novelist and civil rights activist James
Baldwin at Oxford in 1965, *The New York Times Magazine* published
the entire proceedings.

Buckley, Mailer, and the others were not seen as they would be a
decade later—simply as personalities, valued for their style regardless
of their opinions—but as the most articulate and engaging representatives of conflicting political views and movements. Their debates
symbolized and were part of the clash of movements.

Buckley himself became part of this celebrity circle. He became
friendly with Mailer, as he had gotten to be friends earlier with Murray
Kempton, another frequent debating opponent. And the dinner parties
at the Buckleys' apartment in New York were as likely to include
liberals as conservatives. With Mailer, Buckley carried on a kind of
teen-age put-down contest that made audiences think they were personal as well as political enemies.

In a *National Review* article in 1960, he described Mailer as a
"moral pervert." [18] In his debate with Mailer in 1962, he began,
"There is no one whose dismay I personally covet more; because it is
clear from reading the works of Mr. Mailer that only demonstrations
of human swinishness are truly pleasing to him, truly confirm his
vision of a world gone square." And he concluded, "The American
right wing, of whom I am merely one member, [is] clumsily trying to
say what Norman Mailer with his superior skills would be saying so
very much better if only he would raise his eyes from the world's
genital glands." [19]

For his part, Mailer said that Buckley had a "second rate intellect incapable of entertaining two serious thoughts in a row," but that he was also "wonderful company . . . you can't stay mad at a guy who's witty, spontaneous, and likes good liquor."[20] He also expressed his admiration for Buckley's stage presence. "No other act can project simultaneous hints that he is in the act of playing Commodore of the Yacht Club, Joseph Goebbels, Robert Mitchum, Maverick, Savonarola, the nice prep school kid next door, and the snows of yesteryear."[21]

There were opponents on the celebrity circuit whom Buckley disliked. One was Gore Vidal, with whom he had clashed over the Jack Paar show, and another was historian and Kennedy adviser Arthur Schlesinger, Jr. In January 1961, he had debated Schlesinger in Boston, and Schlesinger had tried to set Buckley up for the kill by an extravagant compliment: "Mr. Buckley has a facility for rhetoric which I envy as well as a wit which I seek clumsily to and vainly to emulate." When Buckley published *Rumbles Left and Right,* an anthology of his magazine articles, he got his revenge against Schlesinger.

As he was pondering what he should put on the cover of *Rumbles,* a correspondent reminded him of Schlesinger's compliment, and he thought it would be "mad fun" to include it as a cover blurb for the book.[22] When Schlesinger saw the book, he threatened to sue, and the publisher, after several hostile exchanges, proposed removing the blurb from later printings, but Buckley insisted it be kept, and offered to pay damages in case Schlesinger sued and won. Buckley himself continued to needle Schlesinger. When he met him later that year at a party, he told him, "Your deadline for my next cover blurb is the first of the month," and Schlesinger went into a rage.[23]

Overall, becoming a celebrity drew Buckley farther out of the narrower circle of conservative organizations and student groups to which he had spent much of his time speaking. He had to frame his arguments within the prevailing political assumptions. He had to accept, finally, the growing popular unanimity around such subjects as civil right in the South. And he became less tolerant of the far Right and more tolerant of liberals.

IV

In September 1962, as Buckley was getting caught up in the celebrity whirl of dinners and parties in New York, he and Pat decided to shift their home base. While they still spent weekends and summers in Stamford, they enrolled Christopher at a private school in New York, and they spent all their weekdays at the apartment they rented on the fashionable Upper East Side. Pat, who had been active in Stamford's Junior League, shifted her interests to New York's Metropolitan Museum of Art. And Christopher learned what a celebrity childhood was like. "I was brought down to dinner where people like poor Norman Mailer were and made to read my third-grade compositions," he recalled.

The Buckleys' marriage had worked in spite of Bill's long absences from home. Pat was fiercely loyal and carried grudges against Bill's critics far longer than he did. They called each other "Duckey" and doted not only on their son but on a succession of cocker spaniels. Bill's relationship with Christopher had also begun to blossom once Christopher had come of reading age and Buckley could badger him about his reading habits. Buckley would constantly try to wean him away from comic books with bribes—Christopher recalled being paid five dollars for each book he read—but Christopher, being rebellious, resisted.

Buckley had cherished the times that he spent as a child with his own father—sometimes separated by months when his father was traveling—and he tried to make his times with Christopher memorable. "He believed in a magical childhood, and he clearly believed that I should have one," Christopher said. When they rode together up to Sharon in Buckley's sports car for family get-togethers, he would play recordings of Shakespeare for the six-year-old Christopher and try to explain to him the high points of *Macbeth* and *Hamlet*. On weekends, when Buckley was home, he would take Christopher sailing. When Christopher was seven, Buckley and one of his friends, Reggie Stoops, devised a treasure hunt for him on a small island off Long Island Sound that they called "Treasure Island." They provided Christopher with a treasure map, and he set about following the instructions until he came to the place where the treasure, dime-store jewelry that his mother had purchased for the occasion, was buried.

In the fall of 1960, Buckley devised a real treasure hunt for Christopher. He and Reggie buried a wooden crate with several Georgian silver pieces that Pat had inherited. The plan was that Pat would buy the treasure from Christopher after he found it. But the day before he was to take Christopher out to find the treasure, hurricane Donna blew through the Sound and so altered the geography of Treasure Island that Christopher was never able to find the treasure. For several years afterwards, the treasure hunt was a sore point with Pat until, Buckley said, her "sense of humor caught up with her, as it always does."[24]

V

Buckley's growing celebrity took its toll on *National Review*. Distracted by the column and his speaking schedule and bored with the daily routine of the magazine, Buckley spent increasingly less time in the office, often appearing only on the two days when the current issue was put to bed and the next issue was planned. Without explicitly changing Burnham's title, he put Burnham and his sister Priscilla in charge of the day-to-day running of the magazine.

Burnham was the only one of the original senior editors still working full time on *National Review*. Schlamm had resigned, and Bozell had taken a leave and moved his family to Spain so that he could finish his book on the Warren Supreme Court. And Buckley had broken finally with Kendall, who had joined the faculty at the conservative Catholic University of Dallas after Buckley had helped him negotiate a buy-out of his tenure with Yale.

Kendall provoked the breakup of their friendship. From 1959 to 1961, Kendall wrote several articles from overseas for *National Review* and then protested vociferously—even threatening to resign—over minor editing changes. Then, at their fall 1963 meeting, the *National Review* editors proposed that Kendall, since he had not written for the magazine in two years, be changed from a senior to a contributing editor, as John Chamberlain had been earlier. When Buckley wrote him suggesting the change, Kendall replied, "Dear Sir, I hereby tender my resignation," adding that it would be "too great an honor" to be listed as a contributor.[25]

Kendall fulminated against Buckley and *National Review* in letters to Henry Regnery and Brent Bozell. He wrote Bozell, "The Buckleys consume people as a furnace consumes coal."[26] When Rusher would not accept a free ad from the University of Dallas, Kendall wrote that he felt "about *National Review* much as I would about an ex-wife of mine who'd become a call-girl."[27]

Kendall's letter provoked Buckley, who had stayed judiciously out of the quarrel, to write what would be his last letter to Kendall.

I never had the power to prevent you from being the fool. Our current mendacity [that prevents us from offering free advertisements] . . . is certainly in some measure the result of emoluments paid out over the years to non-performing editors, and as to the reference you make to wives and call-girls, I can only welcome the news that you have finally learned to distinguish between the two.*

Buckley tried to make up for the departure of the old editors by hiring new ones. In 1961, Buckley had hired a new senior editor, William Rickenbacker, the son of Captain Eddie Rickenbacker. Rickenbacker, an investment counselor, was the kind of eccentric Buckley liked to hire. He was fluent in seven languages and could discourse learnedly on a wide range of sujects from Bach to the Common Market. Like Rusher, he had been a Republican rather than a leftist before he became a conservative, and therefore shared little of Burnham's ambivalence toward the conservative Right.

Burnham was consistently skeptical about Rusher, Rickenbacker, and Meyer's pet ventures, such as the New York Conservative Party, which he termed a "good outlet for the frustrations of conservatives." To the consternation of the three editors, Burnham repeatedly urged that *National Review* adopt a more favorable view of Nelson Rockefeller.[28]

The quarrels over politics were supplemented by quarrels over the kind of magazine *National Review* should be. Rusher, Meyer, and Rickenbacker wanted a journal that spoke to, helped organize, and championed the most militant segments of the right wing. Burnham described the different approaches in a letter to Buckley.

Priscilla and I take a more professional point of view toward *National Review*. We want simply to have the best magazine in the world, assuming a general (not too sharply defined) conservative and anti-Communist point of view. Frank, Bill Rickenbacker and Bill Rusher also want a good magazine, of course, but they first of all want a crusade, a political party and a kind of ersatz church, and they want *National Review* itself to be all these things or at least organically and intimately a part of all three, rather than a magazine

---

* Buckley heard from Kendall only once again after this exchange. In 1964, Buckley, who had sponsored Kendall when he joined the Catholic Church, got a telegram from Kendall, addressed "Godson to Godfather," asking him to pray for his godson on the day when the Church had annulled his two marriages. (William F. Buckley, Jr., "Willmoore Kendall," *National Review*, December 31, 1980.) In 1967, Kendall died, the victim of alcoholism and a deteriorating heart condition. In his obituary, Buckley gave Kendall his due as a theorist, but did not recall their friendship: "He was indisputably among the two or three most brilliant political scientists in the United States, recognized as such by his friends (there were few) and foes (they were as numerous as the stars above)." (*National Review*, July 25, 1967.)

—and a magazine which would have a certain aloofness from cru-
sades even if it altogether agreed with them.[29]

Burnham himself sensed the growing strains in the magazine and
blamed them partly on Buckley's absence. In a letter, written in
March 1963 while Buckley was still in Switzerland, Burnham complained that "*National Review* has not really had an editor the last
couple of years." He thought that the conflicts were aggravated because in Buckley's absence there was no "unequivocal deputizing of
administrative authority."[30] Buckley briefly considered making Burnham the executive editor, but Rusher convinced him that such a
move, while resolving the formal basis of the conflict between Burnham and Rickenbacker, would exacerbate the conflict between Meyer
and Burnham.

Buckley did nothing—neither formally elevating Burnham nor re-
suming full-time participation himself. As a result, the conflicts between Burnham and the other editors continued to rage over the next
decade.

VI

Buckley's book on conservatism was originally due April of 1963,
but as of that spring, distracted by his column and speaking schedule,
he had not written a word of it. It was only that fall that he developed
a thesis for the book. In *Up from Liberalism* he had attacked what he
called the "Liberals' fetishistic commitment to democracy," evidenced in their support for black voting rights and for decolonization
in the Third World.[31] In Buckley's new book, which he tentatively
titled *The Revolt Against the Masses,* he proposed to take the argument to a higher plane.

The basic argument of the book, as well as its title, was to be
borrowed from Spanish philosopher José Ortega y Gasset's 1930
work, *The Revolt of the Masses,* which had been reissued in the
United States to great acclaim in 1957.* The principal target of *The
Revolt of the Masses* was the commercialization of culture and the
onset of mass-supported statism, best evidenced in Italian Fascism
and Soviet Communism. Ortega, who was a classical liberal and a
defender of the Spanish Republic, defined the masses not as the work-

---

* Buckley had first read Ortega y Gasset in Willmoore Kendall's political science seminar.
He may have heard of Ortega earlier from his father or from the writings of Albert Jay
Nock, who drew his own concept of the "mass-man" from Ortega.

ing class or the poor but simply as those who conceive of themselves as "average" and "demand nothing special of themselves." According to Ortega, even democracies had been ruled by "specially qualified" minorities on behalf of the great majority, but what distinguished the twentieth century was "the accession of the masses to complete social power." This treatened the viability of Western society. "As the masses by definition neither should nor can direct their own personal existence, and still less rule society in general, this fact means that actually Europe is suffering from the greatest crisis that can afflict peoples, nations, and civilization." [32]

Ortega's theme struck a responsive chord among both the liberal and conservative intellectuals of the fifties, who were rebelling against what they saw as the debasement of American culture—achieved by means of television and advertising—and who saw Eisenhower—a man who apparently preferred golf to serious literature—as the embodiment of mass mediocrity. While Buckley and Russell Kirk, on one side, and Dwight Macdonald and David Riesman, on the other, differed politically on almost every important question of the fifties, they shared a view that American culture and intellectual life were in precipitous decline. [33]

Buckley planned, however, to make a somewhat different use of Ortega's insights than the left-wing critics had. While Macdonald's or Riesman's critique of mass society was primarily cultural, Buckley's would be primarily political. And while Macdonald and the other liberal critics of mass culture could see no alternative to the ascendancy of the mass-man's art, Buckley planned to show that a revolt *against* the masses was brewing.

In November 1963, he outlined the plan of the book in a rambling memorandum to Burnham and to his friend and literary scholar Hugh Kenner. He would show, he wrote, that a "mysterious harmony" existed between the "intellectual revolt against the masses"—evidenced in such phenomena as the "rising relative prestige of the more dogmatic religions" and "the dissipation of the philosophical force of Marxism"—and the "political revolt against the masses." The latter was evidenced in the attack against liberalism. [34]

Buckley again set aside his winter vacation in Switzerland for working on the book. He talked Hugh Kenner into accompanying him and Pat to Saanen, a town that like Saanenmöser was in the vicinity of Gstaad. Anxious to avoid solitary reflection, Buckley hoped that he would be inspired to write the book by daily discussions with Kenner. "The idea was that we would talk it out," Kenner said.

Buckley had first met Kenner, a Canadian-born English professor, at a party in 1959 given by McDowell, Obolensky, publishers of *Up from Liberalism*. They found they shared a common interest in sailing and quickly became close friends. In 1961, Kenner began editing a poetry section for *National Review,* a project he gladly abandoned after several years of hostility from the magazine's readers.* Concerned that Buckley was squandering his own intellectual gifts, Kenner had urged him to take a leave from both *National Review* and his column for a year. "I was sensing that something was happening, that he was simply moving too fast to think, by which I mean that thought had become reflex," Kenner recalled.

Kenner had gone out of his way to encourage Buckley to write *The Revolt Against the Masses.* "This is really your chance to write a book which does NOT play existing controversies by ear," Kenner had written him. "It should be a small classic; at least it should be composed with such an intention." [35]

In Switzerland, Buckley began writing *The Revolt Against the Masses* in a spirit of solemnity and high seriousness. "This very probably will be the last book I will ever write," he wrote Robert Bauman. [36] But again he found it hard to concentrate.

Buckley always followed a schedule of working in the morning on *National Review* and his column, skiing in the midafternoon and then either socializing in the evening or returning to work. That winter, he and Kenner were to meet daily in midmorning to discuss *Revolt Against the Masses.* But when they met, Buckley often changed the subject away from the book. "I brought some stuff over, and we started talking about it," Kenner said, "but it was increasingly hard to hold Bill's attention. It was clear that it wasn't a high priority."

Other times, Buckley suggested that they leave for skiing. That winter there was far less snow than usual, and instead of being able to walk to the ski slopes from the chalet, Buckley and Kenner, whom he was teaching how to ski, had to drive twenty miles or farther over Alpine roads. To get to the slopes by afternoon, they had to leave in the morning.

Buckley spent most of his evenings at dinner parties. According to Kenner, the most memorable was an evening that he and the Buckleys spent with Charlie and Oona Chaplin, who lived in Montreux. The

---

* Kenner said later of his time as poetry editor, "The magazine's readers were not hospitable. *National Review* has some of the dumbest readers in the world." In 1961 Kenner scored an immense coup by getting the eminent poet William Carlos Williams to contribute a poem to the magazine, but for his efforts he got complaints for publishing a poet who had, according to the magazine's readers, once belonged to a Communist front organization.

dinner party at a restaurant in Vevey had been arranged by Buckley's friend James Mason, who was also there. Chaplin was preoccupied with the assassination of President Kennedy, which had occurred three months earlier, and he suggested to his guests that it had been a plot by the CIA or Texas John Birchers.

"I don't trust the FBI. Do you, Mr. Buckley?" Chaplin asked.

"No," Buckley replied. "After all, they let you get out of the country without paying your income tax." [37]

Pat kept kicking Bill under the table, but Chaplin himself was amused by Buckley. "Bill was being masterfully skeptical," Kenner recalled. "He was dissenting quite principally from the things that Chaplin was saying without offending him in any way." Later, Oona Chaplin told Pat, "Mrs. Buckley, you mustn't mind. Don't kick your husband. I've been kicking mine for thirty years, and it simply doesn't work." [38]

In all, Buckley wrote only about ten thousand words of *Revolt Against the Masses* during the two months he and Kenner were in Switzerland—a paltry output for someone who four years earlier had written an entire book while on vacation. When Buckley returned from Switzerland that year, he gave chapters he had done to his secretary to retype, but he never returned to working on them, even though he told *Time* magazine in 1967 that he was still working on the project.

Buckley later faulted the political climate of the mid-sixties for his failure to finish *The Revolt Against the Masses*. The book was based on his belief, Buckley explained,

> that America had reached just the point where it was going to realize that it has to go back to serious thought, and away from these distracting frivolities with which we had been preoccupied. Exactly the opposite happened. Instead of going against the masses, we went right into a situation where the masses tyrannized—the Berkeley campus blowup. So that sort of shook my confidence in the thesis. And instead of finishing the book in 1965, as had been my intention, I just sort of let it sit.

But there were other factors. When Buckley began writing *Revolt Against the Masses,* he encountered philosophical contradictions in his own thinking that he could not resolve. In his first chapter—the only polished part of the draft—Buckley identified the rule of the masses with universal suffrage, or one man, one vote. He contended that by including voters incapable of self-rule in the governing process, the United States "does violence to the principle of enlightened self-government" and encourages "demagogy . . . in places high and low." To achieve enlightened self-government, Buckley proposed eliminating from the voting rolls those Americans who don't know of the United Nations—28 percent by one 1963 poll.

At the same time, Buckley, following Nock and Ortega, insisted that the "mass-men" are not "people who are simply poor, or who do menial work, or who are poorly educated." President Kennedy, as Buckley explained in his memorandum, had been the "complete mass man." [39] In his first chapter, Buckley quoted with approval his own statement, made in a 1956 essay, that he would "sooner be governed by the first two thousand people in the Boston telephone directory, than by the two thousand members of the faculty of Harvard University" as evidence that he would not prefer rule by "the intellectual elite." [40] Both Kennedy and the Harvard faculty knew what the U.N. was. But then what does distinguish the "mass-man" of Ortega and Nock from the worthy elite? In Ortega, it comes down to a psychology of personal initiative and independence—what Riesman in *The Lonely Crowd* would later translate as the "inner-directed personality." But in that case the Harvard faculty might well qualify. Buckley seemed merely to be saying that those members of the elite who were liberals were mass-men by virtue of their beliefs, in which case the category had become meaningless.

The dilemma affected Buckley's discussion of the effects of "mass rule." Macdonald in "Masscult and Midcult" and Herbert Marcuse in *One Dimensional Man* had both tried to show that culture had been debased. But Buckley, unsure whether "mass rule" meant government by sharecropper or government by the Harvard faculty, failed to make a clear case that universal suffrage had been harmful. In *Up from Liberalism,* he had made a racist but arguable case that universal suffrage would threaten southern culture and property, but in *The Revolt Against the Masses,* a chastened Buckley fell back on his favorite whipping boy—the effect of democratic ideology on the United Nations and developing nations. The fact is that what Buckley really objected to was not rule by sharecroppers but rule by the Kennedys and Johnsons—and he failed to make any case that universal suffrage was the cause of their ascendancy.

The Berkeley revolt of fall 1964 posed a related problem for Buckley's thesis. It did not reveal how feeble the revolt against the masses was—after all, the rise of the Left and the Right were correlative— but it did reveal how incoherent the basic categories of *The Revolt*

Against the Masses were. The Berkeley students were not the "masses," either by Buckley's educational criterion or by Ortega's and Nock's psychological one. To Buckley, the problem was their politics, not their qualifications; they not only knew what the United Nations was, they were likely to support it, Lumumba, and Martin Luther King. If Buckley wanted to make his case, he had to argue directly with them.

Buckley might have resolved these contradictions if he had taken the time to reflect upon them. But by that winter, Buckley had created a situation where he had too many other things to do to write a book that required prolonged reflection and rewriting. By 1964, Kenner believed that Buckley "was already moving too fast to do anything but the topical." As Paul Weiss, his philosophy professor at Yale had sensed, Buckley may also have lacked the intellectual capacity for philosophical reflection.

Buckley's abandonment of *The Revolt Against the Masses* represented the abandonment of a deeper rationale for his own politics. And in so far as he left contradictions within his own views unresolved and unexamined, it meant the end of his development as a political thinker.

Buckley himself decided that he did not have a philosophical mind. "He knows he's quick, but doubts he's deep," William Rickenbacker said. He accepted that his intellectual role would be that of a popularizer and controversialist. Kenner said of the decision to lay aside *Revolt Against the Masses:*

> It marked a changeover between the time Bill thought of himself as a sort of political theorist and the later phase in which he became a political commentator. I suspect that [in trying to write *Revolt Against the Masses*] he discovered that he hadn't much more of a genuine nature to say and that he was increasingly simply observing current developments and offering a perspective on them.

In abandoning *Revolt Against the Masses,* Buckley did not abandon the attitude to politics that he had derived from Nock and his father. He still imagined himself a member of Nock's Remnant, he still viewed the greater public with a certain disdain, and he still believed that politics was "something remote, disreputable, and infamous, like slave trading or brothel-keeping," but these views coexisted with a much more positive and optimistic view of himself, the public, and politics, one derived from and reinforced by the wide readership that his column achieved, his numerous speaking engagements, and his appearances on radio and television.

In abandoning theoretical work, Buckley also retained many of the deeper convictions of his youth regarding communism, the welfare state, and popular democracy, but he became willing to take positions on specific issues that appeared to contradict these stands. This would become apparent in his reaction to Barry Goldwater's presidential campaign.

CHAPTER 13

The Boarding Party

At the beginning of November 1963, Barry Goldwater was given an outside chance of winning the Republican nomination and giving Kennedy a close race in the general election. But Kennedy's assassination—by providing an enormous ground swell of sympathy for Lyndon Johnson, Kennedy's successor, and discouraging moderate Rebublicans from making the race—had the ironic effect of making a Republican victory in 1964 far less likely, but Goldwater's nomination far more likely.

Buckley had left for Switzerland just after a reluctant Goldwater announced his candidacy, and he remained there during the first climactic primaries. He was not upset at being an ocean away from the campaign. Unlike other conservatives, Buckley had mixed feelings about Goldwater's running for President. And what efforts he and other *National Review* editors had made to aid the campaign had been rudely rebuffed.

I

Goldwater, Buckley, and *National Review* had grown up together politically, the one adding to the prominence of the other. Goldwater's popularity had clearly benefited *National Review*. In 1961, a letter signed by Goldwater soliciting subscriptions had netted seven thousand new subscribers, an enormous haul for a small political publication. *National Review*'s sharp rise in circulation in the early sixties—from 54,000 in 1961 to 90,000 in 1964—was largely owing to the visibility Goldwater gave to the conservative cause. And the success of Buckley's column—which was placed in more than two hundred papers by early 1964—was largely due to the interest in conservative politics generated by Goldwater.

But Goldwater had equally benefited from his relationship to *National Review* and its editors. Since the 1960 convention, where Goldwater was nominated for President by the South Carolina and Arizona delegations and where he led the opposition to Nixon's "Fifth Avenue Compact" with Rockefeller, *National Review* had treated him as the leader of the conservative movement. They had encouraged his presidential ambitions—and, through YAF, helped organize huge public rallies to dramatize his support.

Buckley had known Goldwater since the late fifties when they periodically shared a stage together. He had written several speeches and ghosted an article on China for Goldwater.[1] Beginning in 1963, Buckley had devoted, he wrote Rusher, "roughly 75 percent of my columns to running interference for Barry Goldwater and cleaning up after him."[2]

Brent Bozell had served as a speech writer for Goldwater in the late fifties and had ghosted the best-selling *The Conscience of a Conservative*. According to one report, Goldwater had so much confidence in Bozell that he never even read the manuscript before sending it to Clarence Manion's small publishing house in Kentucky.[3]

Rusher had known Goldwater since 1955, when Rusher had invited him to address the New York Young Republican Convention, and later, through his ties in the Young Republicans, Rusher had provided an important link between Goldwater and party activists. Rusher and Representative John Ashbrook, a former YR chairman, had thought up the Draft Goldwater Committee while lunching in the House dining room in July 1961. Rusher then convinced Clifton White, a political scientist who became one of the nation's first full-time political consultants, to direct the draft, and himself had become active in the Draft Committee. By the time Goldwater announced his candidacy in

January 1964, the Draft Committee had virtually sealed up the nomination for him.

There had been early signs of strain in the relationship between Goldwater and *National Review*. In 1961 at a *Human Events* banquet, Goldwater failed to list *National Review* among the four newspapers and magazines he thought were most useful to the conservative cause. Goldwater also objected that year to the mailing for the magazine sent out with his endorsement, even though Rusher had cleared the endorsement through Goldwater's office. But nothing prepared Buckley or the editors for what would occur during the presidential campaign.

The first warning sign occurred in spring 1963, when Brent Bozell and his family returned from a year in Spain. Bozell wanted to go back to working for Goldwater, but Goldwater, in Patricia Bozell's words, was "rather cool" to him.[4] In September, Buckley and Bozell set up a meeting with Dr. Charles Kelley, a longtime Goldwater adviser, to see how they could participate in the campaign. When they arrived on the evening of September 15 at Kelley's suite in the Hay-Adams Hotel in Washington, they found two other men already there: Denison Kitchel, a Phoenix lawyer who had moved to Washington the month before to take over Goldwater's campaign, and Bill Baroody, the head of the American Enterprise Institute and a close adviser to Goldwater. Buckley and Bozell both knew Baroody, but they were surprised to find him in Kelley's suite.

At the meeting, Buckley and Bozell volunteered to set up an organization of professors for Goldwater, but Baroody, apparently acting for Kitchel, turned aside each of their suggestions. The meeting broke up without any commitment having been made, and with both Buckley and Bozell angry at Baroody. Then, the next morning, *The New York Times* reported that "the Goldwater-for-President ship has just repelled a boarding party from the forces who occupy the supposedly narrow territory to the right of the Arizona Senator." The story, citing an unnamed source, said that Buckley and Bozell had "cornered some Goldwater aides" in order "to join the campaign organization on a policy planning level," but their offer was cleverly rebuffed.

Feeling that what their candidate needs least is more support from the far right, Goldwater advisers used an old political dodge. They played dumb. They just could not seem to understand what the *National Review* men were getting at. Mr. Buckley and Mr. Bozell reportedly emerged from the conference with no share of the Goldwater command and wondering if they wanted any.[5]

Both Buckley and Bozell were furious—all the more so since they had requested an extremely modest role in the campaign. Buckley telephoned Kitchel and Bozell phoned Goldwater, but both men denied any knowledge of the leak.

No one ever admitted leaking the "boarding party" story to *The New York Times*, but Goldwater campaign aides Dean Burch, Charles Lichenstein, and Ralph de Toledano, as well as Kitchel, believed that Baroody was the most likely person to have done so. Kitchel, who firmly denied talking to the *Times*, acknowledged that prior to the meeting Baroody had described Buckley and Bozell as a "boarding party." "I assume because of his remark to me before the meeting about a boarding party that Baroody was the 'leak,' " Kitchel said.

Baroody, a short, sinewy Lebanese-American, who had been an officer at the Chamber of Commerce, had joined the AEI with the idea that he would turn it into the kind of advisory body for conservative Republicans that Brookings had been for liberal Democrats. Charles Lichenstein, whom Baroody made Goldwater's research director, described him as an "intellectual entrepreneur." Turning Goldwater into a presidential candidate became his pet project, and he didn't want anyone—particularly someone versed in the world of ideas—to displace him. Dean Burch, an Arizonan who became the deputy campaign chairman and later the chairman of the Republican National Committee, described Baroody's perception of Goldwater and of his own role in the campaign.

> Baroody sort of looked on Goldwater as his creation. He'd created this dynamic conservative from Arizona, which was far from true, but he was instrumental, and he was responsible for putting Goldwater in touch with a lot of intellectual conservatives. . . . He was very concerned about who was going to be close to Goldwater. And he was very much opposed to having Buckley close to Goldwater. I think it was probably more professional [competition].

According to journalist Ralph de Toledano, who ran a secret research operation for Baroody during the campaign, Baroody "didn't think too highly" of Buckley. "He thought Bill was sort of a political playboy, not serious."

Baroody was able to win Kitchel's agreement to exclude Buckley. Kitchel was not concerned about professional rivalries, but he was worried that the campaign was positioned publicly too far to the Right, and he preferred that it not be associated with Buckley and *National Review,* which in those days were perceived on the far-Right fringe of politics. Kitchel told journalist Ed McDowell later, "We figured that *National Review* readers would all be with us anyway. And by keeping away from Buckley and Bozell and that crowd, we thought we could appeal to a lot of people who don't like *National Review*— either because they don't understand it or for any number of reasons."[6]

According to Burch, Goldwater himself "felt more kindly toward Buckley than Baroody did." And more often than not Goldwater was forced to apologize to Buckley for what Baroody had done. After the leak in *The New York Times,* Goldwater wrote Buckley a note soliciting his opinions and paid a brief symbolic visit to *National Review*'s offices. In May, after Baroody got Buckley removed from the speakers' platform at a May 12 Madison Square Garden rally for Goldwater that *National Review* had helped to publicize, Goldwater wrote Buckley that "at the last moment, it was decided to limit the individuals on the platform to active Republican political figures."[7] (Goldwater's explanation was particularly lame because of the presence of Chiang Kai-shek supporter Mme. Chennault on the platform.) But while Goldwater tried to assuage Buckley's feelings, he made no effort to countermand Baroody. And, according to former Goldwater aide Stephen Shadegg, "After September, Buckley and Bozell had very little contact with the Senator or with his campaign manager."[8]

Buckley was angered by the "boarding party" story, but he accepted Goldwater's expression of interest at face value. In fact, throughout the next year, Buckley put the best interpretation on the campaign's treatment of him—never suspecting that he was being skewered because of base professional jealousies. In November 1963, he sent a memorandum to Goldwater suggesting that the senator take a European trip with Burnham and novelist John Dos Passos in tow in order to strengthen his credentials as a statesman. Neither Goldwater nor his staff ever responded to Buckley's memo. Then he devised a new scheme for aiding Goldwater.

In January 1964, shortly before he, Pat, and Hugh Kenner left for Switzerland, Buckley had been introduced to Neal Freeman, a handsome young Yale graduate working for Doubleday & Company. He liked Freeman and at the end of an evening's conversation offered him a job as his personal assistant. Freeman, against the advice of his friends, accepted, but when a week later he arrived at *National Review* for work, he still had no idea what he would be doing. His uncertainty grew when he learned that Buckley would be leaving for Switzerland that day. When Buckley came in, he assured Freeman that he had something that would keep him occupied for two months. He wanted him to help make Barry Goldwater's candidacy acceptable to the American people by lining up congressmen and journalists behind the idea of having seventy-three-year-old former President Eisenhower as Goldwater's vice-presidential running mate. On the way to the airport, Freeman inadvertently revealed his skepticism about the plan, but Buckley, intoxicated with his own scheme, thought Freeman was merely questioning the plan's legality. "Don't worry," he told Freeman. "I've checked. It's constitutional. You can run for Vice-President even though you've been elected President twice."

Over the next two months, Freeman recruited several congressmen to endorse the plan. When he gained the support of South Dakota Representative E. Y. Berry, the only American Indian in Congress, he received an ecstatic congratulatory telegram from Switzerland. Later, Buckley got conservative journalist James J. Kilpatrick, a man otherwise known for his dour sobriety, to write an article in *National Review* endorsing the scheme.

Buckley's scheme betrayed his own political naïveté. But it also revealed the extent to which he did not share other conservatives' euphoria with the Goldwater campaign. Without a *deus ex machina* like Eisenhower, Buckley believed, Goldwater would go down to certain defeat and might pull the conservative movement down with him.

II

Buckley's view of Goldwater's chances reflected in part his own pessimism. But it also reflected his growing maturity about conservative politics. In a long piece for *Esquire* after Chambers's death in July 1961, Buckley had gone over their correspondence, and Chambers's insistence on a politics that maneuvered between what was possible and what was merely ideal had had an impact that the experience of the Goldwater campaign would strengthen. Buckley was also forced to test his convictions not simply against those of the other editors, but against a wider public that simply gave Goldwater and his politics no chance at all.

On *National Review,* Buckley and Burnham had been expressing skepticism about Goldwater's campaign for more than a year. They had a low opinion of Goldwater's intelligence and his ability as a presidential candidate. Neither believed until the very end that he would even get the Republican nomination. According to Neal Freeman, Burnham "had been subtly but persistently reminding the editorial board of the hidden virtues of Nelson Rockefeller, and of course, every time he did, Rickenbacker and Rusher would clutch their chests.''

The other editors brooked no criticisms of Goldwater nor doubts about his campaign. ''The rest of us were cheerleaders, led by Bill Rusher,'' Freeman recalled. Rusher was certain that Goldwater would get the nomination, and Frank Meyer was convinced, as late as July 1964, that he would defeat Johnson in November. At the magazine's January retreat, Meyer had wagered $33 that Goldwater would be the next President, while Burnham had bet $120 on Johnson.

The first debate over coverage of Goldwater's campaign occurred after Goldwater announced his candidacy in January 1964. In an editorial, Buckley announced that *National Review* would cover the campaign ''as enthusiastic endorsers of Mr. Goldwater's candidacy; as independent evaluators of his statements and his campaign; and as objective analysts of his chances.''[9]

Rusher recognized that by describing the editors as ''independent evaluators'' and ''objective analysts,'' Buckley was subtly trying to create distance between the magazine and Goldwater's candidacy. In a critical memorandum to the editors, Rusher suggested that they pledge themselves to ''report facts good or bad,'' while offering, if necessary, ''countervailing considerations.''[10] Meyer urged that ''objectivity as a characterization of our view of ourselves always be combined with a phrase signifying our commitment, e.g. objective— but committed to the conservative cause, not neutralist.''[11]

In February 1964, while Buckley was in Switzerland, Burnham wrote him complaining that ''the handling of the campaign continues to trouble me.'' Rickenbacker's copy, he wrote, read ''like a public relations handout.'' Burnham reiterated his position that during the campaign *National Review* must appear and be ''an independent entity in our own essence, speaking with our own voice and authority.'' Goldwater, he wrote, is a ''second-rate'' candidate

> and he seems to be surrounded by third- or fourth-rate persons . . . . Goldwater's own stature doesn't have to be insisted on explicitly; because, however unlofty, he is the best of the available bunch. But I can't see why we shouldn't be sharper and more critical of his organization and the conduct of the campaign from both a policy and a technical point of view.[12]

Buckley agreed with Burnham. In early March, after Goldwater had lost the New Hampshire primary to Henry Cabot Lodge and netted only 23 percent of the vote, Buckley sent the editors in New York a memorandum about the campaign.

The apparent poor showing thus far is about one half a pretty erratic performance by Our Hero. There was no liberal journalist between me and the television screen when Barry Goldwater was on "Meet the Press" last January, and the sinking feeling I then had, I still have. It is a grave wrong, moral and strategic, to let Goldwater down in any way, now that we have him running for President. It is a grave, perhaps graver wrong, strategically and morally, not to leave ourselves the room to say, in private counsels perhaps, subsequently in more public counsels, that the community must not despair of the possibility of nominating and electing a conservative in the years to come merely by the experience of Barry Goldwater back in 1964—*who, after all, did not really have his heart in the campaign, and was not as well qualified to run, or serve, as* (fill in the new hero.) [13]

Rusher feared that Buckley's attitude toward the campaign was being colored by the campaign's treatment of him. Rusher wrote Buckley in Switzerland, warning him not to take the secondhand accounts of Goldwater's negative attitude toward him seriously. "Goldwater's basic attitude toward you borders on the worshipful," Rusher wrote, also expressing a fear that Buckley shared Burnham's "illusions about Rockefeller."

Fortunately the Rockefeller campaign fell on its face—but suppose it hadn't. What did you visualize as the outcome as far as *National Review* was concerned. It is only by accident, as it were, that these questions are moot. I would like, if possible, to avoid facing them unarmed in some future year when Jim Burnham goes whoring after some new false God—possibly Senator Percy of Illinois. [14]

In his reply, Buckley denied that he was even concerned about Goldwater's attitude toward him.

It did not occur to me—truly—that Barry Goldwater was being unfriendly to me. The point is he doesn't want me around, and I say this with all sincerity, *shouldn't* have me around, since my style and personality are different from his. I have always gotten along very well with politicians I seek to help, but I have never tried to become chummy with them, because I don't do this kind of thing well with people I can't talk to in my own language. [15]

Buckley rebuked Rusher for his comments about Burnham and defended his own position on Rockefeller. "My position very simply was that I would not commit myself in 1962 to voting against him in

1964 if he ran against JFK; *tout court*. . . . Rockefeller was opportunistic, and . . . that opportunism . . . would very likely land him right rather than left." [16]

Rusher's concern about Rockefeller turned out, however, to have been entirely warranted. In May, Rockefeller, having been given up for dead, slaughtered Goldwater in Oregon and enjoyed a wide lead in California opinion polls in the weeks before the crucial primary there. At an editorial meeting in late May, Buckley dropped a bombshell. He announced that if Goldwater lost the primary in California, *National Review* ought to call upon him to withdraw from the race in order to avoid a humiliating defeat at the convention. Rusher immediately prepared his letter of resignation in case Goldwater lost the primary.

Fortunately for Rusher and Buckley, Goldwater narrowly won California—on the eve of the election, Rockefeller's second wife had given birth, reminding voters there of his nasty divorce and remarriage. When Buckley found out that Rusher had planned to resign if Goldwater had lost and the editorial had run, he told Rusher to warn him in advance next time. "I am medium-good at finding compromises on these things," he said. [17]

In the wake of Goldwater's victory in California, Buckley defended Goldwater's right to the Republican nomination but, to the consternation of both Meyer and Rusher, insisted that Goldwater did not have a chance in November. In a June 16 column, Buckley wrote, "This is probably Lyndon Johnson's year, and the Archangel Gabriel running on the Republican ticket probably couldn't win." Rusher responded in a private memo, "You are displaying a compulsion to proclaim, on every possible occasion, that Goldwater will be resoundingly defeated in November. . . . What you say about Goldwater's chances in November can have a measurable effect on those chances." [18]

As if to answer Rusher and Meyer, Buckley wrote in his July 2 column, two weeks before the Republican Convention:

> Of course Goldwater could win. But the odds are as the odds are, and there can be no doubt that Mr. Goldwater knows what those odds are. It is not helpful to Goldwater or to the conservative cause to assert apodictically, and pridefully, that he *will* win. Goldwater's supporters should have a less theatrical, but ultimately more alluring standard; that he *should* win. . . . But to suggest that, *ceteris paribus,* he *will* win, is to show a scant regard for political realities.

The convention, which opened in San Francisco on July 13 at the huge Cow Palace proved to be a trying experience for Buckley. On the second night, he was supposed to be the last and featured speaker at a Goldwater rally staged by YAF. Ronald Reagan, with whom Buckley had become friendly four years earlier, was the master of ceremonies. Buckley was waiting offstage—his foot in a cast from a freak accident in his motel room—to be introduced to the packed throng. Reagan introduced Goldwater's sons and then said, "Now I have a big treat for you." At that moment, California Republican Senate candidate George Murphy, who was seated on the stage by Reagan, leaned over and whispered to Reagan that the Goldwater staff wanted the rally wrapped up before Buckley spoke. Reagan, expressing some surprise, told the audience that the rally was running out of time and that it would not be possible to hear from the last speaker, Bill Buckley, who was hobbled by a bad foot.

The incident embarrassed Buckley. He described it later as the most "strident" example of the Goldwater campaign's behavior toward him. But as he had done before, he ascribed serious political motives to the Goldwater camp. In a letter to Reagan after the convention, he said his appearance "was vetoed by Dean Burch. . . . Clearly he didn't want me around during the period when the Goldwater camp was trying hard to keep Eisenhower in tow, since it is apparently the case that Eisenhower goes nuts at the mention of my name."[19] Burch, however, denied any knowledge of the incident.

On July 15, the evening Goldwater was to be nominated, Buckley was chatting with a reporter in the convention press gallery when Rusher called him over from across the barrier separating journalists with passes from those without them. Rusher had just gotten a call from Bill Rickenbacker in New York relaying to Buckley the news his sister Maureen, only thirty-one, had been stricken by a cerebral hemorrhage and was not expected to survive the night. "When he heard my news," Rusher later recalled, "his face seemed to freeze into an expressionless mask. 'Get me to a telephone,' he said quietly."[20] Neal Freeman came into Buckley's suite several hours later and found him "sitting in his underwear looking distraught." At ten that night he took the "red-eye" back to New York. Maureen died two days later.

Maureen had left *National Review* in 1959 when she had her first child, but she had continued to write occasionally and she had edited two anthologies, *An Evening with National Review* and *Relaxing with National Review*. She had also remained close to Bill. "Her death was shattering to him," Patricia Bozell recalled. At a dinner the next week that Pat held for the family, Patricia remembered hearing an anguished cry from Bill as he read a note of condolence from Jim Burnham about Maureen.

Maureen's death cast a pall over Buckley and his brothers and sisters. Prior to it, they had believed that they led charmed lives and that both happiness and success in life would be theirs. "It didn't occur to me before that someone thirty-one years old could die," Buckley said. "Maureen's death made us feel mortal," Patricia Bozell said.

III

Buckley's principal concern in the last months of the campaign was not improving Goldwater's chances—which he deemed completely hopeless—but trying to prevent the demoralization of the conservative movement after November 3. Buckley gave two memorable speeches that fall—one at the Young Americans for Freedom's annual convention and the other at the New York Conservative Party's second anniversary dinner.

Buckley spoke each year at YAF's convention to affirm his link to the organization that he had helped create. Held in September 1964 at the Commodore Hotel in New York City, the convention, as YAF's chairman Robert Bauman saw it, was meant to charge up the delegates for the fall campaign. But Buckley had other things in mind.

Standing at a podium draped with a huge American flag, Buckley declared that "we do not believe in the Platonic affirmations of our own little purities. Our intention is to take the clay God gave us, and mold it into a better world." He then turned to

the role of the conservative movement . . . when to no one's surprise more than our own, we labor under the visitation of a freedom-minded candidate for the Presidency of the United States. I say labor, because the nomination of Barry Goldwater, when we permit ourselves to peek up over the euphoria, reminds us chillingly of the great work that has remained undone; a great rainfall has deluged a thirsty earth, but before we had time properly to prepare it. *I speak of course about the impending defeat of Barry Goldwater.*

As a sepulchral hush fell over the audience, Buckley drove his point home:

Our morale is high, and we are marching. But the morale of an army on the march is that of an army that has been promised victory. But it is wrong to assume that we shall overcome; and therefore it is right to reason to the necessity of guarding against the utter disarray that sometimes follows a stunning defeat: it is right to take thought, even on the eve of the engagement, about the potential need for regrouping, for gathering together our scattered forces.

Buckley explained his own reasons for assuming Goldwater's defeat:

> . . . any election of Barry Goldwater would presuppose a sea change in American public opinion; presuppose that the fiery little body of dissenters, of which you are a shining meteor, suddenly spun off nothing less than a majority of all the American people, who suddenly overcome a generation's entrenched lassitude, suddenly penetrated to the true meaning of freedom in society where the truth is occluded by the verbose mystifications of thousands of scholars, tens of thousands of books, a million miles of newsprint; who suddenly, prisoners all those years, succeeded in passing blithely through the walls of Alcatraz and tripping lightly over the shark-infested waters and treacherous currents, to safety on the shore.

The students listened, disbelieving, and some of them began to weep. "These were kids who came and expected to be told, 'You are going to win, here we are going to win the battle for the Lord,' " Bauman said, "and here they were told that that wasn't the case, and that we weren't going to win the battle for the Lord."

But Buckley, aware of the impression that his words were making, continued to drive home his point:

> The point of the present occasion is to win recruits whose attention we might never have attracted but for Barry Goldwater; to win them not only for November the third, but for future Novembers; to infuse the conservative spirit in enough people to entitle us to look about us, on November fourth, not at the ashes of defeat, but at the well-planted seeds of hope, which will flower on a great November day in the future, if there is a future.

Afterwards, many in the audience were so stunned that they didn't clap. YAF's leaders decided not to publish the speech in their magazine until after the election itself. But Buckley's speech had exactly its desired effect on Bauman and other top YAF leaders. They began thinking about November fourth.

Buckley's speech at the Conservative Party's anniversary dinner, held in the Grand Ballroom of the New York Hilton October 21, was of a completely different character. Speaking to an audience of hardened politicians, who didn't need to be reminded that Goldwater was going to get trounced in two weeks, Buckley mentioned Goldwater's name only once, and then not in the context of the election. Instead, he dwelt on what would be possible for conservatives in the coming decades.

Drawing from the theme of the unfinished *Revolt Against the Masses*, he declared that "there is growing in America a spirit of resistance to the Twentieth Century. . . . In America we are *dragging our feet;* kicking, complaining; hugging on to our ancient moorings." But the revolt against the twentieth century was by no means complete, and if conservatives attempted to hurry it beyond its accepted pace, they might risk sidetracking it. Buckley put into his words what he had learned from Chambers and Burnham and what had been reinforced by the Goldwater experience.

> A conservative is concerned simultaneously with two things, the first being the shape of the visionary or paradigmatic society towards which we should labor; the second, the speed with which it is thinkable to advance towards that ideal society and the foreknowledge that any advance upon it is necessarily asymptotic; not, at least, until the successful completion of the Society for the Abolition of Original Sin. How this movement, considering the contrary tug of history, has got as far as it has got, is something that surpasses the understanding of natural pessimists like myself. Even so, I am guilty of yielding, from time to time, to the temptation to overstress the ideal, often at moments when the prudential should weigh most heavily. I urge you to join with me in trying to resist that temptation.[21]

These two insights—that conservatism, even on the eve of Goldwater's humiliation, was on the rise, but that conservative politics, to succeed, must mediate between the ideal and the prudential—would inform Buckley's politics over the next decades and, through his writings, would influence a great many conservative politicians. Buckley's speech to the New York Conservatives marked his final break with his own radical and pessimistic past.

Buckley's abandonment of radicalism was partly the result of bringing Chambers's—and Burnham's—ideas to bear on events. But it was also the result of his becoming a public figure for whom the conservative movement was merely one audience among several. Buckley could be realistic about conservative prospects in a way that a hardened ideologue like Frank Meyer could not be. But, of course, he could also lose his political mooring in a way that Meyer could not.

IV

On November third, the inevitable occurred. Lyndon Johnson swept the popular vote—61.1 to 38.5 percent—and the electoral college—486 to 52. If it had not been for the segregationist vote in the South, which Goldwater won by his opposition to the Johnson-Kennedy Civil Rights Act of 1964, he would have carried only Arizona.

But Buckley, as he had advised the delegates at the YAF convention, had already turned his attention elsewhere. Several weeks before the final vote, he had had breakfast with Bob Bauman and Marvin Liebman. Bauman, inspired by Buckley's speech, had called up Liebman with a plan for a "conservative umbrella group that could draw in the seniors." Liebman suggested that he see Buckley about the idea. Buckley was enthusiastic about the plan, and the Saturday after Goldwater's defeat, twenty conservatives met at the Buckley family office in Manhattan to plan the American Conservative Union.

Uncharacteristically, Buckley agreed to serve on the organization's board of directors. (Since *National Review* had begun, he had assiduously avoided any other political commitments.) He attended the first meeting of the ACU's board of directors at Washington's Statler Hilton on December 18 and 19, arguing strenuously that members of the John Birch Society should be excluded from the new organization. (The board finally agreed to a compromise proposed by Frank Meyer; Birch Society members were to be excluded from the ACU's board of directors and Advisory Assembly but not from its membership at large.) Only in March, after the organization had been safely launched, did Buckely apologetically withdraw from the board in order not to compromise his fund-raising commitments to *National Review*.

The Goldwater experience had not seriously demoralized him. Indeed, it increased measurably his involvement in electoral politics, the knowledge of which he had previously ceded to Rusher and Clifton White. Toward the end of the 1964 campaign, Buckley invited Clifton White to his apartment in Manhattan for dinner. What happened took White totally by surprise.

Bill wanted to be educated, and I've never seen Bill Buckley keep quiet so long in my life. That evening I talked 90 percent of the time.

He wanted to know exactly what I had done to get the Goldwater nomination, and how I had done it. He decided it must be something significant and worthwhile. He was astonishing.

Of course, White did not know then that within a year, Buckley would try to put some of what he had learned from White into practice in New York City.

CHAPTER 14

Demand a Recount

Buckley's decision to run for mayor of New York was precipitated by his speech at the annual Communion Breakfast of Catholic policemen, sponsored by the Holy Name Society. Held at the New York Hilton after a Mass at St. Patrick's Cathedral on Sunday, April 4, the event attracted more than five thousand New York policemen.

In the wake of angry charges of police brutality being levied by New York black leaders and of violent clashes between police and civil rights demonstrators in the South, Buckley's speech was devoted to defending the police—not by refuting the specific charges against them, but by insisting that the critics of the police, aided by the major newspapers and television networks, were elevating isolated instances into a pattern, while ignoring the everyday dangers the police encountered and the benefits they conferred upon law-abiding citizens. "Policemen, they say, should be human. But when they act human, it is deeply resented that they are not inhuman," he said.

As a case in point, Buckley took the events in Selma, Alabama, where the police had arrested civil rights marchers, led by Dr. Martin Luther King, for refusing to disperse. The police, he argued,

moved, excitedly, humanly, forward: *excessively* yes, and their excesses on that day have been rightly criticized, but were ever the
excesses criticized of those who provoked them beyond the endur-
ance that we tend to think of as human? The television viewer . . .
saw nothing of the policeman's restraint in the face of an order
defied.[1]

While Buckley condemned the killing of Viola Liuzzo, a white civil
rights activist from Detroit, he lamented that the press had covered it
extensively, largely ignoring the "unprovoked killing of a policeman
in Hattiesburg, Mississippi, by a twenty-year-old in his car." He suggested that Liuzzo's death was not surprising.

So the lady drove down a stretch of lonely road in the dead of night,
sharing the front seat with a young Negro identified with the protesting movement; and got killed. Why, one wonders, was this a
story that occupied the front pages from one end to another? . . .
Didn't the killing merely confirm precisely what everyone had been
saying about the South?[2]

The next day the *New York Herald Tribune* reported that to laughter and applause from the police, Buckley had praised the restraint of
the Selma police and had implied that Liuzzo was partly at fault for
her own murder. The reporter omitted Buckley's condemnation of
Liuzzo's murder and his statement that the police had acted "excessively." *The New York Times* story was headlined, "Buckley Praises
Police of Selma/Hailed by 5600 Police Here as He Cites 'Restraint.' "[3] For the next days, the New York papers were filled with
denunciations of Buckley.

Buckley was so outraged by the coverage that he filed a libel suit
against the *Herald Tribune.* A tape recording of the event showed that
the police had neither laughed nor cheered during his statements
about the Selma police and Liuzzo's murder, as the *Tribune* reporter
had claimed. While the *Herald Tribune* did not altogether distort the
thrust of Buckley's remarks, John Leo, listening to the tape for the
National Catholic Reporter, found that the *Tribune* reporter had mis-
quoted Buckley nineteen of the twenty-six times he claimed to be
quoting from his speech.[4] In response to Buckley's suit, the *Tribune*
agreed to reprint Leo's story, along with an apology by the publisher.

The incident did not deter Buckley from speaking at civic events.
On the contrary, it convinced him that he must plunge even deeper
into controversy. Considering later the process of thought that led

him to become a candidate for mayor of New York in 1965, Buckley remarked, "I reached that decision in forty-five minutes after the police crisis speech."

Buckley had a special interest in the 1965 mayoral election. The incumbent, Democrat Richard Wagner, had been stained by scandal —largely the result of his association with Tammany Hall, the New York political machine—and had accumulated growing budget deficits —the deficit in 1965 reaching a record $250 million. He appeared ripe for defeat.

The Republican challenger was expected to be John Lindsay, a tall, handsome Yale graduate who had been elected to Congress from Manhattan's Silk Stocking District in 1958. In seven years Lindsay had compiled a voting record to the left of most Democrats, and in 1964, he had been re-elected with 71 percent of the vote while refusing to back Goldwater against Johnson. For New York's liberal and moderate Republicans, whose voice was John Hay Whitney's *New York Herald Tribune,* Lindsay was the "golden boy" who was being groomed to rescue the Republican Party from the Goldwater extremists. According to their plan, Lindsay would go from congressman to mayor to governor to President.

Lindsay was roundly disliked by New York's conservative Republicans, who saw his election as a far greater evil than the election of another Democrat and were eager to play the role of spoiler. Buckley also wanted to see Lindsay defeated, even if it meant the victory of a Democrat, but although he denied it, others who knew him believed that his dislike of Lindsay went beyond Lindsay's liberal Republicanism. "He had a special animus toward John Lindsay," Conservative Party cofounder Kieran O'Doherty recalled. It might have been based on what was different in their extremely similar backgrounds. Both men had gone to Yale and had even participated in an anti-Wallace demonstration together in 1948; but Lindsay was a Protestant blue blood, a member of the Social Register, and, in Buckley's mind, had enjoyed political success as much on the basis of his social connections and his WASP good looks as on the basis of his intelligence and political acumen.

Buckley wanted not only to cut short Lindsay's rise to the presidency, but to expose what he believed to be his lack of depth and intelligence.

The week after Lindsay's announcement, Buckley wrote a newspaper column proposing a ten-point platform on which a candidate could challenge Lindsay. He also planned to publish it in the next issue of *National Review*. At the Wednesday editorial meeting, Priscilla Buckley innocently proposed a teaser headline across the upper-left-hand corner of the front cover, "Buckley for Mayor." It was meant as a joke, but there was at least one *National Review* reader who didn't take it that way.

When Dan Mahoney, the co-founder of the Conservative Party, saw the teaser on the *National Review* cover, he called Frank Meyer, who was on the state board of the Conservative Party, to see whether he thought Buckley was actually considering a run for mayor. Both Meyer and his wife had talked to Buckley the previous day, and they sensed that he might be interested. Mahoney then contacted the Conservative Party's lawyer, Jim Leff, to see whether Buckley could qualify for the New York ballot even though he was registered in Connecticut. Leff assured Mahoney that he could if he established his residency during the summer. Armed with this information, Mahoney called Buckley on Friday, June 4.

When Mahoney called him, Buckley insisted that the cover line was just a gag, but his interest was piqued when Mahoney assured him that there were no legal obstacles to his running and that a campaign could be adjusted to his already full schedule. *"Is that so?"* Buckley responded.[5] On Monday, June 7, Buckley called Mahoney back and told him that he would run. He had taken very little convincing.

Buckley maintained later that his decision was both spontaneous and innocent. But Neal Freeman, who became Buckey's aide-de-camp during the campaign, insisted that in every respect but one Buckley knew what he was getting into.

> He knew before the rest of us that it was going to be a big deal in the sense that it was going to be a transforming event for him and for the conservative movement. He smelled the possibilities there, and he went after them. What he didn't appreciate was that to run for mayor of a city that large actually requires a little time, that it will interrupt your schedule a little bit. Making concessions to that reality was a difficult personal adjustment.

In the beginning, Buckley envisioned his campaign for mayor as a serious contest of ideas rather than a conventional campaign. He saw politics as a grubby business that was beneath him, even though it increasingly fascinated him. He intended to carry on his regular life, including his column and his editorial duties at *National Review,* while he was campaigning. To protect himself from the demands on his time of Conservative Party activists, he asked his brother Jim to be his campaign manager.

Jim Buckley had left the New Haven law firm of Wiggin and Dana in 1953 and had joined the family business. He was Catawba's traveling troubleshooter. With Jim abroad so much, he and Bill were not as close as they had been when the two were in New Haven, and they tended to see each other only at family get-togethers. But even though Bill had come to rely more on others like Burnham for advice, he retained a deep trust in Jim and a respect for his quiet organizational skills.

Bill called Jim in Hawaii, where he was vacationing, to ask for assistance. "Bill said that he himself couldn't run except under an understanding that it be several hours a day and that for my part it would be even fewer hours a day and that he frankly needed someone to protect him, to be a shield against the eager beavers of the Conservative Party," Jim recalled.

At his first meeting with his campaign committee, held at Marvin Liebman's Madison Avenue office, Buckley laid out the parameters.

> It was a game for all of us and not taken very seriously at that point [Liebman said]. And Buckley said, "Listen, gentlemen, I want this to be a campaign of ideas. After all, we're here to really articulate ideas, and I don't want any of these bumper stickers, balloons, and straw hats. We don't need that kind of stuff. We'll just do it on the ideas. We'll save a lot of money, and it will be terrific.

Buckley carried this same attitude into his opening press conference, held at the Overseas Press Club in Manhattan on June 24. Almost fifty reporters were there, befitting the threat to Lindsay that Buckley's candidacy posed and the novelty of Buckley himself running for office. It was a hot day, and the room was not air-conditioned.

In his speech, Buckley blamed the city's fiscal crisis on the mayor's unwillingness to "offend voting blocs." Buckley proposed to reduce the city's costs by taking a strong hand with labor, abolishing the minimum wage, and instituting a one-year residency requirement for welfare recipients so as to "discourage the thoughtless flow of men and women into New York, whose incapacity to absorb them heightens their own frustrations, adds to the general demoralization, and continues to add to the high overhead of life for which New York is becoming increasingly famous."

Buckley promised to "place no single objective ahead of the necessity to control" the crime rate. He called for "a much larger police force" and for the rejection of the proposal to "encumber" the police with a civilian review board. And he dismissed the argument—then current among black and white liberal civil rights leaders—that black crime was the result of discrimination and should be dealt with as such.

When reporters asked him whether he thought he could win, he refused to follow the politician's script.

REPORTER: Buckley, are you in this campaign to win it or are you in the campaign to, judging from your statement here, perhaps pick away at what you regard as Lindsay's fraud on the party and—

BUCKLEY: No. I am in the campaign to get as many votes as I can get, consistent with maintaining the excellence of my position, so the decision, of course, is up to the people, not me. I will not adapt my views in order to increase my vote by ten people, as you have just seen.

REPORTER: Do you want to be Mayor, sir?

BUCKLEY: I have never considered it.

REPORTER: Do you think that is something that at present should be considered?

BUCKLEY: Not necessarily. What is important is that certain points of view should prevail. Whether you or I administer those points of view is immaterial to me, assuming you are a good administrator.

REPORTER: Do you think you have any chance of winning?

BUCKLEY: No.

REPORTER: How many votes would you consider a satisfactory showing?

BUCKLEY: When the Conservative Party was founded, the first time around, they got 50,000 votes. Against Mr. Kennedy two years later, one year ago, they got 122,000 votes—for Mr. Paolucci. That is a suggestive range.

REPORTER: That is state-wide.

BUCKLEY: That was city-wide.

REPORTER: How many votes do you expect to get, conservatively speaking?

BUCKLEY: Conservatively speaking, one.[6]

Buckley's performance made his Conservative Party supporters very unhappy. By announcing that he would lose before the race even began, Buckley seemed to be throwing away votes. Mahoney worried that with such statements Buckley could "not generate the support that the candidacy would intrinsically merit," but he was unable to persuade him to issue the typical politician's statement that he was in the race to win.

At his press conference a week later, called to introduce his running mates, anti-busing activist Rosemary Gunning, who was running for president of the City Council, and businessman Hugh Markey, running for comptroller, Buckley's defiance of political convention again stole the show.

REPORTER: What would you do if you *were* elected?
BUCKLEY: Demand a recount.[7]

Buckley refused to display what he later called "the usual neurotic confidence of all political candidates."[8] But he also feared that, come November, he might not only lose, but lose big. "I felt no confidence, other than in the cogency of my views, and would have found it personally and professionally embarrassing to go about town speaking nonsense about my own expectations," he wrote later.[9]

In reporting his announcement, the *Herald Tribune* described Buckley as a "right-wing and ultra-conservative debater" and warned that 1965 was not a proper year for "staging esoteric debates."[10] But Buckley's wit and defiance of convention thoroughly charmed the city's press corps and even attracted national media attention to the campaign. While the editors fulminated, the reporters and columnists covered Buckley's press conferences the way they might a good Broadway show. According to *The New Yorker,* the members of the press had a "non-partisan reaction: regardless of what Buckley says, they thoroughly enjoy the way he says it. They seem to be grateful for being spared campaign clichés, and to relish his wit, vocabulary, and rococo style."[11]

Writing in the *New York World-Telegraph* after Buckley's first press conference, Murray Kempton commented:

We have already had candidates for mayor various enough to satisfy every taste except the most refined, and the apparition of William F. Buckley may complete the scale. The truly refined taste, after all, progresses from discontent with each way the thing is being done to the final decision that the thing ought not to be done at all. And Buckley made it plain yesterday that he does not merely disdain the opposition but rather disdains the office itself. . . .

Buckley carried through these indignities as handsomely and containedly as any gentleman ranker offered his first introduction to the men's latrine. He also had the kidney to decline the usual humiliation of soliciting the love of the voters, and read his statement of principles in a tone for all the world that of an Edwardian resident

commissioner reading aloud the 39 articles of the Anglican establishment to a conscript assemblage of Zulus.[12]

II

Buckley thought that he might be able to defeat Lindsay and help
elect the Democrat by drawing away wealthy Manhattan Republicans
concerned about growing deficits. But it took barely a month of campaigning for Buckley and his staff to realize that he would enjoy little
support among these Republicans, who were far more concerned
about defeating Tammany Hall than about electing a Republican who
might be somewhat to their left.

Buckley's greatest base of support, they found, was among just
those New Yorkers whom he knew least: the middle-class Irish, Italians, Poles, and Germans from Queens, the Bronx, Brooklyn, and
Staten Island. Having prospered since the war, these second- and
third-generation Americans no longer felt the pull of New Deal democracy. They were worried about higher taxes rather than unemployment. They wanted a fiscally responsible rather than socially
committed administration. Many of them had started to move into the
Republican column during the 1950s.

They were also vexed by what they saw as the decline of the city,
manifested in both the growing crime rate and the deterioration of the
schools. Looking for a cause for both higher taxes and rising crime
rates, they often found one in the city's black and Puerto Rican population, which had grown measurably in the fifties, while the white
population had shrunk. They saw crime as a result of black lawlessness and higher taxes as the result of the growing sea of black and
Puerto Rican welfare recipients. These middle-class ethnics were in
the first stage of the "white backlash" against the civil rights and
black power movements of the sixties.

They found a spokesman in a thirty-nine-year-old Connecticut resident with an affected accent who talked in polysyllables, but who
addressed precisely the issues they cared about.

Buckley was the only Republican or Democratic candidate willing
to discuss the city's crime rate or its growing welfare rolls. The other
candidates steered away from these issues because of their racial implications. And on a more sophisticated level, he had the same view
of these problems as a middle-class Irish Catholic living in Forest
Hills. He tended to identify checks to black welfare mothers rather
than rebates to private developers as the principal cause of the city's

fiscal crisis. And while identifying the rising crime rate with blacks, he gave little, if any, credence to black charges of police brutality.

Buckley himself was part of the backlash. His resentments were not aroused, however, by the threat of robbery, homicide, or busing, against which he was well insulated, but by the liberal and New Left leaders like James Baldwin who explained black crime as political or social protest, and who believed that the way to eliminate black crime was to eliminate white discrimination against blacks. That kind of reasoning infuriated him and he dug in his heels the same way as when he was confronted by the reasoning of Catholic anti-Communists who believed that the way to fight Soviet Communism was to create social justice at home. He would rarely speak on the subject of blacks and crime during the election without referring derisively to Baldwin's comments.

> Those leaders of the Negro people who cherish resentments, who refuse to deplore misconduct among their race, ought to be publicly and explicitly disavowed by the political leaders of the city. . . . Mr. James Baldwin has said that the Negroes in Harlem who throw garbage out on the streets do so as a form of social protest. It is a much higher form of social protest to denounce such reasoning and the men who make it.[13]

In his speeches, Buckley provided white middle-class audiences with a rationale for their simmering resentment. He connected the city's surplus welfare population not only with its fiscal crisis but with its growing crime rate. In a speech in July to white middle-class Conservative Party supporters in the Bronx, Buckley conjured up an image of the shiftless poor breeding criminal children.

> There are 500,000 people on relief in New York today. What do they contribute—I reduce the argument now to purely material terms—what do they contribute materially to New York? It costs a minimum of $700 to furnish public school education for a child in New York. It costs about $500 per year per person for those on relief; and that much again for public housing. . . . Do we easily justify, in our consciences, luring them into New York by the promise of easy welfare payments? . . . having got their vote, the politicians let them institutionalize themselves as social derelicts, at liberty to breed children who, suffering from inherited disadvantages, alternatively seek surcease in hyperstimulation—in crime and narcotics—and in indolence—as school dropouts or as poolhall conscientious objectors to work; giving that jaded tone to the city

which we recognize as among the most considerable obstacles to its liberation.[14]

He made the institution of a welfare residency requirement and the rejection of the police civilian review board his central issues. And when he described the growing crime rate, it was the growing black crime rate that he was referring to. Testifying in July before the New York City Council, Buckley rejected the argument that the city should try to reduce black crime by pumping money into the ghetto rather than by strengthening the police.

It is one thing to say that the white people of this city . . . should accept—as I believe we should do—a moral responsibility for contributing to the helplessness and despair that breed ignorance and lawlessness [among so many Negroes]. But it is something altogether different—it is a total distortion of civilized thought—to deduce from whatever is the extent of our corporate responsibility for the high rate of Negro crime, that Negro crime is other than criminal. That broken homes, because they are Negro broken homes, are any the less broken. That illegitimacy, because it is Negro illegitimacy, is any the less illegitimate. However understandable it may be that it is a result of *my* delinquency as a parent that my son has become a thief, thievery is wrong; and the supreme duty of civil society is to prevent that thief from marauding against innocent citizens. That is the function of policemen. That and only that. It is the function of *others* to devise the means by which to discharge the debt we have to the Negro people.[15]

During his campaign, Buckley was often accused of racism, and he angrily rejected such charges in the same way as, in the past, he had rejected charges that he was a Fascist, Nazi, or anti-Semite. Buckley believed that he was being called a racist merely because he was openly discussing what he believed to be a racial problem. He told a Conservative Party gathering in October, "The other candidates, sensitive as they are to ethnic sensibilities, do not dare to acknowledge that there is in fact a problem in New York of a kind which cannot be effectively diagnosed except insofar as a racial vocabulary needs to be used."[16]

Buckley had been heavily influenced by sociologists Nathan Glazer and Daniel P. Moynihan's *Beyond the Melting Pot*. Glazer and Moynihan had compared the progress of blacks with that of other American ethnic groups and had reached the conclusion that while blacks had suffered greater oppression, their failure to increase their economic status as quickly as other groups was partly due to the absence of collective self-help, evidenced by the disintegration of the black family. The disintegration of the black family, Glazer and Moynihan argued, was also a principal cause of crime among blacks.

According to Glazer and Moynihan, the solution to the decline of the black family and therefore to blacks' economic status and the growing crime rate did not lie primarily with increased government aid. The "important tasks" on "the agenda of American Negroes," Glazer and Moynihan concluded, were "self-help" tasks, which could be performed only by blacks themselves.[17] Glazer and Moynihan were very critical of the black middle class's failure to finance black community institutions that would encourage proper educational and social values. They had not intended their argument as a polemic against the black civil rights leadership, but against the black middle class of businessmen and professionals—the same group that Harold Cruse would indict in his book *The Crisis of the Negro Intellectual*. They had also not intended their analysis as an argument against economic relief, but rather against an exclusive focus on such relief.

Nonetheless, that is the use Buckley made of their analysis. He cited Glazer and Moynihan to justify his tirades against Congressman Adam Clayton Powell and black militants and to buttress his conviction that increased government spending would not necessarily solve black people's problems or reduce the crime rate.

At the end of July, Buckley got an unexpected chance to explain his views before a black audience. Neal Freeman had accepted an invitation for Buckley to appear along with other mayoral candidates before a group called the One Hundred Men. When Freeman and Buckley arrived at the downtown restaurant where the meeting was held, they were amazed to discover that One Hundred Men was an all-black organization of businessmen and professionals. More than two hundred had crammed the Commuter's Cafe for four hours of candidate interviews, during which, as it turned out, Buckley provided the "evening's fireworks."[18]

Buckley tried, amid scattered boos and mutterings of disapproval, to assure the crowd that he was not a racist.

It is incorrect that the American Conservative is animated by hostility to the legitimate aspirations of the Negro race. The Jew with his crooked nose, the Italian with his accent, they were nothing like the disadvantages you suffered. But socializing the country is not the answer.[19]

He angered the audience further by denouncing Powell. When one man in the audience jumped up to defend the congressman, citing his role in ending segregation in the armed forces, Buckley replied, "Yes, but he wrote a column for the *Daily Worker* 20 years ago and called many of his colleagues in Congress Fascists." When the man continued to protest, Buckley said, "I'm not here to engage in a spitting contest with you, but if any statement in the world is safe to make, it is this: 'Adam Clayton Powell is a scoundrel and an opportunist.' "[20]

Two men walked out in protest, and the audience began to stir, but Buckley remained calm. During the question period, he was asked how he would try as mayor to remove the "obstacles and oppositions and selective discrimination against the black minority." He told the black civic leaders that the burden was theirs not his.

> The *principal* problems that are faced by Negroes today, and that were faced to a lesser extent by other groups, are *not* solved by government. They are solved by the leadership of their own people. Will *you* kindly tell *me* what the government has proposed to do, for instance, about the problem of illegitimacy? . . . The mayor of New York has got to be modest in his pretensions. He must not approach the Negro people and say, "I will transform your life." He must say, "I will give you justice and opportunity," and then it is up to the moral leaders of the community . . . to crack down on discrimination everywhere it shows its hideous head.[21]

After all the candidates had appeared, the black businessmen and professionals voted unanimously to "repudiate" Buckley's candidacy. Informed afterwards of the decision, Buckley commented, "These people are prejudiced against me,"[22] and he did not appear again during his campaign before a predominately black audience.

III

While Buckley was campaigning during the summer, he managed to keep abreast of *National Review,* as well as writing his thrice-weekly column. The magazine had not commented on the John Birch Society since its denunciation in 1962 of Robert Welch's leadership, and Buckley had touched upon the Society only peripherally in his column. But both Buckley and Burnham were upset by the August 1965 issue of *American Opinion* in which the Society not only repeated its insistence that the major branches of government were under Communist domination, but called upon the U.S. to withdraw from Vietnam. The Society's opposition to the war, based upon its conviction that the most important Communist enemy was at home rather than abroad, reflected its own isolationist roots.

In early August, Buckley wrote a column calling the Society's contention "drivel." He and Burnham also insisted that *National Review* run a special issue condemning the John Birch Society over the protests of Rickenbacker and Rusher, who complained that it was "right-wing cannibalism encouraged by the opposition." In marked contrast to the way the magazine had previously presented its criticism of the Society, this time Buckley and the editors featured it on the cover and devoted fourteen pages to it. Instead of targeting Welch, they took aim at the Society itself, describing it as "a grave liability to the conservative and anti-Communist cause." [23]

When Buckley told Mahoney that he was going to be attacking the John Birch Society in his columns, the cautious Mahoney had warned against it, fearing that Birch Society members who were working as volunteers in the lower levels of the mayoral campaign would drop out. (Buckley and Mahoney had been careful to prevent any members of the Birch Society from holding leadership positions.) But Mahoney's fears proved groundless.

While *National Review* got more than fifteen hundred angry letters and as many subscription cancellations, Buckley himself received only a handful of angry letters from conservative activists in New York. On the contrary, the attack on the Society provided Buckley's campaign with ammunition against the growing assaults by his political opponents. By then, Buckley needed the badge of respectability that denouncing the Society merited far more than he needed the legwork of a few conservative activists.

IV

In September, two important events took place that transformed Buckley's chances. First, on September 15, Comptroller Abraham Beame, a short, colorless man known for his attention to fiscal detail, surprised both Buckley and the Conservatives by winning the Democratic primary. Beame was Jewish, and if elected would become New York's first Jewish mayor.

Beame's candidacy failed to diminish Buckley's appeal to ethnic Democrats. While the more colorful Paul O'Dwyer might have been able to hold his own against Buckley, Beame was totally outclassed in debate. And while Beame was a political moderate, he could not hope to create any enthusiasm except among Jewish Democrats; he left a large opening for Buckley among Irish, Italian, Polish, and other ethnic Democrats.

But at the same time, Beame potentially altered the chemistry between Lindsay and Buckley. Against a liberal Democrat, Lindsay might have had to fight Buckley for conservative Republican votes. But against a moderate Democrat, Lindsay could go after the liberal vote and let Buckley and Beame fight over the conservatives.

The second event that transformed Buckley's candidacy took place right after Beame's primary win. The city's daily newspapers went on strike for three weeks. With newspaper coverage unavailable, the television stations stepped in to fill the void. Three televised debates were staged among the candidates, and there were opportunities every day for radio and television interviews. Through the television publicity, Buckley not only reached several million voters for whom he might otherwise have simply been a name on the ballot; he also got a chance to make even the telegenic Lindsay look like a stiff.

Buckley's press secretary, Kieran O'Doherty, believed that the press strike made Buckley's campaign a success. "Were it not for the press strike and the necessary television interviews, I don't know where the campaign would have gone," O'Doherty said. "It was the biggest break he got."

The first televised debate was held on Sunday, September 26, and was broadcast over WCBS-TV. Lindsay was platitudinous ("I ask all New Yorkers to join me, to roll up their sleeves, to care"), Beame was visibly nervous and tedious ("I will go to Washington, where I will be welcomed as a Democrat, and fight for federal aid"), and Buckley was acerbic and witty. Asked if he still would be "flabbergasted" if he were elected, Buckley responded, "Having heard Mr. Beame and Mr. Lindsay, I would be flabbergasted if I weren't elected." [24]

Columnist Rowland Evans and Robert Novak summed up Buckley's performance in the debates: "Buckley's roguish wit and flashy idiom are made for television and this is a television campaign. As a result, New York's liberal voters are being exposed to a larger dose of right-wing ideology than they've ever had before from a mayoralty candidate." [25] *New York Daily News* television critic Edward O'Neill wrote after the second debate, "Love him or hate him, TV fans found it difficult to turn off a master political showman. His rolling eyes, deft handling of the English language and razor-sharp debating techniques were exciting to watch. Even tall, handsome and personable Lindsay found himself being upstaged time and time again."[26]

Buckley's television performances attracted national press attention. Writing in *Life,* political reporter Theodore White commented on the debates.

> On TV Buckley is a star. His haughty face, its puckering and hesitation as he lets loose a shaft of wit, would have made him Oscar Wilde's favorite candidate for anything. In television debate Lindsay is normally flanked by Beame, who wants to talk about budget figures. But when Lindsay can free himself from Beame's figures to loose any of the visions of his task forces, there, on his other flank, is Buckley, puncturing the dream or hope with a witch's shaft of rhetoric.[27]

In late September, buoyed by the first debates, Buckley's candidacy began to gather steam. At the end of September, the *Herald Tribune,* which was the first of the newspapers to return to work, published a poll showing Beame with 44.3 percent, Lindsay with 36.9 percent, and Buckley with 11.2 percent. The poll was the first citywide indication that Buckley had that he was gathering a substantial vote (11 percent of the vote would carry him over 300,000, or twice the showing of any prior Conservative Party candidate) and that he might accomplish what he set out to do by helping Beame defeat Lindsay. Three weeks later, the *New York Daily News,* the newspaper with the best reputation for polling accuracy, had Buckley with 20.4 percent—potentially over 500,000 votes.[28]

Buckley's campaign was being flooded with volunteers—nearly a thousand volunteers were being directed out of the Buckley for Mayor headquarters on 45th Street. And more than $200,000 had been contributed to the campaign, some from pro-Beame Democrats.

Buckley's attitude toward the election had begun to change. When *The New York Times* quoted him on September 5 as saying that he was running "half in fun," he adamantly denied ever having said so. Having early railed against bumper stickers, he now complained to Liebman, who was handling publicity and fund raising, that everywhere he went there were Lindsay posters, but no posters for Buckley. Instead of limiting his campaigning to a day a week, Buckley began to campaign every day. "Bill did go into the thing for a lark," Jim Buckley said. "But I think any sense of its being a lark rapidly disappeared."

Buckley even began to consider the remote possibility that he could win. Neal Freeman recalled:

> There was a moment in September when Bill flirted with the idea that if the liberal vote were to dispose itself in perfect equilibrium between Lindsay and Beame, then he might just sneak through to win at the tape. Intellectually, I don't think Bill ever believed that, but psychologically he flirted with the possibility, if only to keep his engine running.

One of the central tenets of Buckley's campaign had been his opposition to ethnic appeals. His opposition was based both on his disdain for unprincipled politicians, who sought votes by making promises that eventually bankrupted the city, and a certain snobbery toward New York's ethnic groups and the world outside of Manhattan's East Side. Buckley's attitude toward ethnic politics was the same as his attitude toward his own ethnicity: He was not Irish, but American. And his attitude toward New York's boroughs was similar to that of the Stamford commuter. "Every time he went to Queens, he thought he was taking off for Istanbul or something and he fought it," one campaign aide recalled.

But under the impact of his growing support from the middle-class Irish, Italians, and Poles in Queens, Brooklyn, the Bronx, and Staten Island, he began to rethink his attitude toward ethnic politics. The catalyst for this consideration was the Pulaski Day Parade.

On October 1, his aide Neal Freeman called him in the morning in a panic. The *New York Herald Tribune* had run a front-page story headlined, "Pulaski Parade: 'No' by Buckley." According to the story, Buckley was the only mayoral candidate to decline an invitation to the Polish parade, usually an occasion for protest against the Soviet subjugation of the Poles, as well as a purely national celebration. The story quoted a letter from Freeman:

> I am sorry to report that Mr. Buckley will be unable to attend the annual Pulaski Day Parade primarily because he has pledged himself to make no specifically ethnic or nationalist appeals. I hope you will understand his policy: it is to treat the voters of New York as responsible adult-individuals and not as members of monolithic voting blocs.

The *Tribune* article also described the reaction of the Parade Committee:

Of the three candidates, Mr. Buckley was clearly the favorite among some 300 members of the parade committee—that is, until his letter was read. . . . They were relatively silent at the mention of Mr. Beame's and Mr. Lindsay's names, but applauded Mr. Buckley's, then groaned when they heard the letter.

Freeman confessed his own consternation and that of Conservative Party supporters at the Buckley headquarters, particularly Kieran O'Doherty. And while recognizing that Freeman had merely carried out what appeared to be his wishes, Buckley finally realized that he had gone too far in rejecting voting blocs. As he admitted later, he realized that his attitude had been "stuffy." [29]

But he could not repudiate Freeman publicly. Instead, he wrote a letter to the head of the Parade Committee explaining that as a candidate he did not want to "manipulate nationality groups by attending their parades," while affirming his support of the American Friends of the Captive Nations and promising that if he were invited the next year, he would "accept with pride and pleasure." [30]

Buckley's success in the debates and in the polls, along with Beame's apparent lead, created a crisis in Lindsay's organization. Lindsay and his campaign manager, Robert Price, had avoided attacking Buckley on the assumption that it was better to ignore him than to give him the recognition that a public attack would bring. But the television debates had given Buckley whatever recognition he needed, and now Lindsay had to deal with the real political threat that Buckley posed.

Price and Lindsay came to realize, however, that they could turn an attack against Buckley to their advantage. Their strategy against Beame was to run to his left rather than his right (a Lindsay advertisement featured a quotation from columnist Harry Goldman that Lindsay was "somewhat to the left of Beame") in the hope of cutting into Beame's liberal Jewish vote. By attacking Buckley for being a racist and a member of the radical Right, and by posing the election as a choice between Buckley and Lindsay, they could hope to scare Jewish voters who still identified the Right with anti-Semitism.

At the same time, Lindsay's campaign advisers expected that an attack on Buckley's conservatism might help rather than hurt Buckley among non-Jewish ethnic Democrats. But the votes that Buckley got in this manner would have gone to Beame rather than to Lindsay.

Lindsay's lieutenants even tried to hire one former campaign worker to solicit votes for Buckley among potentially pro-Beame Irish Catholics who could never be expected to vote for Lindsay.

In the last month of the campaign, Lindsay repeatedly linked Buckley to Goldwater and accused him of fostering hatred between the races. Lindsay spokesmen like Senator Jacob Javits kept up the offensive. And Lindsay even threatened to file charges with the Fair Campaign Practices Committee, accusing Buckley of "subtle appeals to racial prejudices."

One Buckley proposal gave particular credence to the charges that Lindsay and Javits were making. In a campaign position paper on welfare Buckley suggested that the city institute a "pilot program" to "explore the feasibility of relocating chronic welfare cases outside the city limits." Citing the case of a mother with three illegitimate children, the paper claimed that by sending families to special "rehabilitation centers," the city could not only save money, but also eliminate a source of crime. It added, "Disadvantaged children, and incontinent mothers, might be better off—and certainly New York would be better off—in the country, with special schools, and special supervision aimed at true rehabilitation." [31]

However he tried to soften it, Buckley's proposal smacked of debtors' prisons and poorhouses. It reeked of a certain contempt and intolerance toward the poor—in this case the minority poor. And his opponents were quick to make the most of it. Javits accused Buckley of advocating "sending people on welfare to concentration camps." [32] Lindsay, taking a swipe at Beame as well as Buckley, said, "The vile implications of what Buckley advocates, and Beame sees fit not to condemn, would destroy the last finger of decency for every minority-group member and all citizens of New York." [33]

Buckley's welfare proposal, combined with another proposal for "quarantining" narcotics addicts, prompted an angry exchange with *The New York Times.* On October 23, *The New York Times* editorialized, "For weeks William F. Buckley Jr. has been pandering to some of the more brutish instincts in the community, though his appeals to racism and bigotry have been artfully masked." Buckley fired back a reply to the *Times,* citing his use of Glazer and Moynihan's analysis: "I have not, as it happens, said a single thing about the Negro problem in Harlem that hasn't been said by others whom you have not, so far as I am aware, done one of your hippopotamus-walks over. . . . What brutish instincts am I appealing to? Come, now, my fair-minded friends, tell me." The *Times* responded:

He is no racist himself; yet he delights the prejudices of certain listeners by slurs on Negroes: "I would go to Harlem to a place where garbage is regularly thrown out the window and call a rally and ask the people to stop." He urges a "white blacklash" against Negro leaders ranging from the demagogic Adam Clayton Powell to the vastly more thoughtful Bayard Rustin. . . . Buckley appeals for a definition of the "brutish" instincts to which he is appealing. Those instincts are fear, ignorance, racial superiority, religious antagonism, contempt for the weak and afflicted and hatred for those different from oneself.[34]

Such attacks against Buckley did not slow his ascent at the polls. But while Buckley was rising, Beame appeared to be falling. In the same *Daily News* poll, Beame trailed Lindsay by 5 percent, 42.4 percent to 37.2 percent. In short, Lindsay's strategy appeared to be working: Buckley was gaining but at the expense of Beame.

In his syndicated column, Joseph Kraft explained that Beame had expected to get Jewish Democrats because he was Jewish, and Irish and Italians because of his

reputation as a sharp-pencil man, conservative in fiscal matters and therefore hostile to the welfare projects that benefit the Negroes. But with Buckley in the race, Beame's muted appeal for the backlash vote never had a chance. For the conservative candidate came right out in the open on crime in the streets, drug addiction, protest demonstrations, and all the other code words for racial prejudice. As a result, Beame's normal party standing among the Irish and Italians has plunged.

In the last week of the campaign, Buckley and his staff clashed over how to contend with Beame. In the first debates, Beame had joined Buckley in attacking Lindsay. He had never criticized Buckley. But Beame, feeling the election slipping away and taunted by Lindsay to join his condemnation of Buckley, finally began attacking Buckley.

One of Beame's staff had warned Kieran O'Doherty that they were going to have to attack Buckley in order to prevent the liberal Jewish vote from going to Lindsay. Before Beame's attack, O'Doherty tried to prevent Buckley from responding in kind, but he could not.

I was urging at the last strategy meeting that we've got to do what we can, they are going to attack us, but we've got to take that thing astride and turn around and push the voters over to Beame. Buckley wouldn't do that. He said, "Let Beame take care of himself, I want to hold my vote," and he hit back Beame when Beame attacked him.

At an October 29 press conference, Beame denounced Buckley for campaigning "on a program of fear and prejudice, of hatred of neighbor for neighbor."[35] And, during the radio debate that was held the next evening, Beame inserted himself on Lindsay's side during an angry exchange between the latter and Buckley over Buckley's proposal for rehabilitation centers.

BUCKLEY: You've been calling them "concentration camps." That conjures up Nazi visions of horror specifically aimed at the Jewish people.

LINDSAY: Your remark is offensive and irresponsible and I'll ask you not to make it again.

BUCKLEY: I don't have to take instructions from you on what to say, what not to say. You are trying to do to Jewish voters what the Ku Klux Klan has been trying to do to the white people in the South—keep them scared. You are in there saying in effect to Jewish voters: "Vote for me, vote for me, because over here is an ultra-rightist who is trying to bring bloodshed into the city."

BEAME: There's no one more guilty of prejudice than you and you know it.[36]

By then, Buckley was quite angry with Beame. To O'Doherty's consternation, Saturday evening at Buckley's final rally, before three thousand cheering supporters in Queens, he devoted almost a quarter of his speech to blasting Beame for being "demagogic."

By election eve, Buckley had become the focus of the entire campaign. In *The New York Times,* Richard Witkin wrote, "The biggest issue in the mayoral campaign has turned out to be—not bossism, not time for a change, not crime in the streets—but the role of a third party candidate, who, with his flare for arch phrase-making, has sparked much of the controversy and all of the humor of the campaign."[37]

He was also becoming a national figure. In those days, New York mayoral contests were always followed nationally—the mayor of New York was thought to be the third most important public official in America, after the President of the United States and the governor of New York. But in its closing days, the New York race received more than the usual attention because of the contest between Buckley and Lindsay. Both the Washington newspapers covered it daily, the

major weeklies ran stories regularly on it, and the major political
columnists of the nation, led by Walter Lippmann, weighed in against
Buckley and for Lindsay's side. The New York mayoral election became a reprise of the 1964 Republican presidential primary, only this
time the moderate Republicans were determined to come out victo-
rious.

V

A week before the election, Buckley participated in a pool to guess
his final vote. Even though the *New York Daily News* had him with 18
percent then—about 460,000 votes—he estimated that he would get
only 340,000. Jim Buckley guessed 400,000, and Marvin Liebman,
who was even more worried than Buckley about last-minute slippage,
282,000.[38]

As it turned out, Buckley's estimate was almost exactly correct. He
received 341,226 votes, or 13.4 percent, while Lindsay, with 1,149,106
votes, or 45.3 percent, bested Beame, with 1,046,699, by 4 percent,
or 102,407 votes. To Conservative Party officials like O'Doherty,
Buckley's failure to help defeat Lindsay cast a pall over his vote total.
"I felt like I had ashes in my mouth," Kieran O'Doherty recalled.

Still, Buckley's achievement was significant. He had received far
more votes than any previous Conservative candidate in New York
City. He had held Lindsay to only 45 percent of the vote. The Conservative line had bested the Liberals by almost 60,000 votes. And he
had run what he called a "paradigmatic campaign" that would influence conservatives in the years to come.[39]

Buckley's best comment on the election came later that month
when he was roasted at Saints and Sinners, the New York newspaper-
men's annual banquet. After a host of speakers had twitted him before
a packed dinner audience—the largest Cliff White had ever seen at
the celebrity affair—Buckley rose to respond. "I presume that I am
expected to say something about John Lindsay," Buckley said. "But
I don't believe in kicking a man when he is down." Then he sat down
and would not say another word.

Beame himself blamed Buckley for his defeat. "Do you think Mr.
Buckley was a major factor in your defeat?" a reporter asked him on
election night. "I don't think so. I know so," Beame replied.[40] But the
election results didn't really merit this conclusion.

According to postelection analyses, of the 150,000 or so voters who
deserted Buckley at the last moment, three out of four went to Lind-

say rather than to Beame. If Buckley had kept these voters, and the polls had stayed constant, Lindsay would still have won, if by less. And if Buckley had not run at all, Lindsay would probably have had an easier time defeating Beame.

The breakdown of the vote shows that Lindsay's October strategy worked. By using the specter of the extreme Right, he was able to win almost half of the Jewish and minority vote, while winning the WASP Republican vote handily. But while Buckley and the Conservatives failed to defeat Lindsay, they began to etch out, in the mayoral election, a viable coalition.

Buckley did best in the middle- and upper-middle-class ethnic suburbs—exactly those places that were in the process of changing from the Democratic to the Republican column. He did worst among the two groups that in the years to come would remain the most steadfastly Democratic—minorities and Jews. According to a CBS poll, Buckley got 3.5 percent of the Jewish vote and 1.1 percent of the black vote.[41] And he also did poorly among the East Side upper-class Republicans who in future years would become increasingly uneasy with the conservative drift of Republicanism.

Buckley showed that conservative (as opposed to liberal or moderate) Republicans could attract the votes of white ethnic voters by appealing both to their fiscal conservatism and to their fear that blacks and minorities were wrecking the city's schools, making its streets and subways unsafe, and bankrupting its treasury. Buckley never fully reconciled himself to, or understood, the basis of his political success, but other politicians and political analysts were quick to realize the significance of his appeal.

In his landmark book, *The Emerging Republican Majority,* political scientist and Nixon aide Kevin Phillips would cite Buckley's vote in New York's Catholic assembly districts as a harbinger of the new majority.[42] And in its contours, although not in its size, Buckley's coalition perfectly anticipated the northern urban coalition that Ronald Reagan would create in 1980 and 1984 and that would allow him to carry New York City.

VI

The election changed Buckley's life. Subjected to regular photo stories in *Life* and to national television coverage, he became a celebrity only a notch below Goldwater in public recognition. Neal Freeman was amazed by the difference that the campaign for mayor had made. "It made him a star, and the transformation was quite electric,'' Freeman recalled. "In 1964, you would travel anywhere in the country with Bill Buckley and both of you were anonymous. By 1965, you couldn't walk twenty-five feet in an airport without the autograph hunters.''

Buckley took to his new celebrity, responding graciously to well-wishers, and faithfully answering the hundreds of letters that he began to get each week.

In early 1965, Buckley and Freeman had discussed staging a television show in which Buckley would debate prominent political opponents, but they couldn't find either public or private stations that were interested in it. After the mayoral debates, a major private station, WOR-TV in New York City, agreed to syndicate the new show, to be called *Firing Line*. Buckley's column sales soared, and he was inundated with free-lance writing requests. And he signed a contract with Viking publisher Tom Guinzburg (with whom he had reconciled after their feud at Yale) to write a book on the mayoral campaign.

If the mayoral campaign was a landmark achievement in Buckley's life, the book that he wrote about the campaign was almost as important. During the campaign, he had conceived of a book based on his position papers, but instead of composing a study of urban politics, Buckley wrote a lively account of the campaign, in which he interspersed his own reflections on New York's political history and economic situation. He included the position papers, but only in one uniquely dull chapter. Overall, *The Unmaking of a Mayor,* which he wrote during his two months in Switzerland, was entirely different from his past efforts.

Buckley had shown flashes of literary style in his more personal pieces. His memoir of Chambers was extremely moving. He wrote interesting political travelogues from Mexico and South Africa. Some of the brief obituaries he wrote for *National Review* were prose poems. And in 1965, he published in *Esquire* a stirring account of the trial and imprisonment of Edgar Smith, a New Jersey convict who Buckley believed was innocent. But his political writing, evidenced in his books from *God and Man at Yale* to *Up from Liberalism,* was pedestrian. It was as though his own discomfort with the philosophical approach to politics found expression in his style.

The Unmaking of a Mayor displayed a stylistic brilliance and a skill in narrative that had only been dimly anticipated even by the best of his early writing. Like James Baldwin's *The Fire Next Time* and Normal Mailer's *Advertisements for Myself,* it blended autobiography, reportage, and a novelist's attention to scene and detail with conventional political commentary and analysis. One of the most lively chapters was "Notes (after the Fact) from a Diary (Never Written)" that consisted of imaginary diary entries from the last two months of the campaign.

By allowing his imagination free rein, Buckley was able to impart an immediacy to the clichés of urban crisis.

A modern Justine *could,* in New York City, wake up in the morning in a room she shares with her unemployed husband and two children, crowd into a subway in which she is hardly able to breathe, disembark at Grand Central and take a crosstown bus which takes twenty minutes to go the ten blocks to her textile loft, work a full day and receive her paycheck from which a sizeable deduction is withdrawn in taxes and union fees, return via the same ordeal, prepare supper for her family and tune up the radio to full blast to shield the children from the gamy denunciations her next-door neighbor is hurling at her husband, walk a few blocks past hideous buildings to the neighborhood park to breathe a little fresh air, and fall into a coughing fit as the sulphur dioxide excites her latent asthma, go home, and on the way, lose her handbag to a purse-snatcher, sit down to oversee her son's homework only to trip over the fact that he doesn't really know the alphabet even though he had his fourteenth birthday yesterday, which he spent in the company of a well-known pusher. She hauls off and smacks him, but he dodges and she bangs her head against the table. The ambulance is slow in coming and at the hospital there is no doctor in attendance. An intern finally materializes and sticks her with a shot of morphine and she dozes off to sleep. And dreams of John Lindsay.[43]

By making his writing more personal, Buckley changed his literary persona. He became far more attractive to his readers—appearing in print the way his friends and his colleagues on *National Review* experienced him. In his early books, Buckley appeared to be an arrogant brat. In *The Unmaking of a Mayor,* Buckley portrayed himself as an innocent in the wilds of politics; his humor was often at his own expense. For instance, he recounted his experience the evening of the day in which he had proudly announced his plan for a bicycle path through Manhattan—a proposal that all his advisers had urged him to forgo because it would be seen as flippant.

I remember the evening of that press conference, which I spent at the home of an old Negro election-district boss in Bedford-Stuyvesant, a former Pullman porter of indefatigable political energy and utterly total recall, who had promised to deliver me the entire Bronx, or whatever, and had got together his family and a few lieutenants. We sat about the living room while his warm and hospitable wife in the kitchen below sent up a torrent of sandwiches, cakes, drinks, cigars, as the old gentleman rambled around in his copious memory telling us of this and that. His daughter-in-law, a sophisticated, slightly cynical, more than slightly bemused nurse's aide from a local hospital, told me at one point: "You know, I was for John Lindsay until today." "What," I asked, delighted, "did John Lindsay do today?" "It was that ridiculous bicycle scheme," she said. I paused. But only for a moment, let the devil record. "That *was* ridiculous, wasn't it," I exclaimed—changing the subject, and concluding that as of that moment, I had really and truly become a politician, and how would I formulate *that* sin at my next session with my confessor.[44]

The Bill Buckley of *God and Man at Yale* had charmed older conservatives and inspired younger ones who felt themselves to be part of an embattled Remnant. But the new Buckley could win the sympathy and attract the interest of a far broader range of readers. *The Unmaking of a Mayor* made Buckley into a popular writer.

But while *The Unmaking of a Mayor* was both a political and literary success, it was afflicted by the underlying contradictions that Buckley had failed to resolve while trying to write *The Revolt Against the Masses.* He could not reconcile his philosophical commitment to Nock's elitism with his popular support in the Bronx and Queens. In *The Unmaking of a Mayor,* Buckley attributed the attempt by the press and his political opponents to pillory him to the "prejudice and passion and narrow self-interest [that] are the proximate movers on election day for a heavy percentage of voters." But in defending *his* constituency, maligned as racist by the press and his opponents, he observed that "the people's slogans, their clichés, often sit, however uneasily, or self-consciously, at the top of a structure of values and discriminations which are not lightly to be dismissed, at least not more lightly to be dismissed than the democratic system."[45]

Buckley wanted it both ways. When the newspapers were attacking him, they were appealing to the base prejudices that animate the average voter. When the newspapers accused his constituency of base prejudices, they overlooked the "structure of values and discriminations" that underlay them.

If the campaign for mayor made Buckley into a national celebrity and public figure, it by no means reconciled Buckley to politics as a public vocation. He disliked the messy compromises and the need to appeal to crowds of people. "You know those crowds. . . . How do you suppose de Gaulle stands them?" he said to Murray Kempton just before the end of the campaign.[46] He expressed his dislike for politics in more abstract terms in a speech he gave in December 1965 at *National Review*'s tenth anniversary celebration.

> Politics, it has been said, is the preoccupation of the quarter educated, and I do most solidly endorse this observation, and therefore curse this country above all things, for its having given sentient beings very little alternative than to occupy themselves with politics. It is all very well to ignore [the Johnson administration's] Great Society. But will the Great Society ignore us? . . . Where can we go and feel free *not* to read the *New York Times*? No such freedom exists nowadays, which is the conclusive reason, surely, to deplore this century's most distinctive aggression, which is against privacy, publicly understood.[47]

But Buckley had become fascinated and then thoroughly engrossed by the mayor's race. Whatever he may have proclaimed in public, privately Buckley resolved that in 1970 he would challenge Robert Kennedy for his New York Senate seat. Meanwhile, with the Vietnam War in full swing and the nation bitterly split by protest, he continued to command public attention as the most visible and colorful of the conservatives.

In 1908, after two years working for the General Land Office in Austin, Texas, William F. "Will" Buckley left to join a law practice in Mexico City.

Will Buckley met Aloise Steiner during a business trip to New Orleans in 1917, and they were married on Christmas of that year.

In 1929, the year Will Buckley moved his children and their governesses from Great Elm to Paris. Front row, left to right: Jim, Bill, Patricia, Priscilla, Jane. Back row: Nana, Filipa.

The Buckley family in Sharon, Connecticut, in 1933 after they returned from London. Standing, left to right: John, Will Buckley, Jim. Bottom row: Aloise, Aloise Buckley (with Maureen on her lap and Patricia at her feet), Reid, Priscilla, Jane, and Bill.

The Buckley family spent Christmas 1932 at an inn in Grindelwald, Switzerland. The children—Priscilla, Jane, John, Jim, Aloise, Bill, and Patricia—won a prize for their costumes.

This photo, taken in 1939, shows Bill Buckley sailing with his instructor, Don Carmiencke, and his music teacher, Marjorie Otis Gifford, in the boat his father bought him when he returned from boarding school in England in 1938.

In 1940, during a school vacation at the Buckley's winter home in Camden, South Carolina, Bill and Patricia Buckley entered the Camden Horse Show.

By the end of World War II, John, Jim, and Bill Buckley were all in uniform—
John and Bill in the army and Jim in the navy. Seated, left to right: William F.
Buckley, Sr., Aloise, and Carol. Standing: Jane, Maureen, John, James L., Pa-
tricia, Bill, F. Reid, Priscilla, and Aloise.

Bill Buckley was inducted into the infantry
in July 1944 and was commissioned a lieutenant a year later. Bill's two years in the army
were among the most difficult in his life.

Professor Rollin Osterweis (back row, right),
Yale's debating coach, thought that the 1950
team of Brent Bozell (front, left) and Bill
Buckley (front, right) was the best he ever
coached.

Sheridan Lord, Thomas Guinzburg, and Bill Buckley, who had been roommates at Yale their sophomore year, spent their summer 1948 vacation traveling through Mexico.

In 1949, Buckley met his sister Patricia (left) at Pat Taylor's house in Vancouver, British Columbia, for the July Fourth holiday. Four days later he proposed to Pat.

Bill Buckley and Pat Taylor were married in Vancouver, British Columbia in July 1950 at a ceremony presided over by the archbishop of Vancouver.

Bill Buckley identified with Wisconsin senator Joseph McCarthy, a Catholic and fervent anti-Communist who had drawn the wrath of the Eastern liberal elite. Buckley's first nationally published article and his second book were devoted to defending McCarthy against his critics.

Whittaker Chambers, who joined *National Review* in 1956, exerted a profound influence on Buckley.

National Review's editors liked to poke fun at their liberal opponents. Here, in 1956 (left to right), Priscilla Buckley, Suzanne La Follette, James Burnham, Willmoore Kendall, and Buckley target historian Arthur M. Schlesinger, Jr.

In 1958, Robert Welch founded the John Birch Society, which by the early sixties claimed 100,000 members. Welch believed that Dwight and Milton Eisenhower were Communist agents who helped secure Communist control of the United States.

In 1968, after Buckley and author Gore Vidal appeared together on television during the 1968 presidential conventions, their six-year-old feud erupted into a bitter law suit.

Buckley dances with his sister Maureen at her wedding in 1958. He became extremely fond of the effervescent Maureen after she came to work at *National Review* in 1956.

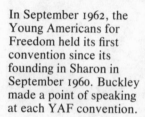

In September 1962, the Young Americans for Freedom held its first convention since its founding in Sharon in September 1960. Buckley made a point of speaking at each YAF convention.

Buckley teaches his son, Christopher, how to ride a motor scooter.

Bill Buckley had always enjoyed a close relationship with Arizona senator Barry Goldwater until Goldwater became the Republican nominee for President in 1964.

In the 1965 New York mayoral contest, Republican governor Nelson Rockefeller (right) backed Congressman John Lindsay. Both men had angered conservatives by refusing to campaign for Goldwater in 1964.

Buckley ran for mayor of New York City that year on the Conservative party ticket with anti-busing activist Rosemary Gunning, the candidate for president of the city council, and businessman Hugh Markey, the candidate for comptroller. Asked at their first joint press conference what he would do if he won, Buckley replied, "Demand a recount."

At the October 1965 Al
Smith Dinner, during the
mayoral campaign, Bill
Buckley shakes hands
with Vice-President
Hubert Humphrey while
Francis J. Cardinal
Spellman looks on.

In 1967, Buckley reached
new heights of celebrity
when he appeared on the
cover of *Time* magazine.
He was also profiled that
year in *Harper's* and *The
Wall Street Journal.*

FIFTY CENTS   NOVEMBER 3, 1967

TIME

WILLIAM BUCKLEY: Conservatism Can Be Fun

VOL. 90 NO. 18
(REG. U.S. PAT. OFF.)

In May 1969, President
Richard Nixon appointed
Buckley a member of the
Advisory Commission on
Information of the United
States Information Agen-
cy, which was chaired by
Buckley's friend Frank
Shakespeare. Buckley had
spearheaded conservative
support for Nixon during
the 1968 campaign.

In November 1970, Jim
Buckley, running as the
Conservative party candi-
date, was elected U.S.
senator from New York.
When Jim announced at
his victory celebration, "I
am the voice of the new
politics," Bill remarked to
friends, "La nouvelle politique, c'est god damn well
moi."

Buckley, who initially
criticized Vice-President
Spiro Agnew's strident
attacks on student demon-
strators and the press,
eventually became a friend
and admirer.

LIFE

KHRUSHCHEV REMEMBERS
The Cuban Missile Crisis

THE BUCKLEYS
A Gifted American Family

The Buckleys at their
family home in Connecticut

DECEMBER 18 · 1970 · 50¢

ALFRED EISENSTAEDT, LIFE MAGAZINE © 1970. TIME INC.

After Jim Buckley's election, *Life* and *Newsweek* both ran features comparing the Buckley family to the Kennedys. Buckley enjoyed the attention, but was not flattered by the comparison to an upwardly mobile Irish Catholic family.

Even though Chilean president Salvador Allende was a Socialist, Buckley believed his government was a beachhead for Soviet Communism in Latin America. When E. Howard Hunt was arrested for the Watergate burglary, Buckley, who had known him since they served together in the CIA, came to Hunt's aid.

UPI

WIDE WORLD

Former Nixon aide Patrick Buchanan (left) and journalist Richard Reeves prepare to join Buckley on his television show *Firing Line*.

In 1980, Henry Kissinger, New York senator Alfonse D'Amato, and Clare Booth Luce joined Buckley at *National Review*'s twenty-fifth anniversary banquet at the Plaza Hotel in New York.

From 1973 to 1976, George Will was *National Review*'s Washington columnist. His criticisms of Nixon and Agnew during the Watergate scandal angered many of the magazine's readers and some of its editors.

At Cadanou's Book Store in Gstaad, Switzerland, John Kenneth Galbraith, David Niven, and Buckley vied to see whose books would be displayed most prominently.

Among Buckley's closest friends and sailing companions were Evan Galbraith (right), a classmate at Yale who became ambassador to France, and Richard Clurman, *Time*'s former chief of correspondents.

When Christopher Buckley returned from working aboard a tramp steamer, his parents were happy to see him, but not the tattoo that he had acquired.

When Ronald Reagan
became president in 1980,
he and Buckley remained
close friends. Here
Reagan greets Buckley at
the White House as John
Cardinal O'Connor looks
on.

In March 1986, Bill and
Pat Buckley attend a state
dinner for Canada's
Conservative party prime
minister Brian Mulroney.

PART FOUR

The Establishment Conservative

He perceived himself as a bridge between us and the administration and not as someone being in the opposition.

—M. Stanton Evans, interview with the author

CHAPTER 15

An Exhilarating Time

In the aftermath of Lyndon Johnson's landslide victory in 1964, political commentators gave up both the Republicans and the conservative movement for lost. Envisioning himself as the heir of Roosevelt's New Deal, Johnson rammed through an overwhelmingly Democratic Congress a program for a Great Society whose scope and cost easily surpassed Roosevelt's.

As the inheritor of Truman's Cold War policies, Johnson also committed the United States to victory over the Communist forces in South Vietnam. While he had pledged in his 1964 campaign not to enlist "American boys to do the fighting for Asian boys," he did precisely that. By the end of 1965, 200,000 Americans would be fighting in Vietnam, and by 1968, 500,000. Johnson, Buckley quipped, was "a man of his most recent word." [1]

Johnson's programs, meant to inspire a new unity among Americans, rent the society in two and destroyed what remained of Roosevelt and Truman's original coalition. His landslide proved the death knell rather than the consummation of Democratic liberalism.

Johnson's foreign policy became the target of a large, militant antiwar movement, centered in the nation's colleges, and Johnson's "War on Poverty" did not calm black resentments against economic and social discrimination. Major riots engulfed northern cities each summer. The spirit of political rebellion fueled a cultural revolt that took root in university towns and in cosmopolitan cities like New York and San Francisco. Avant-garde art went hand in hand with rock 'n' roll; sexual liberation with Third World liberation; marijuana and LSD with Leninist study circles. By the end of Johnson's term, the society was in a kind of turmoil that it had not experienced since the 1930s.

Many conservatives, who had come of age in the quiet of the fifties, were plunged into a turmoil of their own. Some remained shell-shocked from Goldwater's 1964 defeat; others, like Karl Hess, Barry Goldwater's speech writer in 1964, joined forces with the Left against the Vietnam War; the YAF split into right and left wings over the war, the draft, and the legalization of marijuana. But Bill Buckley was strangely at home. "I thought it was an exhilarating time, even though more clearly than at any other time I can think of, the country was really coming apart," he recalled.

Buckley's intense, polemical style thrived in the turmoil of the sixties. He found himself in tune with the prevailing spirit of political iconoclasm and confrontation and with the elevation of political, moral, and aesthetic questions to existential preeminence. *

Even his manner of speech and argumentation, which had seemed at once effete and overly strident in the fifties, fit the times. The same young audiences who pondered the surrealistic lyrics of Bob Dylan's *Highway 61 Revisited* or *Blonde on Blonde* were willing to listen to and enjoy Buckley's elegantly crafted speeches, even if they disagreed with every word he said and had only the vaguest notion what a Gnostic heresy was.

I

Buckley was a regular fixture on college campuses. Students flocked to his lectures the way they did to rock concerts. When Buckley spoke at Rutgers in September 1967, for instance, he was scheduled on a Friday night—the night reserved for big-name entertainment —and was placed in the gymnasium, where a capacity crowd of more than three thousand students came to hear him speak on "The Responsibility of Students." At his speeches, he practiced what he called "rhetorical brinkmanship" in order to gain their attention. At

---

* Yale professor Paul Weiss, reflecting in 1967 on the Buckley of two decades before, called him the "grandfather of the student revolution."

Rutgers, he called a Democratic think tank a "zoo," described Communists as "barbarians," and made fun of Martin Luther King. "Don Giovanni died a nervous wreck for fear there was one woman somewhere he had not seduced. I live in constant fear that I will die before having the opportunity to say no to Martin Luther King."[2]

But he also took his students through winding analyses of constitutional paradoxes. In the mid-sixties, he called on students to pay heed to Aristotle and St. Augustine ("We must acknowledge the superiority of some [minds] to others," he would tell them), and he defended the political repression of civil rights and antiwar protesters on constitutional grounds and according to the theory of political orthodoxy that he had acquired from Willmoore Kendall. One reporter who traveled with Buckley during a speaking tour saw a professor and an entertainer struggling for supremacy within the same person. "One just never knows about Buckley," Larry DuBois noted. "Sometimes one thinks he's really serious about getting through to people. Sometimes one thinks he'd rather be cute, rather caricature their own image of himself instead of get through."[3]

But in the sixties, Buckley became best known not as a writer or speaker but as a television performer. Television was the medium through which he projected his own views and personality onto the canvas of the sixties. Buckley became a regular guest on talk shows like *Today*, as well as the host of *Firing Line*.

The original format of *Firing Line,* which aired on WOR beginning April 30, 1966, was that of a debate between the host and his guest. But it was extraordinary in that Neal Freeman's model was the prize fights that were shown every Friday night on national television. "I was thinking that *Firing Line* ought to be a challenge to the liberal establishment to see if their champions could go three rounds with the boy wonder. It was the fight of the week." And in its first years, Freeman recalled, *Firing Line* was a "bareknuckled intellectual brawl."

The debate between Buckley and his guests often became heated and angry, spurred in part by Buckley's *ad hominem* attacks. The ethic of the boxing ring applied. Buckley was perfectly amiable off camera, but on camera he would do everything he could to discredit his opponent. With liberal and left-wing guests, Buckley was not above trying to discredit their opinions by attacking their past or by likening their views to those of suspected or admitted Communists. It little mattered whether his guests were also his friends.

Brandeis professor and columnist Max Lerner appeared on the show to discuss his support for Communist China's admission to the

United Nations. But he was amazed when Buckley, whom he thought of as a friend, immediately put him on the defensive: "Some people hold it unfortunate that the views of Mr. Lerner have, in large part, been translated into policy over the years. Certainly, the subjugated peoples behind the Iron Curtain have reason to be sorrowful. . . ."

Rather than discuss Lerner's reasons for supporting China's admission to the U.N., Buckley took the oblique tack of associating Lerner's views with those of alleged Communist Owen Lattimore. Lerner found himself arguing about the questions themselves.

> BUCKLEY: . . . are you impatient with a public that says, "Look, I don't want to hear the freshest advice of Owen Lattimore on Far Eastern policy."
> LERNER: I'm not terribly interested in debating Owen Lattimore with you at this point, regardless of the time at our disposal.
> BUCKLEY: I'm not debating Owen Lattimore.
> LERNER: I understand. But you asked me how I felt about him . . .
> BUCKLEY: I don't care how you feel about him.[4]

Buckley could sometimes be brutally insulting. He snarled when he took on Yale historian Staughton Lynd, who had returned in the summer of 1966 from a trip to Hanoi, North Vietnam.

> BUCKLEY: . . . I wonder why . . . you thought that arriving in Hanoi, with a Communist cohort and Communist hosts, anybody would feel any obligation to tell you anything truthful? Were you in a position where you could actually exercise your scholarly apparatus or did they simply treat you in Hanoi the way the average observer would have expected that they would treat you in Hanoi —simply that, here is an American idiot, whom we are in a position to manipulate. . . .[5]

In the show's first year, guests were eager to appear, but after prominent liberals saw how their colleagues were treated, Buckley and Freeman, who was helping to line up guests, found it increasingly difficult to find willing recruits. "After about thirty of them had been carried out on a stretcher," Freeman recalled, "the word went out, 'I won't dignify this protofascist by appearing on his program.' It became increasingly difficult to get big-name liberal guests." Asked why

Robert Kennedy would not appear, Buckley quipped, "Why does baloney reject the grinder?"[6]

Buckley and Warren Steibel, who became the show's producer in its first year, altered the format at the station executive's urging. They made Buckley's lawyer and friend, C. Dickerman Williams, the host. This removed any pretense of Buckley's neutrality—*Firing Line* was now billed as a debate between Buckley and his guest. The new format was useful in preventing open brawls, but its net effect was to loosen rather than tighten the reins on Buckley. "In fact it is easy to be more adversarial if you are not the host," Steibel admitted.

As Freeman recalls, many station executives were "appalled by the level of intensity" of the shows. But what disturbed station executives charmed television audiences. *Firing Line* was an overnight success. Not only conservatives but liberals and leftists regularly watched it. And it was most successful in cosmopolitan settings. In liberal San Francisco, when public station KQED skipped the show one week because tape had been held up in transit, it got a record 180 calls of complaint in the first hour. The liberal TV critic Terrence O'Flaherty of the *San Francisco Chronicle* said of Buckley, "He's a real honest-to-god personality, one of the few live personalities on a dead medium; he's the best thing on the air."[7] In 1968, *Firing Line* won an Emmy, the television industry's highest award.

Firing Line took Buckley's career one step beyond where the mayor's race had left it. In Janaury 1967, *The Wall Street Journal* did a page-one feature. In March 1967, *Harper's* profiled him; and in November, *Time* certified his celebrity by putting him on the cover.

His celebrity was based partly on his being the man whom liberals loved to hate. Norman Mailer wrote him, "I think you are finally going to displace me as the most hated man in America. And of course the position is bearable only if one is number one."[8] In *Harper's,* Larry King wrote about Buckley, "His enemies, laid end to end, would reach from here to Southern Purgatory, to which they variously damn him for inciting radical hatred, dividing the Republican Party, defaming Democracy, and betraying the John Birch Society." But King also described Buckley as "the social darling of so many Establishment liberals."

The Wall Street Journal described his appeal:

The spectacle of William F. Buckley, Jr., spearing a foe . . . holds much the same fascination as the sight of a cat stalking a bird. If you sympathize with the bird, you can still find it possible to admire the grace and ferocity of its pursuer—and certainly the arch-conservative Mr. Buckley has a growing following among liberals who detest his views but frankly admire his panache.[9]

Buckley, who understood that his political and public personality was a facade, was not altogether pleased with his reputation.* In December 1967, he wrote Neal Freeman, "I am a very nice man, but I have a lot of enemies because my tone isn't right." [10] But he was also delighted by the controversy that he was causing. On the wall of his *National Review* office, he posted the hate mail that he was getting from the Left and the far Right. And as he recounted to *Time* interviewer Larry DuBois incidents in which he had angered liberals, Buckley would frequently interject, "What fun," and "That was great fun." [11]

II

In his politics, Buckley continued to call for the obliteration of communism—by any means necessary. In 1965, he argued in *National Review* for a preemptive strike against China's nuclear facilities. Such a strike, Buckley wrote, would "probably have the effect of damping down the trend toward general war." [12] He and Burnham endorsed the use of nuclear weapons in Vietnam to bring the war against the Vietcong to a speedy conclusion.

Buckley's attitude toward the politics of the New Left was little different from that of other conservatives. In 1965, Buckley described New York antiwar marchers as "young slobs strutting their epicene resentment. . . . I wonder how these self-conscious *boulevardiers* of protest would have fared if a platoon of American soldiers who have seen the gore in South Vietnam had parachuted down into their mincing ranks." [13]

He opposed the new civil rights laws passed under the Johnson administration and wanted even the Reverend Martin Luther King's nonviolent civil disobedience suppressed.

---

* Buckley had taken umbrage when his debate victims charged that they had been deceived by his offstage affability. *New York Post* columnist James Wechsler had written of Buckley's debating style, "You allow yourself to become mellow and amiable, then suddenly you discover he is practically calling you a traitor. It's a pretty effective technique, but I've learned to cope with it. I just won't allow myself to get amiable." Buckley replied, "In the first place, I didn't practically call him a traitor; you can't *practically* call anyone a traitor. The real problem is that in America your likes and dislikes are expected to follow ideological lines. In England, it's not considered surprising that people who disagree sharply have social intercourse." (*New York Times Magazine*, September 9, 1965.)

Repression is an unpleasant instrument [he wrote], but it is absolutely necessary for civilizations that believe in order and human
rights. I wish to God Hitler and Lenin had been repressed. And
word should be gently got through to the non-violent avenger Dr.
King, that in the unlikely event that he succeeds in mobilizing his
legions, they will be most efficiently, indeed most zestfully, repressed.[14]

On the other hand, Buckley betrayed a tolerant, even inquisitive,
attitude toward the counterculture. Riding through the East Side on
his Honda, often with a passenger in back, his fashionably long hair
blowing in the wind, Buckley showed the influence of the times. He
published his articles in *Playboy* and *Esquire,* the two most *au courant*
commercial magazines. And while he rejected much of what he heard
and saw in the counterculture, he was seized with curiosity about
what others heard or saw in it.

The way he learned about the Beatles and rock 'n' roll was typical.
Alan Freed, the New York disk jockey who popularized rock 'n' roll,
lived near the Buckleys on Wallacks Point. One summer afternoon in
1964, the Buckleys had Freed and his wife over, and Freed, upon
learning that Buckley had never listened to Elvis Presley or Fats Domino, invited him and Pat to a party at his house the next evening,
where Domino was going to play. The Buckleys arrived too late for
the music, but in time to find the entire band, fully clothed, in the
swimming pool; soon afterwards, Buckley borrowed his son's record
collection and spent an evening listening to it.

At first, he didn't like what he heard. He wrote of the Beatles, "The
Beatles are not merely awful, I would consider it sacrilegious to say
anything less than that they are God-awful. They are so unbelievably
horrible, so appallingly unmusical, so dogmatically insensitive to the
magic of the art, that they qualify as the crowned heads of anti-
music."[15] But in 1968, he changed his mind somewhat: "I mean how
can one prevail against them? The answer is: One cannot. And even
if they are hard to listen to, there is an exuberance there that is quite
unmatched anywhere in the world."[16]

He was even less guarded in his praise of *Hair,* a 1968 rock musical.
Citing a line from André Malraux that Burnham often quoted, Buckley
wrote:

André Malraux once put an end to a hectic discussion about the
shortcomings of modern art by saying simply, "But that's the way
our painters paint." In a sense Malraux was quite right: if this is the

way a creative section of our youth writes musicals, then we must necessarily take them seriously.[17]

III

The way in which Buckley fulfilled and eluded contemporary pre-conceptions about conservatism was most evident in his attitude toward Catholicism. He remained steadfastly opposed to Pope John and his successor's attempts to promote détente and anticolonialism. He denounced American Catholics like Daniel and Philip Berrigan who opposed the Vietnam War in the name of Christianity. And he remained immune to the kind of personal self-examination popular both among believers and nonbelievers in the fifties and sixties.

When two *Mademoiselle* interviewers asked him what "sort of person" he saw himself as, Buckley replied, "I don't study myself very much." When they asked him about Erich Fromm's *Escape from Freedom,* a psychoanalytical study of freedom, Buckley replied:

> It interested me very much. Of course, I, as a practicing Christian, feel that he is really talking about a series of problems for which I have a very orthodox solution. I'm not tortured by the problems that torture a great many other people because I do very sincerely and very simply believe in God and in the whole of the Christian experience. And there are enough resources in it to show me where to go.[18]

He displayed the same openness and lack of dogmatism toward Catholic social doctrine that he did toward the counterculture. Buckley urged the Church to allow married priests; he refused to follow the Church in opposing contraception and divorce; and he applauded the call of Vatican II for tolerance toward other religious beliefs and practices.

In 1966, as liberal organizations were beginning to press for easing the laws forbidding abortion, Buckley chided the Church in his column for lobbying against any change.

> Surely the principal meaning of the religious liberty pronouncements of Vatican II is that other men must be left free to practice the dictates of their own conscience, and if other religions and other individuals do not believe that under certain circumstances abortion is wrong, it would appear to contradict the burden of the Vatican's position to put pressure on the law to maintain the supremacy of one's position.[19]

Buckley, whose Catholicism had always a strain of English Catholic aestheticism, was disturbed by Vatican II's replacement of the Latin Mass with one in each nation's vernacular, but he earnestly tried to adjust. He became a lector—a reader—at St. Mary's, the church in Stamford that he attended every Sunday. But after three years of helping to read the Mass, he gave up. "The proliferation of oddball liturgical stuff offended me," Buckley explained. In an article that year in *Commonweal*,[20] he endorsed Sir Arnold Lunn's wry proposal that each church have one Sunday service in Latin for the "educated few." *

Buckley was aware that his cosmopolitanism and curiosity set him apart from many others who called themselves conservatives. "I feel I qualify spiritually and philosophically as a conservative, but temperamentally I am not of the breed," he told *Time* in 1967.[21]

IV

Buckley followed the same pattern of cultural liberalism and spiritual and political conservatism in the way that he brought up his teenage son, Christopher, during the sixties. As a father, Buckley combined an outward openness and lack of authoritarianism with a determination that Christopher should grow up to be a devout Catholic.

In New York, the Buckleys sent Christopher to St. David's, a strict Catholic school. But at home, Buckley was an extremely lenient parent. Referring to the leader of an LSD cult, Christopher said of his childhood, "I was raised the way I would expect Timothy Leary's children to be raised. I think the last time I was told to be home by a certain hour was when I was fifteen."[22]

In 1967, however, Buckley decided to send Christopher to boarding school and took the boy to see both Taft and Portsmouth Priory. Taft, which was close to Stamford, was a conventional boarding school that was then being touched by the rebellious spirit of the sixties. On the other hand, Portsmouth, ten miles outside of Newport, Rhode Island, was an extremely strict Catholic school set up in 1926 for the upper-class Irish. It was run by Benedictine monks, and the students followed a daily regimen of prayer and study lasting from six-thirty in the morning until ten at night. Unlike Taft students, they were not

---

* Sir Arnold Lunn had written to the London *Times* on the letterhead of the Catholic Mass Society, of which he was the secretary. "It is said that the Latin Mass is only for the educated few. Surely Mother Church, in all her charity, can make a little room even for the educated few?"

allowed to leave on weekends or to visit the town where the school was located. "I loved Taft and loathed Portsmouth and couldn't figure out for the life of me why he wanted to send me there," Christopher said.

But Buckley wanted his son to receive a Catholic education. When Christopher told him that he wanted to go to Taft, his father proposed that they list the pros and cons of each school. "I said OK, and he said, 'Well, the Catholic education for one.' And I said, 'Why is that a pro?' And his answer must have been so convincing that I've blocked it out. By the time we got to the third pro on the Portsmouth side, I knew I was a goner."

V

During the sixties, Buckley became close friends with Garry Wills, who had been his protégé. After his summer at *National Review* in 1957, Wills had gotten a Ph.D. in classics from Yale and had taken a teaching job at Johns Hopkins. In the meantime, he had managed to write books on G. K. Chesterton, Roman culture, and *Politics and Catholic Freedom,* based on Buckley's controversy with *America.* Wills was one of the few people whom Buckley described as a "genius." He saw in Wills not only his own quick wit, but a capacity for scholarship and reflection that he lacked. Wills could be a journalist *and* a scholar. "He was in awe of Garry," John Leonard said. "He was so smart. He was so mature. Bill plays around with his Latin. Garry knew it."

Buckley was equally, if not more, impressed by Wills's moral and religious qualities. Wills had come to *National Review,* like other young recruits, in order to write, but unlike John Leonard or Joan Didion, he never simply wanted to write. He always saw writing as part of a higher moral calling. "Garry burned with the pure moral flame," Leonard recalled. "Everybody else had some career sense, but he wasn't in it to be a writer."

Wills defined himself as a *National Review* conservative. He denounced Eisenhower's invitation to Khrushchev in 1959 and backed Goldwater in 1964. He admired Buckley's politics, seeing him as a moderate fending off the challenges of the extreme Right.* But even

---

* In a letter defending Buckley's stand against the John Birch Society, Wills wrote in 1965, "The pathos of the conservative movement is the futility of most of its demonstrations. Those who keep quietly at their business, who stay balanced even under the severest

then Wills differed with Buckley and the other editors on certain points. As a traditional Catholic, he was not enamored of the free market, nor was he unquestioningly anti-Communist. Having taught catechism at black schools when he was in seminary, he was a proponent of the civil rights movement. He was also an avid defender of Vatican II.

Buckley let himself be influenced by Wills. Under Wills's prodding, he drew a sharp distinction between racist and constitutional opposition to integration. He published Wills's highly favorable review of James Baldwin's *The Fire Next Time* and an article by Wills in which he argued for "preferential hiring" for minorities.[23] He also allowed Wills to praise effusively Vatican II in *National Review*. The "present renewal," Wills wrote, "is not a dissolution of the unchanging original church, but the breakup of a temporal crust over the ancient vitality of the faith."[24]

Wills's "conservative" argument for affirmative action—"those who glory in inherited values and traditions must admit accountability for historic wrongs"—temporarily won Buckley over. In 1964 Buckley wrote a column proposing special measures to aid blacks.[25] And Wills's defense of Vatican II probably contributed to Buckley's willingness to become a lector for three years.

According to Wills, his dissident views only began to cause friction between him and Buckley in 1965, when Wills signed a letter in *The New York Times* protesting Cardinal Spellman's decision to exile antiwar Jesuit priest Daniel Berrigan to Mexico. Wills signed the letter on the same libertarian grounds that he had backed Buckley's criticism of *Mater et Magistra*—believing that dissent was permissible in both cases—but by backing a priest who questioned the basis of anti-Communist foreign policy, Wills had threatened the basis of *National Review*'s and Buckley's politics. "Bill criticized my signing the letter, and we had our first serious argument on this matter," Wills wrote later.[26]

But as late as 1966, Wills and Buckley believed they were close friends and part of the same conservative movement. And when the right-wing book publisher Neil McCaffrey, then the head of Arlington House, offered Wills $7,000 to write a biography of Bill, he accepted.

---

provocation, are doing the finest service possible to the conservative movement. Bill Buckley is a marvelous example." (Buckley Papers.)

In the mid-sixties, Buckley also made two other close friends outside of conservative political circles. Buckley had always been friendly with liberals and left-wingers like Mailer and Kempton, but he had not counted them among his very close friends. Richard Clurman and John Kenneth Galbraith were the first liberal intellectuals whom Buckley really became close friends with.

Buckley's friendship with each reflected his growing celebrity, and probably would not have been possible if Buckley had not denounced the John Birch Society and White Citizens Councils, and distanced himself from those conservatives who believed that Goldwater was the nation's salvation. In 1964, he met Richard Clurman, the chief of correspondents at *Time,* at a dinner party staged by a New York hostess in order to bring the two men together. Clurman immediately discovered a different Buckley from the one he knew by reputation. Clurman had just been through an editors' lunch at *Time* with presidential candidate Barry Goldwater, and he and the other editors had been appalled at Goldwater's inability to answer even routine questions. He asked Buckley, "How does someone with your obvious intellectual gifts become a prime supporter of a very pleasant, but obviously such a limited, man?" According to Clurman, Buckley replied, "Barry Goldwater is a man of tremendously decent instincts, and with a basic banal but important understanding of the Constitution and what it means in American life." "But what would happen if he were elected President of the United States?" Clurman asked. "That might be a serious problem," Buckley quipped.

"At that moment," Clurman later explained, "we became friends."

The next year Buckley met liberal economist John Kenneth Galbraith, who had been ambassador to India during the Kennedy administration. While Buckley was in Switzerland, writing *The Unmaking of a Mayor,* actor David Niven, with whom Buckley had become friendly, invited the Buckleys out to dinner with the Galbraiths. Like Buckley, Galbraith spent about two months each winter in the vicinity of Gstaad, skiing and writing. They shared an admiration for each other's prose and a love of wisecracks, and began to ski together.

When we were first making our way down a difficult trail one afternoon in those early days, I had some difficulty, and when I got to the bottom, Bill said, "How long have you been skiing?" I decided I didn't want to give him anything, so I said, "Thirty years." And reflecting on the general incompetence of my descent, he said, "That's about the same time you've been studying economics."

Galbraith and Niven became Buckley's closest friends in Switzerland, and Galbraith became Buckley's first choice of a debating opponent.

VI

As Buckley's social life expanded, so did his professional life. To Pat Buckley's consternation, the fast pace of his life quickened still further. In 1964, when he had taken on three columns a week, he had announced in *National Review* that he was abandoning the lecture circuit, but he continued to give as many as seventy lectures a year. He had abandoned writing *The Revolt Against the Masses,* but he had not entirely resigned himself to being a popularizer. He spent his 1967 winter in Switzerland preparing an anthology of modern American conservative thought, which was eventually published under the title *Did You Ever See a Dream Walking?* He devoted at least one day every two weeks to *Firing Line* and continued to spend at least two days every two weeks on *National Review.* In addition, he took on a new and potentially perilous career.

In its first seven years, the Omaha radio station that Buckley had bought in 1958 to defray *National Review*'s deficit had lost money each year. Rusher figured that without KOWH, *National Review* would have run a deficit only two years between 1958 and 1965 rather than an average of $55,000 annually. But in 1965, Buckley hired twenty-one-year-old Peter Starr as a salesman for KOWH. Buckley had first met Starr eight years before, when he hired him to take care of his boat, and the two had been regular sailing partners.

The gregarious, charming Starr did so well selling ads that he became the station's general manager within a year, and in 1966, for the first time, KOWH was in the black. Buckley immediately proposed that *National Review* begin buying more radio stations. Rusher and the other *National Review* directors balked at this move.

> At that point, the board of directors under my stimulus gently began easing *National Review* out of the picture [Rusher recalled]. It was not because they didn't want to make a profit or because they didn't think Buckley was going to, but because they more and more began to see some huge electronic dog wagging a small journalistic tail. They insisted on separation, and I remember Bill, even in the board meeting, saying, "You'll be sorry."

In a letter, Rusher commented wryly on Buckley's business sense:

Not long ago and very shrewdly you observed that I do not have
"the dry hole psychology." [The oil wildcatter's idea that if one
hole is dry, oil will gush out of another.] Another way to put it is
that your preferred sort of business enterprise tends to be an extension of your strong natural gambling impulse—an urge to shoot
craps with an idea that appeals to you; the more gimmicky the
better.[27]

But Buckley was undeterred. He and Starr severed the station's
connection to *National Review* and established Starr Broadcasting
Group, with Buckley as chairman and two-thirds owner and Starr as
president and one-third owner. By then, William Casey recalled,
Buckley had become a "wheeler-dealer." Starr, with Buckley's enthusiastic support, began buying radio stations, first one in Sioux
Falls, South Dakota, and then another in Kansas City.

Buckley initially left much of the operation to Starr, under the assumption that Starr knew what he was doing. Buckley thought he
could enjoy the rewards of fast-lane entrepreneurship without suffering either the tedium of detail or the anxiety of teetering between
wealth and Chapter Eleven bankruptcy.

CHAPTER 16

The Most Right, Viable Candidate

Lyndon Johnson's policies not only fueled a rebellion among college students and minorities but they also stoked a growing right-wing movement among middle-class ethnics in the North, white southerners, and the upwardly mobile white Protestants of the prosperous Sunbelt. In northern cities, Irish and Italian Catholics, whose parents or grandparents had often worked their way up from poverty, resented the special favors they saw Johnson conferring on blacks through the War on Poverty. White southerners saw the Texan Johnson doing the Yankees' dirty work in the South by enforcing voting rights and school desegregation. All these groups viewed with alarm the student and black movements' assault upon patriotism and the Protestant ethic.

This revolt was fully evident in Bill Buckley's surprising success in the 1965 New York mayoral contest and Ronald Reagan's resounding defeat of incumbent Democrat "Pat" Brown in the 1966 California's governor's race. As the more astute politicians realized, while the left-wing revolt was more visible and noisy, the right-wing revolt portended a massive repudiation of Democratic liberalism among groups that had been its bulwark in the past.

Two politicians above all were ready to prove liberalism's demise on a national scale: former Vice-President Richard Nixon and former Alabama governor George Wallace. Nixon was the antithesis of the sixties counterculture and New Left: he was anything but a "beautiful person," with wide simian jowls highlighted by a perpetual five-o'clock shadow and small shifty eyes that betokened ulterior motives. Nixon was by no means a *National Review* conservative. Although he had made his mark as a California congressman by doggedly pursuing Alger Hiss on behalf of the House Un-American Activities Committee and had won election to the Senate by "red-baiting" his liberal opponent, Democrat Helen Gahagan Douglas, Nixon had always been a centrist on economic and civil rights issues. In 1960, running against Kennedy, Nixon had received a third of the black vote. And because of his identification with the Eisenhower administration's relatively lean military budgets, he had been perceived as less of a Cold Warrior than his opponent.

But Nixon learned the importance of the Republican right wing in his unsuccessful bid in 1962 to become governor of California. And beginning in 1966, he began actively to court Republican conservatives, including Bill Buckley.

George Wallace, on the other hand, was not the antithesis, but the mirror image, of the New Left rebellion. He was the rebellion turned Right—a rabble-rouser and a demagogue. His defiance of federal integration had propelled him into the Alabama governor's seat in 1962 and into national attention when, in June 1963, he tried to prevent black students from enrolling at the University of Alabama. In 1964, he had run for President in the Democratic primaries on an anti-integration and law-and-order platform, scoring impressively not only in the South but in the North.

Like Nixon, Wallace was not a *National Review* conservative. While he opposed integration on the grounds of states' rights, he was clearly motivated by racism, that is, a belief in the separation of the races, rather than a belief in federalism. And while he shared the conservatives' support for the war and opposition to the Washington bureaucracy, he was an economic populist who prided himself on his appropriations for education, health, and his programs to aid the poor and aged. But Wallace also wanted the support of Buckley—not so much for the votes he commanded but for the legitimacy among conservatives that he conferred.

I

Buckley had first met Nixon in July 1957 through Ralph de Toledano. "Buckley was somewhat impressed meeting the Vice-President of the United States, and Nixon was impressed meeting this great intellectual," Toledano recalled. "They sat there looking at each other, both of them intimidated by the other. Finally, I threw something into the conversation and suddenly it became animated."

Buckley admired Nixon as the man who had defended Whittaker Chambers against Alger Hiss, but he distrusted him on domestic issues—a distrust that was deepened in 1960 when Nixon agreed to Nelson Rockefeller's amendments to the Republican platform. But while Buckley's attitude toward Nixon had not changed markedly since 1960, his attitude toward politics had. He was no longer looking for a paradigmatic conservative. Instead, he was willing to back a nonconservative candidate as long as that candidate was receptive to conservative influence.

Nixon appeared to harbor resentments against Buckley for not supporting him in 1960. Columnists Rowland Evans and Robert Novak reported in October 1965 that Nixon, asked about the John Birch Society, "replied that the Birchers could be handled but that the real menace to the Republican party came from the Buckleyites."[1] In December 1965, when Nixon interviewed *St. Louis Globe-Democrat* reporter Patrick Buchanan, a former Georgetown member of the Young Americans for Freedom, for a job, he asked Buchanan: "You're not as conservative as William F. Buckley, are you?"

But Nixon's resentment was fleeting. He understood that he would have to win over the Republican conservatives if he wanted the nomination. And he hired Buchanan, who thought of Buckley as a hero, to help him win over the Right. "Nixon realized that just as in 1960, he had to make his peace with the Rockefeller wing of the party; in 1968, to be nominated, he had to make his peace with the Goldwater wing of the party," Buchanan recalled.

Buchanan's very first task was to appease *National Review*'s publisher and editor, who had been annoyed by Nixon's remarks to Evans and Novak the previous October. In April, Buchanan sent *National Review* what he later described as a "tortured letter" attempting to explain away what Nixon had said. According to Buchanan, Nixon meant that by repudiating the John Birch Society, Buckley had "made himself a much stronger candidate and a greater threat to the Republican candidate, Rep. Lindsay."[2]

In June, Nixon sent Buckley a complimentary letter about his columns on Vietnam, and in September, Buchanan had lunch with Buckley and Rusher. Meanwhile, Buckley had begun to describe Nixon in his columns as the "apparent designee" of conservative Republicans.[3] In early January 1967, Nixon, spurred by Reagan's victory in California, invited Buckley, Rusher, and Neal Freeman, along with Victor Lasky and Hobart Lewis, to spend a Sunday afternoon with him.

Nixon was living then on Fifth Avenue in the same apartment building as Nelson Rockefeller. When his guests arrived, he served them South African brandy—according to Neal Freeman, a subtle "Nixonian touch" designed to show his ideological sympathies with his guests. Then he treated them to a three-hour review of politics and world affairs, ranging from Southeast Asia to Ronald Reagan's victory. "He gave one of the most brilliant *tour de forces* that I can recall," Lasky said. Freeman was amazed at how Nixon could "interrelate an event in Angola to an event in Taiwan to an event in Bonn." Even Rusher was impressed.

Buckley participated animatedly in the discussion. When it turned to the question of Reagan, Buckley said that he thought it was "preposterous even to consider Reagan as an alternative. . . . Reagan is an ex-actor, who has been in office now for a month," he told Nixon. "The idea of his running for President is loony. The fight is going to be between you and Rockefeller." But Nixon disagreed. "It isn't preposterous," he said. "Anyone who is the governor of California is *ex officio* a candidate for President."

Buckley was completely taken by Nixon. Neal Freeman described his reaction: "I knew when we went down the elevator, early in the evening, that Bill Buckley was going to find some reason to support Richard Nixon. Bill was *very* impressed with how wide-ranging and thoughtful Nixon's conversation had been."

By the spring, Buckley was openly admitting his support for Nixon in interviews that he gave and in the question-and-answer periods during his speeches. When the *Miami News* editors asked him at a meeting in their editorial office whom he considered the "wisest Republican choice" for 1968, he told them Nixon. "The wisest choice would be the one who would win," he said. "No sense running Mona Lisa in a beauty contest. I'd be for the most right, viable candidate who could win."[4]

Nixon, Buchanan, and a new Nixon aide, New York banker Peter Flanigan, continued to shower Buckley with attention. Nixon sent him notes complimenting him on columns and wishing him luck in his candidacy for the board of the Yale Corporation. In September, Nixon appeared on *Firing Line,* and afterwards, he stayed up until one in the morning talking with Buckley and reporter James J. Kilpatrick, who was planning to profile Nixon for *National Review.* Buckley was "astonished" by Nixon's patience in answering Kilpatrick, who after an evening of bourbon was becoming increasingly persistent in his questioning.

In his column, Buckley never explicitly endorsed Nixon, but by framing the choice as one between Nixon and the liberal Rockefeller, Buckley implicitly supported him. "If you say to someone, 'I don't think Reagan is a serious candidate,' and he knows that you loathe Rockefeller, you don't have to say , 'I'm for you,' " Buckley said.

Buckley's decision to go with Nixon was consistent with the approach to politics that he had adopted from Burnham and Chambers. While Buckley continued to admire Nixon's anticommunism ("his anti-Communist resolution is as firm as just about anything in national politics," he wrote in April 1968), he never described Nixon as a conservative candidate.[5] Instead, he believed that Nixon, in contrast to his principal opponents, Romney and Rockefeller, was an electable candidate who would be accountable to conservatives.

Buckley continued to discount Reagan as a candidate, correctly sensing that Reagan was not eager to run and was being pushed in that direction, like Goldwater in 1962 and 1963, by zealous lieutenants and former draft-Goldwater organizer Clifton White. Reagan himself denied to Buckley that he wanted the nomination. Buckley also hesitated to subject Reagan to the intellectual rigors of *Firing Line,* and remained skeptical of both Reagan's credentials to be President and his electability. "Buckley thought that at the time Reagan was not ready for prime-time politics," Neal Freeman recalled.

Neal Freeman attributed Buckley's decision to support Nixon to a combination of Nixon's solicitations and the fact that Buckley expected less of Nixon than he might of a fellow conservative. "Nixon not only courted Buckley assiduously, directly and through surrogates over a number of years, but I think Buckley held Nixon to lower standards ideologically and intellectually because Nixon had never been in Buckley's mind a member of the conservative movement."

Buckley's decision split the *National Review* editorial board and caused his first important political break with Rusher. While Buckley was moving into Nixon's camp, Rusher was drumming up support and building pressure for Reagan's candidacy. The disagreement between the two men reflected their differing political appproaches and estimations of Reagan and Nixon—Rusher was far more sanguine than Buckley about Reagan's abilities and had more or less despised Nixon since 1954, when Nixon had served as the Eisenhower administration's point man against McCarthy.

In the year and a half leading up to the Republican Convention in August 1968, Rusher fired off bimonthly memoranda to *National Review*'s editors on the progress of Reagan's candidacy and the perils of supporting Nixon. These memos were remarkably prescient.

In Rusher's first memo, he predicted that George Romney—then seen as the leading candidate—would fade. In March 1967, Rusher warned that Charles Percy, then being groomed as a candidate, had swung too far to the Left to replace Romney when he faltered. "The question we will have to answer sooner or later," Rusher warned, "is: Nixon or Reagan?"[6]

On the editorial board, Rusher was supported by Rickenbacker and later by Frank Meyer. Burnham initially backed Rockefeller and Percy (until Percy came out against the Vietnam War), but then joined Buckley in Nixon's corner.

Rusher and Rickenbacker could not hope to convince Buckley and Burnham to back Reagan, but at the magazine's quarterly editorial conference in January 1968, they were able to win agreement that the magazine would remain evenhanded toward Nixon and Reagan. Buckley kept his word on the magazine and in his column, but in his public appearances made no secret of his sympathy for Nixon's candidacy. As a result, the principal group that *National Review* could hope to affect—conservative opinion makers—came to associate Nixon with *National Review* in spite of the editors' decision in January.

Rickenbacker, feeling powerless to affect the journal for which he was accountable as a senior editor, resigned after the 1968 election. "I myself *never* voted for Nixon, and began laying plans for a graceful departure from the top rank at *NR* when WFB came out for Nixon in the fall of 1967, long before the editors ever had a chance to discuss it," Rickenbacker said.

Rusher, rather than resign, established a political identity for himself separate from the magazine and Buckley. He eventually began writing a column of his own and appearing regularly on a political debate show called *The Advocates*. It was, however, the end of any active political collaboration between Rusher and Buckley. According to Rusher, their relationship reached a "plateau."

II

As a Nixon supporter, Buckley was worried that Wallace, running as an independent, would insure a Democratic victory by preventing Nixon from winning conservative southern votes. In an April 1967 column he predicted that "Wallace would split the Republican vote, and inevitably the Democrats would prosper, save possibly in one or two states in which Wallace so devastated the Republicans as to take all their votes, permitting him a narrow victory over the Democrats."[7] But Buckley's animus toward Wallace went beyond Wallace's threat to Nixon. Buckley disliked Wallace in a way that he disliked few men in public life.

He saw Wallace as a lower-class demagogue who appealed only to people's base fears and resentments. "Alas, it is his uncouthness that seems to account for his general popularity," he wrote Conservative Book Club president Neil McCaffrey, who was favorably inclined to Wallace.[8] Buckley disliked the way that Wallace used conservative principles of minimal government and federalism to legitimate an essentially racist politics. "My goodness, but he is a dangerous man," Buckley wrote Nancy Reagan. "What I resent most is his abuse of the rhetoric and analysis of conservatism."[9] In a letter to his son, he described Wallace as "Mr. Evil" and a "great phoney."[10]

In 1968, as the election neared, Buckley set out to discredit Wallace among conservatives. He had his sharpest exchange with Wallace on *Firing Line* in January. In that debate, Buckley abandoned the facade of indignation with which he often clothed his performances on the air. Instead he displayed what producer Warren Steibel described as "real animosity."

Wallace was a formidable opponent. Not only was he a clever debater, but he ostensibly shared Buckley's position on a broad range of issues, from the war in Vietnam to the Supreme Court decision on school integration. To establish a difference, Buckley had to attack Wallace from the Right on his economic policy, but from the Left on his racial policy.

In introducing Wallace, Buckley tried to draw him into a discussion of why not one of "two hundred prominent conservatives" queried by *Human Events* backed him for President. But instead of embarrassing Wallace, he became a foil for Wallace's "populism." The moderator, C. Dickerman Williams, had to intervene constantly to calm the discussion as well as to prevent Wallace from monopolizing it.

> WALLACE: Mr. Buckley . . . I run my politics like I do in Alabama. I never went to the County Court Houses to see the county governing body. I just went to the people . . . Now you put too much credit on the support and influence of some fella in a magazine or newspaper or somebody on a college campus that might be conservative or some minister who may be conservative. But actually I go out to the masses of the people with the message that I have . . . and I don't know any prominent conservatives. . . .
>
> WALLACE: Seventy percent of the people last night on a poll on the television stations in St. Louis said they would support me. The fact is that I won the television poll on WIIC in Pittsburgh the other day and defeated Johnson, Kennedy, and Reagan by almost three to one.
>
> BUCKLEY: And they might have given more votes to Perón than they did to you, right? * . . .
>
> WALLACE: That's a real smart answer. The fact that I won a poll is that Perón might have gotten more votes. . . .
>
> BUCKLEY: We know that he got more votes than you got in Alabama.
>
> WALLACE: I got more in Alabama than you got in New York
>
> BUCKLEY: Certainly, I don't claim to be popular in New York. I'm a conservative.

After a break in the show, Buckley took a new tack, accusing Wallace of being a New Dealer rather than a conservative. Wallace demanded that Buckley be specific:

> WALLACE: . . . Name one thing in Alabama that I have supported on the governmental level that you are against.
>
> BUCKLEY: Well, it seems to me that your . . . if I may say so . . . fanatic concern for using public money for certain functions . . . that might otherwise . . .
>
> WALLACE: What . . . name them . . .
>
> BUCKLEY: Well, for instance, you want to take care of the hospi-

---

* Right-wing populist President Juan Perón was elected president of Argentina in 1946 and then established a dictatorship.

talization . . . you want to take care of old people . . .
you want to take care of the poor.

WALLACE: Are you against caring for the poor and old?

BUCKLEY: [*Laughter.*] I knew you would answer that that way. I
hate the poor. [*Laughter.*] My point is that this is a free-
enterprise country and that we have a tradition here of
private philanthropy, of philanthropy conducted by private people and under programs that haven't required
mobilization of the machinery of the state at the federal
or state or local level. That the whole tradition of your
kind of Democrat is one of enormous enthusiasm for
federal handouts. . . .

WALLACE: In the first place, in Alabama we have the highest old
age pension for destitute in our state that you'll find in
most any southern state . . . they're not people who are
. . . have income. I'm for that, myself.

BUCKLEY: You're for what?

WALLACE: Caring for destitute—average age of seventy years old.

BUCKLEY: I am too, except by the government.

Buckley began to ruffle Wallace only when he questioned his position on racial issues. Race was, oddly, Wallace's weak as well as
strong point. His past attempts to block integration were contributing
to his popularity in the North as well as the South, but his popularity,
particularly in the North, was jeopardized by his reputation as a racist. Wallace could not appear to be a racist without threatening his
support in the North. Middle-class Poles in Milwaukee and Irish Catholics in Chicago did not want their opposition to busing and public
housing in their neighborhoods to be construed as racist. And in voting for Wallace, they didn't want to be seen as voting for a racist.
Wallace realized that he could not run against integration, but rather
against what was understood to be the cause of integration—federal
interference in the states and neighborhoods.

But Buckley began to attack Wallace's ambiguity on the race issue.

MODERATOR: . . . Let's get it definitely from Governor Wallace,
whether he is a conservative or pretends to be a conservative. . . .

WALLACE: What do you mean by conservative?

MODERATOR: You give your own definition.

WALLACE: Well, my . . . conservative to me means that you
should allow, on the governmental scene, allow local
people to try to determine policies of local democratic institutions.

BUCKLEY: How can they without the vote?

WALLACE: Without what?

BUCKLEY: The vote. V-o-t-e.

WALLACE: Well . . .

BUCKLEY: What steps would you take to encourage the enfranchisement of the Negro . . .

WALLACE: Well, I've always . . . well, I'll be glad to tell you, I've always made speeches in my state in which I said anybody's entitled to vote regardless of their race or color . . . qualified under the laws of Alabama, and we had Negro citizens by the thousands who voted in 1958, when I first ran for governor, and I might say, in the runoff for governor, that they voted for me.

BUCKLEY: Is that because they didn't have the education you're talking about?

When Wallace tried to make the issue the North versus the South, Buckley pressed the attack, and this time he made Wallace lose his cool. But in doing so, he ended up sounding, he admitted, "like a liberal." It was an important moment in Buckley's political history.

WALLACE: Alabama's been treated almost as a province by the bureaucrats and the Supreme Court of the United States and that's one reason I may be in the presidential race, is I'm tired of Alabama being treated as a province.

BUCKLEY: As a taxpayer, Governor, I don't think a lot of Americans who are paying taxes into Alabama would necessarily adopt that position. Honestly, you're forcing me to sound like a liberal, which has never happened to me before in my entire life. I don't believe strings ought to be attached, but I do believe that Alabama, Alabamans ought to be protected by the Constitution of the United States.

WALLACE: Well, they are protected.

BUCKLEY: Well, they have been inadequately protected . . .

WALLACE: They haven't been inadequately protected.

MODERATOR: Governor, let's get Mr. Buckley to fill in the particulars. In what respect aren't Alabamans protected by the Constitution?

BUCKLEY: They have not been protected, for instance, in Selma, Alabama, it seemed to me notorious, that the rights of certain Negroes were not adequately protected by the sheriff down there.

WALLACE: Well, of course, that's totally untrue, and let me say
. . . my wife received the Negro vote in Selma* . . .
Nobody was killed in Selma. Eight people got
skinned on the head . . . not enough to put on a post-
age stamp. And yet they killed forty-one people in
Detroit. They killed fifty-one in Los Angeles.
["They" refers to black rioters.] So where has all the
trouble erupted in our country? . . .

BUCKLEY: I've always found this one of your most interesting
points. It reminded me of the American capitalist,
you know, who went to the Soviet Union in 1944,
and came back glistening and said the Soviet Union
has no trouble with labor unions. None at all.
[*Laughter.*] Now, one of the reasons of course why
there hasn't been as much crime in the South as there
has been in the North is because you have ways of
dealing with crime which are, to say the least, unusual. The Ku Klux Klan, for instance, seemed to be
a major law enforcer during parts of . . .

WALLACE: Of course, that's totally untrue. I'm not even going
to answer these pseudo-intellectual . . .

BUCKLEY: I'm not a . . .

WALLACE: Yes you are! You're a pseudo-intellectual with a . . .
you got a . . . you just . . . you don't like the people
of Alabama.

BUCKLEY: I like the people of Alabama.

At the end of the debate, Buckley got up quickly from his chair to
avoid having to exchange pleasantries with Wallace, who, as he had
done upon entering the studio, was going from person to person shaking hands. "I remember Bill standing aside so he would go out and he
wouldn't have any contact with him," Warren Steibel said.

The debate was a standoff. Wallace did not see it to his disadvan-
tage to appear as an economic populist. But Buckley, believing that
populism and conservatism were antithetical, was satisfied that he had
discredited Wallace among conservatives. "Wallace took a straight
populist line, and I lapped it up because I was very anti-Wallace. My
design was to show that his hold on conservatism really had to do
with his racism," Buckley recalled.

---

* Wallace, unable by law to succeed himself, had gotten his wife, Lurleen, elected governor
in 1966.

III

In December 1967, ABC television had asked Buckley if he would be a commentator during its coverage of the 1968 Republican and Democratic conventions. ABC News officials told him that they wanted to devote part of their daily coverage to a debate between him and a liberal. The news executives had not selected Buckley's adversary and asked him for suggestions. He gave them eight names, including John Kenneth Galbraith and Norman Mailer. Asked if there was anyone he would not appear with, he said that he would appear with any "non-Communist," but that he preferred not to have to debate Gore Vidal. From his experience on the Jack Paar show and on David Susskind's *Open End* talk show, Buckley was convinced that Vidal would make up facts and quotations in order to discredit a political opponent. He was also disgusted by Vidal's flaunting of his bisexuality.

His relationship with Vidal had already become personally vindictive. In the fall of 1962, after Vidal had attacked Buckley on the Paar show, Buckley had called Vidal a "philosophical degenerate" in a television debate. During a Susskind appearance in July 1964, Vidal had made some derogatory remarks about Buckley's family that Buckley deeply resented. And Buckley had published a review of Vidal's play *Romulus* in *National Review* that referred derisively to Vidal's homosexuality.*

ABC recognized that on the basis of sheer entertainment value, Buckley and Vidal would make the best match. Vidal, sharp-tongued, highly political, and not above hand-to-hand combat, was the perfect opponent for Buckley. Their *ad hominems* promised to drive up ABC's TV ratings, even if they might also raise Buckley's, if not Vidal's, blood pressure to dangerous levels and shed little light on the conventions themselves. In a preview of the convention coverage, the *Washington Post* wrote, "The best show next month will not be on the convention floor or in hotel corridors, but in an ABC studio. In Buckley and Vidal, ABC has a dream television match. They are graceful, shrewd, cool antagonists; paragons of caustic wit and established observers of the American political scene." [11]

---

* After the debate on Susskind's *Open End* in July 1964, the *San Francisco Chronicle* wrote, "Buckley is bile with a smile. Susskind and Vidal rocked back and forth like two old harpies and spat at him with no visible effect on their target nor, I suspect, on the viewers." (July 15, 1964.)

At the Republican Convention, Reagan threw his hat into the ring in a last-minute attempt to stop Nixon. But Buckley was not impressed. During the first day of the convention, Tony Dolan, a young Yale undergraduate who had interviewed Buckley for the *Yale Daily News,* visited him at his room at the Eden Roc Hotel, and confidently predicted that Reagan would win the nomination and the election and create a "Roosevelt-like" change in the country. Buckley raised his hand and said no, the conservatives did not have an intelligentsia to run the country. "Where are the assistant professors?" Buckley asked Dolan.[12]

The convention itself was largely uneventful. Reagan was cut off at the pass by South Carolina Senator Strom Thurmond, who held most of the South in tow for Nixon, and Goldwaterites John Tower and Peter O'Donnell, who did the same with Texas. The only drama was over the vice-presidential selection, which went to the largely unknown Maryland Governor Spiro Agnew, a former Rockefeller supporter.

But the encounter between Buckley and Vidal drew blood from the opening bell. In his opening statement, Vidal had described the Republicans as a "party based almost entirely upon human greed." In response, Buckley made a reference to Vidal's latest satirical novel, *Myra Breckinridge,* which he had not read, but which, he knew, had a transsexual hero.[13]

> It seems to me that the earlier focus of Mr. Vidal on human greed —you remember that he said he found himself wondering whether the party that was devoted to the concept of human greed could ever hope to get a majority of the American people to vote for it. Now the author of *Myra Breckinridge* is well acquainted with the imperatives of human greed. . . .

Laughing demonstratively, Vidal retorted, "If I may say so, Bill, before you go any further, that if there were a contest for Mr. Myra Breckinridge, you would unquestionably win it. I based the entire style polemically upon you—passionate and irrelevant."

And they were off, trading insults and invective. Vidal, who had employed two research assistants to prepare for his clash with Buckley, imputed to Buckley, Reagan, and Nixon views that Buckley believed none of them held. For his part, Buckley prodded Vidal on his "immorality" and the "disdain" he expressed for America by living abroad.

After four days in Miami, Buckley had had enough. He called the ABC producer to suggest the he and Vidal alternate their presentations rather than debate on the air, but the producer rejected Buckley's suggestion on the grounds that it would make the program uninteresting. Buckley was in show business and there was no way out.

In Chicago, where the Democratic Convention was held, Buckley and Vidal became part of the violent turmoil that coursed through the streets. The Democratic Party, split over civil rights, was being torn apart over the Vietnam War. In March, antiwar candidate Senator Eugene McCarthy's strong showing in the New Hampshire presidential primary had helped force Johnson out of the race. New York Senator Robert Kennedy had entered the race to vie with McCarthy for the antiwar vote, while Johnson's Vice-President, Hubert Humphrey, sought to win over party regulars. In April, Martin Luther King was assassinated in Memphis and riots took place across the country. Three weeks later, more than a thousand students at Columbia University took over the administration building, protesting the university's complicity in the war and its indifference toward neighboring Harlem. In June, Kennedy, on the evening of his victory over McCarthy in the California primary, was assassinated. With Humphrey, who was identified with the administration's Vietnam War policy, expected to gain the nomination at the convention, thousands of antiwar protesters had gathered in Chicago's Grant Park across from the Hilton Hotel, where the Democratic candidates were headquartered. Instead of trying to co-opt them, Chicago mayor Richard Daley (himself an opponent of the war) denied them parade permits and tried to disperse them with police. On the climactic night, when Humphrey was outpolling McCarthy inside the convention hall, Chicago's police were turning their nightsticks on the demonstrators, who were chanting defiantly, "Fuck you, LBJ," "Fuck you, Mayor Daley," and "Ho, Ho, Ho Chi Minh, the NLF is going to win." *

Buckley had blamed the assassinations on the spirit of lawlessness that he attributed to the demonstrators in the Chicago streets. "Political assassinations such as that against Robert Kennedy are 'unimaginable,' we keep reassuring ourselves," Buckley wrote in *Esquire*. "But also, in another frame of reference, is the occupation of the office of the President of Columbia University unimaginable." [14]

At the convention, Buckley and his wife had stayed at the Hilton,

---

* The NLF was the pro-Communist National Liberation Front in Vietnam.

across from the park, and had been kept up until three in the morning by the demonstrators' chants. Buckley arrived at the convention the next day in a grim mood. When columnist Murray Kempton visited the ABC trailer, where Buckley was preparing for the evening's bout with Vidal, he found Buckley "occupied only with his embarrassment." He asked Pat Buckley, who was standing beside him, how she was. "I'll tell you how I am," Pat said, referring to Vidal's imputations about Buckley and Myra Breckinridge. "Two hundred million Americans think William F. Buckley is a screaming homosexual and I've got to do something about it." Kempton retreated.

Buckley and Vidal had watched the violent street clashes on television monitors before going on the air. Vidal entered the studio prepared to pillory the Chicago police and his debate opponent, whom he imagined to be in sympathy with them. While Buckley would later privately describe Chicago's Mayor Daley as a Fascist, he was not willing to let Vidal use the police to vindicate the demonstrators, who, in Buckley's mind, had provoked much of the violence.* "Anybody who believes that these characters are interested in the democratic process is deluding himself," he said. Vidal, for his part, compared the Chicago police to those in the Soviet Union: "The police here are brutal. The citizens are paralyzed, and the right of peaceful assembly has been denied by Mayor Daley, who believes in order without law." The demonstrators, Vidal insisted, had been "absolutely well behaved."

At this point, moderator Howard K. Smith intervened, but his question only succeeded in heating up the argument to the boiling point.

SMITH: Mr. Vidal, wasn't it a provocative act to try to raise the Vietcong flag in the park, in the [television news] film we just saw? Wouldn't that invite . . . raising a Nazi flag in World War II would have had similar consequences?

VIDAL: You must realize what some of the political issues are here, the million . . .

BUCKLEY (to Smith, sarcastically): You're so naïve.

VIDAL: People in the United States happen to believe that United States policy is wrong in Vietnam and the Vietcong are correct in wanting to organize their country in their own way politically. This happens to be pretty much the opinion of Western Europe and many other parts of the world. If it is a novelty in Chicago, that is

---

* Buckley wrote to Nancy Reagan in October 1969 of the "unpleasantness of subjection to the fascist dictatorship of Mayor Daley."(Buckley Papers.)

BUCKLEY: too bad. I assume it is the point of American democracy that you can express any point of view you want. . . .

BUCKLEY: And some people were pro-Nazi, and some people were pro-Nazi . . .

VIDAL: Shut up a minute.

BUCKLEY: No I won't. And some people were pro-Nazi, and that answer is that they were well treated by people who ostracized the . . . And I am for ostracizing people who egg on other people to shoot American Marines and American soldiers. I know you don't care because you don't have any sense of identification. . . .

VIDAL: As far as I am concerned, the only sort of pro- or crypto-Nazi that I can think of is yourself. Failing that I would only say we can't have the right of assembly if they're . . .

SMITH: Let's—let's not call names . . .

BUCKLEY: Now listen, you queer, stop calling me a crypto-Nazi . . .

SMITH: Let's stop. . . . Let's . . .

BUCKLEY: . . . or I'll sock you in the goddam face . . .

VIDAL: Oh, Bill, you're so extraordinary . . .

SMITH: Gentlemen, let's stop calling names.

BUCKLEY: . . . and you'll stay plastered. Let the author of *Myra Breckinridge* go back to his pornography and stop making allusions of Naziism to somebody who was in the last war and fought the Nazis. . . .

VIDAL (breaking in): You were not in the infantry . . .

SMITH: Gentlemen, I beg you to . . .

VIDAL: As a matter of fact . . .

BUCKLEY: I was a second lieutenant in the infantry. . . .

VIDAL: You were *not*. You're distorting your military record. . . .

SMITH: Mr. Vidal . . .

Finally Smith got the conversation back on the demonstrators outside, but the damage had already been done. The very thin shell of decorum had cracked completely.

Afterwards, it was Vidal rather than Buckley who was able to separate his on-air performance from his private self. As they were taking off their earphones at the end of the show, Vidal jovially whispered to Buckley, "I guess we gave them their money's worth tonight." But Buckley, who at other times was able to lay aside public controversies, was in no mood to appreciate the entertainment value of the evening.* He felt ashamed at having "blown his cool" and having "misbehaved" on the air. As had occurred during the debate with Wallace, Buckley had lost his composure and begun to react purely emotionally. But where Wallace had caused him to take political positions that were atypical, Vidal had caused him to resort to gutter epithets. He had not merely appeared undignified, but also mean.

Buckley's friends urged him to forget the debate, but he refused. That winter in Switzerland, Buckley spent five weeks writing an account of the debate for *Esquire*—as long as he had taken to write *The Unmaking of a Mayor.* Writer Rebecca West, who was staying with the Buckleys, was amazed. "Bill, you're not going to spend all the time on that man?" she asked him.

Buckley's lengthy account, published that summer, was a careful deliberation on homosexuality and the family in Vidal's works, as well as a recounting of their past appearances together, concluding with a half-apology for having called Vidal a "queer." Vidal, promised a chance to reply by *Esquire,* responded with a piece that not only implied that Buckley was a homosexual and an anti-Semite, but heaped scorn and calumny on Buckley's father. Vidal told the version of the incident at Sharon that he had heard from actress Jayne Meadows Cotter. According to Meadows, the Buckley children (including Bill) had been inspired to invade the Reverend Mr. Cotter's church by their father's ranting and raving the night before at Cotter's wife for having sold a house in Sharon to a Jewish family.

Buckley, who was at his induction physical in North Carolina when the Sharon incident took place, believed that Vidal's article was libelous. Surveying the exchange, *Time* remarked, "Not since [movie star] George Sanders divorced Zsa Zsa Gabor has so much talent been wasted on a nasty spat." [15]

Buckley's battle with Vidal raised the question of what he had lost as well as gained in becoming a public celebrity. That spring he confessed to his friend Hugh Kenner that he was "demoralized" from the encounter with Vidal. In a perceptive letter, Kenner analyzed the problem:

A celebrity is simply one who accepts pay for having no privacy. ABC is now playing the role of Jack Paar, i.e. putting on a show.

---

* At one of their first television debates in the fall of 1962, in which Buckley called Vidal a "philosophical degenerate," Buckley offered to buy Vidal a drink afterwards, but Vidal had rejected the offer. (*Newsweek,* May 13, 1963.)

With part of your mind you assume you will be giving political comment. With another part, you accept Gore Vidal as opposite number despite prior experience. What you have in fact done is accept a role as a Celebrity. You will be playing William F. Buckley, Old Antagonist of Gore Vidal. And you will be conceding the right to have your privacy violated, which means in the first instance being taxed with past statements you never made and leads right up to such imputations—bisexuality, anti-Semitism, etc.—as make up the texture of Gore Vidal's *Esquire* piece.[16]

Kenner was, in fact, saying two different things about Buckley as a celebrity. On one hand, by sacrificing his privacy, Buckley had made himself vulnerable to people like Vidal who were intent on discrediting him and would resort to almost anything, including attacks against his parents, to do so. But on the other hand, he had subordinated his politics to his personality. He was not articulating conservatism, but "playing William F. Buckley," character *extraordinaire*. Indeed, Kenner believed that by this time Buckley had "become a personality and ceased to be an educator."

Both Kenner and John Kenneth Galbraith urged Buckley not to sue Vidal and *Esquire*. "You are talking about a staged row between two highly experienced controversialists," Galbraith wrote him in August. "You first *refused* and then accepted Vidal."[17] Buckley's family, fearful of charges being hurled publicly against their parents and themselves, also advised Buckley not to sue, but he insisted upon doing so. He wrote Galbraith, "If it can be said about me that I'm a crypto-Nazi, then it can be said of every vigorous American conservative. Add to it, also, Vidal sought to revive ancient and slanderous charges against my family."[18]

Buckley's lawsuit against *Esquire* and Vidal dragged on for three years until, finally, after a judge ordered Buckley's suits to court and threw out Vidal's countersuit, Buckley, fearful of a jury trial and further expense, settled with *Esquire* and dropped his suit against Vidal. *Esquire* paid him $15,000 in cash and $100,000 in *National Review* ads and published a statement saying that it did not believe the charges in Vidal's article.*

---

* The depositions in Buckley's suit against Vidal and *Esquire* revealed that Vidal did not have sufficient grounds for his characterization of the Sharon church incident. Buckley was having his induction physical when "the incident" took place, and Jayne Meadows, Vidal's sole source of information, was herself on a USO tour. She later heard about Will Buckley's tirade against her mother from her family, who in turn heard it secondhand from a townsperson who had a relative who worked at Great Elm. Furthermore, one of

One of the most telling comments on the encounter between Buckley and Vidal was written by Buckley's friend Murray Kempton for *Esquire,* but never published because of the ongoing lawsuit. Kempton summed up the paradox of the debate. "The argument is about homosexuality," Kempton wrote. "What makes the thing difficult is that homosexuality, while a proper subject for historical inquiry, almost never provides a useful argument in living controversy." Kempton found a "curious reversal of roles" in the Buckley-Vidal exchange.

> Buckley has taken as his the masculine side of the argument and Vidal is cast in the feminine. Yet no one who at all knows the private Buckley can have failed to detect in him a deep personal kindness, even sentimentality, those qualities we like to admire as womanly.
>
> Vidal's qualities, on the other hand, seem all on the side of what we used to think of as the manly valors; he is detached, tough, cold and calculating in battle. . . . Inevitably, then, Vidal controls the argument; this, like all his more notorious quarrels, ends with the incitement of an excess of someone else's false masculinity by this false femininity of his.

IV

During the summer and fall of 1968, Buckley, when he was not feuding with Vidal, was enjoying his new status as an influential political figure. For the first time, Buckley found his advice actively sought by a presidential candidate. In July, when Nixon had virtually wrapped up the nomination, he had instructed Buchanan to solicit Buckley's suggestion of a vice-presidential candidate. Buckley's recommendation of Johnson's Secretary of Health, Education, and Welfare, John Gardner, a renowned liberal, made Nixon's jaw drop.

For his part, Buckley used his column and *National Review* to secure the conservative vote for Nixon. This meant chipping away at Wallace's vote. In August, he wrote Barry Goldwater, "It seems to me that we ought to have a real chance of winning this year and that the important effort has got to be to discourage Conservatives from voting for George Wallace."[19] And he got both Goldwater and John Ashbrook to publish articles critical of Wallace.

Jane and Priscilla's school friends, who stayed at Great Elm and participated in the incident, was Jewish. It seems unlikely that Will Buckley would have gone on a tirade against allowing Jews in Sharon with his daughters' Jewish classmate at the table. And if he did, it is still unlikely that his children would then have acted on his anger.

Privately, Buckley continued to play a behind-the-scenes role in the campaign, largely through his friend, former CBS executive Frank Shakespeare, who had assumed control of Nixon's media campaign.

On the eve of the election, *National Review* endorsed Nixon. It was the first time the magazine had endorsed a candidate who was not strictly its own, but Buckley bent over backwards to point out that while Nixon was not a *National Review* conservative, he was the next best thing. Nixon, the editorial proclaimed,

> is freed of the subservience to doctrinal middle-of-the-roadism that made Mr. Eisenhower so—never mind. The point is that Mr. Nixon is clearly his own man now, and during the past few years he too has shared some of the disillusions with liberalism which are the way-stations to political maturity. . . . Richard Nixon is capable of giving the country the impluse it needs on the way back to political sobriety.[20]

These were words that Buckley and the magazine's editors would eventually rue.

CHAPTER 17

Verbal Soporifics

When Nixon won in 1968, conservative leaders like John Tower, John Ashbrook, Strom Thurmond, and Barry Goldwater, who had backed Nixon against the worse fate of a liberal Republican, enjoyed a moment of euphoria. Buoyed by Nixon's continuing attention, they began to believe that Nixon was not the lesser of two evils, but "one of us." Frank Shakespeare, a CBS executive who was close to *National Review,* and who had joined Nixon's campaign and then his administration, described the way conservatives justified this identification: "Because conservatives felt so strongly about the nature of communism and the Soviet Union, the aura of Helen Gahagan Douglas and Alger Hiss and all that sort of thing, Nixon was a hero, and he became a conservative hero, and conservatives assumed that because he was a symbol and an image, he was also substance."

Buckley viewed the Nixon years through a coherent strategic framework that he had adopted from Chambers and Burnham. What others believed was deviation by him from conservative principle, he saw as a "dance along the precipice." But he was not immune either to the euphoria or to the illusions about Nixon's politics that Nixon himself actively encouraged. He continued to insist that Nixon was not a "*National Review* conservative," but his use of that phrase increasingly implied that Nixon might, indeed, be another equally acceptable kind of conservative. In the aftermath of Nixon's victory, Buckley proposed Cabinet choices—William Scranton for Secretary of State and (reflecting Burnham's influence) Nelson Rockefeller for Secretary of Defense—suggesting that Nixon had to square accounts with the moderate and liberal wings of the party.

I

Buckley's election support was rewarded with a political appointment through the intercession of Frank Shakespeare, a friend of Buckley since the late fifties. An Irish Catholic conservative in a business dominated by liberal Jews and Protestants, Shakespeare had risen from selling ads to running CBS's New York affiliate. Worried that the country was tearing itself apart, Shakespeare had called Buckley in 1967 to ask him whether he should volunteer in the Nixon campaign. "Frank," Shakespeare remembered Buckley as saying, "I think Nixon is a guy with an awful lot of ability, and I think you should see him and talk with him." Shakespeare ended up masterminding Nixon's brilliantly evasive media campaign, as later portrayed in Joe McGinniss's *The Selling of the President*.

After he won, Nixon made Shakespeare head of the United States Information Agency (USIA), and on Shakespeare's recommendation, he appointed Buckley in May 1969 to be on the Advisory Commission on Information of the USIA, which met monthly to oversee USIA operations. It was the highest part-time appointment that a working journalist could receive, and Buckley found himself on a commission chaired by Frank Stanton, the president of CBS. But it was also one that carried no specific accountability to the administration.

Buckley was bored by the monthly board meetings, which sometimes took place overseas at different USIA stations, but he went out of loyalty to Shakespeare. He never considered himself part of the administration—any more than Stanton and James Michener, the Democrats on the board, did. If Buckley's opinion was affected, it was not by being on the USIA oversight commission, but by being directly wooed by the Nixon White House.

During the first year of his administration, Nixon invited the Buckleys to state dinners and sent Buckley congratulatory notes on his columns. But most importantly, he summoned him periodically to the Oval Office for 30-minute conservations in which only he, Kissinger, and sometimes one of Buckley's friends, Shakespeare or Peter Flanigan, were present.

Buckley was clearly impressed by Nixon's attentions. When *Playboy*'s interviewer asked him in 1970 whether he thought that his appointment to the USIA's Advisory Commission restrained his criticisms of Nixon, Buckley replied:

> I acknowledge that there may be a feeling of restraint deriving not from my appointment to the commission but from the fact that I have seen him once or twice privately. I have discovered a new sensual treat, which, appropriately, the readers of *Playboy* should be the first to know about. It is to have the President of the United States take notes while you are speaking to him, even though you run the risk that he is scribbling, "Get this bore out of here." It's always a little bit more difficult to be rhetorically ruthless with somebody with whom you spend time.[1]

But while Nixon took notes, there is little evidence that he was really interested in what Buckley had to say. His purpose was to win Buckley's favor rather than to solicit advice on how to run the government. Shakespeare realized that he and Buckley were being taken in. As he recalled:

> I became gradually aware of the fact that conservatives were to be given verbal soporifics and occasional things to keep them happy. Conservatives were very clearly not the core, the center, and Nixon thought of Bill Buckley in that framework. Nixon never would have been a friend [of] or relied on a Bill Buckley, but he wanted him to keep thinking well of him, almost a pressure-group handling, if you will.

Kissinger, who was a master himself at manipulating the media, voiced a similar opinion of Nixon's treatment of Buckley. "He liked him, but Buckley would make him uneasy, and he thought he was not really relevant to the decisions that he had to make."

On Nixon's order, other members of the administration sought out Buckley. In Nixon's first year, domestic adviser Daniel P. Moynihan helped draft a Family Assistance Plan that reformed the welfare laws. According to Moynihan's plan, every family of four would be guaranteed $1,600 a year in cash payments and approximately $800 in food stamps—entailing a rise in welfare benefits in sixteen states and supplementing existing benefits in the others.[2] Conservatives had invariably opposed not only the kind of increases in welfare expenditures that this plan entailed, but the guaranteed annual income that it created, and Nixon tried to head off Buckley's and *National Review*'s opposition by dispatching Moynihan to a special *National Review* editorial meeting at Buckley's town house. To the astonishment of the editors, Moynihan stayed for an entire evening. Buckley recalled the event:

> Pat Moynihan called me and said don't take a corporate position on the Family Assistance Plan until you hear me out, so he came with an aide, and talked and wined and dined with *National Review* from five until midnight. He flew up in a White House plane and went back in a White House plane, and he urged as convincingly as he could the merits of the plan.

Moynihan enjoyed the evening himself. "We had this wonderful talk, I went through the plan, and people listened and were sympathetic because they were sympathetic to Nixon." The next day, Buckley sent Moynihan a four-page telegram where he stated some reservations about the plan and included a three-page recipe for the apple soup that Moynihan had enjoyed.

Buckley's most important relationship in the Nixon administration was with Kissinger. Unlike Buckley's relationship with Nixon, it was based on friendship and mutual respect, but as was the case with Nixon, Buckley may have allowed himself to be manipulated.

Buckley and Kissinger had known each other since 1954, when Kissinger, an instructor in government at Harvard and the editor of an academic policy journal, *Confluence,* invited Buckley to contribute an article on McCarthy to a symposium the magazine was having on the subject. Although the magazine claimed not to take sides on issues, Kissinger, out of "cowardice" (as he later admitted), rejected Buckley's defense of the senator. "He was surely offensive to my colleagues, but that was no reason not to publish him," Kissinger said. To atone, he invited Buckley to make yearly presentations before his prestigious international-relations seminar. In 1956, at Kissinger's initiative, they had lunch together at the Yale Club in New York, and became passing friends. Buckley liked the erudite heavyset professor who still had traces of a German accent and whose towering ambition was balanced by a self-effacing wit. They never discussed domestic politics, but they shared, Buckley believed, a hatred of communism.

Kissinger thought of himself as a "historical conservative," modeled after Burke, Disraeli, and Bismarck, and he had had no reservations about printing the more academic and measured Russell Kirk in *Confluence*. In domestic policy, he favored adjustment rather than reaction—one issue of *Confluence* had featured an article by black writer and civil rights proponent Ralph Ellison—while in foreign policy he sought stability against what he perceived as the revolutionary challenge of the Soviet Union. His view of Soviet intentions was closer to that of Burnham than to that of former State Department official and containment advocate George Kennan.

Buckley and Kissinger lunched occasionally over the next decade. As a result of his work for the Council on Foreign Relations, Kissinger had come to the attention of Nelson Rockefeller, and in 1964, he became Rockefeller's chief foreign policy adviser. In February 1968, Kissinger tried to mitigate conservative hostilities to Rockefeller by setting up a private meeting between Rockefeller and Buckley; during the Republican Convention, at Rockefeller's suggestion, he shadowed Buckley, hoping to convince him to hold conservatives in line in case Nixon should falter and Rockefeller's candidacy become viable.

In early August, after the convention, Kissinger wrote Buckley expressing his distaste for Nixon and continued support for Rockefeller. "Miami Beach was a searing experience," Kissinger wrote. "I know I should never be able to convince you of this, but I continue to believe that Rockefeller would have been a better man for conservative values than the eventual nominee."[3] But later that month, Kissinger told Buckley over lunch that he had a "few ideas he thought would be interesting to Nixon, in framing his foreign policy campaign speeches."[4] Buckley volunteered to contact Nixon for Kissinger, and got in touch with Frank Shakespeare. Shakespeare recalled the occasion:

I got a call one day from Bill, and he said, "Frank, there is a hell of a smart guy named Henry Kissinger, and he's been very, very close to Nelson Rockefeller, and he said he wants to meet with Nixon. I think it is something that could be useful to the process. Could you be helpful?" I said, "Sure," and I went in to see John Mitchell, and he said, "Sure, have him in to see me," and the next thing you know Kissinger had met Nixon.*

---

* According the Seymour Hersh, it was Richard Allen and not Buckley (through Shakespeare and Mitchell) who arranged the first contact between Kissinger and Nixon that resulted in Kissinger's providing reports of the Paris peace talks to the Republican candidate. (See *The Price of Power*, 13ff.)

After Nixon had won, Kissinger phoned Buckley again to arrange another meeting with Nixon in order to warn him of new developments in the Vietman War negotiations. Buckley telephoned Nixon and a second meeting was set up. One week later, Kissinger called Buckley. "You will never be able to say again that you have no contact inside the White House."[5]

When Kissinger's appointment as National Security Adviser was announced, *National Review* predicted that he would "render great service."[6]

During his tenure in the White House, Kissinger regularly asked Buckley to come to Washington. Kissinger spared little in his attentions. The first time, he sent the White House jet for Buckley and sent him back on it, accompanied by his aide, Colonel Alexander Haig. One time, wanting to win *National Review* over to his Mideast peace initiative, he invited the entire editorial board to Washington for a briefing. In all, Buckley made at least twenty trips to Washington specifically to see Kissinger and talked to him frequently on the phone.

In calling Buckley to Washington, Kissinger was not seeking his advice. While he had a much higher opinion of Buckley than of other conservatives, most of whom he regarded as ignorant provincials, he didn't believe that Buckley understood foreign policy. "As a type, Buckley is really an artist rather than a foreign policy thinker," Kissinger explained later. "He does not have any detailed strategic view of foreign policy." Instead, Kissinger saw Buckley as both the most reasonable and important leader of the American Right, whom it would be useful to win over.

Kissinger wanted to influence conservatives through Buckley. When the administation was about to take its positions on withdrawing from Vietnam and opening relations with China, Kissinger was very anxious to persuade Buckley that this was a "conservative" course of action. And when the administration took measures that were bound to alienate liberals, like the invasion of Cambodia, he wanted Buckley to rally conservatives behind the administration. "I was hoping he would help mobilize conservatives as a counterweight to the liberal pressures under which we were," Kissinger explained later.

When he was with Buckley, as with his liberal visitors, Kissinger did most of the talking. He defended policies that veered from Buckley's conservative views as having been forced upon the administra-

tion by divisions within the country and the foreign policy establishment—an argument he would later make in *White House Years*.[7]

Kissinger also told Buckley that some of the administration policies
that Buckley objected to were based on secret information, which he
was willing to reveal to him if he promised to tell no one. It was a
technique, Kissinger aide Roger Morris recalled, that Kissinger used
with "no fewer than a couple of dozen different journalists." When
Buckley objected to SALT, Kissinger told him that the decision to
sign a treaty was based on secret information about Soviet submarine
production. According to Buckley, when he went down to Washington to see Kissinger, Kissinger told him:

> Bill, it is a state secret that I will tell you. It is that the Soviet Union
> is bringing out one atomic submarine per month. We can't begin to
> compete with them. We could never get the money to do it. *Any*
> deal that has the effect of interrupting the tremendous leap that they
> are engaged in at this particular moment gives us *ad hoc* advantages
> which you cannot overestimate.

Kissinger also drew Buckley into the labyrinth of White House
intrigue by complaining at length of Secretary of State William Rogers's attempts to subvert a hard anti-Communist policy in Vietnam.
In August, after Kissinger had complained to him of Rogers, Buckley
wrote to Kissinger, proposing that Nixon have Nelson Rockefeller
undertake a series of studies as a prelude to nominating him to replace
Rogers.

> If I read you correctly [Buckley wrote to Kissinger], the republic is
> in very considerable peril . . . we need, as you point out, strong
> pressure, extra-governmental pressure, brought on public policy.
> . . . That pressure, although its provenance would in fact come
> from what one might call the American Right, is best exerted by
> those who are not professionally related to the American Right. . . .
> The ideal man is Nelson Rockefeller.

Kissinger, who knew that Nixon would never allow Rockefeller to
overshadow him, wrote back, "Your basic proposal is not practical
quickly enough."[8]

In the first years, Buckley did not regard Kissinger as a close friend
in the same way as he did Frank Shakespeare, but he did come to

believe that Kissinger was a covert political ally.* After his first audience with the new National Security Adviser, in April 1969, Buckley, acknowledging the distrust that other conservatives harbored for Kissinger, wrote him, "Don't tell anyone my faith in you."[9] "Kissinger I considered one of us," Buckley said later. But other conservatives believed that Kissinger was performing the same public-relations job on Buckley that he performed on liberals he would talk to. "Henry Kissinger is a public-relations genius, and I don't use that word lightly," Frank Shakespeare said. "Henry Kissinger can meet with six different people, smart as hell, learned, knowledgeable, experienced, of very different views, and meet with them back to back, and persuade all six of them that the real Henry Kissinger is just where they are."

David Keene, who was the former head of the Young Americans for Freedom and Vice-President Agnew's chief aide, believed that Kissinger was taking Buckley in. As Keene recalled:

> To give Bill his due, this guy could con the pants off of John Connally. He had one line for liberals, one for conservatives, and all the time he'd swear you to secrecy—"What I'm about to tell you is the highest classified information"—and he'd give you some bullshit, and he'd give somebody else the opposite. Bill was very con-able, partly because he did want to be in, and Kissinger gave everybody that he talked to in those days the sense that they were indeed "in."

During the first years of the Nixon administration, Buckley supported policies that other conservatives found questionable. After Moynihan's visit, *National Review* took no position on the Family Assistance Plan, but in his newspaper column, Buckley, influenced in part by Milton Friedman's support, praised it as a "daring and attractive plan. . . . The appeal of Mr. Nixon's plan is its directness. It accosts, for the first time, the sprawling mass that has grown up around a few humanitarian postulates, grown utterly out of hand, as witnessed in New York City."[10] Buckley generally praised Nixon's Vietnam policies against Burnham's warning that through its program of "Vietnamization," the administration was following the "Gaullist" course of withdrawal. He even supported the administration's tenta-

---

* When Ralph de Toledano criticized his closeness to Nixon, Buckley replied, "It isn't so much that I see virtue, as a certain stability there. We are not friends, you know. The only man for whom I feel friendship [in the administration] is Frank Shakespeare." (Buckley Papers.)

tive opening toward China, without, however, endorsing the idea of recognizing China. His overall appraisal of Nixon's foreign policy was extremely positive. "When I look around the world today and ask myself what it is that I truly care about in international affairs that Nixon has let me down on, I don't come up with anything," Buckley told *Playboy* in May 1970.

Buckley's most revealing assessment of the Nixon administration came after Nixon, in unveiling his deficit budget in 1971, commented to a group of industrialists, "We are all Keynesians now." Nixon's comment struck at the heart of the conservative laissez-faire economics that Buckley had supported for three decades, but instead of condemning Nixon's statement, he tried to justify it. He wrote, "I think Mr. Nixon meant to acknowledge that the mere mention of the word Keynes is not any longer so frightening as it once was." [11]

Buckley's and *National Review*'s defense of Nixon infuriated some conservatives. Ralph de Toledano wrote Buckley in August 1970, "I remember how in 1960 it was me against *National Review* on Nixon and now today *National Review,* in the words of a friend, seems to have become an administration house organ." When conservatives claimed that Nixon was trying to deceive them into thinking he was on their side, Buckley defended Nixon's sincerity. He wrote Hugh Kenner, "I think you are overhard on Nixon. He believes rather intensively, but he has a hell of a time communicating this. Remember, a phony would not have got by Whittaker Chambers." [12]

While Buckley acknowledged the effect of Nixon's attentions, he also insisted that his own positions reflected a strategic outlook on conservatism. When American Conservative Union founder Bob Bauman wrote to Buckley objecting to his support for the Family Assistance Plan, Buckley cited the strategic view that he had learned from Burnham and Chambers. "The conservative has two functions, the paradigmatic and the expediential. It is with reference to the latter function that I tend to prefer the Moynihan plan to the congeries of alternatives." [13]

In December 1970, Buckley was questioned on *Firing Line* by members of the Young Americans for Freedom. This time he added a touch of Kissinger to Chambers and Burnham's view. One of the YAF members asked him, "Bill, one of the gripes that I hear across the country today is that Bill Buckley is not as critical of the nonconservative and often quite liberal policies—domestic and foreign—of the Nixon administration, as he would be, let us say, if Hubert Humphrey won in 1968 and were advocating those same policies." In reply, Buckley set forth his own strategy for conservatives.

I think it's in part true . . . conservatism, as I understand it, is always about two things—it's about the paradigm, how things ought to be—and it's about what can you wrest out of the current situation. The relationship of forces—the phrase is always used by James Burnham—is one that always asks the following question: where are *we* in connection with where *they* are. And when *they,* in the existing situation, become people who, in effect, are saying about America that America isn't worth saving—that it isn't worth fighting wars for—that it isn't worth exerting ourselves in behalf of —*then* one welcomes people who, however imperfect they are in terms of our ideal, nevertheless point up, generally speaking, in the right direction.

Ironically, Buckley's only serious quarrel with the Nixon administration during its first three years was over Vice-President Agnew, the man whom most conservatives came to adopt as their spokesman within the administration. Nixon had been drawn to Agnew because he had a liberal reputation that could attract Democratic votes. Agnew had been elected governor of Maryland in 1966, with strong black and Jewish support, on an antidiscrimination platform, but after the riots prompted by Martin Luther King's assassination in April 1968, Agnew had had a stormy meeting with Maryland's black leaders that had moved him to the Right. A snub from Nelson Rockefeller, whom he had originally backed for the presidency, propelled him into Nixon's camp.

Inept at congressional liaison, Agnew had been groping throughout 1969 for a role as Vice-President, and he found it as the outspoken advocate of right-wing populism. Beginning with a June 7 speech at Ohio State University, Agnew began to pound at the "sniveling hand-wringing power structure" and "the effete corps of impudent snobs who characterize themselves as intellectuals." His immediate targets were the antiwar demonstrators, whom he called "ideological eunuchs," and their supporters in the Democratic Party, whom he identified with the power structure, but in November, at Nixon's behest, Agnew, aided by speech writer Pat Buchanan, turned his populist guns on the "little group of men who enjoy a right of instant rebuttal to every presidential address"—the eastern media elite.

Buckley heard echoes of Wallace's demagoguery in Agnew's speeches. In an October 1969 column, he wrote, "Mr. Agnew is not skilled in polemics and therefore should not engage in them without help." [14] Buckley's comment elicited a frenzied protest from Agnew's office, and in a subsequent column, Buckley explained that he was not attacking the "substance" of Agnew's speeches. "The occasional rhetorical misfires aside, Mr. Agnew is doing okay," he wrote.[15] When Agnew attacked the eastern press's liberal bias in a Des Moines speech written by Buchanan, Buckley leaped to his defense. "Now as a matter of fact, Mr. Agnew wrote a very good speech," Buckley wrote in his column. "It was, moreover, a balanced speech."[16] In a March 1970 column on "The Strategy of Agnewism," Buckley went even further. He wrote that "Agnew's speeches are justly celebrated for their color and for the zest with which they profane the icons of Eastern Seaboard liberalism."[17]

II

During the Nixon years, Buckley seemed to lose the edge of anger that had colored his public politics. His performances on *Firing Line* became comparatively tame. Although he could still be provoked on occasion, he sparred rather than slugged it out with his guests. A perfect example was Daniel Ellsberg, a former Pentagon consultant who leaked the Pentagon's history of the Vietnam War to *The New York Times* and who was being prosecuted by the Nixon administration for violating the Espionage Act. Buckley had condemned Ellsberg, and in the earlier *Firing Line,* he might have tried to destroy him on the air. But when Ellsberg appeared on *Firing Line* in 1972, the hour-long discussion was punctuated by mutual laughter.

BUCKLEY: I have no doubt at all, I can't doubt for a minute that the Kremlin knows much more about our defense setup than I do, for instance.

ELLSBERG: Not thanks to the newspapers. . . .

BUCKLEY: No, no. Thanks to people like Klaus Fuchs. . . .

ELLSBERG: You're not comparing President Nixon to Klaus Fuchs, surely.
[*Laughter.*]

BUCKLEY: Well, the similarities would occur more quickly to you than to me . . .

ELLSBERG: I would not have indicted President Nixon under the espionage statute.
[*Laughter.*]

BUCKLEY: That's, of course, frivolous because the Constitution of the United States—which, incidentally, I urge you to Xerox [*laughter*]—confers on the executive the right to make foreign policy. . . . [18]

As an ally of Nixon, Buckley found his campus speeches sometimes disrupted by protesters. In June 1970, he was interrupted in the middle

of a commencement address at the University of California at Riverside when student protesters commanded the stage and presented him
with a live pig, a symbol of police brutality. As Buckley began to
speak again, a demonstrator exploded a tear-gas canister in the audience. Over the gas, Buckley declared, "Reason may not save us, but
the absence of reason will not save us."[19] But in a column on the
Riverside event, Buckley recounted the presentation of the pig as a
somewhat humorous event and confined himself to wondering
whether he wasn't "playing horse to other people's Lady Godiva."[20]

As he mellowed, his image changed. He appeared tough, but not
rigid and unyielding. Somewhat to his own embarrassment, women
began to find him sexy.*After his speeches, young girls would crowd
the stage like groupies at a rock 'n' roll concert. When he had feminist
Germaine Greer on *Firing Line,* she teased him about his attractive-
ness.

> GREER: I might as well say that if you weren't such a good-
> looking fellow, you wouldn't be in the position that
> you're in today. You exploit it, too. You may not do it
> consciously.
> BUCKLEY: Well, now, wait a minute—
> GREER (to the audience): Don't you agree that he is a pretty
> man?
> BUCKLEY: Well, I [*laughter*]—Let's accept that as a hypothesis.[21]

Buckley's abandonment of his harsher public face had something to
do with his fracas with Vidal, from which Buckley had emerged chastened. But it was also a result of the change in his political status.
Buckley's posture of public hostility had been based on his being an
outsider and a dissenter, but his relationship to the Nixon administration had transformed him into an insider. He was now defending—
and trying to find accommodations with—the status quo rather than
trying to overthrow it.

Even more than before, Buckley attempted to draw a distinction
between the far-Left leadership of the civil rights and antiwar movements and the local leaders and rank and file. He looked for what was

---

* In a March 1973 study for *Psychology Today* of "The Sexual Fantasies of Women," E.
Barbara Hairton described one of the women she had studied: "Dotty was typical of the
group of women who had varied erotic fantasies during intercourse . . . Her fantasy partners were dominant men, intellectuals like William F. Buckley, Jr., or physically forceful
movie stars like Steve McQueen."

positive in the movements. He praised Yale professor Charles Reich's *The Greening of America,* a book that attempted to frame the new culture in terms of a decentralized, communitarian politics. "The best of the troubled youth of today, who for instance have recently discovered Charles Reich in *The Greening of America,* ought to get around to discovering that conservatives have been plugging for many years for the best of what *they,* the Reichians, want." [22]

In May 1969, Buckley joined eleven other journalists in a tour of eight black ghettos that was sponsored by the Urban League and *Time.* To the surprise of the other journalists, Buckley got along remarkably well with the black militants. "Wherever they went, the one who got the most respect and was not treated like some patronizing honky was Bill," said his friend Richard Clurman, *Time*'s chief of correspondents. Buckley's conclusions about what he had seen and heard, while betraying a trace of condescension, were very generous: "The quality and the energy—and the charm—of black leaders in all of these cities is a major marvel. . . . Anyone expecting to hear better speech, better organized ideas, greater enthusiasm in the graduate schools of the Ivy League, has a pleasant surprise coming to him." [23]

Buckley remained most open to the culture rather than the politics of the sixties. On *National Review,* Buckley hired young editors like Chris Simonds who were rock-music fans, and he published—to Meyer's and Rusher's dismay—favorable articles on the Rolling Stones, the Grateful Dead, and the Woodstock rock festival. When a conservative student from Northwestern University wrote him, deploring his and *National Review*'s attitude toward rock music, Buckley printed his letter in "Notes and Asides" and solicited responses from the other editors. He also invited the student to write about the new music for *National Review.*

In 1969, when YAF split over the war and the legalization of marijuana, Buckley intervened to win a hearing for the libertarians who favored marijuana legalization, while denouncing YAF's antiwar faction. That same year, he went to Capitol Hill to testify on behalf of a proposal by New York Congressman Ed Koch to appoint a commission to study the effects of marijuana. Hesitant to discuss something he had never tried, Buckley obtained a sample of Panama Gold from a New York police friend, and, with several friends, sailed out beyond the official limits and lit up. (In 1972, Buckley would come out in favor of decriminalizing marijuana use.)

Simonds attributed Buckley's openness to his love of the new. "Bill was interested in the nonpolitical life-style manifestations [of the counterculture]," Simonds said, "because Bill is fascinated by new things. Bill loves nothing better than to learn something new."

But there were other reasons why Buckley went out of his way to distinguish the cultural from the political manifestations of the sixties. Buckley, who had emerged as a political figure when he was at Yale, was determined that *National Review* be relevant to the young. He believed that winning over college students to conservatism was the way in which *National Review* would create a conservative movement in America. And if there were conservative college students who liked the Rolling Stones, then he believed that *National Review* should reconsider its attitude toward the Rolling Stones.

And Buckley had a more personal reason to take the counterculture seriously. Both his son and his nephews and nieces were devotees. Christopher was sampling both LSD and marijuana by the time he graduated from Portsmouth Priory and was chiding his father about his intolerance toward Martin Luther King, drugs, and rock 'n' roll. John Buckley, Jr., who was then a student at Deerfield, attributed his uncle's change of heart largely to Christopher. "He became tolerant because of Chris," John said.

III

After his mayoral bid, Buckley had publicly brushed aside suggestions that he run for office again. He would run, he told *Time*'s Larry DuBois, in one circumstance: if "voting was by invitation only." [24] But privately he continued to be drawn to politics.

In September 1967, New York Conservatives had formed a committee to draft Bill Buckley to run against incumbent Republican Senator Jacob Javits. Buckley had written a letter to the committee discouraging it, but didn't completely rule out a race until the next winter. Buckley had claimed that the main consideration was that he was a Connecticut resident and would be open to carpetbagging charges again, but other considerations seemed to play an equal, if not greater, part in his decision: the idea of running against Javits did not interest him the way that running against Robert Kennedy had two years earlier. Javits was a proven vote getter—virtually impossible for a Democrat or a Conservative to defeat—and was also Jewish. According to Kieran O'Doherty, Buckley feared an attempt to tie his candidacy to the anti-Semitic Right, and he was worried that he would lose both *Firing Line* and his column. In February, Harry Elmlark had written him that if he ran "we would fold the tent."[25] "I've got my column," he told Kieran O'Doherty. "I can't screw that up."

Buckley saw his column and television show as commanding an audience far greater than that of a politician. His response to a *Playboy* interviewer in 1970 was revealing. "What would you feel about running for a seat in the House?" the interviewer asked Buckley. "God, no," Buckley replied. "Not unless I can have all the seats simultaneously."[26]

When Buckley turned them down, the New York Conservatives turned to Buckley's brother Jim. Jim was a man of sensibility rather than ideology: a conservative rather than a radical in temperament. Soft-spoken, bright but not brillant, a man who not only was, but appeared to be, nice. Based in New York, he had spent most of two prior decades overseeing Catawba's holdings in Israel, the Philippines, and the Spanish Sahara. When he first heard from Bill that the Conservatives were determined to draft him, he was bedridden in Libya with a broken disc.

Jim Buckley was an even less likely candidate than his brother. He was not a cold man, but he was extremely detached. He preferred watching birds—his abiding passion since he was a child—to shaking the hands of working-class voters outside a supermarket. Like Bill, he saw politics as unseemly. But like Bill he was able to turn his eccentricities to political advantage. In an era when the populace had come to distrust politicians, they trusted men who didn't seem made from that mold.

Bill urged Jim to take the plunge. "Nothing is quite the same again" after running for office, Buckley wrote his brother in March. "There is a certain exhilaration in making one's points well, in feeling the response of a crowd in reaction to one's own rhetorical arguments." In conclusion, he advised his brother to become a "lackadaisical candidate."[27]

Jim ran a serious and well-managed but not arduous campaign. He received, however, an astounding 1,139,402 votes, or 17.4 percent, in a three-man race that Javits won. In 1966, the Conservative Party's gubernatorial candidate had received only 510,023 votes.

In 1969, Conservative Party leaders Dan Mahoney and Kieran O'Doherty again began pressuring Bill to run in the 1970 Senate race. Robert Kennedy was dead, and the man Rockfeller had chosen to replace him, upstate Representative Charles Goodell, had surprised party regulars by moving rapidly to the Left once he had assumed higher office. On September 25, 1969, he infuriated Nixon by sponsoring a proposal to withdraw all troops from Vietnam by December 31, 1970. An effective Conservative might be able to pick up most of the Republican vote, it was reasoned, while Goodell and the Democrat would split the liberal vote.

In the fall of 1969, Mahoney brought Clifton White to lunch with Buckley. If Buckley won the Senate, White pointed out, he could command two hundred electoral votes in 1972—enough to mount a significant campaign for President. The prospect of being President did interest Buckley, and he took several weeks to make a final decision, but he finally turned the Conservatives down. "If somebody had said that I could be President, I would have said yes, which is different from saying, 'I can give you a twenty percent chance of being President, if you desert your career and try to climb this particular ladder.' The answer is no, and I said no," Buckley recalled.

Mahoney and O'Doherty then approached Jim Buckley, who initially turned them down flat. But by the spring of 1970, Jim Buckley had begun to have second thoughts. He asked Bill Rusher for advice. He was willing to run, he told Rusher, if he really had a chance of winning. Did Rusher think he did? Rusher contacted Cliff White, who had hired Arthur Finkelstein (later the New Right's foremost pollster) to conduct a statewide poll. Finkelstein discovered that Buckley would begin the election with the allegiance of 25 percent of state voters, no matter who his opponent was. "We can win," he told Jim Buckley at lunch, and Buckley made the decision to run, with White as his campaign manager.

Under White's firm hand, Jim Buckley ran a campaign intended to capture the GOP vote while defusing charges that he was an extremist. He focused his campaign on the need for "stability," backed greater federal authority in protecting the environment, and eschewed the usual right-wing attacks on Medicare, social security, and labor unions. Bill played a largely behind-the-scenes role in the campaign, acting, among other things, as a go-between with the Nixon administration and trying unsuccessfully to win Nelson Rockefeller's blessing for the Conservative Party, if not for Jim Buckley himself.

The administration's role in the campaign was small but important. Nixon could not formally endorse Jim Buckley against a Republican without splitting his own party, but he did whatever he could to show his support for Buckley. On the way back from a campaign trip in Connecticut in October, Nixon stopped at the Westchester County Airport long enough for Conservative Party pickets, who had been advised of the visit, to be photographed surrounding the President with "Nixon and Buckley" signs.

Nixon had Agnew demonstrate more explicitly the administration's displeasure with Goodell and its friendship for Buckley. Agnew denounced Goodell as a "radiclib" and as the "Christine Jorgensen of the Republican Party," referring to a noted transsexual of the time. And with Bill acting as intermediary, the White House arranged that at a luncheon in New York in October, Agnew be photographed with Jim Buckley.

As the Conservatives had hoped, on election day Goodell and his Democratic opponent split the liberal vote, while Buckley got the upstate Republican vote and some of the disaffected middle-class ethnic vote that Buckley had gotten in the mayoral election in 1965. He won with 2,288,190 votes, or 39 percent of the total.

Jim Buckley's victory made Nixon even more eager to appease Bill and the conservatives. The weekend after the election he invited Bill and Mahoney and O'Doherty and their wives to visit him in his retreat in the Bahamas. Buckley managed to discuss with the President his disquiet about Socialist Salvador Allende's victory in Chile, but the event was largely social. Nixon promised Buckley that he would speak at *National Review*'s fifteenth-anniversary celebration the next month—a promise that he broke only because former French president Charles de Gaulle died on that morning and Nixon had to fly to Paris for the memorial service.

When Buckley visited Nixon in the White House after the *National Review* anniversary celebration, Nixon quoted him the articles that the magazine had published in its anniversary issue. "This is an experience that [*Playboy* editor] Hugh Hefner's people ought to look into," Buckley told Buchanan and Nixon.

Nixon also arranged for Buckley to meet Agnew, who had become a sincere admirer of his. Agnew agreed to be the guest speaker at a special *National Review* luncheon planned in December for high-level corporate executives. The event was not only intended to reward prime *National Review* contributors like Jeremiah Milbank and Roger Milliken, but also to draw together under *National Review*'s aegis the leaders of American industry. Thus such notables as Edgar Speer, the president of U.S. Steel, James Roche, the chairman of the board of General Motors, Fred Borch, the chairman of General Electric, and Floyd Hall, the president of Eastern Air Lines, attended.

The luncheon, which became an annual event, was another clear indication that Buckley and *National Review* were no longer a voice of protest against the establishment, but a part of it.

Jim Buckley's election also elevated the Buckley family to the celebrity status enjoyed by the most famous Democratic family, the Kennedys. *Newsweek* ran a box in its story of the 1970 election results, "The Buckleys: An Extraordinary Family." [28] And in the most important tribute of all, *Life,* then the most popular magazine in America, put the Buckley family, as photographed by Alfred Eisenstaedt in Sharon on Thanksgiving 1970, on its cover and ran not only a story on the family but also an article on Will Buckley by Buckley's youngest brother, Reid.

The *Life* story made the comparison with the Kennedys explicit. Under a picture of the Buckleys playing touch football, it wrote, "Without a scorecard, you can scarcely tell the touch football players of Sharon from the Kennedys of Hyannis Port."

Buckley was not pleased by the comparison of his family with an upwardly mobile Irish Catholic family. When one *Newsweek* interviewer asked Buckley about it, he replied testily and somewhat disingenuously, "We do have similarities to the Kennedys. Our wealth, our fecundity, our Catholicism. Other than that the comparison is engaging but misleading. The Kennedys had an Irish Catholic upbringing. I didn't know where Ireland was until I graduated from Yale." [29] But Buckley did not object to the fact that the family was being exalted. Along with his brothers and sisters, he was heady with success. Buckley was confused, however, about what Jim's success meant for him, and in his next book he tried, among other things, to sort out the meaning of his brother's election.

IV

Buckley had the idea for a new book right after the election, and he wrote it in Switzerland in February and March of 1971. The book, which he called *Cruising Speed* and which was serialized in *The New Yorker* before being brought out in hardcover, consisted of a diary kept for a week beginning November 30, but Buckley did not confine himself to reporting that week's events. Instead, the flow of association from present to past and back became the pretext for reflections on the state of the nation and for a far fuller portrait of his life than could have been gleaned from one fall week.

The style was that of *The Unmaking of a Mayor* done one better: the prose appeared effortless, the most subtle connections mere association. As literature, *Cruising Speed* reflected romantic self-expression pioneered by Jack Kerouac and others in the fifties and refined by Norman Mailer and James Baldwin in the sixties.

One sees Buckley as *National Review* editor, *Firing Line* host, columnist, public speaker, friend of the President, brother of the new junior senator, amateur pianist and Bach lover, mentor to scores of high-school and college students who eagerly seek his advice and opinion in hundreds of letters a week, many of which he personally answers, as well as, briefly, father, husband, friend, and bon vivant. The only Buckley missing is the one most familiar to many Americans from Buckley's earlier period: the fierce right-winger determined to do in his opponents.

The Buckley of *Cruising Speed* is above all a nice man. He gives a bearded hitchhiker a ride and, when he discovers that the boy doesn't have a destination or place to stay, puts him up at his house. He responds at length and with respect to long letters from a left-wing history professor. At one point, he even reveals the pain that his unpopularity has caused him. When he speaks at a synagogue in St. Paul, Minnesota, he overhears the young assistant rabbi being asked whether he wants to meet him. The assistant rabbi says, "Hell no," just as he is propelled toward Buckley's hand. Buckley says about the incident,

> I dismissed it as utterly inconsequential, totally understandable, infinitely excusable, etc. etc., even though the sting punctured, and one of these days I will perhaps know enough about myself, though I do not spend much time in conscious introspection . . . to know whether such things are an offense pure and simple against my vanity, or whether, as I would prefer to think, they offend me as ruptures of the membrane of social affections (Garry Wills's term) that makes it possible for people to live together, people by defini-tion being people who disagree on questions trivial and substantial.[30]

He goes so far as to directly plead his case. "I realize that I am, for all my passions, implacably, I think almost *unfailingly* fair, objective, just. . . . I could not conceive, for instance, of disparaging another man's talents simply because I disapprove of the ends to which they are harnessed."[31]

Cruising Speed was also an attempt to justify the life he had chosen, both in view of his brother's Senate race and a decade of doubt about whether he had been correct to abandon scholarship for public life. Jim's victory had somewhat unsettled Buckley. His friends had de-tected a trace of sibling rivalry in his response to his brother's victory. At the victory celebration at the Waldorf Astoria, Buckley had

blanched when his normally modest brother proclaimed from the ros-
trum, "I am the voice of the new politics." Standing amidst friends
and family, Buckley quipped, *"La nouvelle politique c'est god damn
well moi."*

Jim's victory had at once appeared to foreclose his own political
career and had created a need for self-justification and self-celebra-
tion, which he fulfilled through *Cruising Speed.* The book seemed to
say, one friend remarked, "Hey, let's remember the seating order
among Buckley brothers. Jim is a wonderful fellow, but not the most
wonderful fellow."

Through *Cruising Speed,* Buckley also tried to show that his life
was as useful as the life of a scholar and writer of "big books." His
friend John Kenneth Galbraith had chided him to give up public life
the way that Kendall, Meyer, and others had. "Come to the academy
and write *books.* It is only *books* that count," Galbraith had told him
that winter in Switzerland as they skied together.

> But—I answer in hindsight—the theoretical depth is *there,* and if I
> have not myself dug deep the foundations of American conserva-
> tives, at least I have advertised their profundity. How can I hope to
> do better against positivism than Voegelin has done? Improve on
> Oakeshott's analysis of rationalism? . . . What does it take to *sat-
> isfy,* to satisfy *truly, wholly*? . . . A sense of social usefulness. . . .
> How will I satisfy those who listen to me today, *tomorrow*? Hell,
> how will I satisfy *myself* tomorrow, satisfying myself so imper-
> fectly, which is not to say insufficiently, today; at cruising speed?*

Cruising speed was Buckley's metaphor for a life, as he saw it, of
steady, unremitting good works. It was a life that was justifiable even
if it didn't produce electoral victories or big books.

---

* *Cruising Speed,* 229. Eric Voegelin and Michael Oakeshott were both conservative political philosophers. Voegelin's *The New Science of Politics* had an important influence on
American conservatives, and Bill himself was fond of repeating Voegelin's warning
against liberal utopianism: "Conservatives believe that there are rational limits to politics,
that politics should not, in the lofty phrase of Voegelin, attempt to 'immanentize the
eschaton.' " *(Unmaking of a Mayor,* 196–97.)

CHAPTER 18

The Shock of Rejection

While Buckley himself was largely unaffected by the frenzy of the late sixties, two of his closest friends, Brent Bozell and Garry Wills, were very much changed by the times. As Buckley was trying to steer a course between backing Nixon and commending counter-culture theorist Charles Reich, he fell out with both Bozell and Wills. Buckley had moved too much toward the center for Bozell and not far enough for Wills. But in both cases, personal tensions underlay strong political disagreement.

I

Bozell had been Buckley's peer and contemporary at Yale, but in spite of his immense talents, he could never escape Buckley's preeminence. "He was always in Bill's shadow, at Yale and everywhere else," their classmate Bill Ottley said. When *McCarthy and His Enemies* appeared in 1954, the critics treated it as Buckley's book, even though Bozell had done at least half the work and had contributed as much to its overall perspective as Buckley had. Journalist William S. White, reviewing *McCarthy and His Enemies* in *The New York Times,* wrote, "The authors are William F. Buckley, Jr.—who achieved a certain prominence with his only other book, *God and Man at Yale*—and his brother-in-law, L. Brent Bozell, who is a lawyer and has never written a book before. One assumes that Mr. Buckley led this team." [1]

When he was a senior editor at *National Review,* Bozell had displayed at times—especially with regard to the Soviet Union—a certain hard-edged fanaticism. "He was my first realization that you could look wonderful and be bright and intelligent and clear-eyed and be totally bananas," John Leonard recalled. "He really believed in a preemptive nuclear strike on Moscow. I just had this sense of a red-haired guy who could wipe out a city without really being able to imagine there were people in the city."

In the early sixties, looking for time to write his book on the Warren Supreme Court, Bozell took his family to live in Spain, where Buckley's brother Reid lived. There, under the influence of Franco's Falange and the Carlist tradition (a red-bereted conservative clerical movement dating from the 1830s that wanted to restore the line of monarchical succession interrupted by Ferdinand VII), Bozell's political differences with Buckley and *National Review* began to sharpen.

According to Bozell, his first important disagreement with *National Review* was over its describing Pope John's encyclical as a "venture in triviality"and its quip, *"Mater sí, Magistra no."* Bozell was no less opposed to the contents of the encyclical than Buckley was, but he thought Buckley's reaction was impious. "I talked with Bill a little about that. He laughed about it. It was a deep Buckley position. And things began to go badly then," Bozell recalled.

In 1963, Bozell wrote Buckley resigning as a senior editor of *National Review* in order to "give single-minded attention to whatever new thing I decide to do in the future." [2] When he returned to the United States that year, Bozell was intent on establishing an identity distinct from Buckley and *National Review*. He tried to undertake a political career, running for Congress against incumbent Republican Charles Mathias in Montgomery County, Maryland, but his campaign was marked by his looming eccentricity.

Buckley dispatched Neal Freeman to run Bozell's campaign for him. Freeman was immensely impressed with Bozell's oratory—"Brent gave some of the best speeches that Montgomery County or any other county has ever heard," Freeman recalled—but bewildered by his choice of issues. "Brent used to go to the Kiwanis Club and talk about the Gnostic heresy," Freeman recalled. Bozell would gather his campaign staff around the breakfast table in his Bethesda home, including Willmoore Kendall, who was domestic policy expert, and Frederick "Fritz" Wilhelmsen, a University of Dallas political theologian who was in charge of foreign policy. The advisers, Freeman recalled, "thought that the Carlist succession was the number-one foreign policy issue facing America and the biggest domestic issue was the Gnostic heresy, which was spreading across the landscape." (Bozell's other adviser was Howard Hunt, who, according to Freeman, "declined to identify why he was there or who he worked for.")

After being thrashed by Mathias, Bozell set out to establish a new political party. When he presented the proposal at one of the *National Review* editors' evening meetings in New York, Burnham took the lead in pouring cold water on it. Hurt by Burnham and Buckley's rejection and unable to raise money for the new party, Bozell turned to a plan for a new right-wing Catholic journal to be called *Triumph*. An organizing meeting for the new journal was held in Detroit with Russell Kirk (who had converted to Catholicism), Wilhelmsen, and other Catholic conservatives. Kirk described his own reaction. "Brent had already drawn up a dummy magazine, blue and white, and he wanted to know what I thought of it. I said, 'Well, Brent, this is quite impressive, but there is already a magazine just like this. It is called *National Review*.' He didn't like that. It was primarily an anti–*National Review* thing."

Buckley was initially enthusiastic about Bozell's founding a Catholic conservative magazine.* He provided Bozell with fund-raising contacts, and after the second issue of *Triumph* had appeared, he wrote an editorial for *National Review* welcoming "jubilantly the founding of a journal of conservative Catholic opinion."[3] But the relationship between Buckley and Bozell had already begun to sour.

In March 1966, when Buckley wrote a column warning that Catholics should not try to seek legislation that would impose on others their belief that abortion is murder, Bozell wrote a letter to the editor of *National Review* protesting that the column "reeks of relativism. . . . Mr. Buckley writes in this instance as though he had never heard of the natural law."[4] Buckley was stung by the letter. He composed a reply ("Yes, I am angry, because I consider that your letter is pompous, conceited . . . "), but then never sent it.[5]

Triumph's politics became theocratic rather than conservative, with Bozell denouncing America and its constitutional tradition of religious tolerance. In a February 1968 essay repudiating his own book on the

---

* Earlier, in the late fifties, through Burnham's brother Philip, who had been the editor of *Commonweal* and who after retiring from the magazine still had considerable stock in it, Buckley and Burnham had tried unsuccessfully to take over *Commonweal*.

Warren Court, Bozell attacked the American Constitution for being answerable only to itself and not to God. In a letter to the editor, Buckley objected, "All of history concerts to render Mr. Bozell's essay nothing more than an act of piety, history having shown us that great constitutions larded with religious sycophancy have failed in and of themselves to promulgate a free society, let alone a noble society."[6]

In the summer of 1968, after Buckley and Bozell had made an unsuccessful attempt to patch up their differences, Patricia tried to explain Brent to Bill:

> Before *Triumph,* he felt caged by being put (by himself as well, perhaps) in an eternal position of comparison vis-á-vis you. It was a competition neither of you looked for or wanted, and his awareness of your embarrassment at being "ahead" made him set up a defensive barrier against your own. . . . [When he found] his life's work—a defender of the Faith—others' opinions no longer mattered in terms of *personal* self-respect.[7]

The political and personal rift continued to widen. In 1969, Bozell claimed that after Goldwater's defeat the conservative movement had "ceased to be an important political force in America" and repudiated conservatism as an "inadequate substitute for Christian politics."[8] In an editorial, *National Review* described Bozell's analysis as "morbid." "There are those who will not settle for anything less than a mutinous relationship between themselves and their society. . . . To dismiss even contemporary America as one vast plot against the survival of our eternal souls is Manichean and boring."[9] Bozell replied in *Triumph* that while *National Review* had played an important role in the past, "history . . . is moving on to other things, leaving *National Review* to run through its figures."[10]

In 1969, when Buckley decided to include an excerpt from *The Warren Revolution* in his anthology of conservative thought, Bozell responded angrily that he would have denied him permission to reprint the piece "on the grounds that it would be good discipline for you to write your own books." Buckley replied, "I marvel at the behavior of someone who would lead others into Christian habits."[11]

Marvin Liebman, who was close to both Buckley and Bozell, saw the effects of the feud on Buckley. "For Bill, it was very traumatic. The shock of being rejected was very difficult for him," Liebman recalled.

At its peak, *Triumph* had 30,000 subscribers, and a faction that championed its politics in YAF. But both Brent and Patricia Bozell were getting swept up in the hysteria of the late sixties. They increasingly supplemented *Triumph's* polemics against moral decay with political action against the proponents of abortion and pornography.

In 1970, the Bozells founded both a militant anti-abortion organization, Action for Life, and a "broader" organization, the Society for a Christian Commonwealth. One of their sons, Chris, who was enrolled at the University of Dallas, started a neo-Carlist group, Los Hijos de Tormenta, the Sons of Thunder. In June, Brent, swinging a huge wooden cross, led the Sons of Thunder, adorned in red berets and khaki shirts and pants, through the locked plate-glass door of the George Washington University Student Health Service, which, according to Bozell, was counseling abortions. Along with four others, he was arrested and convicted for the action.

The next year, while Brent knelt outside on the pavement, Patricia stormed the stage of the Catholic University auditorium where feminist Ti-Grace Atkinson was speaking. In a speech at Notre Dame earlier, Atkinson had charged that the Catholic Church was "using" Mary in its theory of the virgin birth. When Atkinson, speaking at Catholic University by dint of a court order, declared that Mary would have been better off if she had been "knocked up," Patricia rose from her seat, shouted, "I can't stand this," and striding up to the platform, tried to slap Atkinson. She was arrested.

Publicly, both Buckley and his brother Jim came to their sister's defense. In *National Review,* Buckley cited C. S. Lewis ("the higher the stakes, the greater the temptation to lose your temper") to explain Patricia's actions.[12] But in a letter to Reid, Buckley admitted that he was saddened by Brent "publicly assaulting a hospital [and] by Tish's (God bless her) assault on Ti-Grace Atkinson."[13]

After the two incidents, Bozell became more outspoken in describing the differences between him and Buckley. In an interview with the *Pittsburgh Post-Gazette,* Bozell said that "it is a hindrance to be William Buckley's brother-in-law, because people are under the assumption that I share his views. I do not. He is the right-wing establishment. I consider myself outside the establishment."[14]

At the same time, Brent began to show the first pronounced signs of manic depression, and Patricia, who had begun to suffer from alcoholism in Spain, resumed drinking. Buckley had clung to the conviction that what separated him from Bozell was simply the strength and intractability of Bozell's convictions, but he began to believe that it was, above all, an acute mental illness that stood between them. Outside of performing private acts of kindness—he paid the Bozell

children's tuition at prep schools—there was little that he could do.
"I think [Bozell's deterioration] hurt Bill more than anybody," Neal
Freeman said. "It was a process of Bill trying to reach back for Brent
and Brent going off into another zone."

Freeman and Buckley's other friends believed that the breakup of
the friendship was primarily the result of Bozell's mental condition.

> I was never persuaded that the political differences were all that
> real [Neal Freeman said]. Brent was not only a great telephone
> artist, but he was a great letter writer, and a day without intellectual
> controversy was a day wasted. Because he and Bill had been so
> close, there was a special edge to his disagreements, but Brent
> simply started to fade, and you could see it happening, but you
> couldn't do anything about it.

The breakup of their friendship probably could not have occurred
ten years prior or ten years hence. It was very much a product of the
tumultuous sixties, which exhilarated Buckley and which lifted him to
new heights of celebrity, but in which more troubled, less stable souls
like Bozell capsized. *National Review* editor Jeffrey Hart, who was
briefly an editor of *Triumph,* concluded in a 1973 letter to Buckley
that "the *Triumph* phenomenon was traceable to the prevailing frenzy
of the 1960s—a nice irony, in that the magazine labored to *separate*
itself from American culture generally." [15]

II

At the same time that Bozell was embracing a neo-Carlist politics,
Garry Wills, under the impact of the civil rights and antiwar movements, was developing very wide differences with *National Review*'s
conservatism.

Wills dated his own break with *National Review* from the long
article he wrote for *Esquire* in 1968 on the ghetto riots, "The Second
Civil War." In the article, Wills sympathetically recounted the views
of black militants and called for the police to "contain" rather than
"get tough" with the rioters. Buckley told *Time* reporter Larry Du-
Bois that Wills had "gone over to the militants." [16] And Frank Meyer
tried to prevent Wills from covering the Democratic Convention for
National Review.

By 1968, Wills had not only become sympathetic to black militants,
but adamantly opposed to the Vietnam War. "Garry was very much
on the other side then," Neal Freeman recalled. "He was very much

in tune with the McCarthy-Kennedy wing of the Democratic Party and beginning to be more than a little embarrassed by his historical connection to *National Review*." Buckley printed Wills's descriptive report on the convention over the protests of other editors, and defended its publication in "Notes and Asides" when readers wrote in protesting that it didn't belong in *National Review*. But Wills's convention article was the last political article of his that Buckley would publish in *National Review*.

After the convention, Wills abandoned his biography of Buckley—he told Knopf editor Sophie Wilkins, "I decided that Buckley wasn't important enough"—and began working on a book on Nixon. In *Nixon Agonistes*, Wills attempted to understand the crisis of liberalism, of which he saw Nixon as the ultimate practitioner. In so doing, Wills did not abandon his own identification as a conservative. Instead, he chose to redefine conservatism along the lines that had been sketched out by the "new conservatives" of the early fifties. Wills identified conservatism with Eisenhower rather than with Joe McCarthy or Goldwater and with the responsible use of government power rather than with a mythical free market. In *Nixon Agonistes*, Wills issued a political challenge not merely to Nixon but also to Buckley and *National Review*.

When Wills sent Buckley the draft of *Nixon Agonistes*, Buckley responded that *Nixon Agonistes* was really two books. The first was "the most exciting political book I have ever read. . . . The second . . . a new cosmology. I do not believe you should have combined the two." [17] Frank Meyer's assessment was far less charitable or discerning. In a review that appeared oblivious to most of the book, Meyer described *Nixon Agonistes* as "bilious in its view of Mr. Nixon . . . and the America of self-reliance. . . . The book echoes with the curiously mixed accents of [Bayard] Rustin, Malcolm X, and Tom Hayden." [18]

Both Wills and Buckley realized that the political dispute over civil rights, Vietnam, and the nature of conservatism was threatening their friendship. In May 1970, Wills decided to begin a syndicated column. He wrote Buckley, "I decided the day after Kent State—Nixon has to be stopped. The war has to be. You won't like [the columns]. But I hope you stay 'soft' on their author—as he is on you." Buckley replied a month later:

> Of course, I will maintain, and even cherish my weakness for you. But my disappointment is keen. Not at your taking the stand you have taken, but at some of the rhetoric and argumentation you are

using [in your columns], as for instance, the point that neither Kissinger nor Moynihan should be welcomed back in the academy unless they join your crusade and quit the administration.[19]

In *Cruising Speed* and his columns, Buckley always mixed whatever criticisms he had of Wills with praise and affirmation of their friendship. In one column, he referred to Wills as "my learned, beloved friend Garry Wills, who has taken to the left with alcoholic gusto."[20] Wills reciprocated. Asked in an interview in the *National Catholic Reporter* "Do you still get along with William Buckley?" Wills replied, "I'm still close to him. I admire him very much. My view of him is totally opposed to that of most critics—which is that he is very bright, clever, and brilliant, but morally despicable. Actually, he's the most charitable, kind person I know."[21] When he saw the interview, Buckley wrote Wills, "I consider the publication of your interview in the *National Catholic Reporter,* in which you said what you did about me, the highest achievement of my life."[22]

But politics kept driving them apart. In 1970, Wills submitted to *National Review* what he believed to be a "conservative" argument for opposing the Vietnam War and another for resolving the war in Northern Ireland. Buckley rejected both articles. In a letter, he explained that they were "unnecessarily provocative, in the sense that the special hurt of the conservative community, at losing the brightest of us all, did not seem to me worth stimulating."[23]

Wills reacted angrily. In February 1971, he wrote Buckley:

I have not wanted to quarrel with *National Review.* . . . I wanted to keep old ties, out of old debts and friendships, and hope of mutual instruction. That is why I continued to submit articles—the last two of which were subjected to editorial euthanasia. . . . My personal respect for you continues undiminished and for that reason I must tell you I think the magazine's standards of veracity and honor are scandalously low.[24]

The sniping between Buckley and Wills and between *National Review* and Wills began to intensify. The central issue was Wills's defense of the Berrigan brothers—an issue that combined Catholicism and anticommunism. In a letter, Wills urged Buckley to distinguish between the two Berrigan brothers, Daniel and Philip. Buckley replied that he would do so when Wills began to distinguish between Nixon and Satan. Wills responded, "On distinguishing between Nixon and Satan—that's *easy!* Satan's brighter."[25]

Buckley's public criticism of Wills grew harsh. In an April column, he complained that Wills was "beginning to sound like a slogan writer for the John Birch Society."[26] In a November column, he wrote:

> Garry Wills, in an age when priests are tortured by two of the world's major powers, writes about the "hysterical repression" against the Fathers Berrigan in America. . . . We go whimpering for the approval of the Underground Catholics, whose transfiguration teaches them that the enemy is J. Edgar Hoover and Richard Nixon, in a world that gave us Joseph Stalin and Mao Tse-tung. What overwhelms one is the historical frivolity of these confused, confusing men.[27]

As he had always done with friends, Buckley tried to separate his personal relationship from whatever political disagreement he had with Wills. But while he succeeded in doing so with John Leonard and John Kenneth Galbraith, he did not succeed with Wills. Part of the reason was that Wills, as the controversy continued, evinced what mutual friend Hugh Kenner described as an Oedipal hostility toward Buckley. "Bill was a kind of father figure who Garry had to kick," Kenner said. At one point Kenner invited them to a party at his Santa Barbara home. "We made the mistake of having everybody to dinner at once," Kenner said. "Garry just kept baiting Bill, and it made for a very uncomfortable evening for everybody. Bill is wonderful about that, continually brushing off that kind of thing. But if you knew him, you he could tell he was getting tense."

But Buckley found it more difficult to separate his political disagreement with Wills from his personal feelings about him. Wills hit at the core of Buckley's conviction: the unspoken link between Catholicism and anticommunism that had been forged by Will Buckley during the Mexican Revolution and passed on to his children.

John Leonard, one of *National Review*'s apostates, said,

> The defection of Garry Wills was the most painful of any of these defections. Garry was the future. He was religious. He was the genius they were waiting for. This was the real thing; this was their angel. His defection was the defection of their greatest hope. When Garry said what was happening to blacks was more important than what was reflected in the magazine, and it hurts me personally, morally, he spoke to that best part, that most vulnerable part of the Buckleys. It went from blacks to Nixon to Vietnam. He was saying, not simply I disagree with you, but I am closer to God. A real moral issue was being thrown at them. Coins of soul were being thrown

down. Garry was a soul. And Garry's burned soul scared the shit out of them.

Buckley's break with Wills and the deterioration of his friendship with Bozell meant a change both in his immediate circle of friends and in his interests in life. During the fifties, when he was writing *God and Man at Yale* and founding *National Review,* his closest friends and associates had been conservative political intellectuals like Kendall, Bozell, Schlamm, and Chambers. In the late fifties, both Burnham and Wills, one mentor and the other protégé, had come to occupy a position of similar importance in his life. These were the men with whom he discussed ideas, and to whose judgment he might defer.

Now only Burnham remained. Buckley's other friends among the political intelligentsia were men like Clurman and Galbraith with whom he had fun and sometimes matched wits. They did not challenge his deepest convictions nor provide counsel when he felt uncertain how to respond.

But by then, Buckley had abandoned the deeper intellectual project on which Kendall, Wills, Bozell, and others had been fellow travelers. He was largely falling into the routine of what critic Joseph Epstein called the life of the "celebrity intellectual." [28]

III

Buckley was becoming a member of the establishment that he had long fought. In 1970, he and Clurman organized a luncheon group that became called the Boys Club. Once very month or two, Buckley began having lunch with Clurman, *New York Times* editors A. M. (Abe) Rosenthal and Arthur Gelb, *Newsweek* editor Osborn Elliott, and *Public Interest* editor Irving Kristol. (Later the group added NBC newsman John Chancellor and journalist Theodore White.)

Buckley also became friendly with the group of intellectuals around *Public Interest* and *Commentary* that included not only Kristol, van den Haag, and Moynihan, but also Nathan Glazer and Norman Podhoretz. Appalled by what they saw as the excesses of the student and the militant black movements, these intellectuals had begun to move toward the Right, and in doing so, they began to see Buckley in a different light. "In this transition [away from the Left], Buckley proved to be a very important person," Moynihan said. "Buckley was civil and everybody else was becoming very uncivil." Moynihan, who, unlike Kristol or Podhoretz, never completed the journey from Left to Right, described how he and Nathan Glazer had been impressed by the way Buckley defended their book, *Beyond the Melting Pot,* against the charges of racism leveled by liberals and civil rights leaders. "My God, I was not a racist, I was not a bigot, but all the good guys were calling me a racist, [while] here was this fellow Buckley saying these thoughtful things," Moynihan recalled. "Glazer and I began to notice that we were getting treated in *National Review* with a much higher level of intellectual honesty."

Kristol later attributed Buckley's role in the Boys Club to a change in Buckley. "I don't think the Bill Buckley of 1959 or 1960 would have dreamed of setting up such a luncheon club," Kristol said. But it is equally true that in 1960 Kristol, Rosenthal, and Clurman would not have dreamed of having lunch regularly with the notorious right-wing firebrand. They had changed too.

In 1971, Buckley was invited to become a member of the Bohemian Grove, an annual summer camp meeting of prominent corporate and political leaders. Formerly the preserve of the West Coast elite, the Bohemian Grove gained importance in the sixties and seventies as power and money shifted westward in the country.

In 1967, California's conservative Republican Senator George Murphy had invited him as his guest. At that gathering, Reagan and Nixon, who were both members, met frequently and agreed finally that Reagan would stay out of the primaries unless Nixon faltered. And most of the men who would later become part of the Reagan administration, including George Bush, George Shultz, and Caspar Weinberger, were Grove members.

CHAPTER 19

The Manhattan Twelve

After the November 1970 elections, in which the Republicans did poorly, Nixon began to swing to the center. In January 1971, he introduced neo-Keynesian "full employment" calculations into his budget; he began to reduce military spending (it would fall in real dollars from $98 billion in fiscal year 1969 to $70 billion in FY 1973). Quietly, but not sufficiently so to elude the sight of James Burnham, he endorsed Willy Brandt's *Ostpolitik*—the West German chancellor's attempt to achieve reconciliation with the Soviet Union and East Germany. And there were well-founded rumors of a coming arms control treaty with the Soviet Union and of a rapprochement between the U.S. and China.

Buckley continued to defend Nixon into the spring of 1971, but on July 15, Nixon went too far. On that evening, Buckley and his brother Jim, sitting in the governor's mansion in Sacramento with Reagan, saw Nixon announce on television that he would travel to Peking the next year. Immediately after the speech, Kissinger called Reagan to assure him, in Buckley's words, "that the strategic intentions of the President were in total harmony with the concerns of the conservative community."[1] But in this case, Kissinger failed to convince either

Reagan or the Buckleys. Unfazed by the Sino-Soviet split or by the continuing debate about economic development in China, Buckley continued to see China, like the Soviet Union, as the embodiment of evil in the world. In a column following the speech, Buckley compared Nixon unfavorably to Franklin Roosevelt, who had refused to visit Hitler's Germany. And Buckley, at Burnham's suggestion, began planning a meeting of conservatives to protest Nixon's policies.

I

The meeting was held on a hot July afternoon in the living room of Buckley's East 73rd Street town house—it had formerly been the home of Buckley nemesis Dag Hammarskjöld—and drew the leaders of the Right's principal publications and organizations, then few in number. The participants included Frank Meyer, Rusher, Burnham, and Buckley from *National Review;* Allan Ryskind and Tom Winter from *Human Events;* John Jones and Jeff Bell, staff members of the American Conservative Union; Randy Teague, the executive director of Young Americans for Freedom; Stan Evans, the editor of the *Indianapolis News;* Neil McCaffrey of Arlington House; and Dan Mahoney, the chairman of the New York Conservative Party.

Everyone at the meeting except for Rusher and Evans had been enthusiastic supporters of Nixon in 1968. And even among those most opposed to Nixon's policies, there was some trepidation at opposing a President whom they had considered and many conservatives still did consider "their President."

Neal Freeman, who attended the meeting but did not sign the final statement for professional reasons, thought it was a historic occasion: "It was an extraordinary meeting. It wasn't on a weekend, but people had cleared their schedule and were out of reach of a telephone. We were talking about what for this group was a revolutionary act, and there was much basic philosophical root-seeking conversation."[2]

There was agreement in the group that a public statement critical of the Nixon administration should be issued, but there was considerable disagreement about how critical that statement should be. Among the most militantly anti-Nixon were Meyer, Rusher, Evans, Ryskind, Winter, Teague, and Bell. In June, the ACU had endorsed Agnew but not Nixon for renomination, while YAF had endorsed Reagan for President in 1972. The Washington contingent also tended to be as critical of Nixon's domestic policies as they were of his foreign policy. Among the least willing to make a clear break were Buckley, Burnham, and Mahoney. Freeman recalled "Buckley's discomfort at opposing his President, his party. He was walking on eggs throughout the whole meeting."

Evans was assigned the task of drawing up a statement for the group, and when he returned with a draft, the discussion narrowed to the precise terms of criticism. While Buckley backed Burnham's formulation of "suspending support" of the President, Evans, Rusher, and others wanted to talk of "repudiating" the administration. While Buckley recommended expressing their own policy preferences in "planks," Evans and the Washington contingent wanted the term "demands." And while Buckley preferred focusing on foreign policy, the Washington group wanted a broader emphasis. But the group largely acceded to Buckley's point of view.

The reason was not Buckley's powers of persuasion, but the special place he occupied in the group. He was not only the host, but by far the best known of the conservatives there. As the others realized, without his participation, the group's statement would be ignored. "The only thing that really gave us credibility was Buckley," Stan Evans, who was quite angry at the time, recalled. "Who else had anybody heard of?" As a result, they accorded his opinion greater weight than any of the others. "It was a constant preoccupation to keep Bill on board," Jeff Bell said. "We were negotiating a document that met Bill's requirements but that wouldn't drain all of the sting out of the message," Freeman said.

In the final statement, the twelve signatories declared that they had "resolved to suspend our support of the Nixon administration." Citing Nixon's overtures to China, defense budget reductions, and support of *Ostpolitik*, the signers said, "We touch only lightly on the failures of Mr. Nixon's administration domestically [which] pale into insignificance alongside the tendencies of the administration in foreign policy." But the group stopped short of encouraging "formal political opposition." And it closed on a Buckleyesque turn of phrase: "We reaffirm our personal admiration for Richard Nixon, and our wholehearted identification with the purposes he has over the years espoused as his own and the Republic's. We consider that our defection is an act of loyalty to the Nixon we supported in 1968."[3]

The next week, when Buckley stated the case himself in an essay for *The New York Times Magazine*, "Is Nixon One of Us?," he downplayed Nixon's domestic heresies:

His dalliance with and insecure instrumentation of interventionist fiscal economics reflects nothing more than the regnant confusion among economic theorists, and the acquiescence even by free market economists in the proposition that it is a political necessity to talk imperiously in the economic seas, even though we all know that the President sits on the throne of King Canute.

But he revealed his own fears about the direction of Nixon's foreign policy. The Right will support Nixon, Buckley argued,

provided there is no suspicion—none at all would be tolerated—that Mr. Nixon has been taken in by the other side's reveries, the reveries that are based on the notion that the leadership of the Communist world suddenly stepped forward, as after a speech by Billy Graham, to submit to prefrontal lobotomies, after which they returned to duty at Helsinki, and other pressure points in the world, to push SALT through to international peace and harmony, to tranquilize their legions in Vietnam, Egypt, Chile, West Germany, and Madagascar, whose name I mention only to meet the anapestic challenge. Richard Nixon will have to collapse that suspicion . . . and the tactical question is, how long can he postpone doing so, before the American right comes to the conclusion that he is not one of us.[4]

II

The Nixon administration tried to nip the conservative rebellion in the bud. Buchanan was dispatched to deal with the Washington conservatives, while Kissinger invited Buckley to Washington for a talk.

As Kissinger had done before, he convinced Buckley that the administration's putative hard line—as best represented by Kissinger himself—was being subverted by Rogers and the State Department. Buckley wrote Kissinger after their visit:

My perceptions sharpen, as always they do after visiting with you. Some difficulties I can understand; some of them, indeed, are ontological. Others I cannot understand. For instance, the failure to encourage the right people by promoting them and giving them positions of responsibility. For instance, the failure to refer publicly to the deteriorating military situation. Finally, the acceptance, in a capacity so critical, of someone [Rogers] whose exertions are a greater burden on the commonweal than those of a major enemy power.[5]

But when Buckley set up a meeting between Kissinger, Haig, and a selected group of the Manhattan Twelve, Kissinger failed to convince

Bell, Ryskind, Mahoney, and the others who attended of either his or the administration's commitment to the conservative cause. Bell described the meeting in Kissinger's White House office:

> Kissinger sat there and told us, "Some of ze tings dat I am going to dell you you must not even dell your vives." Can you believe that? We laughed about it afterwards. We had certain information from good sources about what they were saying. We knew for example that they were willing to compromise with the Soviets on missile accuracy. They were willing to compromise away hard target capability. Kissinger and Haig sat there and denied that was true. Kissinger looked over and said, "Al," and he smiled and shook his head . . . so it didn't impress us. We felt it was kind of a patronizing performance by Kissinger and Haig.

In any case, both Kissinger's and Buchanan's efforts to win over the Manhattan Twelve were being subverted by the administration's actions. On August 15, Nixon announced that he was instituting wage-price controls, a measure that he had denounced before and that many conservatives, including Burnham, regarded as "Fascistic." On September 20, Buckley hosted another meeting with Winter, Teague, Evans, Mahoney, and Rusher at his house. At this meeting, Rusher was delegated to get hold of a political consultant to prepare a report on the "possibilities for political action against Mr. Nixon."[6]

Events continued to inflame the conservatives. On October 5, the White House announced that Kissinger would visit Peking that month. On October 12, Nixon announced that he planned to visit Moscow the next May to negotiate the SALT arms control treaty. On October 21, the conservatives held another meeting in New York at which they agreed to draw up a list of demands to present to presidential counselor Charles Colson. Then, with tacit American support, the United Nations voted on October 25 to admit China and to exclude Taiwan. Rusher remarked, "Ever since we've been having these meetings, it has been raining shit."

On November 1, Ryskind presented six pages of demands to Colson. They included the retention of Agnew (who, it was rumored, Nixon planned to drop for Treasury Secretary John Connally), the abandonment of Moynihan's Family Assistance Plan, opposition to *Ostpolitik* and the European Security Conference, no SALT agreement that ceded a Soviet lead in land and sea-based missile launchers, full and stated support of the U.S. defense pact with Taiwan, vigorous prosecution of the war in Southeast Asia, and a "demonstration by action" that American foreign policy was not committed to the "illusion of détente."[7]

On November 30, the group met at the University Club in New York. When they had discussed the possibility of running a candidate against Nixon in the Republican primaries, there had been considerable skepticism, even from militants like Frank Meyer. But the administration's move to the center and the presence of an antiwar Republican, Representative "Pete" McCloskey, in the primaries made them reconsider.

Initially, Buckley opposed the idea. All the major conservative politicians, including Jim Buckley, were lined up firmly behind Nixon, and the only available candidate was Representative John Ashbrook, the chairman of the American Conservative Union and a little-known figure outside of rural Ohio and *Human Events* readers. Buckley feared that Ashbrook would do so poorly against Nixon that he would discredit the conservative challenge to Nixon. But Rusher, Evans, and the militants were convinced that the only way to pressure Nixon to the Right was to run a candidate against him. In the end, Buckley agreed to go along with the majority, and on December 2 a group of the conservatives met with Ashbrook in his Washington office to urge him to run against Nixon.

Ashbrook refused to commit himself at the initial meeting, but he was brought around by the public support of William Loeb, editor of the Manchester, New Hampshire, *Union Leader,* and by the enthusiastic support of conservatives at a private dinner December 13. At that meeting, Rusher contributed $1,000 of his own money to Ashbrook's campaign.[8]

Ashbrook's decision spread consternation through the Nixon camp. "Nixon was paranoid about primary opposition at that point," Agnew's political aide David Keene explained. "Remember the polls at this time showed that [Maine Democratic Senator Edmund] Muskie among others was running neck and neck with or ahead of Nixon." This time the administration sent its most important emissary, Agnew, to convince Buckley and Rusher to quell the revolt.

But Agnew's attitude toward the Ashbrook challenge was ambivalent to say the least. Keene recalled:

> We were viewing it a little bit differently than the Nixon people because to them it was an unmitigated evil, while to us it was a bit of a mixed blessing. We were in the middle trying to be good sol-

diers for Nixon, but Nixon was playing with John Connally. There was all this talk that he would have Connally as his second man and dump Agnew. We felt this could keep us on the ticket.

Agnew and Keene had breakfast with Buckley and Rusher on December 15 at the Waldorf Astoria in New York. According to Keene, Agnew watered down the administration's standard arguments against Ashbrook's candidacy with more implausible arguments of his own in order to send a subliminal message to Buckley and Rusher. He assured them that the Nixon administration was tending to the Right and that it would request a "substantial increase" in the defense budget for fiscal year 1972. But to Buckley and Rusher's surprise, he also argued that Ashbrook's candidacy would hurt his own chances of being on the ticket. If Ashbrook runs, Agnew said, "I'll be through in any case—Nixon will either put Ashbrook as his running mate in order to placate the conservatives, or pick some liberal like Rockefeller because he can no longer have conservative support." Buckley and Rusher tried to assure Agnew that Ashbrook's candidacy would increase "his leverage with Mr. Nixon," but seemingly to no avail.[9]

At the breakfast, Rusher and Buckley also revealed their own disagreement about the purpose of Ashbrook's candidacy. While Buckley conceived of Ashbrook's candidacy as an attempt to pressure Nixon within the framework of the Republican Party, Rusher presented Ashbrook's candidacy as a potential break between Republicans and conservatives. Agnew tried to play Buckley against Rusher. In a letter afterwards to Buckley, he wrote:

> I believe you and Bill Rusher have a basic agreement on the definition of the current difficulties. However, I confess to being reassured because you do not agree on the proper solution. Obviously, nothing is to be accomplished by separating conservatives from the Republican Party. . . . While I have great respect for Bill Rusher's ability and integrity, I hope he can be dissuaded from the course of action he has indicated he was about to pursue.[10]

Buckley took the bait. He replied to Agnew, "My colleague is a very passionate gentleman and that's OK. But it doesn't make for the most purposive discussions." Buckley told Agnew that he had lunched with Ashbrook that day and had

> urged him on making his announcement to declare that he will of course back the candidate of the Republican Party. He is reluctant to do this on the grounds that this will lessen his leverage. I reply

that this will increase his plausibility among regular Republicans in New Hampshire.[11]

When Buckley secured Ashbrook's agreement, he published an editorial in *National Review* promising support for Ashbrook if he were to run. But the editorial revealed Buckley's own hesitancy about the move. A majority of the Manhattan Twelve had voted in favor of Ashbrook's candidacy, the editorial stated, because

> they believe that a lightning rod is needed to attract the real dissent among Republicans, so that Mr. Nixon can feel the shock. Those opposed feared not only the possible futility of a rather hastily conceived venture without any organized backing, but the fallacious impression a meager result might give Nixon (and the nation) that the conservative wing within his own party is either decimated or complacent. *National Review* is not sponsoring Mr. Ashbrook's candidacy. On the other hand, if he runs we will of course endorse him . . . as most closely embodying the opinions of this journal.[12]

The administration was not through trying to pressure Buckley. In late December, Kissinger urged him not to break publicly with the administration. He suggested that Buckley agree to remain on the Advisory Commission of the USIA when his appointment expired the next spring, but Buckley refused. In a letter to USIA official Henry Loomis, Buckley wrote to explain why he would refuse reappointment to the commission: "I am heavily involved as a go-between with the insurrectionary right wing, and whereas I would under no circumstances use my position in the U.S.I.A. to embarrass Mr. Nixon, I do not want Mr. Nixon to use my association with the U.S.I.A. for political purposes."[13]

The administration also tried to use more heavy-handed tactics against Buckley. Top White House aide Peter Flanigan chided Buckley in a telephone call for backing Ashbrook after Nixon had arranged for Agnew to support his brother's Senate bid. When the details of their conversation appeared in Evans and Novak's newspaper column, an angry Buckley reprinted his response to Flanigan in "Notes and Asides":

> The backing of my brother by Richard Nixon in November of 1970 gives his administration zero claim on me to back administration policies when I disapprove of them. I have backed Mr. Nixon on a thousand occasions without having once supposed that for that reason he owed me anything. One of these days you will have to remind

yourself that there are really quite a lot of people in the U.S. who are *not* running for office and for whom patronage from the White House is *not* the supreme ambition . . . [14]

III

At the end of January, Buckley left for Switzerland after having recorded radio spots for Ashbrook to use in New Hampshire. In early February, Rusher wrote to inform Buckley that a poll the campaign took had shown only a 10 percent "hard-core conservative vote" among New Hampshire Republicans. Buckley replied that he was "frankly astonished at the nonchalant way in which we assume that John Ashbrook will fail to do as well as McCloskey." [15]

On February 15, Buckley returned to the U.S. and joined a select group of eighty journalists who were accompanying Nixon and Kissinger to Peking. Buckley was the only conservative columnist in an entourage dominated by network news anchors and the Washington bureau chiefs of major dailies. Nixon's press chief, Ron Ziegler, had originally planned to invite the more supportive Jack Kilpatrick, but Buchanan had insisted on Buckley as the most prominent conservative.

Buckley quipped his way through China. After the Americans had witnessed a three-hour revolutionary ballet, *The Red Detachment of Women,* Buckley was heard to mutter in the lobby, "I think this thing was written by some damned Communist." When the journalists and the Nixon staff were touring the Forbidden City, Buckley remarked loudly enough for Buchanan to hear, as they were standing looking up at one of the great thrones, "How do you think Ashbrook is going to look sitting up there?"

Nixon's staff got in their digs at Buckley too. At Nixon's banquet in Peking, they had Buckley seated between pro-Communist journalists Felix Greene and Wilfred Burchett. When Nixon's top aide, Robert Haldeman, ran into Buckley at a Peking souvenir store, he asked him, "Doing a little trading with the enemy, Bill?" [16]

While in Peking, Buchanan had lunch with Buckley. He knew that Buckley could not be dissuaded from supporting Ashbrook, but he hoped to convince him not to go beyond New Hampshire. Buckley assured him that the campaign would not go to California. But as Buckley's disgust with Nixon's performance in China grew, Buchanan began to doubt that Buckley or the conservatives would keep their word.

While Buckley remained personally cheerful throughout the trip, he became increasingly upset with Nixon. His columns bristled with irony and indignation at Nixon's willingness to cavort with men whom Buckley equated with Nazis. He wrote of Nixon's generous toasts at the first banquet:

Kindly make no mistake about the moral courage all this required. It is unreasonable to suppose that anywhere in history have a few dozen men congregated who have been responsible for greater human mayhem than the hosts at this banquet and their spiritual colleagues, instruments all of Mao Tse-tung. The effect was as if Sir Hartley Shawcross had suddenly risen from the prosecutor's stand at Nuremberg and descended to embrace Goering and Goebbels and Doenitz and Hess, begging them to join with him in the making of a better world.[17]

Writing of the final communiqué—the Shanghai Communiqué— Buckley accused Nixon and Kissinger of abandoning Taiwan while receiving nothing in exchange. The damage, Buckley warned, was not merely geopolitical but moral. "We have lost—irretrievably—any remaining sense of moral mission in the world. . . . When Mr. Nixon, as he regularly did, made reference to the outstanding differences between our two 'systems,' he made it sound as if there are, after all, those who prefer gingham to calico."[18]

He didn't spare even Kissinger. In describing Kissinger's acquiescence in the communiqué he quoted the exact warning about the betrayal of South Vietnam that Kissinger had wanted him to relay to Nixon after the 1968 election. It was the sharpest rebuke Buckley would ever deliver to Kissinger.*

But in spite of his anger and disgust, Buckley never contemplated using Ashbrook's campaign to frustrate Nixon's re-election. He was no longer a radical, but a conservative whose decisions were governed by a strategy of the possible. "I was permanently influenced by Whit-

---

* But he still made excuses for Kissinger. In a telegram to his brother Jim from China, he described Kissinger as appearing "visibly shattered" by the accords. (Buckley Papers.) But Kissinger was not "visibly shattered" by the communiqué itself, the American side of which he had written, but by an acrimonious eleventh-hour battle with Rogers over its terms. As Buckley did not know, the U.S. had already secured from China major concessions in its support for the North Vietnamese—concessions that the U.S. was unable to reveal to the press. Thus, Buckley was simply projecting his own remorse onto Kissinger. (For an account of the China communiqué, see Hersh, *The Price of Power*, Chapter 35. In *Before the Fall*, William Safire also thought that Kissinger felt "guilty" about the communiqué—a misunderstanding based upon his projections. Kissinger himself reveals no remorse or guilt about the accords, in either *White House Years* or the authorized *Kissinger*, by Marvin and Bernard Kalb [Boston: Little, Brown, 1974].)

taker Chambers, when he said he was an 'Orgbureau man,' " Buckley said in recalling his state of mind that winter.*

Suffering from anonymity, poor organization, a dearth of funds (money was being raised by former YAF fund raiser Richard Viguerie's new firm in Falls Church, Virginia), and the outspoken opposition of Goldwater and other prominent conservatives, Ashbrook went down to ignominious defeat in New Hampshire. He received only 9.7 percent of the vote compared to 67.9 percent for Nixon and 22.4 percent for McCloskey. The results were exactly as Buckley feared: they suggested that even within the Republican Party liberal antiwar sentiment was far stronger than conservatism. He wrote Rusher, "As things now appear to me, the Ashbrook candidacy is not amounting to very much. What I fear is a dissipation of our strength."[19] Rusher wrote back, "I can't recall when American conservatism has been in greater disarray."[20]

Ashbrook's dismal showing and the rise of George McGovern, the most liberal of the Democratic candidates, hastened Buckley's return to the Nixon fold. Against the urging of Rusher and pleas from Ashbrook, Buckley kept his word to Buchanan and withdrew his support of Ashbrook's candidacy after New Hampshire. In a public statement, he described Ashbrook's California campaign as "implausible."[21]

After his trip to China, Buckley spent a typical month in Switzerland, enjoying skiing and the company of Niven and Galbraith. Niven's autobiography, *The Moon's a Balloon,* had appeared that winter, and in spite of Galbraith's and Buckley's warnings that a book with that title couldn't sell, it was on its way to becoming a best seller.

At the local bookstore in Gstaad, Cadanou's, the three authors— Buckley's *Cruising Speed* and Galbraith's *Economics, Peace and Laughter* had also just appeared—vied for window space. Buckley was willing to concede first place to Niven, but he was unwilling to let Galbraith upstage him. Before going to China, Buckley had discovered that there were no copies of his book in the store, and he had had six air-expressed to Mme. Cadanou. When he returned, he found

---

* The Nixon administration was taking no chances. The Committee to Re-elect the President instructed the President's supporters nationwide to write letters to editors lambasting Nixon's critics. One form letter concerned Buckley. It read, "Ideologically obsessed, with rigid mind and inflexible attitude, William Buckley sounds like a political Elmer Gantry with his righteous outburst against the Chinese Communist devils. Buckley has no trouble supporting rightist dictators, from Spain to Greece to Brazil, but he appears mentally incapable of recognizing that under Mao the lives of the Chinese masses have been greatly improved." (Jack Anderson, *Washington Post,* May 9, 1973.)

his book in the window, but it had been joined by another Galbraith book, *Ambassador's Journal*. Buckley gave Mme. Cadanou a copy of an anthology of conservative writing that he had done to place alongside Galbraith's books. Galbraith responded with *The New Industrial State,* and Buckley got hold of a German translation of *McCarthy and His Enemies.* At this point, Mme. Cadanou had no more space in her display window, and the two authors gave up.

IV

Starr Broadcasting, which Buckley and Peter Starr had incorporated six years earlier with Buckley as chairman of the board and Starr as president, had grown apace. After buying stations in Sioux Falls and Kansas City in 1968, it took over radio stations in Houston, Memphis, New Orleans, Little Rock, and Dallas, and television stations in Tennessee and Hawaii. To raise money for additional purchases, it had gone public in 1969, with Buckley retaining 11 percent of the stock. Its holdings totaled $14.5 million, and in 1970, the company netted a profit of $376,000. In *Cruising Speed,* Buckley wrote of Starr, "My family apart, I am as fond of Peter as of any human being. Indeed I feel for him that special affection I reserve for anyone who has made me a million dollars."[22]

In 1971, Buckley had been involved in a controversy about his supervision of the stations. A cover story in *New York* magazine accused Buckley of hypocrisy. Starr's stations based their programming decisions strictly on profit. As a result, several stations played rock music and featured disk jockeys and newscasters who romanticized the drug culture and opposed the Vietnam War. For instance, Starr's Kansas City station was converted from a "beautiful music" format to a twenty-four-hour hard-rock format, featuring, in the words of Starr's program director, "total freaks who were really into the scene."[23] Starr's Memphis station editorialized against committing "America's resources to . . . a wider, winless, and unwinnable war."

Earlier on, Buckley had demanded that editors and publishing houses take responsibility for the content of what they print. He had written, for instance, that Simon and Schuster's publication of Jerry Rubin's *Do It* reminded him "of Lenin's dictum that when the last of the bourgeoisie is hanged, a capitalist will sell the rope."[24] But as the article pointed out, Buckley, as the chairman of Starr, had "employed hippie disk jockeys and turned-on disk jockeys and announcers who, when not advertising head shops and skin flicks, read editorials deploring the war in Vietnam."[25]

"What has happened to our Bill?" the article asked. "Has the plump little liberal thought to be hiding in every lean conservative at last emerged? Not exactly. What has actually emerged is the prospect of a tidy capital gains and a gentlemanly six-figure profit."[26]

Buckley himself had uncharacteristically refused to talk to Richard Reingold, the story's author, and had referred him to Peter Starr, and Buckley's reply to the article was unusually brief and evasive, confined to a witty observation on a drawing that accompanied it. But when a *National Review* reader raised the same points in a letter to the magazine, he stated his position in "Notes and Asides":

> It would not occur to me to ask the president [Starr] to suppress music I happen not to like. As regards rock, it happens that—I like it. . . . The stations accept, by and large, the same advertisers accepted by major newspapers. Station managers are individually responsible for rejecting ads and music that are drug-oriented. . . . The news commentators are free to express their individual opinions, except they may not slander, or promote civil disobedience. Corporate opinion is expressed by Peter Starr, who happens to be a political conservative. . . . The Company's earnings, at approximately $1 a share, make it an attractive investment at $18 on the Midwest Exchange. See your local broker.[27]

In the summer of 1972, Buckley and Starr decided to expand their investments well beyond Starr Broadcasting itself. Using a company, Sitco Ltd., that they had formed along with Starr's brother Michael, Starr Broadcasting's vice-president, and Gordon Ryan, the company's counsel, they purchased sixteen drive-ins and one indoor theater in Texas for $6.3 million. If land values continued to rise, the partners expected that they would be able to make a killing in several years.

V

At the Republican and Democratic conventions that summer, Buckley appeared with Galbraith on the morning television show *Today*. Speaking of the orderly Miami convention of the Democrats, Galbraith said, "It is incredible that we should have come from such a nasty and disagreeable business in 1968 to anything that was as agreeable and amiable as it was in these last few days." Buckley responded, "I think that is true. After four years of the Republican administration we have law and order in the Democratic convention.

I think the irresponsiblity of this convention was not behavioral. It was intellectual and philosophical." [28]

After the Republican and Democratic conventions, *National Review* endorsed Nixon for the presidency. The endorsement recalled its tepid endorsement of Eisenhower in 1956—"I prefer Ike." "The editors of *National Review* prefer the reelection of Richard Nixon and Spiro Agnew next November," Buckley wrote. "The fact of a major party's accepting McGovernism, wherein is implicit an indifference toward national independence and a hostility toward individual freedom, is the important datum of this year."

But there was an important difference in Buckley's attitude toward the 1972 election. In 1956, he was uncomfortable with the tactic of voting for the lesser of evils. Indeed, he didn't vote at all. His formulation was an expression of uncertainty as much as it was of distaste for the Republican candidate. In 1972, Buckley was utterly convinced that the tactic was the correct one.

On *National Review,* the only dissenter was Rusher. Meyer had died earlier that year of lung cancer, and Rickenbacker had resigned four years prior, largely because of Buckley's enthusiastic support for Nixon. When Rusher wanted to publish his own view that conservatives would be better off with McGovern—an opponent they could recognize—than with Nixon, Buckley refused, even though at the very beginning he had set up a column in the magazine, "The Open Question," in which editors could dissent from other editors' opinions. Rusher finally had to publish his opinion in the *Los Angeles Times.**

"I felt that his position was eccentric," Buckley said in explaining his action. "And that to have the publisher attached to that position would hurt *National Review*. It would make it sound flaky."

There was also a broader aspect to Buckley's refusal to publish Rusher's dissent. Just as Goldwater's abysmal showing in 1964 had convinced Buckley of the truth of Burnham and Chambers's political conservatism, Ashbrook's showing strengthened Buckley's resolve against symbolic right-wing protests.

But other conservatives shared Rusher's view. In the aftermath of

---

* Rusher, citing Nixon's ability to win conservatives for liberal ends, argued that "conservatism, and therefore America, would on balance be better off . . . under, and in spite of, a President McGovern. At a minimum, we would be compelled to watch the steady disintegration of American society and either resist it or confess our acquiescence in it, rather than have it shielded from our sight by the comforting but wholly meretricious notion that a vote for Mr. Nixon is somehow a vote against it." (*Rise of the Right,* 249.)

Ashbrook's failure, Rusher, Evans, Richard Viguerie, and a new group of younger conservatives resolved to purify the Republican Party of the Nixons and the Rockefellers, even if doing so meant wrecking the party. They would form the leadership of a New Right, for whom Buckley's reformist conservatism would be anathema.

CHAPTER 20

Weak and Devious Men

Buckley and *National Review* gave Nixon little credit for his landslide victory over George McGovern. In a column afterwards, Buckley commented, "No doubt future textbooks on how to score landslide victories will begin with the injunction: Get George Mc-Govern nominated by the opposite party." Buckley warned that if Nixon didn't quickly establish a direction, his popularity would prove fleeting.

> How will . . . voters act in the future? And how will the Congress act toward a President who is disliked for ideological and personal reasons by many Democrats and distrusted by many Republicans . . . Mr. Nixon will fill the void quickly—or he will suffer the fate of Harold Macmillan, who in 1959 won the most triumphant reelection in modern English political history, and eighteen months later everything lay in ruins about him . . . [1]

In the first months of Nixon's second term, Buckley and *National Review* gave his policies the benefit of a doubt. They lauded his last, brutal bombing raid against Hanoi ("When Richard Nixon decided finally to bomb, he decided to bomb definitively"[2]) and praised the domestic program announced in his second inaugural address as "a well-conceived and tough-minded strategy for clearing away the detritus accumulated during a generation of domestic illusion."[3] In March, Buckley even defended the reparations to North Vietnam promised in the Paris Peace Accords.[4] Ignoring the grumbling of other conservatives, Buckley continued to be an unabashed admirer of Henry Kissinger. When Kissinger was appointed Secretary of State in September 1973, *National Review* hailed his appointment as signifying "the expanding role of the intellectual and the verbalist in post-industrial cosmopolitan society." While voicing some reservations about SALT, the magazine termed his achievements as National Security Adviser "spectacular."[5]

But even as the votes from the Nixon landslide were being counted, an issue was surfacing that would not only destroy the Nixon presidency but divide conservatives more deeply and bitterly than the Ashbrook candidacy had. It would also involve Buckley personally in the plight of an old friend.

I

On June 17, 1972, five men had been arrested for breaking into the Democratic National Committee headquarters at the Watergate complex in Washington. The name of former CIA agent Howard Hunt was found in the address books of two of the burglars. Hunt, it was soon learned, was employed as a consultant to White House aide Charles Colson. On September 15, a Washington grand jury indicted the five men plus Hunt and Committee to Re-elect the President (CREEP) counsel G. Gordon Liddy.

Buckley had remained close friends with Howard Hunt for the two decades since Hunt had been his case officer in the CIA. He had also occasionally done favors for Hunt and the CIA—arranging in 1964 for Hunt to stay at his brother Reid's house in Madrid while Hunt was on secret CIA business in Spain. When Hunt once complained about *National Review*'s criticisms of the CIA, Buckley replied good-naturedly, "The best thing I know about the CIA is that you are in it and, indeed, occupy an important position in it."[6]

Through Buckley, Hunt had also become close friends with Brent and Patricia Bozell and with Reid Buckley. One of Hunt's daughters, Kevan, enrolled at Smith, was a friend of Christopher Buckley, whom she visited in Stamford.

In 1970, Hunt had resigned from the CIA and gone to work for a public-relations firm in Washington. Then in July 1971, at the behest of Colson, a fellow Brown University alumnus, he had also become a White House consultant. Acting, he believed, for the national security, Hunt became a member with Liddy—then working as a White House aide—of the infamous White House "plumbers" team. In this capacity, he had helped plan a break-in in September 1971 into the office of Daniel Ellsberg's psychiatrist. At the behest of Liddy, who had gone to work for John Mitchell, the head of the Committee to Reelect the President, Hunt had recruited Cuban exiles and helped plan the Watergate break-in.

In July, when Hunt was summoned for questioning by the U.S. Attorney, Buckley sent Dorothy Hunt, Howard's wife, a note offering to be of assistance. The next month, he wrote Howard Hunt urging him to "write your side of the story for *National Review*."[7] But when Hunt, after his arraignment, proposed that Buckley organize a defense committee on his behalf, he grew exasperated. He wrote Hunt:

> Goddamit, *viejo*, I hardly see how you can complain about having been arraigned on the charge of breaking and entering and seeking to install devices the operation of which is unlawful. I and Jim Burnham and others who know you are perfectly prepared to believe that you acted in pursuit of a grand purpose, but face it, this is an act of faith in you. Neither you nor any member of your team has given us a sliver of hard information on the basis of which we can go to bat for you knowledgeably. I don't really see how you would expect a Committee to Defend Howard Hunt's Right to Set Aside the Law. I think you owe it to yourself and the cause we both serve (forgive the pompous formulation) to confide with Jim Burnham and me, and give us a feel for the situation. Otherwise, we are flying blind.[8]

On December 8, Hunt's wife, Dorothy, carring $10,000 in cash, was killed in an airplane crash. Distraught about his wife's death, Hunt, accompanied by his daughter Kevan, came to see Buckley in New York. Seated in Buckley's living room, Hunt poured out in two hours the story of his last two years. "I was trying to impress on Buckley, 'Look, this was not just a bunch of hooligans acting on their own; this was something with top-level administration backing and, in fact, instigation,' " Hunt recalled.

Hunt told Buckley that he had not seen John Mitchell, but that he knew from Liddy that the break-in was authorized by Mitchell. And he told him not only of the Ellsberg break-in, but of other planned misdeeds. He said that he had no evidence to implicate Nixon directly in the Watergate break-in, but that he assumed Nixon had been aware of what Mitchell, his closest ally in government, was up to.

The morning was a difficult one, not only for Hunt but for Buckley. He was dismayed that Hunt had brought his daughter along, but didn't feel, in the circumstances, that he could say anything to Hunt about it. (Two years later, he would reproach Hunt for "imposing on her a burden she could not possibly shrug off without hurting you."[9]) He was equally troubled by Hunt's revelations, which, if they became public, might, he suspected, force Nixon's resignation. He was appalled by the extent of the administration's malfeasance. Some of it was clearly conventional political "dirty tricks," but other actions clearly exceeded those bounds. One thing Hunt told him, he later admitted, caused him "great torment."

"Hunt said something to me that permitted me to infer that he had instructions along with Liddy to assassinate [columnist] Jack Anderson, and my torment lay in wondering the extent to which I was responsible for finding out whether in fact that had been his instructions."

Hunt's revelations initially immobilized Buckley. He now knew far more about Watergate than the public or anyone else in the media, and he was bound by friendship to one of the conspirators. Hunt himself, convinced that he was targeted for assassination, insisted on calling Buckley from a pay phone to his son Christopher's phone, which Hunt believed was less likely to be tapped. Christopher, who was then going to Yale, had his own quarters and his own phone over the garage at Wallacks Point. In these calls, Hunt told Buckley that there was a safe-deposit box, the contents of which he could not reveal, but which he wanted Buckley and another man who would contact him to open in case of his death. Buckley and the other man would have to decide what to do with what was in the box.

To his son, in whom he confided Hunt's phone messages, Buckley "looked like he was holding the whole world on his shoulders." When Christopher asked him, during a sauna the two were taking, what he thought was in Hunt's safe-deposit box, "that was when he really slumped." To Buckley, it appeared very possible that Hunt's papers implicated not merely Mitchell but Nixon.

For a time, Buckley, compromised by information that he could not reveal, stopped writing about Watergate, but as *National Review*'s editor he could not avoid a position altogether.

II

From the first news of the break-in, most of the Republican and conservative press claimed that the scandal was simply the result of partisan anti-Nixon outrage directed at what were no more than the usual campaign hijinks. On *National Review,* both Rusher and Jeffrey Hart, a Dartmouth English professor who had become a senior editor in 1972, took this position. But from the start, Buckley and Burnham, and therefore *National Review,* had taken a more serious view of the scandal's dimensions. For one thing, Buckley, like his father, had always found the seamy and purely self-interested side of politics reprehensible. Buckley could tolerate, even commend, skullduggery by the CIA in battling communism, but he was quick to condemn such actions when they were intended merely to advance a politician's popularity or income.

In early February 1973, *National Review* editorialized, "This Watergate affair, under its suffocating cover, has acquired a sour, rotting quality that can only be cleaned up by the truth, or at least enough of the truth to provide and adequately and intellectually . . . account for what happened and why." [10]

Buckley continued to be troubled by what Hunt had told him. After consulting his old friend and lawyer, C. Dickerman Williams, he went to see Hunt in prison in March. He asked him point-blank who had originated the idea of assassinating Jack Anderson.

> He was vague about it [Buckley recalled], and all of a sudden I thought that this might have been a hypothesis that was discussed in the same way as the CIA discusses something. There are seven ways to deal with a problem and the nature of the challenge requires that you list all seven, even though you know that the last three are out of the question. I said to myself that I would simply indulge all civilized presumptions.

In April, after details of the Ellsberg break-in had been made public, Buckley felt that he could resume commenting on Watergate himself. His views reflected his growing conviction that Nixon was behaving reprehensibly and was doomed. "Even those who decline to believe that Mr. Nixon had foreknowledge of the affair," Buckley wrote in *National Review,* "believe—many of them—that Nixon's supervision of the Watergate investigation was at least self-serving, at worst criminal." But he urged that Congress censure the President rather than impeach him. "In America the President is the emperor in addition to being the prime minister. . . . If Nixon were impeached, the punishment would be visited primarily on the state," he argued.[11]

In a June 8 editorial, *National Review* suggested for the first time what Buckley had suspected since talking to Hunt: that the Watergate scandal would lead to Nixon's resignation and Agnew's elevation to the presidency. In that editorial, entitled "President Agnew," the editors showed that they were coming to accept the prospect of Agnew replacing Nixon. "In cold political terms," the editorial said, "an incoming Agnew administration could be in a strong position. . . . If Richard Nixon were to leave office within the next year, then Vice President-turned-President Agnew would have nearly three years to gain or lose the nation's trust, affection, and respect."[12]

On the magazine, Watergate sparked vigorous debate among the editors from the very beginning. The chief protagonists were predictably Rusher and Burnham. In a February 1973 letter to Buckley in Switzerland, Rusher explained that while he wanted *National Review* to challenge the media attack on Nixon, Burnham "thinks the present Nixon administration is the most outrageously secretive and byzantine in American history, and that therefore (inferentially) the press is thoroughly justified in its present course."[13]

But the quarrel between Rusher and Burnham soon took second place. *National Review*'s most outspoken commentary on Watergate came from neither Buckley nor the magazine's senior editors, but from its new Washington columnist. George Will ended up offending not merely many Nixon loyalists and conservatives, but also at least two of the editors of *National Review*.

Will, the son of a University of Illinois philosophy professor, had first visited Buckley in 1966, when he was a graduate student in political science at Princeton. Prim and somewhat stuffy, yet quick and witty, Will combined the moral outlook of the small-town Midwest of the fifties with an intellectual sophistication and outward manner shaped by a postgraduate year at Oxford. When they met at *National Review*'s offices, Buckley suggested to Will that he learn to write for popular as well as academic audiences; and as a young professor at the University of Toronto, Will began making periodic contributions to *National Review*. In 1970, he left teaching to become an aide to Colorado Senator Gordon Allott, who had been made chairman of the Senate Republican Policy Committee, and in 1972, he began writing *National Review*'s "Letter from Washington," signed by "CATO." After Allott was defeated for re-election in November, Will approached Buckley about a full-time position with the magazine. Both

Priscilla Buckley and Burnham shared Buckley's admiration for Will, and with their encouragement, Buckley proposed that Will become *National Review*'s regular Washington columnist under his own name and at the same time take over the book section that Elsie Meyer had been editing on a temporary basis since her husband's death.

Even as CATO, Will had stirred considerable controversy on the magazine with his view of Agnew, whom he regarded as a boor and a boob and whose attacks against "elitism" offended his Tory conservatism. In July, Buckley had refused to print a CATO column by Will arguing for Agnew's replacement as Nixon's running mate. "You reach conclusions sharply at variance with the thrust of *National Review*'s policy towards Agnew," Buckley wrote him. "This you are free to do at any time you feel like it, but over your own signature." [14] Will, however, continued sniping at Agnew, prompting complaints from the Vice-President's office. When Will came to New York in December for a *National Review* editorial meeting at Buckley's house, Rusher told him that he would have to mend his fences with Agnew. Will recalled, "One of the persons there said you have to get along with Agnew because he's it. We've chosen."

When word of Will's appointment as Washington columnist and book editor reached the Washington conservatives clustered around *Human Events* and the American Conservative Union, there was considerable protest. The Washington conservatives didn't like Will because of his attacks on Agnew, and they also distrusted his motives. At the same time that he was starting with *National Review,* Will had reached an agreement with *Washington Post* editorial page deputy editor Meg Greenfield to write a weekly column. This raised suspicions about Will's ambitions. "Most of the people felt he was just using *National Review* as a stepping-stone to become the in-house conservative of the *Post,* which to some extent he was from the standpoint of personal ambition," David Keene recalled. These suspicions were augmented by two other factors: having never been a member of YAF or the ACU, Will did not, in his words, have the proper conservative "pedigree," and he was taking over the job of the hardliner whom the Washington conservatives most admired, Frank Meyer.

Will's first columns for the magazine further aggravated his opponents on *National Review*'s editorial staff. In a March column, Will argued that former Treasury Secretary John Connally rather than Agnew should be Nixon's successor. Will's first column on Watergate was harshly critical of Nixon's top aides. Nixon, Will wrote, surrounded himself with a White House staff the size of which was, until recently, exceeded only by its delusions of adequacy. But the unfolding Watergate scandal—the unraveling Watergate cover-up—indicates that the moral turpitude of certain staff members has exceeded even their delusions. Now as they turn on one another, scrambling to avoid being held accountable for what happened, they are doing unprecedented, unforgivable damage to the office and country they were supposed to serve.[15]

In April, Stan Evans, who had been writing a column for the fortnightly *National Review Bulletin,* resigned, largely in protest over Will's columns. "I feel increasingly out of phase with the drift of things at *National Review,* particularly the book section and the political coverage," Evans wrote Buckley.[16] Buckley replied to Evans, "There has been opposition to George Will that frankly mystifies me, knowing his views as I do, and reading his opinions as I do."[17]

But the controversy over Will's coverage reached a peak in June. In the same issue that *National Review* suggested that an incoming "Agnew administration would be in a strong position," Will took his strongest shots yet at the Vice-President.

> Mr. Agnew has been Mr. Nixon's Nixon, the spear-point of Republican partisanship, the instrument of "positive polarization." He is not the ideal instrument for healing a troubled nation. In addition, there are those who believe that Mr. Agnew has certain of the same character traits that have brought Mr. Nixon low. Like Nixon, they will tell you, Agnew has displayed at times in the past a certain morbid hypersensitivity, feelings of insecurity and inferiority regarding the press, the academic community and the establishment generally . . . the feeling here is that a maimed, tainted, impotent Mr. Nixon is preferable to Mr. Agnew.[18]

Rusher flew into a rage at Will's column. In a memo to Buckley, he described it as "simply another blast by the fast-dwindling Connally clique for which Will works as a Stakhonovite spokesman. . . . We must not permit Will to open an unbridgeable gap between *National Review* and Agnew."[19] At the June 15 quarterly meeting of senior editors, Rusher was joined by Jeffrey Hart. They pressed the point and got Buckley's assent to reprimand Will. Will thought he was being censored. In a letter to Buckley, Will expressed his belief that as a columnist he

> could write what I want to write about Agnew or anyone else as long as what I wrote was reasoned. You assert again that I am free

to criticize Agnew. But I very much doubt that anything critical I might say about him will seem to you free of personal animosity on my part. . . . I am convinced you do not understand the choice you are making: when *National Review*'s role as an opinion journal conflicts with its role as instrument of a political movement (and, increasingly, as the instrument of a candidate) the second role is given priority. . . . I flatly reject your contention that my criticism of the Nixon administration has been "gleeful." I read the fate of this administration as nothing short of a national tragedy.[20]

Having gotten Will admonished, but with little effect on his column, Rusher, backed by a flood of readers' complaints, was now determined to get him fired. On August 1, he sent the first of many memos to Buckley recommending that Will be removed from his post, which Buckley ignored.

III

Buckley believed that in not accepting reappointment to the USIA and in backing Ashbrook, he had burned his bridges to Nixon, but that summer, John Scali, the former ABC newsman whom Nixon had made U.N. ambassador, called Buckley to ask him if he wanted to become the public delegate to the United Nations—a part-time position that Eleanor Roosevelt and Moynihan had both held. Scali assured him that Haig, who had become Nixon's deputy, was "terribly enthusiastic" about the idea.[21] Buckley, who had described the U.N. as a "surrealistic organization whose entire role is Aesopian,"[22] demurred, but Scali persisted. He promised Buckley that he would be placed in charge of the U.S. delegation to the Committee on Human Rights.

Buckley said he would think over the offer and, having privately resolved to turn it down, walked back from Scali's office at the Waldorf Astoria to the *National Review,* but on the way he had what he described as

the only experience I ever had in pure, undiluted Walter Mittyism. I saw myself there, in the center of the great assembly at the U.N. . . . holding the delegates spellbound as I read to them from Solzhenitsyn, as I described the latest account of concentration camps in Mainland China, as I pleaded the case of the ballet dancer Panov. I would cajole, wheedle, parry, thrust, mesmerize, dismay, seduce, intimidate. The press of the world would rivet its attention on the

case the American delegate was making for human rights, repristin-
ating the jaded vision of the international bureaucrats.[23]

Having convinced himself that Nixon wasn't simply trying to appease the right wing by appointing him and that he might have some
impact at the U.N., Buckley agreed to serve for one term, from September to December. Over the summer, he was confirmed by the
Senate Foreign Relations Committee. (When the FBI called Rusher to
check routinely on Buckley, it asked him, "Has Mr. Buckley done
anything since 1969 that might embarrass the Nixon administration?"
"No," Rusher replied, "but since 1969 the Nixon administration has
done a great deal that has embarrassed Mr. Buckley."[24]

Buckley's experience, from the first day, confirmed his initial misgivings about the U.N. job. At the orientation in Washington, Buckley
was told that someone must always sit at the U.S. desk in the General
Assembly and appear to be listening to the speaker. "Above all, we
were warned, we must guard against falling asleep." When Buckley
met with Scali to receive his formal assignment, Scali began to hedge
on appointing him as the head of the Third Committee delegation. It
was "my first premonition," Buckley wrote later, "that Walter Mitty
was dead."[25]

The first week, he sent Scali a memorandum, with a copy to Kissinger, outlining what he thought could be accomplished on the Third
Committee. "Unless I am instructed to do otherwise," he wrote, "I
plan to feel free to discuss human rights even if the inference can be
drawn from what I say that I also believe in human rights within the
Soviet Union."[26] Scali called him in the next morning and instructed
him not to send memoranda either to him or to Kissinger and to clear
all his speeches with him. And Scali warned Buckley that détente with
the Soviet Union was the "overarching policy."[27]

Over the next months, Scali and his aides vetoed one after another
of Buckley's speeches as being too "provocative." A column Buckley
wrote describing a speech by Zaire's President Mobutu ("An aide to
General Mobutu placed his speech on the podium, and, after he was
done, retrieved it. Such menial tasks as placing one's own speech on
a podium are inconsistent with the pride of the President of Zaire.")
caused a furor in the White House, which was planning to receive the
offended Mobutu. Buckley's best lines had to be reserved for unofficial addresses.

On United Nations Day, Buckley gave a speech on New York
politics at a buffet lunch organized by New York socialite Mrs. John
Loeb. During the question-and-answer session, a black ambassador

asked Buckley what his views were on a transportation bond referendum. "To tell you the truth," Buckley replied, "I have not studied the issue, which I can divulge in good conscience because I don't have to vote on it, since I vote in Connecticut." Mrs. Loeb interjected, "You see, Mr. Ambassador, in America, we don't vote where we work, we vote where we sleep." "Well," Buckley responded, "even that is not *exactly* correct. If I voted where I slept, I would vote in the United Nations." [28]

IV

Buckley's days at the United Nations provided him with comic relief as the Watergate scandal began to envelop the Nixon administration in a dark cloud of scandal and deceit. In August, Agnew became the subject of an investigation by the U.S. Attorney in Maryland, and in September, a grand jury began meeting to hear evidence that Agnew, as Baltimore county executive, governor, and even as Vice-President, had received kickbacks from building contractors. Agnew denounced the charges as "false, scurrilous, and malicious" and, to the applause of Washington conservatives, insinuated that the media were serving as his chief prosecutor. Both Buckley and *National Review,* assuming that the charges were as Agnew described, rallied to his defense. After Agnew had personally assured him of his innocence, Buckley wrote in his column on September 28, "Mr. Agnew is a man of some backbone and has at least the normal man's indisposition to be pushed around."

At the same time that Agnew was loudly proclaiming his innocence, he had already entered into plea-bargaining negotiations with Justice Department lawyers. On October 10, Agnew resigned from the vice-presidency. Later that day, while still insisting to the press that he was innocent, he appeared in court and pled *nolo contendere* to the charges against him.

Speaking before the New York Conservative Party dinner that week, Buckley took the occasion to express his own disillusionment and to counsel conservatives that they must not identify the fate of their cause with either Agnew or Nixon.

Mr. Agnew, reaching for self-justification, is no more plausible than Alger Hiss. . . . I do not see that it is part of our creed to suggest that no one who believes in our creed can succumb to temptation. . . . He looked us all in the eyes and said he was not guilty, had done nothing wrong, was being persecuted by the Justice Depart-

ment, would not resign: And we believed him. I think it right that
we believed him. But I think it wrong that because we have over
several years now treated Mr. Agnew and the ideas Mr. Agnew is
associated with as inseparable, that we should, in order to attempt
to salvage those ideas, attempt to salvage Mr. Agnew. . . . It is a
terrible irony that at the moment in history when liberalism is sput-
tering in confusion, empty of resources, we should be plagued as
we are by weak and devious men.[29]

Only ten days after Agnew resigned, the "Saturday Night Massacre" took place. Nixon's press secretary, Ron Ziegler, disclosed that
the President had dismissed Special Prosecutor Archibald Cox and
that Attorney General Elliot Richardson and his deputy William Ruck-
elshaus had resigned in protest. In the weeks succeeding, the House
commenced impeachment proceedings, and *The New York Times* and
Time (in its first editorial in fifty years) called for Nixon's resignation.

It had become obvious to Buckley that Nixon would be forced out
of office. In the wake of Nixon's nomination of House Minority
Leader Gerald Ford as Agnew's successor, and the Saturday Night
Massacre, Buckley wrote Reagan,

Our leader is in deep trouble. It is altogether possible he will not
succeed, finally, in extricating himself. I think the moment has come
delicately to insist, in declarations aimed *urbe et orbe,* that Congress must proceed to confirm the Vice President [Gerald Ford] just
in case. Following that, a patient, cautious dissociation would appear to be prudent.[30]

But Buckley was unsure what to do next. On one hand, he thought
conservatives had to dissociate themselves from Nixon as quickly as
possible so that the conservative movement didn't go down with him.
"I thought Nixon should resign, and I thought the conservatives had
to guard against the suspicion that all the liberals wanted him to resign
and none of the conservatives." But Buckley also believed that conservatism, in the public mind, was inextricably identified with Nixon,
and so he balked at doing anything that would deepen Nixon's disgrace and speed his departure.

Buckley was suffering his own form of disillusionment with Nixon,
whom he had helped elect in 1968 and whom he had supported almost
unquestioningly until 1971. His actions over the next six months were
confused and uncertain, so much so that Buckley himself could claim
in retrospect that he called for Nixon's resignation, while Nixon loy-

alists like Pat Buchanan could recall Buckley as one of the few conservatives who didn't "hit us when we were down."

During a lecture in November at Kansas State University, Buckley
first publicly announced his conviction that Nixon would step down.
Speaking before eighteen hundred students jammed into the seats and
aisles and even sitting on the edge of the auditorium stage, Buckley
ignored the immediate controversy and, adopting a professorial manner, devoted the body of his speech to what he called the "assault on
the free market." A local reporter described Buckley's style:

> Buckley read the text of his speech to his audience in much the
> manner of a mother reading a bedtime story to her children. His
> voice would hurry over long phrases and hang onto words he
> wanted to emphasize. His tone would change to comply with the
> personality of the person he was quoting. Most of the audience
> seemed entranced by Buckley's style, but his words were stacked
> upon more words.[31]

During the question-and-answer period, however, Buckley and his
audience sprang to life when a student asked him whether he thought
Nixon would be impeached. "I think it is unlikely Nixon will be impeached," Buckley said. "I think it is probable that he will resign.
And by doing that, rather than hanging by his fingernails onto power,
he would both relieve a Republic that is sorely vexed, and ingratiate
himself with it, as no other act of his at this point would succeed in
doing."[32]

In December, Buckley advised his brother over lunch that he
should call for Nixon's resignation. In a memorandum that he gave
him afterwards, he quipped, "If you see yourself as transfixed by
arrows, I'd be glad to refer to you thereafter as Saint Sebastian." But
Buckley himself did not explicitly call for Nixon's resignation during
that winter. Instead, as he had done in Kansas, he simply predicted
it, as if to predict were to recommend. And he allowed the Nixon
administration to believe that he was still an ally. In December, while
he was urging his brother to act, he even defended Nixon against
accusations that he had cheated on his taxes. On December 13, he
wrote that "the anti-Nixon fervor is comprehensive and undifferen-
tiating." And he complained that Nixon was being victimized by "ma-
levolent pettifoggery."[33]
At the end of December, he had Pat Buchanan on *Firing Line* and

his line of questioning was polite and even deferential. He only touched on resignation once and then in a confused and almost off-hand manner.

BUCKLEY: But what is the point of Nixon saying, "I accept responsibility," when he's going to accept it anyway? If it's up to the public to decide whether to blame him for something then they're going to decide, but he *seemed* to be saying . . . "I will accept responsibility even though I have the option of not accepting it."

BUCHANAN: I don't know what, so to speak, you would have the President of the United States do. He's the leader of—

BUCKLEY: Well, he could invite impeachment or he could invite a vote of censure, that sort of thing.

BUCHANAN: Some of this has gone forward without the invitation —the impeachment . . .

BUCKLEY: No, no, if you're a bank president and you say, "I will accept the responsibility for any malversation committed by my tellers," and a malversation is then proved, then you resign, right?

BUCHANAN: Yes.

BUCKLEY: Or you're docked in your pay. I don't know, something. But this is one of the vexations that people feel Mr. Nixon's always telling us he's going to accept responsibility but somehow one never knows what the force of that acceptance is. . . .[34]

Buckley's reluctance to break openly with Nixon (while urging his brother to do so) may have been indicative of a new cautiousness. But more likely it expressed a reluctance to be at the center of this political controversy. Disillusioned by Nixon's fall, Buckley had withdrawn from the immediate political struggle. In Switzerland that winter, Buckley ignored Watergate. He worked on a book about his three months at the United Nations—published the next year as *United Nations Journal*. And with Evan Galbraith, who had brought his family to visit that winter, he began secretly planning a sail across the Atlantic for the summer after next. (Pat's initial response, when he mentioned the dangerous voyage to her, mixed fear and affection with her usual hyperbole: "If you do, I'll leave you," she said.) Then in March, he took a month-long journalistic sojourn to southern Africa.

Meanwhile, Jim Buckley moved steadily toward breaking with Nixon. At the Conservative Political Action Conference in Washington in February 1974, Jim Buckley, who was the keynote speaker, warned that Nixon's "future and ours cannot reasonably be seen as inextricably intertwined." [35] Then, in March, while Bill was in Rhodesia doing *Firing Line* with Prime Minister Ian Smith, Jim decided to take the fateful step. He telegraphed Bill in Salisbury, "It will happen the day after tomorrow. Sebastian." In his statement, written by Burnham, and delivered at a March 19 press conference, he declared that "in order to preserve the Presidency, Richard Nixon must resign as President." [36]

In his column afterwards, Bill did not endorse Jim's stance, but merely defended his proposal against a Republican congressman's charge that his "willingness to see a man forced out of office without proof of impeachable conduct shows a lack of understanding as to how this Republic was formed and how it operates." Buckley wrote:

> I understand Senator Buckley to perform an act of noblesse oblige. That is to say, to put his country's interests above his own. . . . Maybe Senator Buckley's recommendations are misguided. Certainly they are not outside the spirit of the Constitution, which three times recommends Presidential resignation as a possibility. [37]

It was only in June 1974, three months after Jim's declaration and two months before Nixon resigned, that Buckley publicly took the same stand as his brother: "Mr. Nixon is coaxing us toward one of the great ironies in American political history. All along he has said he would not quit because he was determined to execute the mandate for which he was elected. By not quitting, he is threatening to defeat that mandate." [38] His most direct statement came when the revelations that Kissinger had wiretapped his own employees prompted a public tirade from the Secretary of State. "Only the disappearance from the public scene of Richard Nixon would dissipate that miasma that, for instance, recently caused Mr. Kissinger to go to emotional extremes," he wrote. [39]

V

As Nixon, in Buckley's words, was "going down," Howard Hunt was trying desperately not to return to jail; he had been released at the end of December 1973 while his appeal was being heard.

During his prosecution and imprisonnment, virtually all of Howard Hunt's former friends and colleagues deserted him. The CIA even tried to take away his pension. But Buckley not only took charge of

Hunt's defense, hiring and firing lawyers, but also became his children's guardian and the executor of his wife's estate. When Hunt ran out of money, Buckley paid his lawyer himself. "People were afraid of infection by contact with me," Hunt recalled, "but Bill was not one of these. He rose swiftly to my support."

Buckley was convinced that Hunt had acted from patriotic rather than mercenary motives and was being forced to pay for the crimes of those above him. He suffered, however, for his association with Hunt, which became the subject of Watergate-style gossip. It was assumed that he had something to do with Watergate and—once he had admitted in a casual conversation that Hunt had been his case officer in the CIA—that he was still somehow connected with the CIA. One scandal sheet charged that "Bill Buckley's so-called oil fortune is mostly money deposited by the CIA. . . . He has admitted he has been a long-time deep cover operative for the CIA. Over the years he has participated in several operations in Mexico with E. Howard Hunt, including preparations for the assassination of John F. Kennedy."[40]

After he had admitted being in the CIA, the *Boston Globe* threatened to append this information to his column identification. Buckley responded in his column:

> I like, roughly, in the order described, 1) God, 2) my family, 3) my country, 4) J. S. Bach, 5) peanut butter, and 6) good English prose. Should these biases be identified when I write about, say, Satan, divorce, Czechoslovakia, Chopin, marmalade, and *New York Times* editorials?[41]

When the Watergate tapes were released, there was one embarrassing reference to Buckley and Hunt in them. On January 8, 1973, Nixon had said to Charles Colson in regard to Hunt's bid for clemency: "Hunt's is a simple case. We'll build that son of a bitch up like nobody's business. We'll have Buckley write a column and say, you know, that he, that he should have clemency, if you've given eighteen years of service . . ."

The tape accurately reflected Nixon's attitude toward Buckley, but not necessarily Buckley's attitude toward Nixon. When asked to respond by an Associated Press reporter, Buckley, who had urged after Nixon's resignation that he not be indicted, said, "I don't need to be reminded to write a column urging clemency even for sons of bitches, as Mr. Nixon should know from personal experience."[42]

Buckley's relationship to Hunt and the revelation that he had been in the CIA also led to the final break between Buckley and Garry Wills.

Both men, sensing that a break was imminent, had kept trying to reaffirm their ties. They had continued to exchange gifts and occasional compliments, but Buckley had been increasingly angered by Wills's attacks on Kissinger. Then Wills, spurred by the Hunt-CIA revelations, wrote a series of columns attacking Buckley and *National Review*. In January, he wrote:

Was *National Review,* with four ex-agents of the CIA on its staff, a CIA operation? If so, the CIA was stingy; and I doubt it—but even some on the editorial board raised the question. And the magazine supported Buckley's old CIA boss, Howard Hunt, and publicized a fund drive for him.[43]

Buckley was furious that Wills would suggest that *National Review* was a CIA operation. He circulated the column to the other editors. In the margin, he wrote, "Important for our editorial conference. I think we should smash him."[44] In a column, he wrote in response:

Unfortuntely, Mr. Wills is the exact complement of Mr. Revilo Oliver, who was booted out of the John Birch Society for excessive kookiness sometime after he revealed that JFK's funeral had been carefully rehearsed. Both are classics professors by background. Perhaps one should identify anyone who writes about politics and is also a classics professor as being that?[45]

After Wills's CIA column, Buckley finally broke off the friendship with Wills. When Wills sent him several Chesterton books—an appreciation of Chesterton had been an initial bond between the two men—he thanked him briefly. But he stopped writing letters and notes, and the two men never spent any time together again.

VI

Buckley's view of Nixon's downfall was different from that of Rusher and Evans and many of the younger conservatives in Washington. They blamed George Will, the *Washington Post,* and the liberal media—Evans quipped that he and Rusher had never supported Nixon until "after Watergate."

Hardly a week went by in which Buckley did not receive a letter of protest about Will from one of these conservatives. In April 1974, a young conservative, John Lofton, the editor of the Republican National Committee's *Monday,* wrote Buckley, "Any part you or *National Review* played in making George Will a national spokesman for conservatism was a serious mistake."[46] Several months later, Buckley received protest letters from the directors of both the American Conservative Union and Young Americans for Freedom. "I believe that [Will's] continuance as *National Review*'s Washington Bureau and Book Editor not only damages the credibility of the magazine," the ACU's Ronald B. Dear wrote, "but also provides Will with an unparalleled opportunity to wreak havoc upon the conservative community."[47]

Buckley consistently defended Will against his conservative detractors. To Lofton, he replied, "I think George Will is a man of great talent, and his anti-liberal polemics . . . are as effective as anybody's."[48]

Like Will, Buckley believed that Nixon brought his troubles upon himself. At a speech at the University of Pittsburgh in May, Buckley was asked in the question-and-answer period what could be learned from Watergate.

> Mr. Nixon has been terribly disappointing [he told the students], but he has been terribly disappointing largely in the context of his own choosing. It is . . . impossible for Mr. Nixon to order bacon and eggs in the morning without putting a moral edge on it. This was the trouble of his whole approach: it is that fusion of Quaker rectitude and political exigency.[49]

According to Buckley, Nixon had not done anything different from Roosevelt or Kennedy, but, once accused, he had insisted not only on his innocence but on a standard of rectitude far greater than his predecessors'. Buckley wrote in a column on the eve of Nixon's resignation, "He teased the Puritan conscience of America and loosed the hounds that finally arrived at his door. He demanded loudly that Congress and the Judiciary investigate and track down criminality to its lair. He was giving the public orders for his own execution."[50]

By the time of Nixon's resignation in August, Buckley was convinced that Nixon was taking the conservative movement and the Republican Party down with him. "Nixon's damage to conservative principles has been the major cover-up of the age," Buckley wrote in his newspaper column.[51] When he invited his brother Jim onto *Firing Line* to discuss the subject, Bill ended up taking a more pessimistic view than Jim. When Jim Buckley insisted that Nixon had not betrayed conservatism, Bill countered that "Mr. Nixon's policies were so confusing as regards conservative priorities domestically and internationally that he has left the conservative movement scattered, slightly incoherent, and perhaps even emasculated."[52]

Buckley saw his pessimism confirmed by the results of the 1974 congressional elections, held three months after Nixon resigned and Gerald Ford took office. The Republicans were crushed at the polls. The Democrats won forty-six new seats in the House and four in the Senate, giving them their largest majorities since 1936. Republican conservatives were not spared. In California, right-wing Senate candidate H. L. Richardson got only 37 percent against Democrat Alan Cranston. In Colorado, McGovern's former campaign manager, Gary Hart, easily defeated incumbent Republican Senator Peter Dominick by 59 to 41 percent. *National Review* termed the results a "disaster."

VII

At the same time Republican fortunes were ebbing, Buckley found himself in danger of losing the fortune that Peter Starr had made for him. The drive-ins that he had purchased in 1972 with Peter and Michael Starr and Gordon Ryan for Sitco Ltd. were not panning out. The partners had been banking on rising land prices, but the energy crisis that began in 1973 diminished the drive-ins' return, and rising interest rates forced up Sitco's monthly bank payments in its loans. An investor had offered the partners $10 million for the lands in the fall of 1973, but had backed out, forfeiting a $60,000 deposit, when interest rates continued to spiral. By the summer of 1974, Sitco was $8 million in debt and paying interest charges of $100,000 a month on the theaters. Buckley and his partners, who had personally guaranteed the loans, were facing bankruptcy.[53]

Buckley had allowed Peter Starr a free hand in running Starr Broadcasting and Sitco. Now he felt he had to do something. In July 1974, he met with the Starrs and proposed that they get Starr Broadcasting to buy Sitco. But Buckley didn't seem to understand that this proposal was fraught with peril. Buckley and the Starrs were asking Starr Broadcasting, which was already heavily burdened with a $25 million debt and projecting losses in several of its subsidiaries, to take on an extremely risky land venture. To avoid stockholder charges of "self-dealing," Buckley and the Starrs would have to demonstrate that they were acting to benefit Starr Broadcasting rather than themselves—a virtually impossible task given their own demonstrable stake in the buy-out and the patent risk of the investment. But Buckley convinced himself that the Sitco deal was good for Starr Broadcasting. On the basis of the $10 million offer, Buckley reasoned that if Starr Broadcasting could hold on to Sitco long enough, it would make a healthy profit when land values rose. And Buckley accepted Peter Starr's assurance that "the cash flow of the parent company was more than sufficient simultaneously to meeting the obligations of the company to its seniors *and* to carry the Texas properties." [54]

Buckley also didn't understand the extent to which Peter Starr and his brother had already compromised the relationship between Starr Broadcasting and Sitco. To raise capital for Sitco, Buckley and the Starrs had borrowed $850,000 from Columbia Union National Bank in Kansas City. Without Buckley's knowledge, the Starrs had taken out $450,000 of the $850,000 loan to Sitco as a personal loan to themselves. This meant that when the partners were proposing that Starr Broadcasting assume the debts of Sitco, they were, in effect, proposing that the company take over Peter and Michael Starr's personal debts. And there was another hitch. Columbia Union's Vice-President Glenn Burrus authorized the $850,000 loan to Sitco. But Columbia Union had already loaned Starr Broadcasting money, and Burrus was a director of Starr Broadcasting. With Sitco threatening to go under, Burrus could be charged with conflict of interests in having Starr Broadcasting bail out out Sitco.

In August 1974, Buckley proposed to the Starr board of directors that the corporation take over the theaters and reimburse the partners. According to one director's minutes, Buckley told the directors that the theaters were a "good deal." [55] The Starrs failed to mention that Sitco's liabilities included the personal loans that they had incurred. With Buckley and the Starrs out of the room, the other directors chose a committee of four directors to evaluate the Sitco deal. To avoid charges of impropriety, the board was supposed to choose directors who were "disinterested," but they chose a four-man committee whose chairman was Burrus.

In early October, with Sitco's situation growing worse daily, Buckley feared that he and the Starrs were facing imminent bankruptcy. Buckley began to panic.* Sitting at his typewriter late at night in his Stamford garage office, Buckley composed a confidential memoran-

---

* Buckley later told SEC investigators that he had become "hysterical." (Kronholz, *Wall Street Journal*.)

dum that he sent to the Starrs, his brother Jim, his lawyer Dan Mahoney, and his friend Evan Galbraith. In his memo, Buckley proposed setting up a new Starr board amenable to real-estate purchases and having Starr Broadcasting pay him $100,000 a year that he could transfer back through *National Review* to Sitco. Buckley also suggested that the Sitco partners pledge to indemnify Starr Broadcasting for any loss if it was forced to sell the Sitco "real estate at a value less than that paid for it." [56]

Buckley's memorandum displayed his naïveté and self-delusion. He continued to believe that the Sitco investment would benefit Starr Broadcasting over the long run. And he continued to believe that he could wheel and deal as if he were a private entrepreneur rather than the chairman of a multimillion-dollar public corporation. Buckley's proposal to have Starr Broadcasting pay him a $100,000 salary that would be passed on to Sitco was a perfect example. Buckley, who had taken no salary up to this point, thought the measure justifiable because he was beginning to devote considerable time to the company, but given the nature of the transaction, Buckley could not have avoided charges that he was simply trying to "launder" money to Sitco from Starr.

Starr Broadcasting never paid Buckley a $100,000 salary, but immediately after Buckley's memo, the company did pay *National Review* $30,000 for services it had rendered, which the magazine then gave to Sitco. The company also didn't replace its board, but when three vacancies occurred the next year, the company filled them with Buckley's Yale classmates. While Buckley denied that these actions stemmed directly from his memorandum, they contributed further to the air of impropriety hanging over the Starr-Sitco deal.

As far as Starr Broadcasting's willingness to buy Sitco was concerned, however, Buckley had little basis for worry. Later that month, the special committee of four directors met and recommended that Starr Broadcasting take out an option to buy Sitco and advance $400,000 to the company to defray its immediate debts; and the next year they exercised the option. The Starrs were temporarily saved from bankruptcy, and for the moment, Buckley didn't feel that he had to preoccupy himself with either Sitco and Starr Broadcasting. But the worst was yet to come.

PART FIVE

The Celebrity

Whatever happens in November, Buckley's existence isn't likely to change much, for he leads a life entirely separate from the political confrontations in which he is forever immersing himself.

—Donald Kirk, *Chicago Tribune Magazine*, October 1976

CHAPTER 21

Squire Willy

Nixon's disgrace destroyed the Republicans' credibility and made honesty in government a major political issue. But the factors that had brought about a decline in Democratic liberalism and a rise in Republican conservatism still lurked beneath the surface, waiting for the tide of Watergate to recede. While some conservatives were traumatized by Watergate and the 1974 elections, others set about furthering the gains that conservatives had made since the early sixties.

One group of younger conservatives, angered by the liberal assault on Nixon and by Ford's nomination of Nelson Rockefeller as his Vice-President, began laying the basis for a new right-wing movement in the last months of 1974. They had learned their politics from Buckley and *National Review,* but they were less committed to the Republican Party and were drawn to George Wallace's populism as a means of building a conservative majority. From middle-class backgrounds, they had the same visceral dislike for the eastern establishment as the southern and Midwestern conservatives of the 1920s and 1930s.

Richard Viguerie, who had mastered direct-mail fund raising working for the Young Americans for Freedom under Marvin Liebman, began doing direct mail for a George Wallace presidential bid—an activity that provided him with the rudiments of a mailing list from which to finance other causes and candidates. Howard Phillips, a founder of YAF and director of the Office of Economic Opportunity under Nixon, took over the Conservative Caucus, a lobbying group. Paul Weyrich, backed by the Coors family of Colorado, started the Heritage Foundation and the Committee for the Survival of a Free Congress, an organization that aided conservative candidates. These men and organizations formed the nucleus of what columnist and former Nixon aide Kevin Phillips called the "New Right."

In California, conservatives had also been stirring. In May, Ronald Reagan, who was not going to run for re-election that year, held a meeting of his advisers at his Pacific Palisades home. Reagan was demoralized by the ongoing scandal of Watergate, but John Sears, a young Washington lawyer, argued forcefully that whether Nixon remained or resigned in favor of Ford, Reagan should run for the presidency in 1976.[1] Reagan was not ready to commit himself, but Sears's argument made a strong impression on him and his California advisers.

In the previous crises of conservatism—in 1954, after McCarthy's censure, in 1961, after the rise of the John Birch Society, and in 1965, after Goldwater's defeat—Buckley had been the movement's Moses, leading conservatives out of the political wilderness. But in the wake of Watergate, Buckley, who had helped bring conservatives into the Nixon camp, was among the more demoralized and disheartened.

I

Buckley could derive little consolation from the populist politics of the New Right. When he was younger, he had attacked the establishment, but as a graduate of Yale and son of a millionaire, Buckley had sought a political rather than a social counterrevolution. He didn't want to do away with Skull and Bones or the Council on Foreign Relations, but rather win their adherence to a radically different political outlook. In 1974, he had accepted an invitation to join the Council on Foreign Relations, the organization that had always epitomized for the far Right the eastern upper class's hold over foreign policy.*

Under Burnham and Kissinger's influence, Buckley no longer shared the Right's enmity toward Nelson Rockefeller. When Gerald

---

* Buckley had been nominated for membership in the Council on Foreign Relations in 1965, but was blackballed—by whom, Buckley never found out.

Ford nominated Rockefeller to be his Vice-President in August 1974, Buckley, who had urged him to nominate former U.N. Ambassador George Bush, nonetheless defended Ford's choice. Buckley argued that Rockefeller was a good choice precisely because of his appeal to Democrats and Independents, which would help Ford to "stabilize" the country after the "great dislocation" of Watergate. And he defended Rockefeller against his conservative critics. "Rockefeller likes to be first in all things, and he is not likely to acquiesce silently in the progressive military debilitation of the United States," Buckley wrote in his column.[2]

Buckley also disagreed with a New Right on Wallace's fledgling candidacy. He accepted Wallace's disavowal of racism, but he continued to express skepticism about the New Right's attempt to blend populism and conservatism in the person of Wallace. In a December column, Buckley tried to demonstrate the incompatibility of the two. He took as his example the question of what to do about higher energy costs—which had skyrocketed because of the Arab oil embargo. A conservative, Buckley contended, would pass along higher costs to the consumer in order to encourage more exploration, while a populist "desires a villain," or as Buckley wrote:

> What you come up with in the big oil companies. You start talking about their huge profits. Then you start talking about the problems of the little guy. . . . That's the kind of thing that rolls off George Wallace's tongue as naturally as his talk about the pointyheads in the Supreme Court telling us where to send our children to school.[3]

And Buckley had different political priorities than the New Right conservatives. Buckley had come of age politically during the fifties, when the threat of Soviet Communism was the overriding issue in America. The New Right leaders were coming of age after the Vietnam War when social and economic issues had begun to displace foreign policy. In the mid-seventies, while the majority of Americans supported the Nixon and Kissinger polities of détente with the Soviet Union and while the New Right tried to rally a right wing around such issues as abortion, busing, and high taxes, Buckley devoted an unusual number of columns to defending Chile's anti-Communist regime. Jeff Bell said, "Bill was somewhat aloof from the whole movement away from foreign policy concerns to domestic concerns."

One political issue that absorbed Buckley during the months after Watergate was American policy toward General Augusto Pinochet's regime. In 1973, the squat, mustachioed Pinochet, a conservative autocrat who believed his country had fallen into the hands of Communists, overthrew Chile's elected Socialist President Salvador Allende in a brutal coup that resulted in the death, imprisonment, or exile of about 100,000 Chileans—one out of every one hundred citizens. Torture was widespread. And the political repression came to include not only Communists and Socialists, but Christian Democrats who were initially sympathetic to the coup. Among the public and in the U.S. Congress, there was a tremendous outcry against the coup that ended seventy years of democratic rule in Chile and against the excesses of the new regime. As revelations of the CIA's and Kissinger's complicity in the coup emerged, opponents of the new regime turned their fire on Kissinger.

Buckley had followed the Allende government very closely and had hired a special correspondent in Santiago, Nena Ossa, to provide *National Review* with regular reports. Even though Allende was a Socialist, not a Communist, Buckley saw his regime as a beachhead for Soviet Communism in South America. His election had raised the question of whether Communists could advance to power peacefully. "Chile is the only country in postwar history about which it almost became possible to say that they voted themselves into communism, and for that reason it was hugely important," Buckley said.

In the wake of the coup, Buckley had weighed the Pinochet regime's human rights violations against the alternative of a pro-Communist Chile, toward which he believed the Socialist Allende had inexorably been leading the country. Burnham provided the theoretical perspective in which Buckley and *National Review* saw the coup. "The political choice in Chile was never democracy versus dictatorship," Burnham wrote, "but a right wing authoritarian regime versus the totalist regime to which the victory of the left under existing conditions must have led." *

In one of his first columns after the coup, Buckley disputed an eyewitness estimate that the new junta had executed four or five hundred Chileans and portrayed the new regime as popular. "It is not less true for being a commonplace, that always, everywhere, people prefer an authoritarian government to chaos."[4] Buckley dismissed Democratic arguments that the Nixon administration had helped topple a "democratically elected" government. "Allende was the out-

---

* *National Review*, October 25, 1974. This distinction between authoritarian and totalist regimes, which Burnham claimed that he adapted from British author Brian Crozier, was later popularized by former U.N. Ambassador Jeane Kirkpatrick in a widely read 1979 attack on the Carter administration's human rights policy.

spoken friend of socialist tyranny, and the notion that we should deny to his opponents such help as we gave them, suggests that the United States should be totally indifferent to the growth within Latin America of a government dominated by a man whose idol was Fidel Castro.''[5]

In October 1974, at the suggestion of Nena Ossa, the Chilean ambassador called Buckley to ask him to recommend a public-relations firm that the government could hire. Buckley recommended Marvin Liebman, who had just returned from London, where he had tried unsuccessfully to make a living as a theatrical producer. On October 29, Liebman and Ossa had lunch in New York with Chilean officials to work out the plans for a new organization, and Buckley became intimately involved in the subsequent negotiations between Liebman and the Chilean government.

Buckley and Liebman understood that for a lobbying organization in the U.S. to be effective, it would have to be seen as both nonpartisan and as independent of Chilean funds. But they recognized that they would not be able to raise the $130,000 they needed to launch the new organization from American donors. Liebman decided to accept Chilean funding, but not to register himself as director with the Justice Department. In January, Ossa wrote Buckley that Chilean U.N. Ambassador Mario Arnello had received from the Chilean ambassador funds "to cover three months of a trial period for Friends of Free Chile."[6] In February, Ossa wrote Liebman that they had gotten the "green light" from Pinochet himself.[7] With the Chilean government fully behind the project, Liebman founded the American-Chilean Council, with offices in New York and Santiago. Ossa, whom the Pinochet regime had made head of the National Museum of Fine Arts, served as the ACC's Chilean representative and continued as *National Review*'s correspondent in Chile in spite of her government connections. In a letter, Liebman assured Ossa, "Only Bill and I know the whole story of the ACC."[8]

Buckley's determination to defend Pinochet's regime reflected his own upbringing and the priorities of his generation, but it took him farther from what was becoming the center of conservative agitation. In writing about Pinochet—and in soliciting articles for *National Review*—Buckley also showed a recurring tendency to ignore the canons of objective journalism when he believed that the struggle against communism was at issue. And in helping Liebman and Ossa set up a lobby linked to the Chilean government, Buckley demonstrated a curious ignorance of the law requiring agents of foreign governments to register themselves and their organizations with the Justice Department in Washington.

II

Buckley displayed little apprehension at not being on the cutting edge of conservatism. If anything, he seemed to be losing interest in politics altogether. At the beginning of the new year, 1975, Buckley resolved to do three things before his fiftieth birthday the following November: write a novel, take his sailboat *Cyrano* across the Atlantic, and perform a Bach harpsichord concerto with a symphony orchestra. He would do the first two, but not the third.

Buckley's pessimistic view of conservative prospects may have contributed to his decision to write a novel. "After Watergate, he felt a lot of despair with right-wing politics and with the kind of fellows he had to support for the President," editor and friend Sophie Wilkins said. "Writing with his imagination he was free to have everything according to his heart's desire."

The man who got Buckley started was Sam Vaughan, the mild-mannered president of Doubleday. A liberal, Vaughan had initially made his mark at Doubleday as an editor for Republicans and conservatives. He had become friendly with Buckley when he had commissioned Jeffrey Hart's *The American Dissent,* a history of *National Review* that Doubleday published in 1966. In the fall of 1974, Vaughan had read an interview with Buckley in which Buckley said that if some publisher besides Putnam's, his regular house, came to him with an interesting proposition, he would feel free to do it. Vaughan told his colleagues, "We'll see him as soon as we can and we'll have an idea when we get there."

Vaughan, with editors Betty Prashker and Hugh O'Neill, met Buckley in December at Buckley's favorite Italian restaurant, Paone's, around the corner from *National Review.* According to Buckley, it was Vaughan who first broached the idea of a novel, but Vaughan's recollection is quite different. Vaughan insists that it was Buckley who brought up the idea. "We put a couple of ideas in front of Buckley, which he politely, always politely, brushed on the floor as you would clean crumbs from the table. I can remember asking, What would you like to write that you are not now writing? And he said a novel." When Vaughan asked Buckley what kind of novel he had in mind, he said he would like to write one "like Forsyth." Vaughan thought he was referring to British novelist John Galsworthy's *The Forsyte Saga,* but he was talking about popular spy novelist Frederick Forsyth, the author of the best-selling potboilers *The Day of the Jackal* and *The Odessa File.* Vaughan, who knew that Buckley had been in the CIA, suggested that he consider a novel about "a CIA agent who is out in the world somewhere doing work for his country while his country or part of it decides they are going to dismantle the agency or at least take the lid off it."

Vaughan left lunch in "high excitement." With most authors, Vaughan might have taken his time about offering a contract, but he told Prashker and O'Neill that he wanted to put a contract on Buckley's desk the next afternoon. "It seemed to me it was a bit of a long shot, but a good long shot," Vaughan said. "At the least he would write an interesting book."

The deal was consummated in December before Buckley left for Switzerland. Buckley wrote Alistair Horne just after he signed, "I must do [the novel] in six weeks. I am desolate. I have no ideas, no characters, no plot, no ambition, no inspiration, no nothing, just wads and wads of dough promised to me if I do my duty."[9] But he had a general political purpose in mind. Late that fall, he had seen an anti-CIA suspense movie, *Three Days of the Condor,* and had resolved to write a book in which "the good guys and the bad guys were actually distinguishable."[10] His imagination was sparked by a stray fact picked up in conversation—that fornicating with the queen of England was still a capital crime in Britain—and the outlines of a plot began to take shape in his mind.

Buckley wrote *Saving the Queen* during his two-month stay in Switzerland, going through two drafts before submitting it to Doubleday in March. In a letter, Buckley told Yale professor Thomas Bergin about *Saving the Queen:* "It is without art, but it has what all amateurs owe the reader—an impatient sense of narrative obligation."[11]

Vaughan was surprised by what he got. As he recalled:

> The kind of novel we got is not the kind of novel I thought we would get. I knew something about the contemporary writers he admired like Wilfrid Sheed and Hugh Kenner, some writers of real quality, and I thought we might get a kind of ingenious wordsmith's book, deeply philosophical, witty, but not sturdy. What surprised me when the first draft arrived was the narrative rush, the swiftness of it, the page-turning quality, that he had from the beginning. We didn't get a delicate or arcane or too esoteric novel. What we got was a romp with some ideas at work in it, and a little bit of outrage, especially as far as the British were concerned.

Buckley modeled the hero of *Saving the Queen* on himself. Blackford Oakes is a tall, straw-haired, blue-eyed Yale graduate. He is also a World War II veteran who, faced with being called up for the

Korean War, decides to join the CIA. ("Unless he entered the FBI or a para-military research institute, or developed a sudden, gratifying disability, he might very well go from graduation to a quick refresher course in the latest fighter planes . . . and from there to Korea." [12]) He is bright and witty with "an anarchic stubbornness" in his eyes.[13] What differences exist between Oakes and the author reflect Buckley's ideal of what he might have been: unlike Buckley, Oakes was not stuck in the United States during World War II, but had dueled heroically against German fighters; he is talented at science and math and drawing. As a character, Oakes is an ideal type —Buckley's version of Ian Fleming's James Bond hero—rather than the complex, blemished real heroes of John le Carré or Graham Greene.

Oakes's first mission is to discover how Soviet agents in Britain are learning secrets of American H-bomb development known only to the prime minister and the queen of England. Oakes becomes friends with the queen, and in a climactic scene in her bed, discovers that the queen's cousin, Viscount Peregrine Kirk, is extracting the atom secrets from her and passing them on to the Russians.

Buckley introduced the plot as a flashback, as Oakes waits to testify in the Watergate era before a hostile committee investigating the CIA. *Saving the Queen* was intended as an answer to the agency's critics who charged that it was, in effect, no better than its Soviet counterparts, and to spy novelists like le Carré who implied that there was little difference between the Western and Soviet operatives. Buckley has Oakes put the matter succinctly. Oakes, Buckley wrote,

> felt himself curiously affected by the invisible network being managed at one end by Joseph Stalin, the principal agent—now that Hitler was gone—of human misery; and at the other, by Washington, D.C., a network of its own, protective of human freedoms in design, but, also, necessarily engaged in the same kind of business: lying, stealing, intimidating, blackmailing, intercepting . . . *Quod licet Jovi, non licet bovi* . . . could be used in defense of indefensible propositions. Nevertheless, correctly applied, it was unchallengeable. What it is permitted for Jove to do is not necessarily permitted for a cow to do. We might in secure conscience lie and steal in order to secure the escape of human beings from misery or death; Stalin had no right to lie and steal in order to bring misery and death to others. Yet, viewed without paradigmatic moral coordinates, simpletons would say, simply: *Both sides lied and cheated* —a plague on both their houses.[14]

But in the framework of a novel, Buckley's defense of the CIA is simply another voice in a diverse chorus. When it comes to portraying the men from the other side—Kirk and the Soviet spy chief in London, Boris Bolgin—Buckley's portrayals are curiously human. Kirk is an idealist who despises Stalin but believes in the Marxist-Leninist future. In the end, he commits suicide rather than try to use his association with the queen to blackmail the West into letting him defect. "Okay, you chaps won this one," the sporting Kirk says to Oakes. "And you're right, you Yankee cocksucker, there isn't any point in doing her in for the hell of it."

The message also gets largely subsumed by the "impatient sense of narrative obligation," which Buckley created by using standard spy-novel conventions of hinting at dark deeds ahead and by peppering his politics liberally with easy sex—besides the queen, Oakes makes it with his college girlfriend, Sally, and with Paris whores—and with clever, but sometimes sophomoric repartee. Hugh Kenner, who was surprised by how good *Saving the Queen* was, described it as "not a terribly good spy story," but a "comedy of manners."

III

When Buckley returned to New York in the spring, he made the final arrangements for his voyage across the Atlantic, which he financed through an advance he received from Macmillan on a sailing book. The advance and book contract were part of the settlement of a lawsuit that Buckley had brought against Macmillan and one of its authors, Rev. Franklin Littell, who in a 1969 book, *Wild Tongues,* had described Buckley as "a fascist fellow-traveler."

From the age of thirteen, when his father had bought him a sixteen-foot sailboat, Buckley had been an avid sailor. Buckley was most contented when he was sailing. "He's happy as a pig in mud when he's sitting behind the wheel of his sailboat," Evan Galbraith said. In the beginning, Buckley liked to race. "I am perfectly at home in a small boat, and would, in a small boat race, more often than not come in if not this side of glory, perhaps this side of ignominy," he wrote in 1958.[15] But several poor finishes on his sloop *Suzy Wong,* climaxed by coming in next to last in a summer 1965 race from Marblehead, Massachusetts, to Nova Scotia, convinced him to turn from racing to cruising, and in 1967, he bought a luxurious sixty-foot schooner, *Cyrano,* that slept nine comfortably and was suitable for long voyages.

Buckley had been thinking about sailing across the Atlantic since the early sixties, but he had only begun to take the prospect seriously when he was in Switzerland in 1974. Buckley recruited his son, Christopher, who had graduated from Yale in 1974, and who had increasingly become his father's companion as well as son.* He also recruited old friends Evan Galbraith and Reginald Stoops, Christopher's friend Danny Merritt, and Pat's sister, "Bill" Finucane. (Pat herself did not sail.) They gathered in Miami on May 30 for the trip, but several repairs still needed to be made. Buckley spent the final day dodging a young woman in black who stood on the dock and asked him, every time he got off the boat, if she could have a "session" with him. He repeatedly refused, and he learned later that she then went to New York to enlist the aid of Priscilla Buckley. She was plagued by a demon, she told Priscilla, that had entered her when she had crossed Buckley's path in Saigon a year before, and she could only exorcise the demon by spending a silent half hour with Buckley.

On the trip, the sailors amused themselves by enclosing anti-Communist messages in wine bottles they finished and throwing the bottles overboard in the hope that they would wash up on shore and be forwarded as instructed to *National Review*. Buckley contributed, "*Oiga Fidel: Veniam Videbo Viciam,*" and another traveler wrote, "CIA will guarantee one (1) free assassination upon retrieving this message." [16] To the sailors' delight, one of the bottles came ashore in Fort Lauderdale and its message was sent to *National Review*.

When they landed in Bermuda on the first leg of the journey, McCarthy's former counsel Roy Cohn was standing on the dock. Cohn, clad in bikini drawers and a white T-shirt with "Superjew" emblazoned across it, was accompanied by a heavily muscled young man named Joe, who wore a shirt with a picture of an orgy on it and who was his current boyfriend. "Joe was a catamite," Christopher Buckley said. "He looked like he might have been mixed up with the rough trade. The relationship [between him and Cohn] was very clear."

Buckley, who had remained friendly with Cohn, was embarrassed by Cohn's relationship with Joe. Buckley and his friends hastily convened a conference back on board to figure out how they could politely turn down Cohn's dinner invitation. While they succeeded in crafting several excuses, they were unable to avoid having two lunches with Joe and Cohn, who were staying at the same hotel in Bermuda.

Pat Buckley had feared the worst for her husband, son, and sister,

---

* The previous summer, when Christopher had confessed that he was losing his faith, Buckley had taken him for a week in Taxco, Mexico, where the two had read English Catholic G. K. Chesterton's *Orthodoxy* aloud to each other. "It anchored me," Christopher said later about the experience.

but the thirty-day trip from Miami to Marbella, Spain, by way of
Bermuda and the Azores, was largely uneventful, with the only serious storm between Bermuda and the Azores. For Buckley, however,
the trip was a month-long epiphany. He spent four-hour watches talking with Christopher in a way they never had time to talk on land.
And he left politics behind and concentrated his intelligence and energy on mastering the sea.

When Buckley returned to the United States in July, however, he
discovered that he had become an object of political controversy—
not on the Left, but on the Right.

IV

Buckley had incurred the New Right's wrath not only by his defense of Rockefeller and attacks against Wallace, but by his continued
defense of Kissinger and his advocacy of marijuana decriminalization.
(One cause of friction with the New Right, George Will, was removed
when Will left *National Review* that year to write a column for *Newsweek.**)

Leading the charge against Buckley was Kevin Phillips, the man
who coined the term "New Right," and who came closest to being
the New Right's intellectual. Brought up in a middle-class family in
the Bronx and educated at Colgate and Harvard Law School, Phillips
had first made a name for himself as the author of *The Emerging
Republican Majority*. In 1970, he had left the Nixon administration
and become a syndicated columnist. In July 1975 he began to sketch
out in his column the differences between the Old and the New Right.

Phillips described a New Right that was "populist" rather than
"elitist." He denounced Ford and Rockefeller and called for a presidential ticket in 1976 of Reagan and Wallace. And he began to attack
Buckley, in whose magazine his articles had frequently appeared, as
epitomizing the Old Right. In a column describing a meeting of Howard Phillips's new Conservative Caucus, Kevin Phillips described the
new politics.

---

* On *National Review*, Rusher and Hart had finally convinced Buckley in December 1974,
after Will had made a disparaging remark about Reagan's age, to remove Will's designation as Washington editor. "I showed that column to Buckley," Rusher recalled, "and he
visibly wilted. He said, 'If he is going to write like that, he simply can't remain our
ambassador to the Washington community.' And I said, 'Cheer up, if he finds better
opportunities, he'll step on our face and move upwards.' " But Buckley was not happy
with the decision to remove Will—he wrote "ugh" next to the recommendation in the
minutes. A year later, in December 1975, to Rusher's delight, but Buckley's sorrow, Will
notified Buckley that he was leaving *National Review* for *Newsweek*.

First, today's New Right tends to be overtly populist where the Old Right is generally elitist. Many in the older Buckley-oriented "Conservative Movement" regard ideological conservatism as a surviving high-church religion unhappily now practiced only by the elite handful who have kept uncontaminated by mass culture and politics. . . . Today's "New Right" . . . is designedly anti-elitist—preferring mobilization of Levittown, Georgia, and South Boston to false pretenses of political gentility. Next, it can be said that the critical issues of the Old Right have been national security, free market economics . . . and U.S.-Soviet détente. Those were the themes emphasized by the Buckley-led Manhattan Twelve in their 1971–72 insurgency against Richard Nixon—with little public response. In contrast, the New Right, while favorable to a strong military posture and suspicious of government regulation, puts its principal emphasis on domestic social issues—on public anger over busing, welfare spending, environmental extremism, soft criminology, media bias and power, warped education, twisted textbooks, racial quotas, various guidelines and an ever-expanding bureaucracy.[17]

Phillips became increasingly personal in his attacks on Buckley. In one column, Phillips criticized Buckley for his friendship with John Kenneth Galbraith and membership in the Council on Foreign Relations and for "abandoning Middle America to load up his yacht with vintage wines and sail across the Atlantic." Finally, Buckley struck back in his own column. Describing Phillips as an "eccentric theorist writing orotund stuff," Buckley dismissed the pretensions of the "new" Right.

What is new is that some of the boys are seeking means of co-opting George Wallace into the conservative movement. I do not automatically reject the effort for the simple reason that it is the people who voted for Wallace that are needed—and only George Wallace can deliver them. What is excluded is a concession to George Wallace of a philosophically disreputable kind: the issue, for instance, of metaphysical human equality. Poor Phillips, he flounders about in a circle-squaring futility. If we give in to the worst demands of Wallace populism, we have earned ourselves exactly nothing, save possibly a constitutional amendment to prevent busing. That we should be able to get anyway, and we'd probably get it a lot faster if the New Right, to the extent it is successfully identified with George Wallace, is not seen to be the principal advocate of it.[18]

Phillips threw Buckley's words back at him:

Hell, Wallace isn't going to hook up with Squire Willy and his Companions of the Oxford Unabridged Dictionary. Nor can we expect Alabama truck drivers or Ohio steelworkers to sign on with a politics captivated by Ivy League five-syllable word polishers. . . . Most of the "New Conservatives" I know believe that any new politics or coalition has to surge up from Middle America . . . not dribble down from Bill Buckley's wine rack and favorite philosopher's shelf. . . . There was, of course, a time when Bill Buckley was anti-establishment—back in the long-ago days when he was an Irish *nouveau-riche* cheer leader for Joe McCarthy. But since then, he's primed his magazine with cast-off Hapsburg royalty, Englishmen who part their names in the middle, and others calculated to put real lace on Buckley's Celtic curtains.[19]

Phillips also went after *National Review*. Citing *National Review*'s twentieth-anniversary issue in which the magazine credited Wilhelm Roepke and Eric Voegelin with laying the philosophical foundations of conservatism, Phillips quipped, "So what have they to say to Kansas City and Scranton?" *National Review* editor Jeffrey Hart took up the challenge. In his syndicated column, he denied that "*National Review* was intended to be a mass circulation magazine." Instead it assumed that

out there in Middle America, yes in Kansas City and Scranton, there reside individuals—and perhaps not all that many—who are addicted to good prose and to theoretical perception. . . . The founders of *National Review* also perceived that the intellectual class in modern society possesses unprecedented leverage . . . and they saw that conservatism must therefore be viable as an intellectual as well as a popular and political presence.[20]

But Buckley didn't think Hart's column could persuade Phillips. He wrote Hart: "I doubt that you accomplished much with Kevin, since he really has decided to become a Jimmy Breslin conservative. I have simply nothing to say to someone who is proud of his ignorance of Voegelin. I am ashamed of my superficial knowledge of him."[21]

Buckley did not attempt to answer Phillips again. As far as he was concerned, Phillips had removed himself from serious consideration; and he didn't take Phillips's attacks that seriously. "I don't think Kevin Phillips got anywhere near his heart the way that Garry Wills had," Joe Sobran, who had become an editor of *National Review*, said. "He didn't covet Phillips's esteem the way he had Garry's.

Kevin Phillips was a strategist, a pol. I don't think he was interested in what Kevin thought of him."

But Phillips and the New Right had found a like-minded spirit on *National Review*. And Buckley had to take his own publisher more seriously.

V

Bill Rusher had been veering rightward since the early fifties. Nixon's betrayal of conservatives had not shocked him, but confirmed a growing conviction that the Republican Party was not a fit vehicle for conservatives. Like the New Right conservatives, he regarded Ford's nomination of Rockefeller as the Vice-President and putative successor to the Republican presidency as the last straw. That fall, in the heat of anger, Rusher had written a short book, *The Making of the New Majority Party*, in which he proposed founding a new conservative party to displace the Republican Party.

Rusher was very influenced by Phillips's *The Emerging Republican Majority*, but he translated "Republican" into "conservative." Rusher proposed a party that would unite social conservatives—the erstwhile blue-collar and ethnic Democrats who backed Wallace— with the economic conservatives who invariably voted Republican. Within the Republican Party it was impossible to create this coalition, he argued, because the liberal bloc, while not powerful enough "to impose its will, [is] always able to force the selection of candidates and the adoption of platform planks that [are] calculated to offend its sensibilities as little as possible." [22] It was necessary for conservatives to leave the Republican Party and start their own.

But unlike the New Right populists, Rusher looked to Reagan rather than Wallace as his candidate and to an alliance with social conservatives for immediate tactical ends. This strategy proved more palatable to Buckley. In May, he printed a long excerpt from Rusher's book in *National Review*. But Buckley insisted that a conservative third party could work only if Reagan, denied the Republican nomination, agreed to lead it. Buckley wrote Roger Milliken:

> These are grave times indeed, and I am myself in my current mood attracted to the proposal of a third party, *provided* Reagan (there is no one else who could handle the mission) succeeded simultaneously in winning the Republican primaries. I am not always in agreement with Bill Rusher, but I find a lot in his book, which I assume you have read, most convincing. [23]

Buckley lost interest in Rusher's third party when Reagan announced in July, just after Buckley's return, that he was forming a committee to explore running for President in the Republican Party—an announcement that was tantamount to a declaration of candidacy. From that point, as Rusher continued to agitate for a third party, Buckley's main interest became promoting Reagan's primary challenge against Ford.

VI

Buckley's friendship with Reagan dated back to 1960 when Reagan, the chairman of Democrats for Nixon in California and *National Review* subscriber, introduced him at a Nixon rally in Beverly Hills. Buckley described the incident in an article about Reagan.

> He was to introduce me at a lecture that night in Beverly Hills. He arrived at the school auditorium to find consternation. The house was full and the crowd impatient, but the microphone was dead; the student who was to have shown up at the control room above the balcony to turn on the current hadn't. Reagan quickly took over. He instructed an assistant to call the principal and see if he could get a key. He then bounded onto the stage and shouted as loud as he could to make himself heard. In a very few minutes the audience was greatly enjoying itself. Then word came to him: no answer at the principal's telephone. Reagan went offstage and looked out the window. There was a ledge, a foot wide, two stories above the street level, running along the side of the window back to the locked control room. Hollywoodwise, he climbed out on the ledge and sidestepped carefully, arms stretched out to help him balance, until he had gone the long way to the window, which he broke open with his elbow, lifting it open from the inside and jumping into the darkness. In a moment, the lights were on, the amplifying knobs turned up, the speaker introduced.[24]

They had corresponded and visited each other ever since; and when Reagan ran for governor in 1966, Buckley and *National Review* had championed his candidacy. Reagan himself was in awe of Buckley's intelligence. When asked about him, he would invariably bring up his friend's enormous vocabulary. For instance, in 1967, when a *Time* interviewer asked him about Buckley, he recalled a toast Buckley had given at a dinner in Sacramento just after Reagan was elected governor. A German word, *"Zietgeist,"* was Buckley's toast, and afterwards Reagan had had to ask him what it meant. It became a standing joke between the two men.*

By the early seventies, Buckley had become convinced that Reagan was capable of becoming President, and after Agnew's resignation, Buckley and *National Review* anointed Reagan the leader of conservatism. He saw Reagan as a kind of Frank Capra hero—a *Mr. Smith Goes to Washington* character. Reagan, Buckley told Nixon, "is the only man in America who doesn't care what the *New York Times* said in its editorial page." [25] By 1973, he was urging Reagan in a letter to prepare for 1976.

> I heard it said about you—by a well-wisher—that it will have to be Rockefeller in 1976 because you "refuse to wrap your mind around foreign policy." You must prove such skeptics wrong, and it is not too early to start. You should have someone on your staff who is trained to concentrate full time on such matters. [26]

Buckley never denied that Gerald Ford, who had sat on the dais at *National Review*'s tenth-anniversary banquet, was a conservative, but he doubted whether he had the political and intellectual ability to stand up to the Democratic Congress or the Soviet Union. He described Ford (in terms reminiscent of those he had used for Eisenhower) as a

> genial man of conservative disposition who, however, accepts the coils of détente as he would the fingers of a masseuse, reveling in his presumed contribution to world peace; and who considers himself triumphant when, by raw exercise of the executive veto, he succeeds in reducing from $70 to $60 billion a projected national deficit. [27]

By contrast, he had come to believe that Reagan, if President, could not only stand up to the adversaries of conservatism, but that a Reagan campaign in 1976 could help revive the conservative movement. When asked about the state of the movement, he told an interviewer in November 1975, "As of this moment, as we speak, it's going no-

---

* *Time* interviews. In introducing Barry Goldwater at the *National Review* twentieth-anniversary celebration in December 1975, Buckley said, "Barry Goldwater ran for President the year after the decade of the sixties was destabilized. In a sense it did not matter that he lost—sombody had to lose, and the inertia of the age—what Ronald Reagan would call the *Zeitgeist*—generally stipulates that the loser should be the rightward candidate." (*National Review*, December 5, 1975.)

where. . . . That would change if Reagan were to decide to challenge
Mr. Ford in the primary.''[28]

When Reagan finally announced his candidacy in November 1975,
National Review editorialized, ''He is in our judgment doing the correct thing and the Republic, and the Republican Party, should benefit
from it.''[29]

VII

In November, the same month that Buckley turned fifty, *National
Review* completed its twentieth year of publication. In a retrospective
interview with Richard Viguerie's *Conservative Digest,* Buckley admitted that after the refusal of Americans to aid the Hungarian revolution in 1956, he had had to abandon his vision ''of coming to the
rescue of Eastern Europe.'' But instead of resting his case on political
realism, Buckley showed that he still could not resist endowing the
Soviet devil with magical potency. He thought such a strategy had
become doubly futile, he told the magazine, because the Soviet Union
had achieved military superiority over the U.S.: ''Now, in a period in
which the Soviet Union is actually stronger than we are, militarily, it
becomes pure rodomontade to talk about a total victory over them,
except in philosophical terms, for the very simple reason that we
cannot effect it.''

What, then, could conservatives hope to accomplish? Buckley reverted to a formulation reminiscent of Nock and Chambers. ''More
and more I find that the challenge we face at *National Review,* and all
conservatives face, is to lay down the distinction between their way
of life and our way of life.''[30]

Five years before, in the wake of Jim Buckley's senate victory,
National Review had held a boisterous fifteenth-anniversary celebration at the stylish and contemporary Tavern on the Green. It held its
twentieth-anniversary celebration in the ornate Grand Ballroom of the
Plaza Hotel. The jubilant swinger of 1970 had become a grande dame
of the Right. But the banquet generated no less interest among conservatives: ticket sales had to be halted a week before when all 750
seats were sold. And at the head table were the leading figures of
American conservatism: Bill and Jim Buckley, Reagan, and Goldwater.

Buckley's own speech was as pessimistic as his interview with *Conservative Digest*. He reiterated an argument that he had first made in
an October 1951 article in *Human Events*—that American capitalists
—''a class of self-conscious men benumbed by two generations of

accumulated contempt by academicians, poets, and moralists''—
were sowing the seeds of their own destruction. The American capitalist, Buckley said,

> is the inarticulate, self-conscious bumbling mechanic of the private
> sector, struck dumb by the least cliché of socialism, fleeing into the
> protective arms of the government at the least hint of commercial
> difficulty . . . uniformly successful only in his ambition to grow
> duller and duller as the years go by, eyes left, beseeching popular
> favor and, who knows? perhaps, even, academic favor.

How would Western civilization survive under such a handicap?
Buckley evoked the Remnant:

> Still, the campfires continue to burn, and every now and then you
> hear the chorus singing; the old songs, free of the tormented intro-
> spections of the new idiom; ignorant altogether of the litany of
> reasons why we should hate our own country; axiomatic in their
> demand for human freedom; and the heart stirs, and the blood be-
> gins to run, and, each one of us, in his own ways, continues the
> effort.

Buckley concluded, "We have stood together for one-tenth the life
span of this Republic, and we must resolve to stand with it, and its
ideals, forever.''[31]

VIII

In Switzerland the next winter, Buckley devoted his mornings to
writing the book about his sail across the Atlantic. Called *Airborne,* it
was as much about his relationship with his wife and about his rebellious but adoring son as it was about sailing; and those few technical
passages that concerned sailing were buried amidst entertaining tales
of past shipwrecks. It was a slight book—much of it devoted to string-
ing together anecdotes—but one of Buckley's most entertaining. It
was also the first book he had written that had no bearing whatsoever
on politics.

Like *Cruising Speed,* it was a book about Buckley himself, but it
was not autobiographical in the usual sense. Instead, the book displayed Buckley's delight in his own tastes, whether in sailing companions, wine, or music. Buckley described the kind of people he liked to
sail with:

Your companions on board are a crucial specification. For me, there is one, no-further-questions-asked qualifier: personal rudeness . . . including any sign of impatience (the exception: the captain or the helmsman shouting out impatiently the need for a snatchblock, a flashlight, a scotch and soda).[32]

And the kind of meals he liked to eat:

Rawle could give us anything, beginning with lobster Newburgh and ending with Baked Alaska. We settle on a fish chowder, of which he is surely the supreme practitioner, and cheese and bacon sandwiches, grilled, with a most prickly Riesling picked up at St. Barts for peanuts.[33]

In *Cruising Speed,* these kinds of passages were subordinate to the political message; in *Airborne,* they were the substance of the story. It was Buckley delighting in and enhancing his own celebrity—and no doubt escaping the political disappointments of the preceding years.

While Buckley was in Switzerland, *Saving the Queen* appeared. Although the major reviews were lukewarm—in *The New York Times,* Walter Goodman called it "serviceable entertainment"—it quickly climbed to the top of the best-seller list. Buckley, Niven, and Galbraith continued their friendly competition over whose books were superior. Asked by an interviewer to explain *Saving the Queen*'s success, Galbraith said, "Bill Buckley has a genuine talent for fiction, as his discriminating readers have always known." He called Buckley's decision to write novels "a quantum step in self-recognition."[34]

David Niven had reasons of his own to take Buckley down a notch. When Niven's second book of memoirs had appeared in 1975, he had asked Buckley for a jacket blurb and Buckley had responded with "Probably the best book ever written about Hollywood." When *Saving the Queen* was about to be published, Buckley asked Niven for a blurb, and the actor, busy filming, told Buckley to write it for him. When they were in Switzerland, Buckley told him casually that he had submitted a statement in his name, "Probably the best novel ever written about fucking the Queen. David Niven." "I think that was the only time I ever saw him really caught off balance," Buckley said. "For about half a second, which for him was a long time. Then he started to laugh."[35]

But Niven got his revenge that winter. Buckley and Niven painted together in Switzerland at an atelier they rented, and Niven brought the painter Marc Chagall to visit. Niven, who described Buckley as "the worst amateur painter in the world," had warned him not to show Chagall any of his paintings, but Buckley insisted upon trotting out a collection of paintings, including several of his own. When Chagall came upon a blank canvas, he exclaimed, "I like that one best."

In Gstaad, the Buckleys had become part of a well-known group of winter visitors—members of an international jet set of writers, actors, politicians, and some businessmen—and Pat Buckley had established herself as both a wit and a hostess. Her *bon mots,* like her husband's, were repeated in one dinner conversation after another. Sometimes, like Buckley, she seemed to flout convention. One night, Senator Edward Kennedy and his wife came to dinner. Joan Kennedy passed out early and Ted stayed. At ten-thirty, he asked about the next train, only to be told that the last train was at ten. Kennedy, who a decade earlier had driven his car off the Chappaquiddick bridge, suggested that he borrow the Buckleys' car and return it in the morning. "Hell, no," Pat quipped, "there are two bridges between here and Gstaad."

Buckley kept a certain distance from Gstaad's social whirl, occasionally using his work as an excuse to avoid dinner parties and insulating himself with old friends like Niven, Clurman, John Kenneth Galbraith, and Evan Galbraith. "He's very gregarious, but his idea of being gregarious is not sitting down at a big dinner party with a lot of chance who you sit next to," Evan Galbraith said. In Gstaad, Galbraith recalled, Buckley had once sat next to a woman who complained the whole dinner about having to listen to a Bach concerto. "She sounded as if it was Bach's fault," Buckley said afterwards to Galbraith.

Pat Buckley established her own social life in both Gstaad and New York, centered around lunches, book parties, and charities. Although she was extremely protective and proud of her husband, she insisted on not being treated as an appendage. When the wife of a dentist asked her whether she accompanied her husband on his speaking tours, she responded, "Do you accompany your husband when he drills?"

IX

Through Rusher, Buckley kept in touch that winter with political developments on the Right. Even though Reagan had decided to run as a Republican, Rusher had gone ahead anyway with creating a third party. With backing from Richard Viguerie and Stan and Medford

Evans, he founded the Committee for the New Majority and decided to draw on the ballot gains already achieved by Wallace's American Independent Party and the more openly racist American Party. In February, Rusher and his committee met with the AIP organizers. Afterwards, he wrote Buckley, "One of the principal avenues of attack upon me was my association with you. I found myself in the unfamiliar and not terribly appealing position of having to 'prove' my own conservatism and 'justify' my association with you and other dangerous leftists." [36]

Buckley replied to Rusher:

I confess to find it slightly undignified that you should have to explain your association with me as if to a Jacobinical court. . . . The whole situation sounds to me awfully close to the kooks, and I am troubled about it. . . . In the last analysis if you have to deal with people of that sort, a) you're not going to get anywhere; b) you are simply going to besmirch yourself. [37]

Rusher wrote back that he shared Buckley's concern about "associating with kooks," but he held out the hope that the party could transform itself by nominating Reagan after Reagan lost the Republican nomination. "I have been a prisoner in the Republican Party's chain gang too long," Rusher wrote, "and I intend to try something new this year, even if it only amounts to a change of chain-gangs." [38]

After Reagan had lost both New Hampshire and Florida to Ford, Buckley was not sure what to do. If Reagan were to lose Illinois, he wrote Burnham, should *National Review* "stay in plugging for Reagan until the end? Ease over to Ford? Follow Rusher into whatever of a third party will o' the wisp he comes up with?" [39]

By the time Buckley returned to the U.S. in late March, Reagan had begun to capture primaries in the South. Buckley enthusiastically backed Reagan's presidential bid in his column, without playing an active role in his campaign. He had learned his lesson with Goldwater. In June, as the battle for convention delegates was heating up, he embarked on a sailing trip from Florida to Mexico.

For Buckley, one of the painful aspects of the campaign was Reagan's constant attacks on Kissinger. Throughout Watergate and the first year and a half of the Ford administration, Buckley had continued to defend Kissinger, even when he was criticizing Ford for policies of détente that were initiated by Kissinger. When Roger Milliken complained about Kissinger's effect on American foreign policy, Buckley wrote him in May 1975:

The more I reflect on [our situation], the more convinced I am that the single greatest retreats were conducted under the aegis of Richard Nixon. For this reason alone: that under his tutelage, the entire anti-Communist constituency was virtually disarmed. . . . During this period, I have been in very close touch with Henry Kissinger, and I think you will be surprised by the extent to which his own thinking parallels our own. I am aware he has the reputation of telling his guests what they would most like to hear. But I do not believe he has the talent of a first-rate actor. By which I mean that I think his concern is genuine, and why should it not be? He has no interest in being dominated by the Soviet Union.[40]

He had even disagreed with Burnham on the subject of Kissinger. When Soviet émigré Alexander Solzhenitsyn lumped Kissinger with the proponents of disarmament in a scalding *New York Times Magazine* article in December 1975, Burnham termed the critique "devastating." But Buckley wrote that he was "gravely disappointed" by it.

Mr. Kissinger has never had anything but contempt for those who believe that the choice is between nuclear war and disarmament . . . the Paris Accords were always chancy, but when Solzhenitsyn asks, "Is it possible that the prominent diplomat could not see what a house of cards he was building?" the answer is: that is exactly correct; Kissinger did not anticipate the emasculation of Nixon by the Watergate development of the ensuing summer. . . . What Kissinger says isn't, "We must have détente because the alternative is a nuclear war." What he says is: the American people will not stand up and resist. Under the circumstances, the only alternative is to maneuver.[41]

Buckley continued to act as Kissinger's go-between with the Right. After Kissinger had appeared on *Firing Line* in September 1975, Buckley sent him private evaluations of his tenure from conservative congressmen. And in May, during the primary campaign, Buckley appears to have passed along a message from Kissinger to Reagan. In a note to Kissinger dated May 18, the date of the Michigan primary, Buckley reported:

It is agreed I must call R. Reagan and attempt to persuade him a) to drop his formal, legal position on Panama Canal zone, substituting the substantive-symbolic point; and at the same time urge him to give an anti-Helsinki speech in Michigan to catch the eye of the ethnics (Done: Refractory on point #1, enthusiastic on Point #2).[42]

Not only the New Right but conservatives close to Buckley believed that he was seduced by Kissinger's attentions. After enjoying a private briefing from Kissinger, Burnham had declined Kissinger's further invitations, and he looked askance at Buckley's relationship with Kissinger. Burnham's son recalled, "My father felt very strongly that you don't get seduced by personalities and power. You don't get sucked into things by publicity."

With the primaries completed, Reagan was still one hundred delegates short of the 1,130 he needed to win the nomination from Ford. In mid-July, Reagan's advisers decided to make one last desperate play for delegates. John Sears, Reagan's campaign manager, and David Keene, who had left Jim Buckley's staff to join the campaign, hatched a scheme to pry loose uncommitted Pennsylvania delegates by having Reagan announce before the convention that Pennsylvania's moderate Republican senator, Richard Schweiker, would be his choice for Vice-President. Keene said later:

We wanted to make sure there was some covering fire on the right to protect us, and so I immediately went up to see Bill because I knew that Bill has always had these very strange ideas about the vice-presidency. I said to John Sears, "We can solve this thing with Bill." . . . What we wanted from Bill was a column which would tell the world that it was a smart decision.

Keene did not tell Buckley that the advisers had already made up their minds. Instead, he asked his advice, and when he had steered Buckley into suggesting Schweiker, he asked him to convince Reagan of the choice. Buckley obliged Keene and Sears, and he later wrote a column in defense of Reagan's choice. "It is worth recalling just how traditional, in essence, such a choice actually is," he explained.[43]

X

Reagan's ploy failed to net enough delegates, and at the Republican Convention in August, Ford was nominated to run against the Democratic choice, former Georgia governor Jimmy Carter. Rusher and Viguerie walked out of the convention and began trying to organize support for a slate of candidates on the American Independent Party ticket. But Buckley joined Reagan in backing Ford. Buckley attributed Ford's victory to "that conservative streak in the nation that simply rejects the notion that you throw away an incumbent." And he complimented Ford on having "adopted the Reagan line" at the convention.

> Jerry Ford appears to have been transformed by the experience of Kansas City. He succeeded, with plain but heroic prose, in dissipating some of the hallucinations so painstakingly constructed by Jimmy Carter and the party of everything for everybody paid for by nobody.[44]

Buckley took a dim view of Carter, whose campaign had been based largely on his anti-Watergate pledge that he would never lie to the American people. In 1973, he had had Carter on *Firing Line,* and had learned later to his surprise that Carter had used the occasion to try out a new accent on a national political audience. ("Decided Southern inflections were left, but what had been there before—the deep Southern accent of deep, traditional Georgia—was gone."[45]) At the Democratic Convention, Buckley noted, Carter had embraced liberal stands on full-employment legislation and labor-union prerogatives that were decidedly foreign to a conservative Georgia governor. "His experience as a governor of Georgia who sought popularity with his constituency led him to advocate right-to-work laws. His experience as a presidential candidate led him to oppose right-to-work laws. Is he for that reason a liar?" Buckley wrote in his column.[46] "There's very little Carter would do short of capitulating to the Soviet Union that would surprise me," he told one interviewer.[47]

But Buckley took an even dimmer view of the right-wing alternative to Ford. He wrote of the AIP Convention's choice, former Georgia governor Lester Maddox:

> They nominated Lester Maddox, the former governor of Georgia, whose distinction lies in his expressed preference for hitting a negro over the head with an axe, rather than serve him a plate of fried chicken. . . . The party met as a symbol of resistance to the Ford-Carter national tickets, and they begot a semi-literate segregationist.[48]

Buckley had angered New Right conservatives by defending Reagan's choice of Schweiker, and that fall he did something that angered many of his former allies in the New York Conservative Party. With his brother facing an uphill re-election battle against Daniel Moynihan, Buckley endorsed liberal Democrat Allard Lowenstein, with whom he had become friends years before, in his congressional race in Long Island against incumbent Republican John Wydler. In a column, Buckley praised Lowenstein's "extraordinary integrity and sense of justice."

New York Conservatives felt that Buckley's endorsement damaged his brother's re-election chances. "Bill just blithely ignored the political realities that Allard Lowenstein was a strenuous and successful advocate of the Left liberal position," Conservative Party founder Kieran O'Doherty said. Buckley's move also attracted national conservative ire. *Human Events* termed Buckley's endorsement of Lowenstein an instance of "conservative chic" and described it as the "worst kind of foolishness."*

Buckley's endorsement of Lowenstein reflected not only a certain detachment from conservative politics, but a willingness to thumb his nose at his fellow conservatives just as he had earlier thumbed his nose at the Yale administration or New York liberal intellectuals. Only now Buckley's reference group from which he peered out at the rest of the world was not like-minded conservatives, but the intellectual establishment that he had formerly spurned and that included liberals like Lowenstein and Galbraith as well as Disraeli-type conservatives like Irving Kristol and Henry Kissinger.

---

* In 1978, Buckley again endorsed Lowenstein. "There will be quite a few liberal Democrats in the next Congress," he wrote. "So why not one whose integrity and . . . will at least represent a movement that is grown cynical, bureaucratic, and ineffective." (Column, August 18, 1978.)

CHAPTER 22

A Dirty Business

In the November 1976 elections, both Republicans and conservatives suffered another devastating defeat. Carter edged Ford, and Moynihan easily defeated Jim Buckley. In postelection Gallup polls, only 20 percent of the electorate identified themselves as Republicans, compared to 49 percent as Democrats.

For Buckley, these results confirmed the conservative decline. At a press conference during a speaking visit to the University of Alabama, Buckley volleyed back questions about the election results with a certain wry cynicism.

REPORTER: Would you take a place, if one was offered, in the Carter administration?

BUCKLEY: Not unless he offered me the role of chief critic.

REPORTER: Are you sorry about your brother's losing the New York election?

BUCKLEY: No, my brother will do just very well indeed. It is the people of New York I feel sorry for.

REPORTER: Can Carter possibly deliver all the things he promised to the American people during the election campaign?

BUCKLEY: He has promised to stop inflation, end unemployment
at the same time that he is balancing the budget. The
truth is nobody this side of Paradise could do this—and
Carter knows it.

REPORTER: Will Carter affect the moral tone of the country?

BUCKLEY: He doesn't have the power or the vision to make any
kind of change in American life—and I hope he has
enough sense not to try.[1]

As he had done after the 1974 elections, Buckley turned to fiction
for solace.

I

Buckley had begun a new spy novel during a three-week cruise in
January on the ocean liner *QE2* from New York to Rio de Janiero. In
exchange for giving four lectures, Buckley had gotten room and board
and the time and privacy he needed to write. His only distraction, as
it turned out, had been the sound system of the boat, on which César
Franck's Symphony in D minor had been played over and over again
during the three weeks. In February, he left for Switzerland, where
he finished the novel. More than anything he had written, *Stained
Glass* expressed the dilemma Buckley experienced of being a conservative in a world where the rules were set by others.

Blackford Oakes is again the hero. But he is dwarfed by Count Axel
Wintergrin, a charismatic young German who, having fought the
Nazis during World War II, is now prepared to oust the Soviet Union
from East Germany and reunify his country. Wintergrin is the anti-
Communist archetype, austere, bold, and resolute, and above re-
proach. As he and his movement gain support, he founds a political
party and enters the race for chancellor. With the polls showing that
he might win, the Soviet Union threatens that it will use force to stop
Wintergrin. Fearing that Wintergrin will precipitate a Third World
War, the CIA agrees to work with the Soviet KGB to throttle him.
Ordered by the CIA to help destroy Wintergrin and his movement,
Oakes faces a genuine moral and political conflict between his loyalty
to the CIA and his anti-Communist conviction. Oakes asks himself if
he is "in a dirty business."[2]

Having befriended Wintergrin and gained entry to his inner circle,
Oakes is ordered to assassinate him. But he balks at pushing the
button that would electrocute Wintergrin, and it is only because of his
CIA superior's foresight—he has the device wired to go off anyway
—that Wintergrin is killed.

The moral and political conflict at the center of *Stained Glass* was drawn in large part from the conflict that Buckley had witnessed between Burnham and Schlamm when the Soviet Union invaded Hungary in 1956. Indeed both men appear in *Stained Glass*—Schlamm as an obnoxious West German reporter seeking to embarrass the count and Burnham as the author of *The Machiavellians,* which the count recommends to his staff.

That conflict had been an important event in Buckley's political education. Burnham had contended that the United States could not use force to aid the Hungarians, reasoning, like the CIA in *Stained Glass,* that by aiding actively in liberating Eastern Europe, the United States might bring on World War III. In *Stained Glass,* Oakes finds himself in the same ambivalent situation in which Buckley had found himself in 1957, torn between a politics of reality and one of ideals.

As a fictional character, Oakes remains sophomoric in *Stained Glass.* Even his wit appears forced.* But the moral conflict he faces is genuinely dramatic, as *Stained Glass* moves toward a tragic end. For a moment, Oakes ceases to be a comic-book ideal. Instead of appearing as the resolution of life's problems, Oakes suffers, finally, from the infirmity of thought: he cannot act. One of his CIA accomplices pens a note to him afterwards, "I should have insisted on counting your balls."[3] When Oakes later confronts CIA chief Allen Dulles with the deed, Dulles responds in Burnhamesque fashion. ". . . In this world, if you let them, the ambiguists will kill you. . . . I don't believe the lesson to draw is that *we must not act* because, in acting, we may *prove* to be wrong."[4]

At its best, fiction defies the easy solutions of the debater and the polemicist. In *Saving the Queen,* Buckley had fit his fiction to the requirements of debate; in *Stained Glass,* he allowed his imagination to roam beyond the realm of political certainty. There is no solution in *Stained Glass;* one is left with questions rather than answers, human frailty rather than perfection.

In the person of Wintergrin, Buckley created a symbol that calls forth the underlying religious dimension of the struggle against communism. Wintergrin is a modern Christ, sacrificed by lesser men. As the U.S. and the Soviet Union unite to kill him, Oakes thinks, "He had *always* known. Known right from the beginning. An Axel Wintergrin *could not be permitted to live* in this world."[5] And the book

---

* At dinner with Wintergrin, Oakes tells him of the dinner that he had with Queen Caroline. "Oh, yes. I said to the Queen, I said, 'Ma'am, the grub here is okay, but I can tell you where in Atlantic City you can get better.' " (*Stained Glass,* 152.)

concludes at Christmas—at an annual church service in Wintergrin's chapel given to honor his memory.

Both Vaughan and Sophie Wilkins, who, as Buckley's personal editor and friend, went over the manuscript that summer, recognized *Stained Glass* as superior to its predecessor. "It was closer to the bone than *Saving the Queen*," Vaughan said. "The talk about that decision, killing the count, sticks in the mind and emotions." The readers also responded: *Stained Glass* easily outsold *Saving the Queen*. And it won the American Book Award as the Best Suspense Novel of the year.

II

As Buckley returned to the U.S. in spring 1977, Carter was enjoying widespread popular support—largely the result of his informality and unpretentiousness (he was "Jimmy" to the American people) and his emphasis on human rights in foreign policy. In his inaugural address, Carter had declared that the U.S. "commitment to human rights must be absolute," and he had attempted to demonstrate it by publicly criticizing repressive policies both in the Soviet Union and in Chile and Rhodesia. Where Ford and Kissinger had refused to see Alexander Solzhenitsyn, Carter received Soviet dissident Vladimir Bukovsky.

Kissinger's Realpolitik had rested on the assumption that American policy toward Chile or Rhodesia was inextricably tied to America's Cold War with the Soviet Union: in these countries, the Nixon and Ford administrations backed anti-Communist regimes regardless of their internal practices. Carter rejected this policy. In a May commencement speech at Notre Dame, he declared that "being confident of our own future, we are now free of that inordinate fear of communism which once led us to embrace any dictator who joined us in that fear."

In his columns Buckley had initially praised Carter for speaking out on Soviet violations "with utter dignity," while mildly rebuking him for singling out countries like Chile, Argentina, and Uruguay that "have refused, sometimes by the use of force, to resist Communization."[6] But Carter's Notre Dame speech struck at the heart of Buckley's world view, and he offered a sharp rejoinder in his column the next week.

1. We are *not* confident of our own future, whatever that means, exactly. . . . 2. What is an 'inordinate' fear of Communism . . .

3. To whom did he refer when he spoke of 'embracing' any dictator who 'joined us' in our fear? Franco? Franco's fear was as genuine as anybody's would be whose direct experience of Communists was during a civil war in which a fair percentage of the population was slaughtered.[7]

In his next column, he continued to attack Carter. "President Carter's formulations, in his foreign policy speeches, are so maladroit that one can draw reassurance only from the knowledge that he cannot possibly mean what he says." What particularly angered Buckley was Carter's willingness to invoke sanctions against Ian Smith's white Rhodesian regime and Pinochet's Chile but not against the Soviet Union.

C. S. Lewis spoke about the sin of disproportion [Buckley wrote]. By committing it so egregiously—the hectic concern for human rights in Rhodesia practically defined as the transfer of power from an orderly white community to a disorderly black faction within the black community, contrasted with an increasingly Platonic concern over the systematic repressions in the Soviet empire, and a total absence of criticism of a great Oriental Power with which he seeks anxiously to normalize relations—the President loses coherence, disconcerts his natural allies, and douses water on the flames of home he lit in the first days of his administration when his concern for human rights appeared to be evenhanded, and he had not yet advertised his general bewilderment.[8]

But while Buckley led the conservative charge against Carter's human rights policy, he took Carter's side in the raging debate over the Panama Canal treaties.

In September 1977, Carter signed the two canal treaties, most of whose terms had been negotiated during the Johnson, Nixon, and Ford administrations. The treaties called for joint U.S.–Panamanian administration of the Canal until 2000 and after that sole Panamanian ownership and control, with guarantees of access and priority passage to the U.S. in the event of war.

For many years, Buckley had opposed the U.S. giving up any control over the Canal. In January 1964, as the negotiations were commencing, he had declared, "The land is ours by right of treaty and historical circumstance."[9] During the Republican presidential primary in 1976, he supported Reagan when Reagan tried to make the Ford administration's support of a treaty a major campaign issue. In May both Goldwater and Kissinger tried to convince Buckley—and

hopefully through him, Reagan—of the merits of a treaty. Goldwater
wrote him:

> Unless the U.S. makes some gesture that would indicate a long
> range willingness to change the Panama situation, there will be guer-
> rilla warfare and, frankly, I don't want that and I don't want Ronnie
> to get himself in the position of being elected president with the
> promise to send troops to Panama.[10]

Buckley replied that he had "little to argue with" in Goldwater's
letter, but he still insisted:

> My own feeling though is that we are deeply involved in an age in
> which symbols tend to mean almost everything. Our reputation as a
> pushover nation seems to be deeply embarrassing psychologically.
> . . . It would behoove a great power to give away the Panama
> Canal, were we to find ourselves in such a mood. To be intimidated
> into giving it away is I think something else.[11]

But both Burnham and Kissinger continued to argue with Buckley,
and in October 1976, after a visit to Panama in which he discussed the
Canal with a broad range of Panamanian officials and citizens, Buckley decided to support the treaties. In a column, he noted the Panamanians' "natural pride" and their lack of incentive to destroy the
Canal.

> My own conclusion? Establish that which is necessary for the de-
> fense of the Canal, and require it. Agree that payments from Amer-
> ican shipping will flow into a fund for the generous resettlement of
> the American community in Panama. Require that there be no dis-
> criminatory payment of tolls going through the Canal. Then get out.
> We could stay in. We have a right to stay in. Make that point clear,
> and then get out—while the initiative is still, clearly, our own. That
> is the way great nations should act.[12]

After Carter signed the treaties with Panamian dictator General
Omar Torrijos, conservatives in Washington began to organize against
Senate ratification of the treaties. Both the American Conservative
Union, which was then chaired by Stan Evans, and Howard Phillips's
Conservative Caucus organized massive write-in campaigns against
the treaties. A "truth squad" of Republican congressmen was mobi-
lized to tour cities. And Richard Viguerie sent out four million pieces
of direct mail to raise money for the effort. By the beginning of 1978,

the right-wing effort was beginning to show results in the Senate, as Republicans who had been expected to vote for the treaties continued to sit on the fence.

Even on *National Review,* Buckley found himself isolated. Besides Burnham, none of the other senior editors shared his support for the treaties. But Buckley was not deterred. Rick Brookhiser, who was then a junior editor at the magazine, recalled an editorial conference on the issue.

> Bill came in and said, ''We're going to write about the treaties and we're going to support them.'' And then Jeff [Hart] said, ''Well, I have problems with the treaties at the level of poetry.'' Bill didn't cut him off or anything, he just went back to his thought. Then Burnham said something in support of the treaties, and then Bill said we're going to handle it this way. And I think he said something to Jeff like, ''We'll talk about it later.''

Hart later described the decision to support the treaties in the magazine ''as simply fiat.''

Reagan became the national leader of the campaign against the treaties, using it as the first stage of his 1980 campaign for the presidency. Buckley and Reagan were both concerned that their disagreement over the treaties might endanger their friendship, and they took pains to soften the blow of their difference. After an exchange of correspondence on the issue, Reagan wrote Buckley: ''I must confess we are still disagreeing on the matter of the canal. [But] I assure you it would not in any way affect the friendship I feel for you.'' [13]

In January, the two aired their differences in a public debate. Reagan accepted Buckley's invitation to join him in a special two-hour *Firing Line,* staged at the University of South Carolina. Buckley took along George Will and Burnham as seconds, while Reagan was accompanied by Pat Buchanan and Latin-American expert Roger Fontaine.

Buckley was in a difficult situation for a debater—one that, ironically, recalled his Yale days. The audience was very conservative and supportive of Reagan's rather than his own position. Reagan was able to appeal to sentiment—the imperial nostalgia that had affected Americans after the American defeat in Vietnam—while Buckley had to call on his listeners to rise above sentiment. But just as he had at Yale, he relished the situation. ''If Bill was concerned, he never showed it,'' Neal Freeman recalled. ''He delighted in debate and rebuttal.''

The debate was held in a theater in the round, with the two camps seated facing each other. The *Washington Post* described it as a "Super Bowl of the right." To the audience's applause, Reagan, tanned and relaxed, argued that without control of the Canal, the U.S. could get pushed around in time of war when it needed to send its ships through the Canal. Buckley, somewhat disheveled, his hair fashionably long, his eyebrows popping up and down, his tongue darting, responded that the U.S. would be better off militarily if the Panamanians were not harboring resentment against the U.S. for controlling part of their land. If the U.S. needed to move its Navy quickly through the Canal, Buckley said, "that mobility is more easily effected if we have the cooperation of the local population."

The two men made the most of their own embarrassment at being on opposite sides of a major public issue.

If Lloyds of London had been asked to give odds that I would be disagreeing with Ronald Reagan on a matter of public policy [Buckley began], I doubt they could have flogged a quotation out of their swingingest betting man because judging from Governor Reagan's impeccable record, the statisticians would have reasoned that it was inconceivable that he should make a mistake. But of course it happens to everyone. I fully expect that someday I'll be wrong about something.

After the two debaters had made their opening presentations, they were given seven minutes to question each other. "Well, Bill," Reagan began, "my first question is why haven't you already rushed across the room to tell me that you've seen the light?" "I'm afraid that if I came any closer to you the force of my illumination would blind you," Buckley replied.

When Reagan claimed that it was the Torrijos government, rather than the people of Panama, that was demanding the return of the Canal, Buckley turned his wit on Reagan's argument.

BUCKLEY: But it was before Torrijos became the dictator that the initial riots took place demanding an assertion of sovereignty. How do you account for that?

REAGAN: I think the first time that it was expressed was in 1932 in the Charter of the new Communist Party of Panama that they put as one of their top objectives the taking over of the Canal.

BUCKLEY: Are you saying that the Communists invented patriotism in Panama?

REAGAN: No, no.
BUCKLEY: Yes. Well, you really tried to say that.

In his concluding remarks, Buckley made light of Reagan's recitation of the history of American-Panamanian relations. He recounted the explanation of the Louisiana Purchase that James Thurber had given to two inquiring ladies:

He said, "Louisiana was owned by two sisters called Louisa and Anne Wilmont, and they offered to give it to the United States, provided it was named after them. That was the Wilmont Proviso." . . . Now, intending no slur on my friend Ronald Reagan, the politician in America I admire most, his rendition of recent history and his generalities remind me a little bit about that explanation for the state of Louisiana having been incorporated into this country. He says we, in fact, don't negotiate under threats, and everybody here bursts out in applause. The trouble with that is that it's not true.

Buckley's performance—designed at once to re-establish his credentials as a hardliner and to appeal to American generosity—was masterful and largely defused Reagan's jingoistic appeals.*

Buckley got the last word not only on Reagan but on the press. In his story on the debate, *Washington Post* reporter Ward Sinclair chided Buckley for being wrong. "He says Cortez crossed Panama and was the first to espy the the Pacific Ocean. It was Vasco Núñez de Balboa." Buckley responded in a letter to the *Post*.

What I said in my speech was, "If there is a full-scale atomic war, the Panama Canal will revert to a land mass, and the first survivor who makes his way across the isthmus will relive a historical experience like stout Cortez when, with eagle eyes, he stared at the Pacific and all his men looked at each other with a wild surmise, silent upon a peak in Darien."

The lines are from John Keats. His sonnet "On First Looking into Chapman's Homer." I felt presumptuous enough correcting Ronald Reagan's foreign policy without straightening out Keats's historical solecism. But tell Mr. Sinclair not to worry: It happens all the time, people's inability to tell where I leave off and Keats begins.[14]

---

* Buckley wrote later of Reagan's stand on Panama, "I think, ironically, that Reagan would not have been nominated if he had favored the Panama Canal Treaty, and that he wouldn't have been elected if it hadn't passed. He'd have lost the conservatives if he had backed the treaty, and lost the election if we'd subsequently faced, in Panama, insurrection, as in my opinion we would have." (*Overdrive,* 119.)

Buckley provided conservative legitimacy for Senate Minority Leader Howard Baker and other Republicans who continued to back the treaties. When the treaties passed the Senate 68–32 that spring—only one vote more than was needed for two-thirds ratification—some conservatives blamed Buckley. Stan Evans said,

One can argue that Buckley's participation in the Panama Canal debates might have been the critical factor in getting those treaties passed, because it gave a shelter to the Howard Bakers who otherwise would have had pretty rough going. They would have been in a very exposed position, carrying Jimmy Carter's and Henry Kissinger's position, and the fact that so prominent a conservative as Bill Buckley was in favor of those treaties gave them cover.

To the New Right conservatives, he became, in Alan Crawford's words, a "hate object." Rumors even abounded that Buckley, who had come out in favor of the legalization of marijuana, was "messed up on drugs." Howard Phillips summarized the New Right's disenchantment. "Buckley, for all the good work he has done, is simply not on the cutting edge of American politics anymore. His positions on legalizing marijuana and passage of the Panama Canal treaties were a great disappointment. He really isn't with us anymore." [15]

III

In May 1978, one year after Carter had done so, Buckley was invited to give the commencement address at Notre Dame. Buckley took the opportunity not only to reiterate his opposition to Carter's human rights policy, but to give vent to his own growing pessimism about the direction of American politics and of the West.

Buckley arrived on Saturday afternoon, the day before graduation, to receive an honorary degree and to attend Notre Dame President Rev. Theodore Hesburgh's Baccalaureate Mass. "He was very moved by it," Gerhart Niemeyer, a Notre Dame professor and close friend, recalled. When Pat Buckley, who had accompanied him, made a snide remark about Hesburgh's liberal politics, Buckley rebuked her. "He is a man of God," he said. Later that evening at Niemeyer's, Pat made another crack about Hesburgh, and Buckley, his jaw clenched, repeated, "He is a man of God." It was the sharpest exchange that Niemeyer had ever witnessed between Pat and Bill.

Buckley's speech the next day—given before more than twelve-thousand students and their families at Notre Dame's Athletic and

Convocation Center—was unusually solemn, even grim, with few flashes of the Buckley wit. Quoting extensively from Chambers's letters and from *Witness,* Buckley invoked Chambers's lugubrious and apocalyptical world view. "In the first month that I knew Whittaker Chambers he wrote me that 'it is idle to talk about preventing the wreck of Western civilization. It is already a wreck from within,' " Buckley told the students.

To Buckley, it appeared that the U.S., which in 1956 had resigned itself to containing and not rolling back communism, was now prepared to acquiesce not only in the existence of communism, but in its being merely another social system. "What happened during the Johnson-Nixon years," Buckley told the students, "was a great seizure of self-disgust which fused handily with the new-found exigencies of our foreign policy."

By declaring that Americans' fear of communism had been inordinate, Carter had wiped even the rhetorical slate clean. Buckley summed up his own isolation:

> In the groves of quiet thought we tell ourselves—quietly—that we care . . . about the new holocaust in Cambodia, about the creeping hegemony of Communist thought and techniques in both hemispheres. But ours is a fugitive solicitude, whose expression is damped by the prevailing rhetoric, which is one part evangelistic, one part pharisaic, one part anesthetic.[16]

Buckley's speech took the students aback. "There was no rousing applause," Niemeyer recalled. "The audience was sort of reserved. Some people didn't know what to think of it. It was not the usual commencement speech. It was a very serious speech."

At Notre Dame, Buckley had revealed his own despair about the future of the West, even as conservative Republican candidates, campaigning for the 1978 congressional races, were preparing to demonstrate that conservatism was anything but dead.

IV

Buckley's political pessimism was overshadowed by his business woes. The steps that Buckley had taken to rescue himself and Sitco Ltd. from bankruptcy in 1974 by having Starr Broadcasting buy out the ailing company were coming back to haunt him. In getting Starr Broadcasting to buy out Sitco, Buckley had left himself open to a stockholder suit, but he had not necessarily broken the law. The way

he could break the law would be if Starr Broadcasting failed to disclose all the details of the transaction in the 10-K forms that it was
required to file with the SEC. If those forms were false or inaccurate,
Buckley, as chairman of Starr, was liable, even if he didn't know what
was on them.

In the summer of 1975, Buckley had become worried about the 10-
Ks when two of the company's major lenders complained to him that
Starr Broadcasting had yet to file them that year. Buckley asked his
lawyer Dan Mahoney and Mahoney's firm of Windels, Marx in New
York to check out Starr Broadcasting's finances and its 10-K forms.
Mahoney's report, which he delivered to Buckley in December, was
extremely discouraging. He told Buckley that in the 1974 and 1975
10-K forms that Starr Broadcasting had filed, the company had failed
to disclose several very damaging details of the Sitco transaction,
including the company's assumption through the Sitco deal of the
Starr brothers' personal loans. It was the first Buckley had heard of
the Starrs' personal loans. With Mahoney's help, Starr Broadcasting
filed a revised 10-K. But it was too late.

On its own, the SEC had begun making inquiries about the Sitco
transaction. And in December, a disgruntled stockholder, Paul Solo-
mon, informed Starr's board of directors that he was going to file suit,
charging that Starr's directors had misused company funds in agreeing
to buy Sitco. The SEC, taking note of the stockholder suit and the
revised 10-K, initiated a formal investigation of Starr Broadcasting.
Buckley knew he was in trouble, but he was still acting as if he were
a small-time speculator who could maneuver his way out of trouble.
In the winter of 1976, he called Stephen Umin, a partner in Williams
and Connally, Edward Bennett Williams's prestigious criminal-law
firm in Washington, D.C. Buckley had met Umin seven years before
when Umin agreed to take the case of Edgar Smith, the convicted
murderer who had convinced Buckley of his innocence. Through
working on Smith's behalf, Buckley and Umin had become friends.
But Umin was not a securities lawyer, and had never handled a major
SEC case. Nonetheless, Buckley asked him to take on his case. "I've
got this problem that I want you to talk to my friend Dan Mahoney
about," Buckley told Umin. "In a couple of days you could work it
all out." Umin soon realized that more than a couple of days were
required. "Bill's appreciation of the seriousness of the case was at
ground level," Umin recalled.

Both Umin and Mahoney told Buckley that Starr Broadcasting was
in very big trouble and that Peter Starr had seriously misled him, but
Buckley, torn by friendship for Starr, was initially reluctant to let him

go.* In June 1976, however, under prodding from investment coun-
selors Dillon Read, which had begun overseeing Starr Broadcasting's
finances, Buckley finally fired Starr, who had begun drinking heavily
as the crisis mounted. That put the onus of Starr Broadcasting's troubles on Buckley himself, who had to devote an increasing amount of
time to the company.

In December 1976, Starr's directors began looking for someone to
buy the company, which partly as a result of the drive-in purchases
had lost $7 million over the previous two years. There was growing
stockholder pressure for Buckley, who was presumed to be the target
of a continuing SEC investigation, to step down as chairman. The
next September, when Mr. and Mrs. Roy Disney made their offer to
purchase contingent upon Buckley's stepping down, he resigned.

At the same time that the SEC had begun investigating Starr Broadcasting, it had also launched an investigation of the Buckley family's
oil firm, Catawba, that John Buckley and Benjamin Heath had taken
over after Will Buckley's death in 1958. Like the investigation of Starr
Broadcasting, this one involved charges of self-dealing. In May 1978,
spurred by the SEC investigation, six of the companies that Catawba
controlled ousted Catawba representatives, including John Buckley,
from management positions. Then in September, a despondent John
Buckley, suffering from alcoholism, resigned from Catawba.

Based on the SEC investigations of both Starr and Catawba, Buckley felt that his family was being victimized for political reasons. He
had refused to grant interviews about Starr Broadcasting, but in September 1978, he talked to a *Wall Street Journal* reporter for two and a
half hours. Buckley claimed that he was not responsible for the errors
in Starr's 1975 10-K report. "I can spot a solecism in Webster's dictionary," he said, "but I am no good with figures. I don't understand
them." [17] Buckley also implied that he had not taken a significant role
in Starr's decision making, but the *Journal,* drawing upon documents
from the stockholder suit, including Buckley's late-night memorandum of October 1974, portrayed him as having played an important
role in Starr Broadcasting's decision to take over Sitco. The *Journal*'s
front-page story, entitled "How William Buckley Got Starr Broad-

---

* Buckley came to feel that Starr had not merely misled him, but cheated him. When
Buckley was interviewed by the SEC in the fall of 1978, he learned from the SEC investigators that Starr Broadcasting's management had established an officer's account in his
name. Starr's management had deposited in that account the money it owed Buckley for
renting his yacht for business purposes. But a year later, when Starr Broadcasting owed
him $50,000, the management had deducted from that amount $37,000 it owed him for
Cyrano. (William F. Buckley, Jr., "My Life in Business.") "I was most emphatically
cheated," Buckley said later.

casting to Bail Out His Firm,'' was extremely damning. Without saying so explicitly, the newspaper's account strongly suggested that
Buckley had deliberately and knowingly cheated Starr Broadcasting's
stockholders.

Buckley was in Sydney, Australia, on a lecture tour when the article
appeared, and he didn't read the full version until he reached Singa-
pore a week later. Infuriated, he dashed off a three-thousand-word
reply that he Telexed to New York. ''Miss Kronholz's narrative reads
like a petition for a Reno divorce by Zsa Zsa Gabor documenting the
mental cruelty of her latest husband. It is preposterous in its insinua-
tions,'' Buckley wrote. Buckley insisted that in buying Sitco, Starr
Broadcasting ''made its *own* deal on *its* terms.'' [18]

When Buckley returned to New York two days later, Umin and
Dick Clurman both advised him not to publish the reply because it
would only provoke the SEC and antagonize Starr's management.
Buckley finally submitted a 150-word reply to the *Journal* in which he
assured readers that he would answer the article's charges after the
legal negotiations with Starr were completed. But he couldn't resist a
closing comment: ''Meanwhile, if you care to have the local news, the
headline on page two of this morning's *Straits Times* is Woman Raped
Twice/By Monkey in Jakarta. I know just how the woman feels.'' [19]

On the heels of the Starr controversy, Buckley found himself implicated in another legal action: this one involving the American-Chilean
Council that he had helped Marvin Liebman to found and which he
had served as friend and adviser. While Buckley didn't take the
ACC's money for annual trips to Chile, several *National Review* authors and editors, including Rusher, John Chamberlain, and Jeff Hart,
had their trips financed by the ACC. British writer Robert Moss,
whose trip Buckley and Liebman helped arrange and who produced
National Review's first major piece on the coup, may have knowingly
allowed his political leanings to shape his journalism. Nena Ossa
wrote Liebman after she had met Moss in Santiago in July 1975,
''Fortunately he seems to be enough to the Right to understand that
he cannot possibly write all he sees and hears. His fight against Marxism is much more important than being a journalist. Or so he says to
me.'' *

In September 1976, agents of the Chilean secret police had assassinated Orlando Letelier in Washington. Letelier, a former official of

---

* Several journalists, including William Safire, Robert Novak, Rowland Evans, James J.
Kilpatrick, and Patrick Buchanan, turned down ACC-paid trips to Chile. An incredulous
Liebman wrote Ossa, ''There seems to be a new morality among American journalists.''
(Liebman Papers.)

the Allende government, was a leader of the anti-Pinochet opposition outside of Chile. Democrats in Congress called for sanctions against Chile. In March 1977, *National Review* editor Kevin Lynch, who had also worked for the ACC, suggested that Letelier had been a Cuban agent and that the Chilean government had nothing to do with his killing.[20] In July, the *National Review* speculated on whether Letelier had been an "agent of the U.S.S.R."[21]

As the government investigation of the murder continued to un-cover ties of the killers to the Chilean government, Buckley and *National Review* continued to deny any Chilean link and to try to discredit Letelier. In March 1978, after returning from an ACC trip to Chile, Hart wrote, "At the time that Letelier was blown up by a bomb in Washington, he had become entangled in international terrorism and was receiving funds through Havana."[22] Buckley himself com-mented frequently on the investigation in his column. As late as Sep-tember 1978 he was insisting that "there are highly reasonable, indeed compelling, grounds for doubting that Pinochet had anything to do with the assassination."[23]

That month Liebman had hired Robert Shortley, a former FBI agent, for $2,000 a month to investigate links between Letelier and Cuban or Soviet intelligence. In October, Shortley reported to Lieb-man that "Letelier was not, as some media accounts have indicated, a Cuban or Russian intelligence agent."[24] When Shortley began asking questions around the Justice Department, Justice Department officials had become suspicious and began making inquiries about Shortley's source of funds. This led to an investigation of the ACC and to the charge by the Justice Department that it was a Chilean lobby that was misrepresenting itself as an independent American group.

In December, the Justice Department filed a civil suit charging Liebman and the ACC in court with failing to register as an agent of the Chilean government. Buckley's role in setting up the ACC was spelled out in the Justice Department's brief. Unwilling to contest the Justice Department's suit, Liebman was forced to shut down the ACC.

At the end of 1978, the SEC formally charged Buckley, Peter and Michael Starr, Columbia Union Vice-President Glenn Burrus, and several other directors with failing to disclose the terms of the Sitco deal, and, in a long report on its investigation, suggested that Buckley had also misled other Starr directors in proposing the Sitco purchase.

Buckley had never been so upset in his life. What disturbed him as much as the possible penalties that the SEC might inflict were the terms of the indictment itself, which, in charging fraud, suggested that

Buckley had personally deceived his fellow directors and the stockholders of Starr. "The word 'fraud' bothered him," Dino Pionzio, Buckley's Yale classmate and a Starr board member, recalled. "If they wanted to say that he violated securities regulations in a technical sense, he would be the first to say, 'Yes, I did.' "

In the first week of February 1979, the SEC gave Buckley the choice of signing a "consent decree" to pay the penalty the SEC required or entering into a costly and potentially damaging lawsuit. If Buckley agreed to settle, then the SEC was also willing to negotiate the statements in its final complaint, but if he didn't settle, the agency would publish the initial "dirty complaint."* In this complaint, for instance, the SEC implied that Buckley as well as the Starrs had taken a personal loan from Columbia Union. Buckley had dinner at Paone's with Steve Umin and afterwards they walked up and down the New York streets debating what to do. Umin advised Buckley to sign, not only because of the expense of the suit, but because of the damage that the publication of the SEC's "dirty complaint" would do to his reputation. Buckley finally decided to sign the consent decree.

By signing the SEC's consent decree, Buckley did not signify his guilt or innocence, but he did agree to indemnify Starr's stockholders with $1.4 million in stock and cash and not to become a director of a public corporation for five years. He didn't find it difficult to accept the SEC's restriction on his corporate activity. "I'll see you and raise you five," he told an SEC official.[25]

In an extensive press release issued the next day, Buckley declared his innocence of actual fraud. He said that he didn't read the 10-K forms prepared by Starr Broadcasting's accountants and "didn't even know what a 10-K was until the fall of 1974." He explained that his private memorandum to Mahoney and his brother had been written *"after* the directors had signified their interest by voting to take an option," and that his proposal to alter the board's membership was designed merely to enlist the participation of "land experts" to take advantage of the higher profits offered by land speculation than radio station ownership.

---

* Because it lacks the staff to take all its complaints to court, the Securities and Exchange Commission often uses the threat of publicity to drive its targets into signing a consent decree. Civil libertarians have criticized the SEC for this practice. Monroe Freedman, former dean of the Hofstra Law School, and a National Board member of the American Civil Liberties Union, wrote in 1974, "Another serious problem in securities regulation is prejudicial publicity. Indeed, it has been noted that 'the relief sought by the Commission, even if granted, may not be as significant or as onerous a sanction as the publicity attendant upon the commencement of the proceeding.' " (Monroe Freedman, "A Civil Libertarian Looks at Securities Regulation," *Ohio State Law Journal* 35 [1974].)

With the press release, Buckley also included a letter to Stanley Sporkin, the head of the SEC's enforcement division, protesting his innocence of fraud.

> The world I move about in believes that a "fraud statute" is for the purpose of preventing people from committing a fraud. They understand a fraud to be a *deliberate* misrepresentation, usually for the sake of accumulating money. Now I have not committed a fraud in the accepted understanding of the term. You are about to charge me with having committed a fraud. Not only me, but others, e.g. a gentleman who makes his living as the highly respected president of a black Catholic college in New Orleans on whom I have laid eyes once in my entire life, and who was present at a board meeting of Starr on only a single occasion when I was also there. . . . To hold that I—or Norman Francis [the college president]—were under the law responsible for documents issued under the aegis of the company we allegedly served as directors is, it would appear to me, an eminently specifiable charge. To which I could reply only: if that is what the law says, then I am guilty. But *I* am not the guy who *committed* any fraud. The distinction between those two positions required you exactly one second to apprehend.[26]

Both Buckley's friends and family were convinced that he had been taken in by Starr. "I think Bill was as innocent as the newfound snow and that he got manipulated by people that he trusted. He was the fall guy," his brother John said. "Bill may be very naïve in corporate niceties, especially as viewed through the gimlet eyes of the SEC. Peter Starr would say sign, and he would say where do you sign."

They also thought he had acted unwisely. Dino Pionzio believed that Buckley made a serious mistake in proposing that Starr Broadcasting purchase the theaters. Pionzio said:

> Bill went to great trouble to get independent lawyers, people that gave him evaluations and so forth, who told him that it would be perfectly legitimate to pass [the theaters] on to Starr. But he shouldn't have done that, and when I heard about it, I was a bit upset. It doesn't matter how many opinions you get, how many lawyers you have working on it, you can't have a company that has land that may go into bankruptcy—no matter how good a value you think it is or others tell you it is—pass it on to a public company which you also have control of and call it an arm's-length transaction.

Buckley's lawyer Steve Umin thought he never should have become chairman of Starr Broadcasting. "He was stupid to take on the position of chairman of the board because he didn't have the time and he didn't have the skill," Umin said. "Bill found himself in a world he was totally unequipped to handle."

But the judgment of the press was even less charitable. Just as Buckley feared most, his signing the consent decree was treated as an admission that he had defrauded the stockholders. And much of the press played it up as an instance of hypocrisy on Buckley's part: the crusader for high-toned virtue and free enterprise had been caught committing common vices. *Newsweek*'s story was typical:

> With his patrician accent, elastic eyebrows, and mordant wit, William F. Buckley, Jr. has built a reputation as a media star and conservative theoretician who somehow seems to tower above the grubby everyday world of business. But last week, the Securities and Exchange Commission dashed that elegant image when it charged Buckley and three associates with concocting an elaborate stock-fraud scheme in an effort to save themselves from personal bankruptcy.[27]

Newsweek and other publications gave short shrift to Buckley's claim that he had not known what a 10-K form was. It was, *Newsweek* wrote, "an odd claim for the board chairman of a publicly-held corporation."[28]

The final indignity as far as Buckley was concerned was perpetrated by the *Miami Herald*. In a February 11 column, executive editor John McMullan charged that the SEC and Justice Department were "going easy" on Buckley by not prosecuting him for criminal fraud. In view of Buckley's actions, McMullan asked, "Should the *Herald* continue to run Buckley's column?" And the answer, delivered after several weeks, was no.

V

In those months at the end of 1978 and the beginning of 1979, the magical aura of fulfilled ambition and moral rectitude that had surrounded Bill Buckley since his freshman year at Yale seemed to disappear. The Starr Broadcasting investigation—and indirectly even the Catawba and ACC affairs—had cast aspersions not merely on his political views but on his honesty. "This is the worst week in my life," Buckley had told his son, Christopher, during the week that the SEC publicized its charges against him.

Buckley had also seen his larger family begin to fall apart. He had broken with Brent Bozell—once his closest friend—over *Triumph*'s right-wing Catholicism; Patricia Bozell had begun drinking seriously once again, and Brent had had the first of several attacks of severe manic depression that incapacitated him. John Buckley, lonely and depressed after the collapse of Catawba, was rarely sober. Reid Buckley, once divorced, had produced two little-read novels. Carol Buckley, once divorced, had had serious problems in her life.

On *National Review,* Buckley had endured a great loss. In January 1978, upon returning from the Panama Canal debate, Burnham suddenly lost his vision in one eye—the result of a malfunctioning blood vessel. Then in November, he suffered a massive stroke that temporarily paralyzed his right side and permanently deprived him of his encyclopedic memory. Burnham, who was unable to remember what happened from one day to the next, was forced to withdraw from *National Review,* and the magazine floundered without the kind of political and theoretical guidance that Burnham had provided.

Under the weight of adversity, Buckley's work had also begun to suffer. He was still capable of raising the hackles of both Right and Left—in January 1979, he had broken with much of the Right with a stirring defense of the proposal to create a national holiday honoring Martin Luther King. But often his column and *Firing Line* lacked vigor. Buckley increasingly did *Firing Line* on the road, and while some of these shows were interesting, others appeared only to interest the participants—and sometimes not even the host. In October 1978, Buckley had traveled to Australia where he interviewed Prime Minister Malcolm Fraser, Labor leader Robert Hawke, and three journalists in three separate programs. The shows lacked immediacy and excitement. With Fraser, Buckley appeared mildly deferential. With the journalists, he got into a long argument about aborigines and uranium mining, the details of which eluded most American viewers.

Neal Freeman wrote Buckley, "As you are well aware, the show has lost much of its constituency within the PTV [public TV] system and the long term prospects are decidedly bearish. It's a long hour." [29] Buckley responded to Freeman: "What you say strikes me as distressingly vague. I say this mostly because I have spent so much time in trying to dream up ideas to make the show more exciting. I can't in good conscience tell you that I am optimistic about a *deus ex machina* at the production end." [30]

In Switzerland that winter Buckley tried to put Starr Broadcasting,

Catawba, and the ACC behind him by writing another Blackford Oakes spy novel, but the results were uninspired. *Who's On First*—the first of five books due under a million-dollar contract that Buckley had signed with Doubleday—had a tight and complex plot that ranged from the Soviet invasion of Hungary in 1956 to the Soviet launch of Sputnik the next year; but it didn't have an arresting character like the queen in *Saving the Queen* or Count Wintergrin in *Stained Glass*. Its underlying conflict was also surprisingly conventional, pitting Oakes's loyalty to the CIA and the Cold War against his friendship for and loyalty to two Soviet defectors; and its sentimental resolution —in favor of personal loyalty—suggested not only Buckley's detachment from the political fray, but his unwillingness to think a book through beyond the point at which it was simply entertaining.

When Buckley returned to New York that spring, Reagan was beginning to gear up for another run at the presidency, but Buckley was still distracted by his clash with the SEC. He wrote Alistair Horne in May: "With respect to the SEC matter, I suppose that I will only get it out of my system after I write about it. . . . If it happened that I were as evil as described in one or two of those articles, then people should stick me into Conventry and let me cool off there awhile." [31]

Ken Galbraith and conservative columnist Jack Kilpatrick both advised him not to write the book, but he was determined to do so. In August, Buckley wrote his agent, Lois Wallace, that his prime qualification for writing such a book was that "I find such books extraordinarily boring, and under the circumstances am unlikely to commit one." [32]

Buckley began the book that summer and finished it in Switzerland that winter, as the presidential primaries were beginning. He entitled the thirty-thousand-word manuscript "My Life in Business—Reflections on the SEC, an Incurious Press, and the Public Morality." But unlike his other replies to critics—from *God and Man at Yale* to the mayor's campaign—this one fell flat.

It was largely devoted to a point-by-point refutation of *The Wall Street Journal* and *Newsweek* articles and a paragraph-by-paragraph critique of the SEC report. For someone unfamiliar with the SEC document, Buckley's chapter about it was incomprehensible, not to mention tedious. There was no lively account of the radio business. Nor any sense of the pain, anguish, and confusion of his last years as Starr Broadcasting's chairman of the board.

A certain disingenuousness lingered over the book itself. In his introduction, he claimed that he had written the book in order to discover why the public still treated him with "reverence" when he has been portrayed in the press as "someone who plundered innocent investors for his own benefit."[33] But the manuscript contained no discussion of public moral standards, only of the merits of the SEC's case against him. It was straight "apologia," as columnist Jack Kilpatrick had feared.

Buckley gave the manuscript to numerous friends, including Hugh Kenner, John Kenneth Galbraith, Richard Clurman, and Ernest van den Haag, to read, and they were uniformly against his publishing it. Doubleday president Sam Vaughan had tried to discourage him from writing it ("I kept saying, 'I don't think you should do it, you can't win in the fight' "), but when Buckley finished the manuscript, he still submitted it to Doubleday. Vaughan, placed in a difficult position, refused to publish it. "It wasn't good," Vaughan said. "He might have gotten screwed but that book wasn't going to help him. I thought I would have to say no to him repeatedly, but Dick Clurman and others were also saying no."

Fifteen years earlier, when Buckley had set aside *Revolt Against the Masses,* he had been aware that the book didn't work, but he remained blind to the defects of "My Life in Business," even offering later to send a copy to anyone who was interested. Buckley, however, did give up hope of publishing the book and, in effect, of having the last word on the controversy. For the first time in his life, he had been soundly defeated by an adversary, and he knew it.

CHAPTER 23

The Ventriloquist

Although he had some doubts that Reagan could win, Buckley began publicly backing Reagan for the Republican presidential nomination a full two years before the 1980 primaries.

Buckley's greatest doubt concerned Reagan's age. He didn't know whether the public would accept a sixty-nine-year-old candidate. Reagan, he wrote in 1978, "suffers from the single presumptive disability of being thought too old." [1] And he privately wondered whether Reagan's age would permit him to endure the pace of a presidential campaign. In January 1979, before leaving for Switzerland, Buckley had lunch with Frank Shakespeare and Jim Buckley in New York. When Shakespeare said that he believed that Reagan was not going to win in 1980 because he was "just past that prime," Buckley said nothing, even though he held the same belief. "At that point, if I had had to make a private bet, I would have bet the same thing," he said.

In his speaking engagements, Buckley declared his support of Reagan, but he kept *National Review* from endorsing any of the Republican candidates, and he remained noncommittal in his columns. He wanted to see how Reagan would do in the primaries.

In case Reagan stumbled, Buckley and the other *National Review* editors had fallback positions: Jeff Hart and Priscilla Buckley favored former Treasury Secretary John Connally; Rusher leaned to Illinois Representative Philip Crane. Neal Freeman, who had replaced George Will as the Washington editor, favored Senate Minority Leader Howard Baker. And Buckley's choice was former CIA Director George Bush.

Buckley had known Bush since he and Brent Bozell had campaigned for Bush's father, Prescott, in 1952. Like Buckley, Bush had graduated from Yale and had been a member of Skull and Bones. The two men struck up a friendship that was renewed through occasional visits (Bush moved to Texas soon afterwards to seek his fortune) and periodic letters. Like Reagan, Bush was a longtime *National Review* subscriber, but unlike Reagan, he was first a Republican and second a conservative.

While Buckley made clear to Bush that he was backing Reagan, he let him know that he was his second choice. Speaking on the same platform as Bush to the Young Republican National Federation in June 1979, Buckley said:

> The very last time I saw George was on a summer day last July in a little camp in Northern California [the Bohemian Grove] to which we both belong. He was strolling toward the river to take a swim, a book in his hand. Any book? No, *Stained Glass,* by William F. Buckley, Jr. I knew then that he was running for President, and that I would probably end up supporting him if and when an antecedent commitment of a dozen years' standing should lapse—support George, even if, as Rebecca West said about Anthony Eden, the trouble with him is that he has no redeeming defects.[2]

In his columns in the fall of 1979 and early winter of 1980, Buckley barely mentioned the Republican candidates. He wrote far more about Senator Edward Kennedy, who was challenging Carter in the Democratic primary, and about the dramatic events that were laying the groundwork for a Republican and conservative victory in 1980.

On November 4, 1979, Iranian students took over the American Embassy in Teheran and held its inhabitants hostage. The seizure of American hostages became what journalist Theodore White called a "national humiliation."[3] Buckley was initially preoccupied with defending Kissinger against the charge that by arranging the Shah's medical treatment in the U.S., he had precipitated the hostage take-over, but he also saw the results of the Ayatollah Khomeini's ouster of the Shah as vindicating the hardline attitude toward Third World rebellions that he had taken over the years. "We know the Ayatollah is crazy. The question is, how widespread is the disease," Buckley wrote.[4]

In December,the Soviet Union invaded Afghanistan. The Soviet invasion appeared to confirm conservative predictions of Soviet expansion. It discredited the structure of détente that Nixon and Kissinger had erected, and it created support for the conservative call for a rapid military buildup. In the wake of the Soviet invasion, Buckley called for the U.S. to "undertake a systematic, devoted, evangelical effort to instruct the people of the world that the Soviet Union is animated not by a salvific ideology, but by a reactionary desire to kill and torture, intimidate and exploit others, for the benefit of its own recidivist national appetites for imperialism."[5]

Buckley also gave his attention to the deteriorating economy. At the beginning of 1980, inflation, fueled by rising oil prices, reached a record 18 percent. In spite of attempts by Carter and Federal Reserve Chairman Paul Volcker to remedy the situation by slowing down the economy, the nation suffered continued inflation and growing unemployment, for which many blamed the Carter administration and— forgetting the lessons of the Great Depression—decades of government intervention in the economy.

Buckley's own solution differed from that of many conservatives who were simply calling for tax cuts. Buckley endorsed the proposal of Congressman John Anderson—in nearly every respect, the most liberal of the Republican presidential candidates—to impose a fifty-cent-a-gallon tax on gasoline.

It was only after Bush had upset Reagan in Iowa that Buckley began commenting on the election. Remarking on the loyalty that certain candidates command from voters, Buckley speculated that Reagan "was losing some of his public . . . because of the question of age."[6] In *National Review,* the editors tried to appear neutral between Reagan and Bush. They criticized Reagan's "invisibility" during the Iowa caucus, while they mused about whether Bush, if he won the nomination, would be able to win over "blue collar workers, 'ethnics,' Southerners" in the general election.[7]

Buckley was in Switzerland during the climactic New Hampshire primary. Behind in the polls after Iowa, Reagan began actively campaigning, and Bush, relying on "momentum" rather than specific appeal, saw his advantage slip away. On primary day, Reagan beat Bush two to one and ended his challenge to the nomination. After New Hampshire, Buckley and *National Review* assumed that Reagan would be the nominee. The question now was how he could win in the fall.

I

Buckley and Reagan continued to see each other during the campaign and to talk on the phone regularly, but their relationship was more personal than political. Although Reagan deeply admired Buckley—he read his column and *National Review* closely—he rarely called directly on Buckley for advice. Instead, as he did with other close friends, he liked to swap stories. One exception occurred when, after the New Hampshire primary, he fired campaign manager John Sears and replaced him with Bill Casey. Reagan called Buckley in Italy to explain what he had done and to seek his friend's support.

Buckley knew most of Reagan's campaign officials, and as had occurred in 1968 with Nixon, other people used Buckley as an intermediary with the campaign. But Buckley did not participate actively in Reagan's campaign. Indeed, he played less of a role in Reagan's 1980 campaign then he had played in Nixon's 1968 campaign. Neither John Sears, Reagan's campaign manager through the New Hampshire primary, nor William Casey, who succeeded him, could remember Buckley exercising significant influence over the campaign. This was in part a result of a conscious decision on Buckley's part. Buckley had been burned in 1964 and then disappointed by Nixon's fall, and he had drawn back from becoming too closely identified with any political campaign.

But as was the case in 1964, Buckley could not have had much influence over the campaign, even if he had wanted to. Reagan's political style had always been to delegate authority to subordinates and to intervene only in the most important and pressing matters. He gave Sears and then Casey total authority. They determined where Reagan would go and, to a great extent, what he would say, and they also filled the staff positions. They and the staff they hired jealously protected the candidate from other advisers and from his friends, including Buckley. Buckley discovered this when he tried to get Reagan to hire Tony Dolan as a speech writer.

Dolan was one of the intellectually promising young men whom Buckley had nurtured. When Dolan was in the Army, Buckley gave him his telephone credit-card number for making long-distance calls, and when later Dolan lost his job with the Gannett News Service, Buckley got him a job with the *Stamford Advocate*. Dolan repaid Buckley's confidence in him by winning a Pulitzer Prize for reporting. By 1979, however, Dolan had gotten tired of journalism and wanted to work for the Reagan campaign. Buckley had suggested to Reagan that he hire Dolan as a speech writer, and Reagan had relayed the suggestion to Michael Deaver, but Deaver ignored it. Then Buckley had flown Dolan to Minneapolis to meet with John Sears and his assistant Jim Lake. "They were experts at repelling boarding parties," Dolan recalled. "They were not going to hire someone they could not control."

Buckley didn't fully understand what was happening. "He really does trust people, and it didn't really occur to him that they thought that he was thinking like they did, that he was really trying to put his man with Reagan," his son, Christopher, said. "They didn't want any Buckley people close to the President."

In March 1980, Buckley called Casey, and Casey said that he would talk to Dolan, but nothing happened for several months. Finally, he sent Casey a telegram, and Casey invited Dolan in for an appointment. They hit it off, and Dolan was hired, and soon became Reagan's chief speech writer. Casey said later, "The best thing Buckley did was bugging me into hiring a guy named Tony Dolan."

Buckley used his column to moderate the sectarian zeal of Reagan's followers. Buckley positioned himself not as a camp follower but as a liaison between the conservatives and the more moderate Republicans. And he attached particular importance to reconciling the conservatives with Henry Kissinger. Buckley's opinion of Kissinger, which was already high, had gone up still further with the publication in 1979 of the first volume of Kissinger's memoirs, *White House Years*. As a personal favor, Buckley had helped edit the manuscript and had become convinced of the former Secretary of State's genius.* He put the book in the same class with *Witness* as a "modern classic."[8]

In several columns in spring 1980, Buckley trumpeted the virtues of Kissinger, who was still widely hated by conservatives and whom the Reagan campaign was attacking in order to get at Ford. He described one Kissinger speech assailing the Carter administration's foreign pol-

---

* Kissinger wanted to acknowledge Buckley's considerable editorial assistance in the Foreword to *White House Years*, but Buckley did not want his name mentioned. Buckley appears to have been moved by modesty, but the always defensive Kissinger believed that Buckley didn't want to be associated with his book.

icy as the "best speech delivered over the past season" and defended Kissinger against charges that he had engineered the OPEC oil price rise in 1974 in order to aid the Shah of Iran. He thumbed his nose at the conservatives who feared that Kissinger was maneuvering for a second term as Secretary of State. "Jackie Onassis has been married twice. So why can't Kissinger be secretary of state twice?" he quipped.[9]

Buckley also championed George Bush against conservatives who were angry with him for calling Reagan's supply-side theory "voodoo economics" and for backing the Equal Rights Amendment. In May, Nicholas Brady, a friend of Buckley and Bush's campaign manager in the East, convinced Buckley that the Reagan campaign needed to do something to "conciliate" voters who had supported Bush in the primaries. Buckley called Casey to suggest that the campaign consider naming Bush as Vice-President, and he wrote a column suggesting that Reagan make a "conciliatory gesture" toward Bush. Bush, Buckley wrote, was "the logical choice" for Vice-President. Buckley also suggested the campaign look into nominating Gerald Ford. "Another man who would qualify as validating the ecumenical spirit is Gerald Ford. Would he accept? The conventional wisdom is: No. My own feeling is: Yes." [10]

In a *Firing Line* that month with conservative leaders Daniel Mahoney, Paul Weyrich, and Pat Buchanan, Buckley defended his choice of Bush for Vice-President.

BUCKLEY: It seems to me that Bush is, by virtue of a kind of earned seniority, the obvious candidate, even as Kefauver was the obvious candidate in 1956 to go with Stevenson.

WEYRICH: . . . It seems to me it makes more sense to put somebody out here who is at least compatible in the South and compatible with blue collar workers and can talk to them, as opposed to somebody whom I think is essentially a preppie Republican with an appeal to a narrow group of people who vote in Republican primaries and no place else.

BUCKLEY: Well, he defeated Reagan in Michigan and did so substantially—

WEYRICH: Sure, because Reagan had no funds to expend . . .

BUCKLEY: George Wallace spent nothing, and he won Wisconsin.

WEYRICH: Well, that I think was an extraordinary situation.

BUCKLEY: And Henry Cabot Lodge spent nothing, and he won New Hampshire.

But Buckley did not discuss with Reagan himself the possibility of naming either Bush or Ford; and at the time, Reagan, still smarting from the campaign, appeared unwilling to consider Bush, but Buckley may have helped plant an idea that bore fruit two months later at the Republican Convention in Detroit.

II

Buckley remained curiously detached from the political debates over economic policy within the Republican Party. Much of Reagan's success in the primaries had been the result of his adopting Congressman Jack Kemp's "supply-side economics." Reagan contended that if government cut tax rates 30 percent across the board, the increase in jobs and income would be so dramatic as to offset the potential reduction in tax revenues. Republicans could square the circle. They could cut taxes while curbing the deficit and inflation.

National Review editorialized on behalf of Kemp's economics and against the more traditional Republicans who believed that cutting taxes would widen the deficit and that the only remedy to the deficit and inflation was to reduce spending and the money supply. Buckley claimed to support the supply-side theory, but his own proposals and analysis showed him to be a staunch traditionalist. In one column, Buckley had called for cutting taxes, but then making up "the resulting deficit" through Anderson's gasoline tax.[11]

During June, what was called the "battle for Reagan's mind" became intense among his supporters. Former Ford and Nixon administration officials and corporate executives who had backed John Connally or Bush in the early going tried to move Reagan away from supply-side economics and his more strident foreign policy pronouncements while militant conservatives pressed Reagan to consider Kemp, the principal supply-side spokesman, or Nevada Senator Paul Laxalt for Vice-President. But Buckley stayed clear of these debates. He spent June sailing across the Atlantic.

Buckley had had the idea for another Atlantic crossing while sailing with Dick Clurman the previous year. But a month before setting sail, Clurman had decided that he would go along only on the first leg of the journey, from St. Thomas to Bermuda. "I couldn't imagine spending that month, on the eve of the two political conventions, cut off from the world, the *New York Times,* and in some ways the quadrennial apocalypse of my lifelong professional preoccupations," Clurman later remarked.[12]

During Clurman's leg of the trip, he and Buckley and Evan Galbraith had several discussions about the election. One day, seated on the boat's fantail, eating chicken, the three men talked about what they might like to do in a Reagan administration. Clurman said he would take any senior position on the White House staff. Evan Galbraith insisted that he would not accept an ambassadorship, because ambassadors were just "bullshitters." And Buckley said, "The only position I would consider is the President's spiritual adviser."

Buckley himself compensated for his absence from the political scene by turning the pleasurable sailing jaunt into business. He had made arrangements with Doubleday to write a successor to *Airborne.* He hired a professional photographer, Christopher Little, to go along. He convinced a television crew to make the trip from St. Thomas to Bermuda. And as he had insisted before, every one of the sailors had to keep a journal from which Buckley could draw in writing a book about the trip.

Having sold *Cyrano,* Buckley had chartered a 70-foot yacht, *Sealestial,* to make the journey. Stocked not only with the latest navigational gadgetry, but also with wine and a piano, Buckley and his friends set sail from Bermuda on May 30 and arrived in Portugal one month later. In July, *People* magazine, the mass celebrity weekly, featured photos of Buckley's trip across the Atlantic. The six-page spread was entitled "William F. Buckley, Jr., Braves the High Seas in His Fashion, with Champagne and Scarlatti."

The next winter he would write the story of the trip. *Atlantic High,* like its predecessor, *Airborne,* was filled with charming anecdotes and witty asides, and it also managed to convey Buckley's enthusiasm at sea. But it was a curiously minor and inconsequential book for a man whose political ship, after so many years at sea, appeared to be coming into harbor.

III

After returning to the U.S., Buckley attended the Republican Convention in Detroit. With the nomination sewed up, the only question was whom Reagan would select for Vice-President. Before the convention, Reagan had narrowed the choice to Bush, Baker, and Ford, but some delegates were still calling for Reagan to pick a candidate from the party's Right.

Buckley again threw his weight behind the attempt to unite the conservative and more moderate wings of the party. On the opening day, Representative Phil Crane, who had run unsuccessfully as the candidate of the far Right, gave a speech attacking the idea that Reagan needed "balance" on his ticket. Such a view, Crane said, wrongly assumed that Reagan's ideas were not in the mainstream of "all Americans." In his column, Buckley remarked, "I found this [assertion] a little unsettling because if Reagan's views are those of the political center, then shouldn't we move over to the right." [13]

Buckley praised Kissinger's convention speech as "a forthright declaration of war against the foreign policy of Jimmy Carter," and he dismissed the idea that Kissinger's participation in the negotiations between Reagan and Ford was motivated by the hope of a presidential appointment as "preposterous and documentably untrue." And he praised Reagan's final choice of Bush, after Ford had declined, as "splendid." [14]

After the convention, Buckley acted as an intermediary between Kissinger and Reagan. On August 30, he conveyed to Reagan over the phone a message from Kissinger about the Iranian hostages. Kissinger, Buckley told Reagan, was in touch with the wives of the hostages and had won the agreement of their chief spokeswoman, Louisa Kennedy, to issue a "contradictory statement" if Carter should denounce Reagan's stand on the hostages. Buckley also told Reagan that Kissinger "would be willing to make a public declaration of his non-availability for public office." Reagan greeeted this suggestion "ecstatically." [15]

In his columns, Buckley gently chided Reagan for switching back and forth on the question of whether the U.S. should restore diplomatic relations with Taiwan. "If Ronald Reagan or any member of his staff ever again say, 'We cannot turn back the clock,' I and all my friends and admirers will vote for Carter, and that would mean a Democratic landslide," Buckley wrote. [16]

Buckley responded sarcastically to frequently voiced doubts about Reagan's mental capacity. When Reagan had clinched the nomination, Buckley had written that Reagan is "a man of amiability and discipline, who is simple minded enough to cherish no other ideals than those of the Founding Fathers." [17] But in *National Review,* after the convention, Buckley published as an editorial an anonymous interview with an "American with long involvement in general affairs." The American, Charles Burton Marshall, was an old friend of Buckley and a *National Review* contributor.

Q.—Does Reagan have the necessary knowledge and talents?

A.—No.

Q.—Yet you support him. Your answer astounds me.

A.—Let me go on. Neither did Truman . . . What he did have, among other things, was discernment as to who could help him. He gathered a formidable array of talents about him. . . .

Q.—But back to Reagan. Do you believe he can staff the government with first-rate people?

A.—We can hope. But don't exaggerate. An ascent to second rateness would be a considerable achievement. That is far beyond Carter.[18]

The most difficult column that Buckley had to write that fall was in response to the arrest of Bob Bauman. Bauman, whom Buckley had known since the founding of YAF in 1960, had become the chairman of the American Conservative Union and one of the leading conservatives in Congress. But that September, in the midst of his congressional campaign, he was charged with soliciting sex from a teenaged male prostitute in Washington. Determined to stay in the race, Bauman apologized publicly for his act and assured his constituents that he had rid himself of the homosexual tendencies that alcoholism had brought on. Conservatives initially split over whether Bauman should resign.

Because Bauman was a conservative leader, Buckley felt he had to take a position. At a hotel in Seattle, where he had come for a speaking engagement, he agonized over whether to call for Bauman's resignation. Twenty-five years before, Buckley would have regarded any homosexual as a sinner unworthy of public office, but his attitude had become more liberal under the impact of the counterculture of the sixties and early seventies, the presence of several homosexuals among his closest associates, and the arguments of gay conservatives. In 1974, over the objection of other editors, he had printed David Brudnoy's conservative case for gay rights with a reply from Ernest van den Haag. In 1978, he had printed another debate over gay rights. But Buckley felt that Bauman, who had voted twice against a bill barring discrimination against homosexuals, was guilty not simply of an immoral act, but of hypocrisy.

In his column, Buckley contrasted Bauman's behavior with that of Democrat Fred Richmond, who had also been arrested for homosexual solicitation. Bauman "had ordained standards of conduct which he himself transgressed. . . . Richmond, while repenting his act, never stood as a spokeman for a code of behavior which he expressly violated." Bauman, Buckley concluded, should resign from Congress and from the chairmanship of the ACU as

> an act of contrition. It should never be supposed that sinners cannot effectively rail against sin, else there would be total silence, everywhere. But the cause of Robert Bauman, which he served with such passion . . . exacts of its spokesman a certain spiritual candor, a spirit of meekness toward abiding truths. Bob Bauman is as welcome in my home today as yesterday. But to his friends and supporters he owes an obligation . . . to accept retirement from public life.[19]

Bauman found Buckley's column "personally devastating."[20] He remained defiantly at the helm of the ACU, but was defeated in November in the socially conservative district that he represented. Buckley, however, made good on the offer of friendship that he extended in his column. The next year he tried to get Bauman a job,* he loaned Bauman's wife, Carol, $20,000, and at Bauman's request, he wrote an introduction to Bauman's autobiography, which Bauman's publisher did not use.

IV

In the fall campaign, Reagan sought to move to the center. He assured Chrysler that he would not rescind the government's loan arrangement with the company. And he promised to negotiate arms control with the Soviet Union. Buckley, who understood that to win, Reagan had to convince Americans that he was not an "extremist," did not criticize Reagan for these concessions. On November 4, buoyed by Carter's failure to secure the hostages' release, Reagan won a landslide victory, and the Republicans captured the Senate for the first time since 1952.

Buckley's friends in the administration urged Reagan to appoint Buckley to a high position. When Buckley was in Argentina in late November at a party thrown by David Rockefeller, he received a call from Alfred Bloomingdale, a member of the President's Kitchen Cabinet, inquiring whether he "would agree to serve as Ambassador to

---

* Buckley thought that William Coors, by hiring Bauman, could improve his image with gays, who were boycotting Coors beer to protest an anti-gay statement that Coors had made. Buckley could never get Coors to make the offer—although Bauman would probably have turned down the job.

the United Nations." According to Buckley, he "said no instantly."
When Frank Shakespeare and Bill Casey floated his name as chairman
of the United States Information Agency, Buckley rejected that post
as well. "Bill rejected governing to remain a commentator," his friend
Dick Clurman explained.

But Reagan's election may have reawakened in Buckley the doubts
about his political role that had plagued him after his brother's Senate
victory in 1970. Even though Buckley had articulated both the principles and the tactics of political realism on which Reagan had run, it
was Reagan—an actor of little intellectual accomplishment—and not
Buckley who would now put conservatism to the highest test. An
event the next month may have further contributed to Buckley's
doubts.

Buckley was planning a large banquet in December at the Plaza to
celebrate the magazine's twenty-fifth anniversary and the election of
its most prominent subscriber. Several months earlier, Buckley had
sent an invitation to Reagan, who had been a featured speaker at the
twentieth anniversary, and whom Buckley expected would gladly appear at the twenty-fifth anniversary. He thought the President had
accepted the invitation.

After Reagan's victory, the celebration assumed even greater importance in Buckley's mind: it was to be a vindication of conservatism
and *National Review*'s many years in the political wilderness. But in
November, Roy Cohn, inquiring about the President's attendance at
the celebration, was told by a White House staff member that Reagan
would not be there. Cohn immediately called Buckley, who, Cohn
recalled, became as angry as he had ever heard him.

Chris Buckley, who was present when his father called the White
House, had never seen his father more disappointed.

> My dad had sent three separate invitations and had reminded Nancy
> and Ron about the banquet [Chris recalled]. But with all those things
> going on, Reagan had begun at this point to lose it a little, so he
> could be excused for not remembering things. I remember before
> he called—he hates asking for favors—he was saying, "If he
> doesn't come, I'm not going to his inauguration." I was in the room
> when he made the call to Nancy, and I could tell from his voice.
> Then Reagan got on, and I could tell from my dad's voice. He
> [Reagan] was saying, "If we'd known, I would have done it, but we
> have to be in California." He said, "How about if I do a live TV
> hookup," and my dad was adamant: "We don't do that."

Both Chris Buckley and Tony Dolan were convinced that Reagan's aide Deaver had deliberately lost the invitation. "I'm sure that was Deaver's doing," Dolan said. "Deaver never thought well of Bill. Mike doesn't like conservatives."

Buckley himself was defensive about the President's expected absence. He told a reporter from the *Washington Post*, "The best you can hope for is to be the principal journal that instructs the president of the United States." [21]

The anniversary celebration, held at the gilted Plaza Hotel, was a gala affair even without the President. More than six hundred attended; luminaries included Kissinger, New York Major Ed Koch, Senator-elect Alfonse D'Amato, television's Walter Cronkite and Morley Safer, and almost an entire generation of conservative leaders. George Will summed up the prevailing assessment:

What happened in 1980, I believe, is that American conservatism came of age. In 1964 Barry Goldwater made the Republican party a vessel of conservatism, and, starting before that and particularly after that, *National Review* magazine has filled that vessel with an intellectually defensible modern conservatism. No, the principal architect of this achievement of course is William F. Buckley, the Pope of the conservative movement, operating out of a little Vatican on 35th Street. [22]

The last speaker was Buckley himself. His feelings about Reagan's absence and his uncertainty about his own future loomed large in what he had to say, but he expressed himself humorously. Of the "missing guest," he said:

We have had a merry correspondence for many years, focused in recent months on the role I would play in his Administration. I wrote to him in May to advise him that I could not accept the anticipated invitation to serve him as Secretary of State, or in any other office. He replied that he was very sorry to hear this, as he had in mind for me ambassador to Afghanistan. I replied that I would consider the position if he would provide me with a bodyguard of 15 divisions. That proposal was not resolved.

A few weeks ago I advised him that I had received the periodic form from *Who's Who* asking whether there were any changes I wished to put into my forthcoming entry. I asked the President-elect whether he would acquiesce in my substituting under the designa-

tion "Profession: editor and writer," "Profession: ventriloquist."
He laughed. But laughed longer than I would have done, and this
persuaded me that, as a ventriloquist I was a failure.[23]

Buckley meant the crack about being a ventriloquist as a joke, but
given the widespread doubts about Reagan's intellectual capacity,
Buckley's comments might have appeared denigrating. Afterwards,
Dick Clurman told him that the references to ventriloquy had sounded
bad. But the joke was on Buckley as well as Reagan; if Reagan was a
puppet who lacked a ventriloquist, Buckley in the coming administration was a performer who was lacking his principal prop.

Reagan's victory contributed to Buckley's own celebrity. Immediately after the election, *60 Minutes,* the most popular news show on
television, filmed a 20-minute feature on Buckley. The program aired
in January, the week before Reagan was to be inaugurated. Morley
Safer had interviewed Kissinger and Casey at the *National Review*
banquet. Casey had become offended when Safer had suggested that
there was a "good Bill Buckley and . . . the bad Bill Buckley, who
will, whenever he get the opportunity, skewer an opponent." "What
in the hell does this bad Bill Buckley come from?" Casey asked
Safer.

Safer had also quizzed Buckley about his relationship to the American-Chilean Council. Buckley had been irritated when Safer had
questioned the ACC's practice of paying conservative writers to
travel to Chile and write stories.

> You live on the other side of the track, Morley, where you people
> come from—your CBSes, your *New York Times*es, your *Washing-
> ton Posts.* You can afford to send anybody you want anytime you
> want. People on our side of the track, who live off the charity of our
> readers, we can't send somebody to Chile and pay the round trip or
> —anywhere else. We don't have the money. So what do we do? We
> get honest writers.

But Buckley's best line came when Safer asked him about his
family:

> SAFER: Has there ever been a liberal Buckley?
> BUCKLEY: Well, if there were, I wouldn't reveal it.
> SAFER: What would you do if one came along and openly pro-
>   claimed to be? What would the family do to him or her?
> BUCKLEY: Pray—pray for him.

CHAPTER 24

A Special Relationship

On a cold, bright day in January 1981, Ronald Reagan, standing on the west side of the Capitol and looking out over the Mall, took the oath of office. Bill and Pat Buckley were seated in a reviewing stand with other close friends of the President.

Reagan's speech evoked the broader themes of conservatism: "Government is not the solution to our problem," he declared. "It is the problem." Referring obliquely to the Soviet threat, he said that his administration would "do whatever needs to be done to preserve this last and greatest bastion of freedom." Looking out toward the Lincoln Memorial, he evoked a mood of patriotism and nostalgia. "Standing here, we face a magnificent vista, opening up this city's special beauty and history. At the end of the Mall are those shrines to the giants on whose shoulders we stand."

Buckley felt the special pride of someone who had helped make it all possible, but he was still unsure how he should relate to the new administration. Should he seek to advise the President personally? Or should he confine himself to writing his column and overseeing *National Review,* both of which the President read carefully? And if he were to be invited to advise the President, according to what standards—the paradigm to which he had held Eisenhower accountable, or that mix of the possible and the ideal by which he had judged Nixon?

There was also a deeper question, one that had surfaced during the flap over Reagan's absence at *National Review*'s twenty-fifty-anniversary celebration: Had he, Bill Buckley, fulfilled his own political and personal mandate? Was his life, in some sense, justified?

I

Buckley had several friends in the administration besides Reagan, and numerous protégés. Casey was at the CIA; Tony Dolan and Aram Bashikian, who had written frequently for *National Review,* were on the President's speech-writing staff; and Christopher Buckley was writing George Bush's speeches. Buckley lobbied hard to get a Cabinet post for Evan Galbraith, but Galbraith had to settle for ambassador to France.* He also helped former *National Review* editor Daniel Oliver and Marvin Liebman get administration jobs.

Buckley enjoyed a continuing close relationship with Reagan, the only change being that now he called Reagan "Mr. President" rather than "Ronnie." From time to time, the Reagans invited the Buckleys to attend White House functions and to stay overnight. "When Bill comes to the White House, he hangs his coat on the highest hook," said Dan Oliver. Both husbands and wives talked regularly on the phone. And Buckley began a practice of sending Reagan letters and clippings to the special mailbox set aside for Reagan's personal correspondence.

The relationship between the two men was complicated. On the one hand, they were simply old friends. But in letters to Tony Dolan, Buckley referred to Reagan as "our client"—a term that placed him in the position of a political adviser or consultant. It remained a question for Buckley how he functioned in this capacity.

When the two men were together, Buckley was extremely discreet about offering advice. Casey said, "He can get the President whenever he wants, and the President listens. Whenever there is a big philosophical issue, and people want to weigh in, Buckley can make a phone call. But he is quite cautious about doing it."

Tony Dolan attributed Buckley's reluctance to use his influence to his sense of propriety. "Bill understands the dimensions of the cour-

---

* At the celebration after Galbraith was sworn in, Buckley showed the film of Galbraith, Clurman, and himself discussing presidential appointments on the *Sealestial*.

tesy in the larger sense. You do not intrude unnecessarily on the matters of staff policy and you do not disburb a transcendent relationship, that is, a friendship, for the sake of 'I don't like the way the trade bill is going.' "

Buckley also sensed that Reagan, who was inveterately optimistic and would take action only when intra-administration conflicts had reached crisis proportions, was not really interested in a private brain trust.

In November 1981, Dolan complained to Buckley that Reagan's advisers were trying to sidetrack the larger conservative agenda and to make "this administration another respectable Republican country-club affair interested in managing the economy and monitoring the stock market." "I understand exactly what you say in your letter," Buckley replied, "and it is important that I be aware of it even though I am not in a position to act. Our client and I have a special relationship but it is not one that invites me to come in at him with a point as comprehensive as the one you make, I fear correctly." [1]

II

Buckley knew that he still had important channels of communication with the President through *National Review* and through his column. Several times, Reagan called Buckley or Rusher to discuss what he had read in a column or in the magazine. But Buckley's larger priorities set severe limits on the use of his column and *National Review* to advise the President. Even though Reagan had won by a landslide, Buckley believed that he required active defense against his critics; and Buckley also felt that, to some extent, an attack against Reagan was an attack against the man from whom he had learned his politics. In both his column and *National Review,* the impulse to defend Reagan tended to overwhelm the impulse to advise or criticize him. During Reagan's first year in office, Buckley wrote only one column that was sharply critical of the President—a column attacking his appointment of Terrel Bell, a past proponent of busing, as Secretary of Education (Bell "might as well have been appointed by President McGovern," Buckley wrote). Buckley did call on the administration to break relations with Cuba and to lower tax rates for the rich to 25 percent, but such proposals were so remote from what anyone in the adminstration or Congress contemplated that they did not appear as criticism, but rather as expressions of Buckley's own conservatism.

During that first year, Buckley defended Reagan against Democratic criticisms of his tax bill and budget cuts and his strategy of "quiet diplomacy" toward the violently repressive Argentinean regime; and he defended Reagan against right-wing criticisms of his abrogation of the grain embargo, his nomination of Sandra Day O'Connor to the Supreme Court, and his acquiescence in a record deficit.

Buckley's best columns were those in which he had to defend the administration simultaneously from the Right and the Left. Justifying the administration's decision to aid the Duarte government in El Salvador militarily—a decision that New Right leaders opposed because of Duarte's Social Democratic background and that liberals opposed because of Duarte's past inability to control the right-wing death squads—Buckley wrote:

> Reagan is right: the distinction between the Duartes of this world and the [rebel head Ruben] Zamoras of this world is a distinction with which we need to maneuver. But let us be morally assertive. It is not chauvinistic to announce that the U.S. will not tolerate another Soviet-dominated abscess in the Western hemisphere, and if people don't understand why, then they are moral idiots.[2]

But many of his other columns appeared to be merely apologies for the administration. In a May interview, he rationalized his reluctance to criticize Reagan. "Our job at *National Review* is to focus on the difference between what he does and what he could do, and only reflectively to focus on what he could do and what the paradigm would tell us. It is not hard to speak about the paradigm, but it is hard to say with confidence how far a politician can go."

Buckley's defense of the administration reached a point of absurdity when in early December the Polish government of Wojciech Jaruzelski, with strong Soviet backing, cracked down on the Polish trade-union movement, imprisoning key leaders, including Lech Walesa. The Reagan administration reacted by imposing minor sanctions against the Soviet Union and the Polish government and by encouraging Americans to put a candle in a window to protest Jaruzelski's actions. Conservatives, including those within the administration, were outraged. George Will, an ardent administration supporter, wrote, "The Polish crisis is over. But a crisis of American conservatism is at hand. The administration evidently loves commerce more than it loathes Communism."[3]

Buckley would have been expected to share Will's disquiet, but having taken his usual time off during the third week of December, he did not write anything about Poland until the first week in January 1982, and then rather than criticizing the administration position, he offered a proposal for Bush, on behalf of the U.S. government, to offer a "huge economic transfusion into Poland on the condition only that the money be received, and subsequently deployed, by Lech Walesa and his designates."[4]

At the end of January, when the roar among conservatives had become deafening, Buckley awkwardly joined the administration's right-wing critics. "Primarily, Reagan is a magnetic field," Buckley wrote. "His stands, so long and skillfully articulated, are unambiguous as to concept, flexible in the matter of execution. But in the field of foreign policy there is genuine confusion." Buckley accused the administration of "failure adequately to meet the challenge of the suppression of Poland."[5]

III

Buckley spent the winter of 1982 in Switzerland working on another book like *Cruising Speed,* using a diary of a week in his life as the springboard for reminiscences and reflections. He took a week in mid-November in which he had written three columns, traveled to Tampa on one day and Toledo on another to give speeches, hosted two *Firing Line* programs in Louisville with Kentucky Governor John Y. Brown, attended a harpsichord recital and a ballet (as part of a society benefit for the New York City Ballet), went to several fashionable parties, attended the theater with Ron Reagan, Jr., and his wife, entertained David Niven and his wife in Stamford, tended briefly to *National Review* business (it was the off week when the biweekly magazine was not put together), and answered a voluminous correspondence that could reach six hundred letters a week. He punctuated these events with anecdotes about the people and himself.

There were, however, important differences between the substance of *Cruising Speed* and the new book, which he called *Overdrive.* In *Cruising Speed,* Buckley had used the literary form of a diary as a vehicle for making a political and intellectual statement about the era. *Cruising Speed* both evoked and analyzed the tumultuous time called the sixties. As a diary, it also served a purpose of self-justification, but the author's ego stayed in the background. In *Overdrive,* form became substance, and self-justification became the overweening motif to which the analysis and description of the external world were subordinated.

The constant mention of the author's relationship to the President, his wife, and his children was painful to read. The reader learned that the President attended the fifteenth anniversary of *Firing Line*, that "charter subscriber Ronald Reagan" reads *National Review,* that after the author sent him a film, "El Presidente called to say how impressed he had been by what he had seen," that the Reagans had had Thanksgiving dinner with the Buckleys in 1976, that when Reagan had been elected, the author "saw no reason to lose touch with a very old friend," that during a filming of *Firing Line* the author learned that "my old friend the commander-in-chief is on the line," that the author and his wife took the President's son and his wife to see a play, and that "it would have been unusual if I *hadn't* seen a great deal of Ronald Reagan over the years."[6]

In *Overdrive,* Buckley described his life, but the details he chose were those that celebrity magazines like *People* or *Vanity Fair* coveted. They were the kind of details—the reconstructed Cadillac limousine Buckley owned, the wine he had with lunch ("a half bottle of Côte Rôtie"), the Jacuzzi he had built in his basement ("it is the most beautiful indoor pool this side of Pompeii"), and the names of his chauffeur, cooks, and other servants—that were only of interest because he was a celebrity. Buckley showed no modesty about the trappings of his wealth; instead he celebrated them as tokens of success.

IV

In early April, soon after the Buckleys returned from Switzerland, they left for a five-day vacation in Barbados with the Reagans at actress Claudette Colbert's villa. The house, resting on the edge of the beach, was staffed by black natives wearing Barbadian turbans. Gossip columnist "Suzy" praised the President's choice of company. "If there were a contest for what couple you'd most rather spend the weekend with it would have to be Bill and Pat Buckley."[7]

On the helicopter taking the Reagans and the Buckleys to Colbert's villa, Buckley had teased Reagan that the Secret Srevice would not let him go swimming next day because the beach wasn't sufficiently secure. Reagan said, "Well, Bill, Nancy here tells me that I'm the most powerful man in the Free World. If she's right, then I will swim tomorrow with you." In the water the first day, Buckley asked Reagan if he wanted to earn the *National Review* Medal of Freedom. When the President asked what he would have to do, Buckley responded, "Well, I will proceed to almost drown, and you will rescue me."[8]

Buckley did discuss the perils of the nuclear strategy of mutually assured destruction (MAD) with the President. Buckley's idea, which he later shelved, was that instead of threatening the destruction of the entire Soviet Union, the U.S. should publicly target a Soviet city for attack in case the Soviet Union struck first. Reagan didn't take to Buckley's notion, but he did later make the rejection of MAD a central justification for proposing a "Strategic Defense Initiative" that would intercept Soviet missiles and make a first strike against the U.S. impossible.

During their time together, Reagan gave Buckley several handwritten notes with figures on the unemployment rate, one of which claimed that unemployment had declined by 88,000 in March. Later that month, Buckley used the figures in his column, and the next day Reagan used the same figure in a speech before suburban Chicago schoolchildren. The only problem was that according to the Bureau of Labor Statistics unemployment had risen by 98,000 in March. *The New York Times* branded the figures a "Reaganism."[9]

Back in New York, the Buckleys' social whirl spun even faster than before. Pat Buckley's picture regularly appeared in *W* and in *Women's Wear Daily*'s reports on New York. Like Bill, however, Pat approached her social life as a form of work. She organized charity galas for the Metropolitan Museum and the American Cancer Society and book parties for her husband. Often she got bachelors like Jerry Zipkin, a friend of Nancy Reagan, to escort her, but she increasingly drew Bill himself into the celebrity night life. "He gets dragged, but he tries not to kick and scream," Buckley's friend Richard Clurman said.

Buckley enjoyed dinner parties with people he thought interesting. He was at home with writer Tom Wolfe or record producer Ahmet Ertegun. But he also attended charity dinners that he would have avoided ten years before. At these events, Buckley, who is easily bored, sometimes went through the motions of being sociable. Clurman recalled one New York dinner party given in Buckley's honor at which he was seated next to one of the city's most prominent socialites, a woman whom Buckley had known and talked to for more than two decades. Buckley had arrived at the party somewhat frazzled from an out-of-town speaking engagement. At dinner, he divided himself equally in conversation between his hostess on his left and the prominent socialite on his right. After dinner, Buckley and Clurman escaped before the dancing started, and Buckley asked Clurman on the way out, "By the way, who was that woman I was sitting next to?"

In the long wake of the administration's failure to respond to the Polish coup, Buckley had become more concerned about the drift of the Reagan administation's foreign policy. While he remained supportive overall, he began to pressure the administration from the Right. In his columns, he reinvoked not only Burnham's early strategy of rollback, but also the apocalyptic, religious view of the clash between capitalism and communism that he had inherited from his father and that Chambers had articulated in *Witness*.

In February, Buckley called for the administration to declare war on Cuba. Admitting that the U.S. could not actually invade, Buckley nonetheless insisted "that it is difficult to think of a measure that would give greater heart to the entire anti-communist defense enterprise." [10] In May, he sharply criticized Reagan for offering to negotiate an arms control treaty with the Soviet Union four months after he had broken off talks in protest of the Polish coup.

In the last half of 1982, Buckley joined Evan Galbraith in pressing the administration to follow through on the main item in the list of sanctions it had announced after the coup—its embargo of all American-made parts slated for use in the Soviet–Western European natural-gas pipeline, including parts made by American subsidiaries overseas. When the administration rescinded the embargo in November—under pressure from the State Department, which believed that the action was harming U.S. relations with Western Europe more than it was harming the Soviet Union—Buckley and Galbraith both protested vigorously.

But when Buckley learned from a Wall Street friend of Shultz's that Galbraith was in danger of being fired as ambassador to France, he advised him to keep his peace. "It seems clear to me that this is not one we are going to win," Buckley wrote Galbraith. "If it is so, you should explore a way to exploit our reversal in such a way as to prove that you are a team player." [11]

Buckley had a trying winter in Switzerland. While he worked on a new Blackford Oakes spy novel, he agonized over his friend David Niven, who was then in the last and most debilitating stages of Lou Gehrig's disease. The previous year, Niven, who was suffering mysterious speech impairments and problems with muscle coordination, had gone, at Pat Buckley's urging, to the Mayo Clinic, where his disease was finally diagnosed. That winter, Niven and Buckley would go to paint in the atelier that they rented, and where Buckley also wrote. Niven worked on a painting of clouds that began pink and turned gray. Niven also "exchanged such conversation as he was capable of," Buckley said. By March, Niven was hospitalized.

From Switzerland, Buckley kept in touch with the administration through Tony Dolan. Buckley's criticisms had by no means alienated Reagan, who was himself torn between the different factions in his administration. Buckley's injunction that the President appear to be "the locus of anti-communist thought and action" also struck a responsive chord in Dolan, who kept on his coffee table, next to his Bible, a tribute he, Dolan, had written to Whittaker Chambers. In February 1983, Dolan wrote Buckley to complain about Kissinger's criticisms of the President's "rigid hostility" toward the Soviet Union. To understand the Soviet Union, Dolan wrote, one needed a "phenomenology of evil."

Buckley responded:

> You reach into deep waters, and the question really is whether a vocabulary that does not take into account the anti-Christ is suitable to define such convolutions as we are engaged in. There is no more difficult a point to communicate in a world essentially secular which simply thinks of the Soviet Union as another society given to occasional spasms of barbarism.[12]

A week after Buckley's letter to Dolan, Reagan delivered a speech in Orlando before the National Association of Evangelicals. The speech, drafted by Dolan, quoted Chambers and described the Soviet Union as the "focus of evil in the modern world" and as the seat of an "evil empire." When *New York Times* columnist Anthony Lewis attacked Reagan's speech for using sectarian religion to sell a political program, Buckley responded indignantly, "Mr. Reagan, as leader of the Free World, does well to remind us that we are dealing with men explicitly bound to the proposition that the morality of advancing world revolution is superordinated to any other morality."[13]

Buckley also took aim at the movement for arms control that Reagan's belligerence toward the Soviet Union had spawned in both the U.S. and Western Europe. Buckley was particularly vexed by the American Catholic bishops who were preparing a pastoral letter calling for the administration to initiate steps toward disarmament and questioning the utility—even as deterrent—of nuclear weapons. In April, without great enthusiasm from other editors, Buckley devoted the entire issue of *National Review* to Michael Novak's essay, "Moral Charity in the Nuclear Age," that was intended to answer the bishops.

Buckley introduced Novak's essay in prose that recalled the worst passages of *McCarthy and His Enemies* or *Up from Liberalism*. The bishops' doctrine, Buckley wrote, "is nothing less than an eructation in civilized thought, putting, as it does, the protraction of biological life as the first goal of modern man." [14]

Buckley also welcomed the President's March announcement of a program to create, as an alternative to MAD, a "space shield" that would prevent all nuclear weapons from reaching the U.S. But his initial comment on the new plan—dubbed "Star Wars" by the press and later the "Strategic Defense Initiative" by the administration—betrayed some skepticism about its technological feasibility. "Perhaps we will be taught by the legend of Tantalus that the kind of satisfaction we yearn for is not of this world. Tantalus could not get the fruit he reached for. But Tantalus thirsted—as we should thirst for the fruit of defense against nuclear weapons." [15] But within several months, he had been totally won over and was urging the administration toward "an early scientific breakthrough." [16]

V

That spring, when Buckley returned to the U.S., *Overdrive* appeared after having been excerpted in *The New Yorker*. Buckley's novels after the acclaimed *Stained Glass*—*Who's on First* and *Marco Polo, If You Can*—had been commercial successes, but had been slighted by reviewers. *Overdrive* drew a storm of criticism, as well as a host of parodies. Both the reviewers and the parodists highlighted the work's pomposity and self-absorption. In *The New York Times,* writer Nora Ephron called it "a book about money" and likened it to the "innocent vulgarity" of the memoirs that self-made immigrants wrote late in life. In the *Washington Post,* Grace Lichtenstein wrote that "when parts of this book first appeared in the *New Yorker,* I thought it was a joke, a Buckley parody of how some leftist might view Buckley's preoccupation with material possessions and his aristocratic lifestyle. Alas, it is not an intentional parody. . . . "

Some of Buckley's friends believed that it was intentional self-parody. Irving Kristol said that he found *Overdrive* "a little bit embarrassing but amusing. He can't help but '*épater la bourgeoisie*' so he complains about the length of Cadillacs. I thought he was being a bit willfully *méchant*." But Buckley denied that he was needling his critics. "I attempted to write about life as I experienced it," he said when confronted with this interpretation. "It simply happens to be the case that I have never in my entire life been without servants, maids, and chauffeurs.''

Other friends were appalled by *Overdrive*. John Leonard said:

I thought *Overdrive* was a piece of self-indulgence. He simply doesn't understand to this day that when you talk about getting your limousine customized that people are going to take offense; he doesn't understand it, he resents it. One of the questions you have to ask yourself is how much irony there is in the man. The style is ironic, but I sometimes wonder whether he really gets the irony.

But the most devastating comment on *Overdrive* was made by novelist John Gregory Dunne, a man who had known Buckley slightly— his wife, Joan Didion, had done her first writing for *National Review* —and whose novel *True Confessions* Buckley had praised, while later panning the movie that was made from it. Dunne's review in *The New York Review of Books* betrayed a certain malice, but the review's tone didn't detract from its understanding of its subject. "One inhales and becomes giddy on the high octane of Mr. Buckley's personality," Dunne wrote. "He is so sublimely unselfconscious, so 'blasphemously happy' with his own life that he wants to share with his readers what amounts to a 50,000-word advertisement for himself.''

Dunne suggested that the author was in a deep rut.

[Buckley] seems distracted and disjointed, as he approaches his fifty-eighth birthday. The show has been on the road too long. There have been too many plane trips, too many nights spent in Executive West hotels. Mr. Buckley has spread himself so thin that he has begun to repeat himself, repeatedly. *Overdrive* is *Cruising Speed Redux* as last year's *Atlantic High* is *Airborne Redux*. . . . As might be expected, Mr. Buckley is unrepentant. "The unexamined life may not be worth living," he writes, "in which case I will concede that mine is not worth living." He clearly does not believe it, but his is a performance sorely in need of the very examination he refuses to give it.[17]

Buckley was so stung by Dunne's review that he wrote a long response to his critics in the introduction to the paperback edition of *Overdrive*. But this reply also lacked the verve of earlier pieces. His problem was that the criticism of *Overdrive* was directed not at its politics—it could not be dealt with by an examination of premises— but at its author. Buckley speculated on why so many critics had fastened on his description of his limousine, conveniently ignoring the obvious explanation—that his careful description of its use and manufacture epitomized *Overdrive*'s superficiality. He insisted that his indoor swimming pool was really of "modest dimensions." He responded to Dunne's accusation that he was repeating himself by declaring that he had already planned the successor to *Atlantic High* and that with *Cruising Speed* he had discovered a "literary technique . . . so majestically successful I intend to repeat it ten years hence."

He demanded to be judged as a successful "performing writer." "We seem to concede . . . that only people who are technically qualified can satisfactorily perform on the piano before an audience. . . . I do not see why there should be so much difficulty in applying the same implicit criteria in order to distinguish what one might call the 'performing writer.' . . ."

Buckley didn't appear to understand why the book had upset reviewers—and readers. The problem was personal. Unwilling to recognize ignoble ambitions, vanities, and resentments in himself, he could not recognize their expression in his writing. He was a performing artist who had lost control of his medium, who could no longer shape and anticipate his audience's reactions.

VI

The malaise that had afflicted Buckley's books also had affected *National Review* and *Firing Line*. The magazine still printed well-written articles, and its headlines and short items displayed the same panache as of old, but like Buckley's column, it appeared detached from national politics and exerted very little influence. Those editors who worried about it blamed Buckley's own detachment. Sobran, who wanted the magazine to be politically relevant, was particularly exercised by a 1983 cover story on marijuana.

> *National Review* isn't a very topical magazine [Sobran said]. To have a cover issue on marijuana like we had. *Time* had just done cocaine. Can't we do "ludes" or something? Bill said to me afterwards, "You know five years ago when we ran that other piece on marijuana." Five years, it was almost eleven years ago. For Bill, it was yesterday.

Some readers and former editors complained that the magazine simply suffered from becoming part of the establishment that it once attacked. Dan Oliver thought *National Review* was "less interesting.

It doesn't have that aura of being something that one takes out to read in the park in a brown wrapper. I think what people miss is its being anti-establishment, but it can't be because Bill's establishment now."

With Meyer, Burnham, and Bozell gone, the magazine no longer shaped current political debate by raising it to a higher philosophical level, where the guiding assumptions became apparent. The new editors were talented writers, but they had very little background in philosophy and history, and most of their political experience was with the established Right. Rick Brookhiser, whom Buckley had recruited directly out of Yale, and Joe Sobran had been literature majors in college. Hart was an English professor at Dartmouth. In the five years since Burnham had retired, the editors had engaged in only one major debate—over the meaning of modernism, a literary concept.* There was nothing in the magazine that resembled Meyer and Burnham's heated debates over foreign policy and the welfare state or Meyer and Bozell's exchanges on liberty and virtue. Philosophically, the magazine was simply living off its early capital. "I think *National Review* is not as intellectually good as *The New Republic*," Ernest van den Haag said. "They ought to have articles that are deeper, that are concerned with serious intellectual questions, better intellectual caliber."

Both *Firing Line* and Buckley's column had thrived on controversy. Lacking controversy, *Firing Line* became more intellectual and less political, more of an exploration of issues, conducted under Buckley's patient prodding. Guests like Mortimer Adler, the sponsor of the Great Books, appeared regularly, and even the debates, with friendly antagonists like John Kenneth Galbraith, became predictable. Where the old *Firing Line* teetered precipitously on the edge of intellectual violence, the *Firing Line* of the eighties often risked academic obscurity and dullness. Even when Buckley had an old antagonist on the show, like former Yale chaplain William Sloane Coffin, he was polite and deferential.

Firing Line remained one of the few television shows on which serious questions were discussed at some length, but it was no longer good television. Buckley's audience could ask whether they might not

---

* The debate was set off when Hart, whose cultural views had gone full circle in a decade, wrote a glowing obituary in June 1980 for Henry Miller ("Miller was part of a cultural movement which expanded the individual's options") to which most of the editors, but especially Joe Sobran, took exception. Heated memos passed, and the next year Hart framed the issue in broader terms in "An Intelligent Woman's Guide to Modern American Conservatism," to which Brookhiser, Sobran, and Linda Bridges wrote responses.

get the same out of reading a book or a magazine. And his political audience largely abandoned the show. Pat Buchanan put the difference diplomatically, *"Firing Line* was a masterpiece. He would get the best they had, and he would tear them apart, and he would rarely, if ever, lose. But *Firing Line* has changed. It is much more academic and intellectual than it is combative. Now it is an exploration in issues rather than an engagement." Joe Sobran phrased it more bluntly, *"Firing Line* can be a real snooze."

Even Buckley's column suffered. During the first years of the Reagan administration, conservative activists stopped looking to Buckley's column for guidance. In the beginning, this was because of Buckley's reluctance to criticize the administration. But more important was his detachment from the struggles over policy and power taking place in Washington and the emergence of other conservative columnists who spoke more directly to the activists.

Buckley had to compete with the erudite George Will and with the well-informed Evans and Novak. When he took time with a column, he could write as well as anyone, but some of his columns were done hurriedly. He often relied on crutches like the listing of points or simply summarized articles published elsewhere. Editors who wanted one well-written conservative column in their paper began to opt for Will rather than Buckley. In 1981, the *Boston Globe,* the city's major paper, stopped running Buckley's column in part because the editorial-page editor preferred running George Will.

But Evans and Novak provided even more serious competition. Once liberals, they had moved far to the Right and were now promoting what they called the "Reagan revolution." Their columns were not distinguished by their writing, but by a combination of insider information and impassioned advocacy—both of which were now totally lacking in Buckley's columns.

VII

What had happened to the author of *God and Man at Yale*—the enfant terrible who fearlessly flayed the establishment? Some of Buckley's friends attributed the decline of his work to the absence of friendly and straightforward criticism from his peers.

Burnham had been lost to a stroke since 1978. Buckley had written him right before his debilitating stroke, "With the death of my father, no one else came near to occupying the same role in my life as you have done: as advisor, mentor, friend, companion." [18]

To some extent, Kissinger had come to play the role that Burnham had: he was the man to whom Buckley looked for theoretical guidance. When Christopher Buckley called his father on the phone, Buckley would not interrupt the call except to receive a telephone call from Kissinger. But Kissinger's influence was largely confined to foreign policy; and the two men lacked the intimacy that Burnham and Buckley, who had worked together for two decades, had.

Harry Elmlark, who had supervised Buckley's column from the beginning, had died on Christmas Eve 1980. Elmlark had constantly prodded Buckley to make his column topical. Now at the Universal Press Syndicate, no one ever challenged Buckley. Buckley's executive secretary, Frances Bronson, described the difference.

> Harry was a crusty Democrat, a lovely sounding board. Here [at Universal] it is a much more routinized thing. We're dealing with much younger people. They'll call me and ask about something that is not clear, but no one has ever called Bill about a point. Harry and Bill had a very special relationship. He could call and say, "How can you say that?!"

In *Firing Line,* producer Warren Steibel approved Buckley's turn toward a more academic format. "Bill can be very argumentative, and he can cut people down, but I think what emerged was something more." And Buckley's book editor, Sam Vaughan, reinforced the drift of his work. Vaughan attributed the compulsive narrative of his books to the speed with which he wrote them. "I got the hunch that it came about because of his scheduling. He set himself the task of producing a novel in ten or fifteen or twenty days. However he did it, I didn't want him to lose that."

Other friends blamed the pace of Buckley's life for the decline of his work. Since 1962, when he had begun writing his column, he had taken on one new responsibility after another. In the early eighties, he was writing one book a year, hosting *Firing Line,* editing *National Review,* giving more than fifty speeches a year, writing occasional free-lance pieces for the *New York Times* travel section or book review, keeping up with his correspondence, and enjoying the social life of a New York—and also Washington—celebrity. "He is more a prisoner of his commitments as he approaches sixty than he ever was in his thirties," Hugh Kenner said.

His schedule eliminated the kind of reading that he used to do. In 1982, Gerhart Niemeyer, an old friend, sent Buckley an article on natural law. Buckley wrote him back apologizing that he had "lost the capacity for reading scholarly prose." According to his son, he had "speeded up" as he got older. "It's gotten to where he can't sit through a movie. He'll put on a movie in Stamford after dinner, and five minutes later, he's gone."

Sophie Wilkins despaired that under the pressure of his schedule he would ever write a good novel. "Bill is on a track for doing things as fast as possible, and there is just no time to let the whole person get involved with it."

Buckley had become the victim of his own celebrity. He was swept up—and away—in that luminous world of entertainers, actors and actresses, and wealthy party-goers feted by gossip columnists for their style. Even those aspects of his life that were problematic—like the speed at which he wrote his columns and books—became grist for the celebrity mill.

Joe Sobran saw Buckley as being unable to disentangle his persona from his person. "Ortega y Gasset once said, 'We are all impersonators of ourselves,'" he said. "Bill has been impersonating himself for thirty years." Kenner traced Buckley's immersion in the world of a celebrity to the late sixties:

> I date his becoming a sort of *Today* show property from there. It's a slippery slide. It's hard to say at what point you become a personality and cease to be an educator. I think you reach the point before you realize it. Bill ceased to be a public outrage. He became an ingratiatingly unpredictable personality. He would say the most amazing things to Johnny Carson. And somewhere along the line the possibility of communicating specific encapsulated truths was abandoned.

Above all, Buckley seemed stifled by his own success. He had always functioned best in situations of intellectual and political adversity. He had been raised by his father to conceive of himself as part of an embattled minority that had been called upon to defend truth and goodness against the infidels. His best writing, from *God and Man at Yale* to *Cruising Speed,* had been conceived in a spirit of political combativeness. His public personality, evident at age seven when he wrote the king of England demanding that he pay his war debts, had been forged in the fires of militant opposition. Even his underlying philosophy—pitting the Remnant against the mass-man of mediocrity —assumed defeat and isolation.

With Reagan's victory and the heralding of a new political age,

Buckley's work and personality lost their edge. The most hated man in America became mellow and uninteresting. In *Firing Line,* he often seemed only half awake—not because he was about to fall asleep, but because, lacking combat, he lacked liveliness.

CHAPTER 25

Permanent Things

In November 1984, Ronald Reagan scored another landslide victory. Like the first, it was the result as much of good fortune and a weak opponent as of any underlying political shift toward Reagan's conservatism. Running against Carter's Vice-President, Walter Mondale, allowed Reagan to exploit the issues of Carter's inflation and Iran's Ayatollah Khomeini; and the election itself took place as the business cycle, which had hit bottom during the 1982 election, was on the rise. But it is significant that while Reagan won the presidency and the Republicans narrowly held on to the Senate, the Democrats maintained control of the House of Representatives.

By the beginning of Reagan's second term, the conservative agenda with which Reagan had taken office—lower taxes and higher military spending—had been exhausted; taxes could not be lowered further nor military spending increased without enlarging the record budget deficits that the Reagan fiscal policies had already incurred. With the attempt by new Soviet leader Mikhail Gorbachev to achieve reform at home and new arms accords with the U.S., the conservative foreign policy agenda—based upon the image of an evil empire seeking world domination—began to lose its hold. The remaining conservative initiatives—from a flat tax to the Strategic Defense Initiative (SDI) to support for the Nicaraguan "Contras"—did not enjoy widespread popular support. While liberalism still sputtered, the conservative moment was passing, leaving American politics stalemated.

Like many conservatives, Buckley was oblivious to the shift in the underlying political terrain. Instead of counseling caution and consensus, he called on the President to act as if he had gained an unequivocal conservative mandate from the election. In a postelection column cast in the form of a "secret memo" from Chief of Staff James Baker to the President, Buckley framed the President's choices in his second term: "You have basically two choices: To move dramatically—radically. Or to go gradually. The risk of the latter is far greater than the risk of the former. Because gradual movement is subject to erosion." Buckley wanted the President to press on Congress immediately a far-reaching right-wing agenda, including a return to the gold standard, a freeze on entitlement programs, a declaration of war against Cuba, and the creation of a "defense shield in space." Most of these measures lacked not merely popular support but support within the President's own party.[1]

Reagan's successes in his first term and his second victory also appeared to have removed whatever doubts Buckley had had about the President's ability. In a column, Buckley described Reagan as an "extraordinary president. . . . What he radiates is the kind of idealistic self-assurance that gave what seemed like everlasting life to the movement of Franklin Delano Roosevelt, and it is time everyone realized that this is what Ronald Reagan is up to."[2] At one of the Boys Club meetings, the liberals in the group asked Buckley if he didn't think Reagan was intellectually limited. According to Clurman, Buckley responded that "it was a great mistake to think that, and that actually he was full of substantial views on the most fundamental, basic questions."

Buckley defended Reagan against his critics even more tenaciously than he had during Reagan's first year. In the spring of 1985, Reagan's new Chief of Staff, Donald Regan, and Michael Deaver persuaded Reagan that during a trip to West Germany he should visit a cemetery at Bitburg where former Nazi storm troopers were buried. The gesture was meant as one of reconciliation, but it infuriated not only American Jews, but also veterans' organizations. Buckley defended Reagan's visit on the dubious grounds that Hitler had been defeated and that the Soviet Union was now the principal enemy of freedom. "There was no political vice practiced under Hitler that is not also practiced under the German proconsuls of Stalin and his successors," Buckley wrote.[3]

Buckley's relationship with Reagan remained as close as ever and his potential influence over the President virtually unmatched. In the summer of 1985, a controversy arose about reappointing AFL-CIO head Lane Kirkland to the Bureau for International Broadcasting. Kirkland had been highly critical of the President, and high-ranking White House staff members, including Director of Communications Pat Buchanan, had recommended that Kirkland not be reappointed. But several prominent conservatives, including Jim Buckley, Michael Novak, and Ben Wattenberg, lobbied for Kirkland's reappointment, arguing that Kirkland's support on Capitol Hill was essential to the bureau's funding. Buchanan decided they were right, and told Chief of Staff Don Regan, but Regan reported later that the President was adamant about not reappointing Kirkland. Then Buckley called Buchanan on Saturday to press for Kirkland's reappointment, and Buchanan sent Reagan a message that Buckley was for the reappointment. "It worked," Buchanan said. "He was reading some of the things that Kirkland had said about him just as he okayed the appointment."

I

In November of 1985, Buckley was to be sixty, and in spite of his enthusiasm for the President, he showed continuing signs of disquiet about his own life and work. In March, after Buchanan, who had become a highly successful columnist and television personality after resigning from the Ford administration in October 1974, had joined the administration as the director of communications, Buckley praised Buchanan's idealism and self-sacrifice, calling him a "warrior." But he also indirectly sought to justify his own decision to remain outside the administration and politics.

> It is commonplace in America to suppose that one is not "involved" in politics, at least not seriously involved in politics, if one isn't engaged in public office, or in running for public office. This is, simply, not the case: The editorial page of the *Washington Post* is more influential by a long shot than the votes of fifty congressmen or twenty senators.[4]

Buckley also displayed inordinate defensiveness about the lack of critical acclaim for his novels. That spring, the sixth and most wooden of his Blackford Oakes novels, *See You Later, Alligator,* was published. In May, he printed in "Notes and Asides" a letter to the editor of the *Arkansas Democrat* that criticized that newspaper's book reviewer for calling *See You Later, Alligator* shallow and that gushed about the novel's author. Buckley, the letter said, "has no question done more for our country in a number of important ways than any man this century."[5]

Two weeks later, Buckley excerpted and then replied to a critical review of *See You Later, Alligator* that had appeared in the *St. Louis Post-Dispatch.* "I'm among those who tend to agree with Buckley's politics but find Buckley himself a bit hard to take—too much money, too much Yale," the reviewer, Harry Levins, wrote. "People with names like Blackford Oakes make me uncomfortable, and I squirmed a bit as I spent 351 pages in his company." Buckley's reply was *ad hominem* and—for the Buckley of the 1980s—uncharacteristically venomous.

> If my name had been William Rosenberg, I had attended CCNY and Mr. Levins had felt an allergy to people with such names graduating from such a college, he would have had, one hopes, at least the decency to disguise, if not to surmount, his prejudice; and perhaps even the integrity to disqualify himself as a reviewer of Rosenberg's novels.[6]

II

On June 2, Buckley and ten companions, including his son, Christopher, Evan Galbraith, Dick Clurman, and professional photographer Christopher Little, set out from Honolulu to sail across the Pacific Ocean to New Guinea. The trip, which Buckley had been planning for more than two years, was to be the basis of magazine articles and of a book that Buckley would write in Switzerland the next winter.

The sail aboard the seventy-foot *Sealestial* was rougher than the Atlantic crossings. Squalls with winds higher than fifty miles per hour left the sailors continually drenched. There were also no opulent tourist stops along the way. But Buckley made up for the long stretches of sea by including provisions fit for a luxury cruise. Dick Clurman later wrote:

> We had everything: 300 hours of taped music, from Mozart to Motown, Bach to Basie; 30 movies for nightly, after-dinner viewing; a

potpourri of books from Joseph Conrad and Jane Austen to Elmore
Leonard and Erich Segal; five word processors for the four book-
writers aboard (one, for back-up); 40 cases of wine and champagne.
. . . We had both Old Coke (now "Classic") and New Coke (now
just "Coke"), soft drinks, beer, booze, and liqueurs, freezers
stocked with viands of every description; two ice-cube makers, one
battery-operated so we would never run out. Cigars from "21" and
Dunhill, Swiss chocolates and Tennessee Goo Goo bars.[7]

On the last night aboard the *Sealestial,* after thirty days at sea,
Buckley suddenly announced, "I've got a great idea for our next trip,
June 2, 1990. Rio de Janeiro, Brazil, to Cape Town, South Africa."[8]

That summer, *Life* magazine featured the sail, with a text by Buckley and photographs by Little. Buckley appeared anxious once again
to display his link to the administration. He told the story of the
commander of Johnston Island, where the U.S. stores poisonous gas,
meeting the *Sealestial* as it landed and informing the crew that they
would have to leave in two hours because of island security. But as
he was saying this, Galbraith was called away to the ship's overseas
phone to receive an urgent message from Vice-President George Bush
and then Buckley was called away to receive a message from his wife
that Nancy Reagan would be staying at their house. As the importance
of his visitors began to dawn upon the commandant, Buckley wrote,
his smile went to "half mast."

III

In October, Buckley and *National Review* went to court in Washington to sue the Liberty Lobby for libel. The very fact of the lawsuit
showed how the Right had changed over the prior three decades. The
Liberty Lobby was an outgrowth of the anti-Semitic and racist Right
of the fifties, and *National Review* had long ago dissociated itself and
conservatism from it. Formed in 1955, the Liberty Lobby favored the
deportation of blacks to Africa, bemoaned the influence of Jews and
Jewish organizations on American life, and declared the Holocaust to
have been a hoax.

In 1980, the Liberty Lobby had sued *National Review* for an article
that linked the organization to Lyndon LaRouche's National Caucus
of Labor Committees. Buckley and *National Review* countersued,
charging that in its newspaper, *Spotlight,* the Lobby had "recklessly
and maliciously" libeled *National Review* in articles written in 1979

and 1980. The articles had accused *National Review* of abandoning its political independence to become a "mouthpiece" of the Anti-Defamation League of B'nai B'rith; of advocating the right of "militant sex deviates" to molest children (based on *National Review*'s having printed a debate on gay rights in 1974); and of enjoying a "close working relationship" with the late American Nazi leader George Lincoln Rockwell. In 1983, a federal judge had thrown out the Liberty Lobby's suit against *National Review* and ordered *National Review*'s $16 million suit against the Liberty Lobby to trial.

National Review was represented by Conservative Party founder Dan Mahoney and the Liberty Lobby by Mark Lane—an erstwhile lawyer of the far Left who had become famous for his book attacking the Warren Commission's conclusions about John Kennedy's assassination. On the opening day, the bearded Lane, accompanied by a black legal assistant sitting at the defense table, laid out his case for the racist Liberty Lobby to the six-person all-black jury. Lane argued that *National Review* could not have been injured by the Liberty Lobby since it did not have a respectable reputation to harm.

> *National Review* since its inception has been a racist, pro-Nazi, pro-Fascist publication [Lane charged]. It has no good name. That is what this case is all about. . . . In a demonstration of *chutzpah*, they have come to this city to say "Protect our good name." You must determine what the good name of *National Review* is worth. The figure two cents keeps coming into my mind.[9]

Lane's first witness was Buckley himself. Slouched back in the witness seat as if he were hosting *Firing Line,* but without the benefit of his perennial clipboard, Buckley jousted with Lane for position, disarming him with quips. He responded to one Lane question, "I decline to answer that question; it's too stupid." He asked the judge, "When he asks a ludicrous question, how am I supposed to behave?" When Lane asked Buckley what his general assignment had been in the CIA, Buckley responded, "None of your business." When he asked him, "Have you referred to Jesse Jackson as an ignoramus?" Buckley responded, "If I didn't, I should have."

Lane trotted out quotations from the *National Review* of the fifties and sixties to demonstrate that Buckley was a racist. In 1958, Lane noted, *National Review* had headlined a story about Adam Clayton Powell, "The Jig Is Up." Brandishing a copy of the *American Heritage Dictionary,* to which Buckley had written an introduction, Lane cited the definition of "jig," "A Negro. An offensive term used derogatorily." On the stand, Buckley claimed that he had no idea that the word had a racial connotation.

> LANE: Words are to you what shoes are to a cobbler, isn't that correct?
>
> BUCKLEY: It's a clumsy metaphor because I don't make words like a cobbler makes shoes. I don't make words. I use words.

Mahoney and Buckley sought to establish *National Review*'s respectability by enumerating its ties with public figures, including Nixon, Reagan, and Kissinger. Buckley explained that he had hired Rockwell in 1955 to solicit subscriptions before Rockwell had become a Nazi and had sharply rebuked him after he had. He also noted that in 1969 he had written that the U.S. needed to elect a black President by 1980 and that he and Jesse Jackson had once discussed writing a book together.

After a two-week trial, the jury awarded *National Review* $1,001 in damages for the Liberty Lobby's having alleged that Buckley had a "close working relationship" with Rockwell. While it ruled that *National Review* had been libeled in two of the other instances, it awarded no damages for these. But Buckley's satisfaction from the verdict was lessened by news reports on the trial. He was angered by a *Newsweek* story that portrayed the trial as a battle between "two apostles of conservatism," Buckley and the Liberty Lobby's Willis Carto, and another in *The New York Times* that portrayed it as a fight "between two organs of the conservative movement, *National Review* and the Liberty Lobby."

Buckley wrote *Newsweek,* "No doubt your sleepy reporter, if he disdained the breed of the combatants, would have reported a lawsuit brought by the Black Panthers against the NAACP as just another nigger-fight." He wrote *The New York Times,* "I think that on reflection the author . . . would concede that a journal does not qualify as a 'conservative organ' merely by pointing out, say, the need for an army, navy, air corps, and national anthem in between references to the Zionist conspiracy and worries by its prime mover over the looming 'niggerfication' of America." [10]

IV

In the month spanning his birthday and *National Review*'s December birthday celebration, Buckley himself received even more attention from the press than he had five years earlier, but the kind of attention he received revealed the extent to which he had entered the pantheon of American celebritydom, in which he was valued not for what he said, but for the way he talked, dressed, and lived—indeed, for the apparent contradiction between his life-style and the political movement with which he was identified. In November, *People* ran a story about how Buckley—"America's most peripatetic puritan"— had written a children's book in two hours during a stopover after his sail across the Pacific.[11] *Time* wrote about how Buckley, the conservative, had become a convert to the most modern of gadgets, the computer word processor. And the *Washington Post* ran a two-page birthday feature on Buckley—in its "Style" section.[12]

Buckley scheduled *National Review*'s anniversary celebration for December at the Plaza Hotel. Earlier that fall, he had asked Reagan, Bush, and Kemp to come, and he wanted the banquet to feature presentations by the two leading conservative candidates for 1988. Reagan and Kemp had accepted as soon as they learned of the invitation, but Bush had waited two months before having his chief of staff telephone his regrets that the Vice-President couldn't appear because of his crowded December schedule. Buckley was annoyed with Bush's staff for trying to insulate the candidate, and he believed that Bush was also missing an important opportunity. "Bush has to polish his bombastic style and come up with something that appeals to the Right," he said.

Buckley attended to every detail of the party, including who should sit at what table and whether the names on the seating list should be printed flush left or centered. "I have such a horror of parties that don't work," he explained. Pat Buckley supervised the dinner at the Plaza, contributing her own recipe for the main course of chicken pot pie. And she also organized a brunch the next day for out-of-town guests and New York celebrities.

More than seven hundred invitees paid $175 each to attend the anniversary banquet. Because the President was to be there, each guest had to be surveyed by the Secret Service. As the banquet was to begin, the prominent guests, clad in black tie and ball gowns, waited to be searched on a long line that wound down the corridors of the Plaza. Even an emaciated Roy Cohn, in the last stages of AIDS, had to stand and wait. And, at the last minute, Buckley discovered that the President's entourage of staff and Secret Service would be so large that there would not be any room for television cameras in the banquet hall, except for those from *Firing Line*—a decision that infuriated the networks.

The master of ceremonies was actor Charlton Heston. Heston told the audience of the phone call he'd received from Buckley several weeks before. " 'Chuck,' he said, 'how do you feel about free speech?' Now I thought he was going to quote me an editorial or something. And so I hastened to assure him that of all the freedoms I treasure as an American citizen, the one I hold most precious is free speech. Bill said, 'That's wonderful, Chuck. We'd like you to come East and make one.' "

The speakers at the banquet expressed an abiding optimism about the conservative future. "What will the world look like thirty years from now, when *National Review* celebrates its sixtieth anniversary, in the year 2015, and conservative Presidents have been in office all that time?" Kemp mused. Joe Sobran exulted, "To a group disinclined to expect progress, progress can come as a happy shock. One of our readers has even proved that if you'd rather be right than be President, you can wind up being President." "In a hundred years, there is not a person or a thing in this room that will remain," Rick Brookhiser said. "But our ideas will remain."

Several speakers, including Jeff Hart and Buckley, invoked Whittaker Chambers's words to bear out the conviction that the enemy the U.S. faced was, indeed, an "evil empire." As Hart cited those words, Reagan, sitting next to Priscilla Buckley, leaned over and whispered, "It *is* an evil empire." The speakers also invoked Chambers to contrast the former Communist's pessimism about the West with the mood at the banquet that night. Buckley told the story of trying to convince Chambers that even if the West were "doomed to failure . . . the Republic deserved a journal that would argue the historical and moral case that we *ought* to have survived."

Reagan, speaking from his own presidential dais, set up on the side of the hall and looking across at the sea of seven hundred diners, applauded Buckley and *National Review*. "*National Review* is to the offices of the West Wing of the White House what *People* magazine is to your dentist's waiting room," Reagan said. "I want to assure you tonight: you didn't just part the Red Sea—you rolled it back, dried it up, and left exposed, for all the world to see, the naked desert that is statism."

Buckley was the last to speak, and he praised the President as extravagantly as Reagan had praised him and *National Review*. Calling Reagan's character "the conclusive factor in the matter of American security against ultimate Soviet aggression," Buckley concluded:

What at *National Review* we labor to keep fresh, alive, deep, you are intuitively drawn to. As an individual you incarnate American ideals at many levels. As the final responsible authority, in any hour of great challenge, we depend on you. I was twenty years old when the bomb exploded over Hiroshima. Last week I became sixty. During the interval I have lived as a free man, in a free and sovereign country. I pray that my son, when he is sixty, and your son, when he is sixty, and the sons and daughters of our guests tonight will one day live in a world over which that awful shadow has finally dissipated. Then they will be grateful that, at the threatened nightfall, the blood of their fathers ran strong.[13]

The next year marked the twentieth anniversary of *Firing Line*, and Warren Steibel arranged for a "celebrity roast" to take place as one of the regular weekly shows in January. The host was television critic Jeff Greenfield, whom Buckley had met two decades earlier when Greenfield, a Yale Law School student, had written a critical article on him for the *Yale Alumni Magazine*. Among the celebrities who roasted Buckley were writer Tom Wolfe, John Kenneth Galbraith, and Henry Kissinger.

Buckley sat by himself on the right of his guests. Behind him floated brightly colored balloons, with some of his favorite polysyllabic words, like "sesquipedalian," painted on them. Greenfield twitted Buckley on his defiance of television's standards and on his nervous habits on camera. Television was supposed to be a "visual medium," Greenfield said, "but the only element of visual interest on *Firing Line* is whether Mr. Buckley will ever part his hair with his tongue." Wolfe, wearing his perennial white suit, gave a speech that was mockingly insulting but also extremely penetrating. Wolfe noted how odd it was to be at a "celebrity roast" for Buckley. "You've finally managed to elevate *Firing Line* to Don Rickles and Dean Martin," Wolfe said.

Wolfe read a review of Buckley in which a liberal critic had called him a "national treasure."* "You can imagine the panic that set into Bill Buckley. You know what national treasure is a code word for. It means you're old, toothless, flabby, benign, no longer a threat to anyone. . . . Bill Buckley is in desperate need of insults. He is in desperate need of being thought of as a threat." Wolfe also opened up old wounds. He confided to the audience that to restore his reputation

---

* Conservatives shared this view of Buckley. In a symposium on "The State of Conservatism" organized by the Intercollegiate Studies Institute's *Intercollegiate Review*, Gregory Wolfe wrote, "With the exception of William F. Buckley, Jr., who is now tolerantly treated as a cultural institution, the postwar conservative movement has been defined out of existence." (Spring 1986.)

as "America's foremost polemicist," Buckley had invited Gore Vidal to appear on *Firing Line* the next week. "Are you talking about that queer?" Buckley interrupted Wolfe to ask.

Galbraith needled Buckley about the administration's acceptance of Keynesian economics ("First Keynes, and now Reagan, and now Buckley"), while Kissinger largely made fun of himself and praised Buckley. Buckley spoke briefly at the end. With gray suit rumpled from having slumped in his seat and his tie askew, and his hands shifting nervously from his jacket to pants pockets and back, Buckley said:

> I should acknowledge Jeff Greenfield's words as to the ascendancy of my ideas. He is quite right that I don't stoop to conquer. I merely conquer. . . . Nothing tires an audience more than expressions of gratitude. I'll refrain from expressions of political gratitude to Professor Galbraith to whom all of us owe so much for not exercising political power.

V

After the festivities of the fall and winter, Buckley suffered a letdown from the reception that his newest spy novel, *High Jinx,* received in March. It was either ignored or slighted by critics, and rightly so. It had the fast pace of his earlier spy novels, but in it Buckley appeared to have lost interest in all his major characters except for the Russian agent Boris Bolgin. Sophie Wilkins speculated that he had nothing new to say about Blackford Oakes. "He should not really be condemned to going on with these novels," she said.

But Buckley received some consolation from the fact that Christopher's first novel, *The White House Mess,* which was published at the same time, received glowing reviews and quickly appeared on *The New York Times* and *Washington Post* best-seller lists.

When he had joined Bush's speech-writing staff in 1980, Christopher Buckley had promised not to write a memoir of his experiences, but after working for Bush for a year and a half, he had quit to do the next best thing: write a fictional memoir of the chief aide to a Carteresque Democratic President who serves in office from 1988 to 1992. Buckley's memoir pokes fun at Republicans and Democrats. As it opens, the President-elect and his aide are desperately trying to convince a senile President Reagan to abandon the Oval Office. The writing is lively and taut.

Christopher had not only become an accomplished writer but a man of considerable charm. If Bill Buckley had had to learn to be nice, Christopher appeared to be so naturally. Less outgoing than his father, with a nervous tic that betrayed a sensitivity to the external world, he was possessed of his parents' wit, but not his father's appetite for polemical engagement. Conservative in his politics, he was not a political man.

Bill and Pat's fondest moment came when, at the end of April, Bill's *High Jinx* was fourteenth on the *New York Times* best-seller list and Christopher's book was tenth. Pat had the page framed and prominently displayed in the Buckleys' living room in Stamford.

VI

In mid-March, when Buckley returned to the U.S. from his Swiss vacation, he wrote a column for *The New York Times* proposing his own solution for slowing the city's deadly AIDS epidemic. It was as if he had taken Wolfe's words to heart and was trying consciously to restore his reputation as "America's foremost polemicist." To stop AIDS victims from infecting others, either through donating blood or through anal intercourse, Buckley proposed that AIDS victims be tattooed on the upper forearm and the buttocks. If AIDS victims wanted to marry, their spouses would have to agree to sterilization.[14]

Buckley's column prompted protests from liberals and from the city's gays. The *New York Native,* a gay newspaper, termed the proposal "Buckley's Buchenwald," referring to the Nazi practice of tattooing concentration-camp inmates. A gay coalition staged a demonstration in front of *National Review* with a leaflet that read:

Give Bill
Buckley a
Piece of
Your Mind
Before He
Tattoos
Your . . .

In "Notes and Asides," Buckley printed an angry exchange that he had had with author Robert Massie, whose son was a hemophiliac. Massie accused Buckley of following the Nazi precedent for "keeping track of undesirables marked for destruction." Buckley replied: "Your reliance for emotional effect on the Nazi precedent is disrepu-

table. Because the Nazis used barbed wire to separate human beings
has no bearing on the use of barbed wire to separate cows from
bulls.'' [15] Apparently it didn't occur to Buckley that by his analogy
AIDS victims—spared of being compared with concentration-camp
undesirables—had become cows and bulls.

Buckley delighted in the furor. He posted the demonstration leaflet
on the wall of his study in Stamford. According to one reporter who
accompanied Buckley on the radio and television interviews he did
for *High Jinx,* Buckley got a glint in his eye and uttered a mock ''uh,
oh'' when it became apparent that he would have to defend his views
on AIDS victims.

But unlike other conservatives, Buckley did not intend to stigmatize
homosexuals. That summer, he infuriated New Right conservatives
by featuring on the cover of *National Review* a long criticism of his
position by an anonymous gay conservative.

Buckley also stirred up controversy among conservatives by a
statement he made regarding South Africa. During one of the annual
Firing Line shows in which three journalists question him, *Newsweek*
bureau chief Morton Kondracke asked Buckley whether, if he were a
South African black, he would join the African National Congress
(ANC), the chief anti-apartheid guerrilla organization.

> BUCKLEY: I probably would, yes. I probably would. Unless my
> knowledge of the internal balance of power led me to
> think that [Zulu tribal chief Gatsha] Buthelezi would
> fight a little bit more aggressively than he is now
> doing.
> KONDRACKE: Would you be willing to use violence in order to alter
> the South African regime?
> BUCKLEY: Absolutely. [*Then seeing the technician's signal.*]
> Gentlemen, thank you very much.

Buckley's response angered conservatives, who identified the ANC
with communism and backed the white Botha regime. Buckley tried
to clarify his stand in a column. He acknowledged that the ANC was
controlled by Communists and warned that he did not favor a change
in the present administration's hostility to the ANC, but he still insisted, ''Can you reasonably expect a desperate black South African
to do something else, given existing alternatives?'' Buckley's column
displayed a knowledge of the impulses that had originally led him to
conservatism as well as an ability—lacking in many conservatives—

to empathize with the underdog. But there was undoubtedly an element too of what Rusher called Buckley's tendency to *"épater la
bourgeoisie."*

The column led to rejoinders by *Washington Times* columnist John
Lofton and by Rusher in his own syndicated column. Buckley's position, Lofton wrote, "reveals him to be an armchair revolutionary, a
playpen *putschist.*" [16]

VII

In the wake of *National Review*'s thirtieth anniversary, Buckley
made important changes at the magazine. Priscilla Buckley retired as
managing editor, although she remained as a senior editor, and Buckley chose Rick Brookhiser to replace her. On the magazine, it was
understood that if Brookhiser did well in the job, he would be in a
good position to succeed Buckley when he retired.

Brookhiser's association with Buckley began when as a high-school
student he wrote a letter to *National Review* lamenting the spread of
the antiwar movement, and Buckley printed it in "Notes and Asides."
Buckley had kept track of him at Yale, publishing his articles and
taking him on as an intern for two summers. After graduation he hired
him, and when Brookhiser threatened to go to law school three years
later, he made him the youngest senior editor in the magazine's history. In a letter to Sam Vaughan, Buckley described Brookhiser as a
"cool conservative. . . . He is a young man who was born when the
tide was turning, and therefore he doesn't come at it the same way as
conservatives of my generation come at it." [17]

But lacking passion, Brookhiser's writing also lacked depth; he
tended to tiptoe gracefully on the surface of subjects, and was extremely unlikely to give offense in his writing. Brookhiser's best work
was fair and accurate; his worst, uninteresting. But the qualities of
objectivity that made his writing less interesting made him a promising
person to lead *National Review* in Buckley's absence.

In his first year on the job, *National Review* became more topical.
There were more Washington stories, and more debate within the
magazine about the conservative future. But the magazine continued
to print the kind of conservative fantasy disguised as theory that
would have offended Burnham. In one of these, "The Right to Life
and the Restoration of the American Republic," unsuccessful gubernatorial candidate Lew Lehrman, not content to argue that abortion
was immoral, insisted that the debate over it, already cooling by the
time he wrote, would dominate politics over the next decade and

would be comparable in intensity and historic importance to the debate over slavery prior to the Civil War.

The other younger senior editor on the magazine was Sobran, but there was never any question that he could assume the leadership of *National Review*. A congenitally disorganized person whose desk was invisible under mounds of books and papers, Sobran had proved worse than useless as a functioning editor and had been relegated to writing a biweekly article or review. He lived in the Washington, D.C., suburbs and commuted every other week to editorial meetings.

Sobran was an entirely different person and writer from Brookhiser. A graduate of Eastern Michigan rather than Yale, of lower-middle-class and Eastern European ancestry, Sobran still seethed with the unruly passions of his class and background. Other editors were sometimes offended by his remarks about blacks and other minorities. Twice divorced, he had nonetheless become a champion of the Christian family and an outspoken opponent of gays, feminists, and abortion rights advocates.

At his best, when he was in control of himself, Sobran's writing had the wit, anger, and erudition of the younger Buckley. His weekly book reviews were among the best writing in the magazine. But in his syndicated column, where the *National Review* editors could not restrain him, and where he was expected to write about a range of subjects beyond his own expertise, Sobran allowed his darker impulses freer rein. In the spring of 1986, Sobran embroiled himself and eventually Buckley in a bitter controversy with Jewish neo-conservatives.

Sobran had quarreled with Jewish neo-conservatives before. He had been critical of Israel's hostility toward Palestinian rights and of American reliance upon Israel in the Mideast. But Sobran's views on these subjects were hardly anti-Semitic, being no different than those of some Jewish liberals and members of the Israeli peace movement. But in April 1985, defending Reagan's visit to Bitburg, Sobran appeared to step over the line separating criticism of Israel from anti-Semitism. He took gratuitous swipes at the "Jewish lobby" in Washington and suggested that *The New York Times* "change its name to *Holocaust Update*."

At the beginning of the year, Buckley advised him to be careful in writing about Jews and Israel, but the next April, Sobran ascribed *The New York Times*'s support of the Reagan administration's raid against Libya to the ulterior motives of its Jewish ownership. "One of America's most ardently Zionist newspapers understands that Israel has its own reasons for desiring to pit the United States against the whole

Arab world," Sobran wrote.[18] Then he wrote a column praising *Instauration,* a virulently anti-Semitic and racist magazine, as "often brilliant," and another column criticizing Jews who had complained of the pope's reluctance to recognize Israel for failing to realize that Jews had persecuted Christians as much as Christians had persecuted Jews.[19]

Sobran's columns provoked an angry open letter from Midge Decter, the director of the Committee for the Free World and the wife of *Commentary* editor Norman Podhoretz. Decter accused Sobran of being "little more than a crude and naked anti-Semite."[20] Decter sent a copy of the letter to Buckley and seven other prominent conservatives, and articles on the dispute appeared in the *Washington Times* and *The Nation.* Buckley, who was extremely fond of Sobran, was forced into the fray.

Brookhiser had warned Buckley about Sobran's columns, so he was not surprised when he received Decter's letter. But he took offense at Decter's characterization of Sobran. "I very much regret the tone of your letter," Buckley wrote to Decter. Buckley denied that Sobran was a "crude anything. And beyond that, he is not a naked anti-Semite, nor, in my opinion, a crypto or even a latent anti-Semite." But Buckley acknowledged that if one did not know Sobran, one might be led to conclude that the author of the columns was "animated by anti-Semitism. . . . What Joe needs to know is that certain immunities *properly* attach to pro-Israel sentiment for historical reasons."[21]

Decter wrote Buckley a conciliatory response. "I ought not to have addressed myself to Joe's person but only to his words," she wrote.[22] But she reasserted her conviction that Sobran's columns were crudely anti-Semitic. And other conservatives conveyed their anger to Buckley through the Reverend Richard John Neuhaus, a Lutheran pastor and *National Review*'s religion columnist, who was also on the *Commentary* masthead. At *National Review*'s quarterly editorial conference at the end of May, Buckley, with the support of Hart, Priscilla Buckley, and Brookhiser, tried to explain to Sobran how writings that are "abstractly defensible [could] nonetheless strike non-tendentious people as anti-Semitic." Sobran refused to recognize that he had given grounds for offense—except to say that he should have qualified his praise for *Instauration.* He insisted that he was being victimized by Decter, Podhoretz, and other Jews. But Buckley demanded that he not write any more about Israel and Sobran agreed. Buckley also decided that he would have to make a public statement on the affair, and he composed a long statement for "Notes and Asides" that he read to the other senior editors, including Sobran, before he published it in *National Review*. It was "terribly painful" to do, he said later.

Buckley stated that he did not think Sobran was an anti-Semite, but he acknowledged that Sobran had violated the "prevailing taboos respecting Israel and the Jews. . . . Accordingly I here dissociate myself and my colleagues from what we view as the obstinate tendentiousness of Joe Sobran's recent columns."[23]

Sobran was very hurt by Buckley's statement. He composed a seven-page reply that Buckley was willing to print, but that Hart and Priscilla Buckley counseled against. Sobran agreed to cut it down, and after working several weeks on a reply, he gave up on it. Privately, Sobran compared his experience to that of Chief Justice-elect William Rehnquist, who was then being accused of bigotry by Democrats on the Senate Judiciary Committee. And he compared Buckley unfavorably to Victor Navasky, the editor of *The Nation,* who had come to the defense of Gore Vidal when Podhoretz had accused Vidal of anti-Semitism.

Buckley's stand was criticized by liberals who charged, with some justice, that he had reduced Sobran's anti-Semitism to incorrect decorum toward Israel. In a column in the *Washington Post,* Richard Cohen called on Buckley to fire Sobran. But Midge Decter, who knew Buckley personally and was aware of his loyalty to friends and employees, appreciated the step Buckley had taken in publicly dissociating himself and the magazine from Sobran. "I think he acted splendidly," Decter said. "I know he finds it very difficult to do things like this."

The incident didn't diminish Buckley and Sobran's friendship, and Sobran continued to write regularly for *National Review,* but it cast further doubt upon the kind of leadership that the magazine would have in the years ahead.

VIII

In the summer of 1986, with Reagan's presidency entering its last quarter, Buckley began to press the administration to make a conservative mark on the future. This put Buckley into direct conflict with the President for the first time.

The administration's most important initiatives, Buckley thought, were its Strategic Defense Initiative and its attempt to overthrow the Sandinista government in Nicaragua. In a series of columns in June, he called for the administration to abrogate the 1972 anti-ballistic missile treaty—"that grave strategic millstone around our neck"—in order to open the way for the testing and deploying of SDI.[24] Then in July, he turned to the problem of overthrowing the government of Nicaragua.

To explain why the U.S. needed to overthrow the Sandinista government but not the Pinochet government in Chile, Buckley invoked former Senator William Fulbright's dictum that "the government of the United States has no quarrel with any country, however obnoxious its doctrines, so long as it does not seek to export them. Apply that rule, and you distinguish instantly between Nicaragua and Chile, or the Philippines, or—at least for the present—China."[25] In fact, since 1981, Nicaragua's Sandinista government had stopped sending military aid to El Salvador's rebels.

At the end of June, Reagan finally got Congress to agree to $100 million in aid to the Contras, including $70 million for arms. But in a column, Buckley argued persuasively that "there is no way the Contras can overthrow the existing government." Instead, the Contras would execute "feats of terrorism" against the regime that would greatly diminish the American public's enthusiasm for backing them. Thus, the Reagan policy was self-defeating.

Buckley insisted that Reagan should "acknowledge that there are circumstances under which we would need to engage our military directly" even if doing so would "antagonize marginal congressmen." But how should the military intervene? Buckley ruled out an American blockade because "this means protracted engagements with international protocols that provide for freedom of the seas." Then he also ruled out "oblique military activity over a prolonged period of time" because "it is inconsistent with the American temper to proceed at a fitful pace."[26] This left only one alternative, which Buckley did not state: a massive invasion that would quickly dispatch the Sandinista government.

Buckley's prescription for a cure recalled the military fantasies of Meyer and Schlamm in 1956. While he was calling for the President to state the options more clearly, he could not state them clearly himself.

In July, Buckley became worried that under pressure from the State Department and from Senate Republicans, Reagan was going to make a deal with the Soviet Union that would threaten SDI. That month, Reagan sent Soviet Premier Gorbachev a letter proposing that the ABM treaty be extended for seven and a half years. In August, to aid Republicans in farm states, he worked out an arrangement by which American farmers would be subsidized to sell wheat to the Soviet Union at less than domestic prices. *National Review* hit back in two critical editorials, charging that in offering to extend the ABM treaty, the President was "straying somewhat from his original, unqualified commitment" to SDI, and that in subsidizing Soviet grain imports, the administration had "pre-emptively conceded any future dispute with the Europeans." [27]

Reagan called Buckley to defend his position on the grain exports and the ABM treaty—the first time he had called on his own behalf since becoming President. SDI, Reagan told Buckley, could not be deployed within seven and a half years. But Buckley still contended that by granting any extension to the treaty, the President was legitimizing its use as a tool of disarmament and threatening SDI down the road.

At the end of September, Buckley became alarmed by a succession of events. First, the U.S. arrested a suspected Soviet spy in New York, then the Soviet Union arrested on spying charges American reporter Nicholas Daniloff; when the Soviets released Daniloff, the U.S. released the suspected Soviet spy, and Reagan and Gorbachev announced that they would meet in early October in Reykjavik, Iceland, to prepare the groundwork for a future summit. But here the very depth of his misgivings—and the chorus of criticism from other conservatives—led him to mute his own criticisms of the President.

Instead of accusing the President of appeasing the Soviet Union, Buckley took the indirect approach of saying that *"l'affaire Daniloff"* confirmed that "the democratic free world can't hope to win up against the totalitarian monolith." He blamed Reagan's unwillingness to take a tougher stand and to hold off on the summit on "America's peaceniks." [28] But Reagan was upset by Buckley's charge that the Soviets had forced the U.S. to exchange Daniloff and again called to explain that the release of Daniloff and of the suspected Soviet spy had been "discrete events."

In a column on the pre-summit summit, Buckley, while displaying his disquiet, again pulled his punches. Using the format of an interview with himself, he voiced conservatives' qualms about the meeting, but then let Reagan have the last word.

Q.—Well, are you saying that conservatives have lost their confidence in their Evil Empire anti-Communist leader?
A.—Yup. Many have. Now what's interesting is that some think that withdrawal of confidence is premature—
Q.—Why premature?
A.—Because some conservatives have reason to believe that Reagan is moving in on the Soviet Union, taking special advantage of Soviet weaknesses it does not pay him publicly to advertise.

According to Buckley, Reagan was counting on Soviet fears of SDI to allow him to "dictate . . . the terms of Soviet strategic retreat."[29]

At Reykjavik, Reagan was hopelessly outmaneuvered by Gorbachev, who made it appear that only Reagan's commitment to SDI stood in the way of an agreement—already intimated by the President —to ban all nuclear weapons in ten years. Buckley was stunned by Reagan's performance: not only by the jeopardy in which he placed SDI, but also by his willingness to agree, without consultation with his Joint Chiefs of Staff or American allies, to a plan for eliminating all nuclear weapons, putting the U.S. and its allies at the mercy of the balance of conventional forces. But in his first column after the summit, he barely indicated his misgivings about the President's performance. Instead, he made Reagan's rejection of a compromise on SDI the stuff that heroes are made of.

> Ronald Reagan's faith in his own insights is a continuing inspiration, and I will happily contribute to any monument that would memorialize the chief of these, for instance: "ON THIS PODIUM ON MARCH 23, 1983, PRESIDENT RONALD WILSON REAGAN ANNOUNCED HIS STRATEGIC DEFENSE INITIATIVE, WHICH LED TO LIFTING THE NUCLEAR HOLOCAUST THAT TORMENTED MANKIND DURING MUCH OF THE 20TH CENTURY."
>
> Mr. Reagan saved the day by acting on that insight, but it was a very narrow miss, and the circumstances of the occasion have hugely enhanced the resources of the enemy, foreign and domestic.[30]

In his next column, he urged Republicans not to be defensive about the results of the summit. "The task of the Republican Party reduces to saying Iceland proved that Soviet disarmament proposals aren't on the level."[31] A week later, he was beginning to acknowledge that Reykjavik had been a disaster. In a weak column consisting largely of quotations from *The New York Times,* Buckley concluded, "We are discovering, inch by inch, day by day, that the improvised arrangements in the hot flushes of exchanges between Mr. Reagan and Mr. Gorbachev would have been disastrous in their implications."[32]

In the November elections, the Democrats won back the Senate. *National Review* editorialized, "Reagan's last two years can be like Eisenhower's, from 1958 to 1960, or like what everyone assumed would be Truman's, from 1946 to 1948: a diminuendo or a free fall."[33]

Then the same week, the administration confirmed news reports out of the Mideast that it had been secretly negotiating with and sending arms to Khomeini's Iranian government. While the administration denied that the arms shipments had any bearing on the release of hostages held in Lebanon by pro-Iranian Shi'ite Muslims, there was strong evidence that the administration had, in fact, been exchanging arms for hostages—an act directly at variance with its own pronouncements.

According to one *National Review* editor, Buckley was "incredibly pissed off." Buckley blamed Reagan's chief of staff Don Regan and his national security adviser John Poindexter for the mess, and he tried to put Reagan's motivations in the best light, but he still could not avoid sharply criticizing the administration.

> In defense of Mr. Reagan, it is only fair to acknowledge that it is not easy, in the same room with a wife of a hostage, to adhere to the transcendent position: We do not bargain with terrorists. But no one ever said it was easy to be president, and what we have now is a country that wonders whether it is safe to rely on the word of that government.
>
> Meanwhile, we have got two hostages back, and endangered the lives and liberty of who knows how many more Americans at the hands of terrorists who have learned that terrorism pays.[34]

Then Buckley drew back again. His next column on the Iran deal a week later accepted the administration's claim that "the overriding purpose of Operation Iran was to encourage the 'moderates' within the country." And after making some observations on the operation's effect on U.S.–European relations, he turned to the question, "Is there any role for covert operations?"—which he answered affirmatively.[35]

With Reykjavik, Buckley's initial impulse to defend overwhelmed his critical instincts; it was only a week later that he allowed his deeper misgivings to show through. But Iran appeared to be a case of administration bungling rather than Presidential ineptitude, and Buckley's critical instincts won out. It was only after Operation Iran began to cast a shadow on Reagan's presidency that Buckley closed ranks with the President.

The succession of events—Daniloff, Reykjavik, the November election, Operation Iran—undermined Buckley's confidence in the

President and reinforced his pessimism about the conservative future.
Buckley reverted to formulations that rang of the 1950s rather than
the 1980s. He began to see conservatives again as part of an embattled
minority in a country and world dominated by others. And this perception unleashed an eloquence that had been absent for six years.

On November 18, the Ethics and Public Policy Center, a Washington lobby that had originally made a name for itself defending right-
wing governments against Carter's human rights policies, had its tenth
anniversary banquet at the Washington Hilton Hotel. The Center had
decided to award Buckley the "Shelby Cullom Davis Award," given
each year to an "outstanding leader in public service." The large hall
was filled with Buckley's admirers and with the policy makers, corporate executives, and Washington lobbyists who backed the Center's
work.

The Center's director, Ernest Lefever, had recruited the President
himself to speak in Buckley's honor. Reagan arrived as the banquet
was beginning and joined Buckley and the other speakers and their
wives at the long table on the stage. Before the President spoke, he
and Buckley chatted for a few minutes. "He seemed absolutely airborne," Buckley recalled. Reagan apologized that he was going to
have to leave after he spoke. "I didn't know I was going to speak
before you," he said. "Nancy is in New York, and I was looking
forward to spending the whole evening with you. Sometimes my keep-
ers just overprotect me."

"Yes, and sometimes they don't," Buckley replied.

Reagan's speech matched his mood. It was genial and entirely up-
beat. He made his usual joke about his friend's use of big words:
"You know, I always appreciate the phone calls I get from Bill. I
remember one just before Reykjavik. 'Mr. President,' he said, 'would
you indulge me a timorous moment of matitutinal disquietude?' And I
said, 'Hold the line, Bill, I think my scrambler's still on.' "

Then Reagan described the enduring changes in popular values and
perceptions wrought by conservatives and his administration. In the
seventies, Americans "had lost all sight of the enduring truth [of Judaeo-Christian values]. . . . And with no values to defend they spoke
as if nothing in this great nation were worth defending." But, Reagan
said, Americans had "rediscovered" their "values in these last few
years, and now all the democratic world is discovering them too."
Reagan illustrated his own optimism about the conservative future
with a story about the former heavyweight champion Joe Louis. At a
patriotic rally in Madison Square Garden during World War II, Louis

"stepped to the microphone, spoke one simple line and brought the crowd roaring to its feet. He said, 'We will win, because we're on God's side.' "

Buckley spoke at the end of the evening after a parade of dignitaries, including former U.N. ambassador Jeane Kirkpatrick and former congressman Donald Rumsfeld, had paid homage to him and to Lefever's Center. Pat Buckley was at the head table with him, and Christopher and several of his nieces and nephews were in the audience. Buckley had worked carefully on the speech, and he had even brought several copies with him in case members of the press asked for them. But as he spoke, he veered from the prepared text, interpolating comments on the President's speech.

It was one of his best speeches. It combined wit, anecdote, and Buckley's stubborn insistence on incorporating the most abstract ideas into an after-dinner speech. And it was delivered almost without intonation, in a way that let the intricacies of phrasing rise to the surface. The audience twittered, chuckled, and was utterly spellbound.

Buckley told his own obligatory Galbraith Story.

Last Friday, I received a letter from Professor John Kenneth Galbraith. "Dear Bill," it began. "I've now had two invitations and a telegram from James Goldsmith [chairman of the Center] asking me to attend a dinner later this month celebrating your public ethic. The price, $7,500, seems entirely appropriate for so rare a commodity."

But then he launched into the subject of his speech, the attempt to "bridge between the paradigm and the particular: the criterion and actuality."

That which ought to be, and that which is, are always different, but the relationship between the two should be kinetic: we should know that we ought to strive, and what for. And although the President tells us that we have recovered from the period when "too many had lost all sight of enduring truth," we need to acknowledge, fatalistically, that the assault on the very idea of permanent things is by no means something that happened only yesterday, nor something done only by infamous names.

Buckley returned to the theme of *God and Man at Yale* and *Up from Liberalism:* the tyranny of the laissez-faire theory of knowledge and of ideological pluralism. "Many leaders of thought in America are constrained by a dogmatic egalitarianism to accept the notion that the toleration of pluralism commits us to the proposition that all ideas are equal.'' This dogmatic egalitarianism led to the hypocrisy of academic freedom, ''the right of a mother to kill an unborn child,'' and ''the notion that in exercising his right to attend a black mass, a citizen can consecrate a profanation. . . . Under the banner of pluralism, all we can with philosophical confidence say is that Khomeini's Islamic Fundamentalism is simply their version of our Judaeo-Christian faith.''

Buckley was subtly reproaching Reagan for his unwarranted optimism, while reminding the audience—by the very mention of Khomeini—of the basis for his own current pessimism. He came back to Reagan's reference to Joe Louis and, in the process, to his growing doubts about Reagan and his men in the Oval Office.

> I like to think that I share the ultimate confidence of Joe Louis, as described by the President. But I am often reminded of the little boy with precocious horticultural skills who tended a tiny twenty-foot-square garden in a corner of the slum where he lived. He was visited one day by a priest who exclaimed over the floral enclave. ''That is a beautiful garden you and God built,'' he commented. ''Yeah,'' said the boy, ''but you should have seen it when only God was taking care of it.''

Buckley received a thunderous ovation. Christopher Buckley believed that ''he never spoke better.'' But to Buckley's disappointment, no reporter asked him for a copy of his speech afterwards. And while the event and Buckley's speech were mentioned in several gossip columns, the contents of the speech were not discussed.

The day after Buckley spoke at the banquet, Reagan stumbled and contradicted himself at a press conference on the Iran operation. Then, the next week, Attorney General Ed Meese announced that one of Reagan's National Security Council aides, Lieutenant Colonel Oliver North, had diverted funds from the Iran arms sales to arms for the Contras—in violation of a congressional ban then in effect on military aid to the Nicaraguan rebels. What had been a political embarrassment now had become a scandal.

Buckley and *National Review* again closed ranks behind the President, but unlike some conservatives, they did not defend North or National Security Adviser Poindexter, who resigned at the same time North was fired. They insisted that the scandal was caused by the insubordination of Reagan's aides, and Buckley called on North and

Poindexter to tell their version of events before congressional committees rather than taking the Fifth Amendment. At Buckley's suggestion, Reagan had the White House lawyers contact North's and Poindexter's lawyers to suggest that the two testify, but it was to no avail.

Buckley also contended that the scandal stemmed from the "incoherence" of the administration's policy toward Nicaragua. Knowledgeable observers, Buckley wrote,

> speak of bad advice given to the president in respect of clandestine activity. But surely the worst advice he has got has to do with his continuing schizophrenia on the matter of the Sandinista government. On the one hand, we recognize it, on the other hand we send arms, overt and covert, to the Contras, and finally, we more or less pledge not to use American forces to overthrow that government.[36]

Privately, Buckley despaired over Reagan and the last years of his term. He told associates that in handling the Iran-Contra scandal, Reagan was "incapacitated." He fretted about Reagan's cancer in such a way that it appeared that he was displacing fears of Reagan's dwindling mental capacity onto his body. He worried about Reagan's loss of optimism. "I don't think Reagan can ever recover the kind of leverage he once had," Buckley said. "He has touched pitch."

Epilogue

By removing the magical aura that Reagan had cast over conservative politics, the Iran-Contra scandal revealed the extent to which the conservative movement that Buckley had helped to build was losing its moorings. It was adrift in the world of the late eighties —a world very different from that of the mid-fifties in which it had begun.

The clearest evidence of drift was the lack of a national leader. Since the late fifties, the conservative movement had always had a presidential candidate—first Goldwater, then briefly Agnew, and then Reagan. Now there were claimants to the throne, but no anointed successor. The lack of a leader was symptomatic of the absence of underlying political consensus.

During the fifties, Buckley and *National Review* had generated the conservative movement out of a synthesis of apocalyptical anticommunism and free-market capitalism. Conservatives had stumbled over the Sino-Soviet split and China's turn to the West; and now in the eighties they had not been able to come to terms with Soviet Premier Mikhail Gorbachev's quest for reform at home and arms negotiation abroad. Was Gorbachev's *glasnost* simply a ruse? Were his arms proposals simply part of a publicity offensive designed to divide the West?

Conservatives were even less able to contend with the looming budget and trade deficits that their free-market policies had helped to create. Kevin Phillips was one of the first defectors from the supply-side camp. In *Post-Conservative America* and then in *Staying on Top,* Phillips argued for Japan-style government intervention in the economy to meet Asia's and Western Europe's economic challenge. And while Reagan himself still trumpeted the virtues of the free market, his Treasury Department moved steadily away from the conservatives' free-market doctrine toward the kind of policies Phillips espoused. When the stock market crashed in October 1987, and revealed in one stroke the superficiality of the Reagan recovery, conservatives seemed bewildered—unable to agree on whether to seek further tax cuts or attend to the rising budget deficit.

In the fifties, the conservative movement had been divided between a conservative intellectual elite, led by Buckley and *National Review,* and a base of McCarthyites, segregationists, and anti–New Dealers. ("Our most deeply buried fear," Aloise Buckley Heath wrote of *National Review* in the fifties, "was that Gerald L. K. Smith was the only other conservative in America."[1]) Goldwater and then Reagan had broadened the conservative base and mediated between the politics of the conservative elite and the politics of the larger public. But now the conservative base threatened to split between a fundamentalist hard core, reminiscent of the early fifties, and a more moderate upper-class constituency with little allegiance to the conservative movement. The coalition between economic and social conservatives that the New Right had helped form in the late seventies was sundering.

American conservatives were not returning to the dark days of the early fifties. During the seventies, they had created a network of foundations, think tanks, lobbies, and political action committees that they had expanded during the Reagan years. They had also nurtured the cadre of policy makers and public officials that they had lacked two decades before. And through Reagan administration judicial and agency appointments, they had gained a long-term foothold in government. But conservatives were entering another period of drift and uncertainty like that of the mid-sixties and mid-seventies, when they would have to rethink and rebuild.

Buckley had been singularly responsible for transforming the fractious and irrelevant Right of the early fifties into a conservative movement, and he had helped to steer conservatives through their crisis of confidence after Goldwater's defeat, but he had played a more passive role after Watergate, even becoming briefly a target of New Right criticism. Buckley's influence had revived somewhat during the Reagan years, but he was no longer at the center of conservative politics. This was mostly by choice—he had adopted in the mid-seventies a routine and a pace that precluded ongoing political involvement or reflection. Even as the Reagan administration's crisis was deepening in the winter of 1987, Buckley was off to Switzerland to write a new Blackford Oakes novel.

But Buckley's lack of influence was also the result of the fact that while he had long abandoned the radical tactics of the fifties Right, he was still wedded to priorities and principles of that earlier era. He still clung to the verities of the free market, rejecting any criticisms of the administration's economic policies. On the eve of the October crash, Buckley declared that "supply-side economics [had] done pretty well."[2] And after the crash, *National Review* urged tax cuts and increased incentive for stock speculation.

Buckley also held virtually the same view of the Cold War that he had held when writing *God and Man at Yale*. During the Nixon-Ford years, he had supported Nixon for re-election and defended Kissinger against his critics, but he had never accepted the political premises that led to Nixon's pact with China or Kissinger's willingness to pursue détente. As the Reagan administration had begun to falter in its second term, Buckley's impulse had been to invoke the canons of Cold War anticommunism. In the midst of scandal, he blamed the administration's difficulties on its unwillingness to court open war against the Nicaraguan government. And as the Reagan administration began to contemplate an arms agreement with the Soviet Union, Buckley denounced it as a "suicide pact."[3]

But the plight of conservatism could also revive Buckley. He had excelled as a debater, writer, and politician when he had had to face the hostility of his peers. He had suffered in the eighties not so much from celebrity—he was certainly famous during the sixties—as from the uncritical adulation of his person. With Reagan gone, the lights of celebrity will dim, even for Buckley, and conservatives, including Buckley, will once again become the target for liberal barbs. Buckley could find himself in a familiar role—as a member of an embattled minority standing athwart history and yelling stop.

Notes

PROLOGUE

INTERVIEWS: REID BUCKLEY, THOMAS GUINZBURG, ROLLIN OSTER-
WEIS, PATRICK BUCHANAN, WILLIAM F. BUCKLEY, JR.

1. Lohmann Papers.
2. Quoted by Macdonald in "God and Buckley at Yale."
3. *National Review*, December 31, 1985.
4. Ibid.
5. Chamberlain, *Life with the Printed Word*, 147.
6. *National Review*, December 31, 1980.

CHAPTER ONE

INTERVIEWS: PATRICIA BUCKLEY BOZELL, REID BUCKLEY, BERYL
BUCKLEY MILBURN, JANE BUCKLEY SMITH, ALISTAIR HORNE, JOHN
BUCKLEY, SR., PRISCILLA BUCKLEY, SHERIDAN LORD, STEWART
HOSKINS, WILLIAM F. BUCKLEY, JR., PETER COLEY, WILLIAM
COLEY, ADELAIDE EMORY.

1. *Time* Papers.
2. Will Buckley's records at the University of Texas were obtained through Beryl Buckley Milburn, Will Buckley's niece, and a member of the University of Texas Board of Regents.
3. Priscilla Buckley and William F. Buckley, Jr., eds., *WFB: An Appreciation.*
4. Altman, *Revolution,* 59.
5. Link, *Woodrow Wilson and the Progressive Era,* 108–109.
6. Some of Will Buckley's counterrevolutionary activities are described in Smith, *United States and Revolutionary Nationalism in Mexico,* 177ff.
7. See, for instance, William F. Buckley's address to the Mississippi Valley Historical Association, May 12, 1922, in the Fall Papers.
8. From a privately printed collection of memories edited by Aloise Harding Buckley, *Reminiscences of Aloise Steiner Buckley.* Within the family the recollections are referred to as "Mimi stories."
9. Campbell, ed., *Spectrum of Catholic Attitudes,* 12. One might read this statement as an expression of Bill Buckley's unconscious, infantile hostility toward his father.
10. Aloise Harding Buckley, ed., *Reminiscences.*
11. William F. Buckley, Jr., *Right Reason,* 444.
12. Aloise Harding Buckley, ed., *Reminiscences.*
13. Priscilla Buckley and William F. Buckley, Jr., eds., *WFB: An Appreciation.*
14. See Horne, *The Land Is Bright,* 31.
15. Will Buckley testified on December 6, 1919, before the Senate Foreign Relation's Subcommittee on Mexican Affairs, chaired by his friend and ally New Mexico Senator Albert B. Fall.
16. Priscilla Buckley and William F. Buckley, Jr., eds., *WFB: An Appreciation.*
17. Ibid.
18. Buckley Papers.
19. *Lakeville Journal,* September 19, 1940.

CHAPTER TWO

INTERVIEWS: WILLIAM COLEY, ADELAIDE EMORY, PATRICIA BUCKLEY BOZELL, JANE BUCKLEY SMITH, PRISCILLA BUCKLEY, REID BUCKLEY, JOHN BUCKLEY, SR., PETER COLEY, WILLIAM F. BUCKLEY, JR., ERIC STEVENSON, PHILIP JESSUP, ALISTAIR HORNE, CHARLES AULT, JOHN LAWRENCE, BENJAMIN HEATH, NATHANIEL ABBOTT.

1. Buckley Papers.
2. Priscilla Buckley and William F Buckley, Jr., eds., *WFB: An Appreciation.*
3. Ibid.
4. Quote in Markmann, *The Buckleys,* 43–44.
5. In *Saving the Queen,* Bill's first novel, his hero, Blackford Oakes, attends a British public school on the eve of World War II and is caned for his defiant isolationism. Bill was never caned (Jim had been when he attended a British school in 1933), but his isolationist sentiments were probably not welcomed, even by the Irish Jesuits.
6. For Buckley's account of his years at Millbrook, see his "God and Boys at Millbrook."
7. Priscilla Buckley and William F. Buckley, Jr., eds., *WFB: An Appreciation.*
8. See Wreszin, *The Superfluous Anarchist.*
9. Nock, "Isaiah's Job."
10. Buckley Papers.
11. Ibid.
12. Ibid.
13. Ibid.
14. Ibid. (Letter to Will Buckley.)
15. Ibid.

CHAPTER THREE

INTERVIEWS: REID BUCKLEY, FRANK HARMAN, WILLIAM OTTLEY, WILLIAM CARLIN, THOMAS GUINZBURG, PATRICIA BUCKLEY BOZELL, ROLLIN OSTERWEIS, WILLIAM F. BUCKLEY, JR., BRENT BOZELL, ALAN FINBERG, PAUL WEISS, THOMAS EMERSON, WILLIAM SLOANE COFFIN, EVAN GALBRAITH, THOMAS BERGIN, RICHARD SEWALL, EDWARD CHILTON, CHARLES LICHENSTEIN, CHARLES LINDBLOM, GARRISON ELLIS.

1. Buckley Papers.
2. Ibid.
3. William F. Buckley, Jr., *Cruising Speed,* 142.
4. Macdonald, "Scrambled Eggheads on the Right."
5. For biographical details of Kendall, see Nash, "Willmoore Kendall: Conservative Iconoclast." See also Wills, *Confessions of a Conservative,* Chapter 2.
6. *Yale Daily News,* January 16, 1948.
7. Ibid., April 18, 1948.

CHAPTER FOUR

INTERVIEWS: PAUL WEISS, WILLIAM CARLIN, FRED STANNARD, CHRISTOPHER BUCKLEY, PATRICIA TAYLOR BUCKLEY, REID BUCKLEY, FRANCIS DONAHUE, WILLIAM OTTLEY, THOMAS GUINZBURG, WILLIAM F. BUCKLEY, JR., ROBERT COHEN, JOHN SIMON, ROLLIN OSTERWEIS, PATRICIA BUCKLEY BOZELL, EVAN GALBRAITH, JOHN CHAMBERLAIN, JAMES BUCKLEY, THOMAS BERGIN, HOWARD HUNT.

1. *Yale Daily News,* March 9, 1949.
2. Ibid., March 14, 1949.
3. Ibid., March 10, 1949.
4. *Yale Banner,* 1950, 119.
5. Heath, *Will Mrs. Major Go to Hell?,* 52.
6. Buckley Papers.
7. *Yale Daily News,* September 24, 1949.
8. Ibid., October 15, 1949.
9. Ibid., October 17, 1949.
10. *Harvard Crimson,* June 4, 1949.
11. FBI files. See also Diamond, "God and the FBI at Yale," and reply by Buckley, "Response to Diamond."
12. FBI files.
13. *Yale Daily News,* October 25, 1949.
14. FBI files.
15. *Yale Banner,* 1950, 64.
16. *Yale Daily News,* October 19, 1949.
17. Ibid., December 1, 1949; December 3, 1949.
18. Ibid., January 16, 1950.
19. Ibid., January 17, 1950.
20. Ibid., January 20, 1950.
21. The Alumni Day speech is reprinted in William F. Buckley, Jr., *God and Man at Yale,* 222–27.
22. Griswold Papers.
23. William F. Buckley, Jr., *God and Man at Yale,* 129.
24. Lohmann Papers.
25. Ibid.
26. Hunt, *Undercover,* 69.

CHAPTER FIVE

INTERVIEWS: JOHN BUCKLEY, SR., CHARLES LICHENSTEIN, WILLIAM F. BUCKLEY, JR., ROLLIN OSTERWEIS, JOHN CHAMBERLAIN,

PATRICIA TAYLOR BUCKLEY, HOWARD HUNT, HENRY REGNERY, REID BUCKLEY.

1. William F. Buckley, Jr., *God and Man at Yale,* 186.
2. Ibid., 181.
3. Quoted in ibid., 143.
4. William F. Buckley, Jr., *God and Man at Yale,* 148.
5. Ibid., 151.
6. Ibid., 157.
7. Ibid., 154–55.
8. Ibid., 185.
9. Ibid., lx–lxi.
10. *Human Events,* August 1, 1951.
11. William F. Buckley, Jr., *God and Man at Yale,* New Introduction, ix.
12. Griswold Papers.
13. Eastman, "Buckley versus Yale."
14. Rodman, "Isms and the University."
15. Griswold Papers.
16. Ibid.
17. Ibid.
18. Bundy, "The Attack on Yale."
19. Luce, "God, Socialism, and Yale."
20. Ashburn, "Isms and the University."
21. Hatch, "Enforcing Truth."
22. William F. Buckley, Jr., "The Changes at Yale."
23. Buckley Papers. (Letter to Kevin Corrigan.)
24. Buckley Papers.
25. *America,* November 17, 1951.
26. Fullman, "God and Man and Mr. Buckley."
27. William F. Buckley, Jr., "Father Fullman's Assault."
28. Viereck, "Conservatism under the Elms."
29. William F. Buckley, Jr., *God and Man at Yale,* lix.
30. *Grelmschatka,* June 15, 1951. *Grelmschatka* is a combination of Great Elm and Kamschatka, the elder Buckleys' houses. The newspaper was begun in 1947 by sisters Priscilla and Aloise Buckley and was published irregularly—once every several years—over the next eleven years.
31. Macdonald, "God and Buckley at Yale."

CHAPTER SIX

INTERVIEWS: JOSEPH SOBRAN, PATRICIA BUCKLEY BOZELL, WILLIAM F. BUCKLEY, JR., EUGENE V. CLARK, KIERAN O'DOHERTY.

1. Buckley Papers.
2. See Reeves, *Life and Times of Joe McCarthy,* Chapter 11, for discussion of what he actually said in this speech.
3. Diggins, *Up from Communism,* 217.
4. William F. Buckley, Jr., "Senator McCarthy's Model?"
5. Aloise Harding Buckley, ed., *Reminiscences of Aloise Steiner Buckley.*
6. Priscilla Buckley and William F. Buckley, Jr., eds., *WFB: An Appreciation.*
7. Eastman Papers. (Letter to Max Eastman.)
8. For a description of the split within *The Freeman,* see Chamberlain, *Life with the Printed Word,* and *Time,* January 26, 1953.
9. Buckley Papers.
10. Reeves, *Joe McCarthy,* 451.
11. Buckley Papers.
12. Buckley and Bozell, *McCarthy and His Enemies,* 391.
13. Leo Cherne, cited in Rovere, "Senator McCarthy's Eggheads."
14. Buckley and Bozell, *McCarthy and His Enemies,* 331.
15. Ibid., 3, 329.
16. Ibid., 335.
17. Ibid., 252.
18. Ibid.
19. Ibid., 328.
20. Ibid., 318.
21. Buckley Papers. (Letter to Sam Vaughan.)
22. *Yale Daily News,* April 16, 1954.
23. *New York Times,* April 27, 1954.
24. Macdonald, "McCarthy and His Apologists."
25. *New York Times,* April 4, 1954.
26. Buckley Papers.
27. Ibid. (Letter to Whittaker Chambers.)
28. The speech was reprinted in *U.S. News & World Report,* August 6, 1954.

CHAPTER SEVEN

INTERVIEWS: JAMES BUCKLEY, EVAN GALBRAITH, WILLIAM F. BUCKLEY, JR., HENRY REGNERY, JOHN CHAMBERLAIN, THOMAS BERGIN, PATRICIA BUCKLEY BOZELL, MORRIE RYSKIND, HOWARD HUNT, WILLIAM RUSHER.

1. Buckley Papers.
2. *Die Welt,* September 4, 1978.
3. Chamberlain, *Life with the Printed Word,* 90; Nash, *The Conservative Intellectual Movement,* 145–46.

4. Buckley Papers.
5. William F. Buckley, Jr., "Freedom to Agree."
6. William F. Buckley, Jr., *Right Reason*, 420.
7. Buckley Papers.
8. Ibid.
9. Eastman Papers.
10. Buckley Papers.
11. Ibid.
12. Cited in Diggins, *Up from Communism*, 329.
13. Ibid.
14. Buckley Papers.
15. Chambers, *Witness*, 12.
16. Chambers, *Odyssey of a Friend*, 48.
17. Ibid., 50.
18. Ibid., 55.
19. Buckley Papers.
20. Chambers, *Odyssey of a Friend*, 79.
21. Ibid., 83.
22. Buckley Papers.
23. Priscilla Buckley and William F. Buckley, Jr., eds., *WFB: An Appreciation*.
24. Chambers, *Odyssey of a Friend*, 104.
25. Ibid., 106–7.
26. Ibid., 103–4.
27. McFadden, "*At National Review*," *Maureen Buckley O'Reilly*, 57.
28. Buckley Papers.
29. Ibid.

CHAPTER EIGHT

INTERVIEWS: RUSSELL KIRK, KIERAN O'DOHERTY, PATRICK BUCHANAN, MURRAY KEMPTON.

1. Larson, *Republican Looks at His Party*, vii.
2. Buckley Papers.
3. *National Review*, November 19, 1955.
4. Eastman Papers.
5. *National Review*, November 26, 1955.
6. *Time*, July 6, 1953.
7. See Rovere, *The American Establishment*. See also review by William F. Buckley, Jr., "The Genteel Nightmare of Richard Rovere."
8. *National Review*, November 19, 1955.
9. Ibid.
10. Ibid., November 26, 1955.
11. Ibid., March 21, 1956.

12. Horne, *The Land Is Bright,* 32.
13. *National Review,* July 25, 1956.
14. Ibid., September 29, 1956.
15. Ibid., May 18, 1957.
16. Ibid., June 1, 1957.
17. Ibid., February 29, 1956.
18. Ibid., August 24, 1957.
19. Ibid., September 7, 1957.
20. *Long Island Daily Press*. (In Buckley Papers.)
21. Buckley Papers.
22. Kempton, "Buckley's National Bore."
23. Macdonald, "Scrambled Eggheads on the Right."
24. Fischer, "Editor's Easy Chair."
25. Macdonald, "Scrambled Eggheads on the Right."
26. Kempton, "Buckley's National Bore."
27. Macdonald, "Scrambled Eggheads on the Right."
28. Buckley Papers.
29. *National Review,* August 1, 1956.
30. Ibid.
31. Ibid.

CHAPTER NINE

INTERVIEWS: CHRISTOPHER BUCKLEY, WILLIAM F. BUCKLEY, JR., PRISCILLA BUCKLEY, HUGH KENNER, PATRICIA BUCKLEY BOZELL, JOHN CHAMBERLAIN, JAMES MCFADDEN, WILLIAM CASEY, CLIFTON WHITE.

1. Burnham, "Lenin's Heir."
2. Burnham, *Struggle for the World,* 69.
3. *National Review,* April 11, 1956.
4. Ibid., May 23, 1956.
5. Ibid., August 25, 1956.
6. Ibid., October 13, 1956.
7. Buckley Papers.
8. *National Review,* October 20, 1956.
9. Ibid., November 3, 1956.
10. Ibid., April 6, 1957.
11. McFadden, *Maureen Buckley O'Reilly,* 57.
12. In interviews, both John Chamberlain and Victor Lasky recall Schlamm having a mild stroke right after *National Review* began, and having to go to Florida for several days to recuperate. Chamberlain believes that the tension over his role on the magazine began when he realized, upon his return, that he was not indispensable.
13. Burnham, *Containment or Liberation?,* 241.

14. *National Review,* November 17, 1956.
15. Buckley Papers.
16. Ibid.
17. Ibid.
18. Ibid.
19. *National Review,* January 5, 1957.
20. Ibid.
21. Ibid., January 26, 1957.
22. Ibid., February 23, 1957.
23. Ibid.
24. Buckley Papers.
25. Ibid.
26. Ibid.
27. Ibid.
28. Wills, *Confessions of a Conservative,* 6.

CHAPTER TEN

INTERVIEWS: WILLIAM RUSHER, JAMES MCFADDEN, RICHARD COHEN, BENJAMIN HEATH, PATRICIA TAYLOR BUCKLEY, CHRISTOPHER BUCKLEY, PATRICIA BUCKLEY BOZELL.

1. Chambers, *Odyssey of a Friend,* 189–90.
2. Column, March 10, 1982.
3. *National Review,* December 28, 1957.
4. Buckley Papers.
5. *Time* Papers.
6. William F. Buckley, Jr., "Notes Toward an Empirical Definition of Conservatism," in *The Jeweler's Eye.* (The essay first appeared in October 1963.)
7. *New York Post,* January 15, 1958.
8. *National Review,* January 18, 1958.
9. Priscilla Buckley and William F. Buckley, Jr., eds., *WFB: An Appreciation.*
10. Brent Bozell, *National Review,* November 11, 1958; *National Review Bulletin* (Burnham), November 15, 1958; William F. Buckley, Jr., *Up from Liberalism,* 189.
11. Chambers, *Odyssey of a Friend,* 216.
12. Ibid, 227–28.
13. Ibid, 229.
14. William F. Buckley, Jr., "Notes Toward an Empirical Definition of Conservatism," in *The Jeweler's Eye.*
15. Column, March 24, 1970.
16. William F. Buckley, Jr., *Up from Liberalism,* xv.
17. Ibid., 119.

18. Ibid., 129.
19. Ibid., 125.
20. Ibid., 111, 156.
21. Ibid., 112.
22. Kristol, "On the Burning Deck."
23. William F. Buckley, Jr., 161.
24. Ibid., 169.
25. Ibid., 189.
26. Ibid., 179.
27. Ibid., 193.
28. Chambers, *Odyssey of a Friend,* 247.
29. Buckley Papers.
30. Ibid.
31. William F. Buckley, Jr., xv.
32. Buckley Papers.
33. Ibid.
34. Ibid.
35. Chambers, *Odyssey of a Friend,* 242.
36. Ibid., 213.
37. Ambrose, *Eisenhower,* vol. 2, *The President,* 536.
38. National Review, August, 15, 1959.
39. *New York Times,* September 18, 1959.
40. *National Review,* September 17, 1959.
41. Ibid., October, 24, 1959.
42. Chambers, *Odyssey of a Friend,* 261.
43. Ibid., 265.
44. Ibid., 260.
45. Buckley Papers.
46. Ibid.
47. William F. Buckley, Jr., "Notes Toward an Empirical Definition of Conservatism," in *The Jeweler's Eye.*
48. Buckley Papers.
49. Ibid.
50. Ibid.
51. Ibid.
52. *National Review,* October 22, 1960.
53. William F. Buckley, Jr., "Remarks on a Fifth Anniversary" in *Rumbles Left and Right.*

CHAPTER ELEVEN

INTERVIEWS: WILLIAM OTTLEY, EUGENE V. CLARK, LEE EDWARDS, WILLIAM F. BUCKLEY, JR., RUSSELL KIRK, SCOTT STAN-

LEY, ROBERT BAUMAN, JAMES MCFADDEN, STANTON EVANS,
MARVIN LIEBMAN.

1. Quoted in Mahoney, *Actions Speak Louder*, 288.
2. *Time*, June 23, 1961.
3. *National Review*, January 29, 1961.
4. Ibid., March 25, 1961.
5. Wakefield, "W.F.B. Jr., Portrait of a Complainer."
6. *National Review*, September 9, 1961.
7. Ibid., July 29, 1961.
8. *America*, August 12, 1961.
9. Ibid.
10. Quoted in Wills, *Politics and Catholic Freedom*, 5.
11. *National Review*, August 26, 1961.
12. Ibid.
13. Ibid.
14. Ibid., September 24, 1960.
15. *Time*, March 10, 1961.
16. Buckley Papers.
17. Ibid.
18. Ibid.
19. William F. Buckley, Jr., "Can We Desegregate, Hesto Presto?"
20. *National Review*, October 7, 1962.
21. Group Research Papers.
22. Buckley Papers.
23. Ibid.
24. *National Review*, April 11, 1959.
25. Buckley Papers.
26. Ibid.
27. Ibid.
28. Ibid.
29. Ibid.
30. Ibid.
31. Ibid.
32. *National Review*, April 22, 1961.
33. Buckley Papers.
34. *New York Times*, November 16, 1961.
35. Interviews with Russell Kirk and William F. Buckley, Jr.
36. Rusher, *Rise of the Right*, 121.
37. Buckley Papers.
38. *National Review*, February 3, 1962.
39. Ibid., February 17, 1962.
40. *American Opinion*, March 1962.
41. Buckley Papers.

CHAPTER TWELVE

INTERVIEWS: WILLIAM RUSHER, WILLIAM F. BUCKLEY, JR., MUR-
RAY KEMPTON, CHRISTOPHER BUCKLEY, HUGH KENNER, WILLIAM
RICKENBACKER.

1. Buckley Papers.
2. William F. Buckley, Jr., *Cruising Speed,* 115.
3. William F. Buckley, Jr., "An Evening with Jack Paar," in *Rumbles Left and Right.*
4. Ibid.
5. Ibid.
6. William F. Buckley, Jr., "On Experiencing Gore Vidal."
7. William F. Buckley, Jr., "An Evening with Jack Paar," in *Rumbles Left and Right.*
8. Column, November 4, 1962.
9. Ibid., April 15, 1962.
10. Ibid., August 13, 1963.
11. Ibid., April 15, 1962.
12. Ibid., October 1, 1963.
13. Ibid., November 22, 1963.
14. Ibid., December 7, 1986.
15. Ibid., April 7, 1963.
16. Ibid., December 2, 1962.
17. Ibid., November 25, 1962.
18. *National Review,* December 17, 1960.
19. *Playboy,* January 1963.
20. *Wall Street Journal,* January 31, 1967.
21. Quoted by Larry King, "God, Man, and William F. Buckley, Jr."
22. William F. Buckley, Jr., *The Jeweler's Eye,* 226.
23. *Time* Papers.
24. William F. Buckley, Jr., *Cruising Speed,* 4.
25. Buckley Papers.
26. Ibid.
27. Ibid.
28. Ibid.
29. Ibid.
30. Ibid.
31. William F. Buckley, Jr., *Up from Liberalism,* 119.
32. Ortega y Gasset, *The Revolt of the Masses,* 11, 13, 15.
33. Gilbert, *A Cycle of Outrage,* Chapter 7.
34. Buckley Papers.
35. Ibid.
36. Ibid.
37. William F. Buckley, Jr., *Atlantic High,* 106–7.

38. Ibid., 107.
39. Ibid.
40. William F. Buckley, Jr., "A Reply to Robert Hutchins" in *Rumbles Left and Right,* 103.

CHAPTER THIRTEEN

INTERVIEWS: DENISON KITCHEL, CHARLES LICHENSTEIN, DEAN BURCH, RALPH DE TOLEDANO, NEAL FREEMAN, PATRICIA BUCKLEY BOZELL, VICTOR LASKY, ROBERT BAUMAN, CLIFTON WHITE.

1. *This Week,* September 10, 1961.
2. Buckley Papers.
3. See White, *Suite 3505,* 205.
4. Buckley Papers.
5. *New York Times,* September 16, 1963.
6. *Time* Papers.
7. Buckley Papers.
8. Shadegg, *What Happened to Goldwater?,* 70.
9. *National Review,* January 14, 1964.
10. Buckley Papers.
11. Ibid.
12. Ibid.
13. Ibid.
14. Ibid.
15. Ibid.
16. Ibid.
17. Rusher, *Rise of the Right,* 164.
18. Buckley Papers.
19. Ibid.
20. Rusher, *Rise of the Right,* 167.
21. Reprinted in Mahoney, *Actions Speak Louder,* 392–96.

CHAPTER FOURTEEN

INTERVIEWS: WILLIAM F. BUCKLEY, JR., KIERAN O'DOHERTY, NEAL FREEMAN, JAMES BUCKLEY, MARVIN LIEBMAN, J. DANIEL MAHONEY, WILLIAM RUSHER, CLIFTON WHITE.

1. The speech is quoted in Appendix A in William F. Buckley, Jr., *Unmaking of a Mayor,* 355–59.
2. William F. Buckley, Jr., *Unmaking of a Mayor,* 11–12.
3. *New York Times,* April 5, 1965.

4. *National Catholic Reporter,* May 12, 1965.
5. Mahoney, *Actions Speak Louder,* 28.
6. William F. Buckley, Jr., *Unmaking of a Mayor,* 121–24.
7. Ibid., 132.
8. Ibid.
9. Ibid.
10. *New York Herald Tribune,* June 25, 1965.
11. *New Yorker,* October 30, 1965.
12. *New York World-Telegraph,* June 25, 1965.
13. William F. Buckley, Jr., *Unmaking of a Mayor,* 115–21.
14. Ibid., 40.
15. Ibid., 158.
16. "Harlem Is in New York City," *National Review,* November 2, 1965.
17. Cited in William F. Buckley, Jr., *Unmaking of a Mayor,* 152.
18. *New York Post,* July 28, 1965.
19. Ibid.
20. Ibid.
21. William F. Buckley, Jr., *Unmaking of a Mayor,* 164–66.
22. Ibid.
23. *National Review,* October 19, 1965.
24. *New York Herald Tribune,* September 27, 1965.
25. Ibid., October 27, 1965.
26. *New York Daily News,* October 11, 1965.
27. *Life,* October 29, 1965.
28. *New York Daily News,* October 21, 1965.
29. William F. Buckley, Jr. *Unmaking of a Mayor,* 287.
30. Ibid.
31. Mahoney, *Actions Speak Louder,* 292–93.
32. *New York Times,* October 19, 1965.
33. *New York Herald Tribune,* October 26, 1985.
34. *New York Times,* October 29, 1965.
35. William F. Buckley, Jr., *Unmaking of a Mayor,* 185.
36. Pilot, *Lindsay's Campaign,* 322.
37. *New York Times,* October 26, 1965.
38. Liebman Papers.
39. William F. Buckley, Jr., *Unmaking of a Mayor,* 297.
40. Ibid., 346.
41. Mahoney, *Actions Speak Louder,* 304.
42. Phillips, *The Emerging Republican Majority,* 168.
43. William F. Buckley, Jr., *Unmaking of a Mayor,* 32.
44. Ibid., 257–58.
45. Ibid., 270.
46. Quoted in *Wall Street Journal,* January 31, 1967.
47. *National Review,* January 11, 1966.

CHAPTER FIFTEEN

INTERVIEWS: WILLIAM F. BUCKLEY, JR., NEAL FREEMAN, WARREN STEIBEL, CHRISTOPHER BUCKLEY, JOHN LEONARD, RICHARD CLURMAN, JOHN KENNETH GALBRAITH, WILLIAM RUSHER, WILLIAM CASEY.

1. *National Review,* August 24, 1968.
2. *Time* Papers.
3. Ibid.
4 Buckley Papers.
5. Ibid.
6. *Time,* November 3, 1967.
7. *Time* Papers.
8. Buckley Papers.
9. *Wall Street Journal,* January 31, 1967.
10. Buckley Papers.
11. *Time* Papers.
12. *National Review,* January 12, 1965.
13. Column, April 22, 1965.
14. Ibid., August 19, 1967.
15. William F. Buckley, Jr., "How I Came to Rock."
16. Ibid.
17. Column, May 7, 1968.
18. *Mademoiselle,* June 1961.
19. Column, March 19, 1966.
20. *Commonweal,* November 10, 1967.
21. *Time* Papers.
22. Quoted in Cronkite, *On the Edge of the Spotlight,* 110.
23. *National Review,* "Who Will Overcome," September 22, 1964.
24. *National Review,* May 4, 1965.
25. Wills, *Confessions of a Conservative,* 76–77.
26. Ibid., 67.
27. Buckley Papers.

CHAPTER SIXTEEN

INTERVIEWS: RALPH DE TOLEDANO, PATRICK BUCHANAN, VICTOR LASKY, WILLIAM F. BUCKLEY, JR., NEAL FREEMAN, WILLIAM RICKENBACKER, WILLIAM RUSHER, WARREN STEIBEL, MURRAY KEMPTON, HUGH KENNER.

1. Evans and Novak, October 14, 1965.
2. *National Review,* April 5, 1966.
3. Column, June 25, 1966.
4. *Miami News,* April 18, 1967.
5. Column, April 28, 1968.
6. Buckley Papers.
7. Column, April 22, 1967.
8. Buckley Papers.
9. Ibid.
10. Ibid.
11. *Washington Post,* July 22, 1968.
12. Buckley Papers.
13. Quotations are from William F. Buckley, Jr., "On Experiencing Gore Vidal," and the ABC transcript.
14. William F. Buckley, Jr., *The Governer Listeth,* 91.
15. *Time,* August 29, 1969.
16. Buckley Papers.
17. Later published in *National Review,* October 12, 1972.
18. Buckley Papers.
19. Ibid.
20. *National Review,* November 5, 1968.

CHAPTER SEVENTEEN

INTERVIEWS: FRANK SHAKESPEARE, HENRY KISSINGER, WILLIAM F. BUCKLEY, JR., DANIEL P. MOYNIHAN, ROGER MORRIS, DAVID KEENE, RICHARD CLURMAN, CHRIS SIMONDS, JOHN BUCKLEY, JR., KIERAN O'DOHERTY, PATRICK BUCHANAN.

1. *Playboy,* May 1970. This interview, reprinted in Buckley's *Inveighing We Will Go,* is the most succinct statement of his postradical philosophy.
2. See Moynihan, *Politics of a Guaranteed Income,* Chapter Three.
3. Buckley Papers.
4. William F. Buckley, Jr., *United Nations Journal,* 40.
5. Ibid.
6. *National Review,* December 17, 1968.
7. Kissinger, *White House Years,* 64ff.
8. Buckley Papers.
9. Ibid.
10. See Moynihan, *Politics of a Guaranteed Income,* 370ff.
11. Column, January 20, 1971.
12. Buckley Papers.
13. Ibid.
14. Column, October 28, 1969.

15. Ibid., November 3, 1969.
16. Ibid., November 22, 1969.
17. Ibid., March 7, 1970.
18. *Firing Line,* July 25, 1972.
19. Associated Press, June 19, 1970.
20. Column, June 23, 1970.
21. *Firing Line,* April 1, 1973.
22. William F. Buckley, Jr., *Cruising Speed,* 79.
23. Column, June 3, 1969.
24. *Time* Papers.
25. Buckley Papers.
26. *Playboy,* May 1970.
27. Buckley Papers.
28. *Newsweek,* November 16, 1970.
29. William F. Buckley, Jr., *Cruising Speed,* 23–24.
30. Ibid., 60–61.
31. Ibid., 165.

CHAPTER EIGHTEEN

INTERVIEWS: WILLIAM OTTLEY, JOHN LEONARD, BRENT BOZELL, NEAL FREEMAN, RUSSELL KIRK, MARVIN LIEBMAN, SOPHIE WIL-KINS, HUGH KENNER, DANIEL P. MOYNIHAN, IRVING KRISTOL.

1. *New York Times Book Review,* April 4, 1954.
2. Buckley Papers.
3. *National Review,* September 9, 1966.
4. Ibid., April 4, 1966.
5. Buckley Papers.
6. *Triumph,* February 1968.
7. Buckley Papers.
8. *Triumph,* March 1969.
9. *National Review,* April 8, 1969.
10. *Triumph,* June 1969.
11. Buckley Papers.
12. *National Review,* April 6, 1971.
13. Buckley Papers.
14. *Pittsburgh Post-Gazette,* April 24, 1971.
15. Buckley Papers.
16. Wills, *Confessions of a Conservative,* 76.
17. Buckley Papers.
18. *National Review,* October 20, 1970.
19. Buckley Papers.
20. Column, October 2, 1970.
21. *National Catholic Reporter,* August 7, 1970.

22. Buckley Papers.
23. Ibid.
24. Ibid.
25. Ibid.
26. Column, April 24, 1971.
27. Ibid., November 26, 1971.
28. Epstein, "The Politics of William Buckley."

CHAPTER NINETEEN

INTERVIEWS: NEAL FREEMAN, STANTON EVANS, JEFF BELL, DAVID
KEENE, PATRICK BUCHANAN, WILLIAM F. BUCKEY, JR.

1. William F. Buckley, Jr., "To China with Nixon."
2. Interview, Neal Freeman.
3. *Human Events,* August 7, 1971.
4. Reprinted in William F. Buckley, Jr., *Inveighing We Will Go,* 74–76.
5. Buckley Papers.
6. Moser, *Promise and Hope,* 9.
7. Buckley Papers.
8. Moser, *Promise and Hope,* 11.
9. William Rusher's minutes on the meeting, in Buckley Papers.
10. Buckley Papers.
11. Ibid.
12. *National Review,* December 31, 1971.
13. Buckley Papers.
14. Ibid.
15. Ibid.
16. Safire, *Before the Fall,* 14.
17. Reprinted in *National Review,* March 17, 1972.
18. *National Review,* March 17, 1972.
19. Buckley Papers.
20. Ibid.
21. Ibid.
22. William F. Buckley, Jr., *Cruising Speed,* 105.
23. Reingold, "Bill Buckley: Covert King of Rock Radio."
24. Ibid.
25. Ibid.
26. Ibid.
27. *National Review,* September 10, 1971.
28. Associated Press, August 19, 1972.

CHAPTER TWENTY

INTERVIEWS: HOWARD HUNT, WILLIAM F. BUCKLEY, JR., CHRISTOPHER BUCKLEY, GEORGE WILL, DAVID KEENE, PATRICK BUCHANAN.

1. Column, November 9, 1972.
2. Ibid., February 16, 1973.
3. *National Review* editorial, February 16, 1973.
4. Column, March 6, 1973.
5. *National Review,* September 14, 1973.
6. Buckley Papers.
7. Ibid.
8. Ibid.
9. Ibid.
10. *National Review,* February 2, 1973.
11. Ibid., May 11, 1973.
12. Ibid., June 8, 1973.
13. Buckley Papers.
14. Ibid.
15. *National Review,* "Unraveling," May, 11, 1973.
16. Buckley Papers.
17. Ibid.
18. *National Review,* June 8, 1973.
19. Buckley Papers.
20. Ibid.
21. William F. Buckey, Jr., *United Nations Journal,* xxiv.
22. Column, June 15, 1967.
23. William F. Buckley, Jr., *United Nations Journal,* xxv.
24. Ibid., xxvi.
25. Ibid., 35.
26. Ibid., 68.
27. Ibid., 69.
28. Ibid., 144.
29. Reprinted in *National Review,* November 11, 1973.
30. Buckley Papers.
31. Cathy Claydon, *Olathe* [Kansas] *News,* November 3, 1973.
32. Ibid.
33. Column, December 13, 1973.
34. *Firing Line,* December 20, 1973.
35. *National Review,* February 15, 1974.
36. Ibid., April 12, 1974.
37. Column, April 1, 1974.
38. Ibid., June 12, 1974.
39. Ibid., June 20, 1974.

40. Sherman Skolnick, *Hotline News* (in Buckley Papers).
41. Column, March 20, 1975.
42. Associated Press, November 18, 1974.
43. Column, January 29, 1975.
44. Buckley Papers.
45. Column, March 11, 1975.
46. Buckley Papers.
47. Ibid.
48. Ibid.
49. Ibid.
50. Column, August 7, 1974.
51. Ibid., September 8, 1974.
52. *Firing Line*, September 4, 1974.
53. The details of Sitco's history are in Securities and Exchange Commission files, *SEC vs. The Starr Broadcasting Group, Inc., et al.* See also Kronholz, *Wall Street Journal*, October 24, 1978; and William F. Buckley, Jr., "My Life in Business" (unpublished manuscript).
54. William F. Buckley, Jr., "My Life in Business."
55. Kronholz, *Wall Street Journal*, October 24, 1978.
56. SEC Complaint.

CHAPTER TWENTY-ONE

INTERVIEWS: JEFF BELL, WILLIAM F. BUCKLEY, JR., SOPHIE WILKINS, SAMUEL VAUGHAN, HUGH KENNER, EVAN GALBRAITH, CHRISTOPHER BUCKLEY, JOSEPH SOBRAN, PAT BUCKLEY, JAMES BURNHAM, JR., DAVID KEENE, KIERAN O'DOHERTY.

1. Cannon, *Reagan*, 192.
2. Column, August 24, 1974.
3. Ibid., December 6, 1974.
4. Ibid., October 1, 1973.
5. Ibid., October 11, 1974.
6. Buckley Papers.
7. Liebman Papers.
8. Ibid.
9. Buckley Papers.
10. William F. Buckley, Jr., "The Genesis of Blackford Oakes."
11. Buckley Papers.
12. William F. Buckley, Jr., *Saving the Queen*, 20.
13. Ibid., 27.
14. Ibid., 146–47.
15. William F. Buckley, Jr., "The Threat to the Amateur Sailor" in *Rumbles Left and Right*.
16. William F. Buckley, Jr., *Airborne*, 124.

17. Column, July 7, 1975.
18. Ibid., July 24, 1975.
19. Ibid., August 18, 1975.
20. Ibid., December 23, 1975.
21. Buckley Papers.
22. Rusher, *Making of the New Majority Party,* 15.
23. Buckley Papers.
24. William F. Buckley, Jr., "A Relaxing View of Ronald Reagan."
25. *Chicago Tribune Magazine,* October 17, 1976.
26. Buckley Papers.
27. Column, August 18, 1975.
28. *Conservative Digest,* November 1975.
29. *National Review,* December 5, 1975.
30. *Conservative Digest,* November 1975.
31. Reprinted in *National Review,* December 5, 1975.
32. Wiliam F. Buckley, Jr., *Airborne,* 30.
33. Ibid., 49.
34. *Washington Post,* May 15, 1978.
35. Quoted in Morley, *Other Side of the Moon,* 253.
36. Buckley Papers.
37. Ibid.
38. Ibid.
39. Ibid.
40. Ibid.
41. Column, December 24, 1975.
42. Buckley Papers.
43. Column, August 20, 1976.
44. Ibid., September 6, 1976.
45. Ibid., June 29, 1976.
46. Ibid., September 30, 1976.
47. *Chicago Tribune Magazine,* October 17, 1976.
48. Column, September 2, 1976.

CHAPTER TWENTY-TWO

INTERVIEWS: SAMUEL VAUGHAN, RICHARD BROOKHISER, JEFFREY HART, NEAL FREEMAN, STANTON EVANS, GERHART NIEMEYER, STEPHEN UMIN, WILLIAM F. BUCKLEY, JR., DINO PIONZIO, JOHN BUCKLEY, SR., CHRISTOPHER BUCKLEY.

1. *Huntsville News,* November 1976.
2. William F. Buckley, Jr., *Stained Glass,* 103.
3. Ibid., 331.
4. Ibid., 348.
5. Ibid., 296.

6. Column, March 9, 1977.
7. Ibid., May 26, 1977.
8. Ibid., May 27, 1977.
9. Ibid., January 30, 1964.
10. Buckley Papers.
11. Ibid.
12. Column, October 12, 1976.
13. Buckley Papers.
14. *Washington Post,* January 28, 1978.
15. Crawford, *Thunder on the Right,* 176.
16. *National Review,* June 23, 1978.
17. Kronholz, *Wall Street Journal,* October 24, 1978.
18. Buckley Papers.
19. *Wall Street Journal,* November 13, 1978.
20. *National Review,* March 18, 1977.
21. *National Review Bulletin,* July 15, 1977.
22. Jeffrey Hart, "Letter from Santiago," March 3, 1978.
23. Column, September 1, 1978.
24. Liebman Papers.
25. Quoted in press kit.
26. These quotations and those from the letter to Sporkin were part of the Buckley press kit.
27. *Newsweek,* February 19, 1979.
28. Ibid.
29. Buckley Papers.
30. Ibid.
31. Ibid.
32. Reproduced in Buckley's "My Life in Business" (unpublished).
33. William F. Buckley, Jr., "My Life in Business."

CHAPTER TWENTY-THREE

INTERVIEWS: WILLIAM F. BUCKLEY, JR., TONY DOLAN, CHRISTO-PHER BUCKLEY, WILLIAM CASEY, RICHARD CLURMAN, ROY COHN.

1. Column, January 12, 1978.
2. Buckley Papers.
3. White, *America in Search of Itself,* 21.
4. Column, December 17, 1979.
5. Ibid., January 24, 1980.
6. Ibid., February 20, 1980.
7. *National Review,* February 8, 1980.
8. William F. Buckley, Jr., *Right Reason,* 382.
9. Buckley Papers.
10. Column, May 31, 1980.

11. Ibid., March 17, 1980.
12. William F. Buckley, Jr., *Atlantic High,* 63.
13. Reprinted in *National Review,* August 8, 1980.
14. Ibid.
15. Buckley Papers.
16. Column, August 27, 1980.
17. Ibid., June 6, 1980.
18. *National Review,* September 19, 1980.
19. Column, October 6, 1980.
20. Bauman, *The Gentleman from Maryland,* 69.
21. Washington Post, December 8, 1980.
22. *National Review,* December 31, 1980.
23. Ibid.

CHAPTER TWENTY-FOUR

INTERVIEWS: DANIEL OLIVER, WILLIAM CASEY, TONY DOLAN, WILLIAM F. BUCKLEY, JR., RICHARD CLURMAN, IRVING KRISTOL, JOHN LEONARD, PATRICK BUCHANAN, JOSEPH SOBRAN, FRANCES BRONSON, WARREN STEIBEL, SAMUEL VAUGHAN, HUGH KENNER, GERHART NIEMEYER, CHRISTOPHER BUCKLEY, SOPHIE WILKINS, ERNEST VAN DEN HAAG.

1. Buckley Papers.
2. Column, March 12, 1981.
3. Quoted in Barrett, *Gambling with History,* 299.
4. Column, January 5, 1982.
5. Ibid., January 26, 1982.
6. William F. Buckley, Jr., *Overdrive.*
7. *New York Daily News,* February 4, 1982.
8. *National Review,* December 31, 1985.
9. *New York Times,* April 27, 1982.
10. Column, February 6, 1982.
11. Buckley Papers.
12. Ibid.
13. Column, March 21, 1983.
14. *National Review,* April 1, 1983.
15. Column, April 20, 1983.
16. Ibid., December 9, 1983.
17. Dunne, "Happy Days Are Here Again."
18. Buckley Papers.

CHAPTER TWENTY-FIVE

INTERVIEWS: RICHARD CLURMAN, PATRICK BUCHANAN, WILLIAM F. BUCKLEY, JR., PRISCILLA BUCKLEY, SOPHIE WILKINS, SAMUEL VAUGHAN, MIDGE DECTER, JOSEPH SOBRAN, CHRISTOPHER BUCKLEY.

1. Column, November 26, 1984.
2. Ibid., April 1, 1985.
3. Ibid., May 3, 1985.
4. Ibid., March 6, 1985.
5. *National Review,* May 31, 1985.
6. Ibid., June 14, 1985.
7. Richard Clurman, "Sailing in the Kingdom of Buckley" (unpublished manuscript).
8. Ibid.
9. *Washington Post, Washington Times,* October 9, 1985.
10. Buckley Papers.
11. *People,* November 18, 1985.
12. *Time,* December 9, 1985; *Washington Post,* December 5, 1985.
13. *National Review,* December 31, 1985.
14. *New York Times,* March 18, 1986.
15. *National Review,* April 25, 1986.
16. *Washington Times,* September 22, 1986.
17. Buckley Papers.
18. Column, April 22, 1986.
19. Ibid., May 8, 1986.
20. Buckley Papers.
21. Ibid.
22. Ibid.
23. *National Review,* July 4, 1986.
24. Column, June 23, 1986.
25. Ibid., April 8, 1985.
26. Ibid., July 4, 1986.
27. *National Review,* August 29, 1986.
28. Column, October 8, 1986.
29. Ibid., October 10, 1986.
30. Ibid., October 14, 1986.
31. Ibid., October 16, 1986.
32. Ibid., October 23, 1986.
33. *National Review,* December 5, 1986.
34. Column, November 11, 1986.
35. Ibid., November 18, 1986.
36. Ibid., November 27, 1986.

EPILOGUE

1. Heath, *Will Mrs. Major Go to Hell?*, 140.
2. Column, October 2, 1987.
3. *National Review*, May 22, 1987.

Bibliography

Altman, Ronald. *Revolution*. New York: John Day and Co., 1970.

Ambrose. Stephen. *Eisenhower,* vol. 2, *The President*. New York: Simon and Schuster, 1984.

Ashburn, Frank. "Isms and the University." *Saturday Review,* December 15, 1951.

Barrett, Laurence. *Gambling with History*. Garden City, N.Y.: Doubleday and Co., 1983.

Bauman, Robert. *The Gentleman from Maryland*. New York: Arbor House, 1986.

Beaty, John. *Iron Curtain over America*. Dallas: Wilkinson Publishing Co., 1951.

Buckley, Aloise Harding, ed. *Reminiscences of Aloise Steiner Buckley, 1895–1985*. Privately published, 1986.

Buckley, Christopher. *The White House Mess*. New York: Alfred A. Knopf, 1986.

Buckley, Priscilla, and William F. Buckley, Jr., eds. *WFB: An Appreciation*. Privately published, 1959.

Buckley, William F., Jr. *Airborne*. New York: Macmillan and Co., 1976.

———. *Atlantic High*. Boston: Little, Brown and Co., 1982.

———. "Can We Desegregate, Hesto Presto?" *Saturday Review,* November 11, 1961.

———. "The Changes at Yale." *Atlantic Monthly,* December 1951.

———. *Cruising Speed*. New York: Bantam Books, 1971.

————, ed. *Did You Ever See a Dream Walking?* New York: Bobbs-Merrill Co., 1970.

————. *Execution Eve and Other Contemporary Ballads.* New York: Berkley Publishing Co., 1976.

————. "Father Fullman's Assault." *Catholic World,* August 1952.

————. "Freedom to Agree." *American Mercury,* June 1953.

————. "The Genesis of Blackford Oakes." *Bohemian Club Library Notes,* July 1984.

————. "The Genteel Nightmare of Richard Rovere." *Harper's,* August 1962.

————. "God and Boys at Millbrook." *New York Times Magazine,* October 4, 1981.

————. *God and Man at Yale.* South Bend, Ind.: Gateway, 1951.

————. *The Governor Listeth.* New York: G. P. Putnam's Sons, 1971.

————. *High Jinx.* Garden City, N.Y.: Doubleday and Co., 1986.

————. "How I Came to Rock." *Saturday Evening Post,* August 24, 1968.

————. *A Hymnal: The Controversial Arts.* New York: G. P. Putnam's Sons, 1978.

————. Interview. *Mademoiselle,* June 1961.

————. Interview. *Playboy,* May 1970.

————. *Inveighing We Will Go.* New York: G. P. Putnam's Sons, 1972.

————. *The Jeweler's Eye.* New York: G. P. Putnam's Sons, 1968.

————. *Marco Polo, If You Can.* Garden City, N.Y.: Doubleday and Co., 1982.

————. "On Experiencing Gore Vidal." *Esquire,* August 1969.

————. *Overdrive.* Garden City, N.Y.: Doubleday and Co., 1983.

————. "A Relaxing View of Ronald Reagan." *West,* November 1967.

————. "Response to Diamond." *The Nation,* May 3, 1980.

————. *Right Reason.* Garden City, N.Y.: Doubleday and Co., 1985.

————. *Rumbles Left and Right.* New York: G. P. Putnam's Sons, 1963.

————. *Saving the Queen.* New York: Warner Books, 1976.

————. *See You Later, Alligator.* Garden City, N.Y.: Doubleday and Co., 1985.

————. "Senator McCarthy's Model?" *The Freeman,* May 21, 1951.

————. *Stained Glass.* New York: Warner Books, 1978.

————. *The Story of Henri Tod.* Garden City, N.Y.: Doubleday and Co., 1984.

————. "To China with Nixon." *Playboy,* January 1973.

————. *United Nations Journal.* New York: Anchor Books, 1977.

————. *The Unmaking of a Mayor.* New York: Bantam Books, 1966.

————. *Up from Liberalism.* New York: Honor Books, 1965.

————. *Who's On First.* New York: Avon Publishing Co., 1981.

Buckley, William F., Jr., and L. Brent Bozell. *McCarthy and His Enemies.* Chicago: Henry Regnery, 1954.

Buckley, William F., Jr., and Priscilla Buckley, eds. *Maureen Buckley O'Reilly.* Privately published, 1968.

Buckley, William F., Jr., and Norman Mailer. "The Role of the Right Wing: A Debate." *Playboy,* January and February 1963.

Bundy, McGeorge. "The Attack on Yale." *Atlantic Monthly,* November 1951.

Burnham, James. *Containment or Liberation?* New York: John Day and Co., 1953.

————. "Lenin's Heir." *Partisan Review,* Winter 1945.

————. *The Struggle for the World.* New York: John Day and Co., 1947.

Campbell, Robert, ed. *Spectrum of Catholic Attitudes*. Milwaukee: Bruce Publishing Co., 1969.

Cannon, Lou. *Reagan*. New York: G. P. Putnam's Sons, 1982.

Chamberlain, John. *A Life with the Printed Word*. Chicago: Regnery Books, 1982.

Chambers, Whittaker. *Odyssey of a Friend: Whittaker Chambers' Letters to William F. Buckley, Jr.* New York: G. P. Putnam's Sons, 1969.

———. *Witness*. New York: Random House, 1952.

Crawford, Alan. *Thunder on the Right*. New York: Pantheon, 1980.

Cronkite, Kathy. *On the Edge of the Spotlight*. New York: Morrow and Co., 1981.

Diamond, Sigmund. "God and the FBI at Yale." *The Nation*, April 12, 1980.

Diggins, John. *Up from Communism*. New York: Harper and Row, 1975.

Dunne, John Gregory. "Happy Days Are Here Again." *New York Review of Books*, October 13, 1983.

Eastman, Max. "Buckley versus Yale." *The American Mercury*, December 1951.

Epstein, Joseph. "The Politics of William Buckley." *Dissent*, Fall 1972.

Evans, Rowland, and Robert D. Novak. *Nixon in the White House*. New York: Vintage, 1972.

Fischer, John. "Editor's Easy Chair." *Harper's*, March 1956.

Forster, Arnold, and Benjamin R. Epstein. *Danger on the Right*. New York: Random House, 1964.

Fullman, Christopher E., O.S.B. "God and Man and Mr. Buckley." *Catholic World*, August 1952.

Gilbert, James. *A Cycle of Outrage*. New York: Oxford, 1986.

Glazer, Nathan, and Daniel Patrick Moynihan. *Beyond the Melting Pot*. Cambridge: The M.I.T. Press, 1963.

Hatch, Robert. "Enforcing Truth." *The New Republic*, December 3, 1951.

Heath, Aloise B. *Will Mrs. Major Go to Hell?* New Rochelle, N.Y.: Arlington House, 1969.

Hersh, Seymour M. *The Price of Power: Kissinger in the Nixon White House*. New York: Summit Books, 1983.

Horne, Alistair. *The Land Is Bright*. London: M. Parrish, 1958.

Hunt, E. Howard. *Undercover*. New York: Berkley, 1974.

Kempton, Murray. "Buckley's National Bore." *The Progressive*, July 1956.

King, Larry. "God, Man, and William F. Buckley, Jr.," *Harper's*, March 1967.

Kirk, Russell. *The Conservative Mind*. Chicago: Henry Regnery, 1953.

Kissinger, Henry. *White House Years*. Boston: Little, Brown and Co., 1979.

Kristol, Irving. "On the Burning Deck." *The Reporter*, November 26, 1959.

Kronholz, June. "How William Buckley Got Starr Broadcasting to Bail Out His Firm." *Wall Street Journal*, October 24, 1978.

Larson, Arthur. *A Republican Looks at His Party*. New York: Harper and Brothers, 1956.

Link, Arthur S. *Woodrow Wilson and the Progressive Era*. New York: Harper and Row, 1963.

Luce, Henry. "God, Socialism, and Yale." *Life*, October 29, 1951.

Macdonald, Dwight. "God and Buckley at Yale." *The Reporter*, May 27, 1952.

———. "McCarthy and His Apologists." *Partisan Review*, Spring 1954.

———. "Scrambled Eggheads on the Right." *Commentary*, April 1956.

McFadden, James P. "At *National Review.*" In *Maureen Buckley O'Reilly,* William F. Buckley, Jr., and Priscilla Buckley, eds. Privately published, 1968.

Mahoney, J. Daniel. *Actions Speak Louder.* New York: Arlington House, 1968.

Mailer, Norman. *The Presidential Papers.* New York: Bantam Books, 1964.

Markmann, Charles Lam. *The Buckleys.* New York: Morrow and Co., 1973.

Morley, Sheridan. *The Other Side of the Moon.* New York: Harper and Row, 1985.

Moser, Charles A. *Promise and Hope: The Ashbrook Presidential Campaign of 1972.* Washington, D.C.: Institute of Government and Politics, 1985.

Moynihan, Daniel P. *The Politics of a Guaranteed Income.* New York: Vintage, 1973.

Nash, George H. *The Conservative Intellectual Movement in America Since 1945.* New York: Basic Books, 1976.

———. "Willmoore Kendall: Conservative Iconoclast." *Modern Age,* Spring and Summer 1975.

Nock, Albert Jay. "Isaiah's Job." Reprinted in *Did You Ever See a Dream Walking?,* ed. William F. Buckley, Jr. New York: Bobbs-Merrill Co., 1970.

———. *Memoirs of a Superfluous Man.* South Bend, Ind.: Gateway, 1964.

Ortega y Gasset, José. *The Revolt of the Masses.* New York: W. W. Norton, 1957.

Oshinsky, David M. *A Conspiracy So Immense: The World of Joe McCarthy.* New York: Free Press, 1983.

Phillips, Kevin. *The Emerging Republican Majority.* New Rochelle, N.Y.: Arlington House, 1969.

———. *Post-Conservative America.* New York: Random House, 1982.

Pilat, Oliver. *Lindsay's Campaign.* Boston: Beacon Press, 1968.

Reeves, Thomas. *The Life and Times of Joe McCarthy.* New York: Stein and Day, 1982.

Reingold, Richard. "Bill Buckley: Covert King of Rock Radio." *New York,* June 14, 1971.

Rodman, Selden. "Isms and the University." *Saturday Review,* December 15, 1951.

Rovere, Richard. *The American Establishment.* New York: Harcourt, Brace, and World, 1962.

———. "Senator McCarthy's Eggheads." *The Reporter,* May 11, 1954.

Rusher, William. *The Making of the New Majority Party.* Ottawa: Green Hill Publishers, 1975.

———. *The Rise of the Right.* New York: William Morrow and Co., 1984.

Safire, William. *Before the Fall.* New York: Ballantine Books, 1975.

Shadegg, Stephen. *What Happened to Goldwater?* New York: Holt, Rinehart and Winston, 1965.

Smith, Robert Freeman. *The United States and Revolutionary Nationalism in Mexico.* Chicago: University of Chicago, 1972.

Viereck, Peter. "Conservatism under the Elms." *The New York Times Book Review,* November 4, 1951.

Wakefield, Dan. "W.F.B. Jr., Portrait of a Complainer." *Esquire,* January 1961.

Weinstein, Allen. *Perjury: The Hiss-Chambers Case.* New York: Vintage Books, 1979.

White, F. Clifton. *Suite 3505.* New York: Arlington House, 1967.

———, and William J. Gill. *Why Reagan Won.* Chicago: Regnery Gateway, 1981.

White, Theodore H. *America in Search of Itself*. New York: Warner Books, 1982.
————. *The Making of the President, 1964*. New York: Mentor Books, 1965.
Wills, Garry. *Confessions of a Conservative*. New York: Penguin Books, 1979.
————. *Nixon Agonistes*. Boston: Houghton Mifflin and Co., 1970.
————. *Politics and Catholic Freedom*. Chicago: Henry Regnery Co., 1964.
Wreszin, Michael. *The Superfluous Anarchist*. Providence: Brown University Press, 1970.

MANUSCRIPTS
William F. Buckley, Jr., Papers, Yale University Library
Lucille Cardin Crain Papers, University of Oregon
Max Eastman Papers, Indiana University
Albert B. Fall Papers, Huntington Library
Whitney Griswold Papers, Yale University Library
Group Research Library Papers, Washington, D.C.
Jeffrey Hart Papers, Hoover Institution
Marvin Liebman Papers, Hoover Institution
Carl Lohmann Papers, Yale University Library
Dwight Macdonald Papers, Yale University Library
Henry Regnery Papers, Hoover Institution
Time Papers, Time Inc.

Acknowledgments

I began writing this book in the fall of 1982, two years after Ronald Reagan's landslide election victory. I approached William F. Buckley, and after a correspondence and a meeting in his New York office, he consented to be interviewed and to give me access to his papers at Yale. These papers, which contain Buckley's correspondence since 1951 and *National Review*'s memoranda since its founding, are an invaluable source of information on both Buckley and American conservatism. Buckley's only condition was that I submit quotations from personal letters and from business dealings for his approval. Out of several hundred I submitted, he refused permission to quote in only three instances, and for reasons that were understandable.

Many people were helpful to me in writing this book. Erwin Knoll, the editor of *The Progressive*, first suggested that I write about Buckley. My agent, Kathy Robbins, urged me to use the profile I wrote for *The Progressive* as the basis of a biography and was a source of wisdom and encouragement during the years I worked on it. Sidney Blumenthal, James Gilbert, and Susan Pearson each endured several drafts of the book. Their comments and friendship were invaluable.

My editor at Simon and Schuster, Alice Mayhew, put her faith in the project before it even appeared feasible. Mayhew and editors Ursula Obst and Erika Goldmann provided useful criticisms and suggestions. Eric Rayman provided needed advice, and Henry Ferris and David Shipley speeded the book toward publication.

During the five years I worked on the book, the Alicia Patterson Foundation, the Kaltenborn Foundation, W. H. Ferry, and Stanley Sheinbaum assisted me financially. The fellowship from the Patterson Foundation allowed me to spend a year thinking about the origins of modern American conservatism.

I had to spend two years commuting between my home and the *National Review* office in New York and the Sterling Library at Yale University in New Haven. I want to thank David and Rose Osborne, Walter and Anne Kwass, Pete and Doris Rosenbloom, and Ron Radosh and Allis Wolfe for their warm hospitality. At Yale, librarians Patricia Stark, Gloria Locke, and Judith Schiff were unfailingly helpful. At *National Review,* Frances Bronson and Dorothy McCartney were patient and kind sources of appointments and stray facts and documents. Wes McCune and Gladys Segal at the Group Research Library showed me their voluminous collection. Larry DuBois helped me gain access to the files he had prepared for *Time*'s 1967 cover story; and Mark Dowie shared the files he had prepared, but never used, for an article on Buckley.

Index